Greek Island

THE ROUGH GUIDE

There are more than sixty Rough Guide titles covering
destinations from Amsterdam to Zimbabwe

Forthcoming titles include
Goa • Singapore • Hawaii • London • Moscow • Romania

Rough Guide Reference Series
Classical Music • World Music

Rough Guide Phrasebooks
Czech • French • German • Greek • Italian • Spanish

uide Credits

oy:	Alison Cowan, Peter Casterton, Jules Brown and Amanda Tomlin
s Editor:	Mark Ellingham
.torial:	Martin Dunford, Jonathan Buckley, Graham Parker, Jo Mead, Samantha Cook, Annie Shaw, Lemisse Al-Hafidh and Catherine McHale
Production:	Susanne Hillen, Andy Hilliard, Melissa Flack, Alan Spicer, Judy Pang, Link Hall and Nicola Williamson
Finance:	John Fisher, Celia Crowley and Simon Carloss
Marketing and Publicity:	Richard Trillo (UK); Jean-Marie Kelly (US)
Administration:	Tania Hummel

Acknowledgements

For research on the islands, we're greatly indebted to Nick Edwards, Geoff Garvey, Don Grisbrook, Carol Phile, Andrew Preshous and Mick Rebane, all of whom found places that had slipped by us in the past. Many thanks, too, for the invaluable contributions of readers of the *Rough Guide to Greece* – without whom this book would be nowhere near as sharp or as comprehensive. For their contributions to the ***Contexts*** section, thanks to Pete Raine for the *Wildlife* section, and Nick Edwards for updating the politics. For the advice for disabled travellers, thanks to Alison Walsh. From previous editions, continuing thanks to Richard Hartle, Tim Salmon and Stephen Lees for sharing their long and extensive knowledge of Greece.

Thanks also to Micromap and Melissa Flack for cartography, Helen Fewster and Gareth Nash for proofreading, Andrew Preshous for sterling work on the Basics section, Tania Smith for vital last-minute assistance, and Alison, Peter, Jules and Amanda for relaxed and splendid editing.

This first edition published in 1995 by Rough Guides Ltd, 1 Mercer St, London WC2H 9QJ.

Distributed by the Penguin Group:
Penguin Books Ltd, 27 Wrights Lane, London W8 5TZ
Penguin Books USA Inc., 375 Hudson Street, New York, NY 10014, USA
Penguin Books Australia Ltd, 487 Maroondah Highway, PO Box 257, Ringwood, Victoria 3134, Australia
Penguin Books Canada Ltd, 10 Alcorn Avenue, Toronto, Ontario, Canada M4V 1E4
Penguin Books (NZ) Ltd, 182–190 Wairau Road, Auckland 10, New Zealand.

Rough Guides were formerly published in the US and Canada as Real Guides.

Typeset in Linotron Univers and Century Old Style to an original design by Andrew Oliver.
Printed by Cox and Wyman Ltd (Reading).
Illustrations in Part One and Part Three by Edward Briant; illustrations on p.1 and p.381 by Henry Iles.

448pp, includes index

A catalogue record for this book is available from the British Library

ISBN 1–85828–163–6

Greek Islands

THE ROUGH GUIDE

Written and researched by
**Mark Ellingham, Marc Dubin,
Natania Jansz and John Fisher**

Additional contributions by
Nick Edwards, Geoff Garvey, Don Grisbrook, Richard Hartle,
Carol Phile, Andrew Preshous and Mick Rebane

THE ROUGH GUIDES

CONTENTS

Introduction x

PART ONE BASICS 1

Getting There from Britain 3
Getting There from Ireland 9
Getting There from North America 13
Getting There from Australasia 17
Travellers with Disabilities 19
Visas and Red Tape 21
Insurance 22
Costs, Money and Banks 23
Health Matters 25
Information and Maps 27

Getting Around 29
Accommodation 32
Eating and Drinking 35
Communications: Mail, Phones & the Media 41
Opening Hours and Public Holidays 43
Festivals and Cultural Events 44
Water Sports 48
Police, Trouble and Harassment 48
Directory 50

PART TWO THE GUIDE 53

■ 1 THE ARGO-SARONIC 55

Salamína (Salamis) 56
Éyina (Aegina) 57
Angístri 61

Póros 63
Ídhra 64
Spétses 67

■ 2 THE CYCLADES 71

Kéa 74
Kíthnos 77
Sérifos 79
Sífnos 82
Mílos 87
Kímolos 91
Ándhros 92
Tínos 96
Míkonos 99
Delos 104
Síros 107
Páros 111

Andíparos 117
Náxos 118
Koufoníssi 124
Skhinoússa 125
Iraklía 125
Dhonoússa 125
Amorgós 126
Íos 129
Síkinos 131
Folégandhros 133
Thíra 135
Anáfi 139

■ 3 CRETE 144

Iráklion, Knossos
and Central Crete 146
Eastern Crete 169

Réthimnon and around 178
Haniá and the West 185
Gávdhos 198

■ 4   THE DODECANESE 200

Kássos 200
Kárpathos 202
Rhodes 206
Hálki 218
Kastellórizo (Méyisti) 219
Sími 221
Tílos 225
Níssiros 227
Kós 230

Psérimos 236
Astipálea 237
Kálimnos 239
Léros 241
Pátmos 244
Lípsi 247
Arkí 249
Maráthi 249
Agathoníssi 249

■ 5   THE EAST AND NORTH AEGEAN 251

Sámos 253
Ikaría 265
Foúrni 269
Thímena 269
Híos 270
Psará 281

Inoússes 282
Lésvos 283
Límnos 296
Áyios Efstrátios (Aï Strátis) 301
Samothráki 302
Thássos 304

■ 6   THE SPORADES AND ÉVVIA 310

Skíathos 311
Skópelos 315 .
Alónissos 319

Skíros 323
Évvia 327

■ 7   THE IONIAN 336

Corfu (Kérkira) 338
Erikousa 349
Mathráki 350
Othoní 350
Paxí 350
Andípaxi 352
Lefkádha 352
Meganíssi 357

Kálamos 358
Kástos 358
Kefalloniá 359
Itháki 365
Zákinthos 367
Kíthira 372
Andíkithira 377
Elafónissos 378

PART THREE   CONTEXTS   381

Historical Framework 383
Wildlife 399
Books 404

Language 408
A Glossary of Words and Terms 413
Index 415

MAP SYMBOLS

REGIONAL MAPS

——	Major road
——	Minor road
- - - -	Track or path
+++++	Railway
■■	Chapter division boundary
■--■--	International boundary
⌐	Airport
+	Country church
♣	Monastery or convent
◪	Castle
◆	Ancient site
∩	Cave
♠	Refuge
〰	Mountain range
▲	Peak
☀	Lighthouse

◪	Beach

TOWN MAPS

——	Railway
▬▬	Fortifications
■	Building
✚	Church
◖	Mosque
⊹⊹	Christian cemetery
▢	Park
Ⓜ	Metro station

GENERAL

⌣	Gorge or tunnel
– –	Ferry route

PLACE NAMES: A WARNING!

The art of rendering Greek words in Roman letters is in a state of chaos. It's a major source of confusion with **place names**, for which seemingly each local authority, and each map-maker, uses a different system. The word for "saint", for instance, one of the most common prefixes, can be spelt Áyios, Ágios, or Ághios. And, to make matters worse, there are often two forms of a name in Greek – the popularly used *dhimotikí*, and the old "classicizing" *katharévoussa*. Thus you will see the island of Spétses written also as Spétsai, or Halkídha, capital of Évvia, as Halkís (or even Chalcís, on more traditional maps). Throw in the complexities of Greek grammar – with different case-endings for names – and the fact that there exist long-established English versions of Classical place names, which bear little relation to the Greek sounds, and you have a real mare's nest.

In this book, we've used a modern and largely phonetic **system**, with *Y* rather than *G* for the Greek gamma, and *DH* rather than *D* for delta, in the spelling of all modern Greek place names. We have, however, retained the accepted "English" spellings for the **ancient sites**, and for familiar places like Athens (Athiná, in modern Greek). We have also accented (with an acute) the stressed letter of each word; getting this right in pronunciation is vital in order to be understood.

INTRODUCTION

t would take a lifetime of island-hopping to get to know the more than 160 permanently inhabited Greek islands, let alone the countless smaller gull-roosts which dot
the Aegean and Ionian seas. And what better? At the right time of year or day, the
Greek Islands conform remarkably to their travel-brochure image: any tourist board
in the world would give their eyeteeth for the commonplace vision of these purple-
shadowed isles, floating on a cobalt-and-rose horizon.

Closer to hand, island beaches come in all shapes, sizes and consistencies, from
discreetly framed crescents framed by tree-fringed cliffs straight out of a Japanese
screen painting, to deserted, mile-long gifts deposited by small streams, where you
could imagine enacting Crusoe scenarios among the dunes. But inland there is always
civilization, whether the tiny cubist villages of the remoter outposts, or burgeoning
resorts as cosmopolitan and brazen as any in the Mediterranean.

What amazes most first-time visitors is how little of it all has been spoiled. If you're
used to the big hotel developments and murky waters of the open Mediterranean, as
sampled in Spain, Israel or southern France, then the Aegean islands will come as a
revelation, with their low-key resorts and 30 to 40ft sea-water visibility. This relative
lack of pollution is proclaimed at beachfronts by signs bestowing "Golden Starfish
Awards" – patently self-congratulatory, but with basis in fact at many coves, where live
starfish or octopi curl up to avoid you, and dover sole or rays skitter off across the
bottom. As you might imagine, it's all a paradise for **water-sports**: snorkelling, kayak-
ing, and – on offer now at just about every island – windsurfing. Scuba diving is possible in certain waters, too, while yacht charter, whether bare-boat or skippered, is
increasingly big business, particularly out of Rhodes, Kálimnos, Lefkádha, Póros and
Piraeus; those with the experience to compare them rate the Greek islands on a par
with the Caribbean for quality sailing itineraries. And for the months when the sea is
too cold or blustery to enjoy, many islands – not necessarily the largest ones – offer
superb hiking on old mule-trails between hill villages or up the highest summits.

The islands are extraordinarily rich in **monuments**, too – from both ancient and
medieval times. Although more protected than the Greek mainland from invasions, the
various island groups have been subjected to a staggering variety of foreign influences.
Romans, Arabs, Byzantines, crusading Knights of Saint John, Genoese, Venetians,
French, English, Italians and Ottomans have all controlled numbers of the islands
since the time of Alexander the Great. The high tide of empire has left behind countless monuments: frescoed Byzantine churches and monasteries, the fortified Venetian
capitals of the Cyclades and the Ionians, the more conventional castles of the Genoese
and Knights in the East Aegean and Dodecanese, Ottoman bridges and mosques, and
the Art Deco or mock-Renaissance edifices of the Italian Fascist administration.

A selection from many of these eras is often juxtaposed with – or even superimposed
on – the cities and temples of ancient Greece, which provide the foundation in all
senses for claims of an enduring Hellenic cultural if not racial identity down the centuries; museums, particularly on Crete, Sámos, Rhodes and Límnos, amply document the
archeological evidence. But it was medieval Greek peasants, fisherman and shepherds
who most tangibly and recently contributed to our idea of Greekness with their songs
and dances, costumes, weavings and vernacular architecture, some unconsciously
drawing on ancient antecedents. Much of this has vanished in recent decades, replaced
by an avalanche of tack in the souvenir shops, but enough remains in isolated pockets
for visitors to marvel at its combination of form and function.

Of course, most Greek island-hopping is devoted to more hedonistic pursuits: going
lightly dressed even on a moped, swimming in balmy waters at dusk, talking and drink-

ing under the stars until 3am. Such pleasures amply compensate for certain enduring weaknesses in the Greek tourism "product". If you arrive expecting orthopedic mattresses, state-of-the-art plumbing, cordon bleu cuisine or obsequious service, you'll be disappointed. Except at a very few top-range resorts, Greek island life is simple to the point of basic. Hotel and pension rooms can be box-like; campsites tend to be of the rough-and-ready sort; while food at its best is fresh and simply presented. If you want frills, look elsewhere. The Greek islands offer an enduring escape.

The Greek islanders

To get some understanding of the islanders, it's useful to realize how recent and traumatic were the events that created the modern Greek state and national character. Until well into this century, Crete, the east Aegean and the Dodecanese – nearly half the islands described in this book – remained in Ottoman or Italian hands. Meanwhile, many people from these "unredeemed" territories lived in Asia Minor, Egypt, western Europe or the north Balkans. The Balkan Wars of 1912–13, the Greco-Turkish war of 1919–22 and the organized population exchanges – essentially regulated ethnic cleansing – which followed each of these conflicts, had profound and brutal effects. Orthodox refugees from Turkey suddenly made up a noticeable proportion of Crete's and the east Aegean's population, and with the forced or voluntary departure of their Levantines and Muslims, and during the last war, many of the remaining Greek Jews, these islands gradually lost their multicultural traits.

Even before the rigours of World War II, the Italian occupation of the Dodecanese was characterized by a suppression of Greek Orthodox identity, but in general the war years in most other island groups were not so dire as on the mainland. Neither was the 1946–49 civil war that followed, nor the 1967–74 dictatorship, so keenly felt out in the Aegean, though benign neglect was about the best many islands could subsequently expect until the 1960s. Given the chance to emigrate to Australia, Canada or Africa, many entrepreneurial islanders did so, continuing a trend of depopulation which ironically had accelerated earlier this century, at the time of the first political union with the Greek mainland. The uncomfortably close memory of catastrophe, and a continuing reality of misrule and scarce opportunity at home, spurred yet another diaspora.

The advent of tourism in the 1960s arguably saved a number of islands from complete desolation, though local attitudes towards this deliverance has been decidedly ambivalent. It galls pride to become a class of seasonal service personnel, and the encounter between outsiders and villagers has often been corrosive to a deeply conservative, essentially rural society. Though younger Greeks are adaptable as they rake in the proceeds at resort areas, visitors still need to be sensitive in their behaviour towards the older generations. The mind boggles to imagine the reaction of the black-clad grandparents to nude bathing, or even scanty apparel, in a country where the Orthodox church remains an all-but-established faith and the guardian of national identity. In the presence of Italian-style expresso bars and autoteller cash machines, it's easy to be lulled into thinking that Greece became thoroughly European the moment it joined the EU – until a flock of sheep is paraded along the main street at high noon, or the noon ferry shows up at 3pm, or not at all.

Where and when to go

There is no such thing as a typical Greek island; each has its distinctive personality, history, architecture, flora – even a unique tourist clientele. Landscapes vary from the lush cypress- and olive-swathed Ionians to the bare, minimalist ridges of the Cyclades and Dodecanese, by way of subtle gradations between these extremes in the Sporades and east Aegean. Setting aside the scars from a few of the more unfortunate man-made developments, it would be difficult to single out an island to avoid. All have their adherents and individual appeal. For a thumbnail sketch of each, see the introductions to each of our chapters on the various island groups.

Most islands and their inhabitants are far more agreeable, and resolutely Greek, outside the busiest period of **early July to late August**, when the crowds of foreigners, soaring temperatures and the effects of the infamous *meltémi* can detract considerably from enjoyment. The *meltémi* is a cool, fair-weather wind which originates in high-pressure systems over the far north Aegean, gathering steam as it travels southwards and assuming near-gale magnitude by the time it reaches Crete. North-facing coasts there, and throughout the Cyclades and Dodecanese, bear the full brunt; the wind is less pronounced in the north or east Aegean, where continental landmasses provide some shelter for the islands just offshore.

You won't miss out on warm weather if you come between **late May and mid–June**, or in **September**, when the sea is warmest for swimming. During October you may hit a week's stormy spell, but for most of that month the "little summer of Áyios Dhimítrios", the Greek equivalent of Indian summer, prevails. While the choice of restaurants (and bar and disco diversions) can be limited, the light is softer and going out at midday becomes a pleasure rather than an ordeal.

Moving further out of season, **April** weather is notoriously unreliable, though the air is crystal clear, the landscape green, and there's a good feel to the seaside villages, with everything being freshened up for the season. The sea is swimmable, if a bit cool for prolonged dips, as it is, too, in **October and November**. For these months, the warmest islands are Rhodes and the islets immediately around, and relatively balmy southeastern Crete, where swimming into December is not unheard of. The Ionian islands, by contrast, are best passed over from October to March, as they get the highest rainfall in the country – often for days on end.

Other factors that might affect your timing of a Greek island visit are the level of tourism and the related amenities provided. Service standards, particularly in tavernas, invariably slip under peak-season pressures, and room rates are at their highest from July to September. If you can only visit during mid-summer, reserve a package well in advance, or plan an itinerary off the beaten track, gravitating towards islands with sparser ferry connections and/or no airport. Between November and April, by contrast, you have to contend with pared-back ferry schedules (and very few hydrofoils), and skeletal facilities when you arrive. However, you will find fairly adequate services to the more populated islands, and at least one hotel and taverna open in the port or main town of even the smallest isle.

AVERAGE TEMPERATURES AND RAINFALL																	
	Jan			March			May			July			Sept			Nov	
	°F Max Min		Rain days	°F Max Min		Rain days	°F Max Min		Rain days	°F Max Min		Rain days	°F Max Min		Rain days	°F Max Min		Rain days
Crete (Haniá)	60	46	17	64 48		11	76 56		5	86 68		0	82 64		3	70 54		10
Cyclades (Míkonos)	58	50	14	62 52		8	72 62		5	82 72		0.5	78 68		1	66 58		9
Ionian (Corfu)	56	44	13	62 46		10	74 58		6	88 70		2	82 64		5	66 52		12
Dodecanese (Rhodes)	58	50	15	62 48		7	74 58		2	86 70		0	82 72		1	68 60		7
Sporades (Skíathos)	55	45	12	58 47		10	71 58		3	82 71		0	75 64		8	62 53		12
East Aegean (Lésvos)	54	42	11	60 46		7	76 60		6	88 70		2	82 66		2	64 50		9

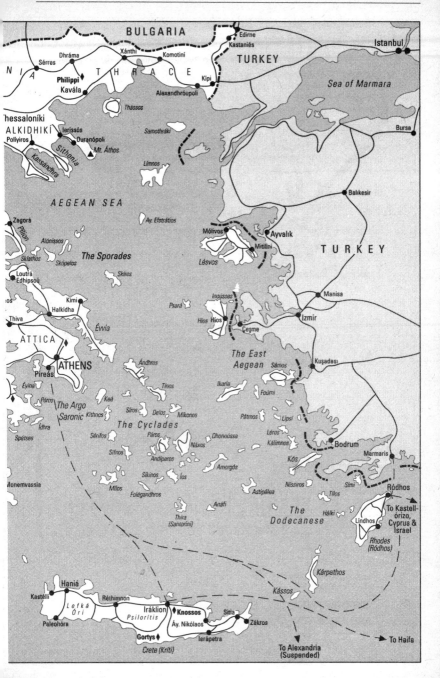

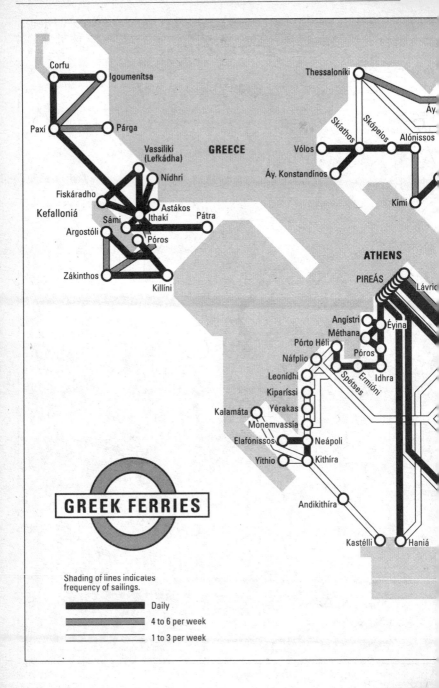

Corfu
Igoumenítsa
Paxí
Párga
Vassiliki (Lefkádha)
Nídhri
GREECE
Thessaloníki
Áy.
Skíathos
Skópelos
Alónissos
Vólos
Áy. Konstandínos
Kími
Fiskáradho
Kefalloniá
Astákos
Ithakí
Pátra
Sámi
Argostóli
Póros
ATHENS
Zákinthos
Killíni
PIREÁS
Lávrio
Angístri
Éyina
Méthana
Pórto Héli
Póros
Náfplio
Idhra
Leonídhi
Spétses
Ermióni
Kiparíssi
Kalamáta
Yérakas
Monemvassía
Elafónissos
Neápoli
Yíthio
Kithíra
Andikithíra
Kastélli
Haniá

GREEK FERRIES

Shading of lines indicates
frequency of sailings.

	Daily
	4 to 6 per week
	1 to 3 per week

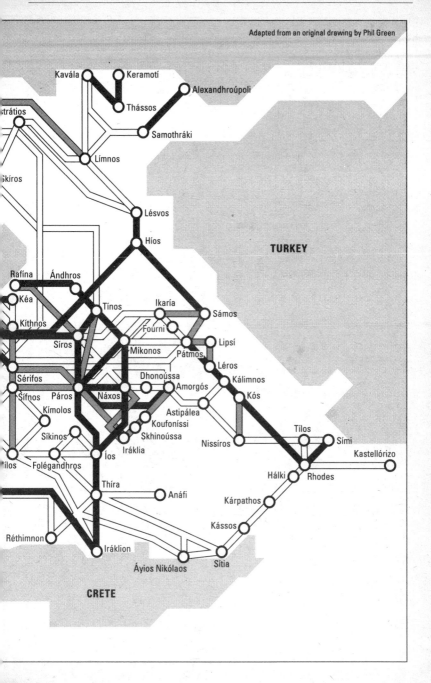

Adapted from an original drawing by Phil Green

TURKEY

CRETE

PART ONE

THE
BASICS

GETTING THERE FROM BRITAIN

It's close on 2000 miles from London to Athens, so for most visitors flying to the Greek islands is the only viable option. There are direct flights to a variety of Greek island and mainland destinations from all the major British airports; flying time is around three and a half hours and the cost of charter flights is reasonable. Sample summer return fares to Athens, gateway to most of the islands, or direct to Corfu, Crete and Rhodes, start from around £160 from London (Manchester £180, Glasgow £200), but there are often bargains to be had, and outside of High Season (which includes Easter), flights can be snapped up for as little as £120 return. Costs can often be highly competitive, too, if you buy a flight as part of an all-in package: see p.5–6 for details of holiday operators.

Road or rail alternatives take a minimum of three days and are only worth considering if you plan to visit the Greek Islands as part of an extended trip through Europe, or in conjunction with Italy. Since the war in former-Yugoslavia, the most popular route is down to southern Italy, then across to Greece by ferry.

BY AIR

Most of the cheaper flights from Britain to Greece are **charters**, which are sold either with a package holiday or as a flight-only option. The flights have fixed and unchangeable outward and return dates, and often a maximum stay of one month.

For longer stays or more flexibility, or if you're travelling out of season (when few charters are available), you'll need a **scheduled** flight. As with charters, these are offered under a wide variety of fares, and are again often sold off at discount by agents. Useful sources for discounted flights are the classified ads in the travel sections of newspapers like the *Independent*, *Guardian*, *Observer* and *Sunday Times*. *Teletext* is also worth checking, while your local travel agent shouldn't be overlooked.

. Although **Athens** is the most promising destination for cheap fares, there are also **direct flights** from Britain to **Thessaloníki**, **Kalamáta**, **Kavála** and **Préveza** on the Greek mainland, and to the islands of **Crete**, **Rhodes**, **Corfu**, **Lésvos**, **Páros**, **Zákinthos**, **Kefalloniá**, **Skiáthos**, **Sámos** and **Kós**. And with any flight to Athens, you can buy a **domestic connecting flight** (on the national carrier, *Olympic*) to twenty or so additional Greek island airports.

CHARTER FLIGHTS

Travel agents throughout Britain sell **charter flights** to Greece, which usually operate from May to October; late-night departures and early-morning arrivals are common. Even the high street chains frequently promote "flight-only" deals, or discount all-inclusive holidays, when their parent companies need to offload their seat allocations. In any case, phone around for a range of offers. Charter airlines include *GB Airways*, *Excalibur* and *Monarch*, but you can only book tickets on these through travel agents.

The greatest variety of **flight destinations** tends to be from London Gatwick and Manchester. In summer, if you book in advance, you should have a choice of most of the Greek regional airports listed above. Flying from elsewhere in Britain (Birmingham, Cardiff, Glasgow or Newcastle), or looking for last-minute discounts, you'll find options more limited, most commonly to Athens, Corfu, Rhodes and Crete.

It's worth noting that **non-EC nationals** who buy charter tickets to Greece must buy a return ticket, of no fewer than three days and no more than four weeks, and must accompany it with an **accommodation voucher** for at least the first few nights of their stay – check that the ticket satisfies these conditions or you could be refused entry. In practice, the "accommodation voucher" has become a formality; it has to name an existing hotel but you're not expected to use it (and probably won't be able to if you try).

The other important condition regards **travel to Turkey** (or any other neighbouring country). If you travel to Greece on a charter flight, you may visit another country only as a day trip; if you stay overnight, you will invalidate your ticket. This rule is justified by the Greek authorities because they subsidize charter airline landing fees, and are therefore reluctant to see tourists spending their money outside Greece. Whether you buy that excuse or not, there is no way around it, since the Turkish authorities clearly stamp all passports, and the Greeks usually check them. The package industry on the east Aegean and Dodecanese islands bordering Turkey, however, does some-

times prevail upon customs officials to back-date re-entry stamps when bad weather strands their tour groups overnight in Anatolia.

Student/youth charters are allowed to be sold as one-way flights only. By combining two one-way charters you can, therefore, stay for over a month. Student/youth charter tickets are available to anyone under 26, and to all card-carrying full-time students under 32.

Finally, remember that **reconfirmation** of return charter flights is vital and should be done at least 72 hours before departure.

SCHEDULED FLIGHTS

The advantages of scheduled flights are that they can be pre-booked well in advance, have longer ticket validities and involve none of the above restrictions on charters. However, many of the cheaper APEX and SuperAPEX fares do have an advance-purchase and/or minimum-stay requirements, so check conditions carefully. Scheduled flights haver an additional advantage in that they are usually daytime flights.

As with charters, discount fares on scheduled flights are available from most high-street travel **agents**, as well as from a number of specialist flight and student/youth agencies. Most discount scheduled fares have an advance-purchase requirement, usually of 14 days.

The biggest choice of scheduled flights is with the Greek national carrier *Olympic Airways*, and *British Airways*, who both fly direct from London Heathrow to Athens (3 times daily) and also to Thessaloníki (daily). *Virgin Airways* also has a daily service to Athens. All these airlines offer a range of special fares and even in July and August can come up with deals as low as £200 return; more realistically, though, you'll pay around £250–325 return for a scheduled flight. You'll also be able to book onward connections to domestic Greek airports. Flights from British regional airports route through Heathrow in the first instance.

East European airways like *ČSA*, *Balkan*, *Malev* and *LOT* are often cheaper – £120 one way, £240 return for much of the year – but nearly always involve delays, with connections in (respectively) Prague, Sofia, Budapest and Warsaw. It is not always possible to book discount fares direct from these airlines, and you'll often pay no more by going through an agent (see box opposite).

PACKAGES AND TOURS

Virtually every British **tour operator** includes Greece in its programme, though with many of the larger groups you'll find choices limited to the established resorts – notably the islands of Rhodes, Kos, Crete, Skiáthos, Zákinthos and Corfu.

If you buy one of these at a last-minute discount, you may find it costs little more than a flight – and you can use the accommodation offered as much or as little as you want. For a rather more low-key and genuinely "Greek" resort, however, it's better to book your holiday through one of the smaller **specialist agencies** listed below and overpage.

SPECIALIST PACKAGE OPERATORS

VILLA OR VILLAGE ACCOMMODATION

These companies are all fairly small-scale operations, offering competitively priced packages with flights and often using more traditional village accommodation. They make an effort to offer islands without over-developed tourist resorts and, increasingly, unspoiled mainland destinations.

Best of Greece, 23–24 Margaret St, London W1N 8LE (☎0171/677 1721). Exclusive, upmarket villa and hotel arrangements from a long-established, very discriminating operator.

CV Travel, 43 Cadogan St, London SW3 2PR (☎0171/581 0851). Quality villas on Corfu and Paxí.

Corfu à la Carte, The Whitehouse, Bucklebury Alley, Newbury, Berks RH16 9NN (☎01635/30621). Selected beach and rural cottages on Corfu, Paxí and Skiáthos.

Grecofile/Filoxenia, Sourdock Hill, Barkisland, Halifax, West Yorkshire HX4 0AG (☎01422/375999). Tailor-made itineraries and specialist packages to unspoiled areas on many islands.

Greek Islands Club, 66 High St, Walton-on-Thames, Kent KT12 1BU (☎01932/220477). Holidays on the Ionian islands, including Kíthira, and the Sporades.

Greek Sun Holidays, 1 Bank St, Sevenoaks, Kent TN13 1UW (☎01732/740317). Good value package holidays, including some fly-drive options, on a wide range of islands.

Island Wandering, 51a London Rd, Hurst Green, East Sussex TN19 7QP (☎01580/860733). One of the best operators around, offering villas and rooms on over forty islands, which they will book for you in any feasible combination, along with inter-island transport. They are particularly strong on the Cyclades and Dodecanese.

Ilios Island Holidays, 18 Market Square, Horsham, West Sussex RH12 1EU (☎01403/259788). Features mainly Ionian and Sporades islands, plus Tínos, Páros and Náxos in the Cyclades.

Kosmar Villa Holidays, 358 Bowes Rd, Arnos Grove, London N11 1AN (☎0181/368 6833). Self-catering apartments on Spétses and other Argo-Saronic isles and Crete.

Laskarina Holidays, St Marys Gate, Wirksworth, Derbyshire DE4 4DQ (☎01629/822203). This company concentrates on a dozen of the less visited islands of the Dodecanese and Sporades.

Continues over

SPECIALIST PACKAGE OPERATORS (cont.)

Manos Holidays, 168–172 Old St, London EC1V 9BP (☎0171/216 8070). Budget packages to most of the major island resorts.

Simply Crete, Chiswick Gate, 598–608 Chiswick High Rd, London W4 5RT (☎0181/994 4462); **Simply Ionian**, same address (☎0181/995 1121). High-quality apartments, villas and small hotels on Crete and the Ionian islands.

Skiathos Travel, 4 Holmesdale Rd, Kew Gardens, Richmond, Surrey TW9 3J2 (☎0181/940 5157). Packages to Skíathos and other of the Sporades, plus some flight-only deals.

Sunvil Holidays, Sunvil House, 7–8 Upper Square, Old Isleworth, Middlesex TW7 7BJ (☎0181/568 4499). Good choice of smaller resorts, including offbeat islands like Límnos.

Voyages Ilena, Old Garden House, The Lanterns, Bridge Lane, London SW11 3AD (☎0171/924 4440). This is a mainland villa specialist but has a few places on Évvia and Hydra (Ídhra).

WALKING HOLIDAYS

All the operators below run trekking groups to both the islands and mainland. Groups generally consist of 10 to 15 people, plus an experienced guide, and the walks tend to be day-hikes from one or more bases, or point-to-point treks staying in village accommodation en route. Camping out is not usually involved.

Explore Worldwide, 1 Frederick St, Aldershot, Hampshire GU11 1LQ (☎01252/344161). This is one of the top hiking companies, and offers a good programme in western Crete.

Ramblers Holidays, Longcroft House, Fretherne Rd, Welwyn Garden City, Herts AL8 6PQ (☎01707/331133). Easy walking tours on Kefalloniá, Itháki and Crete.

Waymark Holidays, 44 Windsor Rd, Slough SL1 2EJ (☎01753/516477). Spring and autumn walking holidays on Sámos, Náxos and Mílos.

SAILING

Dinghy sailing, yachting and windsurfing holidays based on small flotillas of four- to six-berth yachts. Prices start at around £350 per person per week off-season; all levels of experience. Sailing holidays can be flotilla- or shore-based. If you're a confident sailor, it's possible simply to charter a yacht from a broker; the Greek National Tourist Organisation has lists of companies.

Explore Worldwide, 1 Frederick St, Aldershot, Hampshire GU11 1LQ (☎01252/344161). Features a range of island sailing holidays.

Sovereign Sailing, First Choice House, Peelcross Rd, Salford, Manchester M5 2AN (☎ 01293/599944). Independent charters and flotilla holidays on and around the Ionian islands.

Sunsail The Port House, Port Solent, Portsmouth, Hampshire, PO6 4TH (☎01705/210345). Tuition in dinghy sailing, yachting and windsurfing. Clubs include Paxí, Lefkás and Kós.

World Expeditions, 7 North Rd, Maidenhead, Berkshire SL6 1PE (☎01628/74174). Flotilla and bareboat sailing from Páros, Pátmos and Rhodes.

OTHER SPECIALISTS

Peregrine Holidays, 40/41 South Parade, Summertown, Oxford OX2 7JP (☎01865/511642). Natural history tours of Crete and a few other islands, combined with visits to ancient sites.

Skyros Centre, 92 Prince of Wales Rd, London NW5 3NE (☎0171/267 4424). Holistic health, fitness and "personal growth" holidays on the island of Skíros, as well as writers' workshops.

BY TRAIN

Travelling by train from Britain to Greece takes around three and a half days and fares work out more expensive than flights. However, with a regular ticket stopovers are possible – in France, Switzerland and Italy – while with an *InterRail* or *Eurail* train pass you can take in Greece as part of a wider rail trip around Europe.

The most practical route from Britain takes in France, Switzerland and **Italy** before crossing on the ferry from Bari or Brindisi to Pátra (Patras). Because of the war in former Yugoslavia, the increased demand for tickets on the Italian route has put an extra burden on trains and ferries. In summer, you need to book seats on both well in advance.

A rambling alternative from Budapest runs via **Bucharest and Sofia to Thessaloníki**, which is advised as your first stop since Athens is nearly nine hours further on the train.

TICKETS AND PASSES

Regular train tickets from Britain to Greece are not good value. London to Athens costs at least £380 return. If you are **under 26**, however, you can get a **BIJ ticket**, discounting these fares by around 25 percent; these are available through *Eurotrain* and *Wasteels* (see box opposite for addresses). Both regular and *BIJ* tickets have two months' return validity, or can be purchased as one ways, and the Italy routes include the ferry crossing. The tickets also allow for stopovers, so long as you stick to the route prescribed.

Better value by far is to buy an **InterRail pass**, available to anyone resident in Europe for six months. You can buy it from *British Rail* (or any travel agent), and the pass offers unlimited travel on a zonal basis on up to 25 European rail networks. The only extras you pay are supplements on certain express trains, plus half-price fares in Britain (or the country of issue) and on the cross-Channel ferries. The pass includes the ferry from Brindisi in southern Italy to Pátra in Greece. There are several types: to reach Greece from the UK you'll need a pass valid for at least two zones (£209 for a month), though if you're intending to travel further in Europe you can pay up to £249; Greece is zoned with Italy, Turkey and Slovenia.

The equivalent pass for North Americans is the Eurail pass, for details of which, see "Getting There from North America", on p.15.

Finally, anyone over 60 and holding a British Rail Senior Citizen Railcard, can buy a **Rail Europe Senior Card** (£21 for a year). This gives up to fifty percent reductions on rail fares throughout Europe and thirty percent off sea crossings.

BY BUS

The days of £50 Magic Bus returns to Athens are long gone and with charter flights at such competitive rates, it's hard to find good reasons for wanting to spend three or four days on a bus to Greece. However, it's still a considerably cheaper option than taking the train.

Olympic Bus offers the cheapest fares at £100–120 return. *National Express Eurolines* (bookable through any *National Express* office; see box above) has a more reliable reputation, better buses, but higher prices (£200–220 return). Be wary of other operators, who are often cowboy outfits; in recent years there have been a string of accidents and horror stories.

The usual **route** is via France and Italy and then a ferry across to Greece. Stops of about twenty minutes are made every five or six hours, with the odd longer break for roadside café meals.

RAIL TICKET OFFICES

Eurotrain, 52 Grosvenor Gardens, London SW1 (☎0171/730 3402).

International Rail Centre, Victoria Station, London SW1 (☎0171/834 2345).

Wasteels, Victoria Station, London SW1 (☎0171/834 7066).

BUS TICKET OFFICES

National Express Eurolines, 52 Grosvenor Gardens, London SW1 (☎0171/730 0202).

Olympic Bus, 70 Brunswick Centre, London WC1 (☎0171/837 9141).

BY CAR AND FERRY

If you have the time and inclination, **driving to Greece** can be a fine journey. Realistically, though, it's worth considering only if you have at least a month to spare, and want to take advantage of various stopovers en route.

It's important to plan ahead. The **Automobile Association** (AA) provides a comprehensive service offering general advice on all facets of driving to Greece and the names and addresses of useful contact organizations. Their European Routes Service (contact AA on ☎01256/20123 or your local branch) can arrange a detailed print-out of a route to follow. Driving licence, vehicle registration documents and insurance are essential; a green card is recommended.

The most popular **route** is down through France and Italy to catch one of the Adriatic ferries. A much longer alternative through Eastern Europe (Hungary, Romania and Bulgaria) is just about feasible. Driving through former Yugoslavia is not at present an option.

CROSSING THE CHANNEL

Crossing the Channel is easier and cheaper than ever, due to competition between the ferry and Channel tunnel operators.

Le Shuttle runs trains 24 hours · a day through the Channel Tunnel, carrying cars, motorcycles, buses and their passengers, and taking 35 minutes between Folkestone and Calais. At peak times, services are every 15 minutes, and advance bookings unnecessary; during the night, services run hourly. Return fares from May to August cost around £280–310 per vehicle (passengers included), with discounts in the low season.

CROSS-CHANNEL INFORMATION

Hoverspeed, Dover (☎01304/240101); London (☎0181/554 7061). *To Boulogne and Calais.*

Le Shuttle, Customer Services Centre Information and ticket sales (☎01303/271100)

P&O European Ferries, Dover (☎01304/203388); Portsmouth (☎01705/772244); London (☎0181/575 8555). *To Calais*

Sally Line, Ramsgate (☎01843/595522); London (☎0181/858 1127). *To Dunkerque.*

Stena Sealink Line, Ashford (☎01233/647047). *To Calais and Dieppe.*

You can travel a bit cheaper on the main **ferry** or **hovercraft** links between **Dover** and Calais or Boulogne (the quickest and cheapest routes), **Ramsgate** and Dunkerque, or Newhaven and Dieppe. **Fares** on these vary according to season and the size of your car.

The Dover–Calais/Boulogne runs, for example, start at about £180 return low season, £220 return high season for a car with up to five passengers. Taking a **motorbike** costs from £80–90 return.

VIA ITALY

Routes down to Italy **through France and Switzerland** are very much a question of personal taste. One of the most direct is Calais–Reims–Geneva–Milan and then down the Adriatic coast to the Italian port of your choice. Even on the quickest autoroutes (with their accompanying tolls), the journey will involve two overnight stops.

Once in Italy, there's a choice of five **ports** for ferries to Greece. Regular car and passenger ferries link **Ancona**, **Bari** and **Brindisi** with **Igoumenítsa** (the port of Epirus in western Greece) and/or **Pátra** (at the northwest tip of the Peloponnese). Most sail via the island of

FERRIES FROM ITALY TO GREECE

ROUTES

Note: all timings are approximate.

From Ancona *Marlines, Strintzis, ANEK* and *Minoan* to Igoumenítsa (24hr) and Pátra (34hr); daily or nearly so year-round. *Minoan* sails via Corfu, with separate lines for Pátra, Kefalloniá,and Cesme (Turkey) half the year; *Strintzis* and *ANEK* via Corfu; *Marlines* has a summer extension from Pátra to Iráklio (Crete). Most sailings between 8 and 10pm, but there are a number of afternoon departures.

From Bari *Ventouris* to Pátra direct (20hr), nearly daily; to Corfu, Igoumenítsa (12hr) and Pátra (20hr); daily departures year-round between 8 and 9pm. To Pátra via Corfu and/or Igoumenítsa on *Poseidon Lines, Arkadia Lines.*

From Brindisi *Fragline* and *Adriatica* to Corfu, Igoumenítsa (11hr) and Pátra (20hr). *Hellenic Mediterranean Lines* to Corfu and Pátra, three to seven a week depending on season; Igoumenítsa , Kefalloniá, Ithaki, Paxí and Zákinthos, served on separate sailings during summer. *European Seaways* to Corfu, Igoumenítsa and Pátra. *Marlines* to Igoumenítsa and Brindisi. Several ferries leave every day in season, most between 8 and 10.30pm; at least one daily in winter.

From Otranto *R-Lines* to Corfu and Igoumenítsa (9hr); five weekly, May–Oct only.

From Trieste *ANEK* to Igoumenítsa , Corfu and Pátra (43hr). One weekly in summer, tagged on to Ancona service.

FARES

Prices below are one-way high/low season fares; **port taxes** *(£3–5 per person in each direction) are not included. Note that substantial reductions apply on most lines for both* **InterRail** *or* **Eurail** *pass-holders, and those* **under 26***.*

Igoumenítsa from Bari or Brindisi: deck class £28–35/£15–25; car from £36–55/£20–45.

Pátra from Bari or Brindisi: deck class £31–£38/£20–30; car from £36–54/£25–45.

Igoumenítsa from Ancona: deck class £40/50; car from £65/£95.

UK AGENTS

Amathis Travel, 51 Tottenham Court Rd, London W1 (☎0171/636 6158). *Agents for Hellenic Mediterranean.*

Serena Holidays, 40 Kenway Rd, London SW5 (☎0171/244 8422). *For Adriatica Lines.*

Viamare Travel Ltd, Graphic House, 2 Sumatra Rd, London NW6 (☎0171/431 4560). *Agents for ANEK, Arkadia, Fragline, Marlines, R-Lines, Strintzis and Ventouris.*

Corfu, and a few link other Ionian islands en route to Pátra; you can stop over at no extra charge if you get these stops specified on your ticket. Generally, these ferries run year round, but services are greatly reduced out of season.

Ferries also sail – less frequently – from **Trieste** to Pátra, and from **Otranto** to Igoumenítsa. For more details see the "Ferries" box opposite.

Note that crossing to Igoumenítsa is substantially cheaper than to Pátra, and the cheapest of all the crossings are from Brindisi or Otranto to Igoumenítsa. However, drivers will discover that the extra cost in Italian fuel –

around double the British price – offsets the route's savings over those from Bari or Ancona.

In summer, it is essential to **book tickets** a few days ahead, especially in the peak July–August period – and certainly if you are taking a car across. During the winter you can usually just turn up at the main ports (Ancona, Bari, Brindisi, Igoumenítsa/Corfu), but it's still wise to book in advance if possible. A few phone calls before leaving are, in any case, advisable, as the range of fares and operators (from Brindisi especially) is considerable; if you do just turn up at the port, it is worth spending an hour or so shopping around the agencies.

GETTING THERE FROM IRELAND

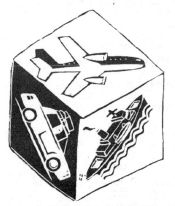

Summer charters operate from Dublin and Belfast to Athens and there are additional services to Míkonos, Rhodes, Crete and Corfu. A high-season charter from Dublin to Athens costs upwards of IR£200 return, while a week's package on one of the above islands costs from IR£440 per person for two weeks.

Year-round **scheduled services** with *Aer Lingus* and *British Airways* operate from both Dublin and Belfast via Heathrow to Athens, but you'll find them pricey compared to charters. Youth and student fares are offered by *USIT* (see below for address).

Travelling via London is an alternative, if flights are in short supply, and may sometimes save you a little money, but on the whole it's rarely worth the time and effort. For the record, budget flights to London are offered by *British Midland*, *Aer Lingus* and *Ryan Air*, while buying a **Eurotrain boat and train ticket** may also slightly undercut plane fares.

FLIGHT AGENTS IN IRELAND

Balkan Tours, 37 Ann St, Belfast BT1 4EB (☎01232/246795). Direct charter flights.

Joe Walsh Tours, 8–11 Baggot St, Dublin (☎01/676 0991). General budget fares agent.

Thomas Cook, 118 Grafton St, Dublin (☎01/677 1721). Mainstream package holiday and flight agent, with occasional discount offers.

USIT. Student and youth specialist. Branches at: Aston Quay, O'Connell Bridge, Dublin 2 (☎01/679

8833); 10–11 Market Parade, Cork (☎021/270 900); Fountain Centre, College St, Belfast (☎01232/324073).

AIRLINES

Aer Lingus, 41 Upper O'Connell St, Dublin (☎01/844 4777); 46–48 Castle St, Belfast (☎01232/245151); 2 Academy St, Cork (☎021/274331).

British Airways, 9 Fountain Centre, College St, Belfast (☎0345/222111); in Dublin, contact *Aer Lingus*.

TRAVELLING VIA ATHENS AND PIREAS

As detailed in the "Getting There" sections, you may well find yourself travelling to the islands via **Athens**. This is not necessarily a hardship. The Greek capital is, admittedly, no holiday resort, with its concrete architecture and air pollution, but it has modern excitements of its own, as well as the superlative ancient sites. A couple of nights' stopover will allow you to take in the Acropolis, Ancient Agora and major museums, wander around the old quarter of Plaka and the bazaar area, and sample some of the country's best restaurants and clubs. And a morning flight into Athens would allow you time to take a look at the Acropolis and Plaka, before heading down to the port of **Pireás** (Piraeus) to catch one of the overnight ferries to Crete or the Dodecanese.

What follows is a brief guide to getting in and out of the city, and some pointers on what to do while you're there. For a full treatment of the city, check the *Rough Guide to Greece*.

ARRIVING

Athens airport – Ellinikón – has two separate terminals: **West** (Dhitikó) which is used by *Olympic Airways* (both national and international), and **East** (Anatolkó) which is used by all the other airlines. The terminals are on opposite sides of the runway, so you have to drive halfway round the perimeter fence to get from one to the other. *Olympic* buses connect the two regularly from around 6am to midnight; taxis are available, too, and should cost no more than 200dr.

Both terminals have money exchange facilities, open 24 hours at the east terminal, 7am to 11pm at the west one; the west terminal also has automatic teller machines that accept *Visa, Mastercard, Cirrus* and *Plus* cards. Insist on some small denomination notes for paying for your bus ticket or taxi ride.

It's about 9km **to central Athens** or to the ferry port of **Pireás** (Piraeus). The easiest way to travel is by **taxi**, which should cost around 1000–1500dr, depending on traffic. Make sure that the meter is switched on, as new arrivals are often charged over the odds. You may find that you have fellow passengers in the cab: this is permitted, and each drop-off will pay the full fare.

If you're happy to carry your bags around, you caould also travel in by **bus**. The blue and yellow #090 and #92 buses connect both terminals with the centre of Athens (Omónia and Síndagma squares). They run every half-hour 6am–9pm, every 40 minutes from 9pm to 12.20am, and every

hour (on the half hour) 1.30–5.30am. Tickets cost 160dr; 200dr between 1.30 and 5.30am.

Bus #19 runs from both airport terminals to **Pireás**, allowing you to get straight to the ferries. It has 12 runs daily between 6am and 9.20pm. Tickets again cost 160dr. Take the bus to the end of the route, Platía Karaïskáki, which fronts the main harbour, and a line of ferry agencies.

All international **trains** arrive at the Stathmós Laríssis, just to the northwest of the city centre. There are hotels in this area or you can take yellow trolley bus (#1) immediately outside to reach Síntagma square.

Baggage

If you are just spending the day in Athens, and want to **store your baggage**, you can do so for 200dr per piece at *Pacific Ltd*, Nikis 26 – just off Síndagma (Mon–Sat 7am–8pm, Sun 7am–2pm). You can also store bags here longer term if you want to take the minimum to the islands.

ACCOMMODATION

Finding **somewhere to stay** in Athens is little problem except at the very height of summer – though it's best to phone ahead. A small selection of places are listed below, or you can book more upmarket rooms through the hotel reservations desk inside the National Bank of Greece on Síndagma square. There is also a **Tourist Office** inside the National Bank, which can supply you with maps of the city.

For a quick stay, **Pláka**, the oldest quarter of the city, is the best area. It spreads south of Síndagma square, in easy walking range of the Acropolis, and has lots of outdoor restaurants and cafés. It's possible to **stay** in the port of Pireás, too, though there's no real need, and you might as well make the most of your time in Athens.

All the listings below are in the Pláka; price categories are for a double room in high season:

4000–6000dr
George's Guest House, Níkis 46 (☎32 26 474).
John's Place, Patróou 5 (☎32 29 719).
Solonion, Spírou Tsangari 11 (☎32 20 008).

6000–8000dr
Dioskouri, Pittákou 6 (☎32 48 165).
Kouros, Kódhrou 11 (☎32 27 431).
Phaedra, Herefóndos 16 (☎32 27 795).

8000–16000dr
Acropolis House, Kódhrou 6 (☎32 22 344).
Adonis, Kódhrou 3 (☎32 49 737).

Myrto, Níkis 40 (☎32 27 237).
Nefeli, Iperídhou 16 (☎32 28 044).

EATING AND DRINKING

Pláka is bursting with touristy restaurants, most very pleasantly situated but poor value. Three with nice sites and good food are *Kouklis* (Tripíodhon 14), *O Platanos* (Dhioyénous 4) and *Iy Klimataria* (Klepsídhras 5). *Eden* (Iiossíou 12) is a decent vegetarian restaurant.

THE CITY AND SIGHTS

Central Athens is a compact, easily walkable area. Its hub is **Síndagma Square** (Platía Sintágmatos), flanked by the Parliament, banks and airline offices, and, as mentioned, the National Bank with the Tourist Office. Pretty much everything you'll want to see in a fleeting visit – the Acropolis, Pláka, the major museums – is within 20–30 minutes' walk of here, square. Just east of the square, too, are the **National Gardens** – the nicest spot in town for a siesta.

Pláka and the Bazaar

Walk south from Síndagma, along Níkis or Filellínon streets, and you'll find yourself in Pláka, the surviving area of the nineteenth-century, pre-Independence, village. Largely pedestrianised, it is a delightful area just to wander around – and it is the approach to the Acropolis.

For a bit of focus to your walk, take in the fourth-century BC **Monument of Lysikrates**, used as a study by Byron, to the east, and the Roman-era **Tower of the Winds** (Aéridhes), to the west. The latter adjoins the Roman forum. Climb north from the Tower of the Winds and you reach **Anafiótika**, with its whitewashed Cycladic-style cottages (built by workers from the island of Anáfi) and the eclectic **Kanellópoulos Museum** (Tues–Sun 8.30am–2.45pm; 400dr).

Head north from the Roman Forum, along Athinás or Eólou streets, and you come to an equally characterful part of the city – the **bazaar** area, which shows Athens in its Near Eastern lights. **Monastiráki square** is worth a look, too, with its Turkish mosque. On Sundays a genuine **Flea Market** sprawls to its west, out beyond the tourist shops promoted as "Athens Flea Market".

The Acropolis and Ancient Agora

Even with a few hours to spare between flight and ferry, you can take in a visit to the **Acropolis** (Mon–Fri 8am–6.45pm/5pm summer/winter, Sat & Sun 8.30am–2.45pm; 1500dr/students 800dr). The complex of temples, rebuilt by Pericles in the Golden Age of the Fifth Century BC, is focused on the famed Parthenon. This, and the smaller Athena Nike and Erechtheion temples are given context by a small museum housing some of the original statuary left behind by Lord Elgin.

If you have more time, make your way down to the **Theatre of Dionysos**, on the south slope (Mon–Sat 9am–2.45pm, Sun 9am–1.45pm; 400dr); and/or to the Ancient (Classical Greek-era) **Agora**, northwest of the Acropolis hill (Tues–Sun 8.30am–2.45pm; 800dr), presided over by the Doric **Thiseion**, or Temple of Hephaestus.

Museums

Athens' major museum is the **National Archeological Museum** (Patissíon 28; Mon 12.30–6.45pm, Tues–Fri 8am–6.45pm; Sat & Sun 8.30am–12.45pm; 1500dr, students 750dr). Its highlights include the Mycenean (Odyssey-era) treasures, Classical sculpture, and, upstairs, the brilliant Minoan frescoes from Thíra (Santoríni).

Two other superb museums are the **Benáki** (Koumbári 1; 8.30am–2pm; closed Tues), a fascinating personal collection of ancient and folk treasures, and the **Museum of Cycladic and Ancient Greek Art** (Neofítou Dhouká 4; Mon & Wed–Fri 10am–4pm, Sat 10am–3pm; 250dr), with its wonderful display of figurines from the Cycladic island civilization of the third millenium BC.

ON TO THE ISLANDS: PIREÁS

Pireás (Piraeus), the port of Athens, is the last stop on the single-line **metro**, which you can board at Omónia or Monastiráki squares. The journey takes about 25 minutes – trains run from 5.30am to midnight – and there's a flat fare of 75dr. If you're travelling by rail from Pátra, the train continues through Athens down to Pireás. **Taxis** cost around 100dr from the city centre or the airport.

You can buy **ferry tickets** from agencies at the harbour in Pireás, or in central Athens (there are several outlets on Leforós Amalías, which runs south of Síndagma square). Wherever you buy tickets, make sure you ask around the agencies and get a ferry that makes a reasonably direct run to your island destination. There may be little choice to obscure islands, but ferries to the Cyclades and Dodecanese can take very different routes.

For the Argo-Saronic islands, you may prefer to take a "Flying Dolphin" **hydrofoil** from the Zéa Marina – a taxi ride (or bus #8) from the metro. These are twice as fast and around twice the cost. Tickets can be bought in advance in Athens – worth doing in high season – or an hour before departure at the quay.

TRAVELLING VIA OTHER MAINLAND PORTS

Although Pireás, the port of Athens, has a wide choice of ferry and hydrofoil connections, certain islands can (or must) be reached from other ports on the mainland. Below is a quick run-through of the more important and useful.

Note also that there are two islands – **Évvia** (northeast of Athens) and **Lefkádha** in the Ionian – that require no ferry, and can be reached by bus, and in Évvia's case by train.

Lávrio

This tiny port, south of Athens (and reachable by bus from the Mavromatéon terminal; 1hr) has daily ferries to **Kéa**, the closest of the Cyclades.

Ráfina

Another small port near Athens (again reachable by bus from the Mavromatéon terminal; 40min). Connections are to the **Cyclades**, **Dodecanese**, **northeast Aegean** and nearby **Évvia**.

Yíthio

This elegant Peloponnese town has ferries most days to the isolated Ionian island of **Kíthira**. It's a 5–6hr haul here by bus (Kifissóu 100 terminal) from Athens, changing at Spárti. Budget hotels in town include the *Kondoyannis* (☎0733/22 518), *Koutsouris* (☎0733/22 321) and *Kranae* (☎0733/22 011), and pricier *Githion* (☎0733/23 452).

Neápoli

A small, undistinguished port at the southern foot of the Peloponnese, with ferry and hydrofoil connections to **Kíthira**, and local boats to the islet of **Elafónissos**. It can be reached by hydrofoil in summer from the Argo-Saronic islands.

Pátra (Patras)

Pátra is the major port of the Peloponnese, and the only real rival to Pireás in terms of traffic. It has ferry connections with Italy and with the main **Ionian islands**. Easiest access from Athens is on the train (Statmós Peloponíssou terminal; 4hr). The city itself is uninteresting, so plan on moving out the same day, if possible. Reasonable budget hotels include the *El Greco* (☎061/272 931), *Esperia* (☎276 476) and *Nicos* (☎061/623 757).

Killíni

This small port, south of Pátra (buses), is the main departure point for the Ionian island of **Zákinthos**, and in summer has boats to **Kefalloniá**. Little point in staying, if you time things right.

Vólos and Áyios Konstandínos

Vólos is a large port city – modern and rather grim – in Thessaly, in central Greece. It is easiest reached from Athens by bus (Mavromatéon terminal; 4hr). Ferries and hydrofoils run regularly to the Sporades – **Skíathos**, **Skópelos** and **Alónissos**. Try to complete your journey the same day.

Áyios Konstandínos is an alternative port for the **Sporades**, again with buses from Athens (Mavromatéon terminal; 2hr 30min).

Kími

This is technically an island port – on Évvia (see Chapter Six) – but is mentioned here as it is the main port for the island of **Skíros** in the Sporades. Kími can be reached by Athens by bus.

Thessaloníki

The northern capital has useful if pricey summer hydrofoils to **Skíathos**, **Skópelos** and **Alónissos** in the Sporades. Also regular ferries to these and **north-east Aegean** islands. It's worth exploring the Byzantine churches and Archeological Museum (with Philip of Macedon's tomb treasure). Hotels are plentiful if mostly uninspiring.

Kavála

The main port of northern Greece (3hr by bus from Thessaloníki) offers fast access to **Thássos**, either direct, or from the nearby shuttle point at Keramotí. There are also links to **Samothráki**, **Límnos** and other **northeast Aegean** islands. The city has a characterful harbour area but hotels are in short supply. Try booking ahead at the *Parthenon* (☎051/223 205), *Akropolis* (☎051/223 543) or *Panorama* (☎051/228 412).

Alexandróupoli

The third northern port (6hr by bus from Thessaloníki) has regular ferries to Samothráki. It's a somewhat unenticing place to stay.

Igoumenítsa

Many ferries from Italy call at Igoumenítsa, stopping at Corfu en route. There are regular shuttles across to **Corfu**, plus daily hops to **Páxi**, augmented in summer by hydrofoils. Hotels are plentiful as nobody stays more than a night.

Párga and Astakós

These two small ports, south of Igoumenítsa, have daily ferries to, respectively, **Páxi** and **Itháki** in the Ionian. Párga is a busy, pleasant resort.

GETTING THERE FROM NORTH AMERICA

Only a few carriers fly directly to Greece from North America, and nobody offers direct flights to any of the Greek islands. Most North Americans choose to travel to a gateway European city, and pick up a connecting flight on from there with an associated airline. If you have time, you may well discover that it's cheaper to arrange the final Greece-bound leg of the journey in Europe, in which case your only criterion will be finding a suitable and good-value North America–Europe flight. For details of onward flights from the UK, see "Getting There from Britain".

In general there just isn't enough traffic on the US–Athens routes to make for very cheap fares. The **Greek national airline**, *Olympic Airways*,

only flies out of New York (JFK), Boston, Montreal and Toronto, though the airline can offer reasonably priced add-on flights within Greece, which are especially useful if you want to head straight on to the Greek islands as they leave from the same Athens terminal that you will fly into.

Another option to consider is picking up a flight to Europe and making your way to Greece by train, in which case a **Eurail Pass** makes a reasonable investment – all the details are covered below. For details of train routes, see "Getting There from Britain".

SHOPPING FOR TICKETS

Discount ticket outlets – advertised in the Sunday travel sections of major newspapers – come in several forms. **Consolidators** buy up blocks of tickets that airlines don't think they'll be able to sell at their published fares, and unload them at a discount. Many advertise fares on a one-way basis, enabling you to fly into one city and out from another without penalty. Consolidators normally don't impose advance purchase requirements (although in busy times you should book ahead just to be sure of getting a ticket), but they do often charge very stiff fees for date changes.

Discount agents also deal in blocks of tickets offloaded by the airlines, but they typically offer a range of other travel-related services like insurance, rail passes, youth and student ID cards, car rentals and tours. These agencies tend to be most worthwhile for students and under-26s, who can benefit from a variety of special deals.

AIRLINES IN NORTH AMERICA

Air Canada (in Canada, call directory inquiries, ☎1-800/555-1212, for local toll-free number; US toll-free number is ☎1-800/776-3000).

Air France (☎1-800/237-2747; in Canada, ☎1-800/667-2747).

Alitalia (☎1-800/223-5730).

British Airways (in US, ☎1-800/247-9297; in Canada, ☎1-800/668-1059).

Canadian Airlines (in Canada, ☎1-800/665-1177; in US, ☎1-800/426-7000).

ČSA Czechoslovak Airlines (☎1-800/223-2365).

Delta Airlines (☎1-800/241-4141).

Iberia (in US, ☎1-800/772-4642; in Canada, ☎1-800/423-7421).

KLM (in US, ☎1-800/374-7747; in Canada, ☎1-800/361-5073).

LOT Polish Airlines (☎1-800/223-0593).

Lufthansa (☎1-800/645-3880).

Olympic Airways (☎1-800/223-1226).

Sabena (☎1-800/955-2000).

Swissair (☎1-800/221-4750).

TAP Air Portugal (☎1-800/221-7370).

TWA (☎1-800/892-4141).

United Airlines (☎1-800/538-2929).

DISCOUNT TRAVEL COMPANIES

Air Brokers International, 323 Geary St, Suite 411, San Francisco, CA 94102 (☎1-800/883-3273). *Consolidator.*

Air Courier Association, 191 University Boulevard, Suite 300, Denver, CO 80206 (☎303/278-8810). *Courier flight broker.*

Airhitch, 2472 Broadway, Suite 200, New York, NY 10025 (☎212/864-2000). *Standby-seat broker. For a set price, they guarantee to get you on a flight as close to your preferred destination as possible, within a week.*

Council Travel, Head Office: 205 E 42nd St, New York, NY 10017 (☎1-800/743-1823). *Student travel organization with branches in many US cities. A sister company, Council Charter (☎1-800/223-7402), specializes in charter flights.*

Discount Travel International, Ives Bldg, 114 Forrest Ave, Suite 205, Narberth, PA 19072 (☎1-800/334-9294). *Discount travel club.*

Educational Travel Center, 438 N Frances St, Madison, WI 53703 (☎1-800/747-5551). *Student/youth discount agent.*

Encore Travel Club, 4501 Forbes Blvd, Lanham, MD 20706 (☎1-800/444-9800). *Discount travel club.*

Interworld Travel, 800 Douglass Rd, Miami, FL 33134 (☎305/443-4929). *Consolidator.*

Last Minute Travel Club, 132 Brookline Ave, Boston, MA 02215 (☎1-800/LAST MIN). *Travel club specializing in standby deals.*

Moment's Notice, 425 Madison Ave, New York, NY 10017 (☎212/486-0503). *Discount travel club.*

New Frontiers/Nouvelles Frontières, Head offices: 12 E 33rd St, New York, NY 10016 (☎1-800/366-6387); 1001 Sherbrook East, Suite 720, Montréal, Quebec H2L 1L3 (☎514/526-8444). *French discount travel firm. Other branches in LA, San Francisco and Québec City.*

Now Voyager, 74 Varick St, Suite 307, New York, NY 10013 (☎212/431-1616). *Courier flight broker.*

STA Travel, Head office: 48 East 11th St, New York, NY 10003 (☎1-800/777-0112; nationwide). *Worldwide specialist in independent travel with branches in the Los Angeles, San Francisco and Boston areas.*

TFI Tours International, Head office: 34 W 32nd St, New York, NY 10001 (☎1-800/745-8000). *Consolidator; other offices in Las Vegas, San Francisco, Los Angeles.*

Travac, Head office: 989 6th Ave, New York NY 10018 (☎1-800/872-8800). *Consolidator and charter broker; has another branch in Orlando.*

Travel Avenue, 10 S Riverside, Suite 1404, Chicago, IL 60606 (☎1-800/333-3335). *Discount travel agent.*

Travel Cuts, Head office: 187 College St, Toronto, Ontario M5T 1P7 (☎416/979-2406). *Canadian student travel organization with branches all over the country.*

Travelers Advantage, 3033 S Parker Rd, Suite 900, Aurora, CO 80014 (☎1-800/548-1116). *Discount travel club.*

UniTravel, 1177 N Warson Rd, St Louis, MO 63132 (☎1-800/325-2222). *Consolidator.*

Worldtek Travel, 111 Water St, New Haven, CT 06511 (☎1-800/243-1723). *Discount travel agency.*

Worldwide Discount Travel Club, 1674 Meridian Ave, Miami Beach, FL 33139 (☎305/534-2082). *Discount travel club.*

Travel clubs are another option – most charge an annual membership fee, which may be worth it for their discounts on air tickets and car rental. Some agencies specialize in **charter flights**, which may be even cheaper than anything available on a scheduled flight, but again there's a trade-off: departure dates are fixed, and withdrawal penalties are high (check the refund policy). Student/youth fares can sometimes save you money, though again the best deals are usually those offered by seat consolidators advertising in Sunday newspaper travel sections.

Don't automatically assume that tickets purchased through a travel specialist will be cheapest – once you get a quote, check with the airlines and you may turn up an even better deal. In addition, exercise caution and *never* deal with a company that demands cash up front or refuses to accept payment by credit card.

For destinations not handled by discounters – which applies to most regional airports – you'll have to deal with airlines' published fares. The cheapest of these is an **APEX** (Advance Purchase Excursion) ticket. This carries certain restrictions: you have to book – and pay – at least 21 days before departure and spend at least seven days abroad (maximum stay three months), and you're liable to penalties if you change your schedule. On transatlantic routes there are also winter **Super**

APEX tickets, sometimes known as "Eurosavers" – slightly cheaper than ordinary Apex, but limiting your stay to between 7 and 21 days. Some airlines also issue **Special APEX** tickets to those under 24, often extending the maximum stay to a year.

Note that fares are heavily dependent on **season**, and are highest from June–September; they drop either side of this, and you'll get the best deals during the low season, November–February (excluding Christmas). Note that flying on weekends ordinarily adds $50 or so to the round-trip fare; price ranges quoted in the sections below assume midweek travel.

FROM THE USA

Non-stop flights to Athens out of **New York** on *Olympic* start at around US$700 round trip in winter, rising to around $1100 in summer for a maximum thirty-day stay with seven-day advance purchase. For about the same price, *Olympic* also flies out of **Boston** once a week in winter, twice a week in summer. *Delta* and *TWA* have daily services from New York to Athens via Frankfurt and while fares cost around $300 more than with *Olympic*, a consolidator or agent might be able to get you a flight for around half the cost the airlines themselves quote; round trips run from around $600 in winter, $900 in summer. *United* flights to Athens are via Paris, and there's a good service from **Washington DC** and **Chicago** – the lowest round-trip winter fare is around $800.

One particularly good deal is on *LOT Polish Airlines*, which flies out of New York and Chicago to Athens several times a week via Warsaw. Fares run from around $700 round trip.

Since all scheduled flights to Athens from the **West Coast** go via New York or another eastern city, you basically end up paying for a transcontinental flight on top of the transatlantic fare: round-trip APEX tickets from Seattle, San Francisco or Los Angeles on *TWA* or *Delta* start at $920 in winter, rising to over $1200 in summer. Most European airlines (including *Air France, British Airways, Iberia, KLM* and *Lufthansa*) also connect the West Coast with Greece via their "homeports" in Europe, but these stopovers often mean a wait of a few hours, sometimes even an overnight stop – be sure to ask your ticket agent.

FROM CANADA

As with the US, air fares from Canada to Athens vary tremendously depending upon where you start your journey. The best-value scheduled fare is on *Olympic*, who fly non-stop out of Montréal and Toronto once a week in winter for CDN$1100 round trip, and twice a week in summer for $1500.

KLM operates several flights a week to Athens via Amsterdam, from Toronto, Montréal, Vancouver and Edmonton – from Toronto, expect to pay around $1150 in winter, $1500 in high season. Travelers from Montréal can also try the European carriers *Air France, Alitalia, British Airways, Iberia, Lufthansa, Sabena, Swissair* and *TAP Air Portugal*, all of which operate several flights a week to Athens via major European cities. One unlikely source for good deals is *Czechoslovak Airline (ČSA)*, which flies out of Montréal to Athens via Prague for around $1100.

Finally, *Air Canada* flies to Vienna with connections to Athens on *Olympic*; flights from Vancouver cost $1600 in winter, $1800 in summer.

RAIL PASSES

A **Eurail Pass** is not likely to pay for itself if you're planning to stick to Greece, though it's worth considering if you plan to travel to Greece across Europe from elsewhere. If you're intent only on the Greek Islands, it's not a lot of use. The pass, which must be purchased before arrival in Europe, allows unlimited free train travel in Greece and sixteen other countries. The **Eurail Youthpass** (for under-26s) costs US$398 for 15 days, $578 for one month or $768 for two months; if you're 26 or over you'll have to buy a **first-class pass**, available in 15-day ($498), 21-day ($648), one-month ($798), two-month ($1098) and three-month ($1398) increments.

You stand a better chance of getting your money's worth out of a **Eurail Flexipass**, which is good for a certain number of travel days in a

---

RAIL CONTACTS IN NORTH AMERICA

CIT Tours, 342 Madison Ave, Suite 207, New York, NY 10173 (☎1-800/223-7987).

DER Tours/GermanRail, 9501 W Divon Ave, Suite 400, Rosemont, IL 60018 (☎1-800/421-2929).

Rail Europe, 226 Westchester Ave, White Plains, NY 10604 (☎1-800/438 7245).

ScanTours, 1535 6th St, Suite 205, Santa Monica, CA 90401 (☎1-800/223-7226).

SPECIALIST TOUR OPERATORS

USA

Above the Clouds Trekking, PO Box 398, Worcester, MA 01602 (☎1-800/233-4499). *Greek trekking holidays.*

Adriatic Tours, 691 West 10th St, San Pedro, CA 90731 (☎1-800/262-1718). *City highlights tours and cruise vacations.*

Archeological Tours, 271 Madison Ave, New York, NY 10016 (☎212/986-3054). *Specialist archeological tours.*

Astro Tours, 216 Fourth Ave South, Seattle, WA 98104 (☎206/467-7777). *Cruise packages to the Greek islands.*

Brendan Tours, 15137 Califa St, Van Nuys, CA 91411 (☎1-800/421-8446). *City highlights, cruise packages and car rental.*

Caravan Tours Inc., 401 N Michigan Ave, Suite 2800, Chicago, IL 60611 (☎1-800/621-8338). *All kinds of packages covering the entire country.*

Classic Adventures, PO Box 153, Hamlin, NY 14464-0153 (☎1-800/777-8090). *Trekking, biking and walking tours in June and September, covering archeological sites and coastal trips.*

Classic Holidays, 790 Boston St, Billerica, MA 01821 (☎1-800/752-5055). *Packages from 8 to 21 days, group tours and cruises.*

Cloud Tours Inc, 645 Fifth Ave, New York, NY 10022 (☎1-800/223-7880). *Affordable escorted tours and Mediterranean cruises.*

Educational Tours and Cruises, 14 (R) Wyman St, Medford, MA 02155 (☎1-800/275-4109). *Custom-designed tours to Greece and the islands, specializing in art, history, food and wine, ancient drama, painting, birdwatching, etc.*

Epirotiki Lines, 551 Fifth Ave, New York, NY 10176 (☎212/949-7273). *Greek cruise specialist.*

Globus Gateway, 92–25 Queens Blvd, Rego Park, NY 11374 (☎1-800/221-0090). *Offers a variety of city and island packages.*

Grecian Travel Inc, 29–11 Ditmard Blvd, Astoria, NY 11105 (☎1-800/368-6262). *For years, a leader in travel to Greece.*

Guaranteed Travel, 83 South St, Box 269, Morristown, NJ 07963 (☎201/540-1770). *Specializes in "Greece-Your-Way" independent travel.*

Hellenic Adventures, 4150 Harriet Ave South, Minneapolis, MN 55409 (☎612/824-2180). *Cruises and city highlights.*

Homeric Tours, 55 E 59th St, New York, NY 10017 (☎1-800/223-5570). *All-inclusive tours from 9 to 23 days, as well as cruises and charter flights.*

Insight International Tours, 745 Atlantic Ave, Boston, MA 02111 (☎1-800/582-8380). *General Greek vacations.*

Odyssey Travel Center, 7735 Old Georgetown Rd, Bethesda, MD 20814 (☎401/657-4647). *Independent package tours, with extensions available to Egypt, Israel and Turkey.*

Topline Travel, 36-01 28 Ave, Long Island City, NY 11103 (☎1-800/221-1289). *Escorted tours of Athens and the islands.*

Triaena Travel, 850 Seventh Ave, New York, NY 10019 (☎1-800/223-1273). *Packages, cruises, apartments and villas.*

Valef Cruises, Box 391, Ambler, PA 19002 (☎215/641-1624). *Yachting trips and charters.*

CANADA

Adventures Abroad, 1027 W. Broadway, Suite 310, Vancouver, British Columbia, VGH 1E3 (☎604/732-9922). *General operator, offering group and individual tours and cruises.*

Auratours, 1470 Peel St, Suite 252, Montréal, Quebec H3A 1TL (☎1-800/363-0323). *General operator, offering group and individual tours and cruises.*

Chat Tours, 241 Bedford Rd, Toronto, Ontario M5R 2K9 (☎1-800/268-1180). *Motorcoach and sea tours, and cruises.*

Trianena Poseidon Tours International, 72 Hutchison St, Montréal, Quebec H3N 1ZL (☎1-800/361-0374). *Custom-made tours, yacht charters and cruises, and apartment and villa vacations.*

Worldwide Adventures, 920 Yonge St, Suite 747, Toronto, Ontario M4W 3C7 (☎1-800/387-1483). *General operator, offering group and individual tours and cruises.*

two-month period. This, too, comes in under-26/first-class versions: 5 days cost $255/$348; 10 days, $398/$560; and 15 days, $540/$740. A further alternative is to attempt to buy an *InterRail* Pass in Europe (see "Getting There from Britain") – most agents don't check residential qualifications, but once you're in Europe it'll be too late to buy a *Eurail Pass* if you have problems. You can purchase *Eurail* passes from one of the agents listed on p.15.

GETTING THERE FROM AUSTRALASIA

It's fairly easy to track down flights from Australia to Athens, less so from New Zealand, but given the prices and most people's travel plans, you'll probably do better looking for some kind of Round-the-World ticket that includes Greece. If London is your first destination in Europe, and you've picked up a reasonably good deal on a flight there, it's probably best to wait until you reach the UK before arranging your onward travel to Greece; see "Getting there from Britain" for all the details.

Note that **prices** given below are in local dollars for published mid-season return fares; travel agents (see box overpage) should be able to get at least ten percent off these. **Students** and anyone **under 26** should try *STA Travel* in the first instance which has a wide range of discounted fares on offer.

FROM AUSTRALIA

Cheapest fares to Athens **from Australia** are with *Aeroflot* ($1650), flying weekly out of Sydney via Moscow, and *Thai* ($2242), which flies from Sydney, Melbourne, Perth or Brisbane via Bangkok. Otherwise, you can fly daily from Perth or Sydney, and several times a week from Melbourne or Brisbane, for $2399 with one of the following: *Olympic* (via Bangkok), *Alitalia* (Bangkok, Rome), *Singapore* (Singapore), *KLM* (Singapore, Amsterdam), *Lufthansa* (Frankfurt) and *United* (Los Angeles, Washington, Paris). *British Airways* and *Qantas* can get you to London via Singapore or Bangkok for the same price, but charge an extra $430 to Athens, while giving you a free return flight within Europe. You can undercut this with their *Global Explorer Pass* ($2499), a **Round-the-World** fare that allows six stopovers worldwide wherever these two airlines fly to (except South America). Also worth considering is *Garuda's* $1685 fare from Sydney, Townsville or Cairns via Jakarta to various European cities, from where you could pick up a cheap onward flight or continue **overland** to Athens. **Departure tax** from Athens, sometimes added to the ticket at the time of purchase, is $33.

FROM NEW ZEALAND

From New Zealand, best deals to Athens are with *Thai* ($2399 via Bangkok) or *Singapore* ($2499 via Singapore), and a very versatile offer with *Lufthansa* ($2899), who can route you through anywhere that Air New Zealand or Qantas fly – including Los Angeles, Singapore, Sydney, Hong Kong or Tokyo – for a stopover. *British Airways/Qantas* can get you to Europe, but not Athens, for $2699, so again you're better off with their *Global Explorer Pass* (see above) at $3099. Surprisingly expensive at $3974 are *Alitalia* (via Rome) and *United* (Los Angeles, Washington, Paris). **Departure tax** from Athens is $42.

AGENTS AND AIRLINES IN AUSTRALASIA

Note: all Australian phone numbers are due to have extra digits added over the next two years.

TRAVEL AGENTS

Adventure World, 73 Walker St, North Sydney (☎02/956 7766); 8 Victoria Ave, Perth (☎09/221 2300).

Flight Centres, *Australia*: Circular Quay, Sydney (☎02/241 2422); Bourke St, Melbourne (☎03/650 2899); plus other branches nationwide.

New Zealand: National Bank Towers, 205–225 Queen St, Auckland (☎09/309 6171); Shop 1M, National Mutual Arcade, 152 Hereford St, Christchurch (☎09/379 7145); 50–52 Willis St, Wellington (☎04/472 8101); other branches countrywide.

Grecian Holidays, 115 Pitt St, Sydney (☎02/231 1277); 71 Grey St, Brisbane (☎07/846 4006).

Grecian Mediterranean Holidays, 49 Ventnor Ave, West Perth (☎09/321 3930).

Grecian Tours Travel, 237a Lonsdale St, Melbourne (☎03/663 3711).

Greek National Tourist Office, 51 Pitt St, Sydney (☎02/241 1663).

Greek Tours, Floor 2, 243 Edward St, Brisbane (☎07/221 9700).

House of Holidays, 298 Clayton Rd, Clayton, Victoria (☎03/543 5800).

STA Travel, *Australia*: 732 Harris St, Ultimo, Sydney (☎02/212 1255); 256 Flinders St, Melbourne (☎03/347 4711); other offices in Townsville, Cairns and state capitals.

New Zealand: Traveller's Centre, 10 High St, Auckland (☎09/309 9995); 233 Cuba St, Wellington (☎04/385 0561); 223 High St, Christchurch (☎03/379 9098); other offices in Dunedin, Palmerston North and Hamilton.

AIRLINES

☎ *008 numbers are toll free, but only apply if dialled outside the city in the address.*

Aeroflot, 388 George St, Sydney (☎02/233 7148). No NZ office.

Alitalia, Orient Overseas Building, 32 Bridge St, Sydney (☎02/247 1308); Floor 6, Trust Bank Building, 229 Queen St, Auckland (☎09/379 4457).

British Airways, 64 Castlereagh St, Sydney (☎02/258 3300); Dilworth Building, cnr Queen and Customs streets, Auckland (☎09/367 7500).

Garuda, 175 Clarence St, Sydney (☎02/334 9900); 120 Albert St, Auckland (☎09/366 1855).
KLM 5 Elizabeth St, Sydney (☎02/231 6333/008 222 747). No NZ office.

Lufthansa/Air Lauda, 143 Macquarie St, Sydney (☎02/367 3800); 109 Queen St, Auckland (☎09/303 1529).

Olympic Airways, *S.A.* Floor 3, 37–49 Pitt St, Sydney (☎02/251 2044). No NZ office.

Qantas, International Square, Jamison St, Sydney (☎02/957 0111/236 3636); Qantas House, 154 Queen St, Auckland (☎09/303 2506).

Singapore Airlines, 17 Bridge St, Sydney (☎02/236 0111); Lower Ground Floor, West Plaza Building, cnr Customs and Albert streets, Auckland (☎09/379 3209).

Thai 75–77 Pitt St, Sydney (☎02/844 0999/008 221 320); Kensington Swan Building, 22 Fanshawe St, Auckland (☎09377 3886).

United 10 Barrack St, Sydney (☎02/237 8888); 7 City Road, Auckland (☎09/307 9500).

TRAVELLERS WITH DISABILITIES

It is all too easy to wax lyrical over the attractions of the Greek islands: the stepped, narrow alleys, the ease of island hopping by ferry, the thrill of clambering around the archeological sites. It is almost impossible, on the other hand, for the able-bodied travel writer to see these attractions as potential hazards for anyone who has some difficulty in walking or is wheelchair-bound or suffers from some other disability.

However, don't be discouraged. It is possible to enjoy an inexpensive and trauma-free holiday in Greece if some time is devoted to gathering **information** before arrival. Addresses of contact organizations are published below and overpage, and the Greek National Tourist Office is a good first step as long as you have specific questions to put to them; they publish a useful questionnaire which you could send to hotels or owners of apartment/villa accommodation. Where possible, try and double check all information, as it's too often outdated.

PLANNING A HOLIDAY

There are **organized tours and holidays** specifically for people with disabilities – both *Thomsons* and *Horizon* in Britain will advise on the suitability of holidays advertised in their brochures. If you want to be more independent, it's perfectly possible, provided that you do not leave home with the vague hope that things will turn out all right, and that "people will help out" when you need assistance. This cannot be relied on. You must either be completely confident that you can manage alone, or travel with an able-bodied friend (or two).

It's important to become an authority on where you must be self-reliant and where you may expect help, especially regarding transport and accommodation. For example, to get between the terminals at Athens airport, you will have to fight for a taxi; it is not the duty of the airline staff to find you one, and there is no trace of an organized line.

It is also vital to **be honest** – with travel agencies, insurance companies, companions and, above all, with yourself. Know your limitations and make sure others know them. If you do not use a wheelchair all the time but your walking capabilities are limited, remember that you are likely to need to cover greater distances while travelling (often over tougher terrain and in hotter weather) than you are used to. If you use one, take a wheelchair with you, have it serviced before you go and carry a repair kit.

Read your travel **insurance** small print carefully to make sure that people with a pre-existing medical condition are not excluded. And use your travel agent to make your journey simpler: **airlines** or bus companies can cope better if they are expecting you, with a wheelchair provided at airports and staff primed to help. A **medical certificate** of your fitness to travel, provided by your doctor, is also extremely useful; some airlines or insurance companies may insist on it.

Make a **list** of all the facilities that will make your life easier while you are away. You may want a ground-floor room, or access to a large elevator; you may have special dietary requirements, or need level ground to enable you to reach shops, beaches, bars and places of interest. You should also keep track of all your other special needs, making sure, for example, that you have extra supplies of drugs – carried with you if you fly – and a prescription including the generic name in case of emergency. Carry spares of any kind of drug, clothing or equipment that might be hard to find in Greece; if there's an association representing people with your disability, contact them early in the planning process.

USEFUL CONTACTS

National Tourist Organization of Greece : See p.27 for addresses. *Offers general advice on terrain and climate. They have nothing specific for disabled visitors except a brief list of hotels which may be suitable.*

In Greece

Association Hermes, Patriarchou 13, Grigouiou E, 16542, Argyroupolis (☎01/99 61 887). *Can advise disabled visitors to Greece.*

continues over

Evyenia Stravropoulou, Lavinia Tours: Egnatía 101, 541 10 Thessaloníki (☎031/240 041). *Will advise disabled visitors and has tested many parts of Greece in her wheelchair. She also organizes tours within Greece.*

In the UK

Holiday Care Service, 2 Old Bank Chambers, Station Rd, Horley, Surrey RH6 9HW (☎01293/774535). *Publishes a fact sheet, and also runs a useful "Holiday Helpers" service for disabled travellers.*

Mobility International, 228 Borough High St, London SE1 1JX (☎0171/403 5688). *Issues a quarterly newsletter on developments in disabled travel.*

Opus 23, Sourdock Hill, Barkisland, Halifax, W Yorks HX4 0AG (☎01422/375999). *Part of Grecofile; will advise on and arrange independent holidays, or for those with carers.*

RADAR, 25 Mortimer St, London W1N 8AB (☎0171/250 3222). *Publish fact sheets and an annual guide to international travel for the disabled.*

Tripscope, Evelyn Rd, London W4 5JL (☎0181/994 9294). *Transport advice to most countries for all disabilities.*

North America

Directions Unlimited, 720 N Bedford Rd, Bedford Hills, NY 10507 (☎1-800/533-5343). *Tour operator specializing in custom tours for people with disabilities.*

Information Center for People with Disabilities, Fort Point Place, 27-43 Wormwood St, Boston, MA 02210 (☎617/727-5540; TDD ☎617/345-9743).

Clearing house for information, including travel, primarily in Massachusetts.

Jewish Rehabilitation Hospital, 3205 Place Alton Goldbloom, Montréal, Quebec H7V 1R2 (☎514/688-9550, ext 226). *Guidebooks and travel information.*

Kéroul, 4545 Ave Pierre de Coubertin, CP 1000, Station M, Montréal, Quebec H1V 3R2 (☎514/252-3104). *Organization promoting and facilitating travel for mobility-impaired people, primarily in Quebec. Annual membership $10.*

Mobility International USA, PO Box 10767, Eugene, OR 97440 (Voice & TDD: ☎503/343-1284). *Information and referral services, access guides, tours and exchange programmes. Annual membership $20 (includes quarterly newsletter).*

Society for the Advancement of Travel for the Handicapped (SATH), 347 5th Ave, New York, NY 10016 (☎212/447-7284). *Non-profit travel-industry referral service that passes queries on to its members as appropriate; allow plenty of time for a response.*

Travel Information Service, Moss Rehabilitation Hospital, 1200 West Tabor Rd, Philadelphia, PA 19141 (☎215/456-9600). *Telephone information and referral service.*

Twin Peaks Press, Box 129, Vancouver, WA 98666; ☎206/694-2462 or ☎1-800/637-2256). *Publisher of the Directory of Travel Agencies for the Disabled ($19.95), listing more than 370 agencies worldwide; Travel for the Disabled ($14.95); the Directory of Accessible Van Rentals and Wheelchair Vagabond ($9.95), loaded with personal tips.*

VISAS AND RED TAPE

UK and all other EC nationals need only a valid passport for entry to Greece; you are no longer stamped in on arrival or out upon departure, and in theory at least enjoy uniform civil rights with Greek citizens. US, Australian, New Zealand, Canadian and most non-EC Europeans receive entry and exit stamps in their passports and can stay, as tourists, for ninety days.

If you are planning to **travel overland**, you should check current visa requirements for Hungary, Romania and Bulgaria, or for newly independent Slovenia and Croatia at their closest consulates; transit visas for most of these territories are at present issued at the borders, though at a higher price than if obtained in advance at a local consulate.

VISA EXTENSIONS

If you wish to stay in Greece for longer than three months, you should officially apply for an **extension**. This can be done in the larger cities like Athens, Thessaloníki, Pátra and Iráklio (Crete) through the *Ipiresía Allodhapón* (Aliens' Bureau); prepare yourself for concerted bureaucracy. In remoter locations you visit the local police station, where staff are usually more cooperative.

Unless of Greek descent, visitors from **non-EC countries** are currently allowed only one six-month extension to a tourist visa, which costs 11,000dr. In theory, **EC nationals** are allowed to stay indefinitely but, at the time of writing, must still present themselves every six months or year, according to whether they have a non-employment resident visa or a work permit; the

first extension is free, but you will be charged for subsequent extensions. In all cases, the procedure should be set in motion a couple of weeks before your time runs out – and, if you don't have a work permit, you will be required to present pink, personalized bank **exchange receipts** (see "Costs, Money and Banks: Currency Regulations" overpage) totalling at least 45,000dr for the preceding three months, as proof that you have sufficient funds to support yourself without working. Some individuals get around the law by leaving Greece every three months and re-entering a few days later for a new tourist stamp. However, with the recent flood of Albanian and ex-Yugoslavian refugees into the country, and a smaller influx of east Europeans looking for work, security and immigration personnel don't always look very kindly on this practice.

If you **overstay** your time and then leave under your own steam – ie are not deported – you'll be given a 22,000dr spot fine upon departure, effectively a double-priced retroactive visa extension – no excuses will be entertained.

CUSTOMS REGULATIONS

For EC citizens travelling between EC countries, limits on goods which have been taxed already have been relaxed enormously. However, **duty-free allowances** are as follows: 200 cigarettes or 50 cigars, two litres of still table wine, one litre of spirits and 60ml of perfume.

Exporting **antiquities** without a permit is a serious offence; **drug smuggling**, it goes without saying, incurs severe penalties.

GREEK EMBASSIES ABROAD

Australia 9 Turrana St, Yarralumla, Canberra, ACT 2600 (☎062/273-3011).

Britain 1a Holland Park, London W11 (☎0171/221 6467).

Canada 80 Maclaren St, Ottawa, ON K2P 0K6 (☎613/238-6271).

Ireland 1 Upper Pembroke St, Dublin 2 (☎01/767254).

New Zealand Cumberland House, 237 Willis St, PO Box 27157, Wellington (☎04/847-556).

USA 2221 Massachusetts Ave NW, Washington DC 20008 (☎202/667-3168).

INSURANCE

UK and other EC nationals are officially enti-tled to free medical care in Greece (see "Health Matters" p.25) upon presentation of an E111 form, available from most post offices. "Free", however, means admittance only to the lowest grade of state hospital (known as a *yenikó nosokomío*), and does not include nursing care or the cost of medi-cations. In practice, hospital staff tend to greet E111s with uncomprehending looks, and you may have to request reimbursment by the NHS upon return home. If you need prolonged medical care, you'll prefer to make use of private treatment, which is expensive.

Some form of **travel insurance**, therefore, is advisable – and essential for **North Americans and Australasians**, whose countries have no formal health care agreements with Greece (other than allowing for free emergency trauma treatment). For medical claims, keep receipts, including those from pharmacies. You will have to pay for all private medical care on the spot

(insurance claims can be processed if you have hospital treatment) but it can all be (eventually) claimed back. Travel insurance usually provides cover for the loss of baggage, money and tickets, too. If you're thinking of renting a moped or motorbike on the islands (most people do), make sure the policy covers motorbike accidents.

EUROPEAN COVER

In Britain, there are a number of low-cost specialist insurance companies including *Endsleigh*, 97–107 Southampton Row, London WC1 (☎0171/436 4451), *Campus Travel*, 52 Grosvenor Gardens, London SW1 (☎0171/730 3402), and *Columbus*, 17 Devonshire Square, London EC2 (☎0171/375 0111). At all of these you can buy two weeks' basic cover in Greece for around £15, £22 for a month.

Most **banks** and **credit card** issuers also offer some sort of vacation insurance, often auto-matic if you pay for the holiday with a card. In these circumstances, it's vital to check what the policy actually covers.

NORTH AMERICAN COVER

Before buying an insurance policy, check that you're not already covered. **Canadians** are usually covered for medical mishaps overseas by their provincial health plans. Holders of official student/teacher/youth cards are entitled to acci-dent coverage and hospital in-patient benefits. **Students** will often find that their student health coverage extends during the vacations and for one term beyond the date of last enrollment. Bank and credit cards (particularly *American Express*) often have certain levels of medical or other insurance included, and travel insurance may also be included if you use a major credit or

---

TRAVEL INSURANCE COMPANIES IN NORTH AMERICA

Access America, PO Box 90310, Richmond, VA 23230 (☎1-800/284-8300).

Carefree Travel Insurance, PO Box 310, 120 Mineola Blvd, Mineola, NY 11501 (☎1-800/323-3149).

International Student Insurance Service (ISIS) – sold by *STA Travel*, see "Getting There from North America" for addresses.

Travel Assistance International, 1133 15th St NW, Suite 400, Washington, DC 20005 (☎1-800/821-2828).

Travel Guard, 1145 Clark St, Stevens Point, WI 54481 (☎1-800/826-1300).

Travel Insurance Services, 2930 Camino Diablo, Suite 300, Walnut Creek, CA 94596 (☎1-800/937-1387).

charge card to pay for your trip. **Homeowners' or renters'** insurance often covers theft or loss of documents, money and valuables while overseas, though conditions and maximum amounts vary from company to company.

After exhausting the possibilities above, you might want to contact a specialist **travel insurance** company; your travel agent can usually recommend one, or see the box opposite. Policies are comprehensive (accidents, illnesses, delayed or lost luggage, cancelled flights, etc), but maximum payouts tend to be meagre. Premiums vary, so shop around. The best deals are usually to be had through student travel agencies – *ISIS* policies, for example, cost $80–105 for a month. If you're transiting through Britain, you may prefer to buy a **British policy** (see above), which is usually cheaper and wider in scope.

Most North American travel policies apply only to items lost, stolen or damaged while in the custody of an identifiable, responsible third party – hotel porter, airline, luggage consignment, etc. Even in these cases you will have to contact the local police within a certain time limit to have a complete report made out so that your insurer can process the claim. Note also that very few insurers will arrange on-the-spot payments in the event of a major expense or loss; you will usually be reimbursed only after going home.

INSURANCE REPORTS

In all cases of loss or theft of goods, you will have to contact the local police to have a **report** made out so that your insurer can process the claim. This can occasionally be a tricky business in Greece, since many officials simply won't accept that anything could be stolen on their turf, or at least don't want to take responsibility for it. Be persistent and if necessary enlist the support of the local tourist police or tourist office.

COSTS, MONEY AND BANKS

The costs of living in Greece have spiralled during the years of EC membership: the days of renting an island house for a pittance are gone forever, and food prices at corner shops now differ little from those of other member countries. However, outside the established resorts, travel in the islands remains reasonably priced, with the cost of restaurant meals, accommodation and public transport as cheap as anywhere in northern or western Europe.

Prices depend on where and when you go. The larger tourist resorts and trendier islands (like Míkonos) are more expensive, and costs everywhere increase in July, August and at Easter. **Solo travellers** invariably spend more than if they were sharing food and rooms. An additional frustration is the relative lack of single rooms.

Students with an *International Student Identity Card* (*ISIC*) can get free – or fifty percent discount off – admission fees at most archeological sites and museums. These, and other occasional discounts, however, are sometimes limited to EC students only.

SOME BASIC COSTS

On most islands you can get by on a **budget** of £16–20/US$24–30 a day, which will get you basic accommodation, breakfast, picnic lunch, and a simple evening meal. Camping would cut costs marginally. On £25–30/$38–45 a day you could be living quite well and also treating yourself to motorbike or car rental.

Inter-island **ferries**, the one other main expense, are quite reasonably priced, helped by government subsidies to preserve island communities. A deck-class ticket from Pireás, the port of Athens, to Crete or Sámos, both 12-to-14-hour trips, costs about £12/US$18. For half the cost, there are dozens of closer islands in reach.

The simplest double **room** can generally be had for £11–17/$16.50–25.50 a night, depending on the location and the plumbing arrangements. Organized **campsites** cost little more than £2.50/US$3.75 per person, with similar charges per tent and perhaps 25 percent more for a camper van. With discretion you can camp for free in the more remote, rural areas.

A basic taverna **meal** with local wine can be had for around £6/US$9 a head. Add a better bottle of wine, seafood, or more careful cooking, and it could be up to £10/US$15 a head – but you'll rarely pay more than that. Sharing seafood, Greek salads and dips is a good way to keep costs down in the better restaurants, but even in the most developed of resorts, with inflated "international" menus you'll often be able to find a more earthy but decent taverna where the locals eat.

CURRENCY

Greek currency is the **drachma** (*dhrahmí*), and the exchange rate is currently around 360dr to the pound sterling, 235dr to the US dollar.

The most common **notes** in circulation are those of 50, 100, 500, 1000 and 5000 (a 10,000 note is due shortly) drachmas (*dhrahmés*), while **coins** come in denominations of 5, 10, 20, 50 and 100dr; you might come across 1dr and 2dr coins, too, though they're rarely used these days.

BANKS AND EXCHANGE

Greek **banks** are normally open Monday–Thursday 8.30am–2pm, Friday 8.30am–1.30pm. Certain branches in larger island towns or tourist centres are open extra hours in the evenings and on Saturday mornings for exchanging money, while outside these times larger hotels and travel agencies can often change money. Always take your passport with you as proof of identity and be prepared for at least one long line – usually you have to line up once to have the transaction approved and again to pick up the cash.

The safest way to carry money is **travellers' cheques**. These can be obtained from banks (even if you don't have an account) or from offices of *Thomas Cook* and *American Express*; you'll pay a commission of 1–2 percent. When exchanging money in Greece using travellers' cheques a **commission** of 400–800dr is charged, so you won't want to change too many small

amounts. You can cash the cheques at most banks and post offices, and (often at poorer rates) at quite a number of hotels, agencies and tourist shops.

Most British banks can issue current account holders with a **Eurocheque** card and cheque-book, with which you can pay for things in some shops and withdraw drachmas from cash machines or Greek banks. An annual fee is payable for this service, plus 2 percent processing charge on the debit facility, but usually there's no commission on straightforward transactions. The current limit is 45,000dr per cheque.

Exchanging money at the **post office** has some considerable advantages in Greece. You miss out on the lines at banks and have access to exchange almost anywhere you go. There are a number of small islands that have no bank but they almost all have a post office. Commissions levied for both cheques and cash tend, at about 300dr per transaction, to be much lower than at banks.

Finally, there is no need to change foreign currency into drachmas **before arrival** unless you're coming in at some ungodly hour at one of the remoter land or sea frontier posts, or on a Sunday. Airport arrival lounges will always have an exchange booth operating for passengers on incoming international flights.

CREDIT CARDS AND ATMs

Major **credit cards** are accepted only by the more expensive shops, hotels and restaurants. They're useful – indeed almost essential – for renting cars, for example, but not much use in the cheaper tavernas or hotels.

If you run short of money, you can get a **cash advance on a credit card**, but be warned that the minimum amount is 15,000dr. The *Emborikí Trápeza* (Commercial Bank) handles *Visa*; the *Ethnikí Trápeza* (National Bank) services *Access/Mastercard* customers. However, there is usually a 2 percent credit card charge, often unfavourable rates and always interminable delays.

It is much easier to use the small but growing network of Greek **cashpoint machines (ATMs)**. The most useful and well distributed are those of the *Trápeza Písteos* (*Credit Bank*), which will accept *Visa* and *American Express*. In the larger towns and airports the *Commercial* and *National* banks have a number of machines catering for a range of card-holders: *Plus System* and *Visa* at the *Commercial* (*Emborikí Trápeza*), *Cirrus* and *Mastercard/Access* at the *National* (*Ethnikí Trápeza*). You will find ATMs, these days, in most towns of any size – and in some of the bigger resorts. They are not yet to be seen, though, on most of the smaller islands.

EMERGENCY CASH

In an emergency, you can arrange to have **money sent** from home to a bank in Greece. Receiving funds via telex takes a minimum of three days and often up to six days, so be prepared for delays. **From the UK**, a bank charge of 3 percent, or minimum £17, maximum £35, is levied. Bank drafts can also be sent, with higher commission rates.

From the US and Canada, funds can be sent via *Western Union* (☎1-800/325-6000) or *American Express MoneyGram* (☎1-800/543-4080). Both companies' fees depend on the destination and the amount being transferred, but as an example, wiring $1000 to Europe will cost around $75. The funds should be available for collection at *Amex*'s or *Western Union*'s local office within minutes of being sent.

CURRENCY REGULATIONS

Greek currency restrictions state that you can't **import** more than 100,000dr to Greece, nor export more than 20,000dr. You are also required to declare foreign banknotes worth more than US$1000: it would makes sense to do this to minimize the hassles if you want to take the currency out again.

If you have any reason to believe that you'll be acquiring large quantities of drachmas – from work or sale of goods – declare everything on arrival, then request (and save) pink, personalized **receipts** for each exchange transaction. Otherwise you may find that you can only re-exchange a limited sum of drachmas on departure. These pink receipts are also essential for obtaining a visa extension (see p.21).

HEALTH MATTERS

There are no required inoculations for Greece, though it's wise to have a typhoid-cholera booster, and to ensure that you are up to date on tetanus and polio. Don't forget to take out travel insurance (see "Insurance" p.22), so that you're covered in case of serious illness or accidents.

The water is safe pretty much everywhere, though you will come across shortages or brackish supplies on some of the drier and more remote islands. Bottled water is widely available if you're feeling cautious.

SPECIFIC HAZARDS

The main health problems experienced by visitors have to do with over-exposure to the sun, and the odd nasty from the sea. To combat the former, wear a hat and drink plenty of fluids in the hot months to avoid any danger of **sunstroke**, and don't underestimate the power of even a hazy sun to **burn**.

For sea-wear, a pair of goggles for swimming and footwear for walking over wet rocks are useful.

HAZARDS OF THE DEEP

In the sea, you may just have the bad luck to meet an armada of **jellyfish**, especially in late summer; they come in various colours and sizes including invisible and minute. Various over-the-counter remedies are sold in resort pharmacies; baking soda or ammonia also help to lessen the sting.

Less vicious but more common are black, spiky **sea urchins**, which infest rocky shorelines year-round; if you step on or graze one, a needle (you can crudely sterilize it by heat from a cigarette lighter) and olive oil are effective for removing spines from your anatomy; they should be extracted, or they will fester.

The worst maritime danger – fortunately very rare – seems to be the **weever fish**, which buries itself in tidal zone sand with just its poisonous dorsal and gill spines protruding. If you tread on one the sudden pain is unmistakably excruciating, and the venom is exceptionally potent. Consequences can range up to permanent paralysis of the affected area, so the imperative first aid is to immerse your foot in water as hot as you can stand. This serves to degrade the toxin and relieve the swelling of joints and attendant pain.

SANDFLIES, MOSQUITOES AND SNAKES

If you are sleeping on or near a **beach**, a wise precaution is to use insect repellent, either lotion or wrist/ankle bands, and/or a tent with a screen to guard against **sandflies**. You are unlikely to be infected by these, but they are potentially dangerous, carrying visceral leishmaniasis, a rare parasitic infection characterized by chronic fever, listlessness and weight loss.

Mosquitoes (*kounóupia*) are less worrying – in Greece they don't carry anything worse than a vicious bite – but they can be infuriating. The best solution is to burn pyrethrum incense coils (*spíres* or *fidhákia* in Greek); these are widely and cheaply available, though smelly. Better if you can get them are the small electrical devices which vaporize an odourless insecticide tablet. Insect repellent is available from most general stores and kiosks.

The **adder** and **scorpion** are found in Greece, though both are shy; just take care when climbing over dry-stone walls where snakes like to sun themselves, and don't put hands/feet in places, ie shoes, where you haven't looked first.

PHARMACIES AND DRUGS

For **minor complaints** it's easiest to go to the local *farmakío*. Greek pharmacists are highly trained and dispense a number of medicines which elsewhere could only be prescribed by a doctor. In the larger towns and resorts there'll usually be one who speaks good English. Pharmacies are usually closed evenings and Saturday mornings, but are supposed to have a sign on their door referring you to the nearest one open. **Homeopathic and herbal** remedies are quite widely available, too, and a few of the larger island towns have homeopathic pharmacies, delineated by the green cross sign.

If you regularly use any form of **prescription drug** you should bring along a copy of the prescription together with the generic name of the drug – this will help should you need to replace it and also avoid possible problems with customs officials. In this context, it's worth being aware that codeine is banned in Greece. If you import any, even the common American Empirin-Codeine compound, you just might find yourself in serious trouble, so check labels carefully.

Contraceptive pills are more readily available every year, but don't count on availability outside of a few large island towns. **Condoms**, however, are inexpensive and ubiquitous – just ask for *profilaktiká* (or more slangy, *plastiká*) at any pharmacy or corner *períptero* (kiosk); the pill, too, can be obtained from a *farmakío*.

Lastly, **hay fever** sufferers should be prepared for the early Greek pollen season, at its height from April to June. If you are taken by surprise, pharmacists stock tablets and creams.

DOCTORS AND HOSPITALS

For serious **medical attention** phone ☎166 – you'll find English-speaking doctors in any of the bigger towns or resorts; the tourist police (☎171 in Athens) or your consulate should be able to come up with some names if you have any difficulty.

In **emergencies**, treatment is given free in **state hospitals** – for cuts, broken bones, etc – though you will only get the most basic level of nursing care. Greek families routinely take in food and bedding for relatives, so as a tourist you'll be at a severe disadvantage.

Somewhat better are the ordinary state-run **outpatient clinics** (*yatría*) attached to most public hospitals and also found in rural locales; these operate on a first-come, first-served basis; usual hours are 8am to noon.

Don't forget to obtain **receipts** for the cost of all drugs and medical treatment; without them, you won't be able to claim back the money on your travel insurance.

INFORMATION AND MAPS

The National Tourist Organisation of Greece (*Ellinikós Organismós Tourismoú*, or *EOT*; *GNTO* abroad) publishes an impressive array of free, glossy, regional pamphlets, which are good for getting an idea of where you want to go, even if the actual text should be taken with an occasional grain of salt. Also available from the EOT are a reasonable fold-out map of the country, a large number of brochures on special interests and festivals, and ferry timetables.

The EOT maintains **offices abroad** in most European capitals, plus major cities in Australia and North America (see box below for details).

TOURIST OFFICES

In Greece, you will find **EOT offices** in most of the larger island towns and resorts. The principal office is in Athens, on Platía Síndagma, inside the National Bank of Greece. Here, in addition to the usual leaflets, you can pick up weekly **schedules for the inter-island ferries** – not 100 percent reliable, but useful as a guideline. EOT staff are very helpful for advice on ferry and bus departures, and often give assistance with **accommodation**.

Where there is no EOT office, you can get information (and often a range of leaflets) from municipally run **tourist offices** or from the **Tourist Police**. The latter are basically a branch (often just a single delegate) of the local police. They can sometimes provide you with lists of rooms to let, which they regulate, and they are in general helpful and efficient.

MAPS

Maps are an endless source of confusion in Greece. Each cartographic company seems to have its own peculiar system of transcribing Greek letters into English – and these, as often as not, do not match the transliterations on the road signs.

The most reliable **general maps** of Greece are the two *Geo Center* maps "Greece and the Islands" and "Greek Islands/Aegean Sea", which

GREEK NATIONAL TOURIST OFFICES ABROAD

Australia
51 Pitt St, Sydney, NSW 2000 (☎02/241-1663).

Britain
4 Conduit St, London W1R 0DJ (☎0171/734 5997).

Canada
1300 Bay St, Main Level, Toronto, ON M5R 3K8 (☎416/968-2220).

1223 rue de la Montagne, QCH 3G, Montréal, Quebec (☎514/871-1535).

Denmark
Copenhagen Vester Farimagsgade 1,2 DK 1606-Kobenhavn V (☎325-332).

Netherlands
Leidsestraat 13, NS 1017 Amsterdam (☎20/254-212).

Norway
Ovre Stottsgate 15B, 0157 Oslo 1 (☎2/426-501).

Sweden
Grev Turigatan 2, PO Box 5298, 10246 Stockholm (☎8/679 6480).

USA
645 Fifth Ave, New York, NY 10022 (☎212/421-5777).

168 North Michigan Ave, Chicago, IL (☎312/782-1084).

611 West 6th St, Los Angeles, CA (☎213/626-6696).

If your home country isn't listed here, apply to the embassy. Note that there are no Greek tourist offices in Ireland or New Zealand.

together cover the country at a scale of 1:300,000. The single fold-up *Freytag-Berndt* 1:650,000 is a good alternative. The *Michelin #980* runs a poor third. All these are widely available in Britain and North America, though less easily in Greece; see the list of map outlets below. *Freytag-Berndt* also publishes a series of more detailed maps on various Greek island groups; these are best bought overseas, from specialist outlets.

Maps of **individual islands** are more easily available on the spot, and while some are wildly inaccurate or obsolete, with strange hieroglyphic symbology, others are reliable and up-to-date. The most comprehensive, though not always the most accurate series, covering most islands of any size and available overseas, is published by *Toubi*.

HIKING/TOPOGRAPHICAL MAPS

Hiking/topographical maps of the islands are hard to obtain. The best are the 1:50,000 sheets published in the Greek mountaineering magazine *Korfes*, and if you're in Athens you can buy back issues at the magazine's office at Platía Kentrikí 16, Aharnés (☎01/24 61 528).

The *Korfes* maps are based on the older maps of the **Army Geographical Service** (*Yeografikí Ipiresía Stratoú*), which cover all areas of the country. You can obtain these in Athens, too, if you visit the *YIS* at Evelpídhon 4, north of Aréos Park, on Monday, Wednesday or Friday from 8am to noon only. All foreigners must leave their passport with the gate guard; EC citizens may proceed directly to the sales hall, where efficient, computerized transactions take just a few minutes. Other nationals will probably have to go upstairs

---

MAP OUTLETS

UK
London
National Map Centre, 22–24 Caxton St, SW1 (☎0171/222 4945);

Stanfords, 12–14 Long Acre, WC2 (☎0171/836 1321);

The Travellers Bookshop, 25 Cecil Court, WC2 (☎0171/836 9132).

Edinburgh
Thomas Nelson and Sons Ltd, 51 York Place, EH1 3JD (☎0131/557 3011).

Glasgow
John Smith and Sons, 57–61 St Vincent St (☎0141/221 7472).

Maps by **mail or phone order** are available from *Stanfords* (☎0171/836 1321).

USA
Chicago
Rand McNally, 444 N Michigan Ave, IL 60611; ☎312/321-1751.

New York
British Travel Bookshop, 551 5th Ave, NY 10176; ☎1-800/448-3039 or ☎212/490-6688.

The Complete Traveler Bookstore, 199 Madison Ave, NY 10016; ☎212/685-9007.

Rand McNally, 150 E 52nd St, NY 10022; ☎212/758-7488.

Traveler's Bookstore, 22 W 52nd St, NY 10019; ☎212/664-0995.

San Francisco
The Complete Traveler Bookstore, 3207 Fillmore St, CA 92123; ☎415/923-1511.

Rand McNally, 595 Market St, CA 94105; ☎415/777-3131.

Santa Barbara
Pacific Traveler Supply, 25 E Mason St, 93101; ☎805/963-4438 (phone orders: ☎805/965-4402.

Seattle
Elliot Bay Book Company, 101 S Main St, WA 98104; ☎206/624-6600.

Washington DC
Rand McNally, 1201 Connecticut Ave NW, Washington DC 20036; ☎202/223-6751.

Note: *Rand McNally* now has more than 20 stores across the US; call ☎1-800/333-0136 (ext 2111) for the address of your nearest store, or for **direct mail** maps.

Canada
Montréal
Ulysses Travel Bookshop, 4176 St-Denis; ☎514/289-0993.

Toronto
Open Air Books and Maps, 25 Toronto St, M5R 2C1; ☎416/363-0719.

Vancouver
World Wide Books and Maps, 736A Granville St V6Z 1G3; ☎604/687-3320.

for an interview; if you don't speak reasonably good Greek, it's best to have a Greek friend get them for you.

As of writing, maps covering Crete, the Dodecanese, the east Aegean, Skiros and most of Corfu are considered militarily sensitive and are not available to the public. Recently, however, a German company, **Harms**, has issued a series of five maps at 1:80,000 scale which cover Crete from west to east and show many hiking routes.

GETTING AROUND

Island-hopping is one of the best features of a Greek holiday – as much a pursuit in itself as a means of transport. The ferry network is extensive, and given time you can reach any of the 166 inhabited isles. Inter-island planes are expensive, at up to four times the cost of a deck-class ferry ticket and twice as much as first or cabin class, but useful for saving time at the start or finish of a visit, getting to or from Athens or Thessaloníki.

Getting around the islands themselves, there are basic bus connections, which most tourists choose to supplement at some stage with moped, bike or car rental.

FERRIES

There are three types of boats carrying passengers around the islands: medium to large-sized **regular ferries** (which operate on the main island routes), **hydrofoils** (run by the *Ceres* "*Flying Dolphins*" and *Dodecanese Hydrofoils*, among other companies), and local **kaíkia** (small boats which in season cover short island hops and excursions). Costs are very reasonable on the longer journeys, though proportionately more expensive for shorter, inter-island connections.

We've detailed **ferry connections** both on our general and chapter maps and in the "Travel Details" at the end of each chapter. Don't take our listings as exhaustive or wholly reliable, however, as schedules are notoriously erratic, and be aware that we have given details essentially for summer departures. **Out-of-season** services are severely reduced, with many islands connected only once or twice a week. However, in spring or autumn those ferries that do operate are often compelled by the transport ministry to call at extra islands, making possible some interesting connections.

The most reliable, up-to-date information is available from the local **port police** (*limenarhío*), who are to be found at Pireás (☎01/42 26 000) and on every substantial island. Their officers rarely speak much English but they keep complete schedules posted – and, meteorological report in hand, are the final arbiters of whether a ship will sail or not in stormy weather conditions. Another excellent resource is *The Thomas Cook Guide to Greek Island Hopping*, which features a comprehensive overview of ferry services, and makes sense of them all with immaculate maps. Alas, the same caveats as above apply to trusting it too completely.

REGULAR FERRIES

On most ferry routes, your only consideration will be getting a boat that leaves on the day, and for the island, that you want. However, when sailing from **Pireás**, the port of Athens, to the Cyclades or Dodecanese islands, you should have quite a range of choice and may want to bear in mind a few of the factors below.

Most importantly, bear in mind that **routes** taken and the speed of the boats vary enormously. A journey from Pireás to Thíra (Santoríni), for instance, can take anything from nine to fourteen hours. Before buying a ticket it's wise to establish how many stops there'll be before your island, and the estimated time of arrival. Many agents act only for one specific boat (they'll blithely tell you that theirs is the only available service), so you may have to ask around to uncover alternatives. Especially in high season, early arrival is critical in getting what may be a very limited stock of accommodation.

The boats themselves have improved somewhat recently, with a fair number of the older tubs consigned to the scrap heap or dumped overseas – just about the only ferries you might want to avoid if you have the choice are the odiferous *Ayios Rafael*, in the north Aegean, and the poorly maintained *Milena* to the Dodecanese. You will more often than not be surprised to encounter a former English Channel or Scandinavian fjord ferry, rechristened and enjoying a new lease of life in the Aegean.

Regular ferry **tickets** are, in general, best bought on the day of departure, unless you need to reserve a cabin berth or space for a car. Buying tickets in advance will tie you down to a particular ferry at a particular time – and innumerable factors can make you regret that. Most obviously there's **bad weather**, which, particularly off-season, can play havoc with the schedules, causing some small boats to remain at anchor and others to alter their routes drastically.

There are only three periods of the year – March 23–25, the week before and after Easter, and mid-August – when ferries need to be booked at least a couple of days in advance. Otherwise, you can always buy a ticket once on board with no penalty, despite what travel agents may tell you. Ticket prices for each route are currently set by the transport ministry and should not differ among ships or agencies.

The cheapest class of ticket, which you'll probably automatically be sold, is **deck class**, variously called *tríti* or *gámma* (third or C class). On the shorter, summer journeys the deck is the best place to be, and your first priority on board will be to stake out some space. On longer, overnight journeys, however, it can be worth paying the extra drachmas for a cabin bunk. Class consciousness has increased of late, so deck-class passengers will find themselves firmly locked out of second-class facilities to prevent them from crashing on the plush sofas. First-class cabin facilities usually cost as much as a plane flight and often the only difference between first and second is a bathroom in the cabin. Most cabins, incidentally, are stuffy and windowless.

Motorbikes and **cars** get issued extra tickets, in the latter case up to four times the passenger fare. If you do drive to Greece, it is only really worth taking your vehicle to larger islands like Crete, Rhodes, Híos, Lésvos, Sámos or Kefalloniá. Even with these, unless you're planning a lengthy stay, you may find it cheaper to leave your car in Pireás and rent another on arrival.

Most ferries sell a limited range of **food** aboard, though it tends to be overpriced and mediocre in quality. Honourable exceptions are the decent, reasonable meals served on longer routes or overnight sailings. On the short hops in the Argo-Saronic, Cyclades and Sporades, it is well worth stocking up with your own provisions.

HYDROFOILS

Hydrofoils – more commonly known as "*Flying Dolphins*" – are roughly twice as fast (and at least twice as expensive) as ordinary ferries. They are a useful alternative to regular ferries if you are pushed for time, though, and their network seems to be growing each year – it's worth asking after services, even if they are not mentioned in this guide. Their drawback is that, owing to their design, they are extremely sensitive to bad weather. Most of the services don't operate – or are heavily reduced – out of season and are prone to arbitrary cancellation if not enough passengers turn up.

At present, hydrofoils operate among the **Argo-Saronic islands** close to Athens, down the **east coast of the Peloponnese** to **Kíthira**, among the **northern Sporades** (Skiáthos, Skópelos and Alónissos), among certain of the **Cyclades** (Ándros, Tínos, Míkonos, Páros, Náxos, Amorgós, the minor islets, Íos, Thíra – and Crete), and in the **Dodecanese** among Rhodes, Kós and Pátmos, with occasional forays in the Ionian islands and up to Sámos or over to Tílos and Níssiros. The principal **mainland ports** are Zéa and Flisvos marinas in Pireás and Paleó Fáliro respectively, Rafína, Vólos, Áyios Konstandínos and Thessaloníki.

Schedules and tickets for the *Ceres* company, which operates most of the "*Flying Dolphin*" lines, are available in Athens from their head office, off Platía Síndagma (☎01/32 20 351), and in Pireás from *Ceres Hydrofoils*, Aktí Miaoúli 69 (☎01/42 80 001); in Vólos from *Tsoulos*, Andonopoúlou 9–11 (☎0421/39 786); and in Thessaloníki from *Strataki*, Iónis Dhragoúmi 1, (☎031/547 047). *Ilios* has offices in Pireás (☎01/42 24 772), while the head office of *Dodecanese Hydrofoils* is at Platía Kíprou 6, Ródhos (☎0241/24 000).

KAÍKIA

In season *kaíkia* (caiques) sail between adjacent islands and to a few of the more obscure ones. These small boats can be extremely useful and often very pleasant. They are no cheaper than mainline services, though, and if classified as tourist agency charters, and not passenger lines, they tend to be quite expensive, with some pressure to buy return fares.

We have detailed the more regular *kaíkia* links in the text of the guide, though many, inevitably, depend on the whims of local boat-owners or fishermen. The only firm information is to be had on the quayside.

Kaíkia and small ferries, despite appearances, have a good safety record; indeed it's the larger, overloaded car-ferries that have in the past run into trouble.

FLIGHTS

Olympic Airways and its subsidiary *Olympic Aviation* operate most **domestic flights** within Greece. They cover a fairly wide network of islands and larger towns, though most routes are to and from Athens, or the northern capital of Thessaloníki. **Schedules** can be picked up at *Olympic* offices abroad (see "Getting There" sections) or through their branch offices or representatives in Greece, which are maintained in almost every town or island of any size.

Fares for flights to and between the islands work out around three to four times the cost of a ferry journey, but on certain inter-island hauls poorly served by boat (Rhodes–Kastellórizo or Kefalloniá-Zákinthos, for example), you might consider the time well bought. For obscure reasons, flights between Athens and Mílos or Kíthira are better value per kilometre.

In addition, de-regulation of airline operations means that there are some **private companies** running internal flights between Athens and major destinations like Corfu and Crete. These often undercut *Olympic* flights by quite a margin and routes are opening up all the time, so it's worth checking options with a local travel agent.

Island flights are often full in peak season; if they're part of your plans, it is worth trying to make **reservations** at least a week in advance. Domestic air tickets are **non-refundable** but you can change your flight details, space permitting, as late as a day before your original intended departure without penalty.

Like ferries, **flights can be cancelled** in bad weather, since many services are on small, 20- to 50-seat turbo-prop planes that won't fly in strong winds. Size restrictions also mean that the 15-kilo baggage **weight limit** is fairly strictly enforced; if, however, you've just arrived from overseas, or purchased your ticket outside Greece, you are allowed the 20-kilo standard international limit. All services operated on the domestic network are **non-smoking**.

TRANSPORT ON THE ISLANDS

Most islands have some kind of bus service, even if only connects the port with the main town or village, and on larger islands there is usually an efficient and reliable network. For visitors, the main drawback is that buses are almost always geared to local patterns and often leave punishingly early to shuttle people to school or work. Luckily, it is almost always possible to rent a moped, a bike, or, on larger islands, a car or jeep. Even if you just get a vehicle for a day, you can get a measure of a small island, and work out where you want to base yourself.

MOPEDS – AND SAFETY

Motorcycles, **scooters**, **mopeds** and **bicycles** are available for rent on most of the islands – in the main town or port, and at larger resorts. Motorcycles and scooters cost from around £10/US$15 a day; mopeds from £6–7/$9–10.5; push-bikes as little as £3/$4.50. Cars or jeeps, when available, cost £37/$40 a day.

All rates can be reduced with bargaining outside of peak season, or if you negotiate for a longer period of rental. To rent motorcycles (usually 125cc) or cars you will need to show a driving licence; otherwise all you need is a passport to leave as security.

Mopeds are good transport for all but the hilliest islands. Before riding off, however, make sure you check your bike's mechanical state, since many are only cosmetically maintained and repaired. Bad brakes and fouled spark plugs are the most common defects. If you break down it's your responsibility to return the machine, so it's worth taking down the phone number of whoever rents it to you in case it gives out and you can't get it back.

A warning should also be given about mopeds and **safety**. There are a string of accidents each year as tourists come to grief on rutted dirt tracks or astride a mechanically dodgy machine. Very few people wear crash helmets – or much else for that matter – so it's best to keep your speed pretty low. In many cases accidents are due to attempts to cut corners, in all senses, by riding two to an underpowered scooter that is simply not designed to propel such a load. Don't be tempted by this apparent economy – and keep in mind, too, that you're likely to be charged an exorbitant price for any repairs if you do have an accident. Above all, make sure your travel insurance policy covers motorcycle accidents.

As far as **models** go, the *Honda 50* and *Suzuki 50* are the standard; on both you shift gear with an easy pedal action. These can carry two people easily enough, though if you have the choice, the so-called *Cub* series, either 75cc or 90cc, give extra power at nominal extra cost. A large *Vespa* scooter is more comfortable on long trips, and has capacious baskets, too, though less stability, especially off paved surfaces. Smaller but surprisingly powerful *Piaggio Si* or *Monte Carlo* models can take one person (and one only) on almost any road and are automatic action.

If you intend to stay for some time in the warmer months, it's worth considering the **purchase** of a moped or motorbike. They are relatively inexpensive to run or repair, do not cause passport problems, can be taken on the ferries very cheaply, and can be resold easily upon departure.

CYCLING

Cycling on the Greek islands is not such hard going as you might imagine, especially if you rent one of the **mountain bikes** that are gradually replacing boneshakers in rental outlets.

If you have your own mountain or touring bike, you might consider bringing it with you on the plane; bikes travel free on most airlines, if within your twenty-kilo limit, and are free too on most of the ferries. Any spare parts you might need, however, are best brought along, since the only specialist bike shops in Greece are to be found in Athens and Thessaloníki.

HITCHING

Hitching carries the usual risks and dangers, but overall the Greek islands are one of the safer places in which to do it. One of the easiest, too, as most island towns are small and involve just a short walk to the main road out.

TAXIS

Greek **taxis** are among the cheapest in western Europe – so long as you get an honest driver who switches the meter on (see p.10 for a warning about Athens). Within city or town limits, use of the meter is mandatory. On smaller islands, and in rural areas, you often need to bargain and fix a price. A reasonable per-vehicle (*not* per-person) charge for a ten-kilometre trip will be the equivalent of about £5/US$7.50.

ACCOMMODATION

There are huge numbers of beds for tourists on the Greek islands, and most of the year you can rely on turning up on pretty much any island and finding a room – if not in a hotel, then in a private house or block of rooms (the standard island accommodation). Almost every island has several campsites, too, which tend to be basic but inexpensive.

Only in July and August, the high season, are you likely to experience problems. At these times, if you don't have a room booked, it is worth striking a little off the tourist trail, turning up at each new place early in the day, and taking whatever is available in the hope that you will be able to exchange it for something better later on. **Out of season**, there is a slightly different problem, as most of the private rooms – and campsites – operate only from April to October, leaving hotels your only option. This means you often have no choice other than to stay in the island's main town(s) or port(s). However, there will often be very little life outside these places, anyway, with all the seasonal bars and restaurants closed. On many of the smaller islands, you will often find just one hotel – and perhaps just one taverna – stays open year-round.

PRIVATE ROOMS

The most common form of island accommodation is **privately let rooms – *dhomátia***. These are regulated and officially classified by the local tourist police, who divide them into three classes (A down to C), according to their facilities. These days the bulk of them are in new, purpose-built low-rise buildings, but a few are still in people's homes, where you'll occasionally be treated to disarming hospitality.

Rooms are almost always scrupulously clean, whatever their other qualities. At their simplest, you'll get a bare, concrete room, with a hook on the back of the door and toilet facilities (cold water only) outside in the courtyard;. At the fancier end of the scale, you get a modern, fully furnished place with an attached, marble-dressed bathroom. Sometimes there's a choice of rooms at various prices – owners will usually show you the most expensive first. Price and quality are not necessarily directly linked, so always ask to see the room before agreeing to take it and settling on the price.

Areas to look for rooms, along with recommendations of the best places, are included in the guide. But as often as not, the rooms find you: owners descend on ferry or bus arrivals to fill any space they have, sometimes waving photos of the premises. In smaller places you'll often see rooms advertised – sometimes in German (*zimmer*); the Greek signs to look out for are *enikiazómena dhomátia* or *enikiázonteh dhomátia*. In the more developed island resorts, where package holidaymakers predominate, *dhomátia* owners will often require you to book in for a stay of at least three days.

If you can't find rooms in an island town or village, ask at the local taverna or *kafenío* (café). Even if there are no official places, there is very

often someone prepared to earn extra money by putting you up.

It has become standard practice for rooms proprietors to ask to **keep your passport** – ostensibly "for the tourist police", but in reality to prevent you skipping out with an unpaid bill. Some owners may be satisfied with just taking down the details, as in hotels, and they'll almost always return the documents once you get to know them, or if you need them for another purpose (to change money, for example).

In **winter**, designated to begin in November and end in early April, private rooms are closed pretty much across the board to keep the hotels in business. There's no point in traipsing about hoping to find exceptions – most rooms owners obey the system very strictly. If they don't, the owners will find you themselves and, watching out for hotel rivals, guide you back to their place.

HOTELS

Hotels are becoming more common on the islands, and you'll find a handful in most of the larger island towns, ports and resorts. In the larger resorts, however, they are often block-booked by package holiday companies.

Like private rooms, hotels are categorized by the tourist police. They range from "Luxury" down to "E-class", and all except the top category have to keep within set price limits. D- and E-class hotels are usually quite reasonable, costing around £10–15/US$15–22.50 for a double room, £7–10/$11–15 for a single. The better-value places tend to be in less touristed areas, as ratings depend partly on location.

VILLAS AND RENTALS

The easiest – and often the most economical – way to arrange a **villa rental** is through one or other of the package holiday companies detailed on p.5–6. They include some superb places, from simple to luxury, and costs, especially if shared between four or so people, can be very reasonable. Several of the companies we list will arrange "multi-centre" stays on two or more islands.

On the islands, a few local travel agents arrange villa rentals, though they are mostly places the above companies couldn't fill. Out of season, you can sometimes get a good deal on a month (or more) villa or apartment rental by asking around locally.

ROOM PRICES

All establishments listed in this book have been **price-graded** according to the scale outlined below. The rates quoted represent the **cheapest available room** in high season; all are prices for a double room, except for category ①, which are per person rates. Out of season, rates can drop by up to fifty percent, especially if you negotiate rates for a stay of three or more nights. Single rooms, where available, cost around seventy percent of the price of a double.

Rented private **rooms on the islands** usually fall into the ② or ③ categories, depending on their location and facilities, and the season; a few in the ④ category are more like plush self-catering apartments. They are not generally available from late October through to the beginning of April, when only hotels tend to remain open.

You should expect rooms in all ① and most ② range accommodation to be without private bath,

though there may a basic washbasin in the room. In the ③ category and above there are usually private facilities.

Some of the cheap places will also have more expensive rooms including en suite facilities – and vice versa, especially in the case of singles tucked in less desirable corners of the building.

Prices for rooms and hotels should by law be **displayed** on the back of the door of your room. If you feel you're being overcharged at a place which is officially registered, threatening to report it to the tourist office or police – who will generally adopt your side in such cases – should be enough to elicit compliance. Small amounts over the posted price may be legitimately explained by tax or out-of-date forms. And occasionally you may find that you have bargained so well, or arrived so far out of season, that you are actually paying less than you're supposed to.

① 1400–2000dr (£4–5.50/US$6–8.50)
② 4000–6000dr (£11–16.50/US$17–25)
③ 6000–8000dr (£16.50–22/US$25–33)

④ 8000–12000dr (£22–33/US$33–50)
⑤ 12000–16000dr (£33–44/US$50–66)
⑥ 16000dr (£44/US$66) and upwards

CAMPING AND YOUTH HOSTELS

Campsites range from ramshackle compounds to highly organized (and rather soulless) *EOT* (Greek Tourist Organisation) – run complexes. Cheap, casual places cost from £2/US$3 a night per person; at the larger sites, though, it's not impossible for two of you and one tent (all separately charged) to add up almost to the price of a basic room. We cover all the best sites in the guide. If you want more details on facilities you can obtain a guide to the main campsites from the EOT.

Generally, you don't have to worry about leaving tents or **baggage** unattended at campsites; the Greeks are one of the most honest races in Europe. The main risk, sadly, comes from other campers, and every year a few items disappear in that direction.

Freelance camping – outside authorized campsites – is such an established element of Greek travel that few people realize that it's officially illegal. Since 1977, however, it has indeed been forbidden by law, and increasingly the regulations are enforced.

If you do camp freelance, therefore, it is vital to exercise sensitivity and discretion. Obviously the police crack down on people camping out

(and littering) on or near popular tourist **beaches**, and they get especially concerned when a large community of campers is developing. Off the beaten track, however, nobody is very bothered, though it is always best to ask permission locally – in the village taverna or café – before pitching a tent.

During **high season**, when everything – even the campsites – may be full, attitudes towards freelance camping are more relaxed, even in the most touristed places.

YOUTH HOSTELS

There are only seven **youth hostels** (*ksenón neótitos*) on the Greek islands: one on Corfu, two on Thíra (Santorini), and four on Crete. These all tend to be fairly easy-going affairs: slightly rundown and a far cry from the institutions you find in northern Europe. It's best to have a valid *IYHF* card, but you can usually buy one on the spot, or maybe just pay a little extra for your bed.

Charges for a dormitory bed are around £4–6/ US$6–9 a night. Most of the hostels have a curfew at 11pm or midnight and the majority of them are only open in the spring and summer months – from Easter to September.

EATING AND DRINKING

Greeks spend a lot of time socializing outside their homes, and sharing a meal is one of the chief ways of doing it. The atmosphere is always relaxed and informal, and pretensions (or expense-account prices) are rare outside of the major island resorts. Greeks are not great drinkers – what drinking they do is mainly done at the café – though in the resorts a whole range of bars, pubs, discos and cocktail joints have sprung up to cater for tourists.

BREAKFAST, PICNIC FARE AND SNACKS

Greeks don't generally eat **breakfast** and the only egg-and-bacon kind of places are in resorts where foreigners congregate; they can be good value, especially in places with lots of competition. More local alternatives are a yogurt or sweet in a patisserie (*zaharoplastía*), or of course you can put together a picnic breakfast with your own ingredients.

Picnic fare is good, cheap and easily available. Staple diet of any picnic is **bread** and the Greek version, available in different shapes and sizes, is good and inexpensive. Try and get to the bakery (*foúrnos*) early when it's served warm from the oven – and try asking for *olikís* (wholemeal), *oktásporo* (eight-grain), or even *enneásporo* (nine-grain). When buying **olives**, go for the fat Kalamáta or Ámfissa ones; they're more expensive, but tastier and more nourishing. *Fétta* **cheese** is ubiquitous – often, these days, imported from Holland or Denmark. It can be very

dry and salty, so it's wise to ask for a piece to taste before buying. If you have access to a fridge, dunking it overnight in a plastic container with water will solve both problems. That sampling advice also goes for other cheeses, the most palatable of which are the expensive gruyère-type *graviéra*. *Kosséri* is another good option, and processed cheese and **cooked meats** are usually available, too.

Yogurts are superlative (and good stomach settlers); honey is also wonderful – and a perfect complement. There's also a good choice of **fruit** particularly watermelon, peaches and grapes, and **salad vegetables**.

Useful expressions in the market are *éna tétarto* (250g) and *éna misó* (500g).

SNACKS

Traditional snacks can be one of the distinctive pleasures of Greek eating, though they are being increasingly edged out by an obsession with *tóst* (toasted sandwiches) and pizzas. However, small kebabs (*souvlákia*) are widely available, and in most larger resorts and towns you'll find *yíros* – doner kebab in *píta* bread with garnish.

Other common snacks include *tirópites* (cheese pies) and *spanokópita* (spinach pies), which can usually be found at the baker's, as can *kouloúria* (crispy baked pretzel rings sprinkled with sesame seeds) and *boutímata* (biscuits heavy on the molasses, cinnamon and butter).

RESTAURANTS

Greek cuisine and **restaurants** are simple and straightforward. There's no snobbery about eating out; everyone does it some of the time, and for foreigners with strong currencies it's fairly inexpensive – around £6–8/US$9–12 for a substantial meal with a bottle of house wine.

In choosing a restaurant, the best strategy is to go where the Greeks go. And they go late: 2pm to 3pm for **lunch**, 9pm to 11pm for **dinner**. You can eat earlier, but you're likely to get indifferent service if you frequent the purely touristic establishments. Chic appearance is not a good guide to quality; you'll mainly be paying for the linen napkins and stemmed wine glasses. Often the most basic are the best, so don't be put off by a restaurant that brings your order in a sheet of paper and plonks it directly on the table-top, as *psistariés* (grills) often do.

It's wise to keep a wary eye on the **waiters** in resort areas. They are inclined to push you into ordering more than you want and then bring things you haven't ordered. They often don't actually write anything down and may work your **bill** out by examining your empty plates. Itemized tabs, when present, may be in totally illegible Greek scribble, so the opportunities for slipping in a few extra drachmas here and there are pretty good, especially in establishments which disdain menus and published prices altogether. The **service charge** is always included, although a small tip (100–150 dr) is standard practice for the "boy" who lays the table, brings the bread and water, and so on.

If you have **children**, have no fears for them. Wherever you go they'll be welcome, and no one gives a damn if they chase the cats or play tag between the tables.

ESTIATÓRIA

There are two basic types of restaurant: the **estiatório** and the *taverna*. Distinctions between the two are slight, though the former is more commonly found in towns and it tends to have slightly more complicated dishes.

An *estiatório* will generally feature a variety of **oven-baked casserole dishes**: *moussakás*, *pastítsio*, stews like *kokinistó* and *stifádho*, *yemistá* (stuffed tomatoes or peppers), the oily vegetable casseroles called *ladherá*, and oven-baked meat and fish. Choosing these dishes is commonly done by going to the kitchen and pointing at the desired trays.

The cooking is done in the morning and then left to stand, which is why the food is often **lukewarm** or even cold. Greeks don't mind this (most believe that hot food is bad for you), and in fact in summertime it hardly seems to matter. Besides, dishes like *yemistá* are actually enhanced by being allowed to cool off and stand in their own juice. Similarly, you have to specify if you want your food with little or no **oil** (*horís ládhi*), but once again you will be considered a little strange since Greeks regard olive oil as essential to digestion (and indeed it is one of the least pernicious oils to ingest in large quantities).

Desserts of the pudding-and-pie variety don't exist, although fruit is always available in season and you may occasionally be able to get a yogurt served at the end of a meal. Watermelons,

melons and grapes are the standard summer fruit. Autumn treats worth asking after in more urban restaurants include *kidhóni* or *ahládhi sto foúrno*, baked quince or pear with some sort of syrup or nut topping.

TAVERNAS

Tavernas range from the glitzy and fashionable to rough-and-ready cabins with a bamboo awning set up by the beach. The primitive ones have a very limited menu, but the more established will offer some of the main *estiatório* dishes mentioned above as well as the standard **taverna fare**. This essentially means *mezédhes* (hors d'oeuvres) and *tis óras* (meat and fish fried or grilled to order).

Since the idea of courses is foreign to Greek cuisine, starters, main dishes and salads often arrive together. The best thing is to order a selection of *mezédhes* and salads to share among yourselves; that, after all, is what Greeks do. Waiters encourage you to take the **horiátiki salad** – the so-called Greek salad, with *fétta* cheese – because it is the most expensive one. If you only want tomato, or tomato and cucumber, ask for *domatosaláta* or *angourodomáta*. *Láhano* (cabbage) and *maroúli* (lettuce) are the typical winter and spring salads.

The most interesting **starters** are *tzatzíki* (yogurt, garlic and cucumber dip), *melitzanosaláta* (aubergine/eggplant dip), *kolokithákia tiganitá* (courgette/zucchini fried in batter) or *melitzánes tiganités* (aubergine/eggplant fried in batter), *yígandes* (white haricot beans in vinaigrette or hot tomato sauce), *tiropitákia* or *spanakópittes* (small cheese and spinach pies), *saganáki* (fried cheese), *okhtapódhi* (octopus) and *mavromatiká* (black-eyed peas).

Of **meats**, *souvláki* (shish kebab) and *brizóles* (chops) are reliable choices. In both cases, pork (*hirinó*) is usually better and cheaper than veal (*moskharísio*). The best *souvláki* is lamb (*arnísio*), but it is not often available. The small lamb cutlets called *païdhákia* are very tasty, as is roast lamb (*arní psitó*) and roast kid (*katsíki*) when obtainable. *Keftédhes* (meatballs), *biftékia* (a sort of hamburger) and the spicy sausages called *loukánika* are cheap and good. *Kotópoulo* (chicken) is also usually a safe bet.

Seaside tavernas of course also offer **fish**, though the choicer varieties, such as *barboúnia* (red mullet), *tsípoura* (gilt-head bream), *fangrí* (sea bream), are expensive. The price is quoted by the kilo, and the standard procedure is to go to the glass cooler and pick your own. The cheapest widely available fish are *gópes* (bogue) and *marídhes* (tiny whitebait, eaten complete with head).

Kalamarákia (fried baby squid) and *okhtapódhi* (octopus) are a summer staple of most seaside tavernas, and occasionally, exotic **shellfish** such as *mídhia* (mussels), *kidhónia* (cherrystone clams) and *garídhes* (small prawns) will be on offer at reasonable prices. Keep an eye out, however, to freshness and season – mussels in particular are a common cause of stomach upsets or even mild poisoning.

Speaking of **seasons**, summer visitors get a relatively poor choice of fish: net trawling is prohibited from mid-May to mid-October, when only lamp-lure and multi-hook line methods are allowed. During these warmer months, such fish as are caught tend to be smaller and dry-tasting, thus requiring the butter sauce often served with fish. Most restaurants import frozen fish.

As in *estiatória*, **desserts** in traditional tavernas are more or less nonexistent, though fruits are usually available, and desserts are increasingly common on menus in more touristed areas. By the same token, tavernas frequented by foreigners are also more inclined to serve **coffee** these days.

SPECIALIST TAVERNAS

Some tavernas specialize. *Psarotavérnes*, for example, feature fish, and *psistariés* serve spit-roasted lamb and goat or *kokorétsi* (grilled offal).

A very few other tavernas concentrate on game (*kinígi*): rabbit, quail or turtle dove in the autumn, when the migrating flocks fly over Greece on their way south.

WINES

Both *estiatória* and tavernas will usually offer you a choice of **bottled wines**, and many have their own house variety, kept in barrels and served out in metal jugs.

Among the **bottled wines**, *Cambas*, *Boutari* the Rhodian *CAIR* products, and the Cretan *Logado* are good inexpensive whites, while *Boutari Nemea* is perhaps the best mid-range red. If you want something better, *Tsantali Agioritiko* is an excellent white or red; *Boutari* do a fine *Special Reserve* red; the Macedonian *Domaine Carras* does both excellent whites and reds; and, in addition, there are various small,

premium wineries whose products are currently fashionable: for example, *Hatzimihali*, *Athanasiadhi* and *Lazaridhi*.

Otherwise, go for the **local wines**. *Retsina* – pine-resinated wine, a slightly acquired taste – is invariably better straight from the barrel. Not as many tavernas keep it as once did, but always ask whether they have wine *varelísio* or *híma* – both mean, in effect, "from the barrel". Non-resinated bulk wine is almost always more than decent.

CAFÉS AND BARS

The Greek eating and drinking experience encompasses a variety of other places beyond restaurants. Most importantly, there is the institution of the **kafenío**, found in every town, village and hamlet in the country. In addition, you'll come across **ouzerís**, **zaharoplastía** and **bars**.

THE KAFENÍO

The **kafenío** is the traditional Greek coffee shop or café. Although its main business is Greek coffee – prepared *skéto* or *pikró* (unsweetened), *métrio* (medium) or *glikó* (sweet) – it also serves spirits such as *oúzo* (aniseed-based spirit), brandy (*Metaxa* brand, in three grades), beer, tea (either herbal mountain tea or British-style *Liptons*) and soft drinks. Another refreshing drink sold in cafés is *kafés frappé*, a sort of iced instant coffee with or without milk or sugar – uniquely Greek despite its French-sounding name. Like Greek coffee, it is always accompanied by a welcome glass of cold water. Standard fizzy soft drinks are sold in all cafés, too.

Usually the only edibles sold in cafés are *glikó koutalioú* (sticky, syrupy preserves of quince, grape, fig, citrus fruit or cherry), and the old-fashioned *ipovríhio*, which is a piece of mastic submerged in a glass of water like a submarine, which is what the word means in Greek.

Like tavernas, *kafenía* range from the plastic and sophisticated to the old-fashioned, spit-on-the-floor variety, with marble or brightly painted metal tables and straw-bottomed chairs. An important institution anywhere in Greece, they are the central pivot of life in the country villages. In fact, you get the impression that many men spend most of their waking hours there. Greek **women** are rarely to be seen in the more traditional places – and foreign women may sometimes feel uneasy or unwelcome in these establishments. Even in holiday resorts, you will find there is at least one café that the local men have kept intact for themselves.

Some *kafenía* close at siesta time, but many remain open from early in the morning until late at night. The chief socializing time is 6–8pm, immediately after the siesta. This is the time to take your pre-dinner *oúzo*, as the sun begins to sink and the heat cools.

OÚZO, MEZÉDHES AND *OUZERÍ*

Oúzo – known as *tsikoudhiá* on Crete – is a simple spirit, averaging 46 percent alcohol, distilled from grape-mash residue left over from wine-making, and then flavoured with herbs such as anis or fennel. If you order *oúzo*, you will be served two glasses, one with the *oúzo*, and one full of water, to be tipped into your *oúzo* until it turns a milky white. You can drink it straight, but

---

A FOOD AND DRINK GLOSSARY

Basics

Aláti	Salt	*Neró*	Water
Avgá	Eggs	*Olikís psomí*	Wholemeal bread
(Horís) ládhi	(Without) oil	*O logariasmós*	The bill
Hortofágos	Vegetarian	*Psári(a)*	Fish
Katálogo/lísta	Menu	*Psomí*	Bread
Kréas	Meat	*Sikalísio psomí*	Rye bread
Lahaniká	Vegetables	*Tirí*	Cheese
Méli	Honey	*Yiaoúrti*	Yogurt

Cooking terms

Ahnistó	Steamed	*Sto foúrno*	Baked
Psitó	Roasted	*Tis óras*	Grilled/fried to order
Sti soúvla	Spit roasted	*Yahní*	Stewed in oil and tomato sauce

Soups and starters

Avgolémono	Egg and lemon soup	*Mavromatiká*	Black-eyed peas
Dolmádhes	Stuffed vine leaves	*Melitzanosaláta*	Aubergine/eggplant dip
Fasoládha	Bean soup	*Skordhaliá*	Garlic dip
Florínes	Canned red Macedonian peppers	*Soúpa*	Soup
		Taramosaláta	Cod roe paté
Kápari	Pickled caper leaves	*Tzatzíki*	Yogurt and cucumber dip
Kopanistí, Ktipití	Spicy cheese purée		

Vegetables

Angináres	Artichokes	*Koukiá*	Broad fava beans
Angoúri	Cucumber	*Maroúli*	Lettuce
Bámies	Okra, ladies' fingers	*Melitzána*	Aubergine/eggplant
Bouréki	Courgette/zucchini, potato and cheese pie	*Papoutsákia*	Stuffed aubergine/eggplant
		Patátes	Potatoes
Briám	Ratatouille	*Piperiés*	Peppers
Domátes	Tomatoes	*Radhíkia*	Wild chicory
Fakés	Lentils	*Rízi/Piláfi*	Rice (usually with *sáltsa* – sauce)
Fasolákia	French beans		
Horiátiki (saláta)	Greek salad (with olives, fétta etc)	*Saláta*	Salad
		Spanáki	Spinach
Hórta	Greens (usually wild)	*Yemistá*	Stuffed vegetables
Kolokithákia	Courgette/zucchini	*Yígandes*	White haricot beans

Fish and seafood

Astakós	Lobster	Kalamarákia	Baby squid	Platís	Skate, ray
Atherína	Sardine-like fish	Kalamária	Squid	Sardhélles	Sardines
Barbóuni	Red mullet	Kidhónia	Cherrystone	Sinagrídha	Dentex
Galéos	Dogfish, squale		clams	Skathári	Black bream
Garídhes	Shrimp	Ksifías	Swordfish	Soupiá	Cuttlefish
Gávros	Mild anchovy	Marídhes	Whitebait	Tsipoúra	Gilt-head bream
Glóssa	Sole	Mídhia	Mussels	Vátos	Skate, ray
Gópa	Bogue	Okhtapódhi	Octopus		

Meat and meat-based dishes

Arní	Lamb	Moskhári	Veal
Biftéki	Hamburger	Moussaká	Aubergine/eggplant, potato
Brizóla	Pork or beef chop		and meat pie
Hirinó	Pork	Sikóti	Liver
Keftédhes	Meatballs	Païdhákia	Lamb chops
Kleftikó	Meat, potatoes and veg cooked	Pastítsio	Macaroni baked with meat
	together in a pot or foil; a Cretan	Patsás	Tripe and trotter soup
	speciality traditionally carried to	Soutzoukákia	Mincemeat rissoles/beef
	bandits in hiding		patties
Kokorétsi	Liver/offal kebab	Stifádho	Meat stew with tomato
Kotópoulo	Chicken	Tsalingária	Garden snails
Kounéli	Rabbit	Youvétsi	Baked clay casserole of
Loukánika	Spicy sausages		meat and (pasta)

Sweets and dessert

Baklavás	Honey and nut pastry	Loukoumádes	Yeast doughnuts in
Bougátsa	Creamy cheese pie		honey syrup and
	served warm with		sesame seeds
	sugar and cinnamon	Pagotó	Ice cream
Galaktobóureko	Custard pie	Pastéli	Sesame and honey bar
Halva	Sweetmeat	Rizógalo	Rice pudding
Karidhópita	Walnut cake		

Fruit and nuts

Fistíkia	Pistachio nuts	Kidhóni	Quince	Portokália	Oranges
Fráoules	Strawberries	Lemóni	Lemon	Rodhákino	Peach
Karpoúzi	Watermelon	Míla	Apples	Síka	(Dried) figs
Kerásia	Cherries	Pepóni	Melon	Stafília	Grapes

Cheese

Fétta	Salty, white	Graviéra	Gruyère-type hard cheese
	cheese	Kasséri	Medium cheese

Drinks

Áspro	White	Kafés	Coffee	Potíri	Glass
Bíra	Beer	Krasí	Wine	Rosé/Kokkinéli	Rosé
Boukáli	Bottle	Limonádha	Lemonade	Stinyássas!	Cheers!
Gála	Milk	Mávro	Red	Tsáï	Tea
Galakakáo	Chocolate milk	Metalikó neró	Mineral water		
Gazóza	Generic fizzy drink	Portokaládh	Orangeade		

its strong, burning taste is hardly refreshing if you do, and many foreigners prefer to mix it with Sprite or lemonade. There are more than a dozen brands of *oúzo* in Greece; the best are reckoned to come from Lésvos, Tírnavos and Sámos, the best-known being the mass-produced *12* label.

Until not long ago, every *oúzo* you ordered was automatically accompanied by a small plate of **mezédhes**, on the house: bits of cheese, cucumber, tomato, a few olives, sometimes octopus or even a couple of small fish. Unfortunately these days you have to ask, and pay, for them.

Though they are confined to the better resorts and select neighbourhoods of the bigger towns, there is a kind of drinking establishment which specializes in *oúzo* and *mezédhes*. These are called **ouzerí**, and are well worth trying for the marvellous variety of *mezédhes* they serve. Several plates of these plus drinks will effectively substitute for a more involved meal at a taverna (though it usually works out more expensive if you have a healthy appetite).

ZAHAROPLASTÍO

A somewhat similar institution to the *kafenío* is the **zaharoplastío**. A cross between café and patisserie, it serves coffee, alcohol, yogurt and honey, sticky cakes, etc, both to consume on the premises and to take away.

The good establishments offer an amazing variety of pastries, cream and chocolate confections, honey-soaked Greco-Turkish sweets like *baklavás*, *kataïfí* (honey-drenched "shredded wheat"), *loukoumádhes*, puffs of batter fried in olive oil, dusted with cinnamon and dipped in syrup (if you have a sweet tooth they'll transport you); *galaktoboúreko* (custard pie), and so on.

If you want a stronger slant towards the dairy products and away from the pure sugar, seek out a **galaktopolío**, where you'll often find *rizógalo* (rice pudding), *kréma* (custard) and home- or at least locally made *yiaoúrti* (yogurt), best if it's *próvio* (from sheep's milk). A sign at either estab-

lishment with the legend *pagotó politikó* or *kaïmáki* means that the shop concerned makes its own Turkish-style ice cream, and the proprietors are probably from Istanbul (Konstantinoúpoli to them, of course) – as good as or better than the usual Italian-style fare.

Both *zaharoplastía* and *galaktopolía* are more family-oriented places than the *kafenío*, and many also serve a basic continental-type **breakfast** of *méli me voútiro* (honey poured over a pat of butter) or jam (all kinds are called *marmeládha* in Greek; ask for *portokáli* – orange – if you want proper marmalade) with fresh bread or *friganiés* (melba-toast-type slivers). You are also more likely to find proper (*evropaïkó*) tea and different kinds of coffee. *Nescafé* has become the generic term for all instant coffee, regardless of brand.

BARS – AND BEER

Bars – *barákia* in the plural – are a recent transplant, once confined to towns, cities and holiday resorts, but now found all over Greece. They range from clones of Parisian cafés to seaside cocktail bars, by way of imitation English "pabs" (*sic*), with videos running all day. Drinks are invariably more expensive than at a café.

They are, however, most likely to stock a range of **beers**, which in Greece are all foreign labels made under licence, since the old Fix brewery closed in the 1980s. *Kronenberg* and *Kaiser* are the two most expensive brews, with the former much preferable and also offering the only dark beer in the country. *Amstel* and *Henninger* are the two ubiquitous cheapies, rather bland but inoffensive. A possible compromise is the sharper-tasting *Heineken*, universally referred to as a "*prássini*" by bar and taverna staff after its green bottle.

Incidentally, try not to be stuck with the one-third litre cans, vastly more expensive (and more of a rubbish problem) than the returnable half-litre bottles.

COMMUNICATIONS: MAIL, PHONES AND THE MEDIA

POSTAL SERVICES

Post offices are open Monday to Friday from about 7.30am to any time between 2pm and 8pm, depending on the size of the town. In the larger towns and resorts, there are usually supplementary weekend opening hours, between 9am and 3pm. At such times you can have money exchanged, in addition to handling mail.

Airmail letters from the islands take three to ten days to reach the rest of Europe, five to fourteen days to get to North America, and a bit more for Australia and New Zealand. The larger the island, on the whole, the quicker the service.

Aerograms are faster and surer. **Postcards** can be inexplicably slow: up to two weeks for Europe, a month to North America or the Pacific. A modest (about 300dr) fee for **express** (*katapígonda*) service cuts letter delivery time by a few days to any destination. **Registered** (*sistiméno*) delivery is also available, but it is quite slow unless coupled with express service.

For a simple letter or card, **stamps** (*grammatósima*) can also be purchased at a *períptero* (corner kiosk). However, the proprietors are entitled to a ten percent commission and never seem to know the current international rates. Ordinary **post boxes** are bright yellow, express boxes dark red; if you are confronted by two slots, *esoterikó* is for domestic mail, *exoterikó* for overseas.

If you are sending large purchases home, note that **parcels** should and often can only be handled in the main island town(s). This way your bundle will be in Athens, and on the plane, within a few days.

RECEIVING MAIL

The **poste restante/general delivery** system is reasonably efficient, especially at the post offices of larger towns. Mail should be clearly addressed and marked *poste restante*, with your surname underlined, to the main post office of whichever town you choose. It will be held for a month and you'll need your passport to collect it.

Alternatively, you can use the **American Express** one-month mail-holding service, free of charge if you carry their cheques or hold their card, but because of new security regulations they will no longer accept delivery of even small packages. *Amex* offices are open Monday to Friday, plus Saturday mornings, and are conveniently spaced (see box below).

AMERICAN EXPRESS OFFICES IN GREECE

Athens: *American Express*, Síndagma/Ermoú 2, PO Box 3325.

Iráklion (Crete): c/o *Adamis Tours*, Avgoústou 23, PO Box 1031.

Kérkira (Corfu): c/o *Greek Skies Travel*, Kapdhistríou 20A, PO Box 24.

Míkonos: c/o *Delia Travel*, at the quay, PO Box 02.

Pátra: c/o *Albatross Travel*, Amalias 48.

Rhodes Town: c/o *Rodhos Tours Ltd*, Ammohóstou 23, PO Box 252.

Skíathos: c/o *Mare Nostrum Hols Ltd*, Papadiamanti 21, PO Box 16.

PHONES

Local calls are relatively straightforward. In many hotel lobbies or cafés you'll find fat, **red pay-phones** which presently take a ten-drachma coin and are for local calls only – you'll generally be asked to give an extra 5dr to the proprietor but pay no extra on the rate. On street corners you'll find call boxes, which work only with **phone cards** (in three sizes: 100, 500 and 1000 units), bought from kiosks, OTE offices and newsagents.

PHONING GREECE FROM ABROAD

Dial the international access code (given below) + 30 (country code) + area code (minus initial 0, see below) + number

Australia ☎0011	New Zealand ☎00
Canada ☎011	UK ☎00
Ireland ☎010	USA ☎011

PHONING ABROAD FROM GREECE

Dial the country code (given below) + area code (minus initial 0) + number

Australia ☎0061	New Zealand ☎0064
Canada ☎001	UK ☎0044
Ireland ☎00353	USA ☎001

GREEK PHONE CODES

Athens ☎01	Kós ☎0242	Pátra ☎061	Skíathos ☎0427
Corfu ☎0661	Míkonos ☎0289	Rhodes ☎0241	Thessaloníki ☎031
Iráklion ☎081	Páros ☎0284	Santoríni ☎0286	Zákinthos ☎0695

USEFUL TELEPHONE NUMBERS

Operator ☎131 (Athens)	Medical emergencies ☎166	Tourist police ☎171
Operator ☎132 (Domestic)	Police/Emergency ☎100	Fire brigade ☎199
Operator ☎161 (International)	Speaking clock ☎141	Road assistance ☎174

If you won't be around long enough to use up a phone card, it's probably easier to make local calls from a *periptero*, or **street kiosk**. Here the phone is connected to a meter, and you pay after you have made the call. Local calls are very cheap (15dr), but **long-distance** ones add up quickly to some of the most expensive rates in the EC – and definitely the worst connections.

For **international** (*exoterikó*) calls, it's better to use either card phones or visit the nearest **OTE** (*Organismós Tiliepikinoníon tis Elládhos*) office, where there's often a slightly better-wired booth reserved for overseas calls only. **Reverse charge (collect) calls** can also be made here, though connections are not always immediate. Be prepared to wait.

In the very largest towns there is at least one branch open **24 hours**, or more commonly 7am to 10pm or 11pm. In smaller towns *OTE* offices can close as early as 3pm, though in a few resorts there are a few *OTE* Portakabin booths. Outgoing **faxes** can also be sent from OTE offices, post offices and some travel agencies – at a price. Receiving a fax may also incur a small charge.

Other options for calls are from a *kafenío* or bar, but make sure the phones are metered: look for a sign saying *Tiléfono meh metrití*. Avoid making long-distance calls from a hotel, as they slap a 50 percent surcharge onto the already outrageous rates.

Calls will **cost**, very approximately, £2.75 for three minutes to all EC countries and most of the rest of Europe, or US$10 for the same time to North America or Australasia. **Cheap rates**, such as they are, apply from 3pm to 5pm and 9pm to 8am daily, plus all weekend, for calls within Greece.

For details of **phone codes and useful numbers**, see the box above.

British Telecom, as well as North American long-distance companies like *AT&T, MCI, Sprint* all enable their customers to make **credit-card calls** while overseas. Most provide service from Greece – contact the company for more details.

THE MEDIA

British newspapers are fairly widely available in Greece for 300–400dr, 700–800dr for Sunday editions. You'll find day-old copies of *The Independent* and *The Guardian*'s European edition in all the resorts as well as in major towns, and a few of the tabloids can be found too. **American and international** alternatives are represented by *USA Today* and the *International Herald Tribune; Time* and *Newsweek* are also widely available. **Local English-language** alternatives include the daily *Athens News*, with a new colour format and improved entertainment listings, and the *Greek Weekly News*, the latter with a good summary of Athens cinema and concert offerings. The expatriate communites in Rhodes and Corfu also put out creditable information sheets.

Among **magazines**, the most enduring is *The Athenian*, an English-language monthly sold in Athens and all major resorts. It's usually worth a read for its cultural/festival listings, updates on Greek life and politics, and often excellent features.

RADIO

If you have a **radio** you may pick up something interesting. Greek music progammes are always accessible despite the language barrier, and with recent challenges to the government's former monopoly of wavelengths, regional stations have mushroomed; the airwaves are now positively cluttered, as every town of more than a few thousand sets up its own studio and transmitter.

The **BBC World Service** can be picked up on short-wave frequencies throughout Greece. For programme times and frequencies (15.07 and 12.09 Mhz are the most common), pick up a copy of "London Calling" from the library of the British Council in Athens.

GREEK TV

Greece's two centralized, government-controlled **TV stations**, ET1 and ET2, nowadays lag behind private channels – Mega-Channel, New Channel, Antenna, Star and Seven-X – in the ratings. On ET1, news summaries in English are broadcast daily at 6pm. Programming on all stations tends to be a mix of soaps (especially Italian and Spanish ones), gameshows, westerns, B-movies and sports. All foreign films and serials are broadcast in their original language, with Greek subtitles. Except for Seven-X, which begins at 7pm, and Mega (a 24-hour channel), the main channels broadcast from breakfast time until the small hours.

Numerous **cable and satellite** channels are transmitted, including Sky, CNN, MTV, Super Channel and Italian Rai. The range available depends on the area you're in.

OPENING HOURS AND PUBLIC HOLIDAYS

It is virtually impossible to generalize about Greek opening hours, except to say that they change constantly. The traditional timetable starts at a relatively civilized hour, with shops opening between 8.30am and 9.30am, and runs through until lunchtime, when there is a long break for the hottest part of the day. Things may then reopen in the mid- to late afternoon.

Tourist areas tend to adopt a slightly more northern timetable, with shops and offices probably staying open right through the day. Certainly the most important arche- ological sites and museums do so.

BUSINESS AND SHOPPING HOURS

Most **government agencies** are open to the public from 8am to 2pm. In general, however, you'd be optimistic to show up after 1pm expect- ing to be served the same day. **Private busi- nesses**, or anyone providing a service – eg film processor, osteopath, electronics repair – is likely to operate on a unitary, 9am–6pm schedule. If someone is actually selling something, then they are more likely to follow a split shift.

Shopping hours during the hottest months are theoretically Monday, Wednesday and

Saturday from approximately 9am–2.30pm, and Tuesday, Thursday and Friday from 8.30am–2pm and 6–9pm; during the cooler months with shorter daylight hours the morning schedule shifts slightly forward, the evening trade a half or even a full hour back. There are so many **excep- tions** to these rules, though, by virtue of holidays and professional idiosyncrasy that you can't count on getting anything done except from Monday to Friday from 9.30am to 1pm or so. It's worth noting that **delis and butchers** are not allowed to sell fresh meat during the afternoon (though some flout this rule); similarly **fishmon- gers** are only open in the morning.

All of the above opening hours will be regu- larly thrown out of sync by any of a vast range of **public holidays and festivals**. The most impor- tant, when almost everything will be closed, are listed in the box overpage.

ANCIENT SITES AND MONASTERIES

All the major **ancient sites** are now fenced off and, like most **museums**, charge admission. This ranges from a token 200dr to a whopping 1500dr, with an average fee of around 500dr. Anomalies are common, with some tiny one-pot museums charging the same as major attractions. At most

PUBLIC HOLIDAYS

January 1	Whit Monday (usually in June)
January 6	August 15
March 25	October 28
First Monday of Lent (February/March, see below)	December 25 & 26
Easter weekend (according to the Orthodox festival calendar, see below)	*There are also a large number of local holidays, which result in the closure of shops and*
May 1	*businesses, though not government agencies.*

VARIABLE RELIGIOUS FEASTS

	Lent Monday	**Easter Sunday**	**Whit Monday**
1995	March 6	April 23	June 12
1996	February 26	April 14	June 3
1997	March 10	April 27	June 16

of them there are reductions of 50–100 percent (the latter applying to EC nationals) for student card holders. In addition, entrance to all state-run sites and museums is **free** to all EC nationals on Sundays and public holidays.

Opening hours vary from site to site. As far as possible, individual times are quoted in the text, but bear in mind that these change with exasperating frequency and at smaller sites may be subject to the whim of a local keeper. The times quoted are generally summer hours, which operate from around April to the end of September. Reckon on similar days but later opening and earlier closing in winter.

Smaller sites generally close for a long lunch and **siesta** (even where they're not supposed to), as do **monasteries**. Most monasteries are fairly strict on visitors' dress, too, especially for women; they don't like shorts on either sex and often expect women to cover their arms and wear skirts, with the necessary wraps sometimes provided on the spot. They are generally open from about 9am to 1pm and 5pm to 8pm (3.30–6.30pm in winter) for limited visits.

FESTIVALS AND CULTURAL EVENTS

Many of the big Greek popular festivals have a religious base so they're observed in accordance with the Orthodox calendar. This is similar to the regular Catholic liturgical year, except for Easter, which can fall as much as three weeks to either side of the western festival. Other festivals are more cultural in nature, including performance of Classical drama in some of the ancient theatres. There's also a full programme of cinema and modern theatre, at its best in the larger island towns but with something on offer in most islands at some point during the year. Outdoor movie screenings are a particularly enjoyable summer pursuit.

EASTER

Easter is by far the most important festival of the Greek year – infinitely more so than Christmas – and taken much more seriously than it is anywhere in western Europe. From Wednesday of Holy Week the state radio and TV networks are given over solely to religious programmes until the following Monday.

The festival is an excellent time to be in Greece, both for the beautiful and moving religious ceremonies and for the days of feasting and celebration that follow. The mountainous island of **Ídhra** with its alleged 360 churches and monasteries is the prime Easter resort, but unless you plan well in advance you have no hope of finding accommodation at that time. Probably the best idea is to make for a medium-sized village where, in most cases, you'll be accepted into the community's celebration.

The first great public ceremony takes place on **Good Friday** evening as the Descent from the Cross is lamented in church. At dusk the *Epitafiós*, Christ's funeral bier, lavishly decorated by the women of the parish, leaves the sanctuary and is paraded solemnly through the streets. In many places, Crete especially, this is accompanied by the burning of effigies of Judas Iscariot.

Late **Saturday** evening sees the climax in a majestic *Anástasi* mass to celebrate Christ's triumphant return. At the stroke of midnight all lights in each crowded church are extinguished and the congregation plunged into the darkness which envelops Christ as He passes through the underworld. Then there's a faint glimmer of light behind the altar screen before the priest appears, holding aloft a lighted taper and chanting "*Avtó to Fós . . .*" (This is the Light of the World). Stepping down to the level of the parishioners, he touches his flame to the unlit candle of the nearest worshipper intoning "*Dévthe, lévethe Fós*" (Come, take the Light). Those at the front of the congregation and on the aisles do the same for their neighbours until the entire church is ablaze with burning candles and the miracle re-affirmed.

Even the most committed agnostic is likely to find this moving. The traditional greeting, as fireworks explode around you in the street, is "*Hristós Anésti*" (Christ is risen), to which the response is "*Alithós Anésti*" (Truly He is Risen). In the week up to Easter Sunday you should wish people a Happy Easter: "*Kaló Páskha*"; after the day, you say "*Hrónia Pollá*" (Many Happy Returns).

The burning **candles** are then taken home through the streets by the worshippers, and it brings good fortune on the house if the candle arrives without having been blown out in the wind. On reaching the front door it is common practice to make the sign of the cross on the lintel with the flame, leaving a black smudge visible for the rest of the year. The Lenten fast is traditionally broken early on Sunday morning with a meal of *mayarítsa*, a soup made from lamb tripe, rice and lemon. The rest of the lamb will be roasted on spits for Sunday lunch, and festivities often take place through the rest of the day.

The Greek equivalent of **Easter eggs** are hard-boiled eggs (painted red on Holy Thursday), which are baked into twisted, sweet breadloaves (*tsouréki*) or distributed on Easter Sunday; people rap their eggs against their friends' eggs, and the owner of the last uncracked egg is considered lucky.

THE FESTIVAL CALENDAR

Most of the other Greek festivals are celebrations of one or another of a multitude of **saints**. The most important are detailed overpage: wherever you are, it is worth looking out for a village, or church, bearing the saint's name, a sure sign of celebrations – sometimes across the town or island, sometimes quiet and local. Saints' days are also celebrated as **name-days**; if you learn that it's an acquaintance's name-day, you wish them "*Hrónia Pollá*" (Many Happy Returns).

Detailed overpage, too, are a scattering of more **secular** holidays, most enjoyable of which are the pre-Lenten carnivals.

In addition to the specific dates mentioned, there are literally scores of **local festivals**, or **paniyíria**, celebrating the patron saint of the village church. With some 330-odd possible name-saints' days you're unlikely to travel around Greece for long without stumbling on something.

It is important to remember the concept of the **paramoní***, or eve of the festival. Most of the events listed below are celebrated on the night before, so if you show up on the morning of the date given you will very probably have missed any music, dancing or drinking.*

January 1

New Year's Day in Greece is the feast day of **Áyios Vassílios**, their version of Santa Claus, and is celebrated with church services and the baking of a special loaf, *vassilópitta*, in which a coin is baked which brings its finder good luck throughout the year. The traditional New Year greeting is "*Kalí Hroniá*".

January 6

The **Epiphany**, when the *kalikántzari* (hobgoblins) who run riot on earth during the twelve days of Christmas are rebanished to the nether world by various rites of the Church. The most important of these is the blessing of baptismal fonts and all outdoor bodies of water. At lakeside, river and seaside locations, the priest traditionally casts a crucifix into the deep, with local youths competing for the privilege of recovering it.

Pre-Lenten carnivals

These span three weeks, climaxing during the seventh weekend before Easter. If you are heading for the Ionian islands, consider a detour to take in the **Pátra Carnival**, which, with its chariot parade and costume parties, is one of the largest and most outrageous in the Mediterranean, with events from January 17 until "Clean Monday", the last day of Lent; on the last Sunday before Lent there's a grand parade.

The **Ionian islands**, especially Kefalloniá, are also good for carnival, while **Skíros** in the Sporades puts on an outrageous "Goat Dance".

March 25

Independence Day and the **Feast of the Annunciation** (*Evangelismós* in Greek) is both a religious and a national holiday, with, on the one hand, military parades and dancing to celebrate the beginning of the revolt against Turkish rule in 1821, and, on the other, church services to honour the news being given to Mary that she was to become the Mother of Christ. There are major festivities on **Tínos**, **Ídhra (Hydra)** and many other places, particularly any monastery or church named Evangelístria or Evangelismós, whose name-day celebration it is.

April 23

The **Feast of St George (Áyios Yióryios)**, the patron of shepherds, is a big rural celebration, with much dancing and feasting at associated shrines and towns. Saint George is also the patron saint of **Skíros**, so this day is celebrated in some style there, too. If April 23 falls before Easter, ie during Lent, the festivities are postponed until the Monday after Easter.

May 1

May Day is the great urban holiday when townspeople traditionally make for the countryside for picnics and to return with bunches of wild flowers. Wreaths are hung on their doorways or balconies until they are burnt on Midsummer's eve. There are also large demonstrations by the left, claiming the *Ergatikí Protomayiá* (Working-Class First of May) as their own.

May 21

The Feast of **Áyios Konstandínos** and his mother, **Ayía Eléni**, the first Orthodox Byzantine rulers. It is widely celebrated as the name-day for two of the more popular Christian names in Greece.

June 29

The **Feast of the Holy Apostles (Ayíi Apostolí), Pétros and Pávlos**. Two more widely celebrated name days.

July 17

The **Feast of Ayía Marína**: a big deal in rural areas, as she's an important protectress of crops.

July 18–20

The **Feast of Profítis Ilías (the Prophet Elijah)** is celebrated at the countless hill- or mountaintop shrines of Profítis Ilías.

July 26

The **Feast of Ayiá Paraskeví** is celebrated in towns and villages bearing the name.

August 6

The **Feast of the Metamórfosi (Transfiguration)** provides another excuse for celebrations. In fact, between mid-July and mid-September there are religious festivals every few days, especially in the rural areas, and with these and the summer heat ordinary business comes to a virtual standstill.

August 15

The **Apokímisis tis Panayías (Assumption of the Blessed Virgin Mary)**. This is the day when people traditionally return to their home village, and in many places there will be no accommodation available on any terms. Even some Greeks will resort to sleeping in the streets. There is a great pilgrimage to **Tínos**, and major festivities at **Páros**, at Ayiássos on **Lésvos**, and at Olímbos on **Kárpathos**.

September 8
The **Yénisis tis Panayías (Birth of the Virgin Mary)** sees special services in churches dedicated to the event (with major festivals 24hr beforehand), and a double cause for rejoicing on **Spétses** where they also celebrate the anniversary of the **Battle of the Straits** of Spétses, which took place on September 8, 1822. A reenactment of the battle takes place in the harbour, followed by fireworks and feasting well into the night.

September 14
A last major summer festival, the **Ípsosi tou Stavroú (Exaltation of the Cross)**.

October 26
The **Feast of Áyios Dhimítrios**, another popular name-day. New wine is traditionally tapped on this day, a good excuse for general inebriation.

October 28
Ókhi Day, the year's major patriotic shindig – a national holiday with parades, folk-dancing and feasting to commemorate Metaxas's apocryphal one-word reply to Mussolini's 1940 ultimatum: "*Okhi!*"(No!).

November 8
Another popular name-day, the **Feast of the Archangels Michael and Gabriel (Mihaíl and Gavriél)**, with rites at the numerous rural monasteries and chapels named after them.

December 6
The **Feast of Áyios Nikólaos**, the patron of seafarers, with many chapels dedicated to him.

December 25
A much less festive occasion than Greek Easter, **Christmas** is still an important religious feast celebrating the birth of Christ, and in recent years it has started to take on more of the trappings of the western Christmas, with decorations, Christmas trees and gifts.

December 31
New Year's Eve, when, as on the other twelve days of Christmas, children go door-to-door singing the traditional *kálanda* (carols), receiving money in return. Adults tend to sit around playing cards, often for money. The *vassilópitta* may be cut at midnight, to mark the start of another year of what can seem like a non-stop round of celebrations.

CULTURAL FESTIVALS

As well as religious festivals, Greece has a full range of **cultural festivals** – highlights of which include **classical drama** in ancient theatres, including that on the island of Thássos. A leaflet entitled "Greek Festivals", available from GNTO offices abroad, includes details of smaller, **local festivals** of music, drama and dance, which take place on a more sporadic basis.

Island-based events include:
Itháki Music Festival (July).
Iráklion (Crete) Festival (early Aug).
Lefkádha Arts Jamboree (Aug).
Réthimnon (Crete) Renaissance Fair (Aug).
Thira (Santoríni) Music Festival (Aug–Sept).
Rhodes Festival (Aug–Oct).

CINEMA

Greek **cinemas** show a large number of American and British movies, always undubbed with Greek subtitles. They are highly affordable, currently 1000–1500dr depending on location, and in summer a number set up outside on vacant lots. An **outdoor movie** is worth catching at least once – indoor shows never quite seem the same once you've seen an open-air screening of Kirk Douglas in *The Odyssey* on Ithaca.

WATER SPORTS

The Greek seashore offers endless scope for water sports, with windsurfing-boards for rent in most resorts and, in larger resorts, waterskiing and parasailing facilities.

The last few years have seen a massive growth in the popularity of **windsurfing** in Greece. The country's bays and coves are ideal for beginners, and boards can be hired in literally hundreds of resorts. Particularly good areas include the islands of Lefkádha, Zákinthos, Náxos, Sámos, Lésvos, Corfu and Crete. You can almost always pay for an initial period of instruction, if you've not tried the sport previously. Rates are very reasonable – about £5/US$7.50 an hour.

Waterskiing is available at a number of the larger resorts, and a fair few of the smaller ones, too. By the rental standards of the ritzier parts of the Mediterranean it is a bargain, with twenty minutes' instruction often available for around £8–10/$12–15. At many resorts, **parasailing**

(*parapént* in Greek) is also possible; rates start at £10/$15 a go.

From ancient times onwards, the combination of navigable waters and natural island harbours have made Greece a tremendous place for **sailing**. Holiday companies offer all sorts of packaged and tailormade cruises (see p.6). Locally, boats and dinghies are rented out by the day or week at many resorts. For more details, pick up the informative brochure "Sailing the Greek Sea" from GNTO offices or contact the *Hellenic Yachting Federation*, Akti Navarchou Kountouridti 7, 18534 Pireás (☎01/41 37 351).

Because of the potential for pilfering submerged antiquities, **scuba diving** is severely restricted, its legal practice confined on the islands to certain coasts around Crete, Kálimnos, Míkonos, and most of the Ionian islands. For more information, contact the *Union of Greek Diving Centres* (☎01/92 29 532).

POLICE, TROUBLE AND HARASSMENT

In an **emergency**, dial ☎100 for the police, ☎171 for the tourist police; in a medical emergency, dial ☎166 for an ambulance.

rooms or on campsites. Unfortunately, the main risk of theft comes from your fellow tourists. Below are a few pointers on offences that might get you into trouble locally, and some advice on sexual harassment – all too much a fact of life given the classically Mediterranean machismo of the culture.

Greece is one of Europe's safest countries, with a low crime rate (though it's creeping up in Athens and other cities), and an almost unrivalled reputation for honesty. If you leave a bag or wallet at a café, you'll most likely find it scrupulously looked after, pending your return. Similarly, Greeks are relaxed about leaving possessions unlocked or unattended on the beach, in

OFFENCES

The most common causes of a brush with authority are nude bathing or sunbathing, and camping outside an authorized site.

Nude bathing is legal on only a very few beaches (on Míkonos, for example), and is deeply offensive to many more traditional Greeks. You should exercise considerable sensitivity to local feeling and the kind of place you're in: it is, for example, very bad etiquette to swim or sunbathe nude within sight of a church. Generally, though, if a beach has become fairly established for nudity, or is well secluded, it's highly unlikely that the police are going to come charging in. Where they do get bothered is if they feel a place is turning into a "hippie beach" or nudity is getting too overt on mainstream tourist stretches. But there are no hard and fast rules; it all depends on the local cops. Most of the time, the only action will be a warning, but you can officially be arrested straight off – facing up to three days in jail and a stiff fine.

Topless (sun)bathing for women is technically legal nationwide, but specific locales often opt out of the "liberation" by posting signs to that effect. It is best to follow their dictates.

Very similar guidelines apply to **freelance camping** – though for this you're still less likely to incur anything more than a warning to move on. The only real risk of arrest is if you are told to move on and fail to do so. In either of the above cases, even if the police do take any action against you, it's more likely to be a brief spell in their cells than any official prosecution.

Drug offences are a far more serious matter, and are treated as major crimes, particularly since there's a growing local use and addiction problem. The maximum penalty for "causing the use of drugs by someone under 18", for example, is life imprisonment and at least a 10-million-drachma fine. Theory is by no means practice, but foreigners caught in possession of small amounts of grass do get long jail sentences if there's evidence that they've been supplying others.

If you get arrested for any offence, you have a right to contact your **consulate** who will arrange a lawyer for your defence. Beyond this, there is little they can, or in most cases will, do.

SEXUAL HARASSMENT

Thousands of women travel independently about the Greek islands without being harassed or feeling intimidated. Greek machismo, however, is strong, if less upfront than in, for example, southern Italy. Most of the hassle you are likely to get is from a small minority of Greeks who migrate to the main resorts and towns in summer in pursuit of "liberated, fun-loving" tourists.

Indigenous Greeks, who are increasingly hospitable as you become more of a fixture in any one place, treat these outsiders, known as *kamákia* (harpoons), with contempt. Their obvious stake-outs are beach bars and discos. Words worth remembering for an unambiguous response include *Pávsteh* (stop it), *afístemeh* (leave me alone) and *fíyeteh* (go away).

Hitching is not advisable for lone women travellers, but camping is generally easy and unthreatening, although away from recognized sites it is often wise to attach yourself to a local family by making arrangements to use nearby private land. On the more remote islands you may feel more uncomfortable travelling alone. The intensely traditional Greeks may have trouble understanding why you are unaccompanied, and might not welcome your presence in their exclusively male *kafenía* – often the only place where you can get a drink. Travelling with a man, you're more likely to be treated as a *kséni*, a word meaning both (female) stranger and guest.

DIRECTORY

ADMISSION FEES Admission fees to major ancient sites and most museums range from 200–1500dr, with an average fee of around 500dr. At most, there are reductions of 50–100 percent (the latter applying to EC nationals) for student card holders. In addition, entrance to all state-run sites and museums is free to all EC nationals on Sundays and public holidays – non-EC nationals will be unlucky to be detected as such on these days. It's free to take photographs, though the use of tripods or video-cameras incurs an extra charge of around 1000dr.

BARGAINING isn't a regular feature of life, though you'll find it possible with private rooms and some off-season hotels. Similarly, you may be able to negotiate discounted rates for vehicle rental, especially for longer periods.

CHILDREN are worshipped and indulged in Greece, perhaps to excess, and present few problems when travelling. Baby foods and nappies/diapers are ubiquitous and reasonably priced, plus concessions are offered on most forms of transport. Private rooms establishments are more likely to offer some kind of babysitting service than the more impersonal hotels.

ELECTRICITY is 220 volt AC throughout the country. Wall outlets take double round-pin plugs as in the rest of continental Europe. North American appliances will require both a step-down transformer and a plug adapter.

DEPARTURE TAX A departure tax is levied on all international ferries – currently 1500dr per person *and* per car or motorbike. To non-EC states (Turkey, Egypt and Israel), it's 4000dr per person. There's also an airport departure tax of 2800–5600dr, depending on destination, but it's always included in the price of the ticket – there's no collection at the airport itself.

FILMS *Fuji* and *Agfa* films are reasonably priced and easy to have processed; *Kodachrome* and *Ektachrome* slide films are expensive, best bought (and processed) outside Greece.

FOOTBALL (soccer) is far and away the most popular sport in Greece – both in terms of participating and watching. The most important (and most heavily sponsored) teams are *Panathanaïkós* and *AEK* of Athens, *Olympiakós* of Pireás, and *PAOK* of Thessaloníki. The only significant island team is the Cretan *Ofí.*

GAY LIFE is still taboo to a certain extent and only high profile in certain areas, like Míkonos, still the most popular European gay resort after Ibiza in Spain. Lesser action occurs on Rhodes; for women, to a modest extent, at Erissós on Lésvos (appropriately). Homosexuality is legal over the age of 17, and (male) bisexuality quite widely accepted.

HIKING Greeks are just becoming used to the notion that anyone should want to walk for pleasure, yet if you have the time and stamina it is probably the single best way to see the country. This guide includes descriptions of a number of hikes. For more detail, you might want to acquire Marc Dubin's *Trekking in Greece* (Lonely Planet). For advice on maps, see p.27.

LAUNDRIES (*plintíria*) are beginning to crop up in most of the main resort towns; sometimes an attended service wash is available for little or no extra charge over the basic cost of 1000–1200dr per wash and dry. Otherwise, ask rooms owners for a *skáfi* (laundry trough), a bucket (*kouvás*), or the special laundry area often available; they freak out if you use bathroom washbasins, Greek plumbing (and wall-mounting) being what they are.

PERÍPTERA are street-corner kiosks. They sell everything from pens to disposable razors, stationery to soap, sweets to condoms, cigarettes to plastic crucifixes . . . and are often open when nothing else is.

USEFUL THINGS TO BRING

An alarm clock (for early buses and ferries); a flashlight (if you camp out); mosquito repellent, sunscreen, and ear plugs for noisy ferries and hotels.

TIME Greek summertime begins at 4am on the last Sunday in March, when the clocks go forward one hour, and ends at 4am the last Sunday in September when they go back. Be alert to this, as scores of visitors miss planes, ferries, etc, every year; the change is not well publicized. Greek time is two hours ahead of Britain, three hours when the countries' respective changes to summertime fail to coincide. For North America, the difference is seven hours for Eastern Standard Time, ten hours for Pacific Standard Time, with again an extra hour for those weeks in April and October. A recorded time message (in Greek) is available by dialling ☎141.

TOILETS Public ones in towns are usually in parks or squares, often subterranean; otherwise try a bus station. Except in areas frequented by tourists, public toilets tend to be pretty filthy – it's best to use the much cleaner ones in restaurants and bars. Note that throughout Greece, you drop paper in the adjacent wastebins, not in the bowl. Blocked toilets and dubious plumbing are common complaints among foreign visitors.

PART TWO

THE

GUIDE

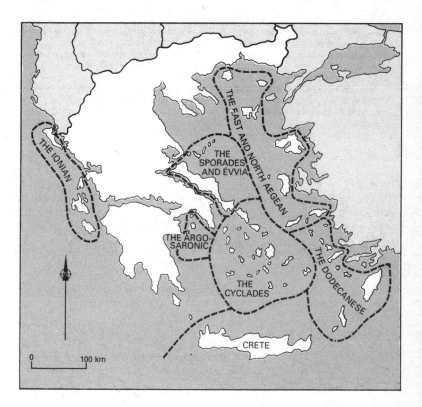

ISLAND ACCOMMODATION: ROOM PRICE SCALES

All establishments in this book have been price-graded according to the scale outlined below. The rates quoted represent the cheapest available room in high season; all are prices for a double room, except for category ①, which are per person rates. Out of season, rates can drop by up to fifty percent, especially if you negotiate rates for a stay of three or more nights. Single rooms, where available, cost around seventy percent of the price of a double.

Rented private rooms on the islands usually fall into the ② or ③ categories, depending on their location and facilities, and the season; a few in the ④ category are more like plush self-catering apartments. They are not generally available from late October through the beginning of April, when only hotels tend to remain open.

① 1400–2000dr (£4–5.50/US$6–8.50)   ④ 8000–12000dr (£22–33/US$33–50)

② 4000–6000dr (£11–16.50/US$17–25)   ⑤ 12000–16000dr (£33–44/US$50–66)

③ 6000–8000dr (£16.50–22/US$25–33)   ⑥ 16000dr (£44/US$66) and upwards

For more accommodation details, see pp.32–34.

FERRY ROUTES AND SCHEDULES

Details of ferry routes, together with approximate journey times and frequencies, are to be found at the end of each chapter in the "Travel details" section. Please note that these are for general guidance only. Ferry schedules change with alarming regularity and the only information to be relied upon is that provided by the port police in each island harbour. Ferry agents in Pireás and on the islands are helpful, of course, but keep in mind that they often represent just one ferry line and won't necessarily inform you of the competition. Be aware, too, that ferry services to the smaller islands tend to be pretty skeletal from mid-September through to May.

In many of the island groups, ferries are supplemented by *Flying Dolphin* hydrofoils – which tend to be twice as quick and twice the price. Most of the major hydrofoil routes are operated from May to early September, with lesser ones sometimes running in July and August only.

CHAPTER ONE

THE ARGO-SARONIC

T
he rocky, volcanic chain of **Argo-Saronic** islands, most of them barely an olive's
throw from the Argolid, differ to a surprising extent not just from the mainland
but from one another. Less surprising is their massive popularity, with Éyina
(Aegina) especially becoming something of an Athenian suburb at weekends.

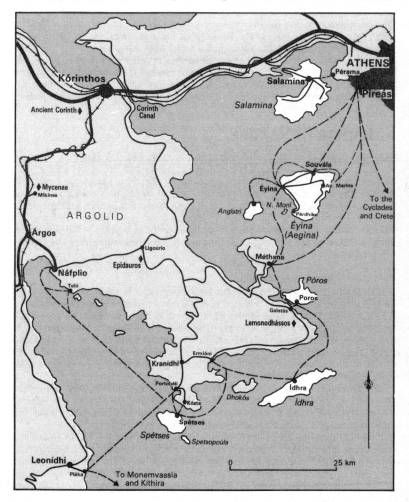

Ídhra (Hydra), Póros and Spétses are not far behind in summer, though their visitors tend to be predominantly cruise- and package-tourists. More than any other group, these islands are at their best out of season, when populations fall dramatically and the port towns return to quiet, provincial-backwater life.

Éyina, important in antiquity and more or less continually inhabited since then, is the most fertile of the group, famous for its pistachio nuts, as well as for one of the finest ancient temples in Greece. Its main problem – the crowds – can be escaped by avoiding weekends, or taking the time to explore its satellite isles, **Angístri** and **Moní**.

The three southerly islands, **Spétses**, **Ídhra** and **Póros**, are pine-cloaked and relatively infertile. They were not really settled until medieval times, when refugees from the mainland – principally Albanian Christians – established themselves here. In response to the barrenness of their new home the islanders adopted piracy as a livelihood, and the seamanship and huge fleets thus acquired were placed at the disposal of the Greek nation during the War of Independence. Today foreigners and Athenians have replaced locals in the rapidly depopulating harbour towns, and windsurfers and sailboats are faint echoes of the warships and *kaíkia* once at anchor.

The closest island of the Argo-Saronic, **Salamína**, is virtually a suburb of Pireás, just over a kilometre offshore to its east, and it almost touches the industrial city of Mégara to the west as well. As you might expect, it is frequented by Athenian weekenders, and is also used as a base for commuting to the capital, but sees very few foreign visitors.

Salamína (Salamis)

Salamína is the quickest possible island hop from Athens. Take the #842 bus from Platía Eleftherias to the shipyard port of Pérama, just west of Pireás, and a ferry (daily 5am–midnight; 100dr) will whisk you across to the little port of Paloukía in a matter of minutes. The ferry crosses the narrow strait where, in 480BC, the Greek fleet trounced the Persian fleet, despite being outnumbered three to one; this battle is said by some to be more significant than the battle of Marathon, ten years earlier. On arrival in Paloukía, you won't be rewarded by desirable or isolated beaches – the pollution of Pireás and Athens is a little too close for comfort – but you soon escape the capital's *néfos* and and city pace.

Paloukía, Salamína and Selínia
PALOUKÍA is really just a transit point. By the ferry dock is a taverna and opposite is a bus station, with services to Salamína Town (3km), the island capital and beyond.

SALAMÍNA TOWN (also known as Kouloúri) is home to 18,000 of the island's 23,000 population. It's a ramshackle place, with a couple of banks, a fishmarket and an over-optimistic (and long-closed) tourist office. Pretty much uniquely for an island town – and emphasizing its absence of tourists – there is no bike or moped rental outlet, and also no hotel (not that you'd want to stay). Fortunately, bus services are excellent, linking most points on the island.

Bus #8 runs to the port at the northwest tip of the island, the **Voudoro peninsula**, where there are ferries across to Lákki Kalomírou, near Mégara on the Athens–Kórinthos road. En route it passes close by the **Monastery of Faneroméni** (6km from Salamína), rather majestically sited above the frustratingly polluted gulf.

Around 6km to the south of Paloukía is a third island port, **SELÍNIA**, which has connections direct to the Pireás ferry dock (winter 9.30am, summer five crossings daily between 8am–2.30pm; 210dr; 30min). This is the main summer resort, with a pleasant waterfront, a bank, several tavernas and two inexpensive hotels, the *Akroyali* (☎01/46 53 341; ②) and *Votsalakia* (☎01/46 71 334; ②), which has a swimming pool and restaurant. Selínia can be reached direct by bus from Paloukía.

Eándio and the south

South from Salamína Town, the road edges the coast towards Eándio (6km; regular buses). There are a few tavernas along the way, but the sea vistas are not inspiring. **EÁNDIO**, however, is quite a pleasant village, with a little pebble beach and the island's best **hotel**, the *Gabriel* (☎01/46 62 275; ③), owned by poet and journalist, Giorgos Tzimas, who is usually only too keen to recite a poem or two. The hotel overlooks the bay, whose waters are again unenticing (probably a health risk) for swimming, but it could be an enjoyable off-season stay.

Two roads continue from Eándio. The one to the southeast runs to the unassuming village resorts of Peráni and Paralía (both around 4km from Eándio). The more interesting route is southeast to Kanákia (8km from Eándio; no buses), over the island's pine-covered mountain, and passing (at around 5km) a monastery – dedicated, like almost all Salamína churches, to Áyios Nikólaos. At the monastery you could turn off the road (left) along a track to the harbour and small-scale resort of Peristéria (5km). This is a much more attractive settlement than the littered beach and scruffy huts of Kanákia itself.

Éyina (Aegina)

Given its current population of a little over 10,000, it seems incredible that **Éyina** (Aegina) was a major power in Classical times – and a rival to Athens. It carried on trade to the limits of the known world, maintained a sophisticated silver coinage system (the first in Greece) and had prominent athletes and craftsmen. However, during the fifth century BC the islanders made the political mistake of siding with their

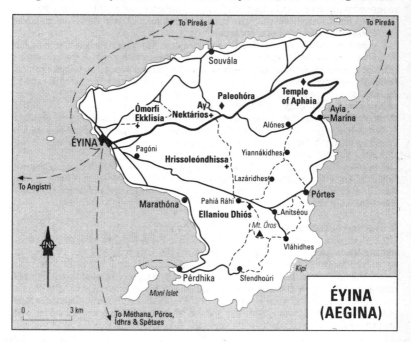

ÉYINA
(AEGINA)

fellow Dorians, the Spartans, which Athens seized on as an excuse to act on a long-standing jealousy; her fleets defeated those of the islanders in two separate sea battles and, after the second, the population was expelled and replaced by more tractable colonists.

Subsequent history was less distinguished, with the familiar central Greece pattern of occupation, by Romans, Franks, Venetians, Catalans and Turks, before the War of Independence brought a brief period as seat of government for the fledgling Greek nation. These days, the island is most famous for its **pistachio orchards**, whose thirsty trees lower the water table several feet annually; hence the notices warning you of the perennial water crisis.

Athenians regard Éyina as a beach annexe for their city, being the closest place to the capital most of them would swim at, though for tourists it has a monument as fine as any in the Aegean in its beautiful fifth-century BC **Temple of Aphaia**. This is located on the east coast, close to the port of **Ayía Marína**, and if it is your primary goal, you'd do best to take one of the ferries that in season run directly to that port. If you plan to stay, then make sure your boat will dock at **Éyina Town**, the island capital. Ferries also occasionally stop at **Souvála**, a Greek weekend retreat between the two ports devoid of interest to outsiders. Hydrofoils, incidentally, are far more frequent, run from the same quay in Pireás as the conventional boats, and cost hardly any more for this particular destination.

Éyina Town

A solitary column of a Temple of Apollo beckons as your ferry or hydrofoil steams around the point into the harbour at **ÉYINA TOWN**. The island's capital, it makes an attractive base, with some grand old buildings from the time (1826–28) when it served as the first capital of Greece after the War of Independence. And for somewhere so close to Athens, it isn't especially overrun by foreign tourists, nor are accommodation prices unduly inflated except on weekends.

The **harbour** is workaday rather than picturesque, but is nonetheless appealing for that: fishermen talk and tend their nets, and *kaíkia* loaded with produce from the mainland bob at anchor. North of the port, behind the small town beach, the rather weather-beaten Apollo-temple column stands on a low hill that was the ancient acropolis and is known, logically enough, as **Kolóna** (Column). Around the temple are rather obscure **ruins** (daily 8.30am–3pm; 400dr), only worth it for the sweeping view from Moní islet on the south to the mainland shore on the northwest. A small museum on the grounds is shut indefinitely owing to structural damage, but on the north flank of Kolóna hill there's an attractive bay with a small, sandy **beach** – the best spot for swimming in the immediate vicinity of the town.

The town's other sights, such as they are, are the frescoed thirteenth-century church of **Ómorfi Ekklisía**, fifteen minutes' walk east of the port, and a house in the suburb of Livádhi, just to the north, where a plaque recalls the residence of **Nikos Kazantzakis**, when he was writing his most celebrated book, *Zorba the Greek*.

Arrival and accommodation

The **bus station** is also on the recently refurbished Platía Ethneyersías, with an excellent service to most villages on the island, while the largest moped and cycle rental place – *Stratos* (☎0297/24 865), with slightly above normal island rates – is in the pink corner building just to the north. There are a few mountain bikes available, but Éyina is large and hilly enough to make motorized cycles worthwhile for anything other than a pedal to the beaches between Éyina Town and Pérdhika. Three **banks** line the waterfront; the **post office** is on Platía Ethneyersías; while the **OTE** lies well inland beyond the cathedral.

Rooms can be hard to come by in Éyina Town, with many of the more comfortable hotels block-booked in the summer months. You would be well advised to phone ahead, or to take whatever you're offered on arrival, at least for the first night. Hard bargaining can be productive, especially out of season and midweek, when rates tend to be two-thirds or less what they are on Friday or Saturday nights. Try the streets inland from Platía Ethneyersías, a couple of hundred metres to the left of the jetty as you disembark; if you really get stuck, there's a **tourist police** post in the same building as the regular police, but reached from a narrow alley just off Ethneyersías, and the unofficial but helpful "Aegina Tourist Board" above a *gelateria* on the corner of Leonárdhou Ladhá and the waterfront.

Best inexpensive accommodation option are rooms, either those inland by the OTE (☎0297/22 334; ②), or those of *Andonis Marmarinos* at Leonárdhou Ladhá 30 (☎0297/22 954; ②), spotless, fairly quiet though not en suite. For more comfort try the *Hotel Marmarinos* nearby at no. 24, run by a branch of the same family (☎0297/23 510; ②–③ midweek, ③–④ weekend). Across the street, *Hotel Artemis* (☎0297/25 195; ④) is appealingly set in a pistachio orchard. Slightly fancier is the *Hotel Areti* on the seafront between Platía Ethneyersías and Kolóna (☎0297/23 593; ②–③ midweek, ③–④ weekend), where ocean views offset a certain amount of traffic noise.

Food and entertainment

When searching for a **meal out**, forego the obvious and touristy glitz outfits on the front in favour of more obscure nooks and crannies. The pistachio nuts for which Éyina is famed make a good snack: they are best unsalted, but are not very cheap.

Directly behind the fish market is a particularly good and inexpensive seafood taverna, the *Psarotaverna Agora,* with outdoor seating on the cobbles in summer. Similar in concept, though not quite as good value, is *Ta Vrehamena,* a little hole-in-the-wall on Leonárdhou Ladhá just seaward from the police station, offering a very limited menu of bulk wine, ouzo and grilled octopus. Just around the corner, the bakery *O Bogris* has good whole grain bread suitable for breakfast or picnics. Next to the *Hotel Areti,* the *Psitopolio Lekkas* is excellent for no-nonsense meat grills by the waterside. At the opposite (south) end of the quay, by the *Trapeza Pisteos* (Credit Bank), *Maridhaki* is a less carnivorous traditional place, dishing up the usual Greek oven standards. Finally, for a mild blowout, *Taverna Votsitsanos,* two blocks straight inland from the centre of the front, has a particularly full menu of fish and oven specialities, with seating in its own garden, the alley or (in winter) indoors.

In terms of **nightlife**, Éyina Town can boast no less than two summer **cinemas**, the *Olympia* and the *Anesis,* and a winter one, the *Titina,* by the park with the medieval tower-house, near OTE. On the corner of Aiándos and Piléos, the *Belle Epoque* bar is worth a visit for its ornate turn-of-the-century architecture.

The Temple of Aphaia

The Doric **Temple of Aphaia** (Mon–Fri 8.30am–7pm, Sat & Sun 8.30am–3pm; 600dr) lies 12km east of Éyina Town, standing among pines that are tapped to flavour the local retsina, beside a less aesthetic radio mast. It is one of the most complete and visually complex ancient buildings in Greece, with superimposed arrays of columns and lintels evocative of an Escher drawing. Built early in the fifth century BC, or possibly at the end of the sixth century, it predates the Parthenon by around sixty years. The dedication is unusual: Aphaia was a Cretan nymph who had fled from the lust of King Minos, and seems to have been worshipped almost exclusively on Éyina. As recently as two centuries ago the temple's pediments were intact and virtually perfect, depicting two battles at Troy. However, like the Elgin marbles they were "bought" from the Turks: this time by Ludwig of Bavaria, which explains their current residence in the Munich Glyptothek museum.

There are buses to the temple from Éyina Town, or you could walk from Ayía Marina along the path that takes up where Kolokotroni leaves off, but the best approach is by rented motorbike, which allows you to stop at the monastery of Áyios Nektários, and the island's former capital of Paleohóra.

Áyios Nektários and Paleohóra

Áyios Nektários, a garishly modern monastery situated around halfway to the Temple of Aphaia, was named in honour of a controversial and high-living worthy who died in 1920 and was canonized in 1961, in a highly irregular fashion.

Paleohóra, a kilometre or so further east, was built in the ninth century as protection against piracy, but it failed singularly in this capacity during Barbarossa's 1537 raid. Abandoned in 1826, following Greek independence, Paleohóra is now utterly deserted, but possesses the romantic appeal of a ghost village. You can drive right up to the site: take the turning signposted for Áyios Nektários and keep going about 400m. Some 20 of Paleohóra's reputed 365 churches and monasteries – one for every saint's day – remain in recognizable state, and can be visited, but only those of Episkopí (locked), Áyios Yióryios and Metamórfosis (on the lower of the two trails) retain frescoes of any merit or in any state of preservation. Nothing remains of the town itself; when the islanders left, they simply dismantled their houses and moved them to Éyina Town.

The East: Ayía Marína and Pórtes

The island's major package resort of **AYÍA MARÍNA**, 15km from Éyina Town, lies on the east coast of the island, south of the Aphaia Temple ridge. The concentrated tackiness of its jam-packed high street is something rarely seen this side of Corfu: signs for Guinness, burger bars and salaciously named ice creams and cocktails. The mediocre beach is packed, overlooked by constantly sprouting, half-built hotels, and the water is frankly filthy. In short, it's only worth coming here for the ferries to Pireás (some five a day in season, with departures in the morning and late in the afternoon).

Beyond the resort, the paved road continues south 8km to **PÓRTES**, a pokey, low-key shore hamlet, dramatically set with a cliff on the north and wooded valleys behind. Among the uneasy mix of new summer villas-in-progress (no short-term accommodation) and old basalt cottages are scattered two or three tiny fish **tavernas** and snack bars, with a functional beach between the two fishing anchorages. Soon the road deteriorates to a steep, rough dirt track climbing to the village of Anitséou, just below an important saddle on the flank of Mount Óros. The road surface improves slightly as it forges west towards the scenic hamlet of **Pahiá Ráhi**, where there's a seasonal taverna. From here, a sharp, paved descent leads to the main west-coast road at Marathóna and a longer, gentler route back to Éyina Town. Just past Pahía Ráhi on the latter option is the signposted side-turning for the **nunnery of Hrissoleóndissa**, which can also be reached from the settlements of Yiannákidhes and Lazáridhes to the east.

Mount Óros

Just south of the saddle between Pahiá Ráhi and Anitséou, mentioned above, are the massive foundations of the shrine of **Ellaníou Dhiós**, with the monastery of Taxiárhes squatting amid the massive masonry. The 532m summit of **Mount Óros**, an hour's walk from the highest point of the road, is capped by a chapel and promises views across the entire island and over much of the Argo-Saronic Gulf.

A few **other paths** cross the largely roadless, volcanic flanks of Óros. From **Anitséou** a one-lane tractor track goes southeast, ending after 15 minutes' walk at the six-house hamlet of **Vláhidhes**, below which stretches the small, shingle beach of **Kípi**, most often visited by boats but also accessible by trail from Vláhidhes. Amazingly in this bulldozer-mad country, another path, initially marked by white paint dots to **Sfendhoúri** hamlet southwest of the peak, still survives. Sfendhoúri itself has a road link with Pérdhika (see below); there is also another direct path from near the Zeus temple to Pérdhika, though this is cut across by a new jeep track.

The West: Marathóna, Pérdhika and Moní islet

The road due south of Éyina Town running along the west coast of the island is served by regular buses (8–10 daily). **MARATHÓNA**, 5km from Éyina, constitutes the only sandy-beach resort on the west coast, though tolerable enough, with its clutch of rooms and tavernas along the shore.

PÉRDHIKA, 9km along and the end of the line, is more scenically set on its little bay and certainly has the best range of non-packaged accommodation on the island, besides the main town. There are **rooms,** and the *Hotel Hippocampus* (0297/61 363; ③). On the pedestrianized esplanade overlooking the water are a dozen **tavernas**, the best being *Toh Proreo*, one of the first encountered, and affiliated with an unusual general store, which boasts log-cabin-like decor.

The only other diversion at Pérdhika is a day-trip to **Moní islet** just offshore (250dr one way; 10min; several departures daily). There was once an EOT-run campsite on Móni, but this is now abandoned and derelict. There are no facilities on the islet and most of it is fenced off as a nature conservation area. It's really only worth the trip for a swim in relatively clear water, as Pérdhika bay itself is of dubious cleanliness and has but the smallest of beaches.

Angístri

Angístri, a half-hour by boat from Éyina, is small enough to be overlooked by most island-hoppers, though it's now in many foreign holiday brochures. Thus the island fosters an uneasy coexistence between Athenian and German old-timers, who bought property here years ago, and British newcomers on package trips. Beaches, however, remain better and less crowded than on Éyina, and out of season the pine-covered island succumbs to a leisurely village pace, with many islanders still making a living from fishing and farming. Headscarves worn by the old women indicate the islanders' Albanian ancestry, and among themselves they still speak *Arvanítika* – a dialect of medieval Albanian with Greek accretions – as do the elders of Póros and Méthana.

The Angístri dock in Éyina Town, separate from the main harbour, is directly opposite the *Ethniki Trapeza* (National Bank). **Boats** from Éyina and Pireás call at both the main villages, Skála and Mílos. **From Pireás**, a direct ferry runs at least twice daily in season, once a day out of season: the journey takes two hours. **From Éyina** (departures from the fish-market harbour), there are boats four or five times a day in season, twice a day out of season.

Skála and Mílos

The essentially modern resort of **SKÁLA** is dominated by dreary modern apartment buildings and hotels with little to distinguish or commend them; they tend to face either inland or the windswept north side of the peninsula over which Skála is rapidly spreading. The popular town beach, the island's only sandy one, nestles against the protected south shore of this headland, below an enormous church that is the local landmark. Between the beach and the ferry dock are two **hotels** with a bit more going for them position-wise: the *Aktaion* (☎0297/91 222; ②–③) and the *Anayennisis* (☎0297/91 332; ②–③); on summer weekends you would be well advised to reserve ahead at one of these. No tavernas demand special recognition. Both **mopeds** and **mountain**

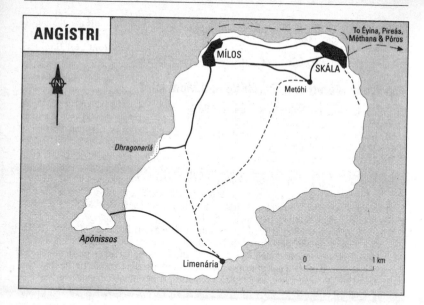

bikes are available for rent at slightly inflated rates (even compared to Éyina); Limenária, the end of the trans-island road, is only 8km distant, so in cooler weather you can comfortably cross Angístri on foot or by pedalling in a couple of hours. A road to the left of the harbour leads within fifteen minutes to the *Angistri Club*, with a disco-bar on the rocks above the sea. From there, it's another ten minutes' walk to a secluded **pebble beach** backed by crumbling cliffs and pine-covered hills; along with Dhragoneriá (see below), this is the best the island has to offer, and is clothing-optional.

Metóhi, the hillside hamlet just above Skála, was once the main village, and in recent years has been completely bought up and restored by foreigners and Athenians; there are no facilities.

Utterly overbuilt Skála threatens in the near future to merge with **MÍLOS**, just 1500m west along the north coast. Once you penetrate a husk of new construction, you find an attractive village centre built in the traditional Argo-Saronic style. Although there's no decent beach nearby, it makes a preferable base to Skála, with plenty of rented **rooms** and some **hotels**. The *Milos Hotel* (☎0297/91 241; ③) is a good, well-positioned choice, and *Ta Tria Adherfia*, in the centre of the village, is the island's best taverna.

The rest of the island

A regular bus service, designed to dovetail with the ferry schedule, connects Skála and Mílos with Limenária on the far side of the island – or you could hike from Metóhi along a winding track through the pine forest, with views across to Éyina and the Peloponnese. The paved west-coast road takes you past the turning for **Dhragoneriá**, an appealing pebble beach with a dramatic backdrop.

LIMENÁRIA is a small farming community, still largely unaffected by tourism. There are two tavernas, a few rooms and a sign pointing to a misleadingly named "beach", which is really just a spot, often monopolized by male naturists, where you can swim off the rocks. A half-hour walk northwest of here, through olive and pine trees, and past a shallow lake, will bring you to a causeway linking Angístri with the tiny islet of **Apónissos**, where there's a seasonal taverna.

Póros

Separated from the mainland by a 350-metre strait, **Póros** ("the ford") only just counts as an island. But qualify it does, making it fair game for the package tours, while its proximity to Pireás also means a weekend invasion by Athenians. Unspoilt it isn't, and the beaches are few and poor, especially compared to neighbouring Ídhra and Spétses. The island town, however, has a bit of character, and the topography is interesting. Póros is in fact two islands, **Sferiá** (which shelters Póros Town) and the more exten-sive **Kalávria**, separated from each other by a shallow engineered canal. According to one local guide book "the canal reminds you of Venice" – a phrase which must have gained much in the translation.

In addition to its regular ferry and hydrofoil connections with Pireás and the other Argo-Saronics, Póros has frequent boats shuttling across from the mainland port of **Galatás** in the Peloponnese: there's a car ferry every 20 minutes. This allows for some interesting excursions – locally to the lemon groves of **Limonódhassos**, **Ancient Troezen**, near Trizini, and the nearby **Devil's Bridge**. Further afield, day-trips to Nápflio or to performances of ancient drama at the great theatre of Epidaurus are possible by car, or by taking an excursion, available from various travel agents in Poros Town.

Póros Town

Ferries from the Argo-Saronics or from Galatás drop you at **PÓROS**, the only town on the island, which rises steeply on all sides of the tiny volcanic peninsula of Sferiá. The harbour and town are picturesque from the sea and the cafés and the waterfront have quite an animation about them. There are no special sights, save for a little **archeolo-gical museum** (Mon–Sat 9am–3pm; free) with a display on the mainland site of Troezen.

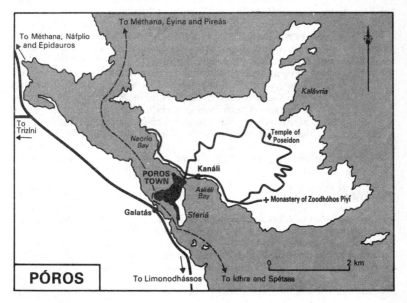

Just back from the waterfront are three **travel agents**: *Marinos Tours* (☎0298/23 423), sole agents for the *Flying Dolphin* hydrofoils, *Family Tours* (☎0298/23 743) and *Saronic Gulf Travel* (☎0298/24 555) all exchange money, sell island maps and arrange accommodation in **rented rooms**. If you want to look around on your own, the quieter and preferable places are in the streets back – and up – from the clocktower, although prices are generally on the high side. Here you'll find two reasonable hotels; *Dimitra* (☎0298/22 697; ④) and *Latsi* (☎0298/22 392; ③). Most of the other hotels are across the canal on Kalávria. Camping is not encouraged anywhere on the island and theré is no official campsite.

Down on the quayside, good-value **restaurants** include *Grill Oasis* and *Mouragio*, at the far end away from the ferry dock, while up in the town the *Three Brothers* taverna (open June–Sept) is pricier but recommended.

Additional facilities around the waterfront include a couple of **moped and bicycle rental** outlets (you can take either across on boats to the mainland), a **bank**, **post office**, **tourist police** (☎0298/22 256; mid-May to end Sept) and a **bookstore**, *Anita's* (by the filling station), which trades secondhand paperbacks.

Kalávria

Most of Póros's **hotels** are to be found on Kalávria, the main body of the island, just across the canal beyond the Naval Cadets' Training School. They stretch for two kilometres or so on either side of the bridge, with some of those to the west ideally situated to catch the dawn chorus – the Navy's marching band. If you'd rather sleep on, head beyond the first bay where the fishing boats tie up. Here, on **Neório Bay** 2km from the bridge, is the pleasant *Hotel Pavlou* (☎0298/22 734; ③).

Alternatively, turn right around **Askéli Bay**, where there is a group of hotels and villas facing good clear water, if not much in the way of beaches. The best island beach is **Kanáli**, near the beginning of the bridge, which usually charges admission – a reflection both of Póros's commercialism and the premium on sand.

The Monastery of Zoodhóhos Piyí and Temple of Poseidon

At the end of the four-kilometre stretch of road around Askéli is the simple eighteenth-century **Monastery of Zoodhóhos Piyí**, whose monks have fled the tourists and been replaced by a caretaker to collect the admission charges. It's a pretty spot, with a couple of summer tavernas under the nearby plane trees.

From here you can either walk up across to the far side of the island through the pines and olives, or bike along the road. Either route will lead you to the few columns and ruins that make up the sixth-century BC **Temple of Poseidon** – though keep your eyes open or you may miss them; look for a small white sign on a green fence to the right of the road coming from the monastery. Here, supposedly, Demosthenes, fleeing from the Macedonians after taking part in the last-ditch resistance of the Athenians, took poison rather than surrender to the posse sent after him. A road leads on and back down in a circular route to the "grand canal".

Ídhra (Hydra)

The port and town of **Ídhra**, with its tiers of substantial stone mansions and white-walled, red-tiled houses climbing up from a perfect horseshoe harbour, is a beautiful spectacle. Unfortunately, thousands of others think so, too, and from Easter until September it's packed to the gills. The front becomes one long outdoor café, the hotels are full and the discos flourish. Once a fashionable artists' colony, established in the 1960s as people restored the grand old houses, it has experienced a predictable metamorphosis into one of the more popular (and expensive) resorts in Greece. But this

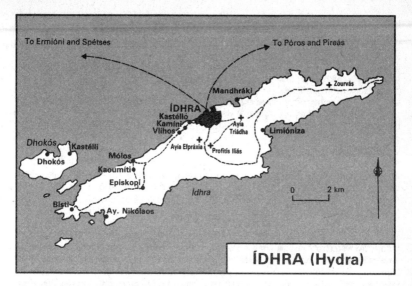

To Ermióni and Spétses

To Póros and Pireás

Zourvás

Mandhráki

ÍDHRA
Kastéllo
Kamíni
Vlíhos

Ayía
Triádha

Limióniza

Dhokós
Kastélli

Ayía Efpráxia

Profitis Iliás

Mólos

Dhokós

Kaoumíti

Episkopí

Ídhra

0   2 km

Bísti

Ay. Nikólaos

ÍDHRA (Hydra)

acknowledged, a visit is still to be recommended, especially if you can get here some time other than peak season.

Ídhra Town

The waterfront of **ÍDHRA TOWN** is lined with mansions, most of them built during the eighteenth century, on the accumulated wealth of a remarkable merchant fleet of 160 ships which traded as far afield as America and, during the Napoleonic Wars, broke the British blockade to sell grain to France. Fortunes were made and the island also enjoyed a special relationship with the Turkish Porte, governing itself, paying no tax, but providing sailors for the Sultan's navy. These conditions naturally attracted Greek immigrants from the less-privileged mainland, and by the 1820s the town's population stood at nearly 20,000, an incredible figure when you reflect that today it is under 3000. During the War of Independence, Hydriot merchants provided many of the ships for the Greek forces and inevitably many of the commanders.

The **mansions** of these merchant families, designed by architects from Venice and Genoa, are still the great monuments of the town. If you are interested in seeking them out, a town map is available locally – or ask the tourist police (see below) for help in locating them. On the western waterfront, and the hill behind, are the **Voulgaris** mansion, with its interesting interior, and the **Tombazis** mansion, used as a holiday hostel for arts students. Higher up, the **Koundouriotis** mansion was once the proud home of George Koundouriotis, a wealthy shipowner who fought in the War of Independence and whose great grandson, Pavlos Koundouriotis, was president of Greece in the 1920s. On the eastern waterfront are the **Kriezis** mansion, the **Tsamados** mansion, now the national merchant navy college which you can visit between lectures, and the **Spiliopoulous** mansion.

Ídhra is also reputedly hallowed by no less than 365 churches – a total claimed by many a Greek island, but here with some justice. The most important is the cathedral of **Panayía Mitropóleos**, built around a courtyard down by the port, and with a distinctive clocktower.

THE MIAOULIA FESTIVAL

On the second or third weekend in June, Ídhra Town celebrates the Miaoulia, in honour of Admiral Andreas Miaoulis whose "fire boats", packed with explosives, were set adrift upwind of the Turkish fleet during the War of Independence. The highlight of the celebrations is the burning of a boat at sea as a tribute to the sailors who risked their lives in this dangerous enterprise.

On an altogether more peaceful note, the International Puppet Theatre Festival takes place here at the end of July, and appeals to children of all ages.

Practicalities

The town is small and compact, but away from the waterfront the streets and alleyways are steep and finding your way around can be difficult. There are several **banks** along the waterfront, the *National Bank* is close to Miaouli; the **tourist police** (☎0298/52 205; mid-May to mid-October, daily 9am–10pm) are on Votsi, oppposite the **OTE**.

Staying on Ídhra means finding a room in the town or, if you're lucky, at Vlihós (see below). There are a number of **pensions and hotels** along, or just behind, the waterfront, often charging up to a third more than usual island rates. Some of the restaurants along the waterfront act as agents for the outlying pensions and hotels, which could save you time and footwork; better still, phone ahead and book. *Hotel Amarylis* at Tombazi 15 (☎0298/53 611; ③) is a small hotel with comfortable rooms and private facilities, or there are a couple of beautifully converted old mansions, *Pension Angelika*, Miaouli 42 (☎0298/52 202; ④) and *Hotel Hydra*, at Voulgari 8 (☎0298/52 102; ④). On the waterfront, but entered from Miaouli, is the slightly rundown but very welcoming *Hotel Sofia* (☎0298/52 313; ②).

There's no shortage of **restaurants** around the waterfront. *Ta Tria Adhelfia* is a good, inexpensive, friendly taverna next to the cathedral. The *Ambrosia Café*, back from the front, serves vegetarian meals and excellent breakfasts, and the new *Veranda Restaurant* (below the *Hotel Hydra*) has stunning views of the sunset. For nightlife, try the **discos** *Heaven*, with impressive views from its hillside site, or the long-established *Kavos*, above the harbour, with a garden for dance breaks.

Beaches around Ídhra Town

The island's only sandy beach is at **MANDHRÁKI**, 2km east of Ídhra Town along a concrete track; it's the private domain of the *Miramare Hotel* (☎0298/52 300; ⑤), although the windsurfing centre is open to all.

On the opposite side of the harbour a coastal path leads around to a pebbly but popular stretch, just before **KAMÍNI**, where there's a good year-round taverna, *George and Anna's*. Continuing along the water on an unsurfaced mule track you'll come to **KASTÉLLO**, another small, rocky beach with the ruins of a tiny fort.

Thirty minutes' walk beyond Kamíni (or a boat ride from the port) will bring you to **VLIHÓS**, a small hamlet with three tavernas, **rooms** and a historic nineteenth-century bridge. **Camping** is tolerated here (though nowhere else closer to town) and the swimming in the lee of an offshore islet is good. Further out is the islet of **Dhokós**, only seasonally inhabited by goatherds and people tending their olives.

The interior and south coast

There are no motor vehicles of any kind on Ídhra, except for two lorries to pick up the rubbish, and no metalled roads away from the port, for the island is mountainous and its interior accessible only by foot or donkey. The net result of this is that most tourists don't venture beyond the town, so with a little walking you can find yourself in a quite different kind of island. A dampener on this is that the pines that formerly covered the island were devastated by forest fires in 1985 and are still recovering.

Following the streets of the town upwards and inland you reach a path which winds up the mountain, in about an hour's walk, to the **Monastery of Profítis Ilías** and the **Convent of Ayía Efpraxía**. Both are beautifully situated; the nuns at the convent (the lower of the two) offer hand-woven fabrics for sale. Further on, to the left if you face away from the town, is the **Monastery of Ayía Triádha**, occupied by a few monks (no women admitted). From here a path continues east for two more hours to the cloister of **Zourvás** in the extreme east of the island.

The donkey path continues west of Vlíhos to **Episkopí**, a high plateau planted with olives and vineyards and dotted by perhaps a dozen summer homes (no facilities). An inconspicuous turning roughly half an hour below leads to Mólos Bay, dirty and sea-urchin-infested, and to the more pleasant farming hamlet of **KAOUMÍTI**. From Episkopí itself faint tracks lead to the western extreme of the island, on either side of which the bays of **BÍSTI** and **ÁYIOS NIKÓLAOS** offer solitude and good swimming.

The south coast, too, if you're energetic and armed with a map, is scattered with coves, the best of which, **LIMIÓNIZA** (beyond Ayía Triádha), is also served by **boat excursions** in season from Ídhra Town.

Spétses (Spetsai)

Spétses was the island where John Fowles once lived and which he used, thinly disguised as Phraxos, as the setting for *The Magus*. It is today very popular, with signs for fast food and English breakfasts lining rather too many of the old town lanes. However, as a whole, the island clings onto its charms quite tenaciously. The architecture of Spétses Town is characterful and distinguished, if less dramatic than that of Ídhra. And, despite a bout of forest fire devastation in 1990, the landscape described by Fowles is still to be seen: "away from its inhabited corner [it is] truly haunted . . . its pine forests uncanny". Remarkably, too, at Spétses's best beach (and arguably the best in the Argo-Saronic), Áyii Anáryiri, development has been limited to a scattering of holiday villas.

Spétses Town

SPÉTSES TOWN (also known as Kastélli) is the island's port – and its only town. It shares with Ídhra the same history of late eighteenth-century mercantile adventure and prosperity, and the same leading role in the War of Independence, which made its foremost citizens the aristocrats of the newly independent Greek state. Pebble-mosaic courtyards and streets sprawl between 200-year-old mansions, whose architecture is quite distinct from the Peloponnesian styles across the straits. As on Ídhra, there are no private cars; horse-drawn cabs connect the various quarters of town, which are strung out along the waterfront.

The sights are principally the majestic old houses and gardens, the finest of which is the magnificent Mexis family mansion, built in 1795 and now used as the **local museum** (daily except Mon 8.30am–2.30pm; 400dr), housing a display of relics from the War of Independence that includes the bones of the Spetsiot admiral-heroine Lascarina Bouboulina.

Just outside the town, Fowles aficionados will notice **Anáryiros College**, a curious Greek recreation of an English public school where the author was employed and set part of his tale; it is now vacant, save for the occasional conference or kids' holiday programme. Like the massive Edwardian **Hotel Possidonion**, another *Magus* setting, on the waterside, it was endowed by Sotirios Anáryiros, the island's great nineteenth-

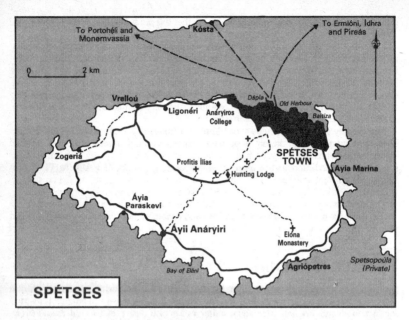

century benefactor. An enormously rich self-made man he was also responsible for planting the pine forest that now covers the island. His former house, behind the *Hotel Roumani*, is a monument to bad taste, decked out like a pharaoh's tomb.

Perhaps more interesting than chasing *Magus* settings, though, is a walk east from the **Dápia**, the cannon-studded main harbour. En route, you pass the smaller "old harbour", where the Athenian rich moor their yachts, and the church of **Áyios Nikólaos** with its graceful belfry and some giant pebble mosaics. At the end of the road you reach the **Baltíza** inlet, where half a dozen boatyards continue to build *kaíkia* in the traditional manner; it was one of these that recreated the *Argo* for Tim Severin's re-enactment of the "Jason Voyage".

Practicalities

A good way to get around the island is by bike and, despite the poor roads, you can reach most points or make a circuit without too much exertion. The most reliable of the **bike and moped rental outlets** is on the road to the old harbour, past the *Rendez-vous* bar.

All kinds of **accommodation** are available in Spétses Town, from the unmissable and unforgettable *Hotel Possidonion* (✆0298/72 208; ⑤; slightly cheaper rooms at the back), where kings and presidents have slept, to more modest **rooms**. Prices are inflated in high season, but the town is smaller and less steep than Ídhra, so hunting around for a good deal is not such hard work. If you don't fancy pounding the streets yourself, try *Pine Island Travel* (✆0298/72 314) or *Meldon Tourist and Travel Agency* (✆0298/74 497), both within 50m of the jetty. Two simple but comfortable places are *Faros* (✆0298/72 613; ④) and *Stelios* (✆0298/72 971; ③). Few places stay open all year – exceptions include the central *Pension Alexandris* (✆0298/72 211; ④) and the *Klimis Hotel* (✆0298/74 497; ④), a quiet and pleasant place run by a formidable matriarch.

In Spétses Town, **food and drink** tend to be a bit on the pricey side. Best options along the waterfront are *Roussos* (formerly *Ta Tzakia*), 300m to the left of the Dápia, and *Taverna Haralambos,* on Baltíza inlet, by the smaller harbour. The only traditional taverna is *Lazaros'* (400m inland and uphill from Dápia: ask for directions), though it can't cope with large parties. For a splurge, try *Trehandiri,* next to the church of Áyios Nikólaos on the way to the old harbour; it's the best of an expensive group of restaurants there. Vegetarian meals are available at *Lirakis,* a rooftop restaurant on the waterfront.

By day, Stambolis's *kafenío,* by the *Flying Dolphin* quáy at Dápia, remains steadfastly traditional. By night, clubbers divide between the **discos** *Coconuts* and *Figaro* – the latter being the summer base of DJs from the trendy Athenian club *Papagayo.*

Spétses has a couple of good **crafts shops**, *Pityousa* (behind the *Hotel Soleil*) and *Gorgona,* opposite; both are upmarket establishments and offer some attractive original work, as well as genuine pieces from the Pireás antique markets.

Around the island

For **swimming** you need to get clear of the town. Beaches within walking distance are at **Ayía Marína** (twenty minutes east, with a taverna), at various spots beyond the **old harbour,** and several other spots half an hour away in either direction. The tempting islet of **Spetsopoúla,** just offshore from Ayía Marína, is, unfortunately, off-limits. It's the private property of shipping magnate Stavros Niarchos, of dubious repute, who maintains it as a pleasure park for his associates; his yacht (the largest in Greece) can sometimes be seen moored offshore.

For heading further afield, you'll need to hire a **bike or moped**, or use the **kaíkia** rides from the Dápia, which run to beaches around the island in summer. A very expensive alternative are the **waterboat taxis**, though they can take up to ten people. **Walkers** might want to go over the top of the island to Áyii Anáryiri, though this is not so fine a walk since the forest fire, which destroyed most of the pines between Ayía Marína and Áyii Anáryiri. The route out of town starts from behind *Lazaros' Taverna.*

West from Spétses Town

Heading west from the Dápia around the coast, the road is paved until the houses run out after a kilometre or so; thereafter it is a dirt track which winds through pine trees and around inlets. The forest stretches from the central hills right down to the shore and it makes for a beautiful coastline with little coves and rocky promontories, all shaded by trees.

VRELLOÚ is one of the first places you come to, at the mouth of a wooded valley known locally as "Paradise", which would be a fairly apt description, except that, like so many of the beaches, it becomes polluted every year by tourists' rubbish. However, the entire shore is dotted with coves and in a few places there are small tavernas – a good one at **ZOGERIÁ**, for instance, where the scenery and rocks more than make up for the inadequate little beach.

Working your way anti-clockwise around the coast towards Áyii Anáryiri you reach **ÁYIA PARASKEVÍ** with its small church and beach – one of the most beautiful coves on Spétses and an alternate stop on some of the *kaíki* runs. There's a basic beach café here in summer. On the hill above is the house John Fowles used as the setting for *The Magus,* the **Villa Yasemia**. It was once owned by the late Alkis Botassis, who claimed to be the model for the *Magus* character – though Fowles denies "appropriat-ing" anything more than his "outward appearance" and the "superb site" of his house.

Áyii Anáryiri

Áyii Anáryiri, on the south side of the island, is the best, if also the most popular, beach: a beautiful, long, sheltered bay of fine sand. Gorgeous first thing in the morn-ing, it fills up later in the day, with bathers, windsurfers and rather manic speedboat-driving waterski instructors. On the right-hand side of the bay, looking out to sea, there's a sea cave, which you can swim out to and explore within. There's a self-service taverna on the beach and, just behind, *Tassos'*, Spétses' finest (and a well-priced) eating establishment: a meal here, prepared with real care and enthusiasm, is not to be missed.

The road and coves continue **east of Áyii Anáryiri**, though often at some distance from each other until you loop back to Ayía Marína.

travel details

Ferries

From the central harbour at **Pireás** at least 4 boats daily run to Ayía Marína (1hr) and 11 to Éyina (1hr 30min); 1–2 daily to Skála and Mílos (2hr); 4 daily to Póros (3hr 30min); 1–2 daily to Ídhra (4hr 30min) and Spétses (5hr 30min). About 4 connections daily between Éyina and Póros; 4–5 daily between Éyina and Angístri; from Angístri about 4 weekly to Paleá Epídhavros, far less frequently to Póros and Méthana.

Most of the ferries stop on the mainland at Méthana (between Éyina and Póros) and Ermióni (between Ídhra and Spétses); it is possible to board them here from the Peloponnese. Some continue from Spétses to Portohéli. There are also constant boats between Póros and Galatás (10min) from dawn until late at night, and boat-taxis between Spétses and Portohéli.

NB There are more ferries at weekends and fewer out of season (although the service remains good); for Éyina and Póros they leave Pireás most frequently between 7.30am and 9am, and 2pm and 4pm. Do not buy a return ticket as it saves no money and limits you to one specific boat. The general information number for the Argo-Saronic ferries is ☎01/41 75 382 or 42 94 533.

Flying Dolphin hydrofoils

Approximately hourly services from the central harbour at Pireás to **Éyina** only 6am–8pm in season, 7am–5pm out (40min).

All hydrofoils going beyond Éyina leave from the **Zéa Marina**: 4–15 times daily to Póros (1hr), Ídhra (1hr 40min), and Spétses (2–2hr 30min). All these times depend upon the stops en route, and frequencies vary with the season.

Éyina is connected with the other three islands twice a day; Póros, Ídhra and Spétses with each other 3–5 times daily. Some hydrofoils also stop at Méthana and Ermióni and all of those to Spétses continue to Portohéli (15min more). This is a junction of the hydrofoil route – there is usually one a day onwards to Toló and Náfplio (and vice versa; 30 and 45min) in season and another (almost year-round) to Monemvassía (2hr). The Monemvassía hydrofoil continues 2–4 times a week to the island of Kíthira.

NB Once again services are heavily reduced out of season, though all the routes between Portohéli and Pireás still run. Hydrofoils are usually twice as fast and twice as expensive as ordinary boats, though to Éyina the price is little different. You can now buy round-trip tickets, so if you need to return on a certain day buy your ticket back when purchasing your outbound leg. In season, it's not unusual for departures to be fully booked for a day or so at a time.

Details and tickets available from the Pireás ticket office at Ákti Themistokléous 8 (☎01/42 80 001, perennially engaged; if you can, try the fax ☎42 83 526). Tickets can also be bought at the departure quays on Aktí Tsélepi in Pireás and at Zéa.

CHAPTER TWO

THE CYCLADES

N amed for the circle they form around the sacred island of Delos, the **Cyclades** (*Kikládhes*) is the most satisfying Greek archipelago for island-hopping. On no other group do you get quite such a strong feeling of each island as a microcosm, each with its own distinct traditions, customs and path of modern development. Most of these self-contained realms are compact enough to walk around in a few days, giving you a sense of completeness and identity impossible on, say, Crete or most of the Ionian islands.

There is some unity. The majority of the islands – Ándhros, Náxos, Sérifos and Kéa notably excepted – are both arid and rocky, and most share the "Cycladic" style of brilliant-white, cubist architecture. The extent and impact of tourism, however, is markedly haphazard, so that although some English is spoken on most islands, a slight detour from the beaten track – from Íos to Síkinos, for example – can have you groping for your Greek phrasebook.

But whatever the level of tourist development, there are only two islands where it has come completely to dominate their character: **Íos**, the original hippie-island and still a paradise for hard-drinking backpackers, and **Míkonos**, by far the most popular of the group, with its teeming old town, selection of nude beaches and sophisticated clubs and gay bars. After these two, **Páros**, **Sífnos**, **Náxos**, and **Thíra** (Santoríni) are currently the most popular, with their beaches and main towns drastically overcrowded at the height of the season. To avoid the hordes altogether – except in August, when nearly everywhere is overrun and escape is impossible – the most promising islands are **Síkinos**, **Kímolos** or **Anáfi**, or even (going to extremes) the minor islets around Náxos. For a different view of the Cyclades, visit **Tínos** and its imposing pilgrimage church, a major spiritual centre of Greek Orthodoxy, or **Síros** with its elegant townscape, and (like Tínos), large Catholic minority. Due to their closeness to Athens, adjacent **Kíthnos** and **Kéa** are predictably popular – and relatively expensive – weekend havens for Greeks. The one major ancient site is **Delos** (Dhílos), certainly worth making time for: the commercial and religious centre of the Classical Greek world, it's visited most easily on a day trip, by *kaíki* or jet boat from Míkonos.

When it comes to **moving on**, many of the islands – in particular Mílos, Páros, Náxos and Thíra – are handily connected with Crete (easier in season), while from Tínos, Míkonos, Síros, Páros, Náxos, Thíra or Amorgós you can reach many of the Dodecanese by direct boat. Similarly, you can regularly get from Míkonos, Náxos, Síros and Páros to Ikaría and Sámos (covered in the East and North Aegean chapter), and there is even a weekly connection from several of the most central Cyclades to Náfplio on the Peloponnese.

Another consideration for the timing of your visit is that the Cyclades often get frustratingly **stormy**, particularly in early spring or late autumn, and it's also the group worst affected by the *meltémi*, which blows sand and tables about with equal ease throughout much of July and August. Delayed or cancelled ferries are not uncommon, so if you're heading back to Athens to catch a flight leave yourself a day or two's leeway.

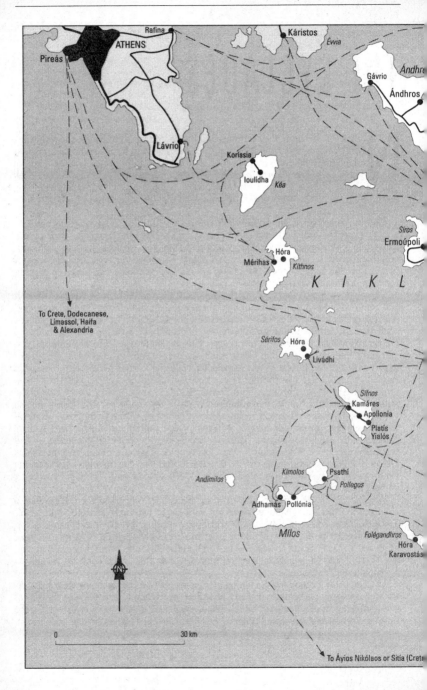

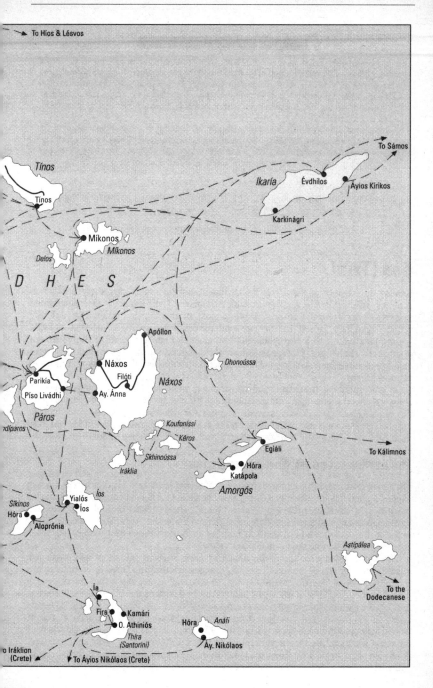

To Híos & Lésvos

To Sámos

Tínos

Tínos

Ikaría   Évdhilos   Áyios Kírikos

Karkinágri

Míkonos

Míkonos

Delos

D H E S

Apóllon

Dhonoússa

Náxos

Filóti

Náxos

Parikía

Píso Livádhi   Ay. Ánna

Koufoníssi

Páros

Kéros

ndíparos

Skhinoússa

Egiáli   To Kálimnos

Iráklia

Hóra

Katápola

Amorgós

Íos

Síkinos   Yialós

Hóra   Íos

Aloprónia

Astípálea

To the
Dodecanese

Ía

Fíra   Kamári

O. Athiniós   Hóra   *Anáfi*

Thíra
(Santoríni)   Áy. Nikólaos

o Iráklion
(Crete)   To Áyios Nikólaos (Crete)

ROOM PRICE SCALES

All establishments listed in this book have been price-graded according to the scale outlined below. The rates quoted represent the cheapest available room in high season; all are prices for a double room, except for category ①, which are per person rates. Out of season, rates can drop by up to fifty percent, especially if you negotiate rates for a stay of three or more nights. Single rooms, where available, cost around seventy percent of the price of a double.

Rented private rooms on the islands usually fall into the ② or ③ categories, depending on their location and facilities, and the season; a few in the ④ category are more like plush self-catering apartments. They are not generally available from late October through the beginning of April, when only hotels tend to remain open.

① 1400–2000dr (£4–5.50/US$6–8.50)   ④ 8000–12000dr (£22–33/US$33–50)
② 4000–6000dr (£11–16.50/US$17–25)   ⑤ 12000–16000dr (£33–44/US$50–66)
③ 6000–8000dr (£16.50–22/US$25–33)   ⑥ 16000dr (£44/US$66) and upwards

For further explanation of our hotel category system, see pp.32–34.

Kéa (Tziá)

Kéa is the closest of the Cyclades to the mainland and is extremely popular in summer, and weekends year-round, with Athenians. Their impact is mostly confined to certain small coastal resorts, leaving most of the interior quiet, although the vistors' presence is felt in the preponderance of expensive apartment or villa accommodation – and a corresponding abundance of supermarkets to the detriment of any remarkably good tavernas. Midweek, or outside peak season, Kéa is a more enticing destination, its rocky, forbidding perimeter enlivened inland by vast oak and almond groves.

As ancient Keos, the island and its strategic well-placed harbour supported four cities – a pre-eminence that continued until the nineteenth century when Síros became the main Greek port. Today tourists account for what sea traffic there is, namely regular ferry connections with Lávrio on the mainland – only a ninety-minute bus ride from Athens – plus useful hydrofoils to and from Zéa, Kíthnos and Rafína.

The northwest coast: Korissía to Otziás

The small northern ferry and hydrofoil port of **KORISSÍA** has fallen victim to uneven expansion and has little beauty to lose; if you don't like its looks upon disembarking, be quick to get a seat on **buses** for Písses (16km), Otziás (6km) or Ioulídha (6km), as they seem to have no fixed schedule other than meeting the boats. There are just three **taxis** on the island, and an identical number of **motorbike-rental** outfits, the latter charging nearly double the normal island rates.

The kindly agents for the *Flying Dolphins* (*Toh Stegadhi* gift shop) sell maps and guides, and can phone around in search of **accommodation**. Three good options are the quiet *Pension Korissia* (☎0288/21 484; ③–④), well inland along the stream bed; *Iy Tzia Mas* (☎0288/21 305; ④), right behind the best end of the otherwise uninspiring port beach; and the somewhat noisy *Karthea* (☎0288/21 204; ③), which does, however, boast single rooms and year-round operation – and a cameo appearance in recent Greek history. When the junta fell in July 1974, the colonels were initially imprisoned for some weeks in the then-new hotel while the recently restored civilian government pondered what to do with them; Kéa was then so remote and unvisited that the erstwhile tyrants were safely out of reach of a vengeful populace.

VOURKÁRI, a couple of kilometres north, is more compact and arguably more attractive than Korissía, serving as the favourite hangout of the well-heeled yachting set. There's no beach to speak of, and little accommodation, merely three fairly expensive and indistinguishable **tavernas** that are better for a seafood treat than ordinary dishes, and the *Vinylio* **bar**, popular with an older crowd. Swimming is better at **Yialiskári**, a small, eucalyptus-fringed beach about halfway back towards Korissía. Across the bay from Vourkári, on a promontory, the Minoan site of **Ayía Iríni** was excavated during the 1960s to reveal the remains of a small settlement, temple and road. There is currently no admission to the public, but you can glimpse the essentials through the perimeter fence.

Another 3km along, **OTZIÁS** has a small beach that's a bit better than that at Korissía, though more exposed to prevailing winds; facilities are limited to a pair of tavernas and a fair number of *garsoniéres* (self-catering units) for rent. Kéa's only functioning monastery, the eighteenth-century **Panayía Kastrianí**, can be reached along a dirt road from Otziás in an hour's walk, or ten minutes by bike. Although more remarkable for its fine setting on a high bluff than for any intrinsic interest, from here you can easily and pleasantly walk on to the island capital, Ioulídha, in another two hours.

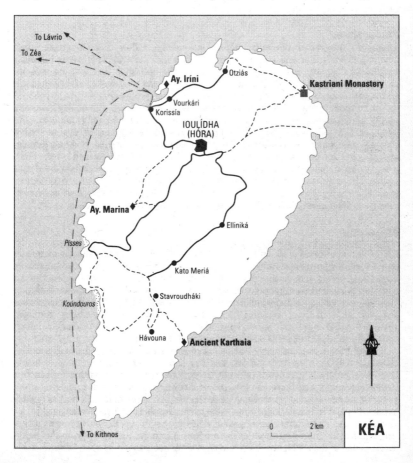

Ioulídha

IOULÍDHA, the ancient Ioulis and birthplace of the renowned early fifth-century BC poets Simonides and Bacchylides, is more usually reached directly from Korissía. With its numerous red-tiled roofs Ioulídha is by no means a typical Cycladic village, but it is beautifully situated in an amphitheatric fold in the hills, and architecturally the most interesting spot on the island. Accordingly it has "arrived" in recent years, with numerous, increasingly trendy bars and bistros well patronized on weekends. The lower reaches stretch across a spur to the **Kástro**, a tumbledown Venetian fortress incorporating stones from an ancient temple of Apollo. Fifteen minutes' walk northeast of town, on the path toward Panayía Kastrianí, you pass the **Lion of Kea**, a sixth-century BC sculpture carved out of the living rock. Six metres long and two high (at the head), it's an imposing beast, with crudely powerful haunches and a bizarre facial expression. There are steps right down to it, but the effect is most striking from a distance. Back in town, the **Archeological Museum** (daily except Mon 8.30am–3pm; free) displays finds from the four ancient city-states of Kéa, though sadly, the best items were long ago spirited away to Athens.

Practicalities

There are two rather dissimilar **hotels** in Ioulídha, either of them quieter than anything down in Korissía, and both much in demand: the somewhat pokey *Filoxenia* (☎0288/22 057; ③), engagingly perched above the shoeshop, but with no en-suite plumbing and saggy beds; or the more comfortable *Ioulis* (☎0288/22 177; ④) up in the *kástro*, with superb views from its terrace and west-facing rooms.

You're spoilt for choice in the matter of **eating and drinking**, with quality generally higher here than near Korissía. The old standby tavernas *Iy Piatsa* and *Iy Ioulidha* – the latter, on the main *platía*, with exceptionally palatable and potent local wine – have recently been joined by *Toh Steki tis Tzias*, serving no-nonsense oven food on a terrace, and an as-yet-unnamed but highly regarded *ouzerí* uphill from (and owned by) the pharmacy; to find it, follow the steps you come to before the arcade that leads into the village centre. The aptly named *Panorama* is the place to linger over a sunset pastry and coffee, while after-dark action seems to oscillate between such bars as *Kamini*, *Leon* and *Kouiz*. Finally, an **OTE, post office** and **bank agent** round out the list of amenities.

The south

About 8km southwest of Ioulídha, reached via a mix of tracks and paths, or by mostly paved road, the crumbling Hellenistic watchtower of **Ayía Marína** sprouts dramatically from the grounds of a small nineteenth-century monastery. Beyond, the paved main road twists around the dramatically scenic head of the lovely agricultural valley at **PÍSSES**, emerging at a large and little-developed beach, albeit of middling cleanliness and with little shade. There are three tavernas behind, plus a pleasant **campsite** (☎0288/31 335) with turfy ground for tents. More substantial development inland consists of studios (☎0288/31 302; ④) lining the access road.

Beyond Písses, road paving – and bus service – fizzles out along the 5km south to **KOÚNDOUROS**, a sheltered, convoluted bay popular with yachters; there's a single taverna behind the largest of several sandy coves, none cleaner or bigger than the beach at Písses. The luxury *Kea Beach* hotel sits out on its own promontory with tennis courts and pool, but the latest curiosity hereabouts is the hamlet of dummy windmills; built as holiday homes, they are "authentic" right down to the masts, thatching and stone cladding.

Besides the very scant ruins of ancient Poiessa near Písses, the only remains of any real significance from Kéa's past are at **ancient Karthaia**, tucked away on the southeastern edge of the island above Póles Bay, and easiest reached by boat. Otherwise, it's a good three hours' round-trip walk from the hamlet of Stavroudháki, some way off the lower road linking Koúndouros, Hávouna and Káto Meriá. Travelling by motorbike, the upper road, which more directly plies between Písses and Káto Meriá, is worth following as an alternative return along the island's summit to Ioulídha; it's paved once you get to Elliniká, and the entire way affords fine views, not least over the thousands of magnificent oaks which constitute Kéa's most distinctive feature.

Kíthnos (Thermiá)

Though perhaps the dullest and certainly the most barren of the Cyclades, a short stay on **Kíthnos** is a good antidote to the exploitation likely to be encountered elsewhere. Few foreigners bother to visit; the island is quieter than Kéa, even in midsummer; while the inhabitants (except in more commercialized Mérihas) are overtly friendly – all factors that compensate for the paucity of specific diversions. Like Kéa, it's a place where Athenians

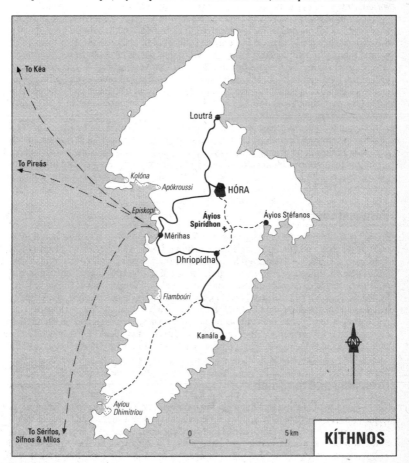

come to buy land for villas, go spear-fishing and sprawl on generally mediocre beaches without having to jostle mass-tourism clients for space. You could use it as a first or, better, last island stop: there are weekly ferry connections with Kéa, more frequent services to and from Sérifos, Sífnos and Mílos, as well as seasonal hydrofoils to Kéa, Zéa and Rafína.

Mérihas and around

In good weather boats dock on the west coast at **MÉRIHAS**, a rather functional ferry and fishing port with most of the island's facilities. This fact almost obliges you to stay here, and makes Mérihas something of a tourist ghetto, but it's redeemed by proximity to the island's best beaches. The closest beach of any repute is **Episkopí**, a stretch of 500m of averagely clean grey sand, with a single taverna, forty minutes' walk north of the town; you can shorten this considerably by sticking to coast-hugging trails and tracks below the road. Far better are the adjacent beaches of **Apókroussi** and **Kolóna**, the latter essentially a sandspit joining the islet of Áyios Loukás to Kíthnos. They lie more than an hour's walk northwest of Episkopí, and are easiest reached by boat-trip from the harbour.

Accommodation proprietors tend to come down to meet the ferries, and a relative abundance of rooms makes for lower prices than on Kéa. Aim to bargain them down to the mid-③ range for something in a garden setting south of the small, gritty town beach behind the (not recommended) *Posidhonio Hotel*; few places have sea views. Studios can also be good value. The best **restaurant** by far is *Toh Kandouni*, a reasonable and tasty grill at the west end of the beach with tables right on the water – or even in the water if you're so inclined; specialities include *sfougáto* fritters and island wine. On the opposite side of the port, the blue-and-white *Kafezaharoplastio O Merihas* is a strategically placed spot for breakfast or some cake, and has rooms upstairs.

Among purveyors of a very modest **nightlife**, *Remezzo* behind the beach is about the best bar in terms of location and music; others tend to play Frank Sinatra covers of *The Girl from Ipanema*, or worse. **Bus service**, principally to Loutrá, Hóra and Driopídha, is marginally more reliable than on Kéa, but still elusive; there are just two **bike-rental** places, one run by Katerini Larentzaki (☎0281/32 248), who also has some rooms. In season, an **OTE** booth functions behind the *Remezzo*.

Hóra and Loutrá

HÓRA is 6km northeast of Mérihas, set in the middle of the island. Tilting south off an east–west ridge, and laid out to an approximate grid plan, it's an awkward blend of Kéa-style gabled roofs, Cycladic churches with dunce-cap cupolas, and concrete monsters. Hóra supports the main **OTE** branch, and a **post office** (the latter open only until noon), but the closest accommodation is at Loutrá (see below). You can **eat** at the taverna run by *Marya Tzoyiou*, or at the grill *Toh Steki*, and there's a single outdoor **bar**, *Apokalypsi*.

The much-vaunted resort of **LOUTRÁ** (3km north of Hóra and named after its thermal baths) is scruffy, its nineteenth-century spa long since replaced by a sterile modern construction. In certain weather conditions, ferries may dock here instead of at Mérihas; facilities include tavernas on the beach, a **pension** (the *Porto Klaras*; ☎0281/31 276; ③) and a few rooms to let.

Driopídha and the south

You're handily placed in Hóra to tackle the most interesting thing to do on Kíthnos: the beautiful **walk south** to Dhriopídha. It takes about an hour and a half, initially following the old cobbled way that leaves Hóra heading due south; critical junctions in the first few minutes are marked by red paint dots. The only reliable water is a well in a valley bottom half an hour along, just before a side trail to the triple-naved **chapel of**

Áyios Sprídhon with recycled Byzantine columns. Just beyond this, you collide with a bulldozed track between Dhriopídha and Áyios Stéfanos, but purists can avoid this by bearing west toward some ruined ridgetop windmills, and picking up secondary paths for the final forty minutes of the hike.

More appealing than Hóra by virtue of spanning a ravine, **DHRIOPÍDHA**'s pleasing tiled roofs are reminiscent of Spain or Tuscany. A surprisingly large place, it was once the island's capital, built around a famous cave, the Katafíki, at the head of a well-watered valley. Behind the main cathedral, there is a single **taverna**, *Iy Pelegra*, serving cheap grills, salad and beer only. For the closest **accommodation**, you must head 6km south to **KANÁLA**, basically some twenty non-descript houses and a church on a sea-washed headland, with tavernas and rooms to rent in season.

From Kanála, a succession of small coves extends up the east coast as far as **ÁYIOS STÉFANOS**, a small coastal hamlet with no facilities opposite a chapel-crowned islet tied by causeway to the body of the island. Southwest of Driopídha, reached by a turning off the road to Kanála, **Flamboúri** is the most presentable beach on the west coast; the double bay of **Ayíou Dhimitríou**, at the extreme southern tip of the island, and reached over a rough road, is not worth the effort.

Sérifos

Sérifos has languished outside the mainstream of history and modern tourism. Little has happened here since the legendary Perseus returned with the Gorgon's head in time to save his mother Danaë from being ravished by the local king Polydectes. Many would-be visitors are deterred by the apparently barren, hilly interior which, with the stark, rocky coastline, makes Sérifos appear uninhabited until your ferry turns into Livádhi bay. The island is recommended for serious walkers, who can head for several small villages and isolated coves in the little-explored interior. Modern Serifots love seclusion, and here, more than anywhere else in the Cyclades, you will find farmsteads miles from anywhere, with only a donkey path to their door. Everyone here seems to keep livestock, and to produce their own wines, and many also cultivate the wild narcissus for the export market.

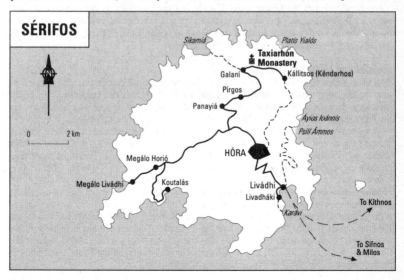

Few islanders speak much English, and many have a deserved reputation of being slow to warm to outsiders. One suspects that the locals still don't quite know what to make of the hordes of trendy northern Europeans who descend on the place for a brief but intense July and August season. American yachties drop anchor here in some numbers as well, to take on fresh water which, despite appearances, Sérifos has in abundance.

Livádhi and the main beaches

Most visitors stay in the port, **LIVÁDHI**, set in a wide greenery-fringed bay and handy for most of the island's beaches. The usually calm bay here is a magnet for island-hopping yachts, whose crews chug to and fro in dinghies all day and night. It's not the most attractive place on Sérifos – and to stay here exclusively would be to miss some fine walks – but Livádhi and the neighbouring cove of Livadháki are certainly the easiest place to find rooms and any other amenities you might need, all of which are very scarce elsewhere.

Unfortunately, the **beach** at Livádhi is nothing to write home about: long, but of hard-packed, muddy sand, the water weedy and prone to intermittent jellyfish flotillas; only the far northeastern end is at all usable. Walk uphill along the street from the *Galanos* bakery, or over the southerly headland from the cemetery, to reach the neighbouring, far superior **Livadháki**. This golden-sand beach, shaded by tamarisk trees, offers snorkelling and other watersports, one rather average taverna and some furtive nudism. If you prefer more seclusion, five minutes' stroll across the headland to the south brings you to the smaller **Karávi** beach, which is cleaner and almost totally naturist, but has no shade or facilities.

A slightly longer 45-minute walk north of the port along a bumpy track leads to **Psilí Ámmos**, a sheltered, white-sand beach considered the best on the island. Accordingly, it's popular, with two rival tavernas, both of which tend to be full in high season. Naturists are pointed – via a ten-minute walk across the headland – towards the beach beyond, the larger and often deserted **Áyios Ioánnis**, but this is rather exposed to weather, has no facilities at all, and only the far south end is inviting. Both beaches are theoretically visited by *kaíkia* from Livádhi, as are two nearby sea-caves, but don't count on it. Additionally, and plainly visible from arriving ferries, two more sandy coves hide at the far southeastern flank of the island, opposite an islet; they are accessible on foot only, by a variation of the track to Psilí Ámmos.

Livádhi and Livadháki practicalities

The **OTE** office is at the foot of the quay. You can **rent a bike or car** from *Blue Bird* next to the single filling station, and there are three **boat-ticket agents**. The public **bus stop** and posted schedule are at the base of the yacht and fishing boat jetty, *not* the ferry dock.

Accommodation proprietors – with the exception of the *Coralli Camping Bungalows*, which regularly sends a minibus – don't always meet ferries, and in high season you'll have to step lively off the boat to get a decent bed. The most rewarding hunting grounds are on the headland above the ferry dock, or Livadháki beach (see below); anything without a sea view will be a notch cheaper. Up on the headland, the *Pansion Cristi* (☎0281/51 214 or 51 775; ④), lower rates June & Sept) has an excellent, quiet position overlooking the bay; the nearby *Areti* (☎0281/51 479; ④) is snootier and a bit pricier. Alternatively, down in the flatlands, the relatively inexpensive seafront *Kyklades Hotel* (☎0281/51 553; ②) has the important virtues of year-round operation and kindly management, though the bay-view rooms get some traffic noise. The *Galanos* (☎0281/51 277; ②), above the eponymous bakery, is useful as a fall back in peak season.

Livadháki, ten to fifteen minutes' walk south, offers more nocturnal peace, choice and quality, though it has a more touristy feel, and the mosquitoes are positively ferocious – bring insecticide coils or make sure your room is furnished with electric vapour pads. One of the oldest and largest complexes of rooms and apartments, close to the beach and with verdant views, is run by *Vaso Stamataki* (☎0281/51 346; ③). Newer and higher-standard choices include the *Helios Pansion* run by Panayiota and Khryssa Gavriel (☎0281/51 066; ③), just above the road as you arrive at Livadháki, or the *Medusa* further along (☎0281/51 127; ③). Near the end of things, beside one of only two public access tracks to the beach and behind the best patch of sand, the *Coralli Camping Bungalows* (☎0281/51 500; bungalows ④) has a restaurant and landscaped tenting-down area, but no prizes for a warm welcome.

The Livádhi seafront has a makeshift road running along its length, filled with traffic, restaurants, shops, and all the services you might need. At the strategic southerly crossroads, the *Galanos* bakery has exceptionally good cheese pies and – if you ask – whole-grain bread under the counter. A butcher plus a handful of fruit shops and **supermarkets** are scattered along the beach, while there's a **pharmacy** at the foot of the quay.

You'll pay through the nose for **meals** in the obvious places near the quay in Livádhi; walk up the beach, and meals get less expensive and more Greek. The two best traditional tavernas are the busy *Stamatis*, and the welcoming restaurant under the *Hotel Cyclades*. At the extreme far northeast end of the beach, *Sklavenis* (aka *Marietta's*) has its loyal adherents for its down-home feel and courtyard seating, but many find the food overly deep-fried and over-priced. Closer to the yacht harbour, *Meltemi* is a good – if slightly expensive – *ouzerí*, something out of the ordinary for the island. For crepes and ice cream, try *Meli*, in the commercial centre, by the port police.

Nightlife is surprisingly lively, though few establishments stay in business more than two consecutive seasons. Two of the most durable are *Vitamin C* and *Froggie's*, the latter presumably named in honour of the island's many noisy amphibians; on the beachfront itself the sound systems of *Karnayio* and *Agria Menta* currently battle it out from adjacent premises.

Hóra

Quiet and atmospheric **HÓRA**, teetering precariously above the harbour, is one of the most spectacular villages of the Cyclades. The best sights are to be found on the town's borders: tiny churches cling to the cliff edge, and there are breathtaking views across the valleys below. At odd intervals along its alleyways you'll find part of the old castle making up the wall of a house, or a marble statue leaning incongruously in one corner. A pleasant diversion is the hour-or-less walk down to Psilí Ámmos: start from beside Hóra's cemetery; to avoid getting lost, aim for the lower of two visible pigeon towers, and then keep close to the phone wires, which will guide you towards the continuation of the double-walled path descending to a bend in the road just above the beach.

Buses connect Livádhi with Hóra, 2km away, some ten times daily, but only manage one or two daily trips to Megálo Livádhi, Galaní, and Kállitsos. You may well want to walk, if you're travelling light, however; it's a pleasant if steep forty minutes up a cobbled way to Hóra, with the *kalderími* leading off from a bend in the road about 300m out of Livádhi. Out of season (by the beginning of October) you'll have no choice, since the bus – like nearly everything else – ceases operation during the winter.

Among two or three **tavernas**, *Stavros* just east of the bus-stop *platía* is the most consistent and can arrange beds, too. The island's **post office** is found in the lowest quarter, and a few more expensive **rooms** for rent lie about 200m north of town, on the street above the track to the cemetery.

The north

North of Hóra, the island's high water table sometimes breaks the surface to run in delightful rivulets swarming with turtles and frogs, though in recent years many of the open streams seem to have dried up. Reeds, orchards, and even the occasional palm tree still take advantage of the unexpected moisture, even if it's no longer visible. This is especially true at **KÁLLITSOS** (Kéndarhos), reached by a ninety-minute path from Hóra, marked by fading red paint splodges along an initial donkey track above the cemetery. Once at Kállitsos (no facilities), a paved road leads west within 3km to the fifteenth-to-seventeenth-century **monastery of Taxiarhón**, designed for sixty monks but presently home only to Makarios, one of the island's two parish priests. He is one of a dying breed of farmer-fisherman monks; if he's about, he'll show you treasures in the monastic church, such as an ivory-inlaid bishop's throne, silver lamps from Egypt (to where many Serifots emigrated), and the finely carved *témblon*. There are no longer any frescoes of note visible.

As you loop back towards Hóra from Kállitsos on the asphalt, the fine villages of Galaní and Panayiá (named after its tenth-century church) make convenient stops. In **GALANÍ** you can get simple **meals** at the central store, which also sells excellent, tawny-pink, sherry-like wine; its small-scale production in the west of the island is highly uneconomic, so you'll find it at few other places on Sérifos. Below the village, trails lead to the remote and often windswept beach of **Sikamiá**, with no facilities and no camping allowed; a better bet for a local swim is the more sheltered cove of **Platís Yialós** at the extreme northern tip of the island, reached by a rough track (negotiable by moped) that branches off just east of Taxiarhón. The church at **PANAYIÁ** is usually locked, but comes alive on its feast day of Ksilopanayía (August 16); traditionally the first couple to dance around the adjacent olive tree would be the first to marry that year, but this led to unseemly brawls – so the priest always goes first these days.

The southwest

A little way south of Panayiá, you reach a junction in the road. Turn left to return to Hóra, or continue straight towards **Megálo Horió** – the site of ancient Sérifos, but with little else to recommend it. **Megálo Livádhi**, further on, is a remote and quiet beach resort 8km west of Hóra, with two tavernas and some rooms. Iron and copper ore were once exported from here, but cheaper African deposits sent the mines into decline and today most of the idle machinery rusts away, though some gravel-crushing still goes on. An alternate turning just below Megálo Horió leads to the small mining and fishing port of **Koutalás**, a pretty if shadeless sweep of bay with a church-tipped rock, a lone taverna and a tiny beach. There's also a direct but rough mule-path from here back to Livádhi, but this shouldn't be attempted without clear local directions or a good map.

Sífnos

Sífnos is a more immediately appealing island than its northern neighbours: prettier, more cultivated and with some fine architecture. This means that it's also much more popular, and extremely crowded in July or August, when rooms are nearly impossible to find. Take any offered as you land, come armed with a reservation, or, best of all, time your visit for June or early in September, though bear in mind that most of the trendier bars and the souvenir shops will be shut for the winter by the middle of the latter month. In keeping with the island's somewhat upmarket clientele, freelance camping is forbidden (and the two designated sites are substandard), while nudism is tolerated only in isolated coves. The locals tend, if anything, to be even more dour and introverted than on Sérifos.

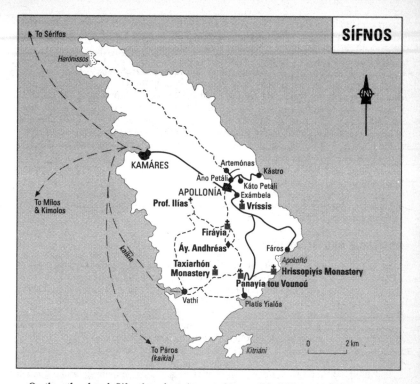

On the other hand, Sífnos' modest size – no bigger than Kíthnos or Sérifos — makes it eminently explorable. The **bus service** is excellent, most of the roads quite decent and there's a network of paths that are fairly easy to follow. Unhappily, one of the best trails was destroyed in late 1992, and plans are mooted to bulldoze yet another unnecessary road straight through the heart of the island from Kamáres to Platís Yialós. Sífnos also has a strong tradition of pottery and was long esteemed for its distinctive cuisine, although most tourist-orientated cooking is average at best. However, the island's shops and greengrocers are well stocked in season.

Ferry connections have improved in recent years, keeping pace with the island's increasing popularity. The main lines head south, via Kímolos to Mílos, with occasional extensions to Thíra, Crete and select Dodecanese, or north, via Sérifos and Kíthnos to Pireás. The only links with the central Cyclades are provided by the unreliable small excursion boat *Aphrodite Express*, which sails to Páros, Náxos, Síros and Míkonos most days but is not for the seasick-prone; and a bona fide ferry, the *Paros Express*, which calls once weekly (at Sérifos too) – usually Tuesday – to deposit you on Síros at a rather uncivilized hour.

Kamáres

KAMÁRES, the port, is tucked away at the foot of high, bare cliffs in the west which enclose a beach. A busy, fairly downmarket resort with concrete blocks of villas edging up to the base of the cliffs, Kamáres has a seafront crammed with bars, travel agencies, ice-cream shops and fast-food places. You can store luggage at the semi-official **tourist office** while hunting for a room (proprietors tend not to meet boats); they also change money and can advise on bed availability throughout the island.

Accommodation is relatively expensive, though bargaining can be productive outside peak season. Try the **rooms** above the *Katzoulakis Tourist Agency* near the quay, as well as the reasonable *Hotel Stavros* (☎0284/31 641; ③), just beyond the church. If desperate, you might try the unofficial *Vangelis* **youth hostel** (①) further inland. At the other end of the scale, there's the good but expensive *Voulis Hotel* (☎0284/32 122; ⑤) across the bay. An extremely scruffy, semi-official campsite appears to have been closed down. You're probably better off anyway at the rooms to let right at the north end of the sands; these are often the last to fill, perhaps because of noise from the adjacent taverna and disco.

The best **restaurants** are the *Meropi*, ideal for a pre-ferry lunch or a more leisurely meal, and the no-name establishment whose decor seems to consist chiefly of a dozen or so retsina barrels (customer self-service). Kamáres also boasts a fair proportion of the island's **nightlife**: try the *Collage Bar* for your sunset cocktail, and move on to the *Mobilize Dancing Club* or the *Cafe Folie*.

Apollonía and Artemónas

A steep twenty-minute bus ride (hourly service until late at night) takes you up to **APOLLONÍA**, the centre of the *hóra*, an amalgam of three hilltop villages which have merged over the years into one continuous community. With white buildings, flower-draped balconies, belfries and pretty squares, it is eminently scenic, though not yet self-consciously so in the Míkonos manner. On the *platía* itself, the **Folk Museum** (open by request; a sign on the door tells you how to find the guard) is well worth a visit. Most of the exhibits celebrate a certain Kyria Tselemende, who wrote a famous local recipe book (fragments of which are kept here), and there's also an interesting collection of textiles, laces, artwork, costumes and weaponry.

Radiating out from the *platía* is a network of stepped marble footways and the main pedestrian street, flagstoned Odhós Styliánou Prókou – lined with shops, churches and restaurants. The garish, cakebox-cathedral of **Áyios Spíridhon** is nearby, while the eighteenth-century church of **Panayía Ouranoforía** stands in the highest quarter of town, incorporating fragments of a seventh-century BC temple of Apollo and a relief of Saint George over the door. **Áyios Athanásios**, next to Platía Kleánthi Triandafílou, has frescoes and a wooden *témblon*. Some 3km southeast, a short distance from the village of Exámbela, you'll find the active monastery of **Vríssis**, dating from 1612 and home to a good collection of religious artefacts and manuscripts.

ARTEMÓNAS, fifteen minutes south of Apollonía on foot, is worth a morning's look around for its churches and elegant Venetian-era and Neoclassical houses alone. **Panayía Gourniá** (key next door) has vivid frescoes; the clustered-dome church of **Kohí** was built over an ancient temple of Artemis (also the basis of the village's name); and seventeenth-century **Áyios Yióryios** contains fine icons. Artemónas is also the point of departure for **Herónissos**, an isolated hamlet with a few potteries behind a deeply indented, rather bleak bay at the northwestern tip of the island. There's a motorable dirt track there or occasional boat trips from Kamáres, though it's only worth the effort on calm days.

Practicalities

The **bank**, **post office**, **OTE** and **tourist police** are all grouped around Apollonía's central plaza. Most of the village's **rooms** establishments are along the road towards Fáros, and thus a bit noisy; the *Margarita* (☎0284/31 701; ③) is comfortable and fairly representative. If you want quieter premises with a better view, be prepared to pay more: your best bet is to head up the stair-street north of the *platía* café, where there's an excellent travel agency, *Aegean Thesaurus* (☎0284/32 190 & 31 145; also in Kamáres at ☎31 804), which can book you into more expensive rooms (③–④). They also sell a worthwhile package consisting of an accurate topographical map, bus/boat schedules and a short text on Sífnos for a few hundred drachmas. Near the central *platía*, there's the popular late-arrival fallback *Sofía* (☎0284/31 238; ③), though most people find somewhere else the next day, as it's a rather cheerless 1970s construction; the *Galini*, 400m south, up in Katavatí (☎0284/31 011; ③), is preferable.

In Hóra there are still a bare handful of quality **tavernas**, the doyen of which is the *Liotrivi* up in Artemónas. Though currently housed in an old olive mill, with orchard seating, and featuring local wine and island specialities, word out is that the owner will shortly move to purpose-built premises and re-open under his own name, *Manganas*. Next to the post office in Apollonía, *Iy Orea Sifnos* is the current incarnation of a taverna which for years has operated on this site, offering chickpea soup on Sundays, local cheese and various vegetarian specialities, all served in a flower-decked garden.

Nightlife in Apollonía tends to be dominated by the thirty-something crowd which, having dined early by Greek-island standards, lingers over its *oúzo* until late. The central *Argo* music bar plays lots of Seventies music and is very popular; try also the *Andromeda* club on the north side of the village, which bills itself as "more than a bar".

The east coast

Most of Sífnos' coastal settlements are along the less precipitous eastern shore, within a modest distance of Hóra and its surrounding cultivated plateau. These all have good bus services, and a certain amount of food and accommodation.

Kástro

An alternative east-coast base which seems the last place on Sífnos to fill up in season, **KÁSTRO** can be reached on foot from Apollonía in 35 minutes, all but the last ten on a clear path beginning at the *Hotel Anthoussa* and threading its way via Káto Petáli hamlet. Built on a rocky outcrop with an almost sheer drop to the sea on three sides, the ancient capital of the island retains much of its medieval character. Parts of its boundary walls survive, along with a full complement of sinuous, narrow streets graced by balconied, two-storey houses and some fine sixteenth- and seventeenth-century churches with ornamental floors. Venetian coats-of-arms and ancient wall-fragments can still be seen on some of the older dwellings; there are remains of the ancient acropolis (including a ram's head sarcophagus by one of the medieval gates), as well as a small **archeological museum** (Tues–Sat 9am–3pm, Sun 10am–2pm; free) installed in a former Catholic church in the higher part of the village.

Besides a fair number of rooms, there are at least two tavernas – the *Star* with the nicest seating, though the food can be dubious. There's nothing approximating a beach in Kástro; for a swim you have to walk to the nearby, rocky coves of **Serália** (to the southeast, and with more rooms) and **Paláti**. You can also hike, from the windmills on the approach road near Káto Petáli, to either the sixteenth-century monastery of **Hrissostómou**, or along a track opposite to the cliff face that overlooks the church of the **Eptá Martíres** (Seven Martyrs); nudists sun themselves and snorkel on and around the flat rocks below.

Platís Yialós

From Apollonía there are almost hourly buses to the resort of **PLATÍS YIALÓS**, some 12km distant, near the southern tip of the island. Despite claims to be the longest beach in the Cyclades, the sand can get very crowded at the end near the watersport facilities rental. Diversions include a pottery workshop, but for many the ugly *Xenia* hotel at the southern end of the beach, and troublesome winds, rule the place out. **Rooms** are expensive, although the comfortable *Pension Angelaki* (☎0284/31 688; ③), near the bus stop, is more reasonably priced. The local **campsite** is rather uninspiring: a stiff hike inland, shadeless, and on sloping, stony ground. Among several fairly pricey **tavernas** are the straightforward *Toh Steki* and *Bus Stop*.

A more rewarding walk uphill from Platís Yialós brings you to the convent of **Panayía tou Vounoú**, though it's easy to get lost on the way without the locally sold map; the caretaker should let you in, if she's about.

Fáros and around

Less crowded beaches are to be found just to the northeast of Platís Yialós (though unfortunately not directly accessible along the coast). **FÁROS**, again with regular bus links to Apollonía, makes an excellent fallback base if you don't strike lucky elsewhere. A small and friendly resort, it has some of the cheapest **accommodation** on the island (☎0284/31 822 & 31 989; both ②) and a few early-evening **tavernas**, the best of which is *Toh Kima*. The closest beaches are not up to much: the town strand itself is muddy, shadeless and crowded, and the one to the northeast past the headland not much better. Head off in the opposite direction, however, through the older part of the village, and things improve at **Glifó**, a longer, wider beach favoured by naturists and snorkellers.

Continuing from Glifó, a fifteen-minute cliffside path – threatened by a proposed road project – leads to the beach of **Apokoftó**, with a good taverna, *Vasilis*, and, up an access road, the *Pension Flora* (☎0284/31 778; ③), with superb views. The shore itself tends to collect seaweed, however, and a rock reef must be negotiated to get into the water. Flanking Apokoftó to the south, marooned on a sea-washed spit and featuring on every EOT poster of the island, is the disestablished, seventeenth-century, **Hrissopiyís monastery**, whose cells are rented out in summer (☎0284/31 255; ②), although you'll need to book well in advance. According to legend, the cleft in the rock appeared when two village girls, fleeing to the spit to escape the attentions of menacing pirates, prayed to the Virgin to defend their virtue.

The interior and Vathí

Apollonía is a good base from which to start your explorations of remoter Sífnos. You can **rent bikes** at *Moto Apollo*, beside the BP station on the road to Fáros, but the island is best explored on foot.

Taking the path out from Katavatí (the district south of Apollonía) you'll pass, after a few minutes, the beautiful empty **monastery of Firáyia** and – fifteen minutes along the ugly new bulldozer track – the path climbing up to **Áyios Andhréas,** where you'll be rewarded with tremendous views over the islands of Síros, Páros, Íos, Folégandhros and Síkinos. Just below the church is an enormous Bronze-Age archeological site.

Even better is the all-trail walk to Vathí, around three hours from Katavatí and reached by bearing right at a signed junction in Katavatí. Part-way along you can detour on a conspicuous side trail to the **monastery of Profítis Ilías**, on the very summit of the island, with a vaulted refectory and extensive views.

Vathí

A fishing village on the shore of a stunning funnel-shaped bay, **VATHÍ** is the most attractive and remote base on the island though, with the recent completion of the road in from Áyios Andhréas, the tranquil days of this little backwater seem numbered. There are a few **rooms** to let – though rarely enough, so freelance camping is tolerated – and one or two tavernas, of which *Okeanis* is best for *mezédhes*, *Manolis* for grills. The two potteries which once functioned here have closed down, but the wonderful, tiny **monastery of the Archangel Gabriel** still watches over the quay.

Well-publicized small boats from Kamáres dock at Vathí (minimum twice daily in season – morning and late afternoon); these are a bit pricey, and most people tend to walk in at least one direction. Rather than retrace your steps to Katavatí, it is theoretically possible to walk back to Platís Yiálos, but be warned that the new road (currently very rough and not yet usable by taxis), has cut the path and caused landslides in several places; even when you reach the pass dividing the two sides of the island, the path's continuation to Platís Yiálos proves steep and hard to find.

Mílos

Mílos has always derived prosperity from its strange geology. Minoan settlers were attracted by obsidian, and other products of its volcanic soil made the island – along with Náxos – the most important of the Cyclades in the ancient world. Today the quarrying of barite, perlite and porcelain brings in a steady revenue, but has left deep and unsightly scars on the landscape. The rocks, however, can be beautiful in situ: on the left as your ferry enters Mílos Bay, two outcrops known as the Arkoúdhes (Bears) square off like sumo wrestlers. Off the north coast, accessible only by excursion boat, the Glaroníssia (Seagull Isles) are shaped like massed organ pipes, and there are more weird formations on the southwest coast at Kléftiko. Inland, too, you frequently come across strange, volcanic outcrops, and thermal springs burst forth at surprising spots.

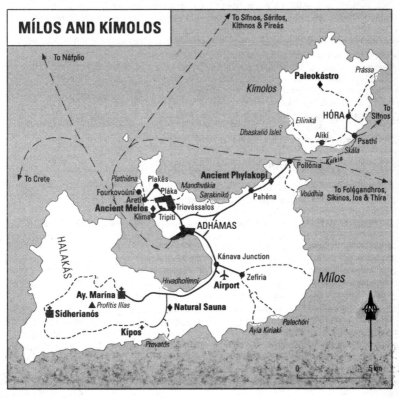

Violated the landscape may be, but as with most weathered volcanic terrain, Mílos is incredibly fertile; away from the summits of **Profítis Ilías** in the southwest and lower hills in the east, a gently undulating countryside is intensively cultivated to produce grain, hay and orchards. The island's domestic architecture, with its lava-built, two-up-and-two-down houses, is reminiscent of Níssiros, while parts of the coast, with their sculpted cliffs and inlets, remind some visitors of Cyprus.

Yet the drab whole is less than the sum of the often interesting parts; Mílos is not and never will become another Santoríni, despite a similar geological history, and is probably the better for it. The locals are reconciled to a very short tourist season lasting from late June to early September, and make most of their money during late July and August; accommodation prices stay uniformly high year-round.

Adhámas

ADHÁMAS is a rather cramped and uninspiring little port, founded by Cretan refugees fleeing a failed rebellion of 1841. Despite sitting on one of the Mediterranean's best natural harbours (created by a volcanic cataclysm similar to, but earlier than, Thira's), it's not a spectacularly inviting place. Most hotel **accommodation** manages to be simultaneously noisy, viewless and relatively expensive. Those that succeed in having only one of these disadvantages include the seafront *Popy* (☎0287/22 393; ④), on the coast road beyond the *Trapatsellis* taverna, and the *Semiramis* (☎0287/22 117; ③), well inland and left off the road to Pláka, with a garden setting. Rooms are concentrated up on the conical hill of the residential district; there is no organized campsite, and you shouldn't attempt to sleep rough. *Trapatsellis* at the start of the tamarisk-lined beach east of the port is easily the best **restaurant** in town, with a full menu of fish and vegetarian specialities, and good local wine from the barrel: dense, unresinated, but not hangover-inducing. *O Kinigos* is a more obvious cheapie near the ferry dock, but the food is greasier.

On the quayside, two travel agencies have information about coastal boat trips, sell maps of the island, and rent out mopeds. Otherwise, Adhámas is the hub of the island's **bus services**, which run hourly to Pláka, four or five times daily in high season to Pollónia, and twice daily to Paleohóri via Zefíria. Incidentally, if you arrive by plane from Athens, the **airport** is 5km southeast of the port, close to Zefíria.

The northwestern villages and ancient Melos

The real appeal of Mílos, however, resides in an area that has been the island's focus of habitation since Classical times, where a cluster of villages huddle in the lee of a crag 4km northwest of the harbour.

PLÁKA (MÍLOS) is the largest of these communities and official capital of the island, a status borne out by the presence of the hospital, **OTE**, **post office**, a part-time **bank** and three **motorbike rental** outfits strewn along the approach road. Unfortunately three or four modern blocks of **rooms** en route overlook this busy boulevard, and so prompt few thoughts of staying. Of three places to **eat**, the *Ouzeri Dhiporto*, a converted general store is the most original, with local specialities such as snails, *pittária* (hollow cheese-laced turnovers) and local wine.

The attractive village of **TRIPITÍ** (meaning "perforated" in Greek), which takes its name from the cliffside tombs of the ancient Melian dead nearby, covers a long ridge a kilometre south of Pláka. Despite semi-desolation (many houses are for sale), it probably makes the best base if you're after a village environment, with its three modest **rooms** establishments, two of which are just down the steep street from the tiny *platía* below the main church. Here also the *Kafenio Iy Hara*, despite a modest appearance, can do simple **meals** to go with its fantastic view of the vale of Klíma (see below); more elaborate and expensive fare is available at the *Ouzeri Methismeni Politea*, at the top of the road to the catacombs. From Tripití, it's possible to walk more or less directly down to Adhámas via Skinópi on the old *kalderími* which begins on the saddle linking Tripití with the hamlet of Klimatovoúni.

TRIOVÁSSALOS and its non-identical twin PÉRAN TRIOVÁSSALOS are more workaday, less polished than Pláka or Tripití. There are "rooms to rent" signs out here as well, but they'll inevitably be noisier. Péran can also offer the idosyncratic taverna *O Hamos,* and a naive pebble-mosaic in the courtyard of Áyios Yióryios church; dating from January 26, 1880, it features assorted animal and plant motifs.

Local sites – and the coast

Pláka boasts **two museums** of moderate interest. Behind the lower car park, at the top of the approach boulevard through the newer district, an **archeological collection** (daily except Mon 8.30am–3pm; 400dr) contains numerous obsidian implements plus a whole wing of finds from ancient Phylakopi (see overpage), with highlights including a votive lamp in the form of a bull and a rather Minoan-looking terracotta goddess. Labelling is scant, but isn't really needed for a plaster cast of the most famous statue in the world, the *Venus de Milo*, the original of which was found on the island in 1820 and appropriated by the French; her arms were knocked off in the melée surrounding her abduction. Up in a mansion of the old quarter, the **Folklore Museum** (Tues–Sun 10am–1pm; 100dr) offers in situ room re-creations but is otherwise a Greek-labelled jumble of impedimenta pertaining to milling, brewing, cheese-making, baking and weaving, rounded off by old engravings, photos and mineral samples.

A stairway beginning near the police station leads up to the old Venetian **Kástro**, its slopes clad in stone and cement to channel precious rainwater into cisterns. Near the top looms the enormous chapel of **Panayía Thalassítra**, where the ancient Melians made their last stand against the Athenians before being massacred in 416 BC. Today it offers one of the best views in the Aegean, particularly at sunset in clear conditions.

From the archeological museum, signs point you towards the **early Christian catacombs** (daily except Wed & Sun 8.45am–1pm; free), 1km south of Pláka and just 400m from Tripití village; steps lead down from the road to the inconspicuous entrance. Although some 5000 bodies were buried in tomb-lined corridors which stretch some 200m into the soft volcanic rock, only the first 50m are illuminated and accessible by boardwalk. They're worth a look if you're in the area, but the adjacent ruins of **ancient Melos**, extending down from Pláka almost to the sea, justify the detour. There are huge Dorian walls, the usual column fragments lying around and, best of all, a well-preserved Roman **amphitheatre** (unrestricted access) some 200m west of the catacombs by track, then trail. Only seven rows of seats remain intact, but these evocatively look out over Klíma to the bay. Between the catacombs and the theatre is the signposted spot where the *Venus de Milo* was found; promptly delivered to the French consul for "safekeeping" from the Turks, this was the last the Greeks saw of the statue until the museum's copy was belatedly forwarded from the Louvre in Paris.

At the very bottom of the vale, KLÍMA is the most photogenic of several fishing hamlets on the island, with its picturesque boathouses tucked underneath the principal living areas. There's no beach to speak of, and only one place to stay, the impeccably sited *Panorama* (☎0287/21 623; ③), whose restaurant currently seems to be resting on its laurels.

Plathiéna, 45 minutes' walk northwest of Pláka, is the closest proper beach, and thus vastly popular in summer. There are no facilities, but the beach is fairly well protected and partly shaded by tamarisks. Head initially west from near the police station on the marked footpath towards ARETÍ and FOURKOVOÚNI, two more cliff-dug, boathouse-hamlets very much in the Klíma mould. Although the direct route to Plathiéna is signposted, it's no longer to go via Fourkovoúni; both hamlets are reached by side turnings off the main route, which becomes a jeep track as you approach Fourkovoúni. By moped, access to Plathiéna is only from Plakés, the northernmost and smallest of the five northwestern villages.

The south

The main road to the south of the island splits at **Kánava junction**, an unrelievedly dreary place at first glance owing to the large power plant here. But opposite this, indicated by a rusty sign pointing seaward, is the first of Mílos' **hot springs**, which bubble up in the shallows and are much enjoyed by the locals.

Taking the left or easterly fork leads to **ZEFÍRIA,** hidden among olive groves below the bare hills; it was briefly the medieval capital until an eighteenth-century epidemic drove out the population. Much of the old town is still deserted, though some life has returned, especially to the wonderfully named *Mama Loula* **taverna**, opposite the magnificent seventeenth-century church.

South of here the road progressively deteriorates into yawning ruts capable of swallowing a motorbike tyre whole, such that it's difficult to imagine a bus making it down the final slope of the 19km to the coarse-sand beach of **Paleohóri**. Actually a triple strand totalling about 800m in length and unarguably the island's best, clothing is optional at the westerly cove, where steam vents heat both the shallow water and the rock overhangs onshore. Although the lower, beachfront **taverna** is hard to resist, the *Artemis* (high season only) stands alluringly at the clifftop. There are also a few **rooms** for rent, but the place is really too remote to be a practical base, and most people bike in for the day, since the bus schedule doesn't permit much time here.

The westerly road from Kánava junction leads past the airport gate to **Hivadholímni**, considered to be the best beach on Mílos bay itself. Not that this is saying much: Hivadholímni is north-facing and thus garbage-prone, with shallow sumpy water offshore; better to veer south to **Provatás**, a short but tidy beach, closed off by colourful cliffs on the east. Being so easy to get at, it hasn't escaped some development. There are two-room establishments plus, closer to the shore, a new luxury complex.

Some 2km west of Provatás, you'll see a highway sign for **Kípos** just before the asphalt fizzles out. Below and to the left of the road, a small **medieval chapel** dedicated to the Kímisis (Assumption) sits atop foundations far older – as evidenced by the early Christian reliefs stacked along the west wall and a carved, cruciform baptismal font in the *ierón* behind the altar screen. At one time a spring gushed from the low tunnel-cave beside the font – sufficiently miraculous in itself on arid Mílos.

For the most part **Halakás**, the southwestern peninsula centred on the wilderness of 748-metre Profítis Ilías, is uninhabited and little built upon, with the exception of the much-venerated **monastery of Sidherianós**. Motorbikes if not cars will take a beating on the maze of rough tracks, and the coast is best explored on the round-the-island day trips on offer from travel agents in Adhámas.

The north coast

From either Adhámas or the Pláka area good roads run roughly parallel to the **north coast** which, despite being windswept and largely uninhabited, is not devoid of interest. **Mandhrákia**, reached from Péran Triovássalos, is another boathouse settlement, and **Sarakinikó**, to the east, is a sculpted inlet with a sandy sea-bed. About 8km from Adhámas, the little hamlet of **Pahéna**, not shown on many maps, has a cluster of rooms and a small beach. About a kilometre beyond this, the remains of three superimposed Neolithic settlements crown a small knoll at **Filakopí** (ancient Phylakopi); the site was important archeologically, but hasn't been maintained and is difficult to interpret.

Pollónia

POLLÓNIA, 12km northeast of Adhámas, must be the windiest spot on the island, hence the name of its longest-lived and best **bar**, *Okto Bofor* (meaning "Force 8 gales"), near the church. The second resort on Mílos after Adhámas, it is, not surprisingly, immensely popular with windsurfers. Pollónia is essentially a small harbour protected by a storm-lashed spit of land on the northeast, where self-catering units are multiplying rapidly, fringed by a long but narrow, tamarisk-fringed beach to the rear, and closed off on the south by a smaller promontory on which the tiny original settlement huddles. Besides the town beach, the only other convenient, half-decent beach is at **Voúdhia**, 3km east, where you will find more of the island's hot springs.

On the quay are a row of three **tavernas**, best of these being *Kapetan Nikolaos* (aka *Koula's*; open year-round). Inland and south of here you'll find another concentration of **accommodation**, more simple rooms and less apartments, most with the slight drawback of occasional noise and dust from quarry trucks. Among the newest and highest-quality units here are the *Kapetan Tasos Studios* (☎0287/41 287; June & Sept ③–④, July–Aug ⑥), with good views of the straits between Mílos and Kímolos. Pollónia has no bank or post office, but there is a helpful **travel agency**, *Blue Waters* (☎0287/41 442) which can change money, rent cars, book accommodation and sell *ANEK* ferry tickets (services to Sitía on Crete). A **motorbike rental** place behind the beach, and a well-stocked **supermarket**, complete the list of amenities.

Getting to Kímolos (see below) may be the main reason you're here. Either the *Tria Adhelfia* or one other *kaíki* makes the trip daily year-round at 6.45am and 2pm, returning from Kímolos an hour later; during high season, there may be additional departures and day trips.

Kímolos

Of the three islets off the coast of Mílos, Andímilos is home to a rare species of chamois and Políegos has more ordinary goats, but only **Kímolos** has any human habitation. Volcanic like Mílos, with the same little lava-built rural cottages, it profits from its geology and used to export chalk (*kimolía* in Greek) until the supply was exhausted. Still a source of fuller's earth, the fine dust of this clay is a familiar sight on the island, where mining still outstrips fishing and farming as an occupation. Rugged and barren in the interior, there is some fertile land on the southeast coast where low-lying wells provide water, and this is where the population of about eight hundred is concentrated.

Kímolos is sleepy indeed from September to June, and even in August sees hardly any visitors. This is probably just as well, since there are fewer than a hundred beds on the whole island, and little in the way of other amenities; such modest facilities as exist are relatively high-priced for what they are.

Psathí and Hóra

Whether you arrive by ferry, or by *kaíki* from Pollónia, you'll dock at the hamlet of **PSATHÍ**, pretty much a non-event except for one good **taverna** midway along the beach, *Toh Kyma*, with sympathetic proprietors. However, rooms here are worth considering, as they are bound to be quieter than anything in Hóra, where the noise of people, animals and vehicles can defeat sleep. **Ferry tickets** are sold only outside the expensive café on end of the jetty, an hour or so before the anticipated arrival of the boat; the Pollónia *kaíki* comes and goes unremarked from the base of the jetty.

Around the bay there are a few old windmills and the dazzlingly white **HÓRA** perched on the ridge above them. Unsung – and neglected – is the magnificent, two-gated **kastro**, a fortified core of roughly the same design as those at Andíparos and Síkinos; the perimeter houses are intact but its heart is a jumble of ruins. Just outside the *kástro* on the north stands the conspicuously unwhitewashed, late-sixteenth-century church of **Hrissostómos**, oldest surviving and most beautiful on the island.

It takes fifteen minutes to walk up to the surprisingly large town, passing the recommended *Maria's* **rooms** (July–Aug only; ②) on the way; you'll also find a certain amount of accommodation, much of it noisy, managed by *Margaro Petraki* (☎0287/51 314; ②), tucked away in the rather unglamourous maze of backstreets. The aptly named *Panorama*, near the east gate of the *kástro*, is the most elaborate and consistently open **taverna**. Self-catering is an easy proposition – and may be a necessity before June or after August – with a well-stocked supermarket, produce stalls and a butcher. Finally, there's a friendly **OTE** office behind Hrissostómos church, and a **post office**.

Around the island

During summer at least, the hamlet of **ALIKÍ** on the south coast is a better bet for staying than Hóra and Psathí, despite its relative remoteness. You should be able to get there in half an hour by following the track that heads levelly south (between a square relay reflector on the left and some power lines on the right) from the west end of Hóra. Alikí is named after the salt pan which sprawls between a rather mediocre beach with no shade or shelter, and a pair each of **rooms** – try *Passamihalis* (☎0287/51 340; ③) – and simple **tavernas**. You can stroll west one cove to **Bonátsa** for better sand and shallow water, though you won't escape the winds; to the east, between Alikí and Psathí, the smaller, more secluded beach of **Skála** is better for camping.

The 700m coarse-sand beach of **Elliniká** is 45 minutes' walk west of Alikí: starting on the road, bear left – just before two chapels on a slope – onto a narrower track which runs through the fields in a valley bottom. Divided by a low bluff, the beach is bracketed by two capes and looks out over Dhaskalió islet towards dramatic bits of Mílos, but again tends to catch heavy weather in the afternoon.

Another road leads northeast from Hóra to a beach and radioactive springs at **Prássa**, 7km away. The route takes in impressive views across the straits to Políegos and there are several shady peaceful coves where you could camp out. Innumerable goat tracks invite exploration of the rest of the island; in the far northwest, on Kímolos' summit, the ruins of an imposing Venetian fortress known as **Paleókastro**.

Ándhros

Ándhros, the second largest and northernmost of the Cyclades, has a number of fine features to offer the visitor, although you have to search them out. Thinly populated but prosperous, its fertile, well-watered valleys have attracted scores of Athenian holiday villas whose red-tiled roofs and white walls stand out among the greenery. Some of the more recently built of these have robbed many of the villages of life and atmosphere, turning them into scattered settlements with no nucleus, and have created a weekender mentality manifest in noisy Friday and Sunday evening traffic jams at the ferry dock. The island neither needs, nor welcomes, independent travellers, and it can be almost impossible to get a bed in between the block-bookings during high season. On the positive side, the permanent population is distinctly hospitable; traditionally working on ships, they are only too happy to practise their English on you. Together with some of the more idiosyncratic reminders of the Venetian period, such as the *peristereónes* (pigeon towers) and the *fráktes* (dry-stone walls, here raised to the status of an artform), it is this that lends Ándhros its charm.

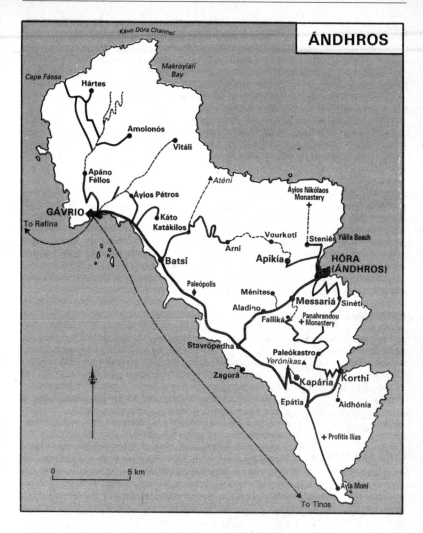

ÁNDHROS

Kávo Dóro Channel

Makroyiáli Bay

Cape Fássa

Hártes

Amolonós

Vitáli

Apáno Féllos

Aténi

Áyios Nikólaos Monastery

Áyios Pétros

GÁVRIO

To Rafína

Káto Katákilos

Vourkotí

Steniés Yiália Beach

Arní

Batsí

Apikía

HÓRA (ÁNDHROS)

Paleópolis

Ménites

Messariá Sinéti

Aladino

Panahrandou Monastery

Falliká

Stavrópedha

Paleókastro

Yerónikas

Zagorá

Kapária Korthí

Epátia

Aidhónia

Profítis Ilías

0   5 km

Ayía Moní

To Tínos

Ferries connect the island with Rafína on the mainland, only an hour from Athens on the bus, and you can loop back onto the central Cycladic routes via Míkonos or Síros. The bus service is poor, and you'd be well advised to consider renting a bike to tour the sights – or face a lot of walking.

Northern and western Ándhros

All ferries arrive at the main port, **GÁVRIO**, a nondescript place whose dirty, windswept beach is usually deserted. The sea in the enclosed harbour is so murky that even the wildfowl aren't interested. A converted dovecote houses a sporadically functioning **tourist office**, and the ferry **ticket agent** only opens half an hour before boats arrive. There's also a part-time **bank**, and a **post office** on the waterfront.

The cheapest **accommodation** is in some rooms in a block behind the hatshop; the *Galaxy* (☎0282/71 228; ③) is also clean and reasonable. *Camping Andros*, 2km down the road, has decent facilities, including a swimming pool and a good café. **Restaurants** worth trying include *Three Star Here* (sic), *O Mourikis* and *O Balmas*, near the port police, while **nightlife** revolves around the *Idhroussa Bar* on Áyios Pétros beach – or you could see if anybody's turned up at the *Disco Marabout.*

The road north begins behind the *Hotel Gavrion Beach.* Around 3km northwest are two beaches named **Féllos**: one, planted with holiday villas but with a taverna behind it; the other hidden beyond the headland and popular with freelance campers. Beyond Ápano Féllos, the countryside is empty except for a few hamlets inhabited by the descendants of medieval Albanians who settled here and in southern Évvia several hundred years ago.

Most traffic heads 8km south down the coast, past *Yiannoulí's* excellent taverna, to **BATSÍ**, the island's main package resort, with large hotels and discos above its fine natural harbour. The beautiful, if crowded, beach curves round the port, and the sea is cold, calm and clean (except near the taxi park). **Hotels** least likely to be inundated by the mostly British package operators include the *Avra* (☎0282/41 216; ②), and the new *Aneroussa Beach Hotel* (☎0282/41 445; ④), perched on a cliff above the south side of the bay. Reasonable fish **meals** can be had at *O Takis.* Except for the open-air cinema, **nightlife**, as typified by *Disco Blue Sky* or *Chaf*, is slick, expensive and geared towards couples. There's also an **OTE** and a **bank**.

From Batsí you're within easy walking distance of some beautiful inland villages. At **KÁTO KATÁKILOS**, one hour inland, three **tavernas** host "Greek nights" organized in Bátsi; a rough track leads to **ATÉNI**, a hamlet in a lush, remote valley, as yet unvisited by the dreaded donkey safaris. **ANO KATÁKILOS** has a couple of undervisited tavernas with fine views across the village. A right-hand turning out of Katákilos heads up the mountain to **ARNÍ**, whose lone taverna is often enshrouded in mist. Another rewarding trip is to a well-preserved, 20-metre-high **Classical tower** at Áyios Pétros, 5km from Gávrio or 9km coming from Batsí.

South of Batsí along the main road are Káto and Áno Apróvato: **Káto** has rooms, a café and a path to a quiet beach, while nearby is the largely unexplored archeological site of **Paleópolis.**

Hóra and around

A minimal bus service links the west coast with **HÓRA** or **ÁNDHROS** town, 35km from Gávrio. With its setting atop a rocky spur cutting across a huge bay, the capital is the most attractive place on the island. Paved in marble and schist from the still-active local quarries, the buildings around the bus station are grand nineteenth-century affairs, and the squares with their ornate wall fountains and gateways are equally elegant. The hill quarters are modern, while the small port acts as a yacht supply station, and below are the sands of Parapórti – a fine beach, if a little exposed to the *meltémi* winds in summer.

The few **hotels** in town are on the expensive side, and tend to be busy with holidaying Greeks: try the *Aigli* (☎0282/22 303; ⑤), opposite the big church on the main walkway. For a less expensive stay, ask around for rooms or check out the seasonal **campsite.** There's a choice of four **tavernas**, the best being the one right by the bus terminus. **Nightlife**, which consists of several bars, together with *Disco Remezzo*, is strongly pitched at a Greek rather than foreign clientele. The **OTE, post office** and various shops are just off the seafront road.

From the square right at the end of town you pass through an archway and down to windswept **Platía Ríva**, with its statue of the unknown sailor scanning the sea. Beyond him lies the thirteenth-century Venetian **Kástro**, precariously joined to the mainland by a narrow-arched bridge, which was damaged by German munitions in the last world war. The **Modern Art Museum** (Wed–Sun 10am–2pm, also 6–8pm in summer; 1000dr) has a sculpture garden and a permanent collection that includes works by Picasso and Braque, as well as temporary exhibits. Don't be discouraged by the stark modern architecture of the **Archeological Museum** (Tues–Sun 8.30am–3pm; 400dr); it turns out to be well laid out and labelled with instructive models. The prize items on view are the fourth-century "Hermes of Ándhros", reclaimed from a prominent position in the Athens archeological museum, and the "Matron of Herculaneum".

Hiking inland and west from Ándhros, the obvious destination is **MÉNITES**, a hill village just up a green valley choked with trees and straddled by stone walls. The church of the **Panayía** may have been the location of a Temple of Dionysus, where water was turned into wine; water still flows continuously from the local rocks. Nearby is the medieval village of **MESSARIÁ**, with the deserted twelfth-century Byzantine church of **Taxiárhis** below. The finest monastery on the island, **Panahrándou**, is only an hour's (steep) walk away, via the village of Fallikά; reputedly tenth-century, it's still defended by massive walls but occupied these days by just three monks. It clings to an iron-stained cliff southwest of Hóra, to which you can return directly with a healthy two- to three-hour walk down the creek valley, guided by red dots. There is a wonderful taverna, *Pertesis*, at Strapouriés, which boasts a view all the way down to the coast and excellent food.

Hidden by the ridge directly north of Hóra, the prosperous nineteenth-century village of **STENIÉS** was built by the vanguard of today's shipping magnates. Today you can splash out at the good fish tavernas here. Just below, at Yiália, there's a small pebbly beach with a café and watersports. Beyond Steniés is **APIKÍA**, a tidy little village which bottles *Sariza*-brand mineral water for a living; there are a few **tavernas** and a very limited number of **rooms**, as well as the new luxury hotel *Dighi Sarisa* (☎0282/23 799 or 23 899; ⑤), just below the spring itself. The road is now asphalted up to Vourkotí and even past this point is quite negotiable via Arní to the west coast. There are some stunning views all along this road but bike riders need to take care when the *meltémi* is blowing – it can get dangerously windy.

Southern Ándhros

On your way south, you might stop at **Zagorá**, a fortified Geometric town – unique in having never been built over – that was excavated in the early 1970s. Located on a desolate, flat-topped promontory with cliffs falling away on three sides, it's worth a visit for the view alone.

The village of **KORTHÍ**, the end of the line, is a friendly though nondescript village set on a large sandy bay, cut off from the rest of the island by a high ridge and so relatively unspoilt – and pleasant enough to merit spending the night at *Pension Rainbow* (☎0282/61 344; ③) or at the austere-looking *Hotel Korthion* (☎0282/61 218; ③). You could also take in the nearby convent of **Zoödhóhou Piyís** (open to visitors before noon), with illuminated manuscripts and a disused weaving factory.

To the north is **PALEÓKASTRO**, a tumbledown village with a ruined Venetian castle – and a legend about an old woman who betrayed the stronghold to the Turks, then jumped off the walls in remorse, landing on a rock now known as "Old Lady's Leap". In the opposite direction out of Korthí are **AIDHÓNIA** and **KAPÁRIA**, dotted with pigeon towers (*peristereónes*) left by the Venetians.

Tínos

The character of **Tínos** is determined largely by the grandiose shrine of **Panayía Evangelístria**, erected on the spot where a miraculous icon with healing powers was found in 1822. A Tiniote nun, now canonized as Ayía Pelayía, was directed in a dream to unearth the relic just as the War of Independence was getting underway – a timely coincidence which served to underscore the age-old links between the Orthodox Church and Greek nationalism. Today, there are two major annual pilgrimages, on March 25 and August 15, when (around noon) the icon bearing the Virgin's image is carried in state down to the harbour over the prostrate forms of the lame and the ill.

The rest of the island, too, smacks of religion and tradition in varying degrees. The Ottoman tenure here was the most fleeting in the Aegean. **Exóbourgo**, the craggy mount dominating southern Tínos and surrounded by most of the island's sixty-odd villages, is studded with the ruins of a Venetian citadel which defied the Turks until 1715, long after the rest of Greece had fallen. An enduring legacy of the long Latin rule is a persistent Catholic minority, which accounts for almost half the population, and a sectarian rivalry that is responsible for the numerous graceful belfries scattered throughout the island; Orthodox and Catholic parishes vying to build the tallest. The sky is pierced, too, by distinctive pigeon towers, even more in evidence here than on Ándhros. Aside from all this, the inland village architecture is striking and there's a flourishing folk-art tradition which finds expression in the abundant local marble. If there are weak points to Tínos, they are that the religious atmosphere tends to dampen nightlife, and that beaches are few and far between. However, the islanders have remained open and hospitable to the relatively few foreigners who touch down here; and any mercenary inclinations seem to be satisfied by booming sales in religious paraphernalia to the Greek faithful.

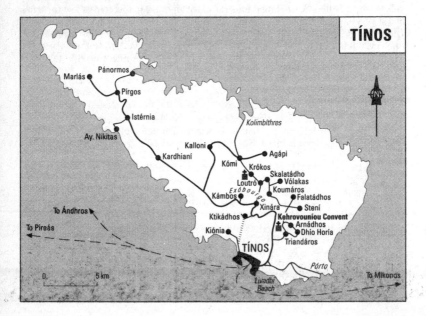

Tínos Town and the southern beaches

Trafficking in devotional articles certainly dominates the busy port town of **TÍNOS**, with the Neoclassical **church** (daily 8.30am–8.30pm) towering above, at the top of Leofóros Megaloháris. Approached via a massive marble staircase, the famous icon inside is all but buried under a dazzling mass of gold and silver *támmata* (votive offerings); below is the crypt (where the icon was discovered) and a mausoleum for the sailors drowned when the Greek warship *Elli*, at anchor off Tínos during a pilgrimage, was torpedoed by an Italian submarine on August 15, 1940. Museums around the courtyard display more objects donated by worshippers, who inundate the island for the two big yearly festivals.

The shrine aside – and all the attendant stalls, shops, and bustle – the port is none too exciting (a beautiful Neoclassical waterfront having been destroyed since the 1960s), with just scattered inland patches of nineteenth-century buildings. You might make time for the **Archeological Museum** (Tues–Sun 8.30am–3pm, closed Mon; 400dr) on the way up to the church, which displays finds, including a fascinating sundial, from the local Roman Sanctuary of Poseidon and Amphitrite (see overpage).

Practicalities

Most **ferries** now dock at the new jetty, 600m north of the old one. There are at least two boats a day from both Pireás and Rafina, with connections to Andhros and Míkonos. When you're leaving, ask your ticket agent which jetty to head for. **Buses** leave from a small parking area in front of a cubbyhole-office on the quay, and are not terribly frequent. A **moped** is a better strategy for exploring, and *Vidalis*, Zanáki Alavánou 16, is a good rental agency, but watch out for the main road to Pírgos, which is in a state of disrepair in some sections and requires care to avoid the potholes. The **tourist police** have an office right opposite the bus terminal.

To have any chance of securing a reasonably priced **room** around the pilgrimage day of March 25 (August 15 is hopeless), you must arrive several days in advance – and even then, be prepared to do a lot of asking around. At other times there's plenty of choice, though you'll still be competing with out-of-season pilgrims, Athenian tourists and the sick and the disabled seeking a miracle cure. Of the hotels, the *Eleana* (☎0283/22 561; ③), east of the quay about 400m inland at the edge of the bazaar, is the best budget option. The conspicuous waterfront *Yannis Rooms* (☎0283/22 515; ③) is just in front of the *Thalia*, all the way around the bay from the old jetty. Slightly pricier options include the *Avra* (☎0283/22 242; ④), a Neoclassical relic on the waterfront, and the *Favie Souzane* just inland (☎0283/22 693 or 22 176; ④). The *Vyzantio*, Zanáki Alavánou 26 (☎0283/22 454; ④), on the road out towards Pórto and the villages, is not especially memorable but it and the *Meltemi* at Filipóti 7, near Megaloháris (☎0283/22 881; ④), are the only places open off-season. Finally, there is a smart new hotel with swimming pool near the beginning of the beach road east of the promontory – *Peolos Bay Hotel* (☎0283/ 23 410 or 23 411; ⑤). Otherwise, beat the crowds by staying at *Tínos Camping* which has tents and a few nice rooms to let (☎0283/22 502; ②); follow the signs from the port, a ten-minute walk.

As usual, most seafront **restaurants** are rather overpriced and indifferent, with the exception of a friendly *Psitopolio* right opposite the bus terminal and the *Zefyros estiatorio* next to the post office. Further round the quay, the *Milos* taverna has a decent selection and reasonable prices. A cluster of places around the bazaar just to the left of Megaloháris as you face the church include *Ta Fanaria*, an inexpensive local hang-out with a limited selection, and *Palea Pallada* and *Peristereonas*, both of them reasonable. Tucked away in a small alley near the seafront off Evangelistrias, *Pigada* does a fine clay-pot moussaka, as well as some more unusual dishes, while *O Kipos*, further inland on the way to the church, has a pleasant garden setting. Wash down your meals with the island's very good barrelled retsina, which is available just about everywhere.

There are quite a few **bars**, mostly in a huddle near the new quay. *Fevgatos* has a pleasant atmosphere, and *Kala Kathoumena* is pretty lively with a mixture of international hits and Greek music, avidly danced to by some of the locals.

Nearby beaches

Most, though not all, of the island's **beaches** are close to town. **KIÓNIA**, 3km northwest (hourly buses), is functional enough but marred by a luxury holiday complex, though there is a campsite here. More importantly, it's the site of the **Sanctuary of Poseidon and Amphitrite**, discovered in 1902, the excavations yielding principally columns (*kiónia* in Greek), but also a temple, baths, a fountain, and hostels for the ancient pilgrims.

LIVÁDHI, though conveniently close (2km) to the port, is rocky and relatively exposed. **PÓRTO**, 8km east, boasts two good beaches to either side of **Áyios Sostís** headland, with another campsite nearby (and four buses daily), but bring food – development here consists of apartments, villas and rooms, and the nearest tavernas are quite a way back towards town, with the exception of the reasonably priced restaurant belonging to *Akti Aegeou* (☎0283/24 248, winter ☎0283/22 048; ⑥) on the first beach of Ayíos Pandelímon.

Northern Tínos

A good beginning to a foray into the interior is to take the stone stairway – the continuation of Odhós Ayíou Nikoláou – that passes behind and to the left of Evangelístria. This climbs for an hour and a half through appealing countryside to **KTIKÁDHOS**, a fine village with a good sea-view taverna, *Iy Dhrosia*, although it tends to be overrun with bus tours in summer. You can either flag down a bus on the main road or stay with the trail until Xinára (see below).

Heading northwest from the junction flanked by Ktikádhos, Tripótamos and Xinára, there's little to stop for – except the fine dovecotes around Kámbos – until you reach **KARDHIANÍ**, one of the most strikingly set and intrinsically beautiful villages on the island, with its views across to Síros from amid a dense oasis. Nestled in the small sandy bay below is a fine little restaurant by the name of *Anemos*, which serves octopus stew and other dishes at good prices. Kardhianí has recently been discovered by wealthy Athenians and expatriates, and now offers the exotic *Toh Perivoli* taverna. **ISTÉRNIA**, just a little beyond, is not nearly so appealing but it does have a pension at the top of the village and a few cafés, perched above the turning for **Órmos Isterníon**, a comparatively small but overdeveloped beach.

Four daily buses along this route finish up at **PÍRGOS**, a few kilometres further north and smack in the middle of the island's marble-quarrying district. A beautiful village, its local artisans are renowned throughout Greece for their skill in producing marble ornamentation; ornate fanlights and bas-relief plaques crafted here adorn houses throughout Tínos. With an attractive shady *platía*, Pírgos is popular in summer, but you should be able to find a **room** easily enough, and you have a choice of two **tavernas**, *Vinia* being the more elegant by far.

The marble products were once exported from **PÁNORMOS** (Órmos) harbour, 4km northeast, with its tiny and surprisingly commercialized beach, but little reason to linger. If you get stuck, there are rooms, a campsite and some tavernas.

Around Exóbourgo

The ring of villages **around Exóbourgo** mountain is the other focus of interest on Tínos. The fortified pinnacle itself, 570m above sea level, with ancient foundations as well as the ruins of three Venetian churches and a fountain, is reached most quickly by steep steps from **XINÁRA** (near the island's major road junction), the seat of the island's Roman Catholic bishop. Most villages in north central Tínos have mixed populations, but Xinára and its immediate neighbours are purely Catholic; the inland villages also tend to have a more sheltered position, with better farmland nearby – the Venetians' way of rewarding converts and their descendants. Yet **TRIPÓTAMOS**, just south of Xinára, is a completely Orthodox village with possibly the finest architecture in this region – and has accordingly been pounced on by foreigners keen to restore its historic properties.

At **LOUTRÓ**, the next community north of Xinára, there's an Ursuline convent and carpet-making school: to visit, leave the bus at the turning for Skaládho. From Krókos, which has a couple of scenically situated restaurants, it's a forty-minute walk to **VÓLAKAS**, one of the highest and most remote villages on the island, a windswept oasis surrounded by bony rocks. Here, half a dozen elderly Catholic basketweavers fashion some of the best examples of that craft in Greece. If the workshops are not open, you can have a drink and buy baskets, at fair prices, in the ground-floor café run by a German–Greek couple.

At Kómi, 5km beyond Krókos, you can take a detour for **KOLIMBÍTHRES**, a magnificent double beach: one wild, huge and windswept, the other sheltered and with a taverna and rooms, but no camping. Any bus marked "Kalloni" passes through Kómi.

From either Skaládho or Vólakas you can traipse on foot to Koúmaros, where another long stairway leads up to Exóbourgo, or skirt the pinnacle towards Stení and Falatádhos, which appear as white speckles against the fertile plain of Livadhéri. From Stení you can catch the bus back to the harbour (seven daily). On the way down, try and stop off at one of the beautiful settlements just below the important twelfth-century **convent of Kehrovouníou**, where Ayía Pelayía dreamed of the icon, and the nuns still float down lavender-tinted corridors and under Lilliputian arches. In particular, **DHÍO HORIÁ** has a fine main square where cave-fountains burble, and **TRIANDÁROS** has a good, reasonable taverna in *Iy Levka*. If you have your own transport, there are some quite wide and fairly negotiable tracks down to some lovely secluded bays on the east of the island from the area of Steni. One such is Santa Margarita; given the lack of tourist development here, it's a good idea to take at least something to drink with you.

This is hardly an exhaustive list of Tíniote villages; armed with a map and good walking shoes for tackling the many old trails that still exist, you could spend days within sight of Exóbourgo and never pass through the same hamlets twice. Take warm clothing too, especially if you're on a moped, since the forbidding mountains behind Vólakas and the Livadhéri plain keep things noticeably cool almost year-round.

Míkonos (Mykonos)

Originally visited only as a stop on the way to ancient Delos, **Míkonos** has become easily the most popular (and the most expensive) of the Cyclades. Boosted by direct air links with Britain and domestic flights from Athens, an incredible 800,000 tourists pass through in a good year, producing some spectacular overcrowding in high summer on Míkonos' 75 square kilometres. But if you don't mind the crowds, or – and this is a much more attractive proposition – you come out of season, the prosperous capital is still one of the most beautiful of all island towns, its immaculately whitewashed houses concealing hundreds of little churches, shrines and chapels.

The sophisticated nightlife is pretty hectic, amply stimulated by Míkonos' former reputation as *the* gay resort of the Mediterranean – a title lost in recent years to places like Ibiza and Sitges in Spain; whatever, the locals take this comparatively exotic clientele in their stride. Unspoilt it isn't, but the island does offer excellent (if crowded and mainly nude) beaches, picturesque windmills, and a rolling arid interior. An unheralded Míkonian quirk is the legality of scuba diving, a rarity in Greece, and dive centres have sprung up on virtually every beach.

Míkonos Town

Don't let the crowds put you off exploring **MÍKONOS TOWN**, the archetypal postcard image of the Cyclades. Its sugar-cube buildings are stacked around a cluster of seafront fishermen's dwellings with every nook and cranny scrubbed and shown off. Most people head out to the beaches during the day, so early morning or late afternoon are the best times to wander the maze of narrow streets. The labyrinthine design was intended to confuse the pirates who plagued Míkonos in the eighteenth and early nineteenth centuries, and it still has the desired effect.

You don't need any maps or hints to scratch around the convoluted streets and alleys of town; getting lost is half the fun. There are, however, a few places worth seeking out if you require more structure to your strolling. Coming from the ferry quay, you'll pass the **Archeological Museum** (Tues–Sat 9am–3pm, Sun 9.30am–2.30pm; 400dr) on your way into town, home to some good Delos pottery – and a superb *souvláki* bar next door. The town also boasts a **Marine Museum** displaying various nautical artefacts (daily 10.30am–1pm & 6.30–9pm; 200dr). Alternatively, behind the two banks there's the **Library**, with Hellenistic coins and late medieval seals, or, at the base of the Delos jetty, the **Folklore Museum** (Mon–Sat 4–8pm, Sun 5–8pm; free), housed in an eighteenth-century mansion and cramming in a larger-than-usual collection of bric-a-brac, including a vast four-poster bed. The museum shares the same promontory as the old Venetian *kástro*, the entrance to which is marked by Míkonos' oldest and best-known church, **Paraportianí**, which is a fascinating asymmetrical hodge-podge of four chapels amalgamated into one.

The shore leads to the area known as "Little Venice" because of its high, arcaded Venetian houses built right up to the water's edge. Its real name is **Alefkándhra**, a trendy district packed with art galleries, chic bars and discos. Back off the seafront, behind Platía Alefkándhra, are Míkonos' two **cathedrals**: Roman Catholic and Greek Orthodox. Beyond, the famous **windmills** look over the area, a little shabby but ripe with photo opportunities. Instead of retracing your steps along the water's edge, follow Énoplon Dhinaméon (left off Mitropóleos) to **Tría Pigádhia** fountain. The name means "Three Wells" and legend has it that should a maiden drink from all three she is bound to find a husband, though these days she'd be more likely to end up with a water-borne disease.

Arrival and information

There is some accommodation information at the **airport**, but unless you know where you're going it's easier to take a taxi the 3km to town and sort things out at the jetty. The vast majority of visitors arrive by boat at the new northern **jetty**, where a veritable horde of room-owners pounce on the newly arrived. The scene is actually quite intimidating and so, if you can avoid the grasping talons, it is far better to go a hundred metres further where a row of offices deal with official hotels, rented rooms and camping information.

The harbour curves around past the dull, central Polikandhrióti beach; behind it is the **bus station** for Toúrlos, Áyios Stéfanos and Áno Méra. Just beyond, next to the **post office**, is the *Olympic Airways* office. Further around the seafront to the southern jetty you'll find the **tourist police** (☎0289/22 482) and *kaíkia* **to Delos**. A second **bus terminus**, for beaches to the south, is right at the other end of the town, beyond the windmills. Buses to all the most popular beaches and resorts run frequently, and until very late in the evening. It is also here that the largest cluster of **motorbike rental** agencies is to be found; prices vary little.

Accommodation

Accommodation **prices** in Míkonos rocket in the high season to a greater degree than almost anywhere else in Greece: a 5000–6000dr town room in early June can reach 15,000dr by August, and hotel rates at the nearby beaches are even more expensive. If you're after **rooms**, it's worth asking at *O Megas* grocery store on Andhroníkou

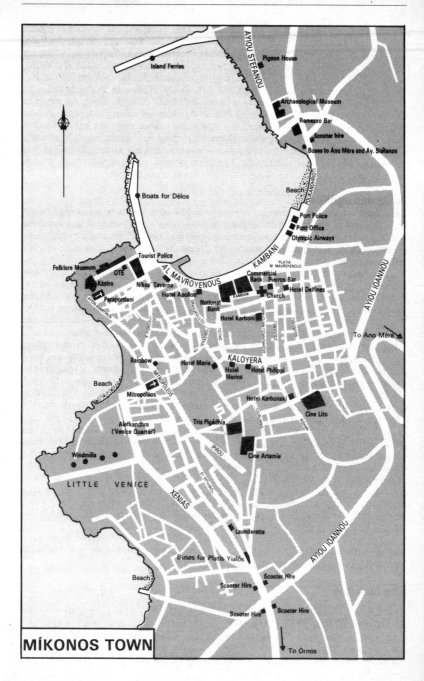

Island Ferries

AYIOU STEFANOU

Pigeon House

Archaeological Museum

Remezzo Bar

Scooter hire

Buses to Áno Méra and Ay. Stéfanos

Boats for Délos

Beach

POULANDHRIOTI

Port Police

Post Office

Olympic Airways

KAMBANI

Tourist Police

Folklore Museum

OTE

AL MAVROYENOUS

PLATIA
M MAVROYENOUS

AY. GERASIMOU

Commercial
Bank

Pierros Bar

Kástro

Níkos' Taverna

AYIOU LOUKA

KAMBANI

Church

Hotel Delfines

Paraportianí

AYÍON ANARGYRON

Hotel Apollon

National
Bank

ENOPLON DHINAMEON

Hotel Karboni

AYIOU IOANNOU

To Áno Méra

Rainbow

MITROPOLEOS

Hotel Maria

KALOYERA

Hotel
Marios

Hotel Phillipi

Beach

Mitropoléos

Hotel Karbonaki

Cine Lito

MATOYANNI

Alefkándhra
('Venice Quarter')

Tría Pigádhia

ZOUGANELI

Cine Artemis

Windmills

IPIROU

LITTLE   VENICE

XÉNIAS

AY. EFRAIM

Launderette

Buses for Platís Yialós

AYIOU IOANNOU

Scooter Hire

Beach

Scooter Hire

Scooter Hire

Scooter Hire

To Órnos

MÍKONOS TOWN

Matoyiánni – they tend to know what's available. One establishment that comes recommended is *Villa Giovani* (☎0289/22 485; ④), near the bus station at the edge of town. Out of season, you could try some of the **hotels in town**, such as *Delfines* on Mavroyéni (☎0289/22 292; ④–⑤), *Karbonis* at Andhroníkou Matoyiánni 53 (☎0289/23 127; ④–⑤), *Apollon* on Mavroyénous (☎0289/22 223; ④–⑤), *Maria* at Kaloyéra 18 (☎0289/22 317; ③–④), *Philippi* at Kaloyéra 32 (☎0289/22 294; ④–⑤), *Karbonaki* at Panahrándou 21 (☎0289/23 127, ③–④), or the *Galini* at Lákka (☎0289/22 626; ③). There are plenty of splurge hotels like *Elysium* (☎0289/23 952; ⑥) on Skholíou Kalón Tehnon and *Petasos* (☎0289/22 608; ⑥). As a last resort, the *Apollo 2001* disco may rent out roof space. Otherwise, there are two **campsites**: *Mykonos Camping* on Paranga beach is infinitely superior to the busier *Paradise Camping* – it is less crowded, has a more pleasant setting and is generally a relaxed and friendly place. Both campsites have regular courtesy minibuses to meet the ferries, so getting in and out of town is no problem.

Eating and nightlife

Even **light meals** and **snacks** are expensive in Míkonos, but there are several bakeries – the best is *Andhrea's*, just off Platía Mavroyénous – and plenty of supermarkets and takeaways in the backstreets, including *Spilia* on Énoplon Dhinaméon, which does decent burgers. For **late-night** snacks, try *Margarita's* on Flórou Zouganéli, or after 3am head for the port, where *The Yacht Club* is open until sunrise.

The area around Kaloyéra is a promising place to head for a **full meal**. The *Edem Garden* at the top of Kaloyéra, is a popular gay restaurant with an adventurous menu, and *El Greco* at Tría Pigádhia is expensive but romantic. Alefkándhra can offer *La Cathedral*, by the two cathedrals on the *platía*, the pricey but well-sited *Pelican*, behind the cathedrals, and *Spiro's* for good fish on the seafront. *Kostas*, also behind the two cathedrals has competitive prices, a good selection including barrelled wine (not easily found on Míkonos) and friendly service. Less than fifty metres further along Mitropoleos, the small *Yiavroutas Estiatorio* is probably the least expensive and most authentically Greek place on the island, again with good barrelled wine. There's something for most tastes in the Lákka (bus station) area: a variety of salads at *Orpheas*, French cuisine at *Andromeda*, and Italian at *Dolce Vita*. Just behind the Town Hall is *Nikos' Taverna* – crowded, reasonable and recommended – and 1km north you can dine by a floodlit pool overlooking the cruise ships at the luxury *Hotel Cavo Tagoo*.

Nightlife in town is every bit as good as it's cracked up to be – and every bit as pricey. *Remezzo* (near the OTE) is one of the oldest bars, now a bit over the hill but a nice place to watch the sunset before the onslaught of the hilarious Greek dancing lessons. *Scandinavia Bar* is a cheap and cheerful party spot, as is the nearby *Irish Bar*, and there are more drinking haunts over in the Alefkándhra area. For classical music, try *Kastro's* for an early evening cocktail, moving on later to the fairly swanky *Montparnasse*. *Bolero's* and *Piano Bar* both have live music, while *Le Cinema* is a newish club worth trying. The **gay** striptease and drag-show scene has shifted to the *Factory* by the windmills; *Manto* and adjacent bars are also popular.

Last but not least, the narcissistic beach ethos of Míkonos is well served by an excellent **gym** for weight-trainers and body-builders: *The Bodywork Gym*, run by Ankie Feenstra, lets you show with pride those well-oiled cuts.

The beaches

The closest **beaches** to town are those to the north, at Toúrlos (only 2km away but horrid) and **ÁYIOS STÉFANOS** (4km, much better), both developed resorts and connected by very regular bus service to Míkonos. There are tavernas and rooms to let (as well as package hotels) at Áyios Stéfanos, away from the beach; *Nikos* taverna at the far end of the bay has a pleasant setting and good prices.

Other nearby destinations include southwest peninsula resorts, with undistinguished beaches tucked into pretty bays. The nearest to town, 1km away, is **Megáli Ámmos,** a good beach backed by flat rocks and pricey rooms, but nearby Kórfos bay is disgusting, thanks to the town dump and machine noise. Buses serve **Órnos** – home to the *Lucky Divers Scuba Club* (☎0289/23 220) – with an average beach, though room prices are over-the-top, and **Áyios Ioánnis**, a dramatic bay with a tiny, stony beach and a chapel.

The south coast is the busiest part of the island. *Kaíkia* ply from town to all of its beaches, which are among the straightest on the island, and still regarded to some extent as family strands by the Greeks. You might begin with **PLATÍS YIALÓS**, 4km south of town, though you won't be alone: one of the longest-established resorts on the island, it's not remotely Greek any more, the sand is monopolized by hotels, and you won't get a room to save your life between June and September. **PSAROÚ**, next door, is very pretty – 150m of white sand backed by foliage and calamus reeds, but covered in sunbathers unless it's dawn, dusk, or out of season. Facilities here include a diving club (☎0289/23 579), waterskiing and windsurfer rental, but again you'll need to reserve well in advance to secure a room between mid-June and mid-September.

A dusty footpath beyond Platís Yialós crosses the fields and caves of the headland, leading to **Paránga** beach, where there's an inexpensive and well-appointed **campsite**. There's some good snorkelling to be done around the east of the bay, cluttered with volcanic rocks, starfish, and sea urchins. More footpaths continue across the clifftops and drop down to **Paradise Beach**, well sheltered by its headland, predominantly nudist, and packed full of beautiful people. The crescent of fine white sand makes it a handsome place

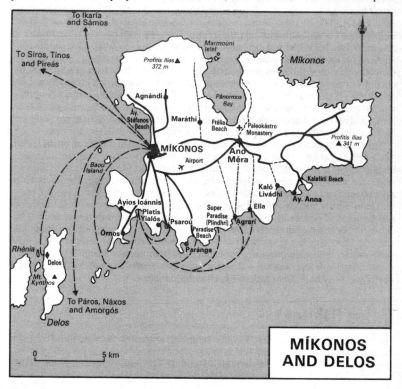

MÍKONOS AND DELOS

to stay; there's an official campsite (April–Oct) with a diving club and two tavernas. The next bay east contains **Super Paradise** (officially "Plindhrí") beach, again, accessible by footpath or by *kaíki*. Once renowned as an exclusively gay, nudist beach, it's now pretty mixed, and a has a good, friendly atmosphere and a couple of tavernas.

Probably the **best beach** on Míkonos, though, is **Elía**, the last port of call for the *kaíkia*. A broad, sandy stretch with a verdant backdrop, it's the longest beach on the island, though split in two by a rocky area. Almost exclusively nudist, it boasts an excellent restaurant, *Matheos*. If the crowds have followed you this far, one last escape route is to follow the bare rock footpath over the spur (look for the white house) at the end of Elía beach. This cuts upwards for grand views east and west and then winds down to **Kaló Livádhi** (seasonal bus service), a stunning beach adjoining an agricultural valley scattered with little farmhouses; even here there's a restaurant (a good one at that) at the far end of the beach. **Lía,** further on, is smaller but delightful, with bamboo windbreaks and clear water, plus another taverna.

The rest of the island

If time is limited, any of the beaches above will be just fine. There are others, though, away from Míkonos Town, as well as a few other destinations worth making the effort for.

East of Elía, roughly 12km by road from the town, **AYÍA ÁNNA** boasts a shingle beach and taverna, with the cliffs above granting some fine vistas; the place achieved its moment of fame as a location for the film *Shirley Valentine*. **TARSANÁ**, on the other side of the isthmus, has a long, coarse sand beach, with watersports, a taverna and smart bungalows on offer. **KALAFÁTI**, almost adjacent, is more of a tourist community, its white-sand beach supporting a few hotels, restaurants and a disco. There's a local bus service from here to Áno Méra (see below), or you can jump on an excursion boat to **Tragoníssi**, the islet just offshore, for spectacular coastal scenery, seals and wild birds. The rest of the east coast is difficult – often impossible – to reach: there are some small beaches, really only worth the effort if you crave solitude, and the region is dominated by the peak of Profítis Ilías, sadly spoiled by a huge radar dome and military establishment. The **north coast** suffers persistent battering from the *meltémi*, plus tar and litter pollution, and for the most part is bare, brown and exposed. **Pánormos Bay** is the exception to this – a lovely, relatively sheltered beach, and one of the least crowded on the island, with a couple of decent tavernas.

From Pánormos, it's an easy walk to the only other settlement of any size on the island, **ÁNO MÉRA**, where you should be able to find a **room**. The village strives to maintain a traditional way of life: in the main square there's a proper *kafenío* and fresh vegetables are sold, *ouzo* and a local cheese are produced, and there's just one hotel; the taverna *Tou Apostoli toh Koutouki* is popular with locals. The red-roofed church near the square is the sixteenth-century **monastery of Panayía Tourlianí**, where a collection of Cretan icons and the unusual eighteenth-century marble baptismal font are worth seeing. It's not far, either, to the late twelfth-century **Paleokástro monastery** (also known as Dárga), just north of the village, in a magnificent green setting on an otherwise barren slope. To the northwest are more of the same dry and wind-buffeted landscapes, though they do provide some enjoyable, rocky walking with expansive views across to neighbouring islands – stroll down to Áyios Stéfanos for buses back to the harbour.

Delos (Dhílos)

The remains of **ancient Delos**, Pindar's "unmoved marvel of the wide world", though skeletal and swarming now with lizards and tourists, give some idea of the past grandeur of this sacred isle a few sea-miles west of Míkonos. The ancient town lies on the west coast

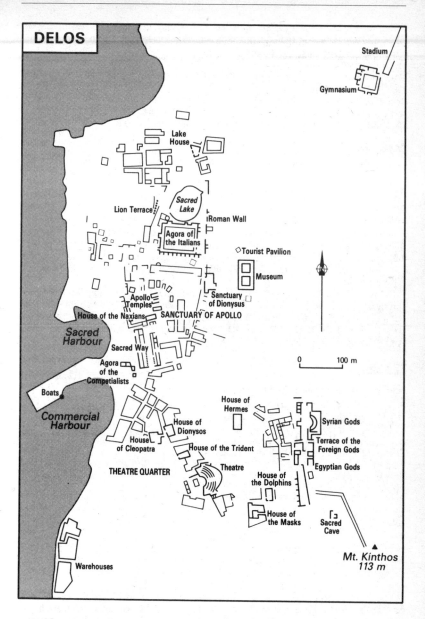

DELOS

Stadium

Gymnasium

Lake House

Sacred Lake

Lion Terrace

Roman Wall

Agora of the Italians

Tourist Pavilion

Museum

Apollo Temples

Sanctuary of Dionysus

House of the Naxians

SANCTUARY OF APOLLO

Sacred Harbour

Sacred Way

Agora of the Competialists

0   100 m

Boats

Commercial Harbour

House of Hermes

Syrian Gods

House of Dionysos

Terrace of the Foreign Gods

House of Cleopatra

House of the Trident

Egyptian Gods

THEATRE QUARTER

Theatre

House of the Dolphins

House of the Masks

Sacred Cave

Mt. Kínthos 113 m

Warehouses

on flat, sometimes marshy ground which rises in the south to **Mount Kínthos**. From the summit – an easy walk – there's a magnificent view of almost the entire Cyclades group; the name of the archipelago means "those [islands] around [Delos]".

The *kaíki* to Delos leaves Míkonos at 9am (2–7 weekly, depending on season; 1500dr round-trip) and returns at 1pm. A larger craft sometimes makes the trip an hour later, and returns an hour later, for a bit more money. During the busier summer months there is also a daily *kaíki* doing return trips from the beaches with pick-up points at Paradise, Paránga, Platís Yialós and Órnes for around 2000dr return. The regular boats will give you only three hours on the island – barely enough time to take in the main attractions. If you want to make a thorough tour of the site, you'll have to come on several morning excursions or take a private afternoon charter tour, both expensive options. In any case, it's a good idea to bring your own food and drink as the tourist pavilion's snack bar is a rip-off.

Some history

Delos' ancient fame was due to the fact that Leto gave birth to the divine twins Artemis and Apollo on the island, although its fine harbour and central position did nothing to hamper development. When the Ionians colonized the island around 1000 BC it was already a cult centre, and by the seventh century BC it had become the commercial and religious centre of the Amphictionic League. Unfortunately Delos also attracted the attention of Athens, which sought dominion over this prestigious island; the wealth of the Delian Confederacy, founded after the Persian Wars to protect the Aegean cities, was harnessed to Athenian ends, and for a while they controlled the Sanctuary of Apollo. Athenian attempts to "purify" the island began with a decree that no one could die or give birth on Delos – the sick and the pregnant were taken to the islet of Rheneia – and culminated in the simple expedient of banishing the native population.

Delos reached its peak in the third and second centuries BC, after being declared a free port by its Roman overlords. In the end, though, its undefended wealth brought ruin: first Mithridates (88 BC), then Athenodorus (69 BC), plundered the treasures and the island never recovered. By the third century AD, Athens could not even sell it, and for centuries, every passing seafarer stopped to collect a few prizes.

The site

Admission 1000dr, including the museum.

As you land, the Sacred Harbour is on your left, the Commercial Harbour on your right; and straight ahead is the **Agora of the Competialists**. Competialists were Roman merchants or freed slaves who worshipped the *Lares Competales*, the guardian spirits of crossroads; offerings to Hermes would once have been placed in the middle of the *agora*, their position now marked by a round and a square base. The **Sacred Way** leads north from the far left corner; it used to be lined with statues and the grandiose monuments of rival kings. Along it you reach three marble steps which lead into the **Sanctuary of Apollo**: much was lavished on the god, but the forest of offerings has been plundered over the years. On your left is the Stoa of the Naxians, while against the north wall of the House of the Naxians, to the right, there stood in ancient times a huge statue of Apollo. In 417 BC the Athenian general Nicias led a procession of priests across a bridge of boats from Rheneia to dedicate a bronze palm tree; when it was later blown over in a gale it took the statue with it. Three **Temples of Apollo** stand in a row to the right along the Sacred Way: the Delian Temple, that of the Athenians, and the Porinos Naos, the earliest of them, dating from the sixth century BC. To the east towards the museum you pass the **Sanctuary of Dionysus**, with its marble phalluses on tall pillars.

The best finds from the site are in Athens, but the **museum** (if it's open) still justifies a visit. To the north is a wall that marks the site of the **Sacred Lake** where Leto gave birth, clinging to a palm tree. Guarding it are the superb **Lions**, their lean bodies masterfully executed by Naxians in the seventh century BC; of the original nine, three have disappeared and one adorns the Arsenale at Venice. On the other side of the lake is the City Wall, built in 69 BC – too late to protect the treasures.

Set out in the other direction from the Agora of the Competialists and you enter the residential area, known as the **Theatre Quarter**. Many of the walls and roads remain, but there is none of the domestic detail that brings such sites to life. Some colour is added by the mosaics: one in the **House of the Trident**, and better ones in the **House of the Masks**, most notably a vigorous portrayal of Dionysus riding on a panther's back. The **Theatre** itself seated 5500 spectators, and, though much ravaged, offers some fine views. Behind the theatre, a path leads past the **Sanctuaries of the Foreign Gods** and up **Mount Kínthos** for more panoramic sightseeing.

Síros (Syros)

Don't be put off by first impressions of **Síros**. From the ferry it looks grimly industrial, but away from the Neórion shipyard things improve quickly. Very much a working island with no real history of tourism, it's probably the most Greek of the

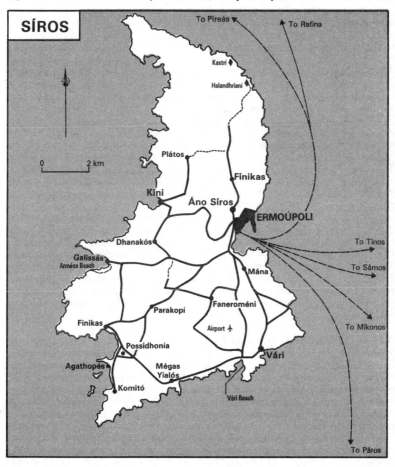

Cyclades; there are few holiday trappings and what there is exists for the benefit of the locals. You probably won't find, as Herman Melville did when he visited in 1856, shops full of ". . . fez-caps, swords, tobacco, shawls, pistols, and orient finery . . .", but you're still likely to appreciate Síros as a refreshing change from having to compete with the beautiful people. Of course, outsiders do come to the island; in fact there's a thriving permanent foreign community, and the beaches are hardly undeveloped, but everywhere there's the underlying assumption that you're a guest of an inherently private people.

Ermoúpoli

The main town and port of **ERMOÚPOLI** was founded during the War of Independence by refugees from Psará and Híos, becoming Greece's chief port in the nineteenth century. Although Pireás outran it long ago, Ermoúpoli is still the largest town in the Cyclades, and the archipelago's capital. Medieval Síros was largely a Catholic island, but an influx of Orthodox refugees during the War of Independence created two distinct communities; almost equal in numbers, the two groups today still live in their respective quarters, occupying two hills that rise up from the sea.

Ermoúpoli itself, the **lower town**, is worth at least a night's stay, with grandiose buildings a relic of its days as a major port. Between the harbour and **Áyios Nikólaos**, the fine Orthodox church to the north, you can stroll through its faded splendour. The **Apollon Theatre** is a copy of La Scala in Milan and once presented a regular Italian opera season; today local theatre and music groups put it to good use. The long, central **Platía Miaoúli** is named after an admiral of the revolution whose statue stands there; in the evenings the population parades in front of its arcaded *kafenía*, while the children ride the mechanical animals. Up the stairs to the left of the Town Hall is the small **Archeological Museum** (Tues–Sun 8.30am–3pm; closed Mon) with three rooms of finds from Síros, Páros and Amorgós. To the left of the clock tower more stairs climb up to **Vrondádho**, the hill that hosts the Orthodox quarter. The wonderful church of the **Anástasi** stands atop the hill, with its domed roof and great views over Tínos and Míkonos; if it's locked, ask for the key at the priest's house.

On the taller hill to the left is the intricate medieval quarter of **Áno Síros**, with a clutch of Catholic churches below the cathedral of Saint George. There are fine views of the town below, and, close by, the **Cappuchin monastery of Saint Jean**, founded in 1535 to do duty as a poorhouse. It takes about 45 minutes of tough walking up Omírou to reach this quarter, passing the Orthodox and Catholic cemeteries on the way – the former full of grand shipowners' mausoleums, the latter with more modest monuments and French and Italian inscriptions. (You can halve the walking time by taking a short cut on to the stair-street named Andhréa Kárga, part of the way along.)

Arrival, facilities and accommodation

The **quayside** is still busy, though nowadays it deals with more touristic than industrial shipping; Síros is a major crossover point on the ferryboat routes. Also down here is the **bus station**, along with the **tourist police** and several **bike rental** places. Between them shops sell the *loukoúmia* (Turkish delight) and *halvadhópita* (sweetmeat pie) for which the island is famed. **Odhós Híou**, the market street, is especially lively on Saturday when people come in from the surrounding countryside to sell fresh produce.

Keeping step with a growing level of tourism, **rooms** have improved in quality and number in recent years; many are in garishly decorated, if crumbling, Neoclassical mansions. Good choices include *Apollon Rooms* at Odhisséou 8 (☎0281/22 158; ③),

Kástro Rooms, Kalomenopoúlou 12 (☎0281/28 064; ③), or *Rooms Paradise*, Omírou 3 (☎0281/23 204; ③) – follow the little white signposts. Close to the seafront and parallel to the market street is the office of Nick Gavalas, at Ándhrou 14 (☎0281/24 451; ②), with rooms and bikes for rent.

A notch up in price and quality is the well-sited *Hotel Hermes* (☎0281/28 011; ④) on Platía Kanári, overlooking the port, or for a slice of good-value opulence, try the *Ksenon Ipatias* (☎0281/23 575; ④), beyond Áyios Nikólaos. At peak times the *Team*

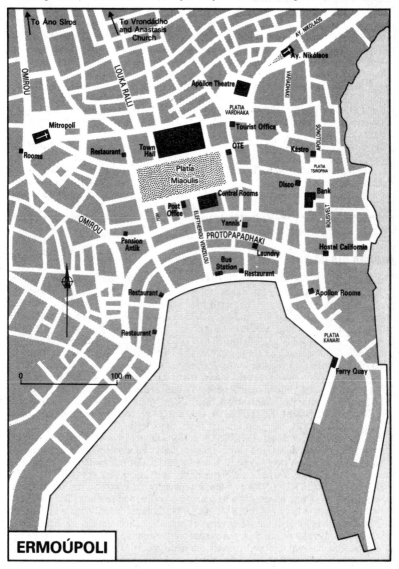

ERMOÚPOLI

Work agency (on the waterfront) may be able to help with accommodation – or place you in their very own *Hotel Europe* (☎0281/28 771; ④), a converted convent. For plusher places around town and hotels of all categories around the island there is a kiosk belonging to the *Syros Hoteliers Association* along the waterfront – turn right after disembarking.

Eating, drinking and nightlife

The most authentic and reasonably priced of the harbour **tavernas** are *Medusa*, at Ándhrou 3, a block in from the water, and *1935*, just inland from the new ferry dock; places actually on the quay tend to be more touristy and expensive. There are one or two exceptions, including the very reasonable *Caro D'Oro* with casseroles and barrelled wine. Highly recommended for an Italian treat is *Il Giardino*, set in a beautifully restored villa opposite the *Apollon*. Just to the left of where the boats dock is an excellent seafront *ouzeri* called *Boubas*. Finally, way up in Vrondádho, at Anastáseos 17, on the corner of Kalavrítou, the cooking at *Tembelis* makes up for the limited seating and grouchy service; *Folia*, at Athanasíou Dhiakoú 6, is more expensive but serves such exotica as rabbit and pigeon. For a musical breakfast, try *Yanni's* near the waterfront.

Incidentally, Síros still honours its contribution to the development of rembétika music; *bouzoúki* great Markos Vamvakaris hailed from here and a *platía* in Áno Síros has been named after him. **Taverna-clubs** such as *Lillis* (up in Áno Síros) and *Rahanos*, with music on weekends, now take their place beside a batch of more conventional disco-clubs down near the Apollon Theatre. There are several more (often expensive) *bouzoúki* bars scattered around the island, mostly strung along routes to beach resorts. The seafront has a rash of lively **bars** – *Tramps* has a relaxed atmosphere and the most eclectic music.

Around the island

The main loop road (to Gallissás, Fínikas, Mégas Yialós, Vári and back), and the road west to Kíni, are good: **buses** ply the routes hourly in season, and run until late. Elsewhere, expect potholes – especially to the **north** where the land is barren and high, with few villages. The main route north from Áno Síros has improved and is quite easily negotiable by bike; en route, the village of Mitikas has a decent taverna just off the road. A few kilometres further on the road forks, with the left turn leading to the small settlement of Sirioúga where there's an interesting cave to explore, while the right fork eventually descends to the north-east coast after passing an excellent *kafenío* with views across to Tinos.

The well-trodden route **south** offers more tangible and accessible rewards. Closest to the capital, fifteen minutes away by bus, is the coastal settlement of **KÍNI**. Though the community is more villas than village, there are two separate beaches, the *Sunset Hotel* (☎0281/71 211; ③–④) and, just away from the seafront, the *Hotel Elpida* (☎0281/71 224; ③). Last but not least, the excellent *Iliovasilema* taverna is just below the *Sunset Hotel*. **GALISSÁS**, a few kilometres south, but reached by different buses, has developed along different lines. Fundamentally an agricultural village, it's been taken over in recent years by backpackers attracted by the island's only **campsites** (*Two Hearts* is the better of the two) and a very pretty beach, much more protected than Kíni's. This new-found popularity has created a surplus of unaesthetic **rooms**, which at least makes bargaining possible, and five bona fide hotels, of which the cheapest is *Petros* (☎0281/42 067; ③). Galissás' identity crisis is exemplified by the proximity of bemused, grazing dairy cattle, a heavy-metal music pub, and upmarket handicrafts shops. Still, the people are welcoming, and if you feel the urge to escape, you can rent a moped, or walk ten minutes past the headland to the nudist beach of **Arméos**, where there's fresh springwater and unofficial camping. Note that buses out are erratically routed; to be sure of making your connection you must wait at the high-road stop, not down by the beach. Dhelfini just to the north is also a fine beach, though it's slowly falling prey to the developers under the translated name of Dolphin Bay.

A pleasant one-hour walk or a ten-minute bus ride south from Galissás brings you to the more mainstream resort of **FÍNIKAS**, purported to have been settled originally by the Phoenicians (although an alternative derivation could be from *fínikas*, meaning "palm tree" in Greek). The beach is narrow and gritty, right next to the road but protected to some extent by a row of tamarisk trees; the pick of the hotels is the *Cyclades* (☎0281/42 255; ③), which also has an acceptable restaurant.

Fínikas is separated by a tiny headland from its neighbour **POSSIDHONÍA** (or Delagrazzia), a nicer spot with some idiosyncratically ornate mansions and a bright blue church right on the edge of the village. It's worth walking ten minutes further south, past the naval yacht club and its patrol boat, to Agathopés, with a sandy beach and a little islet just offshore. Komitó, at the end of the unpaved track leading south from Agathopés, is nothing more than a stony beach fronting an olive grove.

The road swings east to **MÉGAS YIALÓS**, a small resort below a hillside festooned with brightly painted houses. The long, narrow beach is lined with shady trees and there are pedal-boats for hire. **VÁRI** is more – though not much more – of a town, with its own small fishing fleet. Beach-goers are in a goldfish bowl, as it were, with tavernas and **rooms** looming right overhead, but it is the most sheltered of the island's bays, something to remember when the *meltémi* is up. The adjacent cove of **AHLADHI** is far more pleasant and boasts two small good-value hotels, including *Achladi* (☎0281/61 400; ②) on the seafront, and one taverna, all under the same management.

Páros and Andíparos

Gently and undramatically furled around the single peak of Profítis Ilías, **Páros** has a little of everything one expects from a "Greek island" – old villages, monasteries, fishing harbours, a labyrinthine capital – and some of the best nightlife and beaches in the Aegean. Parikía, the *hóra*, is the major hub of inter-island ferry services, so that if you wait long enough you can get to just about anywhere else in the Aegean except the Ionian group; making it a favourite starting point for island wanderings. However, the island is almost as heavily touristed and expensive as Míkonos: in peak season, it's touch-and-go when it comes to finding rooms and beach space. At such times, the attractive inland settlements or the satellite island of **Andíparos** handle the overflow. Incidentally, the August 15 festival here is one of the best such observances in Greece, with a parade of flare-lit fishing boats and fireworks delighting as many Greeks as foreigners, but it's a real feat to secure accommodation around this time.

Parikía and around

PARIKÍA sets the tone architecturally for the rest of Páros, with its ranks of typically Cycladic white houses punctuated by the occasional Venetian-style building and church domes. But all is awash in a constant stream of ferry passengers, and the town is relentlessly commercial. The busy waterfront is jam-packed with bars, restaurants, hotels and ticket agencies, while the maze of houses in the older quarter behind,

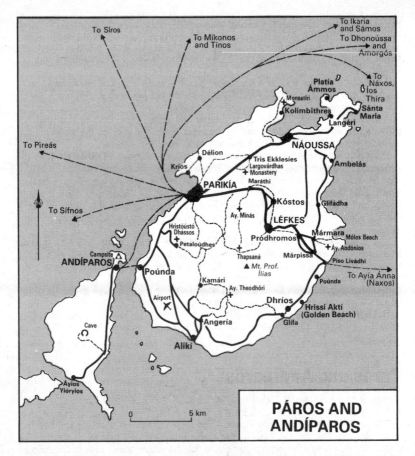

To Síros
To Míkonos
and Tínos
To Ikaria
and Sámos
To Dhonoússa
and
Amorgós

Platía
Ámmos
To
Náxos,
Íos
Thíra
Monastíri
Sánta
María
Kolimbíthres
Langéri

To Pireás
Délion
NÁOUSSA
Tris Ekklesíes
Largovárdhas
Krios
Ambelás
Monastery
PARIKÍA
Maráthi
Kóstos
Glifádha
To Sífnos
Ay. Minás
LÉFKES
Mármara
Mólos Beach
Hristoústó
Dhássos
Pródhromos
Petaloúdhes
Ay. Andónios
Campsite
Thapsaná
Márpissa
Piso Livádhi
ANDÍPAROS
▲ Mt. Prof.
Ílias
Poúnda
To Ayía Ánna
(Naxos)
Kamári
Poúnda
Airport
Ay. Theodhóri
Cave
Dhríos
Hrissí Aktí
(Golden Beach)
Angeriá
Glifa
Alikí
Áyios
Yióryios

0   5 km

**PÁROS AND
ANDÍPAROS**

designed to baffle wind and pirates, has surrendered to an onslaught of chi-chi
boutiques.

Just beyond the central clutter, though, the town has one of the most
architecturally interesting churches in the Aegean – the **Ekatondapilianí**, or "The
One-Hundred-Gated" (daily 9am–1pm & 5–9pm). What's visible today was designed
and supervised by Isidore of Miletus in the sixth century, but construction was
actually carried out by his pupil Ignatius. It was so beautiful on completion that the
master, consumed with jealousy, is said to have grappled with his apprentice on the
rooftop, flinging them both to their deaths. They are portrayed kneeling at the
column bases across the courtyard: with the old master tugging at his beard in
repentance and his rueful pupil clutching a broken head. The church was
substantially altered after a severe earthquake in the eighth century, but its
essentially Byzantine aspect remains, its shape an imperfect Greek cross. Enclosed
by a great wall to protect its icons from pirates, it is in fact three churches
interlocking with one another; the oldest, the chapel of Áyios Nikólaos to the left of
the apse, is an adaptation of a pagan building dating from the early fourth century

BC. Behind Ekatondapiliani, the **Archeological Museum** (daily except Mon 8.30am–2.30pm; 400dr) has a fair collection of antique bits and pieces, its prize exhibits a fifth-century winged Nike and a piece of the *Parian Chronicle*, a social and cultural history of Greece up to 264 BC engraved in marble.

These two sights apart, the real attraction of Parikía is simply to wander the town itself. Arcaded lanes lead past Venetian-influenced villas, traditional island dwellings and the three ornate wall fountains donated by the Mavroyénnis family in the eighteenth century. The town culminates in a seaward Venetian **Kástro**, whose surviving east wall is constructed of masonry pillaged from ancient temples to Demeter and Apollo. The beautiful, arcaded church of Áyios Konstandínos and Ayía Eléni crowns the highest point, from where the fortified hill drops sharply to the quay in a series of hanging gardens.

If you're staying in town, you'll want to get **out into the surroundings** at some stage, if only to the beach. The most rewarding excursion is the hour's walk along an unsurfaced road starting just past the museum up to **Áyii Anáryiri** monastery. Perched on the bluff above town, this makes a great picnic spot, with cypress groves, a gushing fountain and some splendid views.

There are **beaches** immediately north and south of the harbour, though none are particularly attractive when compared to Páros' best. In fact, you might prefer to avoid the northern stretch altogether; heading **south** along the asphalt road is a better bet. The first unsurfaced side track you come to leads to a small, sheltered beach; fifteen minutes further on is **PARASPÓROS**, with a reasonable **campsite** and beach near the remains of an ancient *asklepeion* ("therapy centre"). Continuing for 45 minutes (or a short hop by bus) brings you to arguably the best of the bunch, **AYÍA IRÍNI**, with good sand and a taverna next to a farm and shady olive grove.

Off in the same direction, but a much longer two-hour haul each way, is **PETALOÚDHES**, the so-called "Valley of the Butterflies", a walled-in oasis where millions of Jersey tiger moths perch on the foliage during early summer (June–Sept 9am–8pm; 200dr). The trip pays more dividends when combined with a visit to the eighteenth-century nunnery of **Hristoú stó Dhássos**, at the crest of a ridge twenty minutes to the north. Only women are allowed in the sanctuary, although men can get as far as the courtyard. The succession of narrow drives and donkey paths linking both places begins just south of Parikía, by the *Ksenon Ery*. Petaloúdhes can be reached from Parikía by bus (in summer), by moped, or on an overpriced excursion by mule.

Arrival, information and accommodation

Ferries **dock** in Parikía by the windmill, which houses a summer tourist information centre. Although there's a bus timetable posted here, the **bus stop** itself is 100m or so to the left; routes extend to Náoussa in the north, Poúnda (for Andíparos) in the west, Alikí in the south, and Dhríos on the island's east coast (with another very useful service between Dhríos and Náoussa). The **airport** is around 12km from town, close to Alikí – from where six daily buses run to Parikía.

Most of the island is flat enough for bicycle rides, but mopeds are more common and are available for rent at several places in town. *Polos Tours* is one of the more together and friendly **travel agencies**, issuing air tickets when *Olympic* is shut, acting as agents for virtually all boats and offering free luggage-storage for customers. *Olympic Airways* itself is at the far end of Odhós Probóne, while the **tourist police** occupy a building at the back of the seafront square.

As for **accommodation**, Parikía is a pleasant and central base, but absolutely mobbed in summer. You'll be met off the ferry by locals offering rooms, even at the most unlikely hours, and late at night it's a good idea to capitulate straightaway. If you arrive on an August day without a reservation, consult the tourist office in the windmill itself which can advise on any (rare) vacancies. Avoid persistent offers of rooms or hotels to the north; they're invariably a long walk away from town, and mosquitoes can be a problem. Popular hotels include *Dina* (☎0284/21 325; ④), near Platía Veléntza, and *Kondes* (☎0284/21 246; ④), very close to the windmill by the *ITS Travel Agency*. *Oasis Rooms* (☎0284/21 227; ③–④), near the post office, is fairly reasonable, and there are more rooms to let along the sea front, turning right (south) from the quayside. In the town centre, try *Maria Aliprandi* (☎0284/21 464; ③) or *Mimikos* (☎0284/21 437; ③–④). One of the best deals is to be had at the new branch of *Pension Festos*, managed by young Brits (☎0284/21 635; ③–④).

Eating, drinking and nightlife

Many Parikía **tavernas** are run by outsiders operating under municipal concession, so year-to-year variation in proprietors and quality is marked. However, the following seem to be long-established and/or good-value outfits. Rock-bottom is the *Koutouki Thanasis*, which serves oven food for locals and bold tourists and lurks in a back street behind the (expensive) *Hibiscus*. Also in the picturesque backstreets are *Kyriakos Place* on Lohagou Grivari, which has seats out under a fine tree, and the *Garden of Dionysos* nearby. In the exotic department, *Mey Tey* serves average Chinese food at moderate markup, while Italian dishes can be found at *La Barca Rossa* on the seafront or *Bella Italia* across a waterfront square.

There is a welter of places of varying quality and prices along the seafront towards the bar enclave. Of these, *Asteris Grill House* is very good with some decent specials as well as the usual grilled meats. Further out of town, *Nisiotissa* has a highly entertaining chef-proprietor and is rarely crowded; *Delfini*, on the first paved drive along the road to Poúnda, is long-established and famous for its Sunday barbecue with live music.

Parikía has a wealth of **pubs**, **bars** and low-key **discos**, not as pretentious as those on Míkonos or as raucous as the scene on Íos, but certainly everything in between. The most popular cocktail bars extend along the seafront, all tucked into a series of open squares and offering competing but staggered (no pun intended) "Happy Hours", so that you can drink cheaply for much of the evening. *Kafenio O Flisvos*, about three-quarters of the way south along the front, is the last remaining traditional *oúzo/ mezédhes* outfit among the rash of pizzerias, snack-bars, juice and ice-cream joints. A rowdy crowd favours *Ballos, Apollo's* and the conspicuous *Saloon D'Or*, while the *Pirate Bar* features jazz and blues. *Statue Bar, Evinos* and *Pebbles* are more genteel, the latter pricey but with good sunset views and the occasional live gig. The "theme" pubs are a bit rough and ready for some: most outrageous is the *Dubliner Complex*, comprising four bars, a snack section, disco and seating area. Other popular **dance** floors include *Disco 7* and *Hesperides*.

Finally, a thriving cultural centre, *Arhilohos* (near Ekatondapiliani) caters mostly to locals, with occasional **film** screenings; there are also two open-air cinemas, *Neo Rex* and *Paros*, where foreign films are shown in season.

Náoussa and around

The second port of Páros, **NÁOUSSA** was until recently an unspoiled, sparkling labyrinth of winding, narrow alleys and simple Cycladic houses. Alas, a rash of new concrete hotels and attendant trappings have all but swamped its character, though down at the small harbour, fishermen still tenderize octopuses by thrashing them against the walls. The local festivals – an annual Fish and Wine Festival on July 2, and an August 23 shindig celebrating an old naval victory over the Turks – are also still celebrated with enthusiasm; the latter tends to be brought forward to coincide with the August 15 festival of the Panayías. Most people are here for the local beaches (see below) and the relaxed nightlife; there's really only one sight, a **museum** in the church of Áyios Nikólaos Mostrátos, with interesting icons on display.

Despite encroaching development, the town is noted for its nearby beaches and is a good place to head for as soon as you reach Páros. **Rooms** are marginally cheaper here than in Parikía; track them down with the help of Katerini Simitzi's **tourist office** on the main square. Hotels are much more expensive, though out of season you should haggle for reduced prices at the *Madaki* (☎0284/51 475; ④), the *Drossia* (☎0284/51 213; ④), and the *Stella* (☎0284/51 317; ④). There are two campsites in the vicinity: the relaxed and friendly *Naoussa* **campsite** (☎0284/51565), out of town towards Kolimbíthres (see below), and the newer *Surfing Beach* at Alíki, northeast of Náoussa; both run courtesy mini-buses to and from Parikía.

Most of the harbour **tavernas** are surprisingly good, specializing in fresh fish and seafood. *Diamante* is reasonably priced, *Mouragio* and *Psariana* are average, and *Limanakis* is cheap-ish and traditional; avoid the self-service cafés. There are more places to eat along the main road leading inland from just beside the little bridge over the canal. *Zorbas*, with good barrelled unresinated wine, and the friendly *Glaros* next door are both open 24 hours.

Bars cluster around the old harbour: *Linardo* is the big dance spot, *Agosta* plays more rock, while *Remezzo* is quieter; *Camaron* and *Castello* play Greek pop and traditional music respectively. Before the bridge the adjacent *Island* and *Pirate* bars cater to a more laid-back crowd, with classic tracks, and *Pico Pico* plays world music.

Local beaches

Náoussa has no town beach, but there are some good-to-excellent **beaches** within walking distance, and a summer *kaíki* service also connects them. To the west, an hour's tramping brings you to **Kolimbíthres** (Basins), where there are three tavernas and the wind- and sea-sculpted rock formations from which the place draws its name. A few minutes beyond, **Monastíri** beach, below the abandoned Pródhromos monastery, is similarly attractive, and partly nudist. If you go up the hill after Monastíri onto the rocky promontory, the island gradually shelves into the sea via a series of flattish rock ledges, making a fine secluded spot for diving and snorkelling, as long as the sea is calm. Go northeast and the sands are better still, the barren headland spangled with good surfing beaches: **Langéri** is backed by dunes; the best surfing is at **Sánta María**, a trendy beach connected with Náoussa by road which also has a pleasant taverna named *Aristofanes*; and **Platiá Ámmos** perches on the northeasternmost tip of the island.

The northeast coast and inland

AMBELÁS hamlet marks the start of a longer trek down the **east coast**. Ambelás itself has a good beach, a small taverna, some rooms and hotels, of which the *Hotel Christiana* (☎0284/51 573; ④) is excellent value, with great fresh fish and local wine in the restaurant served by extremely friendly proprietors. From here a rough track leads south, passing several undeveloped stretches on the way: after about an hour you reach **Mólos** beach, impressive and not particularly crowded. **MÁRMARA**, twenty minutes further on, has rooms to let and makes an attractive place to stay, though the marble that the village is built from and named after has largely been whitewashed over.

If Mármara doesn't appeal, then serene **MÁRPISSA**, just to the south, might – a maze of winding alleys and aging archways overhang by floral balconies, all clinging precariously to the hillside. There are rooms here too, and you can while away a spare hour climbing up the conical Kéfalos hill, on whose fortified summit the last Venetian lords of Páros were overpowered by the Ottomans in 1537. Today the monastery of **Áyios Andónios** occupies the site, but the grounds are locked; to enjoy the views over eastern Páros and the straits of Naxos fully, pick up the key from the priest in Máripissa before setting out. On the shore nearby, **PÍSO LIVÁDHI** was once a quiet fishing village, but has been ruined by rampant construction in the name of package tourism. The main reason to visit is to catch a (seasonal) *kaíki* to Ayía Ánna on Naxos; if you need to overnight here, try *Pension Márpissa* (☎0284/41 288; ④), *Hotel Leto* (☎0284/41 283 or 41 479; ④) or the *Magia* (☎0284/41 390; ④), which may also let you sleep on the roof; there's a **campsite** as well.

Inland

The road runs west from Píso Livádhi back to the capital, and while there are regular buses back along it you'd do better, if you have time, to return on foot. A medieval flagstoned path once linked both sides of the island, and parts of it survive in the east between Mármara and the villages around Léfkes. **PRÓDHROMOS**, encountered first, is an old fortified farming settlement with defensive walls girding its nearby monastery. **LÉFKES** itself, an hour up the track, is perhaps the most beautiful and unspoilt village on Páros. The town flourished from the seventeenth century on, its population swollen by refugees fleeing from coastal piracy; indeed it was the island's *hóra* during most of the Ottoman period. Léfkes' marbled alleyways and amphitheatrical setting are unparalleled and, despite the presence of an oversized hotel, a very few rooms, a disco and a taverna on the outskirts, the area around the main square has steadfastly resisted change; the central *kafenío* and bakery observe their siestas religiously.

Half an hour further on, through olive groves, is **KÓSTOS**, a simple village and a good place for lunch in a taverna. Any traces of path disappear at **MARÁTHI**, on the site of the ancient marble quarries which once supplied much of Europe. Considered second only to Carrara marble, the last slabs were mined here by the French in the nineteenth century for Napoleon's tomb. From Maráthi, it's easy enough to pick up the bus on to Parikía, but if you want to continue hiking, strike south for the monastery of **Áyios Minás**, twenty minutes away. Various Classical and Byzantine masonry fragments are worked into the walls of this sixteenth-century foundation, and the friendly couple who act as custodians can put you on the right path up to the convent of **Thapsaná**. From here, other paths lead either back to Parikía (two hours altogether from Áyios Minás), or on up to the island's summit for the last word in views over the Cyclades.

The south of the island

There's little to stop for **south of Parikía** until **POÚNDA**, 6km away, and then only to catch the ferry to Andíparos (see below). What used to be a sleepy hamlet is now a concrete jungle – a far cry from the days when you left the Poúnda church door open to summon the boat over from the smaller island. Neighbouring **ALIKÍ** appears to be permanently under construction, and the **airport** is close by, making for lots of unwelcome noise; the sole redeeming feature is an excellent beachside restaurant, by the large tamarisk tree. The end of the southern bus route is at Angería, about 3km inland of which is the **convent of Áyii Theodhóri**. Its nuns specialize in weaving locally commissioned articles and are further distinguished as *paleomeroloyítes*, or old-calendarites, meaning that they follow the medieval Orthodox (Julian) calendar, rather than the Gregorian calendar.

Working your way around the **south coast**, there are two routes east to Dhríos. Either retrace your steps to Angería and follow the (slightly inland) coastal jeep track, which skirts a succession of isolated coves and small beaches; or keep on, across the foothills, from Áyii Theodhóri – a shorter walk. Aside from an abundant water supply (including a duck pond) and surrounding orchards, **DHRÍOS** village is mostly modern and characterless, lacking even a well-defined *platía*. Follow the lane signed "Dhríos Beach", however, and things improve a bit.

Between here and Píso Livádhi to the north are several sandy coves – Hrissí Aktí (Golden Beach), Tzirdhákia, Mezádha, Poúnda and Logarás – prone to pummelling by the *meltémi*, yet all favoured to varying degrees by campers, and windsurfers making a virtue out of necessity. **HRISSÍ AKTÍ** is now thoroughly overrun with tavernas, room complexes and the whole range of watersports; there are also tavernas at Logarás, but other facilities are concentrated in Dhríos, which is still the focal point of this part of the island.

Andíparos

In recent years the islet of **Andíparos** has become something of an open secret among those who consider Páros to be irredeemably sullied. Inevitably, development has pursued the cognoscenti: there are now at least a dozen places to drink, and in July and August there's a steady stream of vehicles around and through the single village. This is not to say that Andíparos is horrendously commercialized; it isn't – yet. Early in the year it's still a good place to rent a small cottage or apartment, but in high season it can be full of the same young, international crowd you were hoping to leave behind on Páros.

Most of the population of 500 live in the surprisingly large northern **village**, with a long, flagstoned pedestrian street forming its backbone and ending at two squares linked by archways. One has a giant eucalyptus and several cafés; the other is a small, exquisite replica of the *kástro* on Síkinos, with the dwellings on the periphery surviving to their original heights and a central cistern instead of a church. Elsewhere there is the usual complement of Cycladic domes and arches – all in all, a pleasant surprise for those expecting the generally unremarkable architecture of other minor islets.

Andíparos' **beaches** begin right outside town: Psaralidháki, where clothing is optional, is just to the east, and better than "Sunset" beach on the opposite side of the island, though the latter often hosts evening soccer matches. Glífa lies about halfway down the eastern coast, with Livadháki its counterpart to the west. For real seclusion, however, head for Áyios Yióryios on the southwest side, where fine, small sandy coves remain uncluttered despite incipient villa development.

The great **cave** (daily 9.45am–4.45pm; 400dr), inland, just before Áyios Yióryios is the chief attraction for day-trippers. In these eerie chambers the eccentric Marquis de Nointel celebrated Christmas Mass in 1673 while 500 bemused but well-paid Parians looked on; at the exact moment of midnight explosives were detonated to emphasize the enormity of the event. Although electric light and cement steps have diminished its mystery and grandeur, the cave remains impressive. Two buses a day run from the port to the cave. Should you miss them it's a stoney ninety-minute hike from the village, or you can jump on one of the morning boats which will transfer you down the coast to within a short, if tiring, walk of it. In the off-season, you'll have to fetch the key for the cave from the village.

Practicalities

To get here, you have a choice of summer-only **kaíkia** from Parikía (4–5 daily; 1hr) or the year-round, **barge-ferry** (hourly; 15min) from Poúnda, which takes vehicles and is also designed to dovetail with the comings and goings of the Páros buses. If you decide to take in Andíparos as a day-trip from Páros, there is no problem taking rental bikes across on the ferry from Poúnda.

There are two inexpensive **hotels**, the *Mandalena* (☎0284/61 206; ③) and the *Anargyros* (☎0284/61 204; ③) and two slightly more expensive ones, *Galini* (☎0284/61 420; ④) and *Akrogiali* (☎0284/61231; ④), as well as plenty of **rooms**, plus a very popular **campsite** ten minutes' walk northwest along a track, next to its own nudist beach. If you yearn for the quiet life, but with a degree of comfort, try the *Delfini* apartments (☎01/80 53 613 – no local telephone yet; ④) out at Áyios Yióryios; a bus and a mobile food wagon make the journey out here twice daily in high summer.

Of the dozen or so **tavernas** in the village, the *Anargyros*, right on the dock below the namesake hotel, and *Klimataria*, 100m inland, stay open at lunchtime, and *Mario's*, just before the square, features local wine; there's an excellent sweetshop in the eucalyptus-filled *platía* itself. A short-schedule **bank**, a tiny **OTE** booth with morning and evening hours, a **post office**, a **cinema** and several travel agents round out the list of amenities, so that you need never go to Parikía for errands if you don't wish to.

Náxos

Náxos is the largest and most fertile of the Cyclades, and with its green and mountainous interior seems immediately distinct from many of its neighbours. The difference is accentuated by the unique architecture of many of the interior villages: the Venetian occupation (from the thirteenth to the sixteenth century) left towers and fortified mansions scattered throughout the island, while late medieval Cretan refugees bestowed a singular character upon Náxos' eastern settlements.

Today Náxos could easily support itself without tourism by relying on its production of potatoes, olives, grapes and lemons, but has thrown its lot in with mass tourism, so that the island is now almost as busy and commercialized as Páros in season. An airport, which generally acts as a catalyst in such matters, finally opened in 1992; the runway, however, cannot accommodate large jets, and was built atop a former salt-marsh.

Few visitors venture away from the harbour and beach area, though more people trickle inland each year, refusing to be scared off by exaggerated tales of the gruffness of the villagers. And the island certainly has plenty to see if you know where to look: intriguing central valleys, a windy but spectacular north coast, and marvellously sandy beaches in the southwest – these last some of the best in Greece.

Náxos Town

A long causeway, built to protect the harbour to the north, connects **NÁXOS TOWN** (or Hóra) with the islet of Palátia – the place where, according to legend, Theseus abandoned Ariadne on his way home from Crete. The huge stone portal of a **Temple of Apollo** still stands there, built on the orders of the tyrant Lygdamis in the sixth century BC but never completed. Most of the town's life goes on down by the crowded port esplanade or just behind it; move into the back streets and there's an almost medieval atmosphere. Claustrophobic, silent alleys behind the harbour lead up past crumbling balconies and through low arches to the fortified **Kástro**, from where Marco Sanudo and his successors ruled over the Cyclades for the Venetians. Only two of the *kástro*'s original seven towers – those of the Sanudo and Glezos families – remain, although the north gate (approached from Apóllonos) survives as a splendid example of a medieval fort entrance. The Venetians' Catholic descendants, now dwindling in numbers, still live in the old mansions which encircle the site, many with ancient coats-of-arms above crumbling doorways. Other brooding relics survive in the same area: a seventeenth-century Ursuline convent and the Roman Catholic Cathedral – restored in questionable taste in the 1950s, though still displaying a thirteenth-century crest inside. Nearby is one of Ottoman Greece's first

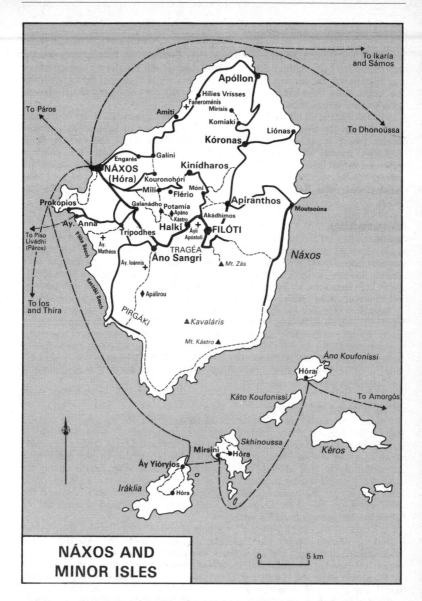

Apóllon
Hílies Vrísses
Faneroménis
Mirísis
Amíti
Komiakí
Liónas
Kóronas
Galíni
Engarés
NÁXOS
(Hóra)
Kinídharos
Kouronohóri
Míli
Flério
Móni
Potamía
Galanádho
Apáno
Kástro
Akádhimos
Prokópios
Ay. Anná
Halkí
Ayií
Apóstoli
FILÓTI
Moutsoúna
Tripodhes
Áno Sangri
TRAGÉA
Ay. Mathéos
Ay. Ioánnis
▲ Mt. Zás
Náxos
Apálirou
PIRGÁKI
▲ Kaváláris
Mt. Kástro ▲

To Páros
To Ikaría
and Sámos
To Dhonoússa
To Piso
Livádhi
(Páros)
To Íos
and Thíra
Pláka Beach
Kastráki Beach

Áno Koufoníssi
Hóra
Káto Koufoníssi
To Amorgós
Kéros
Skhinoússa
Mirsíni
Hóra
Ay Yióryios
Iráklia
Hóra

**NÁXOS AND
MINOR ISLES**

0   5 km

schools, the French School; opened in 1627 for Catholic and Orthodox students alike, its pupils included, briefly, Nikos Kazantzakis. The school building now houses an excellent **Archeological Museum** (daily except Mon 8.30am–3pm; 400dr), whose range of finds – mostly pottery – indicates that Náxos was continually occupied throughout antiquity, from Neolithic to Roman times.

Arrival, information and transport

Large ferries dock along the northerly harbour causeway. All small boats, including the *kaíkia* to Ayía Ánna and the very useful small ferry *Skopelitis*, use the jetty in the fishing harbour, *not* the main car ferry dock. The **bus station** (with a useful left-luggage office) is at its landward end: services run up to five times daily to Apóllon in the far north, via Áno Sangrí, Halkí, Filóti and Apíranthos (for all of which see below), and virtually hourly to the beaches at Ayía Ánna.

In the absence of an official tourist bureau, the "**info**" agency just at the base of the ferry jetty has the most complete and disinterested range of information, probably because they're authorized agents for all the boats calling here; they can also book (expensive) **rooms**. All the campsites and some of the hotel complexes send courtesy minibuses (which park at the town end of the jetty) to meet the ferries during the summer months, and the whole area is swarming with touts. There are two good **bike rental** places: *Nikos Katsaras*, right next to the post office, and another by the bus station.

Accommodation

Rooms can be hard to come by and somewhat overpriced in the old quarter of Hóra, and single rooms are non-existent. If you come up with nothing after an hour of hunting, the southern extension of town offers better value, although you are a long walk from most facilities, and there's significant night-time noise from the clubs and discos. Alternatively, there's little inconvenience involved in staying at Prokópios or Ayía Ánna, with buses in each direction almost hourly between 8am and 7.30pm (and *kaíkia* almost as regularly).

Hotel choices include the *Panorama* on Afitrítis (☎0285/22 330; ④), the nearby *Anixis* (☎0285/22 112; ④), or, as a last resort, the *Dionyssos* (☎0285/22 331; ③) near the *kástro*. Around the back of the *kástro*, the ever friendly and helpful Nikos Katsaras, of bike-rental fame, has opened the *Kastelli* (☎0285/23 082; ④). A fairly bland but cheap option close to the quay is the *Proto* (☎0285/22 394; ③) at Protopapadháki 13, or make your way to the attractive ochre-coloured *Hermes* (☎0285/23 208; ⑤), next to the OTE at the far end of the seafront, for plusher surroundings.

Eating, drinking and nightlife

One of the best quayside breakfast bars is the *Bikini*, which also has a fine bar upstairs with a choice selection of rock music. Further along to the south are a string of relatively expensive but simple oven-food **tavernas** – *Iy Kali Kardhia* is typical, serving acceptable casserole dishes washed down with *híma* wine – which nevertheless offer better value than places in the "Old Market Street" area inland. Much better for the money are *Papagalos*, a mostly vegetarian place in the new southern district, almost all the way to Áyios Yióryios bay; *Karnayio*, behind the *National Bank*, for fish; and *O Tsitas* on the paved street just behind the seafront. A hidden gem is *Toh Roupel*, a wonderful old *kafenío* in a tiny square up Old Market Street.

For local fresh fruit and vegetables, something of a rarity in the Cyclades, there's often a morning **market** outside the Agricultural Bank. Náxos has some very good sandal-makers, particularly Markos Skylakis, who plies his trade near the former market square. The island is also renowned for its wines and liqueurs; a shop on the quay sells the *Prombonas* white and vintage red, plus *kítron*, a lemon firewater in three strengths (there's also a banana-flavoured variant).

Much of the evening action goes on at the south end of the waterfront, and slightly inland in the new quarter. **Nightlife** tends more towards tippling than music clubs, though the misnamed *Day Club* belts out jazz to a well-heeled clientele, and *Jam-Jam* pumps out an average mixture of sounds behind the OTE. The *Ocean Club* is more lively, subsisting on pop-chart fodder, and there are other discos towards Áyios Yióryios – some of them with distinctly uninviting bouncers.

The southwestern beaches

The **beaches** around Náxos Town are considered to be the island's best. For some unusual swimming just to the **north** of the port, beyond the causeway, *Grotta* is easiest to reach. Besides the caves for which the place is named, the remains of submerged Cycladic buildings are visible, including some stones said to be the entrance to a tunnel leading to the unfinished Temple of Apollo.

The finest spots, though, are all **south** of town, the entire southwestern coastline boasting a series of excellent **beaches** accessible by regular bus and *kaíki*. **ÁYIOS YIÓRYIOS**, a long sandy bay fringed by the southern extension of the hotel "colony", is within walking distance. There are several tavernas here and a windsurfing school, plus the first of three **campsites**, with whose touts you will no doubt have become acquainted at the ferry jetty. A word of warning for campers: although this entire coast is relatively sheltered from the *meltémi*, the plains behind are boggy and you should bring along mosquito repellent, as well as plenty of fresh water.

Skipping the bus, a pleasant hour's walk south through the salt marshes brings you to **PROKÓPIOS** beach, with reasonably priced hotels, rooms and basic tavernas, plus the relaxed *Apollon* campsite nearby. Or follow the track a little further to **AYÍA ÁNNA** (habitually referred to as "Ayi'Ánna"), a small fishing and potato-shipping port where there are plenty of **rooms** to let and a few modest tavernas (plus summer *kaíkia* to Píso Livádhi on Páros). The sea-view *Hotel Ayia Anna* (☎0285/24 430; ④) and adjacent *Gorgona* taverna, co-managed by the Kapri family, are both highly recommended. Away from the built-up area, the beach here is nudist, and the busy *Maragas* **campsite** thrives.

Beyond the headland stretch the five lovely kilometres of **PLÁKA** beach, a vegetation-fringed expanse of white sand that comfortably handles the summer crowds of nudists and campers. There are only a couple of buildings right in the middle of Pláka beach, so bring your own provisions. For real isolation, stalk off to the other side of Mikrí Vígla headland, along a narrow footpath across the cliff edge, to **KASTRÁKI** beach – almost as good, and with a single taverna. Be warned, however, that the sea at the southern end of this beach (at Alikó promontory) catches the sewage swept down from Náxos Town. From Kastráki, it's an hour's walk up to the castle of **Apalírou** which held out for two months against the besieging Marco Sanudo. The fortifications are relatively intact and the views are magnificent. Even more remote is **PIRGÁKI** beach, the last stop on the coastal bus route and 21km from Náxos Town; four kilometres further on is Ayiássos beach, where the *Hotel Neraida* (☎0285/75 301; ③) offers decent long-stay terms and has a reasonable but rather slow restaurant.

The rest of the **southern coast** – indeed, virtually the whole of the southeast of the island – is almost completely deserted, and studded by mountains; you'd have to be a very dedicated and well-equipped camper/hiker to get much out of the region.

Central Náxos and the Tragéa

Although buses for Apóllon (in the north) link up the central Naxian villages, the core of the island – between Náxos town and Apíranthos – is best explored by moped or on foot. Much of the region is well off the beaten track, and can be a rewarding excursion if you've had your fill of beaches.

Out of Hóra, you quickly arrive at the neighbouring villages of **GLINÁDHO** and **GALANÁDHO**, forking respectively right and left. Both are scruffy market centres: Glinádho is built on a rocky outcrop above the Livádhi plain; Galánadho displays the first of Náxos' fortified mansions and an unusual "double church". A combined Orthodox chapel and Catholic sanctuary separated by a double arch, the church reflects both the tolerance of the Venetians during their rule and of the locals to established Catholics afterwards. Continue beyond Glinádho to **TRÍPODHES** (ancient Biblos),

9km from Náxos Town. Noted by Homer for its wines, this old-fashioned agricultural village has nothing much to do except enjoy a coffee at the shaded *kafenío*. The start of a long but rewarding walk is a rough road (past the church) which leads down the colourful Pláka valley – past an old watchtower and the Byzantine church of Áyios Mathéos (mosaic pavement) – and ends at the glorious Pláka beach (see previous page).

To the east, the twin villages of **SANGRÍ**, on a vast plateau at the head of a long valley, can be reached by continuing to follow the left-hand fork past Galanádho, a route which allows a look at the domed eighth-century church of **Áyios Mámas** (on the left), once the Byzantine cathedral of the island but neglected during the Venetian occupation and now a sorry sight. Either way, **KÁTO SANGRÍ** boasts the remains of a Venetian castle, while **ÁNO SANGRÍ** is a comely little place, all cobbled streets and fragrant courtyards. A half hour's stroll away, on a path leading south out of the village, is a small Byzantine chapel, **Áyios Ioánnis Yíroulas**, which boasts a breathtaking view down to the sea; the site originally held a Classical temple of Demeter, then a Christian basilica, leaving marble chunks and column fragments scattered around.

The Tragéa

From Sangrí the road twists northeast into the **Tragéa** region, a densely fertile area occupying a vast highland valley. It's a good jumping-off point for all sorts of exploratory rambling, and **HALKÍ** is a fine introduction to what is to come. Set high up, 16km from the port, it's a noble and silent town with some lovely churches. The **Panayía Protóthronis** church, with its eleventh- to thirteenth-century frescoes, and the romantic **Grazia (Frangopoulos) Pírgos**, are open to visitors, but only in the morning. Tourists wanting to stay here are still something of a rarity, although you can usually get a room in someone's house by asking at the store. The olive and citrus plantations surrounding Halkí are crisscrossed by paths and tracks, the groves dotted with numerous Byzantine chapels and the ruins of fortified *pírgi* or Venetian mansions. Between Halkí and Akadhímos, but closer to the latter, sits the peculiar twelfth-century "piggyback" church of **Áyii Apóstoli**, with a tiny chapel (where the ennobled donors worshipped in private) perched above the narthex; there are brilliant thirteenth-century frescoes as well.

A delightful circular path starts from Halkí, heading north to Kalóxilos and, beyond, picking up a track and a road to **MONÍ**. Just before the village, you pass the sixth-century monastery of **Panayía Dhrossianí**, a group of stark grey stone buildings with some excellent frescoes; the monks allow visits at any time, though you may have to contend with coach tours from Náxos Town. Moní itself enjoys an outstanding view of the Tragéa and surrounding mountains, and has three **tavernas**, and some **rooms**, from which you can enjoy both. A dirt road leads on to Kinídharos with its old marble quarry, above the village, and a few kilometres beyond a signpost points you down a rough track to the left, to **FLÉRIO** (also commonly called Melanés). The most interesting of the ancient marble quarries on Náxos, this is home to two famous **koúri**, dating from the sixth century BC, that were left recumbent and unfinished because of flaws in the material. Even so, they're finely detailed figures, over five metres in length: one of the statues lies in a private, irrigated orchard; the other is up a hillside some distance above, and you will need to seek local guidance to find it.

From Flério you could retrace your steps to the road and head back to the *hóra* via Míli and the ruined Venetian castle at Kouronohóri, both pretty hamlets connected by footpaths. If you're feeling more adventurous, ask to be directed south to the footpath which leads over the hill to the Potamía villages. The first of these, **ÁNO POTAMÍA**, has a fine taverna and a rocky track back towards the Tragéa. Once past the valley the landscape becomes craggy and barren, the forbidding Venetian fortress of **Apáno Kástro** perched on a peak just south of the path. This is believed to have been Sanudo's summer home, but the fortified site goes back further if the Mycenean tombs found nearby are any indication. From the fort, paths lead back to Halkí in around an hour.

Alternatively you can continue further southwest down the Potamía valley toward Hóra, passing first the ruined **Cocco pírgos** – said to be haunted by one Constantine Cocco, the victim of a seventeenth-century clan feud – on the way to **MÉSO POTAMÍA**, joined by some isolated dwellings with its twin village **KÁTO POTAMÍA**, nestling almost invisibly among the greenery flanking the creek.

At the far end of the gorgeous Tragéa valley, **FILÓTI**, the largest village in the region, lies on the slopes of Mount Zas (or Zeus) which, at 1000m, is the highest point in the Cyclades. Essentially agricultural, the village's only concession to tourism is a garish fast-food restaurant; otherwise nights out are spent in the very Greek and friendly tavernas and *kafenía*, sampling the region's locally bottled orange and lemonade drinks. Water shortages caused a mass exodus in the 1960s, though Filóti seems to have partly recovered. There are, perhaps as a consequence, plenty of old **houses to rent** and you could do worse than use Filóti as a long-term base; rooms or hotels on the other hand are virtually non-existent. From the village, it's a round-trip walk of two to three hours to the summit of Zás, a climb which rewards you with an astounding panorama of virtually the whole of Náxos and its Cycladic neighbours. From the main Filóti–Apóllon road, take the side road towards Dhánakos until you reach a small chapel on the right, just beside the start of the waymarked final approach trail.

APÍRANTHOS, a hilly, winding 10km beyond, shows the most Cretan influence of all the interior villages. The houses, built mostly of unwhitewashed local stone, present a mottled grey and tan aspect, and the inhabitants are reserved and dignified, though helpful when approached – and reputed to be the best musicians on the island. Among the subdued houses, there are two small **museums** and two Venetian fortified mansions, while the square contains a miniature church with a three-tiered belltower. Ask to be pointed to the start of the spectacular path up over the ridge behind; this ends either in Moní or Kalóxilos, depending on whether you fork right or left respectively at the top.

Apíranthos has a beach annexe of sorts at **MOUTSOÚNA**, 12km east. Emery mined near Apíranthos used to be transported here, by means of an aerial funicular, and then shipped out of the port. The industry collapsed recently and the sandy cove beyond the dock now features a growing colony of vacation villas. The coast south of here is completely isolated, the road petering out into a rutted track – ideal for self-sufficient campers, but take enough water.

Northern Náxos

The route northeast to Apóllon is very scenic and the roads are in good condition all the way. Jagged ranges and hairpin bends confront you before reaching Kóronos, the halfway point, where a road off to the right threads through a wooded valley to **LIÓNAS**, a tiny and very Greek port with a pebbly beach. You'd do better to continue, though, past Skádho, to the high, remote, emery-miners' village of **KOMIAKÍ** – the original home of *kitron* liqueur, and a pleasing, vine-covered settlement which is also the starting-point for perhaps the most extraordinary walk on Náxos. Head up the mountainside path and cross the ridge as far as an improbably long marble *kalderími* or staircase, which descends into the valley. It's overwhelmingly tempting to climb down this Jack-and-the-Beanstalk fixture (though bear in mind that you'll need to come back up at some point): the views are marvellous, the experience exhilarating, and the hamlet at the bottom, **MIRÍSIS**, is enchanting. People from Komiakí migrate downwards in spring and summer to tend and harvest their crops; there are no amenities and all the food is locally produced in this veritable oasis.

Back on the main road, a series of slightly less hairy bends lead down a long valley to **APÓLLON** (Apóllonas), an embryonic and rather tatty resort, with the beach by turns clean and calm, or marred by washed-up tar. There are, however, **rooms** above the shops and tavernas, several **hotels**, and one major attraction – a **koúros**, approached along an unsurfaced road. Lying in situ at a former marble quarry, this largest of Náxos' abandoned stone figures is just over ten metres long, but, compared to those at Flério, disappointingly lacking in detail. Here since 600 BC, it serves as a singular reminder of the Naxians' traditional skill; the famous lions of Delos are also made of Apollonian marble. Not surprisingly, bus tours descend upon the village during the day, but by nightfall Apóllon is a peaceful place; the local festival, celebrated on August 29, is one of Náxos's best, though the place is all but shut a month later.

Apóllon is as far as the bus goes, but with your own transport it's possible to loop back to Náxos Town on the northern coastal route: windswept, bleak, and far removed from the verdant centre of the island. Make sure that you're equipped for this trip, since there are few settlements along the way. Ten kilometres past the northern cape sprouts the beautiful **Ayía** *pírgos*, another foundation (in 1717) of the Cocco family. There's a tiny hamlet nearby, and, 7km further along, a track leads off to **ÁVRAM** beach, an idyllic spot with a family-run taverna and **rooms** to let. Just beyond Híllies Vrísses, the only real village in this region, is the abandoned **monastery of Faneroménis**, built in 1606. Nearby, there's another deserted beach, **AMITÍ**, and then the track leads inland, up the Engarés valley, to Engarés and **GALÍNI**, only 6km from Hóra. The road at last becomes paved here, and on the final stretch back to the port passes a unique eighteenth-century Turkish fountain-house and the fortified monastery of **Ayíou Ioánnou Hrisostómou**, where a couple of aged nuns are still in residence. A footpath from the monastery and the road below lead straight back to town.

Koufoníssi, Skhinoússa, Iráklia and Dhonoússa

In the patch of the Aegean beween Náxos and Amorgós there is a chain of six small islands neglected by tourists and by the majority of Greeks, few of whom have heard of them. **Kéros** – ancient *Karos* – is an important archeological site but has no permanent population, and **Káto Koufoníssi** is inhabited only by goatherds. However, the other four islands – **Áno Koufoníssi**, **Skhinoússa**, **Iráklia** and **Dhonoússa** – are all inhabited, served by ferry, and can be visited. Now just beginning to be discovered by Greeks and foreigners alike, the islets' increasing popularity has hastened the development of better facilities, but they're still a welcome break from the mass tourism of the rest of the Cyclades, especially during high season. If you want real peace and quiet – what the Greeks call *isikhía* – get there soon.

A few times weekly in summer a Pireás-based **ferry** – usually the *Apollon Express* or the tardy *Ergina* – calls at each of the islands, linking them with Náxos and Amorgós and (usually) Páros, Síros, Sérifos and Sífnos. A *kaíki*, the *Skopelitis*, is a reliable daily fixture, leaving Náxos in mid-afternoon for relatively civilized arrival times at all the islets. *Ilios* lines hydrofoil calls on demand at all the islands except Dhonoússa on its twice-weekly foray to Amorgós; you must let the steward, if you're on the hydrofoil,or agent, if you're on the island, know if you want to be picked up or put down.

Koufoníssi and Kéros

Ano Koufoníssi is the most populous island of the group; there is a reasonable living to be made from fishing, and an increasing number of Greek holidaymakers and more adventurous foreigners are being attracted here. The smallest and flattest of the minor islands, it can easily be walked round in a day. The single village of **HÓRA** clusters around the harbour: amenities include a post office, an OTE booth and rooms to let, although they can be in short supply in peak season; an official but rather poorly serviced campsite takes up the slack. Hóra has a number of **eating** and **drinking**

establishments: recommended places are the *Mavros* taverna, a *psistariá* belonging to Dimitris Skopelitis, and the café/restaurant *Soroccos*. *Ta Kalamia* café is also a good spot, as is the *Karnayio Ouzeri*, which offers a fine array of seafood. The best beaches are Fínikas, ten minutes walk from Hóra and blessed with a taverna, and Borí.

Káto Koufoníssi, the isolated islet to the southwest of Áno Koufoníssi, has no accommodation but there is a taverna and some more secluded beaches; local *kaíkia* shuttle people across according to demand.

Kéros is uninhabited and communications are less certain, but if there is a willing group of people keen to visit the ancient site, a boat and boatmen can be hired for around 15,000dr for the day.

Skhinoússa

A little to the west, the island of **Skhinoússa** is just beginning to awaken to its touristic potential, largely due to the energetic efforts being made in that direction by one Yiorgos Grispos.

Boats dock at the small port of Mirsíni, which has one pension (☎0285/71 157; ④) and a couple of cafés; a road leads up to **HÓRA**, the walk takes just over ten minutes. As you enter the village, the well-stocked shop of the Grispos family is one of the first buildings on the left and the aforementioned Yiorgos is a mine of information. Indeed, he is personally responsible for the island's map and postcards, as well as being the boat/hydrofoil agent, having the OTE phone and selling the Greek and foreign press.

Accommodation is mostly in fairly simple rooms, such as *Pension Meltemi* (☎0285/71 195; ④), *Anesis* (☎0285/71 180; ③), *Drossos* and *Nomikos* (no phone; both ③). The main concentration of **restaurants**, cafés and bars is along the main thoroughfare, including a lively *ouzeri* and, further along on the left, the pleasant *Schoinoussa* restaurant – another Grispos family venture.

There are no less than sixteen beaches dotted around the island and accessible by a lacework of trails. Freelance campers congregate on **Tsigoúri beach**, a little over five minutes from Hóra, where there's a large bar and hotel complex under construction by the ubiquitous Grispos. The only other beach with any refreshments is Almirós, which has a simple canteen.

Iráklia

The westernmost of the minor Cyclades, **Iráklia** (pronounced Irakliá by locals) is a real gem, with an atmosphere reminiscent of the Greece of fifteen years ago. There is a small but sprawling settlement at the port with several places to eat, rooms to let and the café/shop *Melissa*, which also acts as a ticket agency for boats and hydrofoils. Hóra, with a few rooms and limited provisions, is the best part of an hour's stroll inland through mountainous terrain; further still, there is a fine cave on the far side of the island. Most visitors stay about fifteen minutes' walk from the port across the hill to the left at Fínikas beach, where there are some **rooms and tavernas** – including one run by the friendly and animated Yiorgos Gavalas, who usually meets ferries at the dock. The beach really is lovely, both deep and wide, with plenty of large bushes and a few trees for shade, and crystal-clear sea – as close as you can get to paradise in modern Greece.

Dhonoússa

Dhonoússa is a little out on a limb in comparison with the others, especially as it is not served by the hydrofoils and the other ferries call far less frequently. Being more northeasterly it is also prone to having its limited connections cut by the winds.

Hóra, where the boat docks, is pleasant enough, and the number of cafés, restaurants and tavernas has now reached double figures; the island has about a hundred rooms for rent, almost all in Hóra. Smaller settlements are dotted around the island and there are several beaches to choose from, including Kéndros and Livádhi to the east, via the hamlets of Haravyí and Mirsíni. The latter has the only springs, orchards and vegetable patches on the island, which may explain the scarcity of fresh produce in these parts.

Amorgós

Amorgós is virtually two islands. Roads through its splendidly rugged terrain are so poor that by far the easiest way of getting between Katápola in the southwest and Egiáli in the northeast is by ferry, *kaíki* or hydrofoil. Hydrofoils in particular dovetail well with the schedules of the main-line ferries, and have greatly lessened the island's isolation; gone are the days when you were sure to get marooned here. Currently all large and most small boats call at both ports, and accept short-hop passengers between one and the other. The bus service between Katápola and Egiáli has also improved, now running five or six times a day.

The island can get extremely crowded in mid-summer, the numbers swollen by Europeans paying their respects to the film location of Luc Besson's *The Big Blue*, although few actually venture out to the wreck of the *Olympia*, at the island's west end, which figured so prominently in the movie. In general it's a low-key, escapist clientele, happy to have found a relatively large, interesting and uncommercialized island with excellent walking.

This may change, however, since the provincial authorities have big plans, including such drastic measures as extensive asphalting of roads, banning ferries from Egiáli altogether and turning its port into a yacht marina. It seems an incongruous fate for an island which, like Folégandhros, has been used as a neglected place of political exile for thousands of years.

The southwest

KATÁPOLA, set at the head of a deep bay, is actually three separate hamlets: Katápola proper on the south flank, Rahídhi on the ridge at the head of the gulf, and Ksilokeratídhi along the north shore. The beach here won't win many awards, unless they're conferred by the two dozen ducks who waddle contentedly across the foreshore, but by virtue of its convenience the place has become a resort of sorts.

There are plenty of small **hotels** and **pensions** and, except in high summer when rooms are almost impossible to find, proprietors tend to meet those boats arriving around sunset – though not necessarily those that show up in the small hours. Among the better places is *Dhimitri's* in Rahídhi (③–④), an enormous compound of interconnecting buildings in an orchard where rooms with bath and use of kitchen vary in price, depending on the season and the number of people. The more obvious *Pension Amorgos* (☎0285/71 013; ③) and fancy *Hotel Minoa* (☎0285/71 480; ④) on the water will be considerably noisier. Best of all is *Tasia Pension* (☎0285/71 313; ②), although it's often booked up by regular guests during the busier months. In Katápola proper, *Mourayio* is the most popular **taverna** with foreigners, though the locals hang out at *O Kamari* mid-quay, whose main attraction seems to be a wide range of sweets. The best bet for a winning combination of food, prices and atmosphere is the *Akrogiali* taverna, while what **nightlife** there is focuses on a handful of cafés and pubs.

Prekas is the one-stop **boat ticket agency**, and a new **OTE** stays open until 11pm. **Moped rental** is available at *Thomas Rentabike* (☎0285/71 007), though the local bus service is more than adequate and walking trails delightful. The **campsite** is well signed between Rahídhi and Ksilokeratídhi; in the latter district are three **tavernas**, of which the middle one – *Vitzentzos* – is by far the best.

Steps, and then a jeep track, lead out of Katápola to the remains of **ancient Minoa**, which are apt to disappoint up close: some Cyclopean wall four or five courses high,

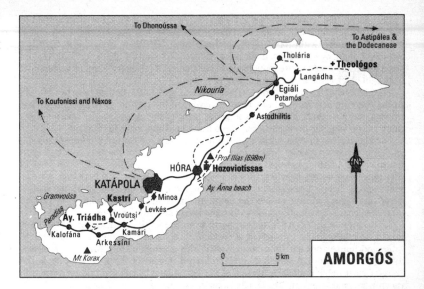

the foundations of an Apollo temple, a crumbled Roman structure and bushels of unsorted pottery shards. It's only the site, with views encompassing Hóra and ancient Arkessíni, that's the least bit memorable. Beyond Minoa the track soon dwindles to a trail, continuing within a few hours to Arkessíni (see below) via several hamlets – a wonderful **excursion** with the possibility of catching the bus back.

The **bus** shuttles almost hourly until 11pm between Katápola and Hóra, the island capital; several times daily the service continues to Ayía Ánna via Hozoviotíssas monastery, and twice a day there's a run out to the "Káto Meriá", made up of the hamlets of Kamári, Arkessíni and Kolofána. **HÓRA**, also accessible by an hour-long path beginning from behind the Rahídhi campsite, is a bleak introverted place, but not without character. Dominated by a rock plug wrapped with a chapel or two, the thirteenth-century Venetian fortifications look down on countless other bulbous churches – including Greece's smallest, **Áyios Fanoúrios**, which holds just three worshippers – and a line of decapitated windmills beyond. Of the half-dozen or so **places to stay**, *Pension Hora* (☎0285/71 110; ④), whose minibus sometimes meets ferries, is the fanciest place, just right of the village entrance, and *Rooms Nomikos* (②), further back by the phone antenna, is the most basic. In addition to the pair of traditional **tavernas**, *Kastanis* and *Klimataria*, there are several noisy bistro-café-pubs, with *Toh Steki* in the upper plaza perennially popular in the late afternoon. On the same square are the island's main **post office** and a **bank**; further up the hill is the main OTE office, with somewhat limited opening hours.

From the top of Hóra, next to the helipad, a wide cobbled *kalderími* drops down to two major attractions, effectively short-cutting the road and taking little longer than the bus to reach them. Bearing left at an inconspicuous fork ten minutes' along takes you towards the spectacular monastery of **Hozoviotíssas** (daily 9am–7pm; donation), which appears suddenly as you round a bend, its vast wall gleaming white at the base of a towering orange cliff. Only three monks occupy the fifty rooms now, but they are quite welcoming, considering the number of visitors who file through; you can see the eleventh-century icon around which the monastery was founded, along with a stack of other treasures. The foundation legend is typical for such institutions in outlandish places: during the Iconoclastic period a precious icon of the Virgin was committed to the sea by beleaguered monks at Hózova, somewhere in the Middle East, and it washed up safely at the base of the palisade here. The view from the *katholikón's* terrace, though, overshadows all for most visitors. To round off the experience, visitors are ushered into a comfy reception room and treated to a sugary lump of *loukoúmi*, a fiery shot of *kítro* and a cool glass of water.

The right-hand trail leads down, within forty minutes, to the pebble **beaches** at **Ayía Ánna**. Skip the first batch of tiny coves in favour of the path to the westernmost bay, where naturists cavort, almost in scandalous sight of the monastery far above. As yet there are no tavernas here, nor a spring, so bring food and water for the day.

For alternatives to Ayía Ánna, take the morning bus out toward modern Arkessíni, alighting at Kamári hamlet (where there's a single taverna) for the twenty-minute path down to the adjacent beaches of **Notiná, Moúros** and **Poulopódhi**. Like most of Amorgós' south-facing beaches, they're clean, with calm water, and here, too, a fresh-water spring dribbles most of the year. For those with their own transport, the road is surprisingly good all the way to the southern tip of the island, leading you past an unbroken chain of magnificent views to some lovely deserted beaches.

Archeology buffs will want to head north from Kamári to Vroútsi, start of the over-grown hour-long route to **ancient Arkessíni**, a collection of tombs, six-metre-high walls and houses out on the cape of Kastrí. The main path from Minoa also passes through Vroútsi, ending next to the well-preserved Hellenistic fort known locally as the "Pírgos", just outside modern **ARKESSÍNI**. The village boasts a single **taverna** with **rooms**, and, more importantly, an afternoon bus back to Hóra and Katápola.

The northeast

The energetically inclined can walk the four to five hours from Hóra to Egiàli. On the Hóra side you can start by continuing on the faint trail just beyond Hozoviotíssas, but the islanders themselves, in the days before the road existed, preferred the more scenic and sheltered valley route through Terláki and Rikhtí. The two alternatives, and the modern jeep road, more or less meet an hour out of Hóra. Along most of the way, you're treated to amazing views of **Nikouriá islet**, nearly joined to the main island and in former times a leper colony. The only habitations on the way are the summer hamlet of **ASFODILÍDHI**, with well water but little else for the traveller, and **POTAMÓS**, a double village you encounter on the stroll down towards Egiáli bay.

EGIÁLI (Órmos), smaller than Katápola, is a delightful beachside place stuck in a 1970s time-warp. Accommodation tends to be reasonably priced: possible places are *Nikitas* (☎0285/73 237; ③) and *Akrogiali* (☎0285/73 249; ③), both above the harbour, and *Lakki* (☎0285/73 244; ④), which has a fine setting along the beach but a rather fierce management style. A couple of kilometres up on the way to Tholária is a new luxury hotel *Aegialis* (☎0285/73 253; ⑥). Behind the *Lakki* there is a very friendly official **campsite**, one of the cheapest in the Cyclades. For **eating out**, the *Korali* has decent fish and the best sunset view, but ultimately loses out to *Toh Limani* (aka *Katerina's*) on the single inland lane, packed until midnight by virtue of its excellent food and barrel-wine, and superb taste in taped music. A few seasonal music **bars**, such as *Selini*, also attempt to compete with *Katerina's*.

The main Egiáli **beach** is more than serviceable, getting less weedy and reefy as you stroll further north. If it's still not to your taste, a trail here leads over various head-lands to an array of clothing-optional bays: the first sandy, the second mixed sand and gravel, the last shingle. There are no facilities anywhere so bring along what you need.

Egiáli has its own **bus service** up to each of the two villages visible above and east, with half a dozen departures daily up and down, but it would be a shame to miss out on the beautiful **loop walk** linking them with the port. **THOLÁRIA**, reached by the path starting at the far end of the main beach, is named after certain vaulted Roman tombs whose exact location nobody seems to know of or care about. A handful of **taverna-cafés**, including a handsome wooden-floored establishment near the church, are more contemporary concerns, and there are now several places to stay, including some fairly fancy **rooms** (reserve through *Pension Lakki* in Egiáli). Or try the *Vigla* (☎0285/73 288; ④), with breakfast included, and the *Thalassino Oneiro* (☎0285/73 345; ③), which has a fine restaurant and an extremely friendly owner. Curling around the head of the vast *kámbos* below is **LANGÁDHA,** home to a sizeable colony of expatriates – something reflected in the German-Greek cooking at *Nikos'* **taverna** at the lower end of the village, which also has some **rooms** (☎0285/73 310; ④), as does *Yiannis'* taverna.

Beyond Langádha, another rocky path leads around the base of the island's highest peak, the 821-metre-high **Kríkelon**, passing on the way the fascinating church of **Theológos**, with lower walls and ground plan dating to the fifth century. Somewhat easier to reach, by a slight detour off the main Tholária–Langádha trail, are the church and festival grounds of **Panayía Epanohóri** – not so architecturally distinguished but a fine spot nonetheless.

Íos

No other island is quite like **Íos**, nor attracts the same vast crowds of young people. The beach is packed with naked bodies by day, and nightlife in the village is loud and long. However, crowded as it is, the island hasn't been commercialized in quite the same way as, say, Míkonos – mainly because few of the visitors have much money. You'll either decide that Íos (short for "Ireland Over Seas", as some would have it) is the island paradise you have always been looking for and stay for weeks, as many people do, or you'll hate it and take the next boat out – an equally common reaction.

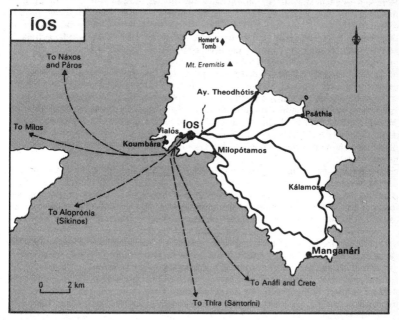

Most visitors stay along the arc delineated by the port – at Yialós, where you'll arrive (there's no airport), in Hóra above it, or at the beach at Milopótas; it's a small area, and you soon get to know your way around. **Buses** constantly shuttle between the three places, with a daily service running roughly from 8am to midnight; you should never have to wait more than fifteen minutes, but at least once try the short walk up (or down) the stepped path between Yialós and the Hóra.

Despite its past popularity, **sleeping on the beach** on Íos is really worth avoiding these days. Violent crime and police raids are becoming more frequent as the island strains under the sheer impact of increasing youth tourism, and the police have been known to turn very nasty. They prefer you to sleep in the official campsites and, given the problem of theft, you should probably take their advice. A further problem is **water shortage**, which occasionally has dire effects, above all, on local toilets. Things can get particularly grim in Yialós, and even in the beachside tavernas only the desperate and foolish dare venture out the back. In the village, you may find a toilet which flushes, although officially water is too scarce to be used for so frivolous a purpose.

Yialós and Hóra

From **YIALÓS** quayside, **buses** turn around just to the left, while Yialós **beach** – surprisingly peaceful and uncrowded – is another five minutes' walk in the same direction. You might be tempted to grab a room in Yiálos as you arrive: owners meet the ferries, hustling the town's **accommodation**. There are also a couple of kiosks by the jetty that will book rooms for you, but you won't find anything below the ④ range in high season and, surprisingly, there are no dormitories; if you're after a budget room, you might do better in Hóra (see below). At the far end of the beach are a couple of the plusher options: *Ios Beach Bungalows* (☎0285/91 267; ⑤) and *Hotel Leto* (☎0286/91 357; ⑥). Beware that the official **campsite** here, to the right of the harbour on a scruffy beach, is the worst of the island's three – and mosquito-ridden. Yialós has all the other essentials: a tourist office, a reasonable supermarket (to the right of the bus stop), and a few fairly authentic **tavernas**. A twenty-minute stroll over the headland at **KOUMBÁRA**, there's a smaller and less crowded beach, largely nudist, with a taverna and a rocky islet to explore.

Most of the less expensive **rooms** are in **HÓRA** (aka Íos Town), a twenty-minute walk up behind the port, though you've got a better chance of getting something reasonable by haggling if you intend to stay for several days. The old white village is becoming overwhelmed by the crowds of tourists, but with any number of arcaded streets and whitewashed chapels, it still has a certain charm. A bevy of expensive fashion and jewellery boutiques have begun to appear recently, reflecting an increased affluence and consumerism among the once avidly anti-materialist clientele.

What the *hóra* is still really about, though, is **nightlife**. Every evening the streets throb to music from ranks of competing discos and clubs – mostly free, or with a nominal entrance charge, though drinks tend to be expensive. Most of the smaller **bars** and pubs are tucked into the thronging narrow streets of the old village on the hill, offering something for everyone – unless you just want a quiet drink. A welcome exception to the techno-pop dancing fodder can be found at the *Taboo* bar, run by two friendly brothers and featuring underground rock, eclectic decor and a clientele to match; *Pegasus* is also recommended. The larger **dancing clubs,** including a branch of Athens' *West Club* and the *Disco Scorpion*, are to be found on the main road to Milopótamos. Finally the *Ios Club*, perched right up on the hill, organizes an annual **festival of live music** for the month of August, showcasing international and Greek acts.

Eating is a secondary consideration but there are plenty of cheap and cheerful *psistariés* and take-away joints: sound choices include *Iy Folia*, near the top of the village, and *Ikoyeniaki Taverna Iy Stani*, at the heart of town.

Around the island

The most popular stop on the island's bus routes is **MILOPÓTAMOS** (universally abbreviated to Milópotas), the site of a magnificent beach and a mini-resort. By day, young people cover every inch of the bus-stop end of the sand; for a bit more space head the other way, where there are dunes behind the beach. There are three busy **campsites**, of which *Far Out*, the furthest away, is probably the best, followed by the nearest, *Stars*, and then *Costas*, but they can all be pretty noisy. There are **rooms** and one good self-service **café**, the *Far Out* – so named for the standard reaction to the view on the ride in. Right at the far end of the bay there is a little quay and a remarkably good and quiet taverna/café called *Drakos*.

From Yialós, daily boats depart at around 10am (returning in the late afternoon) to **MANGANÁRI** on the south coast, where there's a beach and a swanky hotel; you can also get there by moped on the newish road. Predominantly nudist, this is the beach to come to for serious tans, although there's more to see, and a better atmosphere, at **ÁYIOS THEODHÓTIS**, up on the east coast. In high season, a **bus** runs at 10am from Yialós (or ten minutes later from the stop behind the windmills in Hóra), but purists can walk there on a decaying walled track across the heart of the island. This begins just to the north of the windmills; carry water as the hike will take two to three hours. Once there, Áyios Theodhótis boasts a ruined Venetian castle which encompasses the ruins of a marble-finished town and a Byzantine church. In the unlikely event that the beach – a good one and mainly nudist – is too crowded, try the one at **PSÁTHIS**, an hour's stroll to the southeast. Frequented by wealthy Athenians, this small resort has a couple of pricey tavernas, making it better for a day-trip than an extended stay. The other island beach is at **KÁLAMOS**, a three-hour walk along a rough road from Hóra. It's very remote indeed, although at Perivólia – one hour into the walk – there are welcome shady trees and fresh water.

Homer's "tomb", the only cultural diversion on the island, is an expensive one. The story goes that, while on a voyage from Sámos to Athens, Homer's ship was forced to put in at Íos, where the poet subsequently died. Ask at the tourist office in Yialós if you want to visit: you'll need to hire either a donkey or a *kaíki* and, ideally, a guide as it's difficult to find. You can walk, but it's a good three hours' slog to the northeastern tip of the island, passing the Psarápirgos tower on Mount Eremítis, until you reach the site of the ancient town of Plakatos. The town itself has long since slipped down the side of the cliff, but the rocky ruins of the entrance to a tomb remain, as well as some graves – one of which is claimed to be Homer's, but which in reality probably dates only to the Byzantine era.

Síkinos

Síkinos has so small a population that the mule-ride or walk up from the port to the village was only replaced by a bus late in the 1980s and, until the new jetty was completed at roughly the same time, it was the last major Greek island where ferry passengers were still taken ashore in launches. With no dramatic characteristics, nor any nightlife to speak of, few foreigners make the short trip over here from neighbouring Íos and Folégandhros or from sporadically connected Páros, Náxos, or Thíra. In addition to the regular ferries there are unreliable local *kaíkia*, in season only, to and from Íos and Folégandhros. There is no bank on the island, but there is a **post office** up in Kástro-Hóra, near the **OTE**, and you can sometimes change cash at the store in Aloprónia.

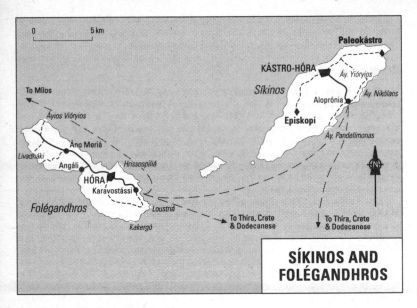

SÍKINOS AND FOLÉGANDHROS

Aloprónia and Kástro-Hóra

Such tourist facilities as exist are concentrated in the little harbour of **ALOPRÓNIA**, with its long sandy beach and the recent additions of an extended breakwater and jetty. More and more formal **accommodation** is being built here, and the days of a discreet slumber under the tamarisks at one end of the beach are probably over. For rooms, try *Flora* (☎0286/51 214 or 51 239; ③, en suite ④); alternatively, the comfortable *Hotel Kamares* (☎0286/51 234; ④), in traditional style, is more affordable than the conspicuous *Porto Sikinos* luxury complex (☎0286/51 247, winter ☎01/41 72 043; ⑤). The **taverna** on the quay is the locals' hangout, while the fancier *Ostria* is affiliated with the *Hotel Kamares*.

The double village of **KÁSTRO-HÓRA** is served by the single island bus, which meets the ferries for transport up the hill, but otherwise schedules are subject to the whim of the driver. In theory, they go up on the hour, and return on the half hour from 7am to 10pm. On the ride up, the scenery turns out to be less desolate than initial impressions suggest. Draped across a ridge overlooking the sea, Kástro-Hóra makes for a charming day trip, though rooms tend to be substandard and poor value, and choices for eating out are similarly limited. A partly ruined monastery, **Zoödhóhou Piyís** ("Spring of Life", a frequent name in the Cyclades), crowns the rock above; the architectural highlight of the place, though, is the central quadrangle of **Kástro**, a series of ornate eighteenth-century houses arrayed defensively around a chapel-square, their backs to the exterior of the village.

Around the island

West of Kástro-Hóra, an hour-plus walk (or hired-mule ride) takes you through a land-scape lush with olives to **Episkopí**, where elements of an ancient temple-tomb have been ingeniously incorporated into a seventh-century church – the structure is known formally as the **Iroön**. Ninety minutes from Kástro-Hóra, in the opposite direction, lies **Paleokástro**, the patchy remains of an ancient fortress. If you turn down and right (south) from this path you'll come to a pair of beaches, **Áyios Yióryios** and **Áyios Nikólaos**, which face Íos; the former cove has a well. With slightly less effort, the pebble beach at **Áyios Pandelímonas** is just under an hour's trail-walk southwest of Aloprónia, and is considered the most scenic and sheltered on the island. All of these beaches are served by excursion *kaíkia* in season.

Folégandhros

The cliffs of **Folégandhros** rise sheer in places over 300m from the sea – until the early 1980s as effective a deterrent to tourists as they always were to pirates. Used as an island of political exile right up until 1974, life in the high, barren interior has been eased since the junta years by the arrival of electricity and the construction of a lengthwise road from the harbour to Hóra and beyond. Development has been given further impetus by the recent exponential increase in tourism and the mild commercialization this has brought.

A veritable explosion in accommodation for most budgets, and slight improvement in ferry arrival times, means there is no longer much need for – or local tolerance of – sleeping rough on the beaches. The increased wealth and trendiness of the heterogenous clientele is reflected in fancy jewellery shops, an arty postcard gallery and a newly constructed helipad. Yet away from the showcase *hóra* and the beaches, the countryside remains mostly pristine, and is largely devoted to the spring and summer cultivation of barley, the mainstay of many of the Cyclades before the advent of tourism. Donkeys and donkey-paths are also still very much in evidence, since the terrain on much of the island is too steep for vehicle roads.

Karavostássi and around

KARAVOSTÁSSI, the rather unprepossessing port, serves as a last-resort base, offering one **hotel**, the *Poseidon* (☎0286/41 205; ③) just behind the pebble shore. Another, the *Vardia Bay,* is under construction on a site overlooking the harbour from the south and will have the added bonus of a good **taverna**, *Iy Kali Kardhia*, just below. The island's first moped-rental place has also made its rather furtive appearance here.

The closest **beach** is the smallish, but attractive enough, sand-and-pebble **Vardhiá**, signposted just north over the headland. Some twenty minutes' walk south lies **Loustriá**, a rather average beach with tamarisk trees and the island's official **campsite** (sporadic water supply).

Easily the most scenic beach on Folégandhros, with an offshore islet and a 300m stretch of pea-gravel, is at **Katergó**, on the southeastern tip of the island. Most people visit on a boat excursion from Karavostássi or Angáli, but you can also get there on foot from the hamlet of Livádhi, a short walk inland from Loustriá. Be warned, though, that it's a rather arduous trek, with some nasty trail-less slithering in the final moments.

Hóra

The island's real character and appeal are to be found in the spectacular **HÓRA**, perched on a cliff-top plateau some 45 minutes' walk from the dock; an hourly high-season **bus** service (6 daily spring/autumn) runs from morning until late at night. Locals and foreigners – hundreds of them in high season – mingle at the cafés and tavernas under the almond, flowering judas and pepper trees of the two main *platías*, passing the time unmolested by traffic, which is banned from the village centre. Toward the cliff-edge, and entered through two arcades, the defensive core of the medieval **kástro** is marked by ranks of of two-storey houses, whose repetitive, almost identical stairways and slightly recessed doors are very appealing.

From the square where the bus stops, a zig-zag path with views down to both coast-lines climbs to the cragtop, wedding-cake church of **Kímisis Theotókou**, nocturnally illuminated to grand effect. Beyond and below it hides the **Hrissospiliá**, a large cave with stalactites, accessible only to proficient climbers; the necessary steps and railings have crumbled away into the sea, although a minor, lower grotto can still be visited.

Practicalities

Hóra **accommodation** seems slightly weighted to favour hotels over rooms, with concentrations around the bus plaza at the east entrance to the village and at the western edge. Recommended rooms places include the purpose-built complex run by *Irini Dekavalla* (☎0286/41 235; ③), east of the bus stop. The nearby *Hotel Polikandia* (☎0286/41 322, winter ☎01/68 25 484; ③) has an engaging proprietress and far lower rates than appearances suggest. The most luxurious facilities are at the cliff-edge *Anemomilos Apartments* (☎ 0286/41 309; winter ☎01/68 23 962; ⑤), whose immaculate appointments and sock-you-in-the-eye views are particularly good value in spring or autumn, when rates drop to the ④ mark. The only hotel within the *hóra* – the *Castro* (☎0286/41 230, winter ☎01/77 81 658; ④) is a bit overpriced, despite recent renovation and undeniable atmosphere, with three rather dramatic rooms looking directly out on an alarming drop to the sea. At the western edge of Hóra near the police station, densely packed rooms outfits tend to block each other's views; the least claustrophobic is the long-established *Odysseas* (☎0286/41 276; ③), which also manages some attractive apartments near the *Anemomilos*. By the roadside on the way to Áno Meriá, the *Fani-Vevis* (☎0286/41 237; ④), in a Neoclassical mansion overlooking the sea, seems to function only in high season.

Hóra's half a dozen **restaurants** are surprisingly varied. The *Ouzeri Folegandhros* in water-cistern plaza, is fun, if a bit eccentrically run, with Greek music in the evenings to balance the New-Age noodlings over breakfast. The latter is probably best taken on the adjacent Platía Kondaríni at *Iy Melissa*, which does good fruit-and-yogurt, omelettes and juices. *Iy Piatsa* has a nightly changing menu of well-executed Greek dishes, while their neighbour and local hangout *O Kritikos* is notable only for its grills. Self-catering is an attractive option, with two well-stocked fruit shops and two supermarkets. Hóra is inevitably beginning to sprawl unattractively at the edges, but this at least means that the burgeoning **nightlife** – two dancing bars and a quantity of musical pubs and *ouzeris* – can be exiled to the south, away from most accommodation. A combination **OTE/ post office** (no bank) completes the list of amenities, though the single **ferry agent** also does money exchange.

The rest of the island

Northwest of Hóra a narrow, cement road threads its way towards **ÁNO MERIÁ**, the other village of the island; after 4km you pass its first houses, clustered around the three churches of Áyios Pandelímonas, Áyios Yióryios and Áyios Andhréas. Two tavernas operate in high season only: *O Mimis*, about halfway along, and *Iy Sinandisi*, at the turning for Áyios Yióryios beach.

Up to six times a day in high season a **bus** trundles out here to drop people off at the footpaths down to the various sheltered beaches on the southwest shore of the island. Busiest of these is **Angáli** (aka Vathí), with five rather basic rooms outfits (no phones; all ②) and three equally simple summer-only tavernas, reached by a fifteen-minute walk along a dirt road from the bus stop.

Nudists are urged to take the paths which lead twenty minutes east or west to **Firá** or **Áyios Nikólaos** beaches respectively; the latter in particular, with its many tamarisks, coarse sand and view back over the island, is Katergó's only serious rival in the best-beach sweepstakes. At Áyios Nikólaos, a lone taverna operates up by the name-sake chapel; Firá has no facilities at all.

Thíra (Santoríni)

As the ferry manoeuvres into the great caldera of **Thíra**, the land seems to rise up and clamp around it. Gaunt, sheer cliffs loom hundreds of feet above, nothing grows or grazes to soften the view, and the only colours are the reddish-brown, black and grey pumice striations layering the cliff face. The landscape tells of a history so dramatic and turbulent that legend hangs as fact upon it.

From as early as 3000 BC the island developed as a sophisticated outpost of Minoan civilization, until around 1550 BC when catastrophe struck: the volcano-island erupted, its heart sank below the sea, and earthquakes reverberated across the Aegean. Thíra was destroyed and the great Minoan civilizations on Crete were dealt a severe blow. At this point the island's history became linked with legends of Atlantis, the "Happy Isles Submerged by Sea". Plato insisted that the legend was true, and Solon dated the cataclysm to 9000 years before his time – if you're willing to accept a mistake and knock off the final zero, a highly plausible date.

These apocalyptic events, though, scarcely concern modern tourists, who are here mostly to stretch out on the island's dark-sand beaches and absorb the peculiar, infernal atmosphere: as recently as a century ago, Thíra was still reckoned to be infested with vàmpires. Though not nearly so predatory as the undead, current visitors have in fact succeeded in pretty much killing off any genuine island life, creating in its place a rather expensive and stagey playground.

Arrival and departure

Ferries dock at the somewhat grim port of **Órmos Athiniós**; **Skála Firás** and **Ía** in the north are reserved for local ferries, excursion *kaíkia* and cruise ships. **Buses**, astonishingly crammed, connect Athiniós with the island capital Firá, and, less frequently, with the main beaches at Kamári and Périssa – disembark quickly and take whatever's going, if you want to avoid a long walk. You're also likely to be accosted at Athiniós by people offering rooms all over the island; it may be a good idea to pay attention to them, given the scramble for beds in Firá especially. If you alight at Skála Firás, you have the traditional route above you – 580 mule-shit-splattered steps to Firá itself. It's not that difficult to walk but the intrepid can also go up by mule or by cable car (summer only, weather permitting), which runs every fifteen minutes between 7am and 8.30pm. The **airport** is located towards the other side of the island, near Monólithos; the shuttle bus service to the *Olympic Airways* office in Firá has been suspended, so you'll need to take a shared taxi.

When it comes to **leaving** – especially for summer/evening ferry departures – get to Athiniós a couple of hours in advance, since unbelievable crowds gather on the dockside. Note, too, that although the bus service stops around midnight, a shared taxi isn't outrageously expensive. Incidentally, **ferry information** from any source is notoriously unreliable on Thíra, so departure details should be quadruple-checked. If you do get stranded in Athiniós waiting for a ferry connection, there's no place to stay, and the tavernas are pretty awful. With time on your hands, it's well worth zigzagging the 3500m up to the closest village, **Megalohóri**. Between Megalohóri and Pírgos village, quite near the junction of the main and Athiniós road, is *Hotel Zorbas* (☎0286/31 433; ④), with very personable Greek and American management. At the centre of Megalohóri, the *Yeromanolis* is a surprisingly reasonable and tasty grill which offers the increasingly rare homemade Santorini wine.

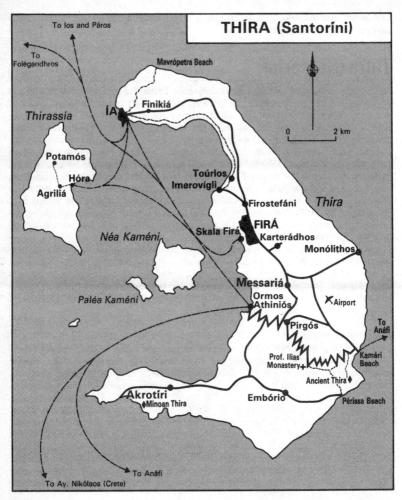

THÍRA (Santoríni)

Firá

Half-rebuilt after a devastating earthquake in 1956, **FIRÁ** (also known as Thíra or Hóra) still lurches dementedly at the cliff's edge. With a stunningly attractive setting, it appears on postcards and tourist brochures and, naturally, you pay the price for its position. Besieged by hordes of day-trippers from the cruise boats, in summer at least, initial impressions of Firá are of gross commercialism; gone are the simple restaurants and bakeries of a decade ago, replaced by supernumerary jewellery and fur boutiques, fast-food places and tourist agencies.

Firá's cliff-top position justifies a visit, but it's not a place to linger. Make time, however, for the **Archeological Museum** (daily except Mon 8.30am–3pm; 400dr), near the cable car to the north of town. An excellent collection, it includes a curious set of erotic Dionysiac figures, and a separate wing to house finds from the Akrotíri site (see below) is due to open soon; there's also the interesting **Museum Megaro** (also known as the Cultural Centre of Gizi Palace; daily 10am–1pm & 5–8pm; 350dr) near the *Kamares* hostel, displaying old engravings, maps and photos.

Practicalities

If you insist on staying here, you'll have to move quickly on arrival, particularly if you want one of the better (and ruinously expensive) **rooms** with views over the caldera; beds are at a premium in summer and by noon nearly everything is full. You'd be well advised to take any reasonable offer, including places just outside the town. You might try **KARTERÁDHOS**, a small village about twenty minutes' walk south of Firá, where there are rooms and the pleasant *Hotel Albatros* (☎0286/23 431; ③), or **MESSARIÁ**, another 2km further, with some more expensive hotels. Otherwise there are three **youth hostels** in the northern part of town, cheap, often full, but not too bad if you have your own bedding and sleep on the roof; the unofficial *Kamares* hostel is cleaner than the official *IYHF* one. Even the *Santorini Camping*, a few hundred metres inland from the central square, with a nice swimming pool and decent restaurant, has to turn away late arrivals in peak season. In the same neighbourhood, single women can stay at the Dominican convent. Out of season it's easier to track down rooms, and prices fall acccordingly; officially, the police only allow hotels to stay open, but you should eventually find someone prepared to put you up.

Restaurants worth trying include *The Roosters*, along 25 Martiou, which is cheap and unpretentious; *Barbara's*, close by the *Loucas Hotel*, is quite the opposite but worth it. Any restaurant overlooking the caldera is going to have prices as high as the cliffs it stands on. As for **nightlife**, *Bizarre* video bar is youth-orientated, with good music and cheap drinks, *Dionysus Disco* boasts free entry, and *Franco's* classical music bar is pricey but great for sunset-watching; *Enigma*, a soul disco, occupies a converted house and garden.

Buses to points further afield leave Firá from the large square straight ahead from the top of the steps, running approximately hourly to Ía, Périssa, Akrotíri, half-hourly to Kamári; timetables are posted in the kiosk at the far end. However, if you want to see the whole island in a couple of days a rented **moped** is useful; *Moto Chris* (☎0286/23 431) at the top of the road that leads down to *Santorini Camping* is particularly recommended.

The north

Once outside Firá, the rest of Santoríni comes as a nice surprise. The volcanic soil is highly fertile, with every available space terraced and cultivated: wheat, tomatoes (most made into paste), pistachios and grapes are the main crops, all still harvested and planted by hand. The island's *visándo* and *nikhtéri* wines are a little sweet for many tastes but are among the finest produced in the Cyclades.

ÍA, 12km from Firá in the northwest of the island, was once a major fishing port of the Aegean, but it has declined in the wake of economic depression, wars, earthquakes and depleted fish stocks. Partly destroyed in the 1956 earthquake, it presents a curious mix of pristine white reconstruction and tumbledown ruins clinging to the cliff face – by any standards one of the most dramatic towns of the Cyclades. Ía is also much the calmest place on the island, and with a **post office**, part-time **bank** and **bike-rental** office there's no reason to feel stuck in Firá. Regular buses ply between Firá and Ía, but the walk in from Imerovígli is rewarding (see below).

Rooms aren't too easy to come by: the local EOT authorities restored, then privatized, some of the old houses as expensive guest-lodges (all ⑥); less expensive choices include the troglodytic *Pension Lauda* (☎0286/71 204; ④), the *Hotel Anemones* (☎0286/71 220; ④), and the *Hotel Fregata* (☎0286/71 221; ④). Quite near the bus terminal, also reachable by the main road that continues round to the back end of the village, is an excellent new hostel, the *Oia* (☎0286/71 465; ①), with a terrace and shady courtyard, a good bar, clean dormitories and breakfast included. Recommended **restaurants** include *Petros* (for fish) and the popular *Neptune*; generally, the further you go along the central ridge towards the new end of Ía, the better value the restaurants. **Nightlife** revolves around sunset-gazing, for which people are bussed in from all over the island, creating traffic chaos; when this pales, there's *Strofi* rock-music bar.

Below the town, 200-odd steps switchback hundreds of metres down to two small harbours: **AMMOÚDHI**, for the fishermen, and **ARMÉNI**, where the ferries dock. Off the cement platform at Ammoúdhi you can swim past floating pumice and snorkel among shoals of giant fish, but beware the currents around the church-islet of Áyios Nikólaos. At Arméni, a single taverna specializes in grilled-octopus lunches.

A satisfying approach to Ía is to walk the stretch from **IMEROVÍGLI**, 3km out of Firá, using a spectacular footpath along the lip of the caldera. Imerovígli has a taverna and one moderate hotel, the *Katerina* (☎0286/22 708; ④); if you carry on to Ía you'll pass Toúrlos, an old Venetian citadel on Cape Skáros, on the way. **FINIKIÁ**, 1km east of Ía, has an excellent unofficial **youth hostel** on the north side of the road, and a couple of recommended restaurants – *Markozanes* and the expensive but varied *Finikias*.

The east and south

Beaches on Santoríni, mostly in the east and south, are bizarre – long black stretches of volcanic sand which get blisteringly hot in the afternoon sun. They're no secret and in the summer the crowds can be a bit overpowering. Closest to Firá, **MONÓLITHOS** has a couple of tavernas but is nothing special. Further south, **KAMÁRI** has surrendered lock, stock and barrel to the package-tour operators and there's not a piece of sand that isn't fronted by concrete villas. Nonetheless it's quieter and cleaner than most, with some beachfront **rooms** available, two inexpensive, co-managed **hotels**, the *Prekamaria* and *Villa Elli* (☎0286/31 266; both ③), and a relatively uncrowded **campsite**.

Things are scruffier at **PÉRISSA**, around the cape. Despite (or perhaps because of) its attractive situation and abundance of cheap rooms, it's noisy and overrun by inconsiderate backpackers. The official **campsite** is very crowded; if you're low on funds, you'd do better to stay in the popular, well-run *Anna* hostel (May–Oct; no phone; ①), at the inland entrance to town; they also have a few double rooms to let. The beach itself extends almost 7km to the west, sheltered by the occasional tamarisk tree, but it tends to be dirty and wind-buffeted.

Kamári and Périssa are separated by the Mésa Vounó headland, on which stood **ancient Thíra** (daily except Mon 9am–3pm), the post-eruption settlement dating from the ninth century BC. Expensive taxis and cheaper buses go up from Kamári, but the best approach is the half-hour walk from Périssa, following a clear **path** up past the hillside chapel. Though impressively large, most of the ruins (dating from between the third and first century BC) are difficult to place, but there are temples and houses with mosaics. The view from the theatre is awesome – beyond the stage there's a sheer drop to the sea. You can continue one hour on the path, soon a cobbled way, down to Kamári, slicing across the switchbacks of the road up. Part way down you pass a huge cave which contains a tiny shrine and a **freshwater spring** – the only one on Thíra and a lifesaver on a hot day.

Inland along the same mountain spine is the monastery of **Profítis Ilías**, now sharing its refuge with Greek radio and TV pylons and antennae of a NATO station. With just one monk remaining to look after the church, the place only really comes to life for the annual Profítis Ilías festival, when the whole island troops up here to celebrate. The views are still rewarding, though, and from near the entrance to the monastery an old footpath heads across the ridge in about an hour to ancient Thíra. The easiest ascent is the half-hour walk from the village of Pírgos.

PÍRGOS itself is one of the oldest settlements on the island, a jumble of old houses and alleys that still bear the scars of the 1956 earthquake. It climbs to another Venetian fortress crowned by several churches and you can clamber around the battlements for sweeping views over the entire island and its Aegean neighbours. By way of contrast **MESSARIÁ**, a thirty-minute stroll north, has a skyline consisting solely of massive church domes that lord it over the houses huddled in a ravine.

Akrotíri

Evidence of the Minoan colony that once thrived here has been uncovered at the other ancient site of **Akrotíri** (Tues–Sat 8.30am–3pm; 1000dr), at the southwestern tip of the island. Tunnels through the volcanic ash uncovered structures, two and three storeys high, first damaged by earthquake then buried by eruption; Professor Marinatos, the excavator and now an island hero, was killed by a collapsing wall and is also buried on the site. Only about three percent of what was the largest Minoan city outside of Crete has been excavated thus far. Lavish frescoes adorned the walls, and Cretan pottery was found stored in a chamber; most of the frescoes are currently exhibited in Athens, but there are plans to bring them back if and when a new museum is built. For now, you'll have to content yourself with the (very good) archeological museum in Firá; Akrotíri itself can be reached by bus from Firá or Périssa, and there are rooms and a basic restaurant at the site. The excellent *Glaros* fish taverna on the way to the beach has excellent food and barrelled wine.

Thirassía and Kaméni

From either Firá or Ía, boat excursions and local ferries run to the charred volcanic islets of **Paleá Kaméni** and **Néa Kaméni**, and to the relatively unspoiled islet of **Thirassía,** which was once part of Santoríni until shorn off by an eruption in the third century BC. Néa Kaméni, with its mud-clouded hot springs and shoe-slicing hike to a volcanically active crater, gets mixed reviews, but everybody seems to enjoy Thirassía. There are three small villages on the islet – including the port with its steep stairs – some tavernas and rooms, and you could enjoy the simple life here while waiting for the once-weekly proper ferry or the islanders' *kaíki* to Ammoúdhi.

Anáfi

A two-hour boat ride to the east of Thíra, **Anáfi** is the end of the line for the three weekly ferries which call there, and something of a travellers' dead end now that the occasional link with Crete and the Dodecanese has been discontinued. Not that this is likely to bother most of the visitors, who intentionally come here for weeks in mid-summer, and take over the island's beaches with a vengeance.

At most other times the place seems idyllic, and indeed may prove too sleepy for some: except for the road up to Hóra, there are no paved roads on Anáfi, nor any bona fide hotels, mopeds, discos or organized excursions; donkeys are still the main method of transport in the interior. Anáfi, though initially enchanting, is a harsh place, its mixed granite/limestone core overlaid by volcanic rock spewed out by Thíra's eruptions.

The harbour and Hóra

Virtually all of the approximately three hundred inhabitants live on the south coast, in the port or the *hóra*. In the minuscule harbour hamlet of **ÁYIOS NIKÓLAOS**, *Toh Akroyiali* is the most permanently open taverna and doubles as the main **ferry agent;** in high season a single pub provides a semblance of nightlife. Most **places to stay** are in Hóra; a bus meets all ferries – as do accommodation proprietors, who seem to have a system for dividing clients up among themselves.

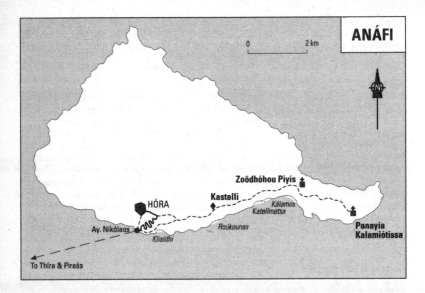

Otherwise **HÓRA**, adorning a conical hill overhead, is a stiff, 25-minute climb up the obvious old mule path which shortcuts the modern road. Exposed and blustery whether or not the *meltémi* is blowing, Hóra can initially seem a rather forbidding ghost town. This impression is slowly dispelled as you discover the hospitable islanders taking their coffee in sheltered, south-facing terraces, or under the anti-earthquake barrel vaulting that features in domestic architecture here.

The modern, purpose-built **rooms** run by *Ioannis Halaris* (☎0286/61 271; ②) or *Manolis Loudharos* (☎0286/61 279; ②), at the extreme east edge of the village, are about the most comfortable – and boast stunning views south over various islets and the distinctive monolith at the southeastern corner of Anáfi. Somewhat simpler are the rooms of the *Gavalas* family (②), looking down over the village from the top of the mule path. Evening **diners** seem to divide their custom between the simple, welcoming *Toh Steki*, with reasonable food and barrel wine served on its terrace, and the more upmarket *Alexandhra's* on the central walkway, which doubles as a bar. Otherwise there are two shops, sporadic fresh produce, a bakery, a **post office** and an OTE station.

East along the coast: beaches and monasteries

The glory of Anáfi is a string of south-facing beaches, currently accessible only by foot or boat, culminating in a pair of intriguing monasteries at the far southeastern tip of the island. The closest to Áyios Nikólaos is **KLISÍDHI**, a short walk along the cliffs to the east of the harbour, where 200m of tan, gently shelving sand gets pounded by a gentle surf; splendidly malapropic signs announce that "Nubbism Is Not Allowed". Above the calamus-and-tamarisk oasis backing the beach, there's a well-patronised **snack bar** (*Toh Kyma*) and adjacent, popular **rooms** (☎0286/61 237; ②).

From a point on the paved road just east of Hóra, the **main path** skirting the south flank of the island is signposted: "Kastélli – Paleá Hóra – Roúkouna – Monastíri". The primary branch of this trail roller-coasters in and out of several agricultural valleys that provide most of Anáfi's produce and fresh water. Just under an hour along, beside a well, you veer down a side trail to **Roúkounas**, easily the island's best beach, with some 500m of broad sand rising to tamarisk-stabilized dunes, which provide welcome shade. A single taverna, *Tou Papa*, operates up by the main trail in season; the suggestively craggy hill of **Kastélli**, an hour's scramble above the taverna, is the site both of ancient Anaphi and a ruined Venetian castle.

Beyond Roúkounas, it's another half hour on foot to the first of the exquisite half-dozen **Katelímatsa** coves, of all shapes and sizes, and 45 minutes to **Kálamos** beach – all without facilities, so come prepared.

The monasteries

Between Katelímatsa and Kálamos, the main route keeps inland, past a rare spring, to arrive at the **monastery of Zoödhóhou Piyís**, some two hours out of Hóra. Masonry from a temple of Apollo which once stood here is plainly visible around the main gate and in a standing structure just behind. According to legend, Apollo caused Anáfi to rise from the waves, pulling off a dramatic rescue of the storm-lashed Argonauts; not surprisingly, he has been venerated on the island ever since.The courtyard, with a welcome cistern, is the venue for the island's major festival, celebrated eleven days after Easter. A family of cheesemakers lives next door and can point you up the start of the spectacular onward path to **Panayía Kalamiótissa**, a little monastery perched atop the abrupt pinnacle at the extreme southeast of the island. It takes another hour to reach, but is eminently worthwhile for the stunning scenery and views over the entire south coast. Kalamiótissa comes alive only during its September 7–8 festival; at other times, you could haul a sleeping bag up here to witness the amazing sunsets and sunrises, with your vantage point often floating in a sea of cloud. There is no water up here, so bring enough with you. It's a full day's outing from Hóra to Kalamiótissa and back; you might wish to take advantage, in at least one direction, of the excursion **kaíki** that runs from Áyios Nikólaos or Klisídhi to Kálamos, on demand, during high season. There is also a slightly larger mail-and-supplies *kaíki* (currently Tuesday and Thursday mornings between 10 and 11am) which takes passengers to and from Thíra (Athiniós), supplementing the main-line ferries to Pireás.

travel details

Ferries

Most of the Cyclades are served by main-line ferries from **Pireás**, but there are also boats which depart from **Lávrio** (for Kéa, and less often, Síros and Kíthnos) and **Rafína**, which has become increasingly important of late, as work proceeds on the new international airport at nearby Spáta. At the moment there are regular services from Rafína to Ándhros, Tínos, Míkonos, Síros, Páros, Náxos and Amorgós, with infrequent extensions of the line into the Dodecanese (of late Pireás-based ships have more regularly included select Cyclades en route to the Dodecanese). All three ports are easily reached by bus from Athens.

The frequency of sailings given below is intended to give an idea of services from April to October, when most visitors tour the islands.

During the winter expect departures to be at or below the minimum level listed with some routes cancelled entirely. Conversely, routes tend to be more comprehensive in spring and autumn, when the government obliges shipping companies to make extra stops to compensate for numbers of boats still in drydock.

AMORGÓS 4–6 ferries weekly to Náxos, Páros, and Síros, some of these continuing to Rafína rather than Pireás; 3–4 weekly to Tínos and Míkonos; 2–3 weekly to Dhonoússa; 2 weekly to Astipálea; 1 a week to Kálimnos, Íos, and Thíra.

ANÁFI 3 weekly to Thíra (1hr 30min) and Pireás (12hr 30min), via Íos, Náxos, Páros; 2 weekly to Síros; 2 weekly *kaíkia* to Thíra (2hr).

ÁNDHROS At least 3 daily to Rafína (2hr), Tínos (2hr), and Míkonos; daily to Síros; 1

weekly to Amorgós and the minor islets behind Náxos.

DHONOÚSSA As for the preceding three, plus 2 weekly to Míkonos, Tínos, Síros; 2 extra weekly to Náxos and Páros; 1 weekly to Íos and Thíra.

ÍOS At least daily to Pireás (10hr), Páros (5hr), Náxos (3hr), Síros and Thíra (2hr); 3 weekly to Crete (Iráklion); 2–6 weekly to Síkinos and Folégandhros; 1–3 weekly to Mílos, Kímolos, Sérifos, Sífnos and Kíthnos; 3 weekly to Anáfi. Irregular seasonal *kaíkia* to Síkinos and Folégandhros.

KÉA 1–3 daily to Lávrio (1¼ 30min); several weekly to Kíthnos.

KÍMOLOS 2 daily *kaíkia* to Mílos (Pollónia) year-round, more in summer; 2–5 weekly to Mílos (Adhámas), Sífnos, Sérifos, Kíthnos, and Pireás (7hr); 1 weekly to Folégandhros, Síkinos, Thíra, eastern Crete (Áyios Nikólaos or Sitía), Kássos, Kárpathos, Hálki, Sími and Rhodes

KÍTHNOS 2–12 weekly to Pireás (3hr 15min); 2–10 weekly to Sérifos, Sífnos, and Mílos; 2–4 weekly to Kímolos, Folégandhros, Síkinos, Íos and Lávrio.

KOUFONÍSSI, SKHINOÚSSA, IRÁKLIA 1–3 weekly to Pireás or Rafína, Náxos, Páros, Síros, Amorgós, Dhonoússa, and each other; 1 weekly to Astipálea and Kálimnos.

MÍKONOS At least 2 daily to Pireás (5hr), Rafína (3hr 30min), Tínos (1hr), Ándhros (3hr 30min) and Síros (2hr); 2–7 weekly *kaíkia* to Delos; 2 weekly to Iráklion (Crete), Thessaloníki, Skíros, Skíathos, Astipálea; 1–2 weekly to Pátmos, Léros, Kálimnos, Kos, Níssiros, Tílos, Rhodes.

MÍLOS At least daily to Pireás (8hr); 5–8 weekly to Sífnos (2hr), Sérifos and Kíthnos; 2 daily *kaíkia* or 4–6 weekly ferries to Kímolos; 2–3 weekly to Folégandhros, Síkinos, Íos and Thíra; 1–3 weekly to Crete (Iráklion or Sitía); 1 weekly to Náxos, Amorgós, Náfplio (Peloponnese), Kássos, Kárpathos, Hálki, Sími and Rhodes (Ródhos).

NÁXOS At least 3 daily to Pireás (8hr), Páros (1hr), Síros, Íos and Thíra; 2–3 weekly to Iráklion, Skhinoússa, Koufoníssi, Dhonoússa, and Amorgós; 1–3 weekly to Ikaría and Sámos; 1–2 a week to Crete (Iráklion), Foúrni, Rafína (6hr 30min). Seasonal *kaíkia* from Ayía Ánna to Páros (Píso Livádhi).

PÁROS At least 3 daily to Pireás (7hr), Andíparos, Náxos, Íos, Thíra, and Síros; almost daily to Iráklion (Crete); 3–6 weekly to Ikaría and

Sámos; 3 weekly to Amorgós and the islets behind Náxos, and Rafína (5 hr), 3 or 4 weekly to Síkinos and Folégandhros; 3 weekly to Rhodes, Kárpathos, Thessaloníki; 2 weekly to Skíathos, Skíros, Anáfi. Seasonal small ferries to Sífnos and Náxos (Ayía Ánna).

SÉRIFOS and SÍFNOS 5–12 weekly to Pireás (4hr 30min/6hr) and each other; 4–11 weekly to Mílos; 4–6 weekly to Kímolos; 2–3 weekly to Folégandhros, Síkinos, Íos, and Thíra (Santoríni); once weekly to Síros; once weekly to eastern Crete and select Dodecanese; daily (June–Aug) from Sífnos to Páros.

SÍKINOS and FOLÉGANDHROS 2–4 weekly with each other, and to Pireás (10hr), Kíthnos, Sérifos, Sífnos, Mílos; 1–3 weekly to Íos, Thíra, Síros, Páros, Náxos, and Kímolos; 1 weekly to eastern Crete (Áyios Nikólaos or Sitía), Kássos, Kárpathos, Hálki, Sími and Rhodes; unreliable seasonal *kaíkia* to Íos.

SÍROS At least 2 daily to Pireás (4hr), Tínos (1hr), Míkonos (2hr), Náxos, and Páros; 4 weekly to Rafína (3hr 30min), Amorgós and the islets behind Náxos; 2 weekly to Íos, Síkinos, Folégandhros and Thíra; 2 weekly to Ikaría, Sámos, Astipálea; 1–2 weekly to Pátmos, Léros, Kálimnos, Kos, Níssiros, Tílos, Rhodes.

THÍRA At least daily to Pireás (10–12hr), Páros, Íos and Náxos; 3–6 weekly to Iráklion, Crete (5hr); 3–5 weekly to Síkinos and Folégandhros; 3 weekly to Thessaloníki; 2–3 weekly to Siros, Anáfi, Mílos, Kímolos, Sífnos, Sérifos and Kíthnos; 2 weekly to Skíros, Skíathos; Astipálea, Kálimnos, Kos and Rhodes; 1 weekly to Náfplio (Peloponnese), Crete (Áyios Nikólaos or Sitía), Kárpathos, Kássos, Hálki and Rhodes; also weekly to Amorgós and minor islets. Regular shuttle *kaíki* from Ía to Thirassía.

TÍNOS At least 2 daily to Pireás (5hr), Rafína (4hr), Ándhros, Síros and Míkonos; 4 weekly to Páros; 2 weekly to Náxos, Thíra, Iráklion (Crete), Skíros, Skíathos, Thessaloníki; 1–2 weekly to Páros, Náxos, Amorgós and minor islets between last two. Unreliable *kaíkia* to Delos.

Other services

To simplify the lists above, certain strategic **hydrofoil** and **small-boat services** have been omitted. Of these, the *Skopelítis* plies daily in season between Míkonos and Amorgós, spending each night at the latter and threading through all of the minor isles between it and Náxos, as well as Náxos and Páros (Píso Livádhi), in the course of a week. Note that this boat has no café or restaurant on board, so take provisions for what can be quite lengthy journeys. The *Aphrodite Express* follows an intricate route linking Náxos, Míkonos, Síros, Páros, Sífnos and Mílos; the popular *Ios Express* links Thíra (Skála Firás), Íos, Náxos, Páros and Míkonos daily in season. The *Paros Express* is actually a small car ferry, based on Síros despite its name, which does a very useful weekly circle route linking that island with Páros, Náxos, Íos, Thíra, Síkinos, Folégandhros, Sífnos, Sérifos and Kíthnos. The *Katamaran*, a small-capacity (and expensive) jet-boat, operates almost daily during summer out of Rafína and connects Síros, Tínos, Míkonos, Páros and Náxos with either the minor isles and Amorgós or a selection from among Íos, Síkinos, Folégandhros, Thíra and Anáfi (☎0294/22 888 for details). Another jetboat, the *Nearchos*, links Páros, Íos and Thíra with either Iráklion or Réthimnon on Crete on an almost-daily basis. In summer there are *Ilio Line* hydrofoils (*Delfini I, II, III, IV, V*), based in Rafína, which venture out at least once a week as far down as Mílos in the western Cycladic chain, rather more frequently through the central islands. A recent, welcome development is the appearance of *Ceres* "Flying Dolphins" between Zéa (Pireás), Kéa and Kíthnos – twice daily Friday to Monday in high season, once daily mid-week.

International ferries

Between May and October, *Minoan Lines* links Páros with Kuşadası (Turkey) and Ancona (Italy) twice weekly. One domestic stopover – either on Páros or Kefalloniá – may be allowed.

Flights

There are **airports** on **Páros**, **Míkonos**, **Thíra**, **Síros**, **Mílos** and **Náxos**. In season, or during storms when ferries are idle, you have little chance of getting a seat on less than three days' notice. The Athens–Mílos route is probably the best value for money; the other destinations seem deliberately overpriced, in a usually unsuccessful attempt to keep passenger volume manageable. Expect off-season (Oct–April) frequencies to drop by at least eighty percent.

Athens–Páros (6–11 daily; 45min)

Athens–Míkonos (4–8 daily; 50min)

Athens–Thíra (4–5 daily; 1hr)

Athens–Síros (3–4 daily; 35min)

Athens–Mílos (3 daily; 45min)

Athens–Náxos (3–5 daily; 45min)

Míkonos–Thíra (4 weekly; 40min)

Míkonos–Iráklion (3 weekly; 1hr 10min)

Míkonos–Rhodes (4 weekly; 1hr 10min)

Thíra–Iráklion (2–3 weekly; 40min)

Thíra–Rhodes (4 weekly; 1hr)

CHAPTER THREE

CRETE

Crete (Kríti) is a great deal more than just another Greek island. Often, especially in the cities or along the developed north coast, it doesn't feel like an island at all, but rather a substantial land in its own right: a mountainous, wealthy and surprisingly cosmopolitan one. But when you lose yourself among the mountains, or on the less-known coastal reaches of the south, it has everything you could want of a Greek island and more: great beaches, remote hinterlands and hospitable people.

In **history**, Crete is distinguished above all as the home of Europe's earliest civilization. It was only at the beginning of this century that the legends of King Minos and of a Cretan society that ruled the Greek world in prehistory were confirmed by excavations at Knossós and Festós. Yet the **Minoans** had a remarkably advanced society, the centre of a maritime trading empire as early as 2000 BC. The pre-Classical artworks produced on Crete at this time are unsurpassed anywhere in the ancient world, and it seems clear, that life on Crete in those days was good. This apparently peaceful culture survived at least three major natural disasters. Each time the palaces were destroyed, and each time they were rebuilt on a grander scale. Only after the last destruction, probably the result of a eruption of Thíra (Santoríni) and subsequent tidal waves and earthquakes, do significant numbers of weapons begin to appear in the ruins. This, together with the appearance of

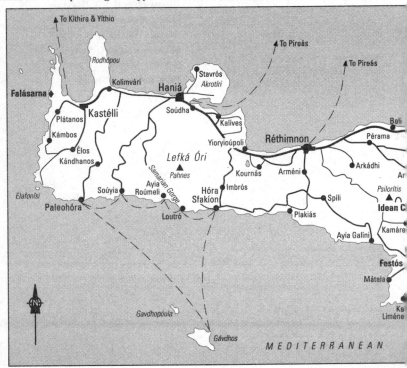

the Greek language, has been interpreted to mean that Mycenaean Greeks had taken control of the island. Nevertheless, for nearly 500 years, by far the longest period of peace the island has seen, Crete was home to a culture well ahead of its time.

The Minoans of Crete came originally from Anatolia; at their height they maintained strong links with Egypt and with the people of Asia Minor, and this position as meeting point and strategic fulcrum between east and west has played a major role in Crete's subsequent history. Control of the island passed from Greeks to Romans to Saracens, through the Byzantine Empire to Venice, and finally to Turkey for more than two centuries. During World War II, the island was occupied by the Germans and attained the dubious distinction of being the first place to be successfully invaded by paratroops.

Today, with a flourishing agricultural economy, Crete is one of the few islands which could probably support itself without **tourists**. Nevertheless, tourism is heavily promoted. The northeast coast in particular is overdeveloped, and though there are parts of the south and west coasts that have not been spoiled, they are getting harder to find. By contrast, the high mountains of the interior are still barely touched, and one of the best things to do on Crete is to **rent a vehicle** and explore the remoter villages.

Where to go

Every part of Crete has its loyal devotees and it's hard to pick out highlights, but generally if you want to get away from it all you should head west, towards **Haniá** and the smaller, less well-connected places along the south and west coasts. It is in this part of the island that the White Mountains rise, while below them yawns the famous **Samarian Gorge**. The far east, around **Sitía**, is also relatively unscathed.

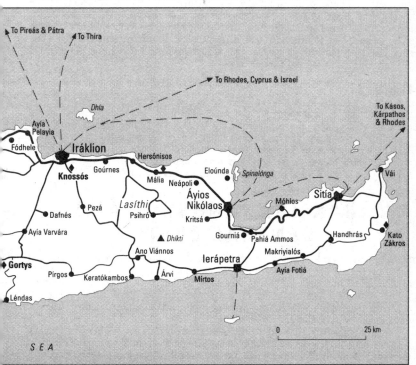

Whatever you do, the first main priority is to leave **Iráklion** (Heraklion) as quickly as possible, having paid the obligatory, and rewarding, visit to the **archeological museum** and nearby **Knossós**. The other great Minoan sites cluster around the middle of the island: **Festós** and **Ayía Triádha** in the south (with Roman **Górtys** to provide contrast), and **Mália** on the north coast. Almost wherever you go, though, you'll find a reminder of the island's history, whether it's the town of **Gourniá** near the cosmopolitan resort of **Áyios Nikólaos**, the palace of **Zákros** in the far east or the lesser sites scattered around the west. Unexpected highlights include Crete's Venetian forts, dominant at **Réthimnon**, and magnificent at **Frangokástello**; its Byzantine churches, most famously at **Kritsá**; and, at Réthimnon and Haniá, the cluttered old quarters full of Venetian and Turkish relics.

Climate

Crete has by far the longest summers in Greece and you can get a decent tan here right into October and swim at least from May until November. Several annual harvests, also make it the most promising location for finding **casual work**. The cucumber greenhouses and pickling factories around Ierápetra have proved to be winter lifelines for many long-term Greek travellers. The one seasonal blight is the *meltémi*, which blows harder here and more continuously than anywhere else in Greece – the best of several reasons for avoiding an **August** visit.

IRÁKLION, KNOSSÓS AND CENTRAL CRETE

Many visitors to Crete arrive in the island's capital, **Iráklion** (Heraklion), but it's not a beautiful city, nor one where you'll want to stay much longer than it takes to visit the **archeological museum** and nearby **Knossós**. Iráklion itself, though it has its good points – superb fortifications, a fine market, atmospheric old alleys, and some interesting lesser museums – is for the most part an experience in survival: modern, raucous, traffic-laden, overcrowded and expensive.

The area immediately around the city is less touristy than you might expect, mainly because there are few decent beaches of any size on this central part of the coast. To the west, mountains drop straight into the sea virtually all the way to Réthimnon, with just two significant coastal settlements – **Ayía Pelayía**, a sizeable resort, and **Balí**, which is gradually becoming one. Eastwards, the main resorts are at least 40km away, at **Hersónissos** and beyond, although there is a string of rather unattractive development all the way there. Inland, there's agricultural country, the richest on the island, and a series of wealthy but rather dull villages. Directly behind the capital rises **Mount Ioúktas** with its characteristic profile of Zeus; to the west the Psilorítis massif spreads around the peak of **Mount Ída** (Psilorítis), the island's highest. On the south coast there are few roads and little development of any kind, except at **Ayía Galíni** in the southwest, a nominal fishing village long since swamped with tourists, and **Mátala**, which has thrown out the hippies that made it famous and is now crowded with package-trippers. **Léndas** has to some extent occupied Mátala's old niche.

Despite the lack of resorts, there seem constantly to be thousands of people trekking back and forth across the centre of the island. This is largely because of the superb archeological sites in the south: **Festós**, second of the Minoan palaces, with its attendant villa at **Ayía Triádha**, and **Górtys**, capital of Roman Crete.

Iráklion

The best way to approach **IRÁKLION** is by sea; that way you see the city as it should be seen, with Mount Ioúktas rising behind and the Psilorítis range to the west. As you get closer, it's the city walls that first stand out, still dominating and fully encircling the oldest part of town; finally you sail in past the great fort defending the harbour entrance. Unfortunately, big ships no longer dock in the old port but at great modern concrete wharves alongside, which neatly sums up Iráklion itself. Many of the old parts have been restored from the bottom up, but they're of no relevance to the dust and noise characterizing the city today. These renovations invariably look fake, far too polished and perfect alongside the grime that seems to coat even the newest buildings.

Orientation, arrival and information

Virtually everything you're likely to want to see in Iráklion lies within the walled city, and even here the majority of the interest falls into a relatively small sector, the northeastern corner. The most vital thoroughfare, **25 Avgoústou**, links the harbour with the commercial city centre. At the bottom it is lined with shipping and travel agencies, and rental outlets, but as you climb these give way to banks, restaurants and stores. **Platía Venizélou** (or Fountain Square), off to the right, is crowded with cafés and restaurants; behind Venizélou is **El Greco Park**, with the OTE office and more bars, while on the opposite side of 25 Avgoústou are some of the more interesting of Iráklion's older buildings. Further up 25 Avgoústou, **Kalokerinoú** leads down to Haniá Gate and out of the city westwards; straight ahead, Odhós 1821 goes nowhere very much, but adjacent 1866 is given over to the animated **market**. To the left, Dhikeosínis, a major shopping street, heads for **Platía Eleftherías**, paralleled by the touristy pedestrian alley, Dedhálou, the direct link between the two squares. Eleftherías is very much the traditional centre of the city, both for traffic, which swirls around it constantly, and for life in general: ringed by more expensive tourist cafés and restaurants and in the evening alive with hordes of strolling locals.

Points of arrival

Iráklion **airport** is right on the coast, 4km east of the city. The #1 bus leaves for Platía Eleftherías every few minutes from the car park in front of the terminal; buy your ticket (130dr) at the booth before boarding. There are also plenty of taxis outside, and prices to major destinations are posted; it's about 1000dr to the centre of town.

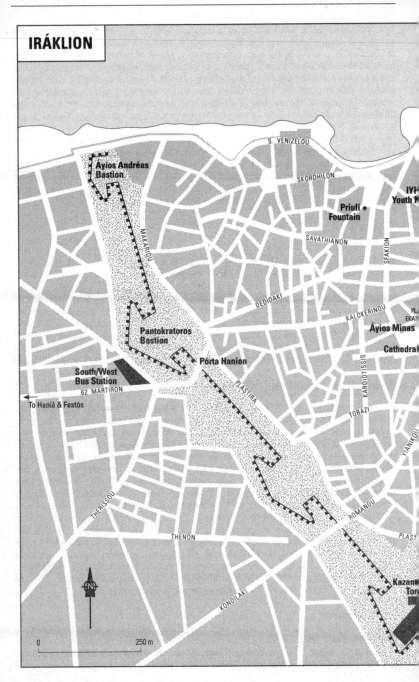

IRÁKLION

S. VENIZELOU

SKORDHILON

Áyios Andréas
Bastion

Priuli
Fountain

IYH
Youth

SAVATHIANON

SFAKION

MAKARIOU

DEDIDAKI

KALOKERINOU

PL
EKAT

Áyios Minas

Pantokratoros
Bastion

KARDIOTISSIS

Cathedral

Pórta Hanion

PLASTIRA

South/West
Bus Station

62 MARTIRON

TOBAZI

To Haniá & Festós

YIANIKOU

THERISSOU

ROMANOU

PLAST

THENON

Kazan
Tom

KONDILAKI

N

0   250 m

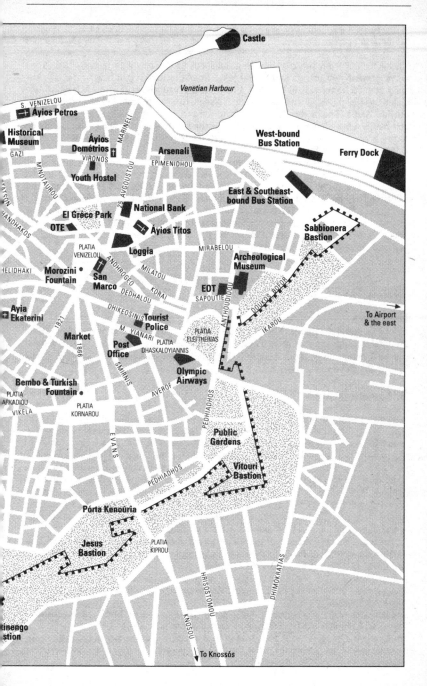

There are three main **bus stations** and a small terminus. Services along the coastal highway to or from the **east** (Mália, Áyios Nikólaos, Sitía, etc) use the terminal just off the main road between the ferry dock and the Venetian harbour; the #2 local bus to Knossós runs from the city bus stop, adjacent to the east bus station. Main road services **west** (Réthimnon and Haniá) leave from a terminal right next to the east bus station on the other side of the road. Buses for the **southwest** (Festós, Mátala or Ayía Galíni) and along the inland roads west (Tílissos, Anóyia) operate out of a terminal just outside Haniá Gate, a very long walk from the centre along Kalokerinoú (or jump on any bus heading down this street). The **southeast** (basically Ierápetra and points en route) is served by a small terminus just outside the walls in Platía Kíprou at the end of Odhós Evans on Trikoúpi.

From the wharves where the **ferries** dock, the city rises directly ahead in steep tiers. If you're heading for the centre, for the archeological museum or the tourist office, cut straight up the stepped alleys behind the bus station onto Doukos Bofor and to Platía Eleftherías. This will take about fifteen minutes. For accommodation, though, and to get a better idea of the layout of Iráklion's main attractions, it's simplest to follow the main roads by a rather more roundabout route. Head west along the coast, past the major east-bound bus station and on by the Venetian harbour before cutting up towards the centre on 25 Avgoústou.

> The telephone code for Iráklion is ☎081

Information

Iráklion's **tourist office** (Mon–Fri 8am–2.30pm; ☎228 825) is just below Platía Eleftherías, opposite the archeological museum at Zanthoudhídhou 1. The **tourist police** – more helpful than most – are on Dhikeosínis, halfway between Platía Eleftherías and the market.

Accommodation

Finding a **room** can be difficult in season. The best place to look for inexpensive rooms is in the area around Platía Venizélou, along Handhákos and towards the harbour to the west of 25 Avgoústou. Other concentrations of affordable places are around El Greco park and by the bottom of the market (slightly more expensive and noisy) and off Kalokerinoú, down towards Haniá Gate. Better hotels mostly lie closer to Platía Eleftherías, to the south of Platía Venizélou and near the east- and west-bound bus stations. The dusty park between the main bus station and the harbour is always crowded with the sleeping bags of those who failed to find, or couldn't afford, a room; if you're really hard up, crashing here has the advantage that local farmers come around recruiting casual labour in the mornings, but a pleasant environment it's not.

There are no **campsites** near to Iráklion now that *Camping Iraklion* has closed. The nearest sites are both found to the east of the city: *Creta Camping* at Gouves(16km), and *Caravan Camping* at Hersonisos (28km).

Atlas, Kandanoleon 11 (☎288 989). Rather run-down old pension in convenient but noisy alley between Platía Venizélou and El Greco park. Pleasant roof garden and freshly squeezed orange juice for breakfast. ②.

Dedalos, Dedhálou 15 (☎244 812). Very centrally placed on the pedestrianized alley between Venizélou and Eleftherías. Decent balcony rooms with private bath. ④.

Marin, Doukos Bofor 12 (☎224 736). A short distance along from the *Kris* and two other more expensive hotels, the *Lato* and the *Alaira*, but the best value of the lot. Very convenient for the bus stations and the archeological museum. ④.

Metropol, Karterou 48 (☎242 330). Quieter area near cathedral. Dated 1960s-style hotel but one of the best of the moderate hotels; rooms with shower are good value, more so as price also includes breakfast. ④.

Mirabello, Theotokopoulou 20 (☎285 052). Good-value, family-run place in a quiet street close to El Greco park. ③.

Olympic, Platía Kornarou (☎288 861). Overlooking busy *platía* and the famous Bembo and Turkish fountains. One of the many hotels built in the 1960s, but one of the few that has been refurbished. ⑤.

Paladion, Handhákos 16 (☎282 563). Very basic and cheap, near Platía Venizélou with stuffy rooms upstairs, but a pleasant garden at the back with rooms off it. No private facilities. ②.

Rea, Kalimeráki 1 (☎223 638). A friendly, comfortable and clean hotel in quiet street. Some rooms with washbasin, others with own shower. One of the best of the cheaper hotels. ②.

Rent Rooms Vergina, Hortatson 32 (☎242 739). Basic but pleasant rooms (with washbasins) in quiet street around a courtyard with an enormous banana tree. ②.

Youth hostel, Vironos 5 (☎286 281). The original youth hostel which has operated since 1963. Family run, very friendly and helpful with plenty of space and up to 50 beds on the roof if you fancy sleeping out under the stars. In addition to dormitories, family and double rooms are also available. Hot showers, breakfast (400dr) and TV. ①.

The Town

From the port, the town rises overhead, and you can cut up the stepped alleys for a direct approach to Platía Eleftherías (Liberty Square) and the archeological museum. The easiest way to the middle of things, though, is to head west along the coast road, past the main bus stations and the *arsenali*, and then up 25 Avgoústou, which leads into **Platía Venizélou**. This is crowded with Iráklion's youth, patronizing outdoor cafés (marginally cheaper than those on Eleftherías) and with travellers who've arranged to meet in "Fountain Square". The **fountain** itself is not particularly spectacular at first glance, but on closer inspection is really a very beautiful work; it was built by Venetian governor Francesco Morosini in the seventeenth century, incorporating four lions which were some 300 years old even then. From the *platía* you can strike up Dedhálou, a pedestrianized street full of tourist shops and restaurants, or continue on 25 Avgoústou to a major traffic junction. To the right, Kalokerinoú leads west out of the city, the **market** lies straight ahead, and Platía Eleftherías is a short walk to the left up Dhikeosínis.

Platía Eleftherías and the archeological museum

Platía Eleftherías is very much the traditional heart of the city: traffic swirls around it constantly, and in the evening strolling hordes jam its expensive cafés and restaurants. Most of Iráklion's more expensive shops are in the streets leading off the *platía*.

The **Archeological Museum** (Mon 12.30–7pm, Tues–Sat 8am–7pm, Sun 8.30am–3pm; 1000dr) is nearby, directly opposite the EOT office. Almost every important prehistoric and Minoan find on Crete is included in this fabulous, if bewilderingly large, collection. The museum tends to be crowded, especially when a guided tour stampedes through, but it's worth taking time over. You can't hope to see everything, nor can we attempt to describe it all (several good museum guides are sold here; best is probably the glossy one by J A Sakellarakis) but highlights include the **town mosaics** in Room 2 (galleries are arranged basically in chronological order), the famous **inscribed disc** from Festós in Room 3 (itself the subject of several books), most of Room 4, especially the magnificent bull's head **rhyton** (drinking vessel), the **jewellery** in Room 6 (and everywhere) and the engraved **black vases** in Room 7. Save some of your time and energy for upstairs, where the **Hall of the Frescoes**, with intricately reconstructed fragments of the wall paintings from Knossós and other sites, is especially wonderful.

Walls and fortifications

The massive **Venetian walls**, in places up to fifteen metres thick, are the most obvious evidence of Iráklion's later history. Though their fabric is incredibly well preserved, access is virtually nonexistent. It is possible, just, to walk on top of them from St Anthony's bastion over the sea in the west as far as the tomb of Nikos Kazantzakis, Cretan author of *Zorba the Greek*. His epitaph reads: "I believe in nothing, I hope for nothing, I am free." At weekends, Iraklians gather here to pay their respects and enjoy a free view of the soccer matches below. If the walls seem altogether too much effort, the **port fortifications** are very much easier to see. Stroll out along the jetty (crowded with courting couples after dark) and you can get inside the sixteenth-century **castle** (Mon–Sat 8am–4pm, Sun 10am–3pm; 400dr) at the harbour entrance, emblazoned with the Venetian Lion of St Mark. Standing atop this, you can begin to understand how Iráklion (or Candia as it was known until the seventeenth century) withstood a 22-year siege before finally falling to the Ottomans. On the landward side of the port, the Venetian **arsenali** can also be seen, their arches rather lost amid the concrete road system all around.

Churches, icons and the Historical Museum

From the harbour, 25 Avgoústou will take you up past most of the rest of what's interesting. The **church of Áyios Títos**, on the left as you approach Platía Venizélou, borders a pleasant little *platía*. It looks magnificent principally because, like most of the churches here, it was adapted by the Turks as a mosque and only reconsecrated in 1925; consequently it has been renovated on numerous occasions. On the top side of this *platía*, abutting 25 Avgoústou, is the Venetian **City Hall** with its famous loggia, again almost entirely rebuilt. Just above this, facing Platía Venizélou, is the **church of San Marco**, its steps usually crowded with the overflow of people milling around in the *platía*. Neither of these last two buildings has found a permanent role in its refurbished state, but both are generally open to house some kind of exhibition or craft show.

Slightly away from the obvious city-centre circuit, but still within the bounds of the walls, there are a couple of lesser museums worth seeing if you have the time. First of these is the collection of **icons** in the **church of Ayía Ekateríni** (daily except Sun 10am–1pm, Tues, Thurs & Fri also at 4–6pm; 400dr), an ancient building just below the undistinguished cathedral, off Kalokerinoú. This excellent display might inspire you to seek out less-known icons in churches around the island. The finest here are six large scenes by Mihalis Damaskinos (a near-contemporary of El Greco) who fused Byzantine and Renaissance influences. Supposedly both Damaskinos and El Greco studied at Ayía Ekateríni in the sixteenth century when it functioned as a sort of monastic art school.

The **Historical Museum** (Mon–Fri 9.30am–4.30pm, Sat 9.30am–2.30pm; 600dr) is some way from here, down near the waterfront opposite the stark *Xenia* hotel. Its display of folk costumes and jumble of local memorabilia includes the reconstructed studies of both Nikos Kazantzakis and Emanuel Tsouderos (Cretan statesman and Greek prime minister). There's enough variety to satisfy just about anyone, including the only El Greco painting on Crete, *View of Mount Sinai and the Monastery of St Catherine*.

The beaches

Iráklion's **beaches** are some way out, whether east or west of town. In either direction they're easily accessible by public bus: #6 west from the stop outside the *Astoria* hotel in Platía Eleftherías; #7 east from the stop opposite this, under the trees in the centre of the *platía*.

Almirós (or Amoudhári) to the west has been subjected to a degree of development, taking in a campsite, several medium-size hotels and one giant one (the *Zeus Beach*, in the shadow of the power station at the far end), which makes the beach hard to get to without walking through or past something built up.

Amnissós, to the east, seems the better choice, with several tavernas and the added amusement of planes swooping in immediately overhead to land. This is where most locals go on their afternoons off; the furthest of the beaches is the best, although new hotels are encroaching here, too. Little remains here to indicate the once-flourishing port of Knossós aside from a rather dull, fenced-in dig. If you're seriously into antiquities, however, you'll find a more rewarding site in the small villa, known as **Nirou Hani** (daily except Mon 8.30am–3pm) at Háni Kokkíni, the first of the full-blown resort developments east of Iráklion.

Eating

Big city as it is, Iráklion disappoints when it comes to eating. The cafés and tavernas of *platías* **Venizélou** and **Eleftherías** are essential places to sit and watch the world pass, but their food is expensive and mediocre. One striking exception is *Bouyatsa Kirkor*, by the fountain in Venizélou, where you can sample authentic *bouyatsa*; alternatively, try a plate of *loukoumades*, available from a number of cafés at the top of Dhikeosinis. The cafés and tavernas on **Dedhálou**, the pedestrian alley linking the two main *platías*, are very run of the mill, enticing you in with persistent waiters and faded photographs of what appears to be food.

A more atmospheric option is to head for the little alley, **Fotíou Theodosáki**, which runs through from the market to Odhós Evans. It is entirely lined with the tables of rival taverna owners, certainly authentic and catering for market traders and their customers as well as tourists. Compared to some, they often look a little grimy, but they are by no means cheap, which can come as a surprise. Nearby, at the corner of Évans and Yiánari, is the long-established taverna *Ionia*, which is the sort of place to come to if you are in need of a substantial, no-nonsense feed, with a good range of Greek dishes.

Other good tavernas are more scattered. Still near the centre, just off Eleftherías at **Platía Dhaskaloyiánnis** (where the post office is), are some inexpensive and unexceptional tavernas; but the *platía* is a pleasant and relaxing venue, if not for a meal then to sit at one of its cafés. Nearer Venizélou, try exploring some of the back streets to the east, off Dedhálou and behind the *loggia*. The *Taverna Giovanni*, on the alley Korai parallel to Dedhálou, is one of the better tavernas in Iráklion: a friendly place with a varied menu that uses fresh, good quality ingredients but with reasonable prices and a good atmosphere both inside and out. It also caters for vegetarians.

The **waterfront** is lined with fish tavernas with little to recommend them. Instead, walk across the road to *Ippokambus*, which specializes in *mezédhes* at moderate prices. It is deservedly popular with locals and is often crowded late into the evening – you may have to wait in line or turn up earlier than the Greeks eat. Even if you see no space it is worth asking as the owner may suddenly disappear inside the taverna and emerge with yet another table to carry further down the pavement.

Should you have a craving for **non-Greek food**, there is Italian at the *Loukoulos* and Chinese at the *New China Restaurant*, both with leafy courtyards and both in the same street as the *Taverna Giovanni*. There is also the *Curry House* just off Dedhálou, which advertises both Indian and Mexican food, but don't expect the real thing. You can eat decent pizza at many tavernas in the centre, or far better at the excellent *Tartuffo* on Dhimokratias (the road towards Knossós) near the *Galaxy* hotel. Go early, as it's usually packed with locals.

For **snacks and takeaways,** there's a whole group of *souvlaki* stalls clustering around 25 Avgoústou at the entrance to El Greco park, which is handy if you need somewhere to sit and eat. For cheese or spinach pies or some other pastry, sweet or savoury, there are no shortage of *zaharoplastía*, such as the *Samaria* next to the Harley Davidson shop across from the park. If you want to buy your own food, the **market** on Odhós 1866 is the place to go; it's an attraction in itself, which you should see even if you don't plan to buy.

Drinking, nightlife and entertainment

Iráklion is a bit of a damp squib as far as **nightlife** goes, certainly when compared to many other towns on the island. If you're determined, however, there are a few city-centre possibilities, and plenty of options if all you want to do is sit and **drink**. In addition, there are a number of **cinemas** scattered about, for which check the posters on the boards by the tourist police office. Most enjoyable is the open-air cinema on the beach to the west of the city.

Bars
Bars tend to fan out into the streets around Handhákos, and while you will stumble on many places by following the crowds, *Odysseia* (Handhákos 63), *Jasmin* (tucked in an alley mid-way down Handhákos) and *El Azteca* (Psavomilingou 32, west of Handhákos), a Mexican bar serving *tacos*, are all good places for which to aim.

The most animated place is a *platía* behind Dedhálou (up from the *Giovanni*), where there are several trendy bars (including *Flash* and *Notos*) with outdoor tables and popular with students in term time. Enjoy a game of backgammon here during the day or early evening; later it can get get extremely lively with many distractions. In and around Platía Venizélou, there are many bars, again some are very fashionable, with *De Facto* being one of the most popular. This is one of the new breed of *kafenío* emerging in Iráklion, attracting younger people; the drinks are cocktails rather than *raki*, the music is western or modern Greek and there are prices to match. Another is the *Idaean Andron*, on Pardhikari around the corner from the *Selena* hotel, which has a nice atmosphere, and there are more along Kandanoléon, off El Greco park.

Iráklion looks a great deal better than you'd expect from above, and there are fancier **roof-top places** above most of the restaurants in Platía Eleftherías, the *Cafe-Bar Dore* for example. This serves food as well, and while it's not exactly the sort of place to wear cut-offs and T-shirt, it's no more expensive than the restaurants in the *platía* below. Many hotels around the city have roof-top bars which welcome non-residents; those just above the bus stations and harbour, such as the *Alaira* have particularly stunning views.

Less elevated romance is to be had at the *Onar* café (Handhákos 36b, north of Venizélou); there's a small terrace and they serve a wide variety of teas as well as great ices, just the thing when you're winding down around around midnight. *Tasso's* is a popular hang-out for young hostellers, lively at night and with good breakfasts to help you recover in the morning; similar bars in the area include the *Utopia*, further down Handhákos, and the *Bonsai*, next to *Christakos Rooms*.

Clubs and discos
For **discos** proper, there is a greater selection even if they are all playing "techno" at the moment, interspersed with Greek music (and not the Greek music you get for tourists). *Trapeza* is still the most popular, down towards the harbour at the bottom of Doukos Bofor, below the archeological museum. *Makao* also has a following and is on the opposite side of the street to *Trapeza*; or try *Genesis* next door. Another cluster of nightclubs can be found on Ikarou, about a twenty-minute walk away. Retrace your steps towards

the archeological museum, but before emerging onto Platía Eleftherías turn left down-hill and follow the main road, Ikarou. Here you'll find the *Minoica*, the *Korus Club* and the *Athina*, again playing similar music and popular with the young Iraklions.

Listings

Airlines *Olympic*, on Platía Eleftherías (☎229 191), is the only airline with a permanent office in Iráklion. Charter airlines flying in to Iráklion mostly use local travel agents as their representatives.

Airport For airport information call ☎282 025. Bus #1 runs from Platía Eleftherías to the airport every few minutes.

Banks The main branches are on 25 Avgoústou, many of which have 24hr cash machines (not always working); there's also a *VISA* machine at *Ergo Bank* on Dhikeosínis.

Car and bike rental 25 Avgoústou is lined with rental companies, but you'll find cheaper rates on the backstreets and it is always worth asking for discounts. Good places to start – out of dozens – include *Eurocreta* (Sapotie 2; ☎226 700) for cars and *Motor Speed* (Ariadnis; ☎224 812) for bikes, both near the archeological museum; *Blue Sea* (Kosma Zotou 7, near the bottom of 25 Avgoústou; ☎241 097); *Ritz* in the *Hotel Rea* for cars (Kalimeráki 1; ☎223 638); and *Sun Rise* (25 Avgoústou 46; ☎221 609) for cars and bikes.

Ferry tickets Available from *Minoan Lines* (25 Avgoústou 78; ☎224 303), *Kavi Club* near the tourist office (☎221 166), or any of the travel agents listed below.

Hospital Most central is the hospital on Apollónion, southwest of Platía Kornarou, between Alber and Moussoúrou.

Laundry There's a launderette in the backstreets below the archeological museum (Mon–Fri 9am–2pm & 5–7pm, Sat 9am–2pm).

Left luggage Offices in the east-bound and southwest bus stations (daily 6am–8pm; 200dr per bag per day), as well as a commercial agency at 25 Avgoústou (daily 7am–11pm; 450dr per bag per day); you can also leave bags at the youth hostel (even if you don't stay there) for 200–300dr per bag per day. If you want to leave your bag while you go off on a bike for a day or two, the rental company should be prepared to store it.

Newspapers and books For English-language newspapers, novels as well as local guides and maps, Dedhálou is the best bet. *Planet International Bookstore* at the corner of Handhákos and Kidonias, behind Platía Venizélou, has a huge stock of English-language titles.

Pharmacies Plentiful on the main shopping streets – at least one is open 24hr on a rota basis, check the list on the door of any.

Post office Main office in Platía Dhaskaloyiánnis, off Eleftherías (Mon–Fri 7.30am–8pm). There's also a temporary office (a van) at the entrance to El Greco Park (daily 7.30am–7pm), handy for changing money.

Taxis Major taxi ranks in Platía Eleftherías and El Greco Park or call ☎210 102 or 210 168. Prices displayed on boards at ranks.

Telephones The OTE head office is in El Greco Park – often long waits, though an efficient 24hr service.

Travel agencies Budget operators and student specialists include the extremely helpful *Blavakis Travel* (Platía Kallergon 8, just off 25 Avgoústou by the entrance to El Greco Park; ☎282 541) and *Prince Travel* (25 Avgoústou 30, ☎282 706). For excursions around the island, villa rentals etc, the bigger operators are probably easier: *Irman Travel* (Dedhálou 26; ☎242 527) or *Creta Travel Bureau* (20–22 Epiménidhou; ☎243 811). The latter is also the local *American Express* agent.

Knossós

KNOSSÓS, the largest of the Minoan palaces, reached its cultural peak more than 3000 years ago, though a town of some importance persisted here well into the Roman era. It lies on a low, largely man-made hill some 5km southeast of Iráklion; the surrounding hillsides are rich in lesser remains spanning 25 centuries, starting at the beginning of the second millennium BC.

Barely a hundred years ago the palace existed only in mythology. Knossós was the court of the legendary King Minos, whose wife Pasiphae bore the Minotaur, half-bull, half-man. Here the labyrinth was constructed by Daedalus to contain the monster, and youths were brought from Athens as human sacrifice until Theseus arrived to slay the beast, and with Ariadne's help, escape its lair. The discovery of the palace, and the interplay of these legends with fact, is among the most amazing tales of modern archeology. Heinrich Schliemann, the excavator of Troy, suspected that a major Minoan palace lay under the various tumuli here, but was denied the necessary permission to dig by the local Ottoman authorities at the end of the last century. It was left for Sir Arthur Evans, whose name is indelibly associated with Knossós, to excavate the site, from 1900 onwards.

The Site

April–Sept Mon–Fri 8am–7pm, Sat & Sun 8.30am–3pm; Oct–March daily 8.30am–3pm; 1000dr, students 500dr.

As soon as you enter the **palace of Knossós** through the West Court, the ancient ceremonial entrance, it is clear how the legends of the labyrinth grew up around it. Even with a detailed plan, it's almost impossible to find your way around the site with any success. The best advice is not to try; wander around for long enough and you'll even-

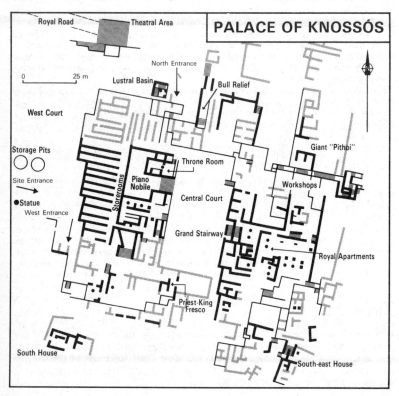

tually stumble upon everything. If you're worried about missing the highlights, you can always tag along with one of the constant guided tours for a while, catching the patter and then backtracking to absorb the detail when that particular crowd has moved on. You won't get the place to yourself, whenever you come, but exploring on your own does give you the opportunity to appreciate individual parts of the palace in the brief lulls between groups.

Knossós was liberally "restored" by Evans, and these restorations have been the source of furious controversy among archeologists ever since. It has become clear that much of Evans's upper level – the so-called *piano nobile* – is pure conjecture. Even so, his guess as to what the palace might have looked like is certainly as good as anyone else's, and it makes the other sites infinitely more meaningful if you have seen Knossós first. Without the restorations, it would be almost impossible to imagine the grandeur of the multistorey palace or to see the ceremonial stairways, strange, top-heavy pillars and gaily painted walls that distinguish the site. For some idea of the size and complexity of the palace in its original state, take a look at the cutaway drawings (wholly imaginary but probably not too far off) on sale outside.

Royal Apartments

The superb **Royal Apartments** around the central staircase are not guesswork, and they are plainly the finest of the rooms at Knossós. Unfortunately, extensive renovations are currently taking place and these mean that the apartments are likely to be closed for some time, although glimpses can be had through the wooden railings. The **Grand Stairway** itself is a masterpiece of design: not only a fitting approach to these sumptuously appointed chambers but also an integral part of the whole plan, its large well bringing light into the lower storeys. Light wells such as these, usually with a courtyard at the bottom, are a constant feature of Knossós and a reminder of just how important creature comforts were to the Minoans, and of how skilled they were at providing them.

For evidence of this luxurious lifestyle you need look no further than the **Queen's Suite**, off the grand **Hall of the Colonnades** at the bottom of the staircase. Here, the main living room is decorated with the celebrated **dolphin fresco** (a reproduction; the original is now in the Iráklion archeological museum) and with running friezes of flowers and abstract spirals. On two sides, it opens out onto courtyards that let in light and air; the smaller one would probably have been planted with flowers. In use, the room would have been scattered with cushions and hung with plush curtains, while doors and further curtains between the pillars would have allowed for privacy, and for cool shade in the heat of the day. This, at least, is what they'd have you believe, and it's a very plausible scenario. Remember, though, that all this is speculation and some of it is pure hype; the dolphin fresco, for example, was found in the courtyard, not the room itself, and would have been viewed from inside as a sort of *trompe l'oeil*, like looking through a glass-bottomed boat. Whatever the truth, this is an impressive example of Minoan architecture, the more so when you follow the dark passage around to the queen's **bathroom**. Here is a clay tub, protected behind a low wall (and again probably screened by curtains when in use), and the famous "flushing" toilet (a hole in the ground with drains to take the waste away – one flushed it by throwing a bucket of water down).

The much-pored over **drainage system** was a series of interconnecting terracotta pipes running underneath most of the palace. Guides to the site never fail to point these out as evidence of the advanced state of Minoan civilization, and they are indeed quite an achievement, in particular the system of baffles and overflows to slow down the runoff and avoid any danger of flooding. Just how much running water there would have been, however, is another matter; the water supply was, and is, at the *bottom* of the hill, and even the combined efforts of rainwater catchment and hauling water up to the palace can hardly have been sufficient to supply the needs of more than a small elite.

Going up the Grand Stairway to the floor above the queen's domain, you come to a set of rooms generally regarded as the **King's Quarters**. These are chambers in a considerably sterner vein; the staircase opens into a grandiose reception chamber known as the **Hall of the Royal Guard**, its walls decorated in repeated shield patterns. Immediately off here is the **Hall of the Double Axes**, believed to be have been the ruler's personal chamber, a double room that would allow for privacy in one portion while audiences were held in the more public section. Its name comes from the double-axe symbol carved into every block of masonry.

The Throne Room and the rest of the palace

Continuing to the top of the Grand Stairway, you emerge onto the broad **Central Court**. Open now, this would once have been enclosed by the walls of the buildings all around. On the far side, in the northwestern corner of the courtyard, is the entrance to another of Knossós's most atmospheric survivals, the **Throne Room**. Here, a worn stone throne sits against the wall of a surprisingly small chamber; along the walls around it are ranged stone benches, and behind there's a reconstructed fresco of two griffins. In all probability this was the seat of a priestess rather than a ruler (there's nothing like it in any other Minoan palace), but it may just have been an innovation wrought by the Mycenaeans, since it seems that this room dates only from the final period of Knossós's occupation. The Throne Room is now closed off with a wooden gate, but you can lean over this for a good view, and in the antechamber there's a wooden copy of the throne on which everyone perches to have their picture taken.

The rest you'll see as you wander, contemplating the legends of the place which blur with reality. Try not to miss the giant *pithoi* in the northeast quadrant of the site, an area known as the palace workshops; the storage chambers which you see from behind the Throne Room and the reproduction frescoes in the reconstructed room above it; the fresco of the Priest-King looking down on the south side of the central court, and the relief of a charging bull on its north side. This last would have greeted you if you entered the palace through its north door; you can see evidence here of some kind of gate house and a lustral bath, a sunken area perhaps used for ceremonial bathing and purification. Just outside this gate is the **theatral area**, an open space a little like a stepped amphitheatre, which may have been used for ritual performances or dances. From here the **Royal Road**, claimed as the oldest road in Europe, sets out. At one time, this probably ran right across the island; nowadays it ends after about a hundred yards in a brick wall beneath the modern road. Circling back around the outside of the palace, you get more idea of its scale by looking up at it; on the south side are a couple of small reconstructed Minoan houses worth exploring.

Practicalities

The #2 local **bus** sets off every ten minutes from the Iráklion's city bus stop (adjacent to the east bus station), runs up 25 Avgoústou (with a stop by Platía Venizélou) and out of town on Odhós 1821 and Évans.

At Knossós, outside the fenced site, is the *caravanserai* where ancient wayfarers would rest and water their animals. Head out onto the road and you'll find no lack of watering holes for modern travellers either – a string of rather pricey tavernas and tacky souvenir stands. There are several **rooms** for rent here, and if you're really into Minoan culture, there's a lot to be said for staying out this way to get an early start. Be warned that it's expensive and unashamedly commercial.

Beyond Knossós

If you have transport, the drive beyond Knossós can be an attractive and enjoyable one, taking minor roads through much greener country, with vineyards draped across low hills and flourishing agricultural communities. If you want specific things to seek out, head first for **MIRTIÁ**, an attractive village with a small **Kazantzakis Museum** (daily except Sun 9am–4pm; 400dr) in a house where the writer's parents once lived. **ARHÁNES**, at the foot of Mount Ioúktas, is a much larger place that was also quite heavily populated in Minoan times. None of the three sites here are open to the public, but one of them, **Anemospília**, has caused huge controversy since its excavation in the 1980s. Many traditional views of the Minoans, particularly that of Minoan life as peaceful and idyllic, have had to be rethought in the light of the discovery of an apparent human sacrifice. From Arhánes you can also drive to the top of Mount Ioúktas to enjoy the panoramic views. At **VATHÍPETRO**, south of the mountain, is a Minoan villa (with wine press in situ) which can be explored (daily 8.30am–3pm).

Southwest from Iráklion: sites and beaches

If you take a **tour** from Iráklion (or one of the resorts), you'll probably visit the Górtys, Festós and Ayía Triádha sites in a day, with a lunchtime swim at Mátala thrown in. Doing it by public transport, you'll be forced into a rather more leisurely pace, but there's still no reason why you shouldn't get to all three and reach Mátala within the day; if necessary, it is easy enough to hitch the final stretch. **Bus services** to the Festós site are excellent, with some nine a day to and from Iráklion (fewer run on Sunday), five of which continue to or come from Mátala; there are also services direct to Ayía Galíni. If you're arriving in the afternoon, plan to visit Ayía Triádha first, as it closes early.

The route to Áyii Dhéka

The road from Iráklion towards Festós is a pretty good one by the standards of Cretan mountain roads, albeit a dull one, too. The country you're heading towards is the richest agricultural land on the island, and right from the start the villages en route are large and business-like. In the largest of them, Ayía Varvára, there's a great rock outcrop known as the *Omphalos* (Navel) of Crete, supposedly the very centre of the island.

Past here, you descend rapidly to the fertile fields of the Messará plain, where the road joins the main route across the south near the village of **ÁYII DHÉKA**. For religious Cretans Áyii Dhéka is something of a place of pilgrimage; its name, "The Ten Saints", refers to ten early Christians martyred here under the Romans. In a crypt below the modern church you can see the martyrs' tombs. It's an attractive village to wander around, with several places to eat and even some **rooms** along the main road.

Górtys

Daily 8.30am–3pm; 400dr.

Within easy walking distance of Áyii Dhéka, either through the fields or along the main road, sprawls the site of **Górtys**, ruined capital of the Roman province that included not only Crete but also much of North Africa. Cutting across the fields will give you some idea of the scale of this city at its zenith in approximately the third century AD; an enormous variety of other remains, including an impressive **theatre**, are strewn across your route. Even in Áyii Dhéka you'll see Roman pillars and statues lying around in people's yards or propping up their walls.

There had been a settlement here from the earliest times, but the extant ruins date almost entirely from the Roman era. Only now is the site being systematically excavated, by the Italian School. At the main entrance to the fenced site, alongside the road, are the ruins of the still impressive **basilica of Áyios Títos**; the eponymous saint converted the island to Christianity and was its first bishop. Beyond this is the **Odeion** which houses the most important discovery on the site, the **Law Code**. These great inscribed blocks of stone were incorporated by the Romans from a much earlier stage of the city's development; they're written in an obscure early Greek-Cretan dialect, and in a style known as *boustrophedon* (ox-ploughed), with the lines reading alternately in opposite directions like the furrows of a ploughed field. At ten metres by three metres, this is reputedly the largest Greek inscription ever found. The laws set forth reflect a strictly hierarchical society: five witnesses were needed to convict a free man of a crime, only one for a slave; raping a free man or woman carried a fine of a hundred staters, violating a serf only five. A small **museum** in a loggia (also within the fenced area) holds a number of large sculptures found at Górtys.

Míres

Some 20km west of Górtys, **MÍRES** is an important market and focal point of transport for the Messará plain: if you're switching buses to get from the beaches on the south coast to the archeological sites or the west, this is where you'll do it. There are good facilities including a **bank**, lots of **restaurants** and plenty of **rooms**, though there's no particular reason to stay unless you are waiting for a bus or looking for work (it's one of the better places for agricultural jobs). Heading straight for Festós, there's usually no need to stop.

Festós

Mon–Fri 8am–7pm, Sat & Sun 8.30am–7pm; 800dr, Sun free.

The **Palace of Festós** was excavated by the Italian, Federico Halbherr (also responsible for the early work at Górtys), at almost exactly the same time as Evans was working at Knossós. The style of the excavations, however, could hardly have been more different. Here, to the approval of most traditional archeologists, reconstruction was kept to an absolute minimum – it's all bare foundations, and walls which rise at most a metre above ground level. This means that despite a magnificent setting overlooking the plain of Messará, the palace at Festós is not as immediately arresting as those at Knossós or Mália. Much of the site is fenced off and, except in the huge central court, it's almost impossible to get any sense of the place as it was; the plan is almost as complex as at Knossós, with none of the reconstruction to bolster the imagination.

It's interesting to speculate why the palace was built halfway up a hill rather than on the plain below; certainly not for defence, for this is in no way a good defensive position. Psychological superiority over the peasants or reasons of health are both possible, but it seems quite likely that it was simply the magnificent view that finally swayed the decision. The site looks over Psilorítis to the north and the huge plain, with the Lasíthi mountains beyond it, to the east. Towards the top of Psilorítis you should be able to make out a small black smudge: the entrance to the Kamáres cave (see p.169).

On the ground closer at hand, you can hardly fail to notice the strong similarities between Festós and the other palaces: the same huge rows of storage jars, the great courtyard with its monumental stairway, and the theatral area. Unique to Festós, however, is the third courtyard, in the middle of which are the remains of a **furnace** used for metalworking. Indeed, this eastern corner of the palace seems to have been home to a number of craftsmen, including potters and carpenters. Oddly enough, Festós was much less ornately decorated than Knossós; there is no evidence, for example, of any of the dramatic Minoan wall paintings.

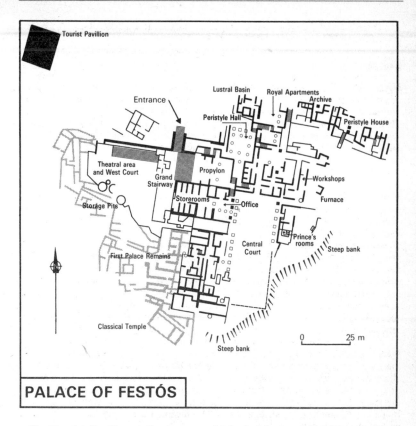

PALACE OF FESTÓS

The **Tourist Pavilion** at Festós serves drinks and food and also has a few beds, though these are very rarely available (thanks to advance bookings) and expensive when they are. The nearby village of **ÁYIOS IOÁNNIS**, along the road towards Mátala, has a few more **rooms**, including some at *Taverna Ayios Ioannis*, which is also a good place to eat.

Ayía Triádha

Daily 8.30am–3pm; 400dr.

Some of the finest artworks in the museum at Iráklion came from **Ayía Triádha**, about a 45-minute walk (or a short drive) from Festós. No one is quite sure what this site is, but the most common theory has it as some kind of royal summer villa. It's smaller than the palaces, but if anything even more lavishly appointed and beautifully situated. In any event, it's an attractive place to visit, far less crowded than Festós, with a wealth of interesting little details. Look out in particular for the **row of stores** in front of what was apparently a marketplace, and for the remains of the **paved road** that once led down to the Gulf of Messará. The sea itself looks invitingly close, separated from the base of the hill only by Timbáki airfield (mainly used for motor racing these days), but if you try to drive down there, it's almost impossible to find your way around the unmarked dust tracks. There's a fourteenth-century **church** at the site, worth visiting in its own right for the remains of ancient frescoes.

Mátala

MÁTALA has by far the best-known **beach** in Iráklion province, widely promoted and included in tours mainly because of the famous **caves** cut into the cliffs above its beautiful sands. These are believed to be ancient tombs first used by Romans or early Christians, but more recently inhabited by a sizeable hippie community. You'll still meet people who will assure you that this is *the* travellers' beach on Crete. Not any more it isn't. Today, the town is full of package tourists and tries hard to present a respectable image; the cliffs are now cleared and locked up every evening.

A few people still manage to evade the security, or sleep on the beach or in the adjacent campsite, but on the whole the place has changed entirely. The last ten years have seen the arrival of crowds and the development of hotels, discos and restaurants to service them; early afternoon, when the tour buses pull in for their swimming stop, sees the beach packed to overflowing. All of which is not to knock Mátala too much; as long as you're prepared to accept it for what it is – a resort of some size– you'll find the place more than bearable. The town beach *is* beautiful, but if the crowds get excessive, you can climb over the rocks in about twenty minutes (past more caves, many of which are inhabited through the summer) to another excellent stretch of sand, known locally as "Red Beach". In the evening, when the trippers have gone, there are waterside bars and restaurants looking out over invariably spectacular sunsets.

The chief problems concern prices and crowds: rooms are both expensive and oversubscribed, food is good but not cheap. If you want a **place to stay**, try looking up the little street to the left as you enter town, just after the *Zafíria* hotel (☎0892/42 112; ④), where there are several rooms for rent, such as *Matala View* and *Red Beach* (both ③). If these are full, then everywhere closer in is likely to be, too, so head back out on the main road, or try the **campsite**, *Camping of Matala* (☎0892/42 720), next to the beach above the car park; *Komos Camping* is a nicer site, but a few kilometres out of Mátala. There are places to **eat and drink** all over the main part of town. Also impossible to miss are most other **facilities**, including stores, currency exchange, car and bike rental, travel agents, post office, and an OTE office in a temporary building in the car park behind the beach.

Around Mátala: Pitsídhia and Kalamáki

One way to enjoy a bit more peace is to stay at **PITSÍDHIA**, about 5km inland. This is already a well-used option, so it's not quite as cheap as you might expect, but there are plenty of rooms, lively places to eat and even music bars. If you decide to stay here, the beach at **KALAMÁKI** is an alternative to Mátala. Both beaches are approximately the same distance to walk, though there is a much better chance of a bus or a lift to Mátala. Kalamáki itself is beginning to develop somewhat, with a number of rooms and a couple of tavernas, but so far it's a messy and unattractive little place. The beach stretches for miles, surprisingly wild and windswept, lashed by sometimes dangerously rough surf. At the southern end (more easily reached by a path off the Pitsídhia–Mátala road) lies **Kómmos**, once a Minoan port serving Festós and now the site of a major archeological excavation. As yet there's not a great deal to see, but this is another good beach.

Iráklion's south coast

South of the Messará plain are two more beach resorts, Kalí Liménes and Léndas, with numerous other little beaches along the coast in between, but nothing spectacular. **Public transport** is very limited indeed; you'll almost always have to travel via Míres (see p.160). If you have your own transport, the roads in these parts are all passable, but most are very slow going; the Kófinas Hills, which divide the plain from the coast, are surprisingly precipitous.

Kalí Liménes

While Mátala itself was an important port under the Romans, the chief harbour for Górtys lay on the other side of Cape Líthinon at **KALÍ LIMÉNES**. Nowadays, this is once again a major port – for oil tankers. This has rather spoiled its chances of becoming a major resort, especially when aggravated by the lack of a paved road and proper facilities. Some people like Kalí Liménes: the constant procession of tankers gives you something to look at, there are a number of places offering **rooms** – the best is the *Kanavourissia Beach* (③), a kilometre or so east of the village – the coastline is broken up by spectacular cliffs and, as long as there hasn't been a recent oil spill, the beaches are reasonably clean and totally empty. But (fortunately) not too many share this enthusiasm.

Léndas

LÉNDAS, further east along the coast, is far more popular, with a couple of buses daily from Iráklion and a partly justified reputation for being peaceful (sullied by considerable summer crowds). Many people who arrive think they've come to the wrong place: at first sight, the village looks filthy; the beach is small, rocky and dirty; and the rooms are frequently all booked. A number of visitors leave without ever correcting that initial impression, but the attraction of Léndas is not the village at all but on the other (west) side of the headland. Here, there's an enormous, excellent sandy beach, part of it usually taken over by nudists, and a number of taverna/bars overlooking it from the roadside. It's a couple of kilometres by car from Léndas, along a rough track; if you're walking, you can save time by cutting across the headland. Camping on the beach, or with luck getting one of the few **rooms** (②–③) at the tavernas, is a considerably more attractive prospect than staying in the village. After you've discovered the beach, even Léndas begins to look more welcoming, and at least it has most of the **facilities** you'll need, including a shop which will change money and numerous places to eat.

Once you've come to terms with the place, you can also explore some less good but quite deserted beaches eastwards, and the scrappy remains of **ancient Lebena** on a hilltop overlooking them. There was an important *Asclepieion* (temple of the god Asclepios) here around some now-diverted warm springs, but only the odd broken column and fragments of mosaic survive.

East of Iráklion: the package-tour coast

East of Iráklion the startling pace of tourist development in Crete is all too plain to see. The merest hint of a beach is an excuse to build at least one hotel, and these are outnumbered by the concrete shells of resorts-to-be. It's hard to find a room in this monument to the package-tour industry, and expensive if you do.

Goúrnes and Goúves

As a general rule, the further you go, the better things get: when the road detours all too briefly inland, the real Crete of olive groves and stark mountains asserts itself. You certainly won't see much of it at **GOÚRNES**, where there used to be a US Air Force base, or at nearby Kato Goúves, where there's a **campsite**, *Camping Creta* (☎0897/41 400), which will be quiet until the Greek air force move in next door. From here, however, you can head inland to the old village of **GOÚVES**, a refreshing contrast, and just beyond to the **Skotinó Cave**, one of the largest and most spectacular on the island (about an hour's walk from the coast).

Not far beyond Goúrnes is the turning for the direct route up to the Lasíthi plateau, and shortly after that you roll into the first of the big resorts, Hersónisos (or, more correctly, Límin Hersonísou; Hersónisos is the village in the hills just behind, also overrun by tourists).

Hersónisos (Límin Hersonísou)

HERSÓNISOS was once the port that served the Minoan city of Knossós, and more recently just a small fishing village; today it's the most popular of Crete's package resorts. If all you want is plenty of bars, tavernas, restaurants and Eurodisco nightlife then come here. The resort has numerous small patches of sand beach between rocky outcrops, but a shortage of places to stay in peak season.

Along the modern seafront, a solid line of restaurants and bars is broken only by the occasional souvenir shop: in their midst you'll find a small pyramidal **fountain** with broken mosaics of fishing scenes. This is Roman and the only real relic of the ancient town of Chersonesos. Around the headland above the harbour and in odd places along the seafront, you can see remains of Roman harbour installations, mostly submerged.

Beach and clubs excepted, the only distraction is **Lychnostatis** (daily 9.30am–2pm; 1000dr), an open-air "museum" of traditional Crete, on the coast on the eastern edge of the town next to the *Caravan* campsite.

A short distance inland are the three **hill villages** of Koutoulafari, Piskopiano and "old" Hersónisos, which all have a good selection of tavernas, and are worth searching out for accommodation.

Practicalities

Hersónisos is well provided with all the back-up **services** you need to make the holiday go smoothly. Banks, bike and car rental, post office and OTE are all on or just off the main drag, as are the taxi ranks. **Buses** in either direction leave every half-hour.

Finding somewhere to stay can be difficult in July and August. Much of the **accommodation** here is allocated to package-tour operators and what remains is not that cheap. To check for availability of accommodation generally, the quickest and best option is to visit the very helpful **tourist office** on Giaboudaki, just off the main street towards the harbour. Reasonably priced central options include the *Crystal* on Giaboudaki (☎0897/22 546; ③) and the *Nancy* on Ayía Paraskevis (☎0897/22 212; ③), but be prepared for a fair amount of noise. At the eastern end of town, is a good **camp-site**, *Caravan Camping* (☎0897/22 025), and almost opposite, on the inland side of the main road, is a **youth hostel** (☎0897/23 674; ①). The hostel is well run by the very helpful and friendly American-born Greek Kostas Zikos, who is a mine of information on the general area, including bus and ferry schedules.

Despite the vast number of **places to eat**, there are few in Hersónisos worth recommending, and the tavernas down on the harbour front should be avoided. One of the few Greek tavernas that stands out is *Kavouri* along Arheou Theátrou, but it is more expensive. Better to head out of town on the Piskopiano road where, near the junction to Koutoulafari, the friendly *Fengari Taverna* serves good Greek food at a reasonable price. Sitting at your table overlooking the street below you can marvel at the steady trek of clubbers heading down the hill to the bars and nightclubs of Hersónisos. The hill villages have the greatest selection of tavernas, particularly Koutoulafari, where a more relaxed evening is had in its narrow streets and small *platías*.

Hersónisos is reknowned for its **nightlife** and there is no shortage of it. Most of the better bars and clubs are along the main road. Especially popular are *La Luna*, with up-to-date music, and the *Hard Rock Cafe*, which also has live music on a Sunday. *Aria*, a large glass-fronted disco, is the biggest on Crete and always attracts. *Club 99* is also worth a visit. If you fancy a quiet drink then you have come to the wrong resort. There is an open-air **cinema** at the *Creta Manis* hotel.

Stalídha

STALÍDHA is a Cinderella town, sandwiched in between its two louder, brasher and some would say uglier sisters of Mália and Hersónisos, but it is not quiet or undeveloped. This rapidly expanding beach resort, with more than sixty tavernas and bars and a few discos, can offer the best of both worlds with a friendlier and more relaxed setting, a better beach (and usual array of water sports) and very easy access to its two livelier neighbours. If you're content soaking up the sun, then make sure you find somewhere to stay at the English end of the resort where two sunbeds and an umbrella only set you back 1000dr. At the German end it can be twice the price.

Finding a **place to stay** can be difficult as most rooms are already booked by the package companies. Try the travel agencies in the village first, as they will know what is available, but expect to pay 5000–8000dr for a room or studio. Finding **somewhere to eat** is less difficult as there are plenty of rather ordinary tavernas. One of the better and most popular is *Maria's Taverna*, in the centre of resort.

Stalídha is completely overshadowed by its neighbours when it comes to **nightlife**, though you can dance at *Bells* disco, on the main coast road, or at *Rhythym*, on the beach; the *Sea Wolf Cocktail Bar* and *Akti Bar* are near each other along the beach.

Mália

Much of **MÁLIA** is taken up by the package industry, so in the peak season finding a place to stay is not always easy. You're best off, especially if you want any sleep during the night, trying one of the numerous **rooms** (③) signposted in the old town. Tracking back from here, along the main Iráklion road, there are a number of reasonably priced **pensions** on the left including the *Argo* (☎0897/31 636; ③). Further along this road, on the right opposite the *Mobil* station, lies the **youth hostel** (☎0897/31 555; ①), which is rundown, unwelcoming and not especially clean – strictly a desperation option. To save time, it would be sensible in the first instance to call in at one of the travel companies in Mália, for example, *Foreign Office* (☎0897/31 217) on the main road.

Eating in Malia is unlikely to be a problem as **restaurants** jostle for your custom at every step, especially along the beach road. None of these are particularly good, but that's the price of mass production. The best places are around Platía Áyíou Dhimitríou, a pleasant square beside the church in the centre of the old town. Try a meal at *Totto-Lotto*, or even better at *Taverna Minos Knossos*, after an aperitif at the *Ouzeri Kapilla*, where they serve excellent local wine from the wood. There are a number of other welcoming tavernas off the *platía*.

The beach road comes into its own when the profusion of **bars**, **discos** and **clubs** erupt into a pulsating cacophony during the hours either side of midnight. *Zoo* is a new club, and once past midnight, one of the internal walls parts to reveal an even larger dance area. *Zig Zag* and *Cloud 9* are the other really popular clubs in Mália. *Desire*, along the beach road, concentrates on rock and has good-quality live music some nights. Unfortunately, a good night's clubbing and dancing is frequently spoilt by drunken groups of youths pouring out of the bars. The situation has got so bad that tour operators have threatened to pull out of the resort if action isn't taken to deal with the hooligans.

The Palace of Mália

Tues–Sun 8.30am–3pm; 400dr, Sun free.

The archeological site lies forty minutes' walk east of Mália town on the main road. Any passing bus should stop, or you could even rent a bike for a couple of hours as it's a pleasant, flat ride. Much less imposing than either Knossós or Festós, the **Palace of Mália** in some ways surpasses both. For a start, it's a great deal emptier and you can wander among the remains in relative peace. While no reconstruction has been attempted, the palace was never reoccupied after its second destruction, so the ground plan is virtually intact. It's a great deal easier to comprehend than Knossós and, if you've seen the reconstructions there, it's easy to envisage this seaside palace in its days of glory. There's a real feeling of an ancient civilization with a taste for the good life, basking on the rich agricultural plain between the Lasíthi mountains and the sea.

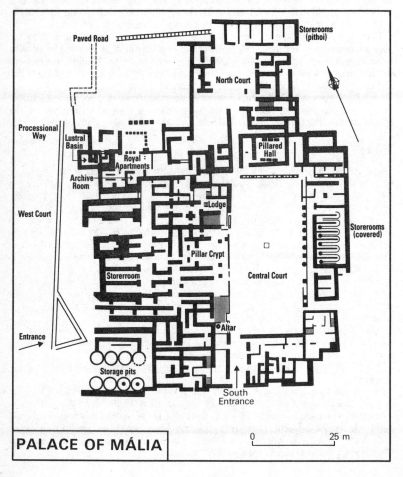

PALACE OF MÁLIA

0   25 m

From this site came the famous gold pendant of two bees (which can be seen in the Iráklion museum or on any postcard stand), allegedly part of a horde that was plundered and whose other treasures can now be found in the British Museum in London. The beautiful leopard's-head axe, also in the museum at Iráklion, was another of the treasures found here. At the site, look out for the strange indented stone in the central court, which probably held ritual offerings; for the remains of ceremonial stairways; and for the giant *pithoi* which stand like sentinels around the palace. To the south and east, digs are still going on as a large town comes slowly to light.

Moving on

Leaving the archeological zone, you can follow the dirt track that runs around it to a lovely stretch of near-deserted sand. Considering its position this is an amazingly little-visited patch of beach. You can walk back along the shore to Mália from here, or take a bus (every half-hour in either direction) from the stop on the main road.

Head **east**, and it's not long before the road leaves the coast, climbing across the hills towards Áyios Nikólaos. If you want to escape the frenetic pace of all that has gone before, try continuing to **SÍSI** or **MÍLATOS**. These little shore villages are bypassed by the main road as it cuts inland, and so far have seen only the beginnings of a tourist industry; each has a few villa/apartments and a few tavernas, and there's a **campsite** at Sísi (☎0841/71 247), the more developed of the two. The beaches aren't great, but they make for a refreshing change of pace.

West of Iráklion: around Psilorítis

Most people heading **west from Iráklion**, speed straight out on the new coastal highway, non-stop to Réthimnon. If you're in a hurry this is not such a bad plan; the road is fast and spectacular, hacked into the sides of mountains which for the most part drop straight to the sea. On the other hand, there are no more than a couple of places where you might consider stopping. By contrast, the old roads inland are agonizingly slow, but they do pass through a whole string of attractive villages beneath the heights of the Psilorítis range. From here you can set out to explore the mountains and even walk across them to emerge in villages with views of the south coast.

The coastal route towards Réthimnon

Leaving the city, the **new highway** runs behind a stretch of highly developed coast, where the hotels compete for shore space with a cement works and power station. As soon as you reach the mountains, though, all this is left behind and there's only the clash of rock and sea to contemplate. As you start to climb, look out for **Paleókastro**, beside a bridge which carries the road over a small cove; the castle is so weathered as to be almost invisible against the brownish face of the cliff.

Ayía Pelayía and Fódhele

Some 3km below the highway, as it rounds the first point, lies the resort of **AYÍA PELAYÍA**. It looks extremely attractive from above (less so close up), but it is also very commercial: not somewhere to roll up without a reserved room, though out of season you might find a real bargain at an apartment.

Not far beyond Ayía Pelayía, there's a turning inland to the village of **FÓDHELE**, allegedly El Greco's birthplace. A plaque from the University of Toledo acknowledges the claim and, true or not, the community has built a small tourist industry on that basis. There are a number of craft shops and some pleasant tavernas where you can sit outside along the river: there's also "El Greco's house" and a picturesque Byzantine church. None of this amounts to very much but it is a pleasant, relatively unspoiled village if you simply want to sit in peace for a while. A couple of **buses** a day run here from Iráklion, and there's the odd tour; if you arrive on a direct bus, the walk back down to the highway (about 3km), where you can flag down a passing service, is not too strenuous.

Balí and Pánormos

BALÍ, on the coast approximately halfway between Iráklion and Réthimnon, also used to be tranquil and undeveloped, and by the standards of the north coast it still is in many ways. The village is built around a couple of small coves, some 2km from the highway (a hot walk from the bus), and is similar to Ayía Pelayía except that the beaches are not quite as good and there are no big hotels. There are, however, lots of **rooms** (more every month it seems) and a number of "modest hotels" (brochure-speak). You'll have plenty of company. The last and best beach, known as "Paradise", no longer really deserves the name; it's a beautiful place to splash about, surrounded by mountains rising straight from the sea, but there's rarely a spare inch on the sand.

Continuing along the coast, the last stop before you emerge on the flat stretch leading to Réthimnon is at PÁNORMOS. This, too, is an attractive village with a small sandy beach and a few rooms, but again there are crowds, mostly arriving by boat on day trips from Réthimnon.

Inland towards Mount Psilorítis

Of the **inland routes** the old main road (via Márathos and Dhamásta) is not the most interesting. This, too, was something of a bypass in its day and there are few places of any size or appeal, though it's a very scenic drive. If you want to dawdle, you're better off on the road which cuts up to Tílissos and then goes via Anóyia. It's a pleasant ride through fertile valleys filled with olive groves and vineyards, a district (the Malevísi) renowned from Venetian times for the strong, sweet Malmsey wine.

Tílissos and Anóyia

TÍLISSOS has a significant archeological site (daily 8.30am–3pm; 400dr) where three Minoan houses were excavated; unfortunately, its reputation is based more on what was found here (many pieces in the Iráklion museum) and on its significance for archeologists than on anything which remains to be seen. Still, it's worth a look, if you're passing, for a glimpse of Minoan life away from the big palaces, and for the tranquillity of the pine-shaded remains.

ANÓYIA is a much more tempting place to stay, especially if the summer heat is becoming oppressive. Spilling prettily down a hillside close below the highest peaks of the mountains, it looks traditional, but closer inspection shows that most of the buildings are actually concrete; the village was destroyed during the war and the local men rounded up and shot – one of the German reprisals for the abduction of General Kreipe. The town has a reputation as a handicrafts centre (especially for woven and woollen goods), skills acquired both through bitter necessity after most of the men had been killed, and in a conscious attempt to revive the town. At any rate it worked, for the place is thriving today – thanks, it seems, to the number of elderly widows keen to subject any visitor to their terrifyingly aggressive sales techniques.

Quite a few people pass through Anóyia during the day, but not many of them stay; it shouldn't be hard to find a **room** in the upper half of town. On the other hand, there's almost nowhere to eat: one **taverna** on the main road where it loops out of the lower village, and a *souvláki* place near the top of the town, both of which serve barbecued lamb, the local speciality. Vegetarians are advised to buy their own bread and cheese (local cheese is also excellent).

Mount Psilorítis and its caves

Heading for the mountains, a rough track leads 13km from Anóyia to the **Nídha plateau** at the base of Mount Psilorítis. Here there's a taverna that used to let rooms but seems now to have closed to the public altogether, though it's still used by groups of climbers. A short path leads from the taverna to the celebrated **Idhéon Ándron** (Idean Cave), a rival of that on Mount Dhíkti (see next page) for the title of Zeus's birthplace and certainly associated from the earliest of times with the cult of Zeus. Unfortunately, there's a major archeological dig going on inside, which means the whole cave is fenced off, with a miniature railway running into it to carry all the rubble out. In short, you can see nothing.

The taverna also marks the start of the way to the top of **Mount Psilorítis** (2456m), Crete's highest mountain, a climb that's not for the unwary, but for experienced, properly shod hikers is not at all arduous. The route is well marked with the usual red dots and it should be a six- to seven-hour return journey to the chapel at the summit; in spring, thick snow may slow you down.

If you're prepared to camp on the plateau (it's very cold, but there's plenty of available water) or can prevail on the taverna to let you in, you could continue on foot next day down to the southern slopes of the range. It's a beautiful hike, at least while the road they're attempting to blast through is out of sight, and also relatively easy, four hours or so down a fairly clear path to **VORÍZIA**. If you're still interested in caves, there's a more rewarding one above the nearby village of **KAMÁRES**, a climb of some three hours on a good path. Both Vorízia and Kamáres have a few **rooms** and some tavernas, at least one daily **bus** down to Míres, and alternate (more difficult) routes to the peak of Psilorítis if you want to approach from this direction.

EASTERN CRETE

Eastern Crete is dominated by **Áyios Nikólaos**, and while it is a highly developed resort, by no means all of the east is like this. Far fewer people venture beyond the road south to **Ierápetra** and into the eastern isthmus, where only **Sitía** and the famous beach at **Vái** ever see anything approaching a crowd. Inland, too, there's interest, especially on the extraordinary **Lasíthi** plateau, which is worth a night's stay if only to catch its abidingly rural life.

Inland to the Lasíthi plateau

Leaving the palace at Mália, the highway cuts inland towards Neápoli, soon beginning a spectacular climb into the mountains. Set in a high valley, **NEÁPOLI** is a market town little touched by tourism. There is one hotel, some rooms, a modern church and a couple of museums. Beyond the town, it's about twenty minutes before the bus suddenly emerges high above the Gulf of Mirabéllo and Áyios Nikólaos, the island's biggest resort. If you're stopping, Neápoli also marks the second point of access to the **Lasíthi Plateau**.

Scores of bus tours drive up here daily to view the "thousands of white-cloth-sailed windmills" which irrigate the high plain, and most groups will be disappointed. There are very few working windmills left, and these operate only for limited periods (mainly in June). This is not to say the trip is not justified, as it would be for the drive alone, and there are many other compensations. The plain is a fine example of rural Crete at work, every inch devoted to the cultivation of potatoes, apples, pears, figs, olives and a host of other crops; stay in one of the villages for a night or two and you'll see real life return as the tourists leave. There are plenty of easy rambles around the villages as well, through orchards and past the rusting remains of derelict windmills. You'll find rooms in the main town of **TZERMIÁDHO**, and at Áyios Konstandínos, Áyios Yióryios (where there's a folk museum and the friendly *Hotel Dias*; ☎0844/31 207; ③) and Psihró.

Psihró and the Dhiktean cave
PSIHRÓ is much the most visited, as it's the base for visiting Lasíthi's other chief attraction, the **Dhiktean Cave**, birthplace of Zeus (daily 10.30am–5pm; 400dr; watch out for slippery stones inside). In legend, Zeus's father, the Titan Kronos, was warned that he would be overthrown by a son and accordingly ate all his offspring; however, when Rhea gave birth to Zeus in the cave, she fed Kronos a stone and left the child concealed, protected by the Kouretes, who beat their shields outside to disguise his cries. The rest, as they say, is history (or at least myth). There's an obvious path running up to the cave from Psihró and, whatever you're told, you don't have to have a guide if you don't want one, though you will need some form of illumination. On the other hand, it is hard to resist the guides, who do make the visit much more interesting, and they're not expensive if you can get a small group together (about 500–600dr each). It takes a Cretan imagination to pick out Rhea and the baby Zeus from the lesser stalactites and stalagmites.

    Buses run around the plateau to Psihró direct from Iráklion and from Áyios Nikólaos via Neápoli. Both roads offer spectacular views, coiling through a succession of passes guarded by lines of ruined windmills.

Áyios Nikólaos and around

ÁYIOS NIKÓLAOS ("Ag Nik" to the majority of its British visitors) is set around a supposedly bottomless salt lake, now connected to the sea to form an inner harbour. It is supremely picturesque, has some style, exudes confidence and exploits this to the full. The lake and port are surrounded by restaurants and bars, which charge above the odds, and whilst still very popular, some tourists are distinctly surprised to find themselves in a place with no decent beach at all.

Practicalities

The greatest concentration of **stores** and **travel agents** are on the hill between the bridge and Platía Venizélou. The main **ferry agent** is *Massaros Travel* (☎0841/22 267), on Koundoúrou near the **post office**. The **tourist office** (daily 8.30am–9.30pm; ☎0841/22 357), situated between the lake and the port, is one of the best on the island for information about accommodation.

Accommodation

The town is no longer packed solid with tourists, so it is much easier to find a place to stay, though in the peak season you will not have so much choice. One thing in your favour is that there are literally thousands of **rooms**, scattered all about town. The tourist office normally has a couple of boards with cards and brochures about hotels and rooms, including their prices. If the prices seem very reasonable it is because they are for the low season. There is no longer a youth hostel, and the nearest **campsite**, *Gournia Moon*, is 17km away at Pahiá Ámmos (see p.173).

Atlantis, (☎0841/28 964) Nothing special but handy hotel next to the bus station; it has a snack bar below for breakfast. ②.

Dias, Latous 6 (☎0841/28 263). If you can afford the extra then this is one of the best-value hotels around. ③.

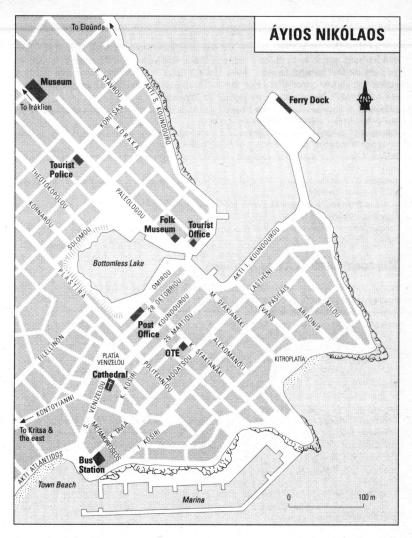

ÁYIOS NIKÓLAOS

To Eloúnda

Museum

To Iráklion

E. STAVROU

KORITSAS

KORAKA

AKTI S. KOUNDOUROU

Ferry Dock

Tourist
Police

THEOTOKOPOLOU

KORNAROU

PALEOLOGOU

SOLOMOU

PLASTIRA

Folk
Museum

Tourist
Office

Bottomless Lake

AKTI I. KOUNDOUROU

LASTHENI

PASIFAIS

EVANS

ARIADNIS

MILOU

OMIROU

28 OKTOBRIOU

KOUNDOUROU

M. SFAKIANAKI

Post
Office

25 MARTIOU

ALEXOMANÓLI

FILELLINON

OTE

MODATSOU

K. SFAKIANAKI

KITROPLATÍA

PLATÍA
VENIZELOU

POLITEHNIOU

Cathedral

VENIZELOU

K. KOSIRI

KONTOYIANNI

S. METAMORFOSSOS

K. TAVLA

KOSIRI

To Kritsa &
the east

AKTI ATLANTIDOS

Bus
Station

Town Beach

Marina

0   100 m

Green House, Modatsou 15 (☎0841/22 025). Probably the best cheap place to stay in town; clean
with shared facilities. ②.

Katerina, Stratigou Koraka 30 (☎0841/22 766). A pension close to the *Marilena* and another good
choice in the same price bracket. ②.

Lida, Salaminos 3a (☎0841/22 130). All rooms in this friendly hotel have a shower, balcony and a
partial sea-view. ④.

Loukas, Platía Venizélou 13 (☎0841/23 169). A very central location in the heart of the shopping
area of Áyios Nikólaos. ③.

Marilena, Erithrou Stavrou 14 (☎0841/22 681). One of the cheaper pensions and excellent value. ②.

Eating and drinking

At least when it comes to eating there's no chance of missing out, even if the prices are fancier than the restaurants. There are tourist-oriented **tavernas** all around the lake and harbour and little to choose between them, apart from the different perspectives you get on the passing fashion show. Have a drink here perhaps or a mid-morning coffee and choose somewhere else to eat. The places around the Kiroplatía are generally fairer value, but again you are paying for the location.

Ellinikon, on Kapetan Kozyri. A small *kafenío* with loads of character that serves traditional mountain dishes, freshly made with village raki or wine.

Ikaros and **Loukakis**, on the Elounda road, a few minutes' walk away from the port. Very competitively priced and good value tavernas, next to each other on the waterfront.

Itanos, Kyprou 1. Serves Cretan food and wine, and has a terrace across the road opposite; popular with the locals.

Pelagos, on Koraka, just back off the lake behind the tourist office. A stylish fish taverna, serving good food but at a price.

Taverna Alouasi, Paleologou 40. Serves good, traditional Cretan food in and under a plant-covered trellised courtyard, and is reasonably cheap.

Trata, corner of Sfakianaki and Tselepi. Good restaurant, with a tempting roof garden for sultry nights. Slightly more expensive than *Itanos*, but also popular with the locals.

The coast north of Áyios Nikólaos

North of Áyios Nikólaos, the swankier hotels are strung out along the coast road, with upmarket restaurants, discos and cocktail bars scattered between them. **ELOÚNDA**, a resort on a more acceptable scale, is about 8km out along this road. Buses run regularly, but if you feel like renting a moped it's a spectacular ride, with impeccable views over a gulf dotted with islands and moored supertankers. Try *Olous Travel*, next to the post office, if you want a **room** here.

Just before the village a track (signposted) leads across a causeway to the "sunken city" of **Oloús**. There are restored windmills, a short length of canal, Venetian salt pans and a well-preserved dolphin mosaic, but of the sunken city itself no trace beyond a couple of walls in about two feet of water. At any rate swimming is good, though there are sea urchins to watch out for.

From Eloúnda, *kaíkia* run to the fortress-rock of **Spinalónga**. As a bastion of the Venetian defence, this tiny islet withstood the Turkish invaders for 45 years after the mainland had fallen; in more recent decades, it served as a leper colony. As you watch the boat which brought you disappear to pick up another group, an unnervingly real sense of the desolation of those years descends over the place. **PLÁKA**, back on the mainland, used to be the colony's supply point; now it is a haven from the crowds, with a small pebble beach and a couple of ramshackle tavernas. There are boat trips daily from Áyios Nikólaos to Oloús, Eloúnda and Spinalónga, usually visiting at least one other island along the way.

Inland to Kritsá and Lató

The other excursion everyone from Áyios Nikólaos takes is to **KRITSÁ**, a "traditional" village about 10km inland. Buses run at least every hour from the bus station, and despite the commercialization it's still a good trip: the local crafts (weaving, ceramics and embroidery basically, though they sell almost everything here) are fair value and it's also a welcome break from living in the fast lane at "Ag Nik". In fact, if you're looking for somewhere to stay around here, Kritsá has a number of advantages: chiefly availability of **rooms**, better prices, and something at least approaching a genuinely Greek atmosphere; try *Argyro* (☎0841/51 174; ②) on your way to the village. There are a number of decent places to eat, too, or just to have a coffee and a cake under one of the plane trees.

On the approach road, some 2km before Kritsá, is the lovely Byzantine **church of Panayía Kirá** (Mon–Sat 9am–3pm, Sun 9am–2pm; 400dr), inside which are preserved perhaps the most complete set of Byzantine frescoes in Crete. The fourteenth- and fifteenth-century works have been much retouched, but they're still worth the visit. Excellent (and expensive) reproductions are sold from a shop alongside. Just beyond the church, a metalled road leads off towards the archeological site of **Lató** (daily except Mon 8.30am–3pm), a Doric city with a grand hilltop setting. The city itself is extensive, but neglected, presumably because visitors and archeologists on Crete are concerned only with the Minoan era. Ruins aside, you could come here just for the views: west over Áyios Nikólaos and beyond to the bay and Oloús (which was Lató's port), and inland to the Lasíthi mountains.

The eastern isthmus

The main road south and then east from Áyios Nikólaos is not a wildly exciting one, essentially a drive through barren hills sprinkled with villas and above the occasional sandy cove. Five kilometres beyond a cluster of development at Kaló Hório, a track is signed on the right for the **Moní Faneroméni**. The track is a rough one and climbs dizzily skywards for 6km, giving spectacular views over the Gulf of Mirabélo along the way. The view from the monastery itself must be the among the finest in Crete. To get into the rather bleak-looking monastery buildings, knock loudly. You will be shown up to the chapel, built into a cave sanctuary, and the frescoes are quite brilliant.

Gourniá, Pahiá Ámmos and Móhlos

Back on the coast road, another 2km brings you to the site of **Gourniá** (daily except Mon 8.30am–3pm; 400dr), slumped in the saddle between two low peaks. The most completely preserved Minoan town, its narrow alleys and stairways intersect a throng of one-roomed houses centred on a main square and the house of the local ruler. Although less impressive than the great palaces, the site is strong on revelations about the lives of the ordinary people ruled from Knossós. Its desolation today (you are likely to be alone save for a dozing guard) only serves to heighten the contrast with what must have been a cramped and raucous community 3500 years ago.

It is tempting to cross the road here and take one of the paths through the wild thyme to the sea for a swim. Don't bother – the bay and others along this part of the coastline act as a magnet for every piece of floating detritus dumped off Crete's north coast. There is a larger beach, and rooms to rent, in the next bay along at **PAHIÁ ÁMMOS**, about twenty minutes' walk, where there is also an excellent fish taverna, *Aiolus*; or in the other direction, there's the campsite of *Gournia Moon*, with its own small cove and its own swimming pool.

This is the narrowest part of the island, and from here a fast new road cuts across the isthmus to Ierápetra in the south. In the north, though, the route on towards Sitía is one of the most exhilarating in Crete. Carved into cliffs and mountainsides, the road teeters above the coast before plunging inland at Kavoúsi. Of the beaches you see below, only **MÓHLOS** is at all accessible, some 5km below the main road. This sleepy village has a few rooms, a hotel or two and a number of tavernas; if you find yourself staying the night, try the rooms at *Limenaria* (☎0841/94 206; ②). Nearer Sitía the familiar olive groves are interspersed with vineyards, and in late summer the grapes, spread to dry in the fields and on rooftops, make an extraordinary sight in the varying stages of their slow change from green to gold to brown.

Sitía

SITÍA is the port and main town of the relatively unexploited eastern edge of Crete. It's a pleasant if unremarkable place, offering a plethora of waterside restaurants, a long sandy beach and a lazy lifestyle little affected even by the thousands of visitors in peak season. There's an almost Latin feel to the town, reflected in (or perhaps caused by) the number of French and Italian tourists, and it's one of those places you may end up

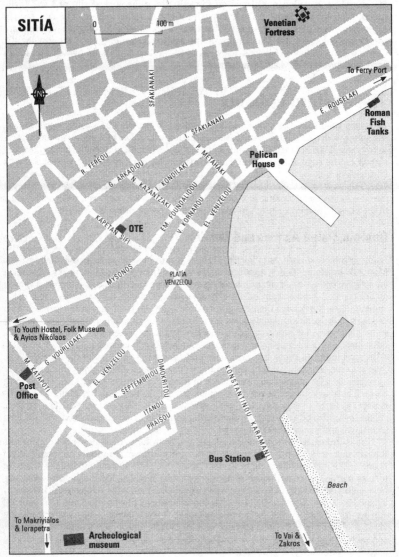

SITÍA

0   100 m

Venetian Fortress

To Ferry Port

SFAKIANAKI

Roman Fish Tanks

E. ROUSELAKI

I. SFAKIANAKI

P. METAHAKI

Pelican House

R. FEREOU

G. ARKADIOU

N. KAZANTZAKI

I. KONDILAKI

EM. FOUNDALIDOU

V. KORNAROU

EL. VENIZELOU

KAPETAN SIFI

OTE

MYSONOS

PLATÍA VENIZELOU

To Youth Hostel, Folk Museum & Ayios Nikólaos

M. KATAPOTI

G. VOURLIDAKI

EL. VENIZELOU

4. SEPTEMBRIOU

DIMOKRITOU

ITANOU

PRAISOU

KONSTANTINOU KARAMANLI

Post Office

Bus Station

Beach

To Makriyiálos & Ierapetra

Archeological museum

To Vai & Zakros

staying longer than you intended. For entertainment, there's the **beach**, providing good swimming and windsurfing; or in town a mildly entertaining **folklore museum** (Tues, Thurs & Fri 9am–1pm & 5–8pm, Wed 9am–1pm, Sat 5–8pm; closed Mon & Sun), a Venetian fort and Roman fish tanks to explore, and an interesting **archeological museum** (Tues–Sat 8.45am–3pm, Sun 9.30am–2pm; 400dr). Look out, too, for the town's resident pelicans, Níkos and Alítis.

Practicalities

There are plenty of cheap pensions and **rooms**, especially in the streets around the OTE, a good **youth hostel** (☎0843/22 693; ①) on the main road as it enters town, and rarely any problem about sleeping on the beach (though it is worth going a little way out of town to avoid any danger of being rousted by police). For rooms, try *Pension Venus*, Kondhiláki 60 (☎0843/24 307; ②), *Hotel Arhontiko*, Kondhiláki 16 (☎0843/28 172; ②), and *Hotel Nora*, Rouselaki 31 (☎0843/23 017; ②), near the ferry port; if you have problems finding somewhere to stay, the **tourist police** at Mysonos 24 in the centre of town may be able to help.

For **food**, the waterside places are expensive enough to make you careful about what you eat; best value here is *Remegio*, or there are cheaper options in the streets behind, including a couple of excellent ice-cream parlours. **Nightlife** centres on a few bars and discos near the ferry dock and out along the beach. The one major excitement of the year is the August **Sultana Festival** – a celebration of the big local export, with traditional dancing and all the locally produced wine you can consume included in the entrance to the fairground.

Onward to Vái beach and Palékastro

Leaving Sitía along the beach, the Vái road climbs above a rocky, unexceptional coastline before reaching a fork to the **Monastery of Toploú**. The monastery's forbidding exterior reflects a history of resistance to invaders, but doesn't prepare you for the gorgeous flower-decked cloister within. The blue-robed monks keep out of the way as far as possible, but their cells and refectory are left discreetly on view. In the church is one of the masterpieces of Cretan art, the eighteenth-century icon *Lord Thou Art Great*. Outside you can buy enormously expensive reproductions.

Vái beach itself features alongside Knossós or the Lasíthi plateau on almost every Cretan travel agent's list of excursions. Not surprisingly, it is now covered in sunbeds and umbrellas, though it is still a superb beach. Above all, it is famous for its palm trees, and the sudden appearance of the grove is indeed an exotic shock. Lying on the fine sand in the early morning, the illusion of a Caribbean island is hard to dismiss. As everywhere, notices warn that "Camping is forbidden by law"; for once the authorities seem to mean it and most campers climb over the headlands to the south or north. If you do sleep out, watch your belongings since this seems to be the one place on Crete with crime on any scale. There's a café and an expensive taverna at the beach, plus toilets and showers. By day you can find a bit more solitude by climbing the rocks or swimming to one of the smaller beaches which surround Vái. **Ítanos**, twenty minutes' walk north by an obvious trail, has a couple of tiny beaches and some modest ruins of the Classical era.

PALÉKASTRO, some 9km south, is in many ways a better place to stay. Although its beaches can't begin to compare, you'll find several modest places with rooms, a number of reasonable restaurants (good rooms and food at the *Hotel Hellas*; ☎0843/61 240; ②), and plenty of space to camp out without the crowds; the sea is a couple of kilometres down a dirt track. Palékastro is also the crossroads for the road south to Zákros.

Zákros

ZÁKROS town is a little under 20km from Palékastro, at the end of the paved road. There are several tavernas and a hotel, the *Zakros* (☎0843/61 284; ③), in the village that seems to have seen better days, but the Minoan palace is actually at Káto Zákros, 8km further down a newly paved road to the sea. Most buses run only to the upper village, but in summer, a couple every day do run all the way to the site. Part way along you can, if on foot, take a short cut through an impressive **gorge** (the "Valley of the Dead", named for ancient tombs in its sides) but it's usually not difficult to hitch if your bus does leave you in the village.

The **palace of Zákros** (daily except Mon 8.30am–3pm; 400dr) was an important find for archeologists; it had been occupied only once, and abandoned hurriedly and completely. Later, it was forgotten almost entirely and as a result was never plundered or even discovered by archeologists until very recently. The first major excavation began only in 1960; all sorts of everyday objects (tools, raw materials, food, pottery) were thus discovered intact among the ruins, and a great deal was learned from being able to apply modern techniques (and knowledge of the Minoans) to a major dig from the very beginning. None of this is especially evident when you're at the palace, except perhaps in a particularly simple ground plan, so it's as well that it is also a rewarding visit in terms of the setting. Although the site is some way from the sea, parts of it are often marshy and waterlogged: partly the result of eastern Crete's slow subsidence, partly the fault of a spring which once supplied fresh water to a cistern beside the royal apartments, and whose outflow is now silted up. Among the remains of narrow streets and small houses higher up, you can keep your feet dry and get an excellent view down over the central court and royal apartments. If you want a more detailed overview of the remains, buy the guide to the site on sale at the entrance.

The village of **KÁTO ZÁKROS** is little more than a collection of tavernas, some of which rent out rooms around a peaceful beach and minuscule fishing anchorage. It's a wonderfully restful place, but it is often unable to cope with the volume of visitors seeking rooms in high season. The *Poseidon* (☎0843/93 316; ③) has good views.

Ierápetra and the southeast coast

From Sitía, the route south is a cross-country roller-coaster ride until it hits the south coast at **MAKRIYIALÓS**. This little fishing village has one of the best beaches at this end of Crete, with fine sand which shelves so gently you feel you could walk the 340km to Africa. Unfortunately, in the last few years it has been heavily developed, so while still a very pleasant place to stop for a swim or a bite, it's not somewhere you're likely to find a cheap room.

From here to Ierápetra, there's little reason to stop; the few beaches are rocky and the coastal plain submerged under ranks of polythene-covered greenhouses. One exception, however, is **Dasaki Butterfly Gorge**, which although affected by forest fires in recent years is certainly worth a visit. Beyond here, beside the road leading in to Ierápetra, are long but exposed stretches of sand, including the appropriately named "Long Beach", where you'll find a campsite, *Camping Koutsounar* (☎0842/61 213), which has plenty of shade.

Ierápetra

IERÁPETRA itself is a cheerless modern supply centre for the region's farmers. It also attracts an amazing number of package tourists and not a few backpackers looking for work, especially out of season. The tavernas along the tree-lined front are scenic enough and the beach, its remotest extremities rarely visited, stretches for a couple of miles to the east. But as a town, most people find it pretty uninspiring. Although there has been a port here since Roman times, only the **Venetian fort** guarding the harbour and a crumbling minaret remain as reminders of better days. What little else has been salvaged is in the one-room **museum** (Tues–Sat 8.30am–2.30pm; 400dr) near the post office.

If you want to stay, head up Kazantzakís from the chaotic bus station, and you'll find **rooms** at the *Four Seasons* (☎0842/24 390; ③); nearby is the *Cretan Villa*, Lakerda 16 (☎0842/26 522; ③), a beautiful 180-year-old house. More central, and also good value, is the *Hotel Ersi*, Platía Eleftherías 20 (☎0842/23 208; ②). You'll find places to **eat and drink** all along the waterfront (the better places being towards the Venetian fort); there is a clutch of bars and fast-food places along the central Kyrba, behind the promenade.

West from Ierápetra

Heading west from Ierápetra, the first stretch of coast is grey and dusty, the road jammed with trucks and lined with drab ribbon development. There are a number of small resorts along the beach, though little in the way of public transport. If travelling under your own steam, there is a scenic detour worth taking at Gra Ligiá. The road, on the right, is signed for Anatolí and climbs to Máles, a village clinging to the lower slopes of the **Dhíkti range**. Here would be a good starting point if you wanted to take a walk through some stunning mountain terrain. Otherwise, the dirt road back down towards the coast (signed Míthi) has spectacular views over the Libyan Sea, and eventually follows the Mírtos river valley down to Mírtos itself.

Mírtos and Árvi

MÍRTOS is the first resort that might actually tempt you to stop, and it's certainly the most accessible, just off the main road with numerous **buses** to Ierápetra daily and a couple direct to Iráklion. Although developed to a degree, it nonetheless remains tranquil and inexpensive, with lots of young travellers (many of them sleeping on the beach, to the irritation of locals). If you want a **room**, try *Rooms Angelos* (☎0842/51 106; ②) or *Rooms Mertini* (☎0842/51 386; ②), though there are plenty of others. Just off the road from Ierápetra are a couple of excavated **Minoan villas** you might want to explore: Néa Mírtos and Pírgos.

After Mírtos the main road turns inland towards Áno Viánnos, then continues across the island towards Iráklion; several places on the coast are reached by a series of rough side tracks. That hasn't prevented one of them, **ÁRVI**, from becoming a larger resort than Mírtos. The beach hardly justifies it, but it's an interesting little excursion (with at least one bus a day) if only to see the bananas and pineapples grown here and to experience the microclimate (noticeably warmer than neighbouring zones, especially in spring or autumn) that encourages them.

Beyond Árvi

Two more villages, **KERATÓKAMBOS** and **TSOÚTSOUROS**, look tempting on the map. The first has a rather stony beach and only the most basic of rooms available, but it's popular with Cretan day-trippers and great if you want to escape from the tourist grind for a spell. The second is developed and not really worth the tortuous thirteen-kilometre dirt road in.

If you hope to continue across the south of the island, be warned that there are no buses, despite completion of the road towards Míres after years of work. It's an enjoyable, rural drive, but progress can be slow; there's very little traffic if you're trying to hitch.

RÉTHIMNON AND AROUND

The relatively low, narrow section of Crete which separates the Psilorítis range from the White Mountains in the west seems at first a nondescript, even dull part of the island. Certainly in scenic terms it has few of the excitements that the west can offer, there are no major archeological sites as in the east and many of the villages seem modern and ugly. On the other hand, **Réthimnon** itself is an attractive and lively city, with some excellent beaches nearby. And on the south coast, in particular around **Plakiás**, are beaches as fine as any Crete can offer, and as you drive towards them the scenery and villages improve by the minute.

Réthimnon

In the past ten years or so, **RÉTHIMNON** has seen a greater influx of tourists than perhaps anywhere else on Crete, with the development of a whole series of large hotels extending almost 10km along the beach to the east. For once, though, the middle of town has been spared, so that at its heart Réthimnon remains one of the most beautiful of Crete's major cities (with only Haniá as a serious rival), with an enduringly provincial air. A wide sandy beach and palm-lined promenade border a labyrinthine tangle of Venetian and Turkish houses lining streets where ancient minarets lend an exotic air to the skyline. Dominating everything from the west, is the superbly preserved outline of the fortress built by the Venetians after a series of pirate raids had devastated the town.

The Town

With a beach right in the heart of town, it's tempting not to stir at all from the sands, but Réthimnon repays at least some gentle exploration. For a start, you could try checking out the further reaches of the **beach** itself. The waters protected by the breakwaters in front of town have their disadvantages, notably crowds and dubious hygiene, but less sheltered sands stretch for miles to the east, crowded at first but progressively less so if you're prepared to walk a bit.

Away from the beach, you don't have far to go for the most atmospheric part of town, immediately behind the **inner harbour**. Almost anywhere here, you'll find unexpected old buildings, wall fountains, overhanging wooden balconies, heavy, carved doors and rickety shops, many still with local craftsmen sitting out front, gossiping as they ply their trades. Look out especially for the **Venetian loggia**, now being converted into a library (it used to house the town museum); the **Rimóndi fountain**, another of the more elegant Venetian survivals; and the **Nerandzes mosque**, best preserved of several in Réthimnon, whose minaret you can climb (daily 11am–7pm; closed Aug) for excellent free views over the town and surrounding countryside. Simply by walking past these three, you'll have seen many of the liveliest parts of Réthimnon. Ethníkis Andistásis, the street leading straight up from the fountain, is also the town's **market** area.

The old city ends at the Porta Guora at the top of Andistásis, the only surviving remnant of the city walls. Almost opposite are the quiet and shady **Public Gardens**. These are always a soothing place to stroll, but most visitors only bother in the latter half of July, when the **Réthimnon Wine Festival** is staged here. Though touristy, it's a thoroughly enjoyable event, with spectacular local dancing as the evening progresses and the barrels empty. The entrance fee includes all the wine you can drink, though you'll need to bring your own cup or else buy one of the souvenir glasses and carafes on sale outside the gardens.

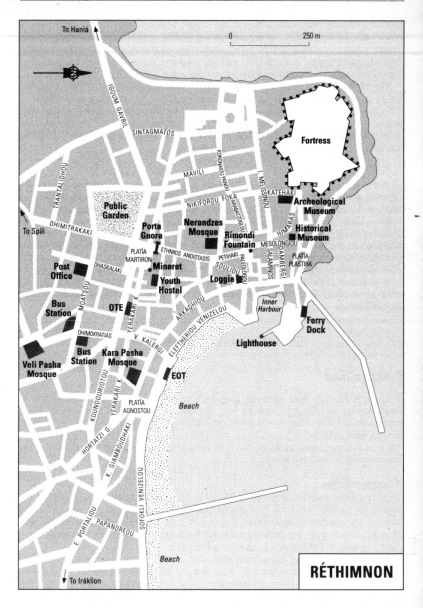

To Haniá

0   250 m

To Spili

To Iráklion

RÉTHIMNON

Map labels:
- IGOUM GAVRIL
- SINTAGMATOS
- TRANDALIDHOU
- MAVILI
- KORNAROU PANOU
- I. MELISSINOU
- SKATEHAKI
- Fortress
- DHIMITRAKAKI
- Public Garden
- NIKIFOROU FOKA
- SARADZOGLOU
- Archeological Museum
- Porta Guora
- Nerandzes Mosque
- Rimondi Fountain
- MESOLONGIOU
- Historical Museum
- HIMARAS
- DAMBERGI
- SALAMINOS
- PLATÍA MARTIRON
- ETHNIKIS ANDISTASIS
- PETIHAKI
- PALEOLOGOU
- PLATÍA PLASTIRA
- DHASKALAKI
- Minaret
- SOULIOU
- Post Office
- MOATSOU
- Youth Hostel
- Loggia
- Inner Harbour
- Bus Station
- OTE
- YERAKARI K.
- ARKADHIOU
- Ferry Dock
- DHIMOKRATIAS
- V. KALERGI
- ELEFTHERIOU VENIZELOU
- Lighthouse
- Bus Station
- Kara Pasha Mosque
- Veli Pasha Mosque
- KOUNDOURIOTOU
- YERAKARI K.
- EOT
- PLATÍA AGNOSTOU
- Beach
- HORTATZI G.
- K. GIAMBOUDHAKI
- SOFOKLI VENIZELOU
- E. PORTALIOU
- PAPANDREOU
- Beach

The museums and fortress

Heading in the other direction from the fountain, you can approach the mighty fortress via two interesting museums. The **Historical and Folk Art Museum** (daily except Mon 9am–1pm), on Mesolongíou, is small but tremendously enjoyable. Gathered within its two modest rooms are musical instruments, old photos, basketry, farm implements, an explanation of traditional bread-making techniques, smiths' tools, traditional costumes and jewellery, lace, weaving and embroidery, pottery, knives and old wooden chests. It makes for a fascinating insight into a fast disappearing rural (and urban) lifestyle, which had often survived virtually unchanged from Venetian times to the 1960s, and is well worth a look.

The **archeological museum** (daily except Mon 8.30am–3pm; 400dr, Sun free) occupies a newly converted building almost directly opposite the entrance to the fortress. This was built by the Turks as an extra defence for the entry, and later served as a prison, but it's now entirely modern inside: cool, spacious and airy. Unfortunately, the collection is not particularly exciting, and really only worth seeing if you're going to miss the bigger museums elsewhere on the island.

The massive **Venetian Fortress** (daily 9am–4pm; 200dr) is a must, however. Said to be the largest Venetian castle ever built, this was a response, in the last quarter of the sixteenth century, to a series of pirate raids (by Barbarossa among others) that had devastated the town. Inside now is a vast open space dotted with the remains of all sorts of barracks, arsenals, officers' houses, earthworks and deep shafts, and at the centre a large domed building that was once a church and later a mosque. It was designed to be large enough for the entire population to take shelter within the walls, and you can see that it probably was. Although much is ruined, it remains thoroughly atmospheric, and you can look out from the walls over the town and harbour, or in the other direction along the coast to the west. It's also worth walking around the outside of the fortress, preferably at sunset, to get an impression of its fearsome defences, plus great views along the coast and a pleasant resting point around the far side at the *Sunset Taverna*.

The telephone code for Réthimnon is ☎0831

Practicalities

Réthimnon has two **bus stations** diagonally opposite each other at the corner of Dhimokratías and Moátsou, one for long-distance and north-coast services, the other for trans-island and village buses. From here walk north towards the sea; the waterside **tourist office** (Mon–Fri 8am–3.30pm; ☎29 148) will be in front of you when you get to the beach. If you arrive by **ferry**, you'll be even more conveniently placed, over at the western edge of the harbour.

Accommodation

There's a great number of places to stay in Réthimnon, and only at the height of the season are you likely to have difficulty finding somewhere; though you may get weary looking. The greatest concentration of **rooms** is in the tangled streets west of the inner harbour, between the Rimóndi fountain and the museums; there are also quite a few places on and around Arkadhíou and Platía Frakidaki.

There are a couple of **campsites** 4km east of town. Take the bus for the hotels (marked *Scaleta/El Greco*) from the long-distance bus station to get there. *Camping Elizabeth* (☎28 694) is a pleasant, large site on the beach, with all facilities. Only a few hundred metres further east along the beach is *Camping Arkadia* (☎28 825), a bigger and slightly less friendly site.

Anna, Katehaki (☎25 586). Comfortable pension in a quiet position on the street that runs straight down from the entrance to the fortress to Melissinou. ④.

Atelier, Himáras 32 (☎24 440). Pleasant rooms close to *Rooms George*, run by a talented potter, who has her studio in the basement and sells her wares in a shop on the other side of the building. ③.

Barbara Dokimaki, Plastíra 14 (☎22 319). Strange warren of a rooms place, with one entrance at the above address, just off the seafront behind the *Ideon*, and another on Dambergi, opposite *Corina*; some excellent rooms. ③.

Byzantine, Vosporou 26 (☎55 609). Excellent-value rooms in a renovated old Byzantine palace. The tranquil patio bar is open to all. ④.

Corina, Dambergi 9 (☎26 911). Very friendly pension with a couple of good balcony rooms at the front, several darker ones behind. ③.

Ideon, Platía Plastíra 10 (☎28 667). Hotel with a brilliant position just north of the ferry dock; little chance of space in season, though. ⑥.

Leo, Vafíou 2 (☎29 851). Good hotel with lots of wood and traditional feel. Price includes breakfast, and there's a good bar. ④.

Réthimnon Haus, V. Kornarou 1 (☎23 923). Very pleasant, upmarket rooms place in an old building just off Arkadhíou. Bar downstairs. ③.

Rooms George, Makedonias 32 (☎27 540). Decent rooms (some with fridge), near the archeological museum. ③.

Vrisinas, Heréti 10 (☎26 092). Pension in a narrow street parallel to Kalérgi, worth checking as you walk from the bus station, but often full. Lovely rooms, though some are noisy. ③.

Youth hostel, Tombázi 41 (☎22 848). Cheapest beds in town are in the youth hostel dormitories (or on the roof). It's large, clean, very friendly and popular, and there's food, showers, clothes-washing facilities and even a library of books in an assortment of languages. ①.

Zania, 3 Pavlou Vlastou (☎28 169). Pension right on the corner of Arkadhíou by the old youth hostel building; a well-adapted old house, but only a few rooms. ③.

Eating and drinking

Immediately behind the town **beach** are arrayed the most touristy restaurants. One that maintains its integrity (and reasonable prices) is *Taverna Samaria*, almost opposite the tourist office. Around the **inner harbour**, there's a second, rather more expensive group of tavernas, specializing in fish, though as often as not the intimate atmosphere in these places is spoilt by the stench from the harbour itself: *O Zefyros* and *Seven Brothers* are two of the less outrageously pricey of these.

The cluster of *kafenía* and tavernas **by the Rimóndi fountain** and the newer places spreading into the surrounding streets generally offer considerably better value. A couple of the old-fashioned *kafenía* serve magnificent yoghurt and honey. Places to try include *Kyria María* at Moshovitou 20, tucked down an alley behind the fountain (after the meal, everyone gets a couple of Maria's delicious *tiropitákia* with honey on the house); *Agrimi*, a reliable standard on Platía Petiháki; and the *Zanfoti kafenío* overlooking the fountain, relatively expensive, but a great place to people-watch over a coffee, and with good yogurt and honey, too. Slightly cheaper places in the surrounding back-streets include *Stelios Soumbasakis*, a simple, friendly taverna at Nikiforou Foka 98, corner of Koronaíou; and *Taverna Haroulas Kargaki*, Melissinou by Mesolongíou, for big, cheap breakfasts plus standard taverna fare at reasonable prices. A good lunchtime stop close to the archeological museum is *O Pontios*, Melissinou 34, a simple place with tables outside and an enthusiastic female proprietor. A noisier evening alternative is *Taverna O Gounos* at Koroneou 6 in the old town, where the family running it perform live *lyra* every night. When things get really lively the dancing starts.

If you want takeaway food, there are numerous **souvláki** stalls, including a couple on Arkadhíou and Paleológou and *O Platanos* at Petiháki 44, or you can buy your own ingredients at the **market** stalls set up daily on Andistásis below the Porta Guora. There are small general stores scattered everywhere, particularly on Paleológou and Arkadhíou; east along the beach road you'll even find a couple of mini supermarkets. The **bakery** *I Gaspari*, on Mesolongíou just behind the Rimóndi fountain, sells the usual cheese pies, cakes and the like, and it also bakes excellent brown, black and rye bread. There's a good *zaharoplasteío* on Petiháki.

Nightlife

Nightlife is concentrated in the same general areas as the tavernas. At the west end of Venizélou, approaching the inner harbour, a small cluster of noisy **music bars** rock the beach – *Rouli's* is one of the liveliest. Several glitzier bar/discos, including *Fortezza* and *Metropolis*, gather on an alley between the inner harbour and Arkadhíou. Larger **discos** are mostly out to the east, among the big hotels, but there are one or two in town. *Odysseas*, on Venizélou right by the inner harbour, is a touristy Cretan music and dancing place, with live performances every evening from 9.30pm.

Around Réthimnon

While some of Crete's most drastic resort development spreads ever eastwards out of Réthimnon, to the west a sandy coastline, not yet greatly exploited, runs all the way to the borders of Haniá. But of all the short trips that can be made out of Réthimnon, the best known and still the most worthwhile is to the **monastery of Arkádhi**.

Southeast to Arkádhi

The **monastery of Arkádhi** (daily 6am–8pm), some 25km southeast of the city and immaculately situated in the foothills of the Psilorítis range, is also something of a national Cretan shrine. During the 1866 rebellion against the Turks, the monastery became a rebel strongpoint in which, as the Turks gained the upper hand, hundreds of Cretan guerrillas and their families took refuge. Surrounded and, after two days of fighting, on the point of defeat, the defenders ignited a powder magazine just as the Turks entered. Hundreds (some sources claim thousands) were killed, Cretan and Turk alike, and the tragedy did much to promote international sympathy for the cause of Cretan independence. Nowadays, you can peer into the roofless vault where the explosion occurred and wander about the rest of the well-restored grounds. The sixteenth-century Rococo church survived, and is one of the finest Venetian structures left on Crete; other buildings house a small museum devoted to the exploits of the defenders of the (Orthodox) faith. The monastery is easy to visit by public bus or on a tour.

West to Yioryoúpoli and beyond

Leaving Réthimnon to the west, the main road climbs for a while above a rocky coastline before descending (after some 5km) to the sea, where it runs alongside sandy **beaches** for perhaps another 7km. An occasional hotel and a campsite (*George*) offer accommodation, but on the whole there's nothing but a line of straggly bushes between the road and the windswept sands. If you have your own vehicle, there are plenty of places to stop here for a swim, and rarely anyone else around – but beware of some very strong currents.

If you want to stay for any time, virtually the only base is **YIORYOÚPOLI** at the far end, where the beach is cleaner, wider and further from the road. It's not exactly unknown, but neither is it heavily developed. If you're after a base for a few days that's peaceful but not too quiet, there are a lot of **rooms** for rent and several **hotels**, well used in mid-season. Most of the better rooms are found by heading for the main *platía* and then looking along the road down towards the beach. More central possibilities include *Rooms Voula* (☎0825/61 359; ③), above a gift shop to the east of the *platía*, or the *Paradise Taverna* (☎0825/61 313; ③), which has rooms and is a good place to eat, off the southeast corner of the *platía*.

Within walking distance inland is **Kournás**, Crete's only lake, set deep in a bowl of hills and almost constantly changing colour. There's a taverna on the shore with a few rooms for rent, or you could try for a bed in the nearby village of Moúri.

Beyond Yioryoúpoli, the main road heads inland, away from a cluster of coastal villages beyond Vámos. It thus misses the Dhrápano peninsula, with some spectacular views over the sapphire Bay of Soudha, several quiet beaches and the setting for the film of *Zorba the Greek*. **KÓKKINO HORIÓ**, the movie location, and nearby **PLÁKA** are indeed postcard-picturesque (more so from a distance), but **KEFALÁS**, inland, outdoes both of them. On the exposed north coast there are beaches at **ALMIRÍDHA** and **KALÍVES**, and off the road between them. Both have quite a few apartments but not many rooms available; Almirídha, though, makes an enjoyable lunch stop.

South from Réthimnon

There are a couple of alternative routes south from Réthimnon, but the main one heads straight out from the centre of town, an initially featureless road due south across the middle of the island towards Ayía Galíni. About 23km out, a turning cuts off to the right for Plakiás and Mírthios, following the course of the spectacular Kourtaliótiko ravine.

Plakiás and the south coast

PLAKIÁS has undergone a major boom and is no longer the pristine village all too many people arriving here expect. That said, it's still quite low key, there's a satisfactory beach and a string of good tavernas around the dock. There are hundreds of **rooms**, but at the height of summer you'll need to arrive early if you hope to find one; the last to fill are generally those on the road leading inland, away from the waterside. Try *Rooms Nefeli* (③) at the end of the road inland behind *Candia Tours*. If needed, there's a **youth hostel** (☎0832/31 306; ①) on the edge of town. The beach is long and nobody is likely to mind if you sleep out on the middle section – but Damnóni (see below) is far better if that's your plan.

Once you've found a room there's not a lot else to discover here. You'll find every facility strung out around the waterfront, including a temporary post office, bike rental, money exchange, supermarket and even launderette. Places to eat are plentiful, too. The attractive **tavernas** on the waterfront in the centre are a little expensive; you'll eat cheaper further inland, or around the corner at one of the tavernas facing west (*Julia's Place*, here, has good vegetarian food).

Mírthios
For a stay of more than a day or two, **MÍRTHIOS**, in the hills behind Plakiás, also deserves consideration. It's no longer a great deal cheaper, but at least you'll find locals still outnumbering the tourists and something of a travellers' scene based around another popular **youth hostel** (☎0832/31 202; ①), with a friendly taverna and several rooms for rent. The Plakiás bus will usually loop back through Mírthios, but check; otherwise, it's less than five minutes' walk from the junction. It takes twenty minutes to walk down to the beach at Plakiás, a little longer to Damnóni, and if you're prepared to walk for an hour or more, there are some entirely isolated coves to the west – ask directions at the hostel.

Damnóni
Some of the most tempting beaches in central Crete hide just to the east of Plakiás, though unfortunately they're now a very poorly kept secret. These three splashes of yellow sand, divided by rocky promontories, are within easy walking distance and together go by the name **DAMNÓNI**. At the first, Damnóni proper, there's a taverna

with showers and a wonderfully long strip of sand, but there's also a lot of new development including a number of nearby rooms for rent and a huge new German hotel, which has colonized half of the main beach. At the far end, you'll generally find a few people who've dispensed with their clothes, while the little cove which shelters the middle of the three beaches (barely accessible except on foot) is entirely nudist. Beyond this, Ammoúdhi beach has another taverna (with good rooms for rent) and a slightly more family atmosphere. All these are considerably more attractive than Plakiás's own beach, though you'd have less far to walk, and probably spend less, staying in the village of **LEFKÓYIA**, 2km away. The disadvantages are that Lefkóyia is not itself on the coast, and besides a couple of tavernas and four or five places renting **rooms**, it has no facilities at all.

Préveli and "Palm Beach"

Next in line comes **PRÉVELI**, some 6km southeast of Lefkóyia. It takes its name from a **monastery** (daily 8am–1pm & 3–7pm) high above the sea which, like every other in Crete, has a proud history of resistance, in this case, accentuated by its role in the last war as a shelter for marooned Allied soldiers awaiting evacuation off the south coast. There are fine views and a monument commemorating the rescue operations, but little else to see. The evacuations took place from **"Palm Beach"**, a sandy cove with a small date-palm grove and solitary drink stand where a stream feeds a little oasis. The beach usually attracts a summer camping community and is now also the target of day-trip boats from Plakiás. Sadly, these two groups between them have left this lovely place filthy, and despite a belated clean-up campaign it seems barely worth the effort. The climb down from the monastery is steep, rocky and surprisingly arduous; if you do come, it's a great deal easier on the boat.

Spíli and Ayía Galíni

Back on the main road south, **SPÍLI** lies about 30km from Réthimnon. A popular coffee break for tours passing this way, Spíli warrants time if you can spare it. Sheltered under a cliff are narrow alleys of ancient houses, all leading up from a *platía* with a famous 24-spouted fountain. If you have your own transport, it's a worthwhile place to stay, peacefully rural at night but with several good **rooms** for rent. Try the *Green Hotel* (☎0832/22 056; ③) or the pleasant and cheaper *Rooms Herakles* (☎0832/22 411; ②) just behind.

The ultimate destination of most people on this road is **AYÍA GALÍNI**. If heading here was your plan, maybe you should think again since this picturesque "fishing village" is so busy that you can't see it for the tour buses, hotel billboards and British package tourists. It also has a beach much too small for the crowds that congregate here. Even so, there are some saving graces – mainly some excellent restaurants and bars, plenty of rooms and a friendly atmosphere that survives and even thrives on all the visitors. Out of season, it can be quite enjoyable, and from November to April the mild climate makes it an ideal spot to spend the winter. A lot of long-term travellers do just that, so it's a good place to find work packing tomatoes or polishing cucumbers. If you want somewhere to stay, start looking at the top end of town, around the main road: the good-value *Hotel Minos* (☎0832/91 292; ②) with superb views is a good place to start, but there are dozens of possibilities, and usually something to be found even at the height of summer.

The coastal plain east of Ayía Galíni, hidden under acres of polythene greenhouses and burgeoning concrete sprawl, must be among the ugliest regions in Crete, and Timbáki the dreariest town. Since this is the way to Festós and back to Iráklion, however, you may have no choice but to grin and bear it.

The Amári Valley

An alternative route south from Réthimnon, and a far less travelled one, is the road which turns off on the eastern fringe of town to run via the **Amári Valley**. Very few buses go this way, but if you're driving it's well worth the extra time. There's little specifically to see or do (though hidden away are a number of frescoed Byzantine churches), but it's an impressive drive under the flanks of the mountains and a reminder of how, in places, rural Crete continues to exist regardless of visitors. The countryside here is delightfully green even in summer, with rich groves of olive and assorted fruit trees, and if you **stay** (there are rooms in Thrónos and Yerákari) the nights are cool and quiet. It may seem odd that many of the villages along the way are modern; they were systematically destroyed by the Germans in reprisal for the 1944 kidnapping of General Kreipe.

HANIÁ AND THE WEST

The substantial attractions of Crete's westernmost quarter are all the more enhanced by its relative lack of visitors; and despite the now-rapid spread of tourist development, the west is likely to remain one of the emptier parts of the island. This is partly because there are no big sandy beaches to accommodate resort hotels, and partly because it's so far from the great archeological sites. But for mountains and empty (if often pebbly) beaches, it's unrivalled.

Haniá itself is one of the best reasons to come here, perhaps the only Cretan city which could be described as enjoyable in itself. The immediately adjacent coast is relatively developed and not overly exciting; if you want beaches head for the **south coast**. **Paleohóra** is the only place which could really be described as a resort, and even this is on a thoroughly human scale; others are emptier still. **Ayía Rouméli** and **Loutró** can be reached only on foot or by boat; **Hóra Sfakíon** sees hordes passing through but few who stay; **Frangokástello**, nearby, has a beautiful castle and the first stirrings of development. Behind these lie the **Lefká Óri** (White Mountains) and, above all, the famed walk through the **Gorge of Samariá**.

Haniá

HANIÁ, as any of its residents will tell you, is the spiritual capital of Crete, even if the nominal title has passed (in 1971) to Iráklion. For many, it is also by far the island's most attractive city, especially if you can catch it in spring, when the Lefká Óri's snow-capped peaks seem to hover above the roofs. Although it is for the most part a modern city, you might never know it as a tourist. Surrounding the small outer harbour is a wonderful jumble of half-derelict Venetian streets that survived the wartime bombardments, and it is here that life for the visitor is concentrated. Restoration and gentrification, consequences of the tourist boom, have made inroads of late, but it remains an atmospheric place.

Arrival and orientation

Large as it is, Haniá is easy to handle once you've reached the centre; you may get lost wandering among the narrow alleys of the old city but that's a relatively small area, and you're never far from the sea or from some other obvious landmark. The **bus station** is on Kidhonías, within easy walking distance from the action – turn right out of the

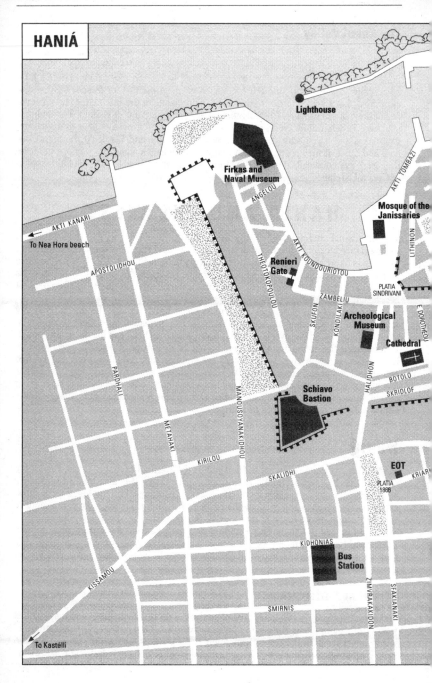

HANIÁ

Lighthouse

Firkas and
Naval Museum

ANGELOU

AKTI TOMBAZI

Mosque of the
Janissaries

AKTI KANARI

To Nea Hora beach

LITHINON

AKTI KOUNDOURIOTOU

APOSTOLIDHOU

THEOTOKOPOULOU

Renieri
Gate

PLATIA
SINDRIVANI

ZAMBELIU

SKUFON

KONDILAKI

Archeological
Museum

E. DOROTHEOU

Cathedral

PARDHALI

METAHAKI

MANOUSOYANAKIDHOU

HALIDHON

BOTOLO

SKRIDLOF

Schiavo
Bastion

KIRILOU

SKALIDHI

EOT

KRIAR

PLATIA
1866

KISSAMOU

KIDHONIAS

Bus
Station

ZIMVRAKAKIDON

STAKIANAKI

SMIRNIS

To Kastélli

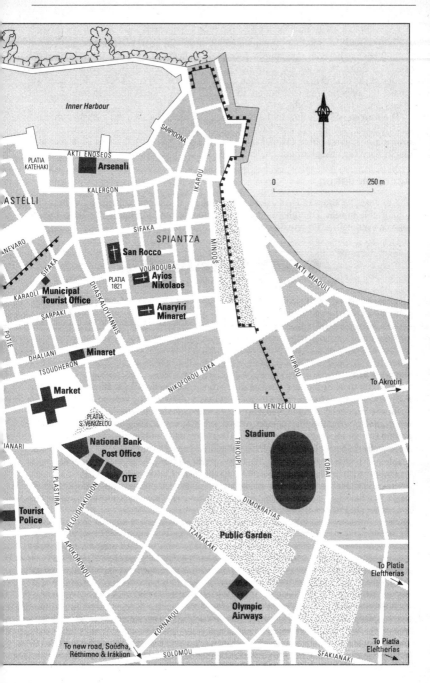

Inner Harbour

PLATIA
KATEHAKI

AKTI ENOSEOS

SARPIDONA

Arsenali

KALERGON

ASTÉLLI

SIFAKA

SPIANTZA

San Rocco

VOURDOUBA

PLATIA
1821

Ayios
Nikolaos

Municipal
Tourist Office

DHASKALOYIANNIS

Anaryiri
Minaret

SARPAKI

MINDOS

IKAROU

AKTI MIAOULI

DHALIANI

Minaret

TSOUDHERON

NIKOFOROU FOKA

KIPROU

To Akrotiri

Market

PLATIA
S. VENIZELOU

EL VENIZELOU

IANARI

National Bank
Post Office

OTE

Stadium

TRIKOUPI

KORAI

N. PLASTIRA

VELOUDHAKIDHON

DIMOKRATIAS

Tourist
Police

TZANAKAKI

Public Garden

APOKORONOU

To Platía
Eleftherías

KORNAROU

Olympic
Airways

To new road, Soúdha,
Réthimno & Iráklion

SOLOMOU

SFAKIANAKI

To Platía
Eleftherías

0   250 m

station, then left down the side of Platía 1866 and you'll emerge at a major road junction opposite the top of Hálidhon, the main street of the old quarter leading straight down to the Venetian harbour. Arriving by **ferry**, you'll anchor about 10km from Haniá at the port of Soúdha: there are frequent buses which will drop you by the **market** on the fringes of the old town, or you can take a taxi. From the **airport** (about 15km) taxis will almost certainly be your only option, though it's worth a quick check to see if any sort of bus is meeting your flight.

The **tourist office** is now in the new town, just off Platía 1866 at Kriári 40 (suite 14/15, 4th floor; Mon–Fri 7.30am–2.30pm). This is complemented by an extremely helpful **municipal tourist office** (Mon–Fri 8.30am–1.30pm; ☎59 990) at Sifaka 22, a couple of blocks from the inner harbour.

Accommodation

There must be thousands of **rooms to rent** in Haniá and, unusually, quite a few comfortable **hotels**. Though you may face a long search for a bed at the height of the season, eventually everyone does seem to find something.

HANIÁ AND THE TELEPHONE
The telephone code for Haniá is ☎0821

At the time of writing, the Haniá phone system is being modernized and some numbers listed may have changed. Many starting with a "2" digit, for example, now begin with "9". Other innovations are far too complex and brain-taxing to list here; if in doubt, contact the tourist office.

Harbour area

Perhaps the most desirable rooms of all are those overlooking the harbour, and, surprisingly, such rooms are sometimes available at reasonable rates: be warned that this is often as they're very noisy at night. Most are approached not direct from the harbourside itself but from Zambelíu, the alley behind, or from other streets leading off the harbour further around (where you may get more peace). The nicest of the more expensive places are here, too, usually set back a little, so they're quieter, but often with views from the upper storeys.

Amphora, Theotokopóulou 20 (☎43 132). Large, traditional hotel, and beautifully renovated; worth the expense if you get a view, but probably not for the cheaper rooms with no view. ⑥.

Artemis, Kondiláki 13 (☎91 196). One of many in this touristy street running inland from Zambelíu. ③

Lucia, Akti Koundouriótou (☎90 302). Harbour-front hotel with balcony rooms; less expensive than you might expect for one of the best views in town. ③.

Meltemi, Angelou 2 (☎40 192). First of a little row of pensions in a great situation on the far side of the harbour; perhaps noisier than its neighbours, but ace views and a good café downstairs. ③

Piraeus, Zambelíu 10 (☎94 665). One of the oldest hotels in Haniá; basic and somewhat run-down but friendly, English-speaking and excellent value even for a room with a balcony over the harbour. ③

Rooms George, Zambelíu 30 (☎43 542). Old building with steep stairs and eccentric antique furniture; rooms vary in price according to position and size. ③.

Rooms Eleonora, Theotokopóulou 13 (☎50 011). One of several in the backstreets around the top of Angelou: prices are lower at nearby *Eugenia*. ③.

Rooms Stella, Angelou 10 (☎73 756). Creaky, eccentric old house, close to the Lucia, with plain, clean rooms above a ceramics shop. ③.

Thereza, Angelou 8 (☎40 118). Beautiful old house in a great position with stunning views from roof terrace and some rooms; classy decorations, too. A more expensive pension than its neighbours but deservedly so; unlikely to have room in season unless you book. ④.

The old town: east of Hálidhon

In the eastern half of the old town, rooms are far more scattered, and in the height of the season your chances are much better over here. **Kastélli**, immediately east of the harbour, has some lovely places with views from the height. Take one of the alleys leading left off Kaneváro if you want to try these, but don't be too hopeful since they are popular and often booked up.

Fidias, Sarpáki 8 (☎52 494). Signposted from the cathedral. Favourite backpackers' meeting place: rather bizarrely run, but extremely friendly pension and has the real advantage of offering single rooms or fixing shares. ③.

Kastelli, Kaneváro 39 (☎57 057). Not the prettiest location, but comfortable, modern, reasonably priced pension and very quiet at the back. Alex, who runs the place, is exceptionally helpful and also has a few apartments and a beautiful house (for up to 5 people) to rent. ③.

Kydonia, Isódhion 15 (☎57 179). Between the cathedral *platía* and Platía Sindrívani, in the first street parallel to Hálidhon. Rather dark, but good value for so central a position. ③.

Lito, Episkópou Dorothéou 15 (☎53 150). Pension very near the cathedral; another street with several options. ③.

Marina Ventikou, Sarpáki 40 (☎57 601). Small, personally run rooms place in quiet corner of old town. Others nearby. ③.

Monastiri, Áyíou Markou 18, off Kaneváro (☎54 776). Pleasant rooms, some with a sea view in the restored ruins of a Venetian monastery. ③.

Nikos, Dhaskaloyiánnis 58 (☎54 783). One of a few down here near the inner harbour; relatively modern rooms all with shower. ③.

Youth hostel and campsites

Youth hostel, Dhrakoniánou 33 (☎53 565). The youth hostel is a long way from anywhere you might otherwise visit and is not much of a place: four or five rooms with about eight metal bunks in each, but it is at least cheap and friendly, with a good view inland. You get here on the *Ay. Ioannis* bus (every 15min; last one at midnight) from the *platía* opposite the market – ask for Platía Dhexamení. Organizes cheap guided tours to the Samarian Gorge and other places. ①.

Camping Ayía Marína (☎48 555). About 8km or so west of Haniá, on an excellent beach at the far end of Ayía Marína village. This is beyond the range of Haniá city buses, so to get here by public transport you have to go from the main bus station. Check before turning up, because the site is earmarked for redevelopment.

Camping Hania (☎31 686). A smaller, cheaper site behind the beach some 4km west of Haniá, just about in walking distance if you follow the coast around, but much easier reached by taking the local bus (see "Beaches" overpage). There's a large sign to warn you where to get off. The site is lovely, if rather basic in terms of facilities; small, shady and just a short walk from some of the better beaches.

The City

Haniá has been occupied almost continuously since Neolithic times, so it comes as a surprise that a city of such antiquity should offer little specifically to see or do. It is, however, a place which is fascinating simply to wander around, stumbling upon surviving fragments of city wall, holes in which ancient Kydonia is being excavated and odd segments of Venetian or Turkish masonry.

Kastélli and the harbour

The port area is as ever the place to start, the oldest and the most interesting part of town. It's at its busiest and most attractive at night, when the lights from bars and restaurants reflect in the water and crowds of visitors and locals turn out to promenade. By day, things are quieter. Straight ahead from Platía Sindrivani (also known as Harbour Square) lies the curious domed shape of the **Mosque of the Janissaries**, until recently the tourist office, but currently without a function. The little hill that rises behind the mosque is **Kastélli**, site of the earliest habitation and core of the Venetian and Turkish towns. There's not a great deal left, but it's here that you'll find traces of the oldest walls (there were two rings, one defending Kastélli alone, a later set encompassing the whole of the medieval city) and the sites of various excavations. Beneath the hill, on the **inner (eastern) harbour**, the arches of sixteenth-century Venetian arsenals survive alongside remains of the outer walls; both are currently undergoing restoration.

Following the esplanade around in the other direction leads to a hefty bastion which now houses Crete's **Naval Museum** (Tues, Thurs & Sat 10am–2pm & 4–6pm). The collection is not exactly riveting, but wander in anyway for a look at the seaward fortifications and the platform where the modern Greek flag was first flown on Crete (in 1913). Walk around the back of these restored bulwarks to a street heading inland and you'll find the best-preserved stretch of the outer walls.

The old city

Behind the harbour, lie the less picturesque but more lively sections of the old city. First, a short way up Hálidhon on the right, is Haniá's **Archeological Museum** (daily except Mon 8.30am–3pm; 400dr, Sun free), housed in the Venetian-built church of San Francesco. Damaged as it is, especially from the outside, this remains a beautiful building and a fine little display, covering the local area from Minoan through to Roman times. In the garden, a huge fountain and the base of a minaret survive from the period when the Turks converted the church into a mosque; around them are scattered various other sculptures and architectural remnants.

The **Cathedral**, ordinary and relatively modern, is just a few steps further up Hálidhon on the left. Around it are some of the more animated shopping areas, particularly **Odhós Skrídlof** (Leather Street), with streets leading up to the back of the market beyond. In the direction of the Spiántza quarter are ancient alleys with tumbledown Venetian stonework and overhanging wooden balconies; though gentrification is spreading apace, much of the quarter has yet to feel the effect of the city's modern popularity. There are a couple more **minarets**, too, one on Dhaliáni, and the other in Platía 1821, which is a fine traditional *platía* to stop for a coffee.

The new town

Once out of the narrow confines of the maritime district, the broad, traffic-choked streets of the **modern city** have a great deal less to offer. Up Tzanakáki, not far from the market, you'll find the **Public Gardens**, a park with strolling couples, a few caged animals (including a few *kri-kri* or Cretan ibex) and a café under the trees; there's also an open-air auditorium which occasionally hosts live music or local festivities. Beyond here, you could continue to the **Historical Museum** (Mon–Fri 9am–1pm), but the effort would be wasted unless you're a Greek-speaking expert on the subject; the place is essentially a very dusty archive with a few photographs on the wall. Perhaps more interesting is the fact that the museum lies on the fringes of Haniá's desirable residential districts. If you continue to the end of Sfakianáki and then go down Iróön Politehníou towards the sea, you'll get an insight into how Crete's other half lives. There are several (expensive) garden restaurants down here and a number of fashionable café-bars where you can sit outside.

The beaches

Haniá's beaches all lie to the west of the city. For the packed **city beach**, this means no more than a ten-minute walk following the shoreline from the naval museum, but for good sand you're better off taking the local bus out along the coast road. This leaves from the east side of Platía 1866 and runs along the coast road as far as **Kalamáki beach**. Kalamáki and the previous stop, **Oasis beach**, are again pretty crowded but they're a considerable improvement over the beach in Haniá itself. In between, you'll find emptier stretches if you're prepared to walk: about an hour in all (on sandy beach virtually all the way) from Haniá to Kalamáki, and then perhaps ten minutes from the road to the beach if you get off the bus at the signs to *Aptera Beach* or *Camping Hania*. Further afield there are even finer beaches at **Ayía Marína** to the west, or **Stavrós** (see p.193) out on the Akrotíri peninsula (reached by *KTEL* buses from the main station).

Eating

You're never far from something **to eat** in Haniá: in a circle around the harbour is one restaurant, taverna or café after another. All have their own character, but there seems little variation in price or what's on offer. Away from the water, there are plenty of slightly cheaper possibilities on Kondiláki, Kaneváro and most of the streets off Hálidhon. For snacks or lighter meals, the cafés around the harbour on the whole serve cocktails and fresh juices at exorbitant prices, though breakfast (especially "English") can be good value. For more traditional places, try around the market and along Dhaskaloyiánnis (*Singanaki* here is a good traditional bakery serving *tiropitta* and the like, with a cake shop next door). Fast food is also increasingly widespread, with numerous *souvláki* places on Karaolí; at the end of the outer harbour, near the naval museum; and around the corner of Plastíra and Yianári, across from the **market** (see "Listings", overpage, for details of the market and supermarkets)

Boúyatsa, Sífaka 4. Tiny place serving little except the traditional creamy *boúyatsa*: eat in or take away.

Dino's, inner harbour by bottom of Sarpidóna. One of the best choices for a pricey seafood meal with a harbour view; *Apostolis*, almost next door, is also good.

Karnáyio, Platía Kateháki 8. Set back from the inner harbour near the port police. Not right on the water, but one of the best harbour restaurants nonetheless.

Kings, Kondiláki. The first of numerous good places as you head up Kondiláki from Zambelíu. Again, some vegetarian food.

Le Saladier, Kaneváro just off Platía Sindriváni. French-run joint offering salads of every kind.

Lito, Episkópou Dorothéou 15. Café/taverna with live music (usually Greek-style guitar), one of several in this street.

Meltemi, Angelou 2. Slow, relaxed place for breakfast, and where locals (especially expats) sit whiling the day away or playing *tavli*.

Neorion, Sarpidóna. Café to sit and be seen in the evening; some tables overlook the harbour. Try an expensive but sublime lemon *graníta*.

Pafsilipon, Sífaka 19. Good, standard taverna. Tables on the street and also on the raised pavement opposite. House speciality is *toúrta*.

Tamam, Zambelíu just before Renieri Gate. Young, fashionable place with adventurous Greek menu including much vegetarian food. Unfortunately only a few cramped tables outside, and inside it's very hot. Slow service.

Tasty Souvlaki, Hálidhon 80. Always packed despite being cramped and none-too-clean, which is a testimonial to the quality and value of the *souvláki*. Better to take away.

Taverna Ela, top of Kondiláki. Live Greek music to enliven your meal.

Toh Dhiporto, Skridhlóf 40. Long-established, very basic taverna amid all the leather shops. Multilingual menu offers such delights as "Pigs' Balls", or, more delicately, *Testicules de Porc*.

Vasilis, Platía Sindriváni. Perhaps the least changed of the harbourside cafés. Reasonably priced breakfasts.

Bars and nightlife

There are NATO air force and navy bases out on Akrotíri, which means there are some **bars** in Haniá that are a lot heavier than you'd expect, full of servicemen. Over the last couple of years, some of these places have been closed and others tamed, however, and the troops have been on their best behaviour in the face of local opposition to their presence: tourists and young locals predominate in most places.

The smartest and newest places are on and around **Sarpidóna**, in the far corner of the inner harbour: bars like *Fraise*, on Sarpidóna; and late night disco-bars such as *Berlin Rock Café*, on Radimánthus, just around the corner at the top of Sarpidóna. Heading from here around towards the outer harbour, you'll pass others including the *Four Seasons*, a very popular bar by the port police, and then reach a couple of the older places including *Remember* and *Scorpio* behind the *Plaza*. *Fagotto*, Angelou 16, is a pleasant, laid-back jazz bar, often with live performers. **Discos** proper include *Ariadni*, on the inner harbour (opens 11.30pm, but busy later), and *Agora Club*, a big, bright place on Tsoudherón behind the market, which doesn't really get going until 2am. Tucked down a passage near the Schiaro Bastion (Skalidhi and Hálidhon) *Anayennisi Club* is a new place that becomes frenetic after midnight.

A couple of places that offer more traditional entertainment are the *Café Kriti*, Kalergón 22, at the corner of Androgéo, basically an old-fashioned *kafenío* where there's **Greek music and dancing** virtually every night, and the *Firkas* (the bastion by the naval museum), with Greek dancing at 9pm every Tuesday; pricey but authentic entertainment. It's also worth checking for events at the open-air auditorium in the public gardens, and for performances in restaurants outside the city, which are the ones the locals will go to. Look for posters, especially in front of the market and in the little *platía* across the road from there.

For **films**, you should also check the hoardings in front of the market. There are open-air screenings at *Attikon*, on Venizélou out towards Akrotíri, about 1km from the centre, and occasionally in the public gardens.

Listings

Airlines *Olympic*, Tzanakáki 88 (☎57 701; Mon–Fri 9am–4pm). There's a bus from here connecting with their flights. For airport information phone ☎63 245.

Banks The main branch of the *National Bank* is directly opposite the market. Convenient smaller banks for exchange are next to the bus station, at the bottom of Kaneváro just off Platía Sindrivani, or at the top of Hálidhon. There are also a couple of exchange places on Hálidhon, open long hours, and a post office van parked through the summer in the cathedral *platía*.

Bike and car rental Possibilities everywhere, especially on Hálidhon, though these are rarely the best value. For cars try *Hermes*, Tzanakáki 52 (☎54 418), friendly and efficient; for bikes and cars *Duke of Crete*, Sífaka 3, (☎21 651), Skalídhi 16 (☎57 821) and branches in Ayía Marína and Plataniás (discount for cash).

Boat trips Various boat trips are offered by travel agents around town, mostly round Soúdha Bay or out to beaches on the Rodhópou peninsula. *Domenico's* on Kaneváro offers some of the best of these.

Ferry tickets The agent for *Minoan* is *Nanadakis Travel*, Hálidhon 8 (☎23 939); for *ANEK* on Venizélou, right opposite the market (☎23 636).

Launderette There are three, at Kaneváro 38 (9am–10pm), Episkópou Dorothéou 7 and Áyii Dhéka 18. All do service washes.

Left luggage The bus station has a left luggage office.

Market and supermarkets If you want to buy food or get stuff together for a picnic, the market is the place to head. There are vast quantities of fresh fruit and vegetables as well as meat and fish, bakers, dairy stalls and general stores for cooked meats, tins and other standard provisions. There are also several small stores down by the harbour *platía* which sell cold drinks and a certain amount of food, but these are expensive (though they do open late). A couple of large supermarkets can be found on the main roads running out of town, for instance *Inka* on the way to Akrotíri.

Post office The main post office is on Tzanakáki (Mon–Fri 7am–8pm, plus Sat for exchange 8am–2pm). In summer, there's a handy Portakabin branch set up in the cathedral *platía*.

Taxis The main taxi ranks are in the cathedral *platía* and, especially, Platía 1866. For radio taxis try ☎29 405 or ☎58 700.

Telephones OTE headquarters (daily 6am–midnight) is on Tzanakáki just past the post office. It's generally packed during the day, but often blissfully empty late at night.

Tourist police Kareskáki 44 (☎94 477). Town and harbour police are on the inner harbour.

Travel agencies For cheap tickets home (*Magic Bus* and student/charter flights) *Bassias Travel*, Skridhlóf 46 (☎44 295), is the place, very helpful for regular tickets, too. They also deal in standard excursions. Other travel agents for tours and day trips are everywhere.

Around Haniá: the Akrotíri and Rodhopoú peninsulas

Just north of Haniá, the **Akrotíri peninsula** loops around to protect the Bay of Soúdha and a NATO military base and missile-testing area. In an ironic twist, the peninsula's northwestern coastline is fast developing into a luxury suburb; the beach of Horafákia, long popular with jaded Haniotes, is surrounded by villas and apartments. **STAVRÓS**, further out, has not yet suffered this fate, and its **beach** is absolutely superb if you like the calm, shallow water of an almost completely enclosed lagoon. It's not very large, so it does get crowded, but rarely overpoweringly so. You can rent rooms here, and there are two tavernas.

Inland are the **monasteries of Ayía Triádha** and **Gouvernétou** (both daily 9am–2pm & 5–7pm). The former is much more accessible and has a beautiful seventeenth-century church inside its pink-and-ochre cloister; it's also one of the few Cretan monasteries in which genuine monastic life continues. Beyond the latter, you can clamber down a craggy path to the abandoned ruins of the monastery of Katholikó and the remains of its narrow (swimmable) harbour.

West to Rodhopoú

The coast to the west of Haniá was the scene of most of the fighting during the German invasion in 1941. As you leave town, an aggressive diving eagle commemorates the German parachutists, and at Máleme there's a big German cemetery; the Allied cemetery is in the other direction, on the coast just outside Soúdha. There are also beaches and considerable tourist development along much of this shore. At **AYÍA MARÍNA** there's a fine sandy beach, and an island offshore said to be a sea monster petrified by Zeus before it could swallow Crete. Seen from the west, its "mouth" still gapes open.

Between **PLATANIÁS** and **KOLIMBÁRI** an almost unbroken strand unfurls, by no means all sandy, but deserted for long stretches between villages. The road here runs through mixed groves of calamus reed (Crete's bamboo) and oranges; the windbreaks fashioned from the reeds protect the ripening oranges from the *meltémi*. At Kolimbári, the road to Kastélli cuts across the base of another mountainous peninsula, **Rodhopoú**. Just off the main road here is a monastery, **Goniá** (daily 9am–2pm & 5–7pm; respectable dress), with a view most luxury hotels would envy. Every monk in Crete can tell tales of his proud ancestry of resistance to invaders, but here the Turkish cannon balls are still lodged in the walls to prove it, a relic of which the good fathers are far more proud than of any of the icons.

South to the Samarian Gorge

From Haniá the **Gorge of Samariá** (May to mid-Oct; 1000dr for entry to the national park) can be visited as a day trip or as part of a longer excursion to the south. At over 16km, it's Europe's longest gorge and is startlingly beautiful. **Buses** leave Haniá for the top at 6.15am, 7.30am and 8.30am, plus 1.30pm, and you'll normally be sold a return ticket (valid from Hóra Sfakíon at any time). It's well worth catching the early bus to avoid the full heat of the day while walking through the gorge, though be warned that

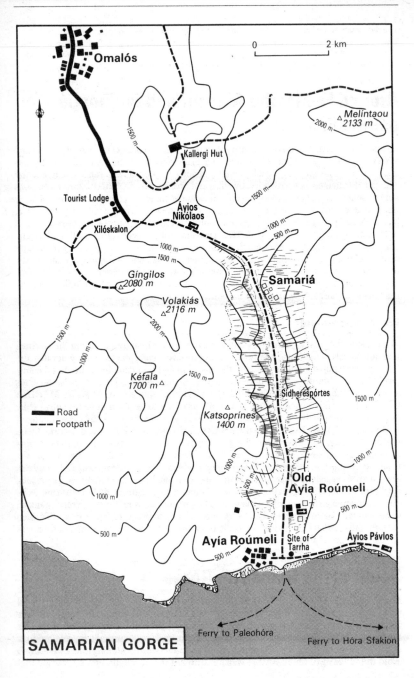

0   2 km

Omalós

Melíntaou
△ 2133 m
2000 m

1500 m

Kallergi Hut

Tourist Lodge

1500 m

Áyios
Nikólaos

Xilóskalon

1000 m
500 m

1000 m

1500 m

Samariá

Gíngilos
△2080 m

1500 m

Volakiás
△ 2116 m

2000 m

1000 m

Kéfala △
1700 m

1500 m

1500 m

Sidheréspórtes

1000 m

Road
Footpath

△
Katsoprínes
1400 m

1000 m

500 m

Old
Ayia Roúmeli

1000 m

500 m

1000 m

500 m

Ayía Roúmeli

Site of
Tarrha

Áyios Pávlos

500 m

500 m

SAMARIAN GORGE

Ferry to Paleohóra   Ferry to Hóra Sfakion

you will not be alone – there are often as many as five coachloads setting off before dawn for the nail-biting climb into the White Mountains. There are also direct early-morning buses from Iráklion and Réthimnon, and bus tours from virtually everywhere on the island. Despite all the crowds, the walk is hard work, especially in spring when the stream is a roaring torrent. Early and late in the season, there is a danger of flash floods, which are not to be taken lightly. In 1993, a number of walkers perished when they were washed out to sea. If in doubt, phone the Haniá Forest Service (☎0821/67 140) for information.

Omalós

One way to avoid the early start would be to stay at **OMALÓS**, in the middle of the mountain plain from which the gorge descends. There are some ordinary **rooms** for rent and a couple of surprisingly fancy **hotels**; try the *Neos Omalos* (☎0821/67 269; ③). But since the village is some way from the start of the track, and the buses arrive as the sun rises, it's almost impossible to get a head start on the crowds. Some people sleep out at the top (where there's a bar-restaurant and kiosks serving drinks and sand-wiches), but a night under the stars here can be a bitterly cold experience. The one significant advantage to staying up here would be if you wanted to undertake some other climbs in the White Mountains, in which case there's a **mountain hut** (☎0821/ 24 647; ①) about ninety minutes' walk from Omalós or from the top of the gorge.

Through the gorge

The **Gorge** itself begins at the *Xilóskala*, or "wooden staircase", a stepped path plunging steeply down from the southern lip of the Omalós plain. Here, at the head of the track, opposite the sheer rock face of Mount Gíngilos, the crowds pouring out of the buses disperse rapidly as keen walkers march purposefully down while others dally over breakfast, contemplating the sunrise for hours. You descend at first through almost alpine scenery: pine forest, wild flowers and very un-Cretan greenery – a verdant shock in the spring, when the stream is also at its liveliest (and can at times be positively dangerous). Small churches and viewpoints dot the route, and about halfway down you pass the abandoned village of **Samariá**, now home to a wardens' station, with picnic facilities and filthy toilets. Further down, the path levels out and the gorge walls close in until at the narrowest point (the *Sidherespórtes* or "Iron Gates") one can practically touch both tortured rock faces at once, and, looking up, see them rising sheer for almost a thousand feet.

At an average pace, with regular stops, the walk down takes five or six hours, and the upward trek considerably longer. It's hard work (you'll know all about it next day), the path is rough, and solid shoes vital. On the way down, there is plenty of water from springs and streams (except some years in September and October), but nothing to eat. The park that surrounds the gorge is the only mainland refuge of the Cretan wild ibex, the *kri-kri*, but don't expect to see one; there are usually far too many people around.

Villages of the southwest coast

When you finally emerge from the gorge, it's not long before you reach the village of **AYÍA ROUMÉLI**, which is all but abandoned until you reach the beach, a mirage of iced drinks and a cluster of tavernas with **rooms** for rent. If you want to get back to Haniá, buy your boat tickets now, especially if you want an afternoon on the beach; the last boat (connecting with the final 6.30pm bus from Hóra Sfakíon) tends to sell out first. If you plan to stay on the south coast, you should get going as soon as possible for the best chance of finding a room somewhere nicer than Ayía Rouméli.

Loutró

For tranquillity, it's hard to beat **LOUTRÓ**, two-thirds of the way to Hóra Sfakíon, and accessible only by boat or on foot. The chief disadvantage of Loutró is its lack of a real beach; most people swim from the rocks around its small bay. If you're prepared to walk, however, there are deserted beaches along the coast to the east. Indeed, if you're really into walking there's a coastal trail through Loutró which covers the entire distance between Ayía Rouméli and Hóra Sfakíon, or you could take the daunting zigzag path up the cliff behind to the mountain village of Anópoli. Loutró itself has a number of tavernas and rooms, though not always enough of the latter. Call the *Blue House* (☎0825/91 127) if you want to book ahead; this is also the best place to eat. There is also space to camp out on the cape by a ruined fort, but due to a long history of problems, you should be aware that campers are not very popular in the village.

Hóra Sfakíon and beyond

HÓRA SFAKÍON is the more usual terminus for walkers traversing the gorge, with a regular boat service along the coast to and from Ayía Rouméli. Consequently, it's quite an expensive and not an especially welcoming place; there are plenty of rooms and some excellent tavernas, but for a real beach you should jump straight on the evening bus going toward Plakiás. Plenty of opportunities present themselves en route, one of the most memorable at **Frangokástello**, a crumbling Venetian attempt to bring law and order to a district that went on to defy both Turks and Germans. Its square, crenellated fort, isolated a few kilometres below a chiselled wall of mountains, looks like it's been spirited out of the High Atlas or Tibet. The place is said to be haunted by ghosts of Greek rebels massacred here in 1829; every May, these *dhrossoulítes* (dewy ones) march at dawn across the coastal plain and disappear into the sea near the fort. The rest of the time Frangokástello is peaceful enough, with a superb beach and numbers of tavernas and rooms, but it's on its way to development. Slightly further east, and less influenced by tourism or modern life, are the attractive villages of **SKALOTÍ** and **RODHÁKINO**, each with basic lodging and food.

Soúyia

In quite the other direction from Ayía Rouméli, less regular boats also head to **SOÚYIA** and on to Paleohóra. Soúyia, until World War II merely the anchorage for Koustoyérako inland, is low key with a long, grey pebble beach and mostly modern buildings (except for a church with a sixth-century Byzantine mosaic as the foundation). Since the completion of the new road to Haniá, the village has started to expand; even so, except in the very middle of summer, it continues to make a good fallback for finding a room or a place to camp, eating cheaply and enjoying the beach when the rest of the island is seething with tourists.

Kastélli and the western tip

Apart from being Crete's most westerly town, and the end of the main road, **KASTÉLLI** (Kíssamos, or Kastélli Kissámou as it's variously known) has little obvious attraction. It's a busy town with a rocky beach visited mainly by people using the boat that runs twice weekly to the island of Kíthira and the Peloponnese. The very ordinariness of Kastélli, however, can be attractive: life goes on pretty much regardless of outsiders, but there's every facility you might need. The **ferry agent's office** in Kastélli is right on the main *platía* (*Ksirouksakis*; ☎0822/22 655), and nothing else is far away apart from the dock, a wearying two-kilometre walk (or inexpensive taxi ride) from town.

Falásarna to Elafonísi

To the west of Kastélli lies some of Crete's loneliest, and, for many visitors, finest coastline. The first place of note is ancient **Falásarna**, city ruins which mean little to the non-specialist, but they do overlook some of the best beaches on Crete, wide and sandy with clean water. There's a handful of tavernas and an increasing number of rooms for rent; otherwise, you have to sleep out, as many people do. This can mean that the main beaches are dirty, but they remain beautiful, and there are plenty of others within walking distance. The nearest real town is **PLÁTANOS**, 5km up the recently paved road, along which there are a couple of daily buses.

Further south, the western coastline is still less discovered and the road is surfaced only as far as Kámbos; there is little in the way of official accommodation. **SFINÁRI** has several houses which rent rooms, and a quiet pebble beach a little way below the village. **KÁMBOS** is similar, but even less visited, its beach a considerable walk down a hill. Beyond them both is the **monastery of Hrissoskalítissa**, hard to get to down a rough dirt road (though increasingly visited by tours from Haniá or Paleohóra), but well worth the effort for its isolation and nearby beaches; the bus gets as far as Váthi, from where the monastery is another two hours' walk away.

Five kilometres beyond Hrissoskalítissa, the road bumps down to the coast opposite the tiny uninhabited islet of **Elafonísi**. You can easily wade out to the island with its sandy beaches and rock pools, and the shallow lagoon is warm and crystal-clear. It looks magnificent, but daily boat trips from Paleohóra and coach tours from elsewhere on the island ensure that, in the middle of the day at least, it's far from deserted. Even bigger changes are now on the horizon here as Greek and German companies have bought up large tracts of land to create a monster tourist complex. If you want to stay, and really appreciate the place, there are a couple of seasonal tavernas, but bring some supplies unless you want to be wholly dependent on them.

A round trip

If you have transport, a circular drive from Kastélli, taking the coast road in one direction and the inland route through Élos and Topólia, makes for a stunningly scenic circuit. Near the ocean, villages cling desperately to the high mountainsides, apparently halted by some miracle in the midst of calamitous seaward slides. Around them, olives ripen on the terraced slopes, the sea glittering far below. Inland, especially at **ÉLOS**, the main crop is the chestnut, whose huge old trees shade the village streets.

In **TOPÓLIA**, the chapel of Ayía Sofía is sheltered inside a cave which has been known since Neolithic times. Cutting south from Élos, a partly paved road continues through the high mountains towards Paleohóra; on a motorbike, with a sense of adventure and plenty of fuel, it's great: the bus doesn't come this way, villagers still stare at the sight of a tourist, and a host of small, seasonal streams cascade beside or under the track.

Kándhanos and Paleohóra

Getting down to Paleohóra by the main road, which is paved the whole way, is a lot easier, and several daily buses from Haniá make the trip. But although this route also has to wind through the western outriders of the White Mountains, it lacks the excitement of the routes to either side. **KÁNDHANOS**, at the 58-kilometre mark, has been entirely rebuilt since it was destroyed by the Germans for its fierce resistance to their occupation. The original sign erected when the deed was done is preserved on the war memorial: "Here stood Kándanos, destroyed in retribution for the murder of 25 German soldiers".

When the beach at **PALEOHÓRA** finally appears below it is a welcome sight. The little town is built across the base of a peninsula, its harbour on one side, the sand on the other. Above, on the outcrop, Venetian ramparts stand sentinel. These days Paleohóra has become heavily developed, but it's still thoroughly enjoyable, with a main street filling, in the evening, with tables as diners spill out of the restaurants, and with a pleasantly chaotic social life. A good place to eat with some good imaginative vegetarian specials is *The Third Eye*, just out of the centre towards the sandy beach. There are scores of places to stay (though not always many vacancies) and there's also a fair-sized **campsite**; in extremis, the beach is one of the best to sleep out on, with showers, trees and acres of sand. Nearby discos and a rock'n'roll bar, or the sound-track from the open-air cinema, combine to lull you to sleep. When you tire of Paleohóra and the excellent windsurfing in the bay, there are excursions up the hill to Prodhrómi, for example, or along a five-hour coastal path to Soúyia.

You'll find a helpful **tourist office** (daily 9.30am–1pm & 5.30–9pm) in the town hall on Venizélos, in the centre of town; they have full accommodation lists and a map (though you'll hardly need this). The **OTE, banks** and **travel agents** are all nearby; the **post office** is on the road behind the sandy beach. **Boats** run from here to Elafonísi, the island of Gávdhos, and along the coast to Soúyia and Ayía Rouméli.

Gávdhos

The island of **Gávdhos**, some fifty kilometres of rough sea south of Paleohóra, is the most southerly landmass in Europe. Gávdhos is small (about 10km by 7km at the most) and barren, but it has one major attraction: the enduring isolation which its inaccessible position has helped preserve. There are now a few package tours (travel agents in Paleohóra can arrange a room if you want one), and there's a semi-permanent community of campers through the summer, but if all you want is a beach to yourself and a taverna to grill your fish, this remains the place for you.

travel details

Ferries

Áyios Nikólaos and Sitía 1–3 ferries a week to Kássos, Kárpathos, Hálki, Rhodes and the Dodecanese; 1-2 weekly to Thíra, Folégandhros, Mílos, Sífnos and Pireás.

Haniá 1 or 2 ferries daily to Pireás (12hr).

Hóra Stakíon 5 ferries daily to Loutró/Ayía Rouméli; 3 weekly to Gávdhos in season.

Iráklion 2 ferries daily to Pireás (12hr); 3 ferries weekly to Thessaloníki; at least one daily ferry to Thíra (4hr), also fast boats and hydrofoils (2hr 30min); daily ferries to Páros in season; most days to Míkonos and Íos; at least twice weekly to Náxos, Tínos, Skíros, Skíathos, Kárpathos and Rhodes. Ferries to Ancona (Italy) twice weekly and Çeşme (Turkey) weekly and weekly to Limassol (Cyprus) and Haifa (Israel).

Kastélli (Kíssamos) 1–3 ferries weekly to Kíthira, Yíthio (8hr), Monemvassía and Pireás.

Paleohóra 3 boats a week in season to Gávdhos. Also daily sailings to Elafonísi and Soúyia.

Réthimnon 3 ferries a week to Pireás (12hr); weekly service and seasonal day trips to Thíra.

Buses

Áyios Nikólaos–Sitía (7 daily 6.30am–8pm; 2hr).

Haniá–Réthimnon–Iráklion (30 daily 5.30am–9.30pm; 3hr total).

Haniá–Hóra Sfakíon (4 daily 8.30am–3.30pm; 2hr).

Haniá–Paleohóra (5 daily 8.30am–5pm; 2hr).

Iráklion–Áyios Nikólaos (27 daily 6.30am–7.30pm; 1hr 30min).

Iráklion–Ierápetra (7 daily 7.30am–6.30pm; 2hr 30min).

Iráklion–Ayía Galíni (7 daily 6.30am– 4.15pm; 2hr 15min).

Iráklion–Festós (9 daily 7.30am–5.30pm; 1hr 30min).

Kastélli–Haniá (15 daily 5am–7.30pm; 1hr 30min).

Réthimnon–Spíli–Ayía Galíni (7 daily 6.30am–5pm; 45min/1hr 30min).

Flights

Haniá Several flights a day to Athens, one weekly to Thessaloníki.

Iráklion Many daily flights to Athens; 4 weekly to Rhodes, 2 weekly to Míkonos, and 3 weekly to Thessaloníki.

CHAPTER FOUR

DODECANESE

T he most distant of the Greek islands, the **Dodecanese** (*Dhodhekánisos*) lie close to the Turkish coast – some, like Kós and Kastellórizo, almost within hailing distance of the shore. Because of this position, and their remoteness from Athens, the islands have had a turbulent history: they were the scene of ferocious battles between German and British forces in 1943–44, and were only finally included in the modern Greek state in 1948 after centuries of occupation by Crusaders, Turks and Italians. Even now the threat (real or imagined) of invasion from Turkey is very much in evidence. When you ask about the heavy military presence, locals talk in terms of "*when* the Turks come", rarely "*if . . .*".

Whatever the rigours of the occupations, their legacy includes a wonderful blend of architectural styles and of eastern and western cultures. Medieval Rhodes is the most famous, but almost every island has its Classical remains, its Crusaders' castle, its traditional villages, and abundant grandiose public buildings. For these last the Italians, who occupied the islands from 1912 to 1943, are mainly responsible. In their determination to beautify the islands and turn them into a showplace for fascism they undertook public works, excavations and reconstruction on a massive scale; and if historical accuracy was sometimes sacrificed in the interests of style, only the expert is likely to complain. A more sinister aspect of the Italian administration was the attempted forcible Latinization of the populace: spoken Greek and Orthodox observance were banned in public from 1920 to 1943. The most tangible reminder of this policy is the great number of older people whose preferred language is Italian rather than Greek.

Aside from this frequently encountered bilingualism, the Dodecanese themselves display a marked topographic and economic schizophrenia. The dry limestone outcrops of **Kastellórizo**, **Sími**, **Hálki**, **Kássos** and **Kálimnos** have always been forced to rely on the sea for their livelihoods, and the wealth generated by the maritime culture – especially in the nineteenth century – fostered the growth of attractive port towns. The sprawling, relatively fertile giants, **Rhodes** (Ródhos) and **Kós**, have recently seen their traditional agricultural economies almost totally displaced by a tourist industry attracted by good beaches and nightlife, as well as the Aegean's most exciting ensembles of historical monuments. **Kárpathos** lies somewhere in between, with a (formerly) forested north grafted on to a rocky limestone south; **Tílos**, despite its lack of trees, has ample water, though the green volcano-island of **Níssiros** does not. **Léros** shelters softer contours and more amenable terrain than its map outline would suggest, while **Pátmos** and **Astipálea** at the fringes of the archipelago boast architecture and landscapes more appropriate to the Cyclades.

The largest islands in the group are connected almost daily with each other, and none (except for Astipálea) is hard to reach. Rhodes is the main transport hub, with services to Turkey, Israel, Cyprus and (very sporadically) Egypt, as well as connections with Crete, the northeastern islands, the Cyclades and mainland. Kálimnos is an important secondary terminus, with useful ferry and hydrofoil services.

Kássos

Barren and depopulated since an 1824 Ottoman massacre and subsequent emigration, **Kássos** attracts few visitors despite being a regular port of call for the ferries. What is

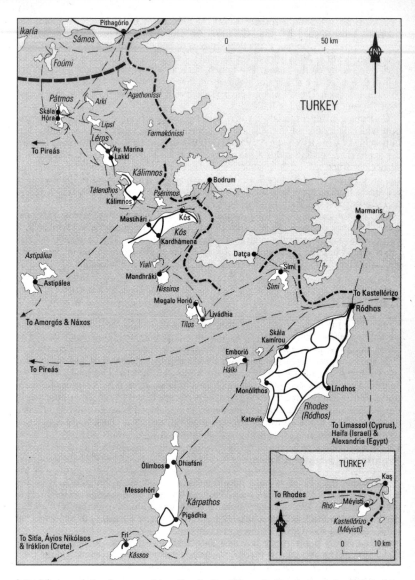

left of the population is grouped together in five villages in the north, under the shadow of Kárpathos, leaving most of the island accessible only to those on foot. There's little sign here of the wealth brought into other islands by emigrant workers, nor, since the island has little to offer them, by tourists; the crumbling houses which line the village streets and the disused terraces covering the land poignantly recall better days.

It's just ten minutes' walk from the port at Emborió to **FRÍ**, the capital; indeed the furthest village, **PÓLIO**, is only 3km away. There are two **hotels** in Frí, the *Anagenissis*

(☎0245/41 323; ④) and the *Anessis* (☎0245/41 201; ③) and in summer a few rooms, for example, those owned by Elias Koutlakis (☎0245/41 303; ②) or Katerina Markou (☎0245/41 613; ②). Among a half-dozen places to **eat** in Frí, *Kassos* is good for basic oven dishes, while *Milos* specializes in grilled fish; otherwise, fresh produce can be hard to come by on the island. The **beach**, such as it is, is at Ammoúa, on the other side of the underused airstrip; in high season, there are excursion boats to a better one on Armathiá islet. There's a large **cave** (Seláï), with impressive stalactites, southwest of Frí, beyond the hamlet of Kathístres.

Continuing inland, especially if you're seeking isolation, is more rewarding; the single **bus** which links five of the villages will give you a head start in your wanderings. Between **AYÍA MARÍNA** and **ARVANITOHÓRI**, the dirt track across the island leaves the paved road heading south. Civilization is soon left behind as you are wrapped in a silence disturbed only by the goat bells and an occasional wheeling hawk; smallholdings and olive groves are still sporadically tended, but no one stays long. After about an hour the Mediterranean appears to the south of the island, an expanse of water ruffled by the odd ship en route to Cyprus and the Middle East.

The higher fork leads to the mountain chapel and monastery of **Áyios Yióryios**, while the other drops gradually down to the coast, finally emerging at **Helathrós**, a beautiful cove at the end of a cultivated but uninhabited valley. The beach is small and sandy, the swimming great after the rigours of the walk, and seabirds of every kind circle the cliffs. With plenty of supplies, it could be a great place to camp.

Kárpathos

Alone of the the major Dodecanese, **Kárpathos** was held by the Venetians after the Byzantine collapse and so has no castle of the crusading Knights of Saint John. The island has always been something of a backwater and, despite a magnificent coastline of cliffs and rocky promontories constantly interrupted by little beaches, has succumbed surprisingly little to tourism. This has a lot to do with the appalling road system, the dearth of interesting villages and the high cost of food, which offsets reasonable room prices. Most visitors come here for a glimpse of the traditional village life that prevails in the isolated north of the island and for the superb, secluded beaches. Although there's an airport which can take direct international flights, only a few charters use it, and visitors are concentrated in a couple of resorts in the south.

Pigádhia (Kárpathos Town)

PIGÁDHIA, the capital, is now more often known simply as Kárpathos. It curves around one side of Vróndis Bay, with a harbour where boats dock right in the heart of town, while a three-kilometre-long sickle of sandy beach stretches out to the west and north. The place itself is almost entirely modern, and there's really nothing to see, but it does offer just about every facility you might need.

As you get off the ferry you'll almost inevitably be met by people offering **rooms**, and you might as well take up an offer – standards seem generally good, and the town is small enough that no location is going to be too inconvenient. If you do want to seek out somewhere yourself, walk into town and follow the signs up past the *Hotel Coral* to *Anna's Rooms* (☎0245/22 313; ②) or the *Artemis Pension* (②), both good value and very well positioned. Nearby *Vittoroulis Furnished Apartments* (☎0245/22 639; ③) are available only on a weekly basis, but worth it if you are staying that long. Other, simpler rooms establishments include *Sofia's* (☎0245/22 154; ②), *Konaki* (☎0245/22 908; ②), on the upper through-road west of the town hall, and the *Filoxenia* (☎0245/22 623; ②). Hotels include the *Avra* (☎0245/22 388; ②) and the more comfortable *Karpathos*

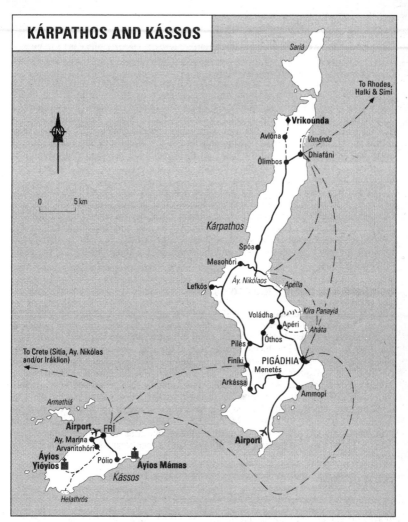

KÁRPATHOS AND KÁSSOS

Sariá

To Rhodes,
Halki & Sími

◆ **Vrikoúnda**

Avlóna ● ↗ *Vanánda*

Ólimbos ● ● Dhiafáni

0   5 km

Kárpathos

Spóa ●

Mesohóri ●
Áy. Nikólaos   *Apélla*
Lefkós ●

Kíra Panayiá
Voládha ●   ● Apéri   *Aháta*
Pilés ●   ● Óthos
To Crete (Sitía, Ay. Nikólas
and/or Iráklion)   Finíki ●   **PIGÁDHIA**
Menetés

Arkássa ●
Ammopí ●

Armathiá

Airport ▸ FRÍ
Ay. Marína ●
Arvanitohóri ●   **Airport** ✈
Áyios   Pólio
Yióyios   ● *Áyios Mámas*
Kássos

Helathrós

(☎0245/22 347; ③). More expensive places are generally further out and tend to be occupied by package groups as far as the ruined fifth-century basilica of **Ayía Fotiní** – though development is gradually spreading beyond here; *Toh Limanaki* taverna, at the southern end, is good but opens only at lunchtime.

Most of the waterfront **tavernas** are much of an expensive muchness, with some notable exceptions: the *Psistaria Olympia* is good for meat-lovers, while fish aficionados should head for *Iy Kali Kardhia*, at the north end on the way to the beach. Places inland tend to work out less expensive: try *Mike's*, inland up a pedestrian way from the stylish *Kafenio Cafe*, for friendly service. Live **music** can be heard nightly at *Kafenio Halkia*, in one of the few surviving old buildings next to the church on Apodhímon Karpathíon; the limited menu of supper dishes seems to be a secondary consideration.

Services and transport

There's an **OTE** office (Mon–Sat 7.30am–3.10pm, Sun 9am–2pm) on Platía Pémptis Oktovríou at the west end of Apodhímon Karpathíon; the *Olympic* office is right by this; and the **post office** is directly south, on Ikosiogdhóïs Oktovríou, the main inland street running parallel to Apodhímon Kapathíon.

If you want to get out and explore the island there are four **buses** a day to Pilés, via Apéri, Voládha and Óthos, four to Ammopí, and one or two to Arkássa and Fíniki. **Taxis** aren't too expensive to get to these villages on the paved roads, but can charge a fortune to go anywhere further afield. Places up by the post office like *Holiday* (☎0245/22 813) or *Circle* (☎0245/22 690) rent **cars**, while *Hermes* (☎0245/22 090) does **bike rental** and repairs. Be warned that the only fuel on the island is to be found just to the north and south of town, and the tanks on the small bikes are barely big enough to complete a circuit of the south, let alone head up north; the latter is expressly forbidden by most outfits, in any case.

The north is better explored by boat or on a **tour**: *Olympos Travel* (☎0245/22 993), on the front near the port, offers very good deals on all-in trips (from around 4500dr to Ólimbos), though the rival boat (*Chrisovalandou Lines*; pay on board for best deals) is much more attractive. *Olympos* and other agents can also offer trips to Kássos and to isolated east coast beaches. Less well-publicized is the fact that you can use these boats to travel one-way between the north and the south, paying about one-third of the going rate for day trips.

Southern and central Kárpathos

The flat southern extremity of Kárpathos, towards the airport, is extraordinarily desolate – its natural barrenness has been exacerbated by fires. There are a couple of empty, sandy beaches, but they're not at all attractive and are exposed to any wind that may be blowing. The nicest beach here is the tiny cove by the *Hotel Poseidon*, which has some shelter. You're better off in this direction going no further than **AMMOPÍ**, just 7km from Pigádhia. This, together with the recent development at Arkássa (see below), is the closest thing on Kárpathos to a developed beach resort: two sandy coves serviced by a couple of tavernas and a few rooms places. It's scattered and not exactly pretty, but as yet is far from overwhelming. Heading across the island, there's a steep climb up to **MENETÉS**, a lovely village on the ridge of the hills with handsome old hilltop houses, a tiny folklore museum and a spectacularly sited church. There's a good taverna here, *Manolis*, and a memorial with views back to the east.

The west coast

Beyond Menetés, you immediately start to descend to **ARKÁSSA** on the west coast, with excellent views across to Kássos as you come down. Arkássa has recently been heavily developed, with hotels and restaurants dotted along a rocky coast and beaches both south past the headland and north at Fíniki, neither a very long walk; most places are aimed squarely at the package market, but you could try *Rooms Irini* (☎0245/61 263; ②). Signs point along a cement road to Ayía Sofía, just five minutes' walk, where you can see a whitewashed chapel. Around this are various remains of **ancient and Byzantine Arkessia**, above all several mosaic floors with geometric patterns. Some are part-buried, including one running diagonally under the floor of a half-buried chapel, emerging from the walls on either side. Various bits of marble, broken statuary and columns are propped up in and around this chapel.

The tiny fishing port of **FINÍKI**, just a couple of kilometres away, boasts a small beach, three or four tavernas, and several rooms establishments lining the road to the jetty; *Fay's Paradise* (☎0245/61 308; ②) is noted for the squid and stuffed cabbage in the attached taverna. The continuation of the road up the west coast isn't too bad, and it's gradually being improved as the tarmac encroaches round the southern half of the island, currently running out halfway to the attractive resort of **LEFKÓS** (Paraliá Lefkoú). Although this is a delightful place for flopping on the beach, it necessitates some advance planning: there are only three buses weekly, no vehicle rental, and Lefkós marks the furthest point you can reach from Pighádhia on a small motorbike and return safely before running out of gas. Your efforts will be rewarded by striking topography of cliffs, hills, islets and sandspits surrounding a triple bay. The *Sunlight Restaurant* has garnered an enviable tamarisk-shaded position on the southern cove, and several **rooms** places (no phones; ③) dot the promontory overlooking the two more northerly and progressively wilder bays.

Back on the main road, you climb higher to **MESOHÓRI** through one of the few sections of pine forest not scarred by fire. The village tumbles down towards the sea around narrow, stepped alleys; the road ends at the top of town, where a snack bar represents the only tourist facility of any sort. Alternatively, you can carry on to Spóa, overlooking the east coast.

The centre and the east coast

The centre of Kárpathos supports a quartet of villages – **APÉRI, VOLÁDHA, ÓTHOS** and **PILÉS** – blessed with superb hillside settings and ample running water. In these settlements nearly everyone has "done time" in North America, then returned home with their nest eggs: New Jersey, New York and Canadian car plates tell you exactly where repatriated islanders struck it rich. From Apéri, the largest and wealthiest of them, you can bike 7km along a very rough road to the dramatic and isolated pebble beach of **Aháta**, with a spring but no other facilities. Óthos is almost at the highest point of the island and is dwarfed by a huge wind generator up above it, while Pilés is perhaps the prettiest of these villages, with great views to the west.

Beyond Apéri, the road up the **east coast** is extremely rough in places, but a beautiful drive, passing above beaches most easily accessible by boat trips from Pigádhia. **Kíra Panayiá** is the first encountered, via a rutted side road; there's a surprising number of villas, rooms and tavernas in the ravine behind the 150m of fine gravel and turquoise water. **Apélla** is the best of the beaches you can – just about – reach by road, but has no amenities. The end of this route is **SPÓA**, high above the shore, where the road stops by a snack bar at the edge of the village; there's also a good traditional *kafenío* a short way down. **Áyios Nikólaos**, 5km below, is an excellent beach with tavernas, and an ancient basilica to explore.

Northern Kárpathos

Although connected by road with Spóa, much the easiest way to get to northern Kárpathos is by boat – inter-island ferries call at Dhiafáni once a week or there are smaller tour boats from Pigádhia daily. These take a couple of hours, and are met at Dhiafáni by buses to take you up to Ólimbos, the traditional village that is the main attraction of this part of the island.

High in the mountains, **ÓLIMBOS** straddles two small peaks, the ridges above studded with windmills, a couple of them still operational though most are now ruined. Although the road and electricity, together with a growing number of tourists, are dragging the place into the twentieth century, it hasn't fully arrived yet. The women here are immediately striking in their magnificent **traditional dress** and after a while you notice that they also dominate the village: working in the gardens, carrying goods on their shoulders, or tending the mountain sheep. Nearly all Ólimbos men emigrate or work outside the village, sending money home and returning only on holidays. The long-isolated villagers also speak a unique dialect, said to maintain traces of its Doric and Phrygian origins. Traditional music is still heard regularly and draws crowds of visitors at festival times.

The number of day trippers is increasingly changing the atmosphere here; it's still a very picturesque place, full of photo oportunities, but the traditions are dying fast (or at least they're hard to find in season). On the whole, it's only the older women and those who work in tourist shops who wear traditional dress nowadays and during the day you'll almost certainly see more visitors than locals. This might be a good reason to stay, either as an organized excursion or in one of an increasing number of **rooms** places: the *Ólimbos* (☎0245/51 252; ②), near the village entrance, is a good bare-bones option, while *Hotel Aphrodite* (☎0245/51 307; ②) offers both en suite facilities and a southerly ocean view. There are also plenty of places to **eat** – *Parthenonas*, on the square by the church, is excellent; try their *makaroúnes*, a local dish of homemade pasta with onions and cheese.

From the village, the west coast and tiny port and beach at **Frísses** are a dizzy drop below, or there are various walks up into the mountains. It's also possible to walk between Ólimbos and Spóa or Messohóri in the south, a six-to-seven hour trek made less scenic by the aftermath of fires. Perhaps the most attractive option, however, and certainly the easiest, is to walk back down a ravine through extensive unburnt forest to Dhiafáni. A small stream trickles alongside most of the way, and there is a spring; at your approach, snakes slither into hiding and partridges break cover. The hike takes around 90 minutes downhill – too long to accomplish in the standard three or four hours allowed on day trips if you want to explore Ólimbos as well. By staying overnight in Ólimbos, you could also tackle the trail north to the Byzantine ruins at **Vrikoúnda**, via Avlóna hamlet; Ólimbos was originally founded as a refuge from pirates that plagued the coast here.

Dhiafáni

Although its popularity is growing – and will do so exponentially on completion of the new dock – rooms in **DHIAFÁNI** are still inexpensive, and life slow. There are plenty of places at which to stay and eat, shops that will change money and even a small travel agency. Try the garrulously friendly *Pansion Delfini* (0245/51 391; ②) or *Pansion Glaros* (0245/51 259; ②; high season only), up on the southern hillside. Back on the front, the favourite taverna is *Anatoli*, easily recognizable by the folk reliefs that sprout from its roof.

There are boat trips to various nearby beaches – as well as to the uninhabited islet of **Sariá** or through the narrow strait to Trístomo anchorage and the ruins of Vrikoúnda (see above) – or there are several in walking distance. Closest is **Vanánda**, a stoney beach with an eccentric campsite snack bar in the spring-fed oasis behind. To get there, follow the pleasant signposted path north through the pines, but don't believe the signs that say ten minutes – it's over half an hour away.

Rhodes (Ródhos)

It's no accident that **Rhodes** is among the most-visited Greek islands. Not only is its east coast lined with numerous sandy beaches, but the kernel of the capital is a beautiful and remarkably preserved medieval city, the legacy of the crusading Knights of Saint John who used the island as their main base from 1309 until 1522. Unfortunately this showpiece is jammed to capacity with up to 50,000 tourists a day, ten months of the year. The island revels in cheap drink (extended duty-free status was one of the conditions of Dodecanese incorporation into Greece in 1948), and can seem swamped, particularly in August as *smörgåsbord*, fish fingers and pizza jostle alongside *moussaká* on menus.

Blessed with an equable climate and strategic position, Rhodes was important from earliest times despite a lack of many good harbours. The best natural port spawned the ancient town of Lindos which, together with the other city states, Kameiros and Ialyssos, united in 408 BC to found the new capital of Rhodes at the northern tip of the island. The cities had always allied themselves promiscuously with Alexander, Persians, Athenians or Spartans as prevailing conditions suited them, generally escaping retribution for backing the wrong side by a combination of seafaring, audacity, sycophancy and its burgeoning wealth as a trade centre. Following the failed siege of Demetrius Polyorkites in 305 BC, Rhodes prospered even more, displacing Athens as the major venue for rhetoric and the arts in the east Mediterranean. The town, underneath virtually all of the modern city, was laid out by one Hippodamus in the grid layout much in vogue at the time, with planned residential and commercial quarters.

Decline set in when Rhodes became involved in the Roman civil wars, and Cassius sacked the town; by late imperial times, it was a backwater, a status confirmed by numerous Barbarian raids during the Byzantine period. The Byzantines were compelled to cede the island to the Genoese, who in turn handed it over to the Knights of St John. The second great siege of Rhodes, during 1522–23, saw Ottoman sultan Süleyman the Magnificent oust the stubborn knights, who departed for Malta; the town once again lapsed into relative obscurity, though heavily colonized and garrisoned, until the Italian seizure of 1912.

Ródhos Town

RÓDHOS TOWN divides into two unequal parts: the compact old walled city, and the amorphous new town which sprawls around it in three directions. Throughout, the tourist is king. In the **modern district**, especially the part west of Mandhráki yacht harbour, the few buildings which aren't hotels are souvenir shops, car rental or travel agencies and bars – easily a hundred in every category. Around this to the north and west stretches the **town beach** (standing room only for latecomers), complete with deckchairs, parasols and showers. At the northernmost point of the island an art deco combined **aquarium** and **museum** (daily 9am–9pm; 400dr) with apparently rotting stuffed fish and an extraordinary collection of grotesque freaks of nature (a Cyclopean goat, an eight-legged calf, etc) offer some distraction.

Simply to catalogue the principal monuments and attractions cannot do full justice to the infinitely more rewarding **medieval city**. There's an enormous amount of pleasure to be had merely in slipping through the nine surviving gates and strolling the streets, under flying archways built for earthquake resistance, past the warm-toned sandstone and lava walls splashed with ochre and blue paint, and over the *hokhláki* (pebble) pavement, the little stones arranged into mosaics in certain courtyards.

First thing to meet the eye, and dominating the northeast sector of the city's originally fourteenth-century fortifications, is the **Palace of the Grand Masters** (Tues–Sat 8am–6pm, Sun 8.30am–3pm; 800dr, includes medieval exhibit). Destroyed by an ammunition depot explosion in 1856, it was reconstructed by the Italians as a summer home for Mussolini and Victor Emmanuel III ("King of Italy and Albania, Emperor of Ethiopia"), neither of whom used it much. The exterior is as authentic as possible, but inside things are on an altogether grander scale: a marble staircase leads up to rooms paved with Hellenistic mosaics from Kós, and the movable furnishings rival many a northern European palace. The ground floor is home to the splendid **Medieval Exhibit** (Tues–Sat 8am–2.30pm), whose collection highlights the importance of Christian Rhodes as a trade centre. The Knights are represented with a display on their sugar-refining industry and a gravestone of a Grand Master; precious manuscripts and books precede a wing of post-Byzantine icons, moved here permanently from the church of Panayía Kástrou. On Tuesday and Saturday afternoons, there's a supplementary tour of

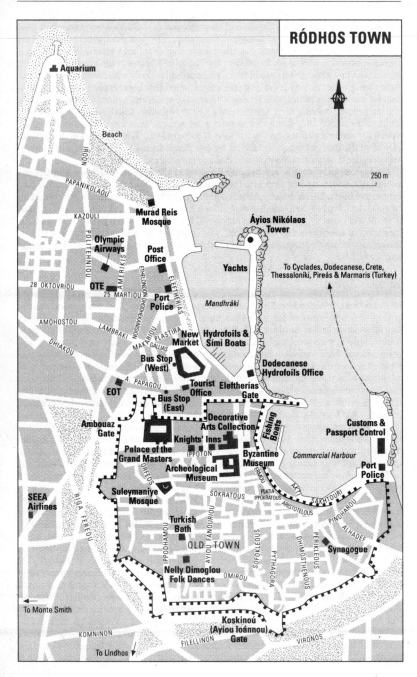

RÓDHOS TOWN

⚓ Aquarium

Beach

IROON

PAPANIKOLAOU

KAZOULI

POLITEHNIOU

Murád Reis
Mosque

Olympic
Airways

Post
Office

AMERIKIS

ETHELONDON DHODHEKANISSOU

ELEFTHERIAS

Áyios Nikólaos
Tower

Yachts

To Cyclades, Dodecanese, Crete,
Thessaloníki, Pireás & Marmaris (Turkey)

OTE

28 OKTOVRIOU

25 MARTIOU

Port
Police

Mandhráki

AMOHOSTOU

LAMBRAKI

DHIAKOU

MAKARIOU

PLASTIRA

GALLIAS

New
Market

Hydrofoils &
Sími Boats

Bus Stop
(West)

A. PAPAGOU

EOT

Tourist
Office

Bus Stop
(East)

Eleftherías
Gate

Dodecanese
Hydrofoils Office

Ambouaz
Gate

Decorative
Arts Collection

Knights' Inns

IPPOTON

Palace of the
Grand Masters

ORFEOS

Archeological
Museum

Byzantine
Museum

Fishing
Boats

Customs &
Passport Control

Commercial Harbour

ERMOU

Port
Police

SEEA
Airlines

RIGA FEREOU

Suleymaniye
Mosque

SOKRATOUS

PLATIA
IPPOKRATOUS

AKTI

SACHTOURI

ARISTOTELOUS

PINDHAROU

Turkish
Bath

IPPODHAMOU

AYIOU FANOURIOU

OLD TOWN

SOFOKLEOUS

PYTHAGORA

DHIMOSTHENOUS

PERIKLEOUS

AL HADEF

Synagogue

Nelly Dimoglou
Folk Dances

OMIROU

To Monte Smith

KOMNINON

Koskinoú
(Ayíou Ioánnou)
Gate

FILELLINON

VIRONOS

To Líndhos

0   250 m

the **city walls** (one hour, starting 2.45–3pm), beginning from a gate next to the palace – the only permitted access, incidentally.

The heavily restored **Street of the Knights** (Odhós Ippotón) leads due east from the Platía Kleovoúlou in front of the Palace; the "Inns" lining it housed the Knights of St John, according to linguistic and ethnic affiliation, until the Ottoman Turks compelled them to leave for Malta after a six-month siege in which the defenders were outnumbered thirty to one. Today the Inns house various government offices and cultural institutions vaguely appropriate to their past, but the whole effect of the renovation is predictably sterile and stagey (indeed, nearby streets were used in the filming of *Pascali's Island*).

At the bottom of the grade, the Knights' Hospital has been refurbished as the **Archeological Museum** (Tues–Sat 8.30am–6pm, Sun 8.30am–3pm; 600dr), though the arches and echoing halls of the building somewhat overshadow the contents – largely painted pottery dating from the sixth and seventh centuries. Behind the second storey sculpture garden, the Hellenistic statue gallery is more accessible: in a rear corner stands the so-called "Marine Venus", beloved of Lawrence Durrell, but lent a rather sinister aspect by her sea-dissolved face – in contrast to the friendlier *Aphrodite Bathing*. Virtually next door is the **Decorative Arts Collection** (Tues–Sun 8.30am–3pm; 400dr), gleaned from old houses across the Dodecanese; the most compelling artefacts are carved cupboard doors and chest lids painted with mythological or historical episodes in naïve style.

Across the way stands the **Byzantine Museum** (Tues–Sun 8.30am–3pm; 400dr), housed in the old cathedral of the Knights, who adapted the Byzantine shrine of Panayía Kástrou for their own needs. Medieval icons and frescoes lifted from crumbling chapels on Rhodes and Hálki, as well as photos of art still in situ, constitute the exhibits; it's worth a visit since most of the Byzantine churches in the old town and outlying villages are locked, although the collection has been severely depleted by transfers of the best items to the Palace of the Grand Masters.

If you leave the Palace of the Grand Masters going straight south, it's hard to miss the most conspicuous Turkish monument in Rhodes, the candy-striped **Süleymaniye mosque**, rebuilt in the nineteenth century on foundations 300 years older. The old town is in fact well sown with mosques and *mescids* (the Islamic equivalent of a chapel), many of them converted from Byzantine shrines after the 1522 conquest, when the Christians were expelled from the medieval precinct and founded new quarters outside. A couple of these mosques are still used by the sizeable **Turkish-speaking minority** here, some of them descended from Muslims who fled Crete between 1913 and 1923. Their most enduring civic contribution is the imposing **hamam** or Turkish bath on Platía Ariónos up in the southwest corner of the medieval city, although sadly this is shut indefinitely.

Heading downhill and east from the Süleymaniye mosque, **Odhós Sokrátous**, once the heart of the Ottoman bazaar, is now the "Via Turista", packed with fur and jewellery stores and milling tourists. Beyond the fountain in Platía Ippokrátous, Odhós Aristotélous leads into the Platía ton Evreón Martirón (Square of the Jewish Martyrs), renamed in memory of the large local community that was almost totally annihilated in early 1944. You can visit the ornate **synagogue** on Odhós Simíou just to the south, maintained essentially as a memorial to the 2000 Jews of Rhodes and Kós sent from here to the deathcamps.

About a kilometre southwest of the new town, overlooking the west-coast road, the sparse remains of **Hellenistic Rhodes** – a restored theatre and stadium, plus a few columns of an Apollo temple – perch atop Monte Smith, the hill of Áyios Stéfanos renamed after a British admiral who used it as a watchpoint during the Napoleonic wars. The wooded site is popular with joggers and strollers, but for summer shade and greenery the best spot is the **Rodini park**, nearly two kilometres south of town on the road to Lindos. On August evenings a wine tasting festival is held here by the municipal authorities.

Arrival, orientation and information

All international and inter-island **ferries** dock at the middle of Rhodes' three ports, the commercial harbour; the only exceptions are local **boats** to and from Sími, and the **hydrofoils**, which use the yacht harbour of Mandhráki. Its entrance was supposedly once straddled by the Colossus, an ancient statue of Apollo built to celebrate the end of the 305 BC siege; today two columns surmounted by bronze deer are less overpowering replacements.

The **airport** is 17km southwest of town, near the village of Paradhíssi; public urban buses make the trip just six times daily. Those arriving at an unsociable time of day on a charter may find that the night taxi fare into town is barely any less than the cost of hiring a car for a day at the airport counter.

Orange-and-white *KTEL* **buses** for both the west and east coasts of Rhodes leave from two almost adjacent terminals on Odhós Papágou, within sight of the so-called New Market (a tourist trap). Between the lower eastern station and the **taxi** rank at Platía Rimínis there's a helpful **municipal tourist office** (Mon–Fri 8am–7pm, Sat 8am–6pm), while some way up Papágou on the corner of Makaríou is the **EOT office** (Mon–Fri 7.30am–3pm); both dispense bus and ferry schedules plus information sheets on archeological site times and admissions.

Accommodation

Inexpensive pensions abound in the old town, contained almost entirely in the quad bounded by Odhós Omírou to the south, Sokrátous to the north, Perikléous to the east and Ippodhámou to the west. Even in peak season, lodging is the one thing in Rhodes that's still reasonably priced. At crowded times, or late at night, it's prudent to accept the offers of proprietors meeting the ferries and change base next day if necessary.

Andreas, Omírou 28D (☎0241/34 156). Perennially popular, this hotel is the best, most imaginative of the old-house restorations. All rooms have sinks, and there is a terrace bar with a view, and French and English is spoken. ③.

Apollo, Omírou 28C (☎0241/35 064). Basic but clean and friendly rooms place. Self-catering kitchen makes this good for longer stays. ②.

Casa de la Sera, Thisséos 38 (☎0241/75 154). Another Jewish-quarter renovation, with wonderful floor tiles in the en suite rooms and a breakfast bar. ④.

Kastro, Platía Ariónos (☎0241/20 446). Vassilis the proprietor is a famous eccentric artist renowned for his royalist leanings, but the hotel is fine for budget rooms; expect some noise from nearby restaurants. ②.

ROOM PRICE SCALES

All establishments listed in this book have been price-graded according to the scale outlined below. The rates quoted represent the cheapest available room in high season; all are prices for a double room, except for category ①, which are per person rates. Out of season, rates can drop by up to fifty percent, especially if you negotiate rates for a stay of three or more nights. Single rooms, where available, cost around seventy percent of the price of a double.

Rented private rooms on the islands usually fall into the ② or ③ categories, depending on their location and facilities, and the season; a few in the ④ category are more like plush self-catering apartments. They are not generally available from late October through the beginning of April, when only hotels tend to remain open.

① 1400–2000dr (£4–5.50/US$6–8.50)	④ 8000–12000dr (£22–33/US$33–50)
② 4000–6000dr (£11–16.50/US$17–25)	⑤ 12000–16000dr (£33–44/US$50–66)
③ 6000–8000dr (£16.50–22/US$25–33)	⑥ 16000dr (£44/US$66) and upwards

For more accommodation details, see pp.32–34.

FLATTERY WILL GET YOU ROUND THE WORLD!

"The excellence of the TV series is only surpassed by the books. All who have had any involvement in Rough Guides deserve accolades heaped upon them and free beer for life."
Diane Evans, Ontario, Canada

"I've yet to find a presentation style that can match the Rough Guide's. I was very impressed with the amount of detail, ease of reference and the smooth way it swapped from giving sound advice to being entertaining."
Ruth Higginbotham, Bedford, UK

"What an excellent book the Rough Guide was, like having a local showing us round for our first few days."
Andy Leadham, Stoke, UK

"Thank you for putting together such an excellent guidebook. In terms of accuracy and historical/cultural information, it is head and shoulders above the other books."
John Speyer, Yorba Linda, California

"We were absolutely amazed at the mass of detail which the Rough Guide contains. I imagine the word Rough is a deliberate misnomer!"
Rev. Peter McEachran, Aylesbury, UK

"I have rarely, if ever, come across a travel guide quite so informative, practical and accurate! Bravo!"
Alan Dempster, Dublin, Ireland

"The Rough Guide proved to be a very popular and useful book and was often scanned by other travellers whose own guides were not quite so thorough."
Helen Jones, Avon, UK

"My husband and I enjoyed the Rough Guide very much. Not only was it informative, but very helpful and great fun!"
Felice Pomeranz, Massachusetts, USA

"I found the Rough Guide the most valuable thing I took with me – it was fun to read and completely honest about everywhere we visited."
Matthew Rodda, Oxford, UK

"Congratulations on your bible – well worth the money!"
Jenny Angel, New South Wales, Australia

"Our Rough Guide has been as indispensable as the other Rough Guides we have used on our previous journeys."
Enric Torres, Barcelona, Spain

We don't promise the earth, but if your letter is really useful (criticism is welcome as well as praise!), we'll certainly send you a free copy of a Rough Guide. Legibility is a big help and, if you're writing about more than one country, please keep the updates on separate pages. All letters are acknowledged and forwarded to the authors.

Please write, indicating which book you're updating, to:

Rough Guides, 1 Mercer St, London WC2H 9QJ, England,
or
Rough Guides, 3rd floor, 375 Hudson St, New York, NY 10014-3657, USA

Travel the world
HIV *Safe*

Travel *Safe*

HIV, the virus that causes AIDS, is worldwide.

You're probably aware of the dangers of getting it from unprotected sex, but there are many other risks when travelling.

Wherever you're visiting it makes sense to take precautions. Try to avoid any medical or dental treatment, but if it's necessary, make sure the equipment is sterilised. Likewise, if you really need to have a blood transfusion, always ask for screened blood.

Make sure your travelling companions are aware of the risks and the necessary precautions. In fact, you should take your own sterile medical pack, available from larger high street pharmacies.

Remember, ear and body piercing, acupuncture and even tattoos could be risky, because they all involve puncturing the skin. And although you might not normally consider any of these things now, after a few drinks - you never know.

Of course, the things that are dangerous at home are just as dangerous when you travel. So don't inject drugs or share works.

Avoid casual sex and always use a good quality condom when having sex with a new partner (and each time you have sex with them).

And it's not just a 'gay disease' either. In fact, worldwide, it's most commonly transmitted through sex between men and women.

For information in the UK:

Ring for the TravelSafe leaflet on the Health Literature Line freephone 0800 555 777, or pick one up at a doctor's surgery or pharmacy.

Further advice on HIV and AIDS: National AIDS Helpline: 0800 567 123. (Cannot be reached from abroad).

The Terrence Higgins Trust Helpline (12 noon–10pm) provides advice and counselling on HIV/AIDS issues: 0171 242 1010.

MASTA Travellers Health Line: 0891 224 100.

Travel *Safe*

Travel the world HIV *Safe*

Iliana, Gavála 1 (☎0241/30 251). This former Jewish mansion exudes a Victorian boarding-house atmosphere, but is clean and quiet enough with private facilities. ③.

Minos, Omírou 5 (☎0241/31 813). Modern and hence a bit sterile, but with great views, this pension is managed by an English-speaking family. ③.

S. Nikolis, Ippodhámou 61 (☎0241/34 561). A range of establishments at the top of the old town. Hotel rates (⑤) include a huge breakfast, or there's the option of self-catering apartments, a simple pension (③) or a youth hostel (①). Booking essential for hotel and apartments, but accepted only with credit-card number.

Eating and drinking

Eating well for a reasonable price is a challenge, but not an insurmountable one. As a general rule, the further back from Sokrátous you go, the better value you'll find.

Aigaion, corner Eskhílou and Aristofánous. Run by a welcoming Kalymniot family, this *ouzeri* features brown bread and curiosities such as *foúski* (soft-shell oyster).

Le Bistrot, Omírou 22–24. Open for lunch and supper daily except Sun, this is a genuine French-run bistro with excellent if pricey food. Always full, with a loyal expatriate clientele.

Mikis, in alley behind Sokrátous 17. Very inexpensive hole-in-the-wall place, serving only fish, salads and wine.

Nireas, Platía Sofkléous 22. Another good, family-run Greek *ouzeri*; reservations advised in the evenings.

O Meraklis, Aristotélous 32. This *pátsas* (tripe-and-trotter soup) kitchen is only open 3–7am for a clientele of post-club lads, Turkish stallholders, night-club singers and travellers just stumbled off an overnight ferry. Great free entertainment, and the soup's good, too.

O Yiannis, in Koskinoú village. *Mézedhes* and wine here works out very reasonably for a group; you can get the last bus out here, but will have to take a taxi back.

Palia Istoria, Mitropóleos 108, corner of Dhendhrínou, in south extension of new town, Álmoss district. Reckoned to be the best *ouzeri* on Rhodes, but very expensive.

Sea Star, Platía Sofokléous. The Nireas' rival, with seafood offered by a colourful proprietor.

Yiannis, Apéllou 41, below *Hotel Sydney*. Fair portions of Greek oven food, dished out by a family long resident in New York.

Nightlife

Except for some low-key pubs around Platía Dhoriéos, such as *Mango Bar*, Rhodes old town is tomb-silent at night. Most of the action is in the new town, particularly along Dhiákou. Theme night and various drinks-with-cover gimmicks predominate; for sheer tackiness none can match *Tropical Oasis* near the EOT, where loud music videos, a "Dancing Waters" show and several bars with exorbitant prices surround a pool to which admission is allegedly free. More sedate are the **folk dances** (Mon–Fri at 9.20pm, April–Oct; 2500dr, students 1250dr) presented by the *Nelly Dimoglou Company*, performed in the gardens of Andhroníkou, near Platía Ariónos. There are also three cinemas: the *Rodou* in Makaríou 45, the *Dhimotikou* in Efstathiádhi and the *Esperia* on Ikostipémptis Martíou, all in the new town.

Listings

Airlines *British Airways*, Platía Kíprou 1 (☎0241/27 756); *KLM*, Ammohóstou 3 (☎0241/21 010); *Olympic*, Iérou Lóhou 9 (☎0241/24 571); *SEEA*, Pávlou Melá 17 (☎0241/21 998). Scheduled flights are exorbitant; there's a very faint chance of picking up an unclaimed return charter seat to northern Europe – ask at the various group tour offices.

Bike rental Mopeds will make little impact on Rhodes' huge area, and gain you scant respect from motorists. Sturdier Yamaha 125s, suitable for two persons, go for as little as 3500dr a day. There are plenty of outlets, especially around Odhós Dhiákou.

Bookstores *Academy*, Iónos Dhragoúmi 7, *Moses Cohen*, Thevréli 83D, both in the new town.

Car rental Prices are the island standard of £33/US$50 per day, but can be bargained down to about £27/US$40 a day, all-in, out of season. Among the more flexible local outfits are *Holiday Autos*, Yioryíou Leónidos 38 (☎0241/74 532), *Orion*, next door at no. 36 (☎0241/22 137); *MBC*, Ikostipémptis Martíou 29 (☎0241/28 617) and *Kosmos*, Papaloúka 31 (☎0241/74 374).

Exchange Most bank branches are in the new town, keeping weekday evening and Saturday morning hours; at other times use the ATMs of the *Commercial Bank*, *Credit Bank*, *Ionian Bank* (with a useful branch in the old town), or *National Bank*.

Ferries Tourist office handouts list the bewildering array of representatives for the seven boat and two hydrofoil companies which operate here. A recommended general travel agency in the old town is *Castellania*, Evripídhou 1–3, corner Platía Ippokrátous; schedule information is available at the *limenarheio*, on Mandhráki esplanade near the post office.

Phones At the corner of Amerikís and Ikostipémptis Martíou in the new town, open daily 6am–11pm. Many of the booths offer long-distance phone service, but beware of possible surcharges on the basic OTE rates.

Post office Main branch with outgoing mail, poste restante and exchange windows on Mandhráki harbour, open Mon–Fri 7.30am–8pm; mobile office on Órfeos in the old town, open shorter hours.

The east coast

Heading down the coast from the capital you have to go some way before you escape the crowds from local beach hotels, their numbers swelled by visitors using the regular buses from town or on boat tours out of Mandhráki. Nostalgia buffs might look in at the decayed, all-but-abandoned spa of **Thérmes Kallithéas**, dating from the Italian period. Located 3km south of Kallithéa resort proper, down an unsigned road through pines, the spa is set in a palm grove and is illuminated at night to create a hugely enjoyable spectacle of mock-orientalia. The former fishing village of **FALIRÁKI**, which draws a youngish package clientele, is all too much in the mode of a Spanish *costa* resort, while the scenery just inland – arid, scrubby sand-hills at the best of times – has been made that much more dreary by fire damage that stretches way beyond Líndhos. **TSAMBÍKAS**, 26km south of town, is the first place at which most will seriously consider stopping. Actually the very eroded flank of a much larger extinct volcano, the hill has a monastery at the summit offering unrivalled views along some 50km of coastline. A steep, 1500-metre-long cement drive leads to a small car park and a snack bar, from which concrete steps lead to the summit. The monastery here is unremarkable except for the happier consequences of the September 8 festival: childless women climb up – sometimes on their knees – to be relieved of their barrenness, and any children born afterwards are dedicated to the Virgin with the names Tsambikos or Tsambika, names particular to the Dodecanese.

From the top you can survey **KOLÍMBIA** just to the north, once an unspoiled beach stretching south from a tiny cove ringed with volcanic rocks but now backed by a dozen, scattered low-rise hotels. Shallow **Tsambíkas bay** on the south side of the headland warms up early in the spring, and the excellent beach, though protected by the forest service from development other than a couple of tavernas, teems with people all summer. If it's too much, you can walk further south over another cape to the relatively deserted bay of **Stégna**. This, however, gets a fair bit of traffic from the many tourists staying in **ARHÁNGELOS**, a large village just inland overlooked by a crumbling castle and home to a dwindling leather crafts industry. Though you can disappear into the warren of alleys between the main road and the citadel, the place is now firmly caught up in package tourism, with a full complement of banks, tavernas, mini-marts and jewellery stores. A more peaceful overnight base on this stretch of coast would be **HARÁKI**, a pleasant if undistinguished, two-street fishing port with mostly self-catering accommodation (generally ③) overlooked by the stubby ruins of **Feraklós castle**. You can swim off the town beach if you don't mind an audience from the handful of waterfront cafés and tavernas, but most people head north a kilometre beyond the castle – the last stronghold of the Knights to fall to the Turks – to the secluded **Agáthi beach**. At Haráki, on the right as you face the sea, past the military outpost, is *Efterpi*, the best restaurant on this coast; the Turkish chef used to cook at the Istanbul Hilton.

Líndhos

LÍNDHOS, the island's number-two tourist attraction, erupts 12km south of Haráki.
Like Ródhos Town itself, its charm is heavily undermined by commercialism and
crowds, and there are only two places to stay that are not booked semi-permanently by
tour companies. These are *Pension Electra* and *Pension Katholiki*, next door to each
other on the way to the north beach, but both are of a low standard and overpriced at
③. Recommendable eating places are similarly thin on the ground, although *Agostino's*,
by the southerly beach car park, is notable for bulk wine, real country sausages and the
fact that it counts some locals among its customers. Otherwise, the village is now a
mess of bars, crêperies, package villas, bad restaurants and travel agents – the last
redeemed by car rental rates 25–30 percent less than in Ródhos Town.

At midday dozens of coaches park nose-to-tail on the access road, with even more on
the drive down to the beach. Back in the village itself, traditional houses not snapped
up by the package outfits have been bought and refurbished by wealthy British and
Italians and, although high-rise hotels have been prohibited, the result is not much
better – a curiously lifeless, fake resort.

Nevertheless, if you arrive before or after the tours, when the pebble streets
between the immaculately whitewashed houses are relatively empty, you can still
appreciate the beautiful, atmospheric setting of Líndhos. The **Byzantine church** is
covered with eighteenth-century frescoes, and several of the older fifteenth-to-
eighteenth-century mansions are open to the public; entrance is free but you may come
under pressure to buy something, especially the lace for which the village is noted.

On the bluff above the town, the ancient acropolis with its scaffolding-swaddled Doric
Temple of Athena is found inside the Knights' **castle** (daily 8.30am–5pm; 800dr) – a
surprisingly felicitous blend of two cultures. Though the ancient city of Líndhos and its
original temple date from at least 1100 BC, the present structure was begun by the
tyrant Kleovoulos in the sixth century BC and completed over the next two centuries.

Líndhos' sandy coves, though numerous, are overrated, overcrowded and can be
polluted; if you do base yourself here, better, quieter beaches are to be found south of
Lárdhos (see p.217). At the southern flank of the acropolis huddles the small, sheltered
Saint Paul's harbour, where the apostle is said to have landed on a mission to evangel-
ize the island, though he would doubtless turn in his grave faced with today's ranks of
topless sun-worshipppers.

The west coast

Rhodes' west coast is the windward flank of the island, so it's damper, more fertile and
more forested; most beaches, however, are exposed and decidedly on the rocky side.
None of this has deterred development and as in the east the first few kilometres of the
busy shore road down from the capital have been surrendered entirely to industrial
tourism. From the aquarium down to the airport the asphalt is fringed by an uninter-
rupted line of Miami-beach-style mega-hotels, though such places as Triánda, Kremastí
and Paradhísi are still nominally villages, and appear so in their centres. This was the
first part of the island to be favoured by the package operators, and tends to be
frequented by a decidedly middle-aged, sedate clientele that often can't be bothered to
stir much out of sight of the runways.

Neither the planes buzzing over Paradhísi or the giant power plant at Soroní are
much inducement to pause, and you probably won't want to until reaching the important archeological site of **KAMEIROS**, which with Líndhos and Ialyssos was one of
the three Dorian powers that united in the fifth century BC to found the powerful city-
state of Rhodes. Soon eclipsed by the new capital, Kameiros was abandoned and only
rediscovered in the last century. As a result it is a particularly well-preserved Doric
townscape, doubly worth visiting for its beautiful hillside site (Tues–Sun 8.30am–3pm;

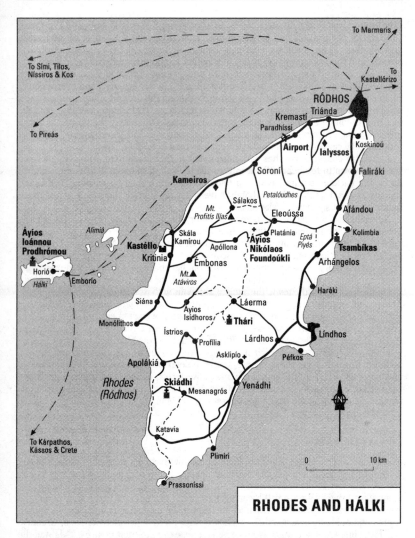

To Marmaris

To Símí, Tílos,
Níssiros & Kos

To
Kastellórizo

RÓDHOS
Triánda
Kremastí
Paradhíssi

To Pireás

Airport   Ialyssos   Koskinoú

Soroní   Faliráki

Kameiros

Petalóudhes

Sálakos

Mt.   Eleoússa   Afándou
Profítís Ilías

Áyios   Alimiá   Skála   Platánia   Eptá   Kolímbia
Ioánnou   Kamírou   Apóllona Áyios   Piyés
Prodhrómou   Kastéllo   Nikólaos   Tsambíkas
                          Kritinía   Foundoúkli
Horió   Émbonas   Arhángelos
Hálki   Emborió   Mt.
                          Atáviros   Haráki

                          Siána   Láerma
                                   Áyios
                          Isidhoros   Thári
Monólithos   Líndhos
              Ístrios   Lárdhos
                      Profília
                          Asklipío   Péfkos
         Apolákiá

    Rhodes   Skiádhi
    (Ródhos)   Mesanagrós   Yenádhi

              Katavía

To Kárpathos,
Kássos & Crete
                          Plimíri
                                        0   10 km

              Prassoníssi

RHODES AND HÁLKI

400dr). While none of the individual remains are spectacular, you can make out the foundations of a few small temples, the *stoa* of the *agora*, and a water catchment basin. Because of the gentle slope of the site, there were no fortifications, nor was there an acropolis.

On the beach below Kameiros there are several tavernas, ideal while waiting for one of the two daily buses back to town (if you're willing to walk 4km back to Kalavárda you'll have a better choice of service). There are more tavernas clustered at **SKÁLA KAMÍROU** 15km south, a tiny anchorage which somewhat inexplicably is the hapless target of coach tours come to see Ye Olde Authentic Fishing Village (decals on the windows of several restaurants attest to the fact). Less heralded is the daily *kaíki* that leaves for the island of **Hálki** at 2.30pm, weather permitting, returning early the next morning; on Wednesdays and Sundays, there are day trips departing at 9am and returning at 4pm.

A couple of kilometres south of Skála, the "Kastello", signposted as **Kástro Kritinías**, is from afar the most impressive of the Knights' rural strongholds, and the access road is too rough for tour buses to pass. Close up it proves to be no more than a shell, with only a chapel and a rubbish-filled cistern more or less intact inside – a glorious shell, though, with fine views west to assorted islets and Hálki. You make a "donation" to the formidable woman at the car park in exchange for fizzy drinks, seasonal fruit or flowers.

Mountain villages

Beyond Kritinía itself, a quiet hillside village with a few rooms and tavernas, the main road winds south through the forest to **SIÁNA**, the most attractive mountain settlement on the island, famous for its aromatic pine-sage honey and *soúma*, the local firewater. Bus tours also stop in at the church on the square, with heavily restored eighteenth-century frescoes. The tiered, flat-roofed farmhouses of **MONÓLITHOS**, 4km southwest at the end of the public bus line, are scant justification for the long trip out here, and food at the two **tavernas** is indifferent owing to the tour-group trade, but the view over the bay is striking, and you could use the village as a base by staying in rooms or at the pricier *Hotel Thomas* (☎0246/61 291; ③). Diversions in the area include yet another **Knights' castle** 2km west of town, photogenically perched on its own pinnacle and enclosing a couple of chapels, and the fine gravel beach of **Foúrni**, five bumpy, curvy kilometres below the castle, its 800-metre extent unsullied except for a seasonal drinks stand. Beyond the headland, to the left as you face the water, are some caves that were hollowed out by early Christians fleeing persecution.

The interior

Inland Rhodes is hilly, and still mostly wooded, despite the depredations of arsonists. You'll need a vehicle to see much here, especially as the main enjoyment is in getting away from it all: no one site justifies the tremendous expense of a taxi or the inconvenience of trying to make the best of the sparse bus schedules.

In retrospect it will probably be the scenery which stands out, along with the last vestiges of the old agrarian life in the slowly depopulating villages. Young Rhodians that do remain in the interior stay largely to help with the grape harvest in late summer (when there's some chance of work for foreigners too). If you have time to spare, and a bit of Greek at your command, traditional hospitality in the form of a drink at the *kafenío*, or perhaps more, is still very much alive.

Ialyssos and the Valley of the Butterflies

Starting from the west coast, turn inland at Triánda for the five-kilometre uphill ride to ancient **Ialyssos** on Filérimos hill. Important as this city was, its visible remains are few; most conspicuous are a subterranean chapel covered with faded frescoes and a Doric fountain. The pine-covered slopes here also shelter the grounds of Filérimos monastery (which you can visit) and a Byzantine-cum-Turkish castle, but the whole ensemble won't take more than an hour of your time.

Beyond Paradhísi, another side turning leads within 7km to **Petaloúdhes**, the "Valley of the Butterflies" (daily June–Sept 9am–6pm; 200dr). Actually a rest stop for Jersey tiger moths, it might more accurately be christened the "Valley of the Tour Buses", but is an appealing place, with liquidambar trees shading and wooden bridges crossing a small stream. Do not imitate the practice of clapping or shouting to launch the tree-roosting moths into flight – this stresses them and interferes with their reproduction.

Eptá Piyés to Profítis Ilías

From the Kolímbia bus stop on the east coast road, it's a three-kilometre walk or drive inland to **Eptá Piyés** (daily April–Nov 9am–6pm; 200dr), a superb oasis with a tiny reservoir for swimming and an unusual streamside taverna. Continuing inland, you reach **ELEOÚSSA** after another 9km, in the shade of the dense forest at the east end of Profítis Ilías ridge. Two other undisturbed villages, Platánia and Apóllona, nestle on the south slopes of the mountain overlooking the start of the burned area, but most people keep straight on 3km further to the late Byzantine church of **Áyios Nikólaos Foundoúkli** (St Nicholas of the Hazelnuts). The partly shaded site has a fine view north over cultivated valleys, and locals descend in force for picnics on weekends; the frescoes inside, dating from the thirteenth to the fifteenth centuries, could use a good cleaning but various scenes from the life of Christ are recognizable.

Negotiating an unsignposted but fairly obvious welter of dirt tracks gets you finally to **Profítis Ilías**, where the Italian-vintage chalet-hotel *Elafos/Elafína* (✆0246/22 225; ⑤) hides in deep woods just north of the 798-metre marker, Rhodes' third-highest point. There's good, gentle strolling around the summit and the namesake monastery, and the lodge's snack bar is generally open in season.

Atáviros villages

All tracks and roads west across Profítis Ilías more or less converge upon the main road from Kalavárda bound for **ÉMBONAS**, a large and architecturally nondescript village backed up against the north slope of 1215-metre Mount Atáviros, roof of the island. Émbonas, with its two pensions and rather carnivores-oriented tavernas (of which *Skevos* is the best), is more geared to handling tourists than you might expect, since it's the venue for summer "folk-dance tours" from Ródhos Town. The village also lies at the heart of the island's most important wine-producing districts, and CAIR – the vintners' cooperative – produce a range of generally excellent varieties: the white *Ilios*, the red *Chevaliers*, and the premium label *Emery*. To see what Émbonas would be like without tourists, carry on clockwise around the peak past the Artámiti monastery, to less-celebrated **ÁYIOS ISÍDHOROS**, with as many vines and tavernas (try *Snag* (sic) *Bar Ataviros*), a more open feel, and the **trailhead** for the five-hour return ascent of Atáviros.

Thári Monastery

There's a mediocre road from Áyios Isídhoros to Siána, and an even worse one that runs the 12km east to Láerma, but the latter is worth enduring if you've any interest at all in Byzantine monuments. In **LÁERMA** proper, the church of Áyios Yióryios, just above the plane-shaded fountain, looks modern but actually contains fourteenth-century frescoes; get the keys from the adjacent *kafenío*. This is just an appetizer for the **monastery of Thári**, lost in pine forests five well-marked kilometres south. The oldest religious foundation on the island, the monastery was re-established as a living community of half a dozen monks in 1990 by a charismatic abbot from Pátmos. The striking *kathólikon* consists of a long nave and short transept surmounted by barrel vaulting. Despite two recent cleanings, the damp of centuries has smudged the frescoes, dating from 1300 to 1450, but they are still exquisite: the most distinct, in the transept, depict the Evangelist Mark and the Archangel Gabriel, while the nave boasts various acts of Christ, including such rarely illustrated scenes as the storm on the Sea of Galilee, meeting Mary Magdalene, and healing the cripple.

The monastery, dedicated to the Archangel Michael, takes its name from the legend of its foundation. A princess, kidnapped by pirates, was abandoned here by her captors; she saw the Archangel in a dream, and he promised her eventual deliverance. In gratitude, she vowed to build as many monasteries in his honour as the gold ring cast from her hand travelled in cubits. Upon being reunited with her parents the deed was done, but the ring was lost in some bushes, and never found. Thus "Thári" comes from *tharévo*, "I hazard, guess, venture", after the family's futile search for the heirloom. In their pique, apparently only one cloister was founded.

The far south

South of a line connecting Monólithos and Lárdhos, you could easily begin to think you had strayed onto another island – at least until the still-inflated prices brought you back to reality. Gone are the five-star hotels and roads to match, and with them most of the crowds. Gone too are most tourist facilities and public transport. Only one daily bus runs to Kataviá, along the east coast, where deserted beaches are backed by sheltering dunes that offer scope for private camping. Tavernas grace the more popular stretches of sand but there are still relatively few places to stay.

A new auxiliary airport is planned for the area, however, so this state of affairs won't persist indefinitely. Already massive construction is beginning behind the sandier patches south of **LÁRDHOS**, solidly on the tourist circuit despite an inland position between Láerma and the peninsula culminating in Líndhos. The beach 2km south is gravelly and the water can be dirty, but is well served by the best of the island's three campsites and the outriders of the small *Lárdhos Bay* complex. Four kilometres east, **PÉFKOS** (*Péfki* on some maps) is a low-key package resort on the beach road to Líndhos; the sea is cleaner than at Lárdhos but beaches are minimal.

Asklipío

Nine kilometres beyond Lárdhos, a paved side road heads 4km inland to **ASKLIPÍO**, a sleepy village guarded by a crumbling castle and graced by the Byzantine church of **Kímisis Theotókou**, whose frescoes are in far better condition than Thári's owing to the drier local climate. To gain admission, call at the priest's house behind the apse, or if that doesn't work, haul on the belfry rope. The building dates from 1060, with a ground plan nearly identical to that of Thári, except that two subsidiary apses were added during the eighteenth century, partly to conceal a secret school in a subterranean crypt. The frescoes themselves are somewhat later than Thári's, though the priest claims that the final work at Thári and the earliest here were executed by the same hand, a master from Híos.

The format and subject matter of the frescoes is rare in Greece: didactic "cartoon strips" which extend completely around the church in some cases, and extensive Old Testament stories in addition to the more usual lives of Christ and the Virgin. There's a complete sequence from Genesis, from the Creation to the Expulsion from Éden; note the comically menacing octopus among the fishes on the Fifth Day. A seldom-encountered *Revelation of John the Divine* takes up most of the east transept, and pebble mosaic flooring decorates both the interior and the vast courtyard.

To the southern tip

Returning to the coast road, there are ample facilities at **YENÁDHI**, though tour operators have yet to arrive. The shore is empty again until **PLIMÍRI**, which consists of a single **taverna** on a sheltered, sandy bay; just off the crumbling jetty, a ten-year-old wreck attracts expert scuba divers. Beyond Plimíri the road curves inland to **KATAVIÁ**, nearly 100km from the capital. There are several tavernas at the junction that doubles as the *platía*, and a few rooms to rent; the village, like so many in the south, is three-quarters deserted, the owners of the closed-up houses off working in Australia or North America.

From Kataviá a rough, marked track leads on to **Prassoníssi**, Rhodes' southern-most extremity and site of a lighthouse automated only in 1989. From May to October you can stroll across the wide, low sandspit to visit, but winter storms swamp this tenuous link and render Prássonissi a true island. Even in summer the prevailing northwesterly winds drive swimmers to the lee side of the spit, leaving the exposed shore to the world-class windsurfers who come to train here. In season the scrubby junipers rustle with tents and caravans; water comes from two **tavernas** flanking the access road. The outfit next to the old windmill is more characterful, but beware of their fish grills, which are tasty but among the most expensive in Greece.

The southwest coast

West of Kataviá, the island loop road emerges onto the deserted, sandy southwest coast, and soon deteriorates in a long, yet-to-be-improved stretch. If freelance camping and nudism are your thing, this is the place to indulge, though you'll need your own transport, or lots of supplies and a stout pair of shoes. Just before the road shapes up again, there's a turning for the fourteenth-century hilltop monastery of **Skiádhi**, which houses a miraculous icon of the Virgin and Child; in the fifteenth century a heretic stabbed the painting, and blood was said to have flowed from the wound in the Mother of God's cheek. The offending hand was, needless to say, instantly paralysed; the fissure, and suspicious brown stains around it, are still visible. You can stay the night upon arrangement with the caretaker, but as with the beaches below you'll have to bring your own kit and on weekends you'll have plenty of (local) company.

The nearest town is modern and unexciting **APOLAKIÁ**, a few kilometres inland but equipped with a couple of **rooms** and **tavernas** plus a general store, ideal for those beachcombers undaunted by the logistics of staying in southern Rhodes. At the central, badly marked roundabout, there always seem to be a few visiting motorists scratching their heads over maps: northwest leads to Monólithos, due south goes back to Kataviá, and the northeast option is a paved scenic road cutting quickly back to Yennádhi. Just a bit further on is the proudly featured side track to an irrigation dam just north, oddly scenic as these things go and plainly visible from Siána overhead.

Hálki

Hálki, a tiny (20 square kilometres) limestone speck west of Rhodes, is a member of the Dodecanese in its own right, though all but three hundred of the population have decamped (mostly to Rhodes or to Tarpon Springs, Florida) in the wake of a devastating sponge blight early in this century. Depsite a renaissance of tourism in recent years, the island is tranquil compared to Rhodes, with a slightly weird, hushed atmosphere; the big event of the day is when someone catches a fish.

The first hint of development came in 1983, when UNESCO designated Hálki as the "isle of peace and friendship", and made it the seat of an annual summer international youth conference. (Tílos was approached first but declined the honour.) As part of the deal, 150 crumbling houses in the harbour town of Emborió were to be restored as guest lodges for the delegates and other interested parties, with UNESCO footing the bill. In the event, only one hotel was actually finished, after the critical lack of fresh water which had hampered all previous attempts at tourist development was supposedly remedied by the discovery of undersea aquifers by a French geological team. By 1988 the rest of the grandiose plans had still not been seriously acted on. The only tangible sign of "peace and friendship" was an unending stream of UNESCO and Athenian bureaucrats and their dependents occupying every available bed at unpredictable intervals and staging drunken, musical binges under the guise of "ecological conferences". The islanders, fed up with what had obviously turned out to be a scam, sent the freeloaders packing at the end of that year.

Emborió

Since then, in conjunction with specialist tour operators, most of the designated houses in **EMBORIÓ** have been restored, but all are pretty much block-booked by the companies themselves and occupied by a rather staid, well-mannered clientele; independent travellers will be lucky to find anything at all. Places to start hunting include *The Captain's House* (☎0241/45 201; ③), where the English co-manager, Christine Sakelaridhes, can point you in likely directions, *Pension Kleanthi* (☎0241/37 648 or 57 334; ③), and *Hotel Manos* (☎0241/45 295; ②). Of the several **tavernas** on Emborío waterfront, *Maria's* and *Yiannis* are about the most reliable, while *Omonia* offers more authenticity.

There's a **post office** (the best place to change money), three stores, a bakery, and two **beaches** nearby. Póndamos is sandy and minute, with *Nick's Taverna*, which serves good lunches to beach-goers and also has rooms (☎0241/57 295; ②); Yialí, north of Emborío, is larger and pebbly.

The rest of the island

Three kilometres inland lies the old pirate-safe village of **HORIÓ**, abandoned in the 1950s but still crowned by the Knights' castle. Across the way, the little church of **Stavrós** is a venue for one of the two big island festivals on September 14. There's little else to see or do here, though you can spend a few enjoyable hours **walking** across the island. A newly bulldozed dirt road picks up where the cement "Tarpon Springs Boulevard" mercifully ends; the latter was donated by the expatriate community in Florida to ensure easy Cadillac access to the Stavrós *paniyíri* grounds, though what Hálki really needed (and still needs) is a proper sewage system and salt-free water supply. At the end of the walk you'll come to the monastery of **Ayíou Ioánniou Prodhrómou**. The caretaking family there can put you up in a cell (except around August 29, the other big festival date), but you'll need to bring supplies. The terrain en route is monotonous, but compensated by views over half the Dodecanese and Turkey.

Kastellórizo (Méyisti)

Kastellórizo's official name, Méyisti (biggest), seems more an act of defiance than a statement of fact. While the largest of a tiny group of islands, it is in fact the smallest of the Dodecanese, barely more than three nautical miles off the Turkish coast but over seventy from its nearest Greek neighbour (Rhodes). At night you find its lights quite outnumbered by those of the Turkish town of Kaş, across the bay.

Less than a century ago there were 16,000 people here, supported by a fleet of schooners which made fortunes transporting goods, mostly timber, from the Greek towns of Kalamaki (now Kalkan) and Andifelos (Kaş) on the Anatolian mainland. But the advent of steam power and the Italian seizure of the Dodecanese in 1912 sent the island into decline. Shipowners failed to modernize their fleets, preferring to sell their ships to the British for the Dardanelles campaign, and the new frontier between the island and republican Turkey, combined with the expulsion of all Anatolian Greeks in 1923, deprived any remaining vessels of their trade. During the 1930s the island enjoyed a brief renaissance when it became a major stopover point for French and Italian seaplanes, but events at the close of World War II put an end to any hopes of the island's continued viability.

When Italy capitulated to the Allies in the autumn of 1943, a few hundred British commandos occupied Kastellórizo until displaced by a stronger German force in the spring of 1944. At some stage during the hasty departure of Commonwealth forces, the fuel dump caught fire and an adjacent arsenal exploded, taking with it more than half of the 2000 houses on Kastellórizo. Enquiries have concluded that the retreating Allies did some looting, though it was probably Greek pirates engaging in some pillaging of their own who accidentally or deliberately caused the conflagration. In any event the British are not especially popular here; islanders were further angered by the fact that an Anglo-Greek committee delayed for many years the payment of reparations to 850 surviving applicants in Athens; furthermore, those who had emigrated to Australia, and the few who chose to stay on the island after 1945, were strangely ineligible for such benefits. Even before these events most of the population had left for Rhodes, Athens, Australia and North America. Today there are less than 200 people living permanently on Kastellórizo, and they are largely maintained by remittances from emigrants and by subsidies from the Greek government, which fears that the island will revert to Turkey should their numbers diminish any further.

Kastellórizo Town

The remaining population is concentrated in the northern harbour, **KASTELLÓRIZO** – the finest, so it is said, between Beirut and Pireás – and its little "suburb" of **Mandhráki**, just over the fire-blasted hill with its half-ruined castle of the Knights. The castle now houses the local **museum** (Tues–Sun 7.30am–2.30pm; free), with displays including plates from a Byzantine shipwreck, frescoes rescued from decaying churches, and a reconstruction of an ancient basilica. The surviving quayside mansions, with their tiled roofs, wooden balconies and long, narrow windows, have obvious counterparts in Anatolian villages across the water. One street behind the waterfront, though, all is desolation – abandonment having succeeded where the 1944 fire failed.

Despite its apparently terminal plight, Kastellórizo may have a future of sorts. During the 1980s the government dredged the harbour to accommodate cruise ships, completed an airport for flights to and from Rhodes, and briefly contemplated making the island an official port of entry, a measure calculated to appeal to the many yachties who call here. Each summer, too, the population is swelled by returnees of "Kassie" ancestry, some of whom celebrate traditional weddings in the **Áyios Konstandínos** cathedral, betwen the port and Mandhráki, with its ancient columns pilfered from Patara in Asia Minor. Perhaps the biggest boost for the island's tourism industry in recent years has come from its use as the location for the film *Mediterraneo*, which has resulted in a tidal wave of Italian visitors.

Practicalities

Despite its recent strut in front of the cameras, Kastellórizo is not prepared for more than a few dozen visitors; water and fresh produce, apart from fish, can be in short supply. **Pensions** tend to be fairly basic, with long climbs up and down stairs to a single bathroom. If you're not met off the boat, the best budget option is the restored mansion-pension of the Mavrothalassitis family (☎0241/49 202; ②), or try *Paradhisos* (☎0241/49 074; ②) at the west end of the seafront, *Barbara* (☎0241/49 295; ②), at the opposite end of things, or the more modern *Kristallo* (☎0241/41 209; ②). More luxury is available, at a price, at the *Hotel Meyisti* (☎0241/49 272; ⑥).

Waterfront **tavernas** have had a long and detrimental acquaintance with the yacht market; much better restaurants are to be found inland. Especially recommended are *Iy Orea Meyisti*, run by the Mavrothalassitis family (they of the pension), and *Ouzeri O Meyisteas*, behind the disused municipal market building, which specializes in reasonably priced and generous helpings of goat chops.

The **post office** is at the far end of things, behind *Hotel Meyisti*; there's no OTE or bank. Most ferry companies are represented by one of several grocery stores, while the only travel agency, *DiZi Travel*, has a monopoly on **flights** back to Rhodes.

Kastellórizo has traditionally depended heavily on produce smuggled across from Kaş and lately it has been possible to arrange a ride over **to Turkey** on the supply boat

Varvara, run by the *Taverna Apolavsi*. It's a bit of a racket, however: since Kastellórizo is not an official port of entry/exit, non-"Kassies" must pay a hefty "special visa fee" to customs; the ride itself, though, may be free – if the *Varvara*'s crew were going shopping anyway.

The rest of the island

Swimming is complicated by the total absence of beaches and the abundance of sea urchins and razor-sharp limestone reefs everywhere; the easiest access is beyond the graveyard at Mandhráki. Perseverance is rewarded by clear waters graced by a rich variety of marine life. Over on the east coast, accessible only by boat, is the grotto of **Perastá**, famed for its stalactites and the strange blue light effects inside; rubber-raft trips give you just two hours there or, for more money, you can take it in as part of a day tour that includes Rho islet (see below).

Heat (infernal in summer) permitting, you can hike forty minutes west of the port on a track, then a path, passing country chapels along the way to **Paleokástro**, site of the Doric city. From the heights you've tremendous views over the elephant's-foot-shaped harbour and surrounding Greek islets across to Turkey. Until her death in 1982, "The Lady of **Rhó**", on the **islet** of that name, resolutely hoisted the Greek flag each day in defiance of the Turks on the mainland. Should you take a *kaíki* day trip out here, her grave is the first things you see when you dock; from the tomb a path heads southeast for 25 minutes to the islet's southerly port. The islet has no facilities – just one caretaker, four dogs and hundreds of goats – so bring your own food and water.

Sími

Sími's most pressing problem, lack of water, is in many ways also its greatest asset. If the rain cisterns don't fill in winter, brackish water must be imported at great expense from Rhodes. So, however much it might want to, the island can't hope to support more than two or three large hotels. Instead hundreds of people are shipped in daily during the season from Rhodes, relieved of their money and sent back. This arrangement suits both the islanders and those visitors lucky enough to stay longer. Many foreigners return regularly, or even own houses here – indeed since the mid-1980s the more desirable dwellings, ruined or otherwise, have been sold off in such numbers that the island has essentially become the Ídhra of the Dodecanese.

Sími Town

The island's capital – and only proper town – consists of **Yialós**, the port, and **Horió**, on the hillside above, collectively known as **SÍMI**. Incredibly, less than a hundred years ago the town was richer and more populous (30,000) than Ródhos Town. Wealth came from expertise in shipbuilding and sponge-diving nurtured since pre-Classical times. Under the Ottomans, Sími, like many of the Dodecanese, enjoyed considerable autonomy in exchange for a yearly tribute in sponges to the sultan; but the 1919–22 war, the advent of synthetic sponges, and the gradual replacement of the crews by Kalymniotes spelt doom for the local economy. Vestiges of both activities remain, but the souvenir-shop sponges are mostly of North American origin today, and now many of the magnificent nineteenth-century mansions are roofless and deserted, their windows gaping blankly across the fine natural harbour. The 3000 remaining Simiotes are scattered fairly evenly throughout the mixture of Neoclassical and more typical island dwellings, though despite the surplus of properties many outsiders have preferred to build anew, rather than restore shells accessible only by donkey or on

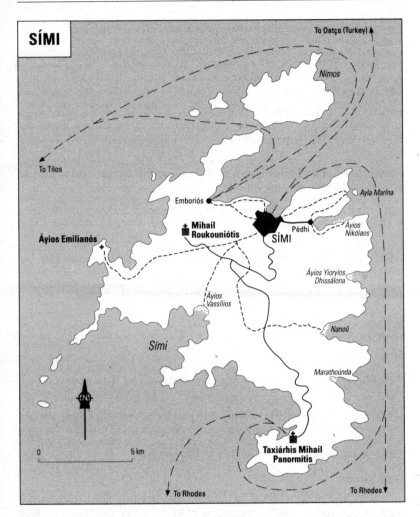

foot. As on Kastellórizo, a wartime ammunition blast – this time set off by the retreating Germans – levelled hundreds of houses up in Horió. Shortly afterwards, the official surrender of the Dodecanese to the Allies was signed here on May 8, 1945: a plaque marks the spot at the present-day *Restaurant Les Katerinettes* (not otherwise recommended), and each year on that date there's a fine festival with music and dance.

The **port**, a protected historical area since the early 1970s, is deceptively lively, especially between noon and 4pm when the Rhodes-based excursion boats are in, but one street back from the water, the more peaceful pace of village life takes over. Two massive stair-paths, the Kalí Stráta and Katarráktes, effectively deter many of the day-trippers and are most dramatically climbed towards sunset; the massive ruins along the lower reaches of the Kalí Stráta are lonely and sinister after dark, home only to wild figs and nightjars.

Follow blue arrows through Horió to the excellent local **museum** (Tues–Sun 10am–2pm; 400dr). Housed in a fine old mansion at the back of the village, the museum concentrates on Byzantine and medieval Sími, with exhibits on frescoes in isolated churches and a gallery of medieval icons. On the way back to central Horió, the nineteenth-century pharmacy, with its apothecary jars and wooden drawers full of exotic remedies, is worth a look.

At the very pinnacle of things a **castle of the Knights** occupies the site of Sími's ancient acropolis, and you can glimpse a stretch of Cyclopean wall on one side. A dozen churches grace Horió; that of the Ascension, inside the fortifications, is a replacement of the one blown to bits when the Germans torched the munitions cached there. One of the bells in the new belfry is the nose-cone of a thousand-pound bomb, hung as a memorial.

Arrival and services

There are daily **excursion boats** from Mandhráki in Ródhos Town, but you'll come under considerable pressure at the quay to buy an expensive return ticket – not what you want if you're off island-hopping and don't plan to return to Rhodes. Either insist on a one-way ticket, or better still, buy tickets through travel agents on Rhodes or take the islanders' own unpublicized and significantly cheaper boat, the *Symi I*, which sails to Rhodes in the morning, returning between 2pm and 6pm after shopping hours are done. Twice a week there are mainline ferries as well.

The **OTE** and **post office** are open the standard Monday to Friday hours; there are full-service **banks** and designated exchange agents for odd hours. In summer an unmarked green-and-white van shuttles between Yialós and Pédhi via Horió at regular intervals until 11pm; in winter, it is replaced by a blue van. There are also three taxis, though this is a perfect island for boat and walking excursions. *ANES*, the outlet for *Symi I* tickets, and *Psihas*, the agent for all big inter-island **ferries**, are one alley apart in the market place.

Accommodation

The **accommodation** situation for independent travellers is tough, though not nearly so bad as on Hálki. Studios, rather than simple rooms, predominate, and package operators control most of these; if there are any vacancies, proprietors meet arriving boats. Best value are rooms with kitchen facilities let by the English-speaking *Katerina Tsakiris* (☎0241/71 813; ③), with a grandstand view over the harbour; reservations usually essential. Rather more basic are two standbys down by the market area, the *Glafkos* (☎0241/71 358; rooms ②, studios ③) on the square, and the fairly cramped, last-resort *Egli* (☎0241/71 392; ②). With a bit more to spend, there are rooms, studios and houses managed by the *Jean & Tonic* bar (☎0241/71 819; ③–④), or the *Hotel Horio* (☎0241/71 800; ④) and the adjacent *Hotel Fiona* (☎0241/72 088; ④) are good, traditional-style outfits at the top of the Kalí Stráta up in Horió. If money's no object, the *Aliki* (☎0241/71 665; ⑤), a few paces right from the clocktower, is also a famous monument. Failing all of these, the best strategy is to appeal for help from *Sunny Land* (☎0241/71 320), the first agency you encounter after disembarking: their weekly rates for villas, houses and apartments are highly competitive even if you don't stay a full seven days.

Eating and drinking

You're best off avoiding entirely the north and west side of the port, where menus, prices and attitudes tend to have been terminally warped by the day-trade. Exceptions are *Tholos*, an excellent female-run *ouzeri* out beyond the Haráni boatyard, and two places with unbeatable views – *Elpidha*, an *ouzeri*-café near *Sunny Land*, which looks straight across the water at *Tembeloskala*, another good *ouzeri*-bar. Matters improve perceptibly as you press further inland or up the hill. At the very rear of what remains of Sími's bazaar, *O Meraklis* has polite service and well-cooked dishes; *Neraïdha*, well back from the water near the OTE, is delicious and still reasonably priced despite its discovery by tours. Up in Horió, *Georgios* is a decades-old institution, serving what can only be described as large portions of Greek *nouvelle cuisine* in a pebble-mosaic court-yard – excellent value, but open for dinner only.

Nearly half a dozen **bars** satisfy the urge for a drink in Yialós. With a large ex-pat community, a few bars are run by foreigners: in Horió, *Jean & Tonic* caters to a mixed clientele; down at Yialós, *Vapori* is the oldest bar on the island, welcoming customers with desserts, breakfast and free newspapers.

Around the island

Sími has no big sandy beaches, but there are plenty of pebbly stretches at the heads of the deep narrow bays which indent the coastline. **PÉDHI**, 45 minutes' walk from Yialós, still has much of the character of a fishing hamlet, with enough water in the plain behind – the island's largest – to support a few vegetable gardens. The beach is average-to-poor, though, and the giant *Pedhi Beach* hotel (packages only) has consider-ably bumped up prices at the three local tavernas, of which the most reasonable and authentic is *Iy Kamares*. Many will opt for another twenty minutes of walking via goat track along the south shore of the almost landlocked bay to **Áyios Nikólaos**, the only all-sand beach on Sími, with sheltered swimming and a mediocre taverna. Alternatively, a marked path on the north side of the inlet leads within an hour to **Ayía Marína**, where you can swim out to a monastery-capped islet.

Around Yialós, you'll find tiny **Nós** "beach" ten minutes past the boat yards at Haráni, but there's sun here only until lunchtime and it's packed with day-trippers. You can continue along the coastal track here past tiny gravel coves and rock slabs where nudists disport themselves, or cut inland from the Yialós *platía* past the abandoned desalination plant, to the appealing **Emborió** bay, with two tavernas – *Maria's* is the best. Inland from this are a Byzantine mosaic fragment and, nearby, a catacomb complex known locally as *Dhodheka Spilia*.

Plenty of other, more secluded coves are accessible by energetic walkers with sturdy footwear, or those prepared to pay a modest sum for the taxi-boats that leave daily in season from 10am, with the last trip out around noon or 1pm. These are the best way to reach the southern bays of **Marathoúnda** and **Nanoú**, and the only method of getting to the spectacular, cliff-girt fjord of **Áyios Yióryios Dhissálona**. Dhissálona lies in shade after 1pm, and Marathoúnda lacks a taverna, making Nanoú the most popular destination for day-trips. The beach at Nanoú consists of 200m of gravel sand and pebbles, with a scenic backdrop and a taverna behind – the latter prob-ably the most reasonable of Sími's far-flung eateries.

On foot, you can cross the island – which has retained patches of its natural juniper forest – in two hours to **Áyios Vassílios**, the most scenic of the gulfs, or in a little more time to **Áyios Emilianós**, where you can stay the night (bring supplies) in a wave-lashed cloister at the island's extreme west end. On the way to the latter you might look in at the monastery of **Mihaíl Roukouniótis**, Sími's oldest, with lurid eighteenth-century frescoes and a peculiar ground plan: the *kathólikon* is actually two stacked churches, the currently used one built atop an earlier structure abandoned to the damp. The less intrepid can explore on guided walks led by Hugo Tyler (☎0241/71 670), which are generally met by a boat for the ride home.

The Archangel is also honoured at the huge monastery of **Taxiárhis Mihaíl Panormítis**, Sími's biggest rural attraction and generally the first port of call for the excursion boats from Rhodes. You get a quick half-hour tour with them; if you want more time, you'll have to come on a "jeep safari" from Yialós, or arrange to stay the night (for a donation), in the *ksenónas* set aside for pilgrims. There are numbers of these in summer, as Mihaíl has been adopted as the patron of sailors in the Dodecanese.

Like many of Sími's monasteries, it was thoroughly pillaged during the last war, so don't expect too much of the building or its treasures. An appealing pebble court surrounds the central *kathólikon*, tended by the single remaining monk, lit by an improbable number of oil lamps and graced by a fine *témblon*, though the frescoes are recent and mediocre. The small museum (100dr) contains a strange mix of precious antiques, junk (stuffed crocodiles and koalas), votive offerings, models of ships named *Taxiarhis* or *Panormitis*, and a chair piled with messages-in-bottles brought here by Aegean currents – the idea being that if the bottle or toy boat arrived, the sender got his or her wish. A tiny beach, a shop/*kafenío* and a taverna round out the list of amenities; near the latter stands a memorial commemorating three Greeks, including the monastery's abbot, executed in February 1944 by the Germans for aiding British commandos.

Tílos

The small, blissfully quiet island of **Tílos**, with a population of only 350 (shrinking to 80 in winter), is one of the least visited of the Dodecanese, although it can be visited as a day trip by hydrofoil once or twice a week. Why anyone should want to come for just a few hours is unclear: while it's a wonderful place to rest on the beach or go walking, there is nothing very striking at first glance. After a few days, however, you may have stumbled on several of the seven small castles of the Knights of Saint John which stud the crags, or gained access to some of the inconspicuous medieval chapels, some fres-

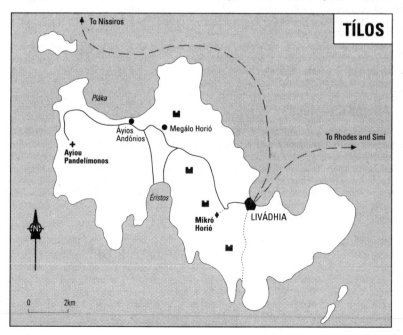

coed or pebble-mosaiced, clinging to hillsides. Though rugged and scrubby on the heights, the island has ample water – mostly pumped up from the agricultural plains – and groves of oak and terebinth near the cultivated areas. The volcano on neighbouring Níssiros has contributed pumice beds and red-lava-sand beaches to the landscape as well. From many points on the island you've fine views across to Sími, Turkey and Níssiros.

The single paved road runs the seven kilometres from Livádhia, the port village, to Megálo Horió, the capital and only other significant habitation. When boats arrive a rust-coloured **minibus** links the two, and accommodation proprietors from Éristos lay on their own vehicles, but at other times you can walk, charter said minibus or rent a motorbike.

Livádhia

Of the two settlements, **LIVÁDHIA** is more equipped to deal with tourists and is closer to the best hikes. The port town retains an overall feel of traditional Greece – though a rash of building sites behind Livádhia's long pebble beach is an ominous sign. If there are vacancies, **room** and **hotel** owners meet the ferries, but in high season it may be worth phoning ahead. Budget options include *Stamatia's* (☎0241/44 334; ②), on the waterfront but rather pokey, or the recently refurbished and good-value *Hotel Livadhia* (☎0241/44 266; ②), which also runs *Studios Sofia* just behind (③). Nearby is the *Pension Periyali* (☎0241/44 398; ②), and east down the beach, then inland, is *Kastello* (☎0241/44 292; ③).

Of the seafront **tavernas**, *Sofia's* is a convivial meeting place, but you'll probably get a better meal at *Irina* (aka *Yiorgos*); the best place for fish grills is *Blue Sky*, an unmissable place perched above the ferry dock. For breakfast or pre-dinner drinks, *Omonia* – under the trees strung with fairy lights, near the post office – is enduringly popular. **Nightlife** on Tílos is restricted to two bars: *La Luna* at the ferry pier and a music pub in Mikró Horió (see below).

The **post office** is the only place to change money; **OTE** consists of a phone box in the larger of two grocery stores; and two agencies at the jetty divide the **ferry-ticket** trade between them. There's also a bakery, and plenty of other produce sold off pickup trucks.

Around the island

From Livádhia you can walk an hour north to the pebble bay of **Lethrá**, or slightly longer south to the sandy cove of **Thóloú**; the path to the latter begins by the cemetery and the chapel of **Áyios Pandelímon** with its Byzantine mosaic court and then curls around under the hard-to-climb castle of **Agriosikiá**; once up on the saddle, a cairned route leads to the citadel in twenty minutes. It's less than an hour west by trail up to the ghost village of **Mikró Horió**, whose 1500 inhabitants abandoned it in the 1950s. The only intact structures are the castle-guarded church (locked except for the August 15 festival) and an old house which has been restored as a music pub.

Megálo Horió and around

The rest of Tílos' inhabitants live in or near **MEGÁLO HORIÓ**, with an enviable perspective over its vast agricultural *kámbos*, and overlooked in turn by the vast Knights' castle which encloses a sixteenth-century chapel. The castle was built on the site of ancient Tílos, and is reached by a stiff, half-hour climb that begins at the *Ikonomou* supermarket before threading its way through a vast jumble of cisterns, house foundations and derelict chapels.

Your choices for **accommodation** are the *Pension Sevasti* (☎0241/44 237; ③), *Milio Apartments* (☎0241/44 204; ③), or *Studios Ta Elefandakia* (☎0241/44 213; ③). The restaurant attached to the *Pension Sevasti* is the most reliably open at lunchtime and has the best view. Two more fortresses stare out across the plain: the easterly one of **Massariá** helpfully marks the location of a cave where Pleiocene midget-elephant bones were discovered in 1971. A trail goes there from the road, ending just beyond the spring-fed cypress below the cave-mouth, which was hidden for centuries until a World War II artillery barrage exposed it. The bones themselves have been transferred to a small museum in Megálo Horió, which isn't currently open to the public.

Below Megálo Horió, a sign points left for the 75-minute walk to the one-kilometre-long **Éristos** beach, behind which are two **tavernas** with **rooms** (②), the *Tropikana* and *Navsika*. Both are set well back from the sand, hidden among orchards, but the food is nothing exceptional.

The far northwest

The main road beyond Megálo Horió hits the coast again at **Áyios Andónios**, with a single hotel/taverna (the *Australia*, ☎0241/44 296; ③) and an exposed, average beach. At low tide you can find more lava-trapped skeletons strung out in a row – human this time, presumably tide-washed victims of a Nissirian eruption in 600 BC, and discovered by the same archeologists who found the miniature pachyderms.

There's better swimming at isolated **Pláka** beach, 2km west of Áyios Andónios, and the road finally ends 8km west of Megálo Hório at the fortified fifteenth-century monastery of **Ayíou Pandelímonas**, deserted except from July 25 to 27, when it hosts the island's biggest festival. The tower-gate and oasis setting, over 200 forbidding metres above the west coast, are more memorable than the damaged frescoes within; to guarantee access, you need to visit with the regular Sunday morning tour, as there's no caretaker.

Níssiros

Volcanic **Níssiros** is noticeably greener than its southern neighbours Tílos, Hálki, and Sími, and unlike them has proved attractive and wealthy enough to retain more of its population, staying lively even in winter. While remittances from abroad (particularly Astoria, New York) are inevitably important, much of the island's income is derived from quarrying; offshore towards Kós the islet of Yialí is a vast lump of gypsum and pumice on which the miners live as they slowly chip it away.

The main island's peculiar geology is potentially a source of even more benefits: DEI, the Greek power company, spent much of the years between 1988 and 1992 sinking exploratory **geothermal wells** and attempting to convince the islanders of the benefits of cheap electricity. Mindful of the DEI's poor behaviour in similar circumstances on Mílos, however, the locals rallied against the project, fearing noxious fumes, industrial debris and land expropriation as in the Cyclades. In 1991 DEI bulldozed a new road of dubious necessity around the southwest flank of the island, damaging farmland and destroying a beautiful 500-year-old *kalderími* in the process; metal litter from unsuccessful test bores also did little to endear them to the local populace.

In 1993, a local referendum went massively against the projects, and DEI, together with its Italian contractor, took the hint and packed up. The desalination plant, reliant on expensive power from the fuel-oil generator, scarcely provides enough fresh water to spur a massive growth in package tourism. The relatively few tourists who stay the night, as opposed to the day-trippers from Kós, still find peaceful villages with a minimum of concrete eyesores, and a friendly population.

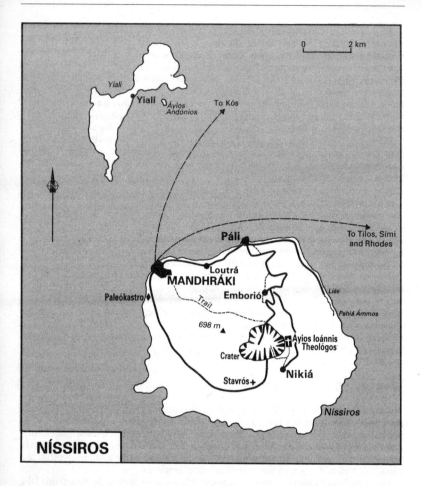

NÍSSIROS

Mandhráki

MANDHRÁKI is the port and capital, the wood balconies and windows on its tightly packed white houses splashed in bright colours, with blue swatches of sea visible at the ends of the narrow streets. Except for the drearier fringes near the ferry dock, the bulk of the place looks cheerful, arrayed around the community orchard or *kámbos* and overlooked by two ancient fortresses which also protect it somewhat from the wind.

Into a corner of the first of these, the predictable Knights' castle, is wedged the little monastery of **Panayía Spilianí**, built on this spot in accordance with the instructions of the Virgin herself, given in a vision to one of the first Christian islanders. Its prestige grew after raiding Saracens failed to discover the vast quantities of silver secreted here, in the form of a rich collection of Byzantine icons. On the way up to the monastery, you might stop in at the house restored for the **Historical and Popular Museum** (no set hours).

As a defensive bastion, the 2600-year-old Doric **Paleókastro**, twenty minutes' well-signposted walk out of the Langadháki district, is infinitely more impressive than the Knights' castle, and one of the more underrated ancient sites in Greece.

Practicalities

You'll see a handful of hotels and tavernas on your left as you disembark; best of the mid-range options, helpful and friendly, are the *Hotel/Restaurant Three Brothers* (☎0242/31 344; ③) and the *Romantzo* (☎0242/31 340; ③). In all honesty, though, these are best passed up in favour of establishments in the town proper. Just beyond the public toilets is the simple pension *Maria Intze* (②), across from *Enetikon Travel*, the main **travel agency**. A more popular budget option is the basic but clean *Pension Iy Dhrosia* (☎0242/31 328; ②), tucked right under the castle on the shore; enquire at Mihalis Orsaris's butcher shop on the main street. If it's full, the same management has slightly more expensive rooms inland. Also set back from the sea, but overlooking the *kámbos*, is Mandhráki's luxury accommodation, the *Porfiris* (☎0242/31 376; ③), with gardens and a pool.

Eating options include *Kleanthis*, a popular local hangout at lunchtime, and adjacent *Mike's* which looks tacky, but isn't particularly. The inland *Taverna Nissiros* is inexpensive and always packed after dark, whereas the *Karava*, next to *Enetikon*, is pricey and empty – a sea view and good menu compensate; the excellent *Taverna Irini* on the old *platía* does a fine *souvlaki* and fresh seafood dishes. Island **specialities** include pickled caper greens, *pittiá* (chickpea croquettes), and *soumádha*, an almond-extract drink nowadays only available from one family or two tavernas (*Romantzo* and *Karava*). The focus of **nightlife**, oddly enough, is not the shore but various bars and cafés near the lively inland Platía Ilikioménis such as *Cactus Bar*.

There's a short-hours OTE near the same *platía*, a **bank agent** and a **post office** at the harbour. Also by the jetty is a small **bus station**, with (theoretically) early morning and early afternoon departures into the interior and another four or so as far as Páli. In practice these are subject to cancellation, so you might consider renting a **moped**: the half-day or overnight rates offered by an inland tourist shop are better than the *Hotel Romantzo's* somewhat expensive full-day rates.

Beaches – and Páli

Beaches on Níssiros are in even shorter supply than water – the tour agency here can successfully market excursions to a beach on **Áyios Andónios** islet, just next to the mining apparatus on Yialí. Closer at hand, the black-rock beach of **Hokhláki**, behind the Knights' castle, is impossible if the wind is up, and the town beach at the east edge of the harbour would be a last resort in any weather. Better to head out along the main road, passing the half-abandoned spa of **Loutrá** (hot mineral-water soaks by prior arrangement) and the smallish **White Beach**, 2km along and dwarfed by an ugly new namesake hotel (☎0242/31 498; generally fully booked by tour groups), whose guests crowd onto the beach.

A kilometre further, 45 minutes' walk in all from Mandhráki, the fishing village of **PÁLI** makes a more attractive proposition as a base. Here you'll find the *Hotel Hellenis* (☎0242/31 453; ③), two **rooms** places (fanciest at the west end of the quay) and arguably the best and cheapest **taverna** on the island, *Afroditi*, featuring white Cretan wine and homemade desserts. Another dark-sand beach extends east of Páli to an apparently abandoned new spa, but to reach Níssiros's best beaches, continue in that direction for an hour on foot (or twenty minutes by moped along the road), past an initially discouraging seaweed- and cowpat-littered shoreline, to the delightful cove of **Liés**, where the track ends. A ten-minute scramble past a headland to the idyllic expanse of **Pahiá Ámmos**, as broad and sand-red as the name implies, is well worth it.

The interior

It is the **volcano** which gives Níssiros its special character and fosters the growth of the abundant vegetation – and no stay would be complete without a visit. When excursion boats arrive from Kós or Rhodes, the *Polyvotis Tours* coach and usually one of the public buses are pressed into service to take customers up the hill, but if you want to get up there without the crowds it's best to use either the morning and afternoon scheduled buses, a moped or your own feet to get up and back. Tours tend to set off at about 10.30am and 2.30pm, so time yourself accordingly for relative solitude.

Winding up from Páli, you'll first pass the virtually abandoned village of **EMBORIÓ**, where pigs and cows far outnumber people, though the place is slowly being bought up and restored by Athenians and foreigners. New owners are surprised to discover natural **saunas**, heated by volcano steam, in the basements of the crumbling houses; at the outskirts of the village there's a public one in a cave, whose entrance is outlined in white paint. If you're descending to Páli from here, an old cobbled way offers an attractive shortcut.

NIKIÁ, the large village on the east side of the volcano's caldera, is a more lively place, and its spectacular situation offers views out to Tílos as well as across the volcanic crater. Of the three **kafenía** here, the one on the engaging, round *platía* is rarely open, while the one in the middle of town usually has food. There is also **accommodation**, but it tends to be substandard and expensive. By the bus turnaround area, signs point to the 45-minute **trail** descending to the crater floor; a few minutes downhill, you can detour briefly to the eyrie-like **monastery of Áyios Ioánnis Theológos**, with a shady tree and yet another perspective on the volcano. The picnic benches and utility buildings come to life at the annual festival, the evening of September 25. To **drive** directly to the volcanic area you have to take the unsignposted road which veers off just past Emborió.

Approaching from any direction a sulphurous stench drifts out to meet you as the fields and scrub gradually give way to lifeless, caked powder. The sunken main **crater** is extraordinary, a Hollywood moonscape of grey, brown and sickly yellow; there is another, less visited double-crater to the west, equally dramatic visually, with a clear trail leading up to it. The perimeters of both are pocked with tiny blow-holes from which jets of steam puff constantly and around which little pincushions of pure sulphur crystals form. The whole floor of the larger crater seems to hiss, and standing in the middle you can hear something akin to a huge cauldron bubbling away below you. In legend this is the groaning of Polyvotis, a titan crushed here by Poseidon under a huge rock torn from Kós. When there are tourists around a small café functions in the centre of the wasteland.

Since the destruction of the old trail between the volcano and Mandhráki, pleasant options for walking back to town are limited. If you want to try, backtrack along the main crater access road for about 1km to find the start of a clear but unmarked path which passes the volcanic gulch of **Káto Lákki** and the monastery of **Evangelistrías** on its two-hour course back to the port.

Kós

After Rhodes, **Kós** is easily the most popular island in the Dodecanese, and there are superficial similarities between the two. On Kós as on Rhodes, the harbour is guarded by an imposing castle of the Knights of Saint John, the waterside is lined with grandiose Italian public buildings, and minarets and palm trees punctuate extensive Hellenistic and Roman remains.

Though sandy and fertile, the hinterland of Kós lacks the wild beauty of Rhodes' interior, and it must also be said that the main town has little charm aside from its antiquities, and is overrun by high-rise hotels. Rhodes-scale tourist development imposed on an essentially sleepy, small-scale island economy, with a population of only 22,000, has resulted most obviously in even higher food and transport prices than on Rhodes. While Rhodes is a provincial capital in its own right, Kós is purely and simply a holiday resort, although there's also a strong military presence here – which itself exacerbates pressure on scarce food and housing resources and effectively puts large tracts of the island off-limits. Except for its far west end, this is not an island that attracts many independent travellers, and in high season you'll be lucky to find any sort of room at all.

Kós Town

The town of **KÓS** spreads in all directions from the harbour; apart from the **castle** (Tues–Sun 8.30am–3pm; 400dr), its sole compelling attraction lies in the wealth of Hellenistic and Roman remains, many of which were only revealed by an earthquake in 1933, and restored afterwards by the Italians. The largest single section is the ancient **agora**, linked to the castle by a bridge or reached by a signposted walkway from Platía Eleftherías next to the **Archeological Museum** (same hours as the castle; 400dr). The **Casa Romana** (same hours; admission free), a palatial Roman house at the rear of town, and the sections of the ancient town bracketed by the **odeion** and the **stadium** are more impressive up close. Both have well-preserved fragments of mosaic floors, although the best have been carted off to the Palace of the Grand Masters in Rhodes – and what remains tends to be under several inches of protective gravel.

There are, in fact, so many broken pillars, smashed statues and fragments of bas-relief lying around among the ruins here that nobody knows quite what to do with them. The best pieces have been taken for safekeeping into the castle, where most of them are piled up, unmarked and unnoticed. A couple of pillars, now replaced by scaffolding, were once even used to prop up the branches of **Hippocrates' plane tree**. This venerable tree has guarded the entrance to the castle for generations, and although not really elderly enough to have seen the great healer, it has a fair claim to being one of the oldest trees in Europe. Just next door is the imposing eighteenth-century **mosque of Hatzi Hassan**, its ground floor – like that of the Defterdar mosque on Platía Eleftherías – taken up by rows of shops.

Kós also boasts a rather bogus **"old bazaar"**: a lone pedestrianized street, today crammed with tatty tourist boutiques, running from behind the overpriced produce market on Eleftherías as far as Platía Dhiagóras and the isolated minaret overlooking the inland archeological zone. About the only genuinely old thing here is a capped **Turkish fountain** with an inscription, found where the walkway cobbles cross Odhós Venizélou.

Arrival, transport and services

Large **ferries** anchor just outside the harbour at a special jetty by one corner of the castle; **excursion boats** to neighbouring islands sail right in and dock all along Aktí Koundouriótou. **Hydrofoils** dock beyond the main archeological zone, on Aktí Miaoúli. Virtually all ferry and excursion boat agents sit within 50m of each other at the intersection of Vassiléos Pávlou and the waterfront. Important exceptions include the head office of *Stefamar*, out on Avérof, for boats to Kálimnos, Psérimos and Níssiros, and the booking office for *Nearhos Mamidhakis (Dodecanese Hydrofoils)*, on Platía Iróön Politehníou (the round plaza at the back of the harbour).

The **airport** is 26km west of Kós Town in the centre of the island; an *Olympic Airways* shuttle bus meets *Olympic* flights, but if you arrive on any other flight you'll have to either take a taxi or head towards the giant roundabout outside the airport gate and find a *KTEL* bus – they run from here to Mastihári, Kardhámena and Kéfalos as

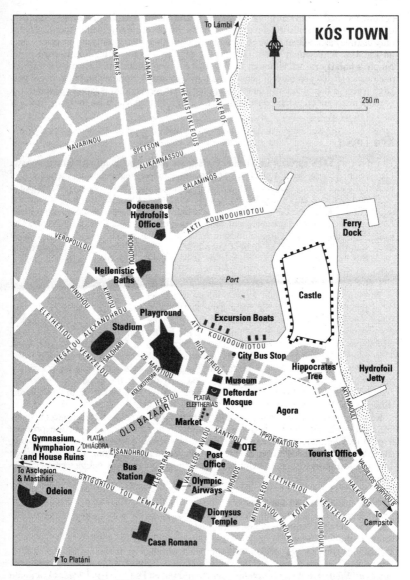

KÓS TOWN

To Lámbi

N

0   250 m

To Lámbi

AMERKIS
KANARI
THEMISTOKLEOUS
AVEROF
NAVARINOU
SPETSON
ALIKARNASSOU
SALAMINOS

Dodecanese Hydrofoils Office
AKTÍ KOUNDOURIOTOU
Ferry Dock

VEROPOULOU
IRODHOTOU
KIPPOU
PINDHOU

Hellenistic Baths
Port
Castle

ELEFTHERIOU
MEGALOU VENIZELOU
ALEXANDHROU
ISALDHARI
25 MARTIOU
KOLOKOTRONI
IFESTOU

Playground
Stadium
Excursion Boats
AKTÍ KOUNDOURIOTOU
RIGA FEREOU
• **City Bus Stop**
Hippocrates Tree
Hydrofoil Jetty
AKTÍ MIAOULI

■ **Museum**
■ **Defterdar Mosque**
PLATÍA ELEFTHERIAS
Agora
OLD BAZAAR

Market
XANTHOU
IPPOKRATOUS

Gymnasium, Nymphaion and House Ruins
PLATÍA DHIAGORA
PISANDHROU
VASSILEOS PAVLOU
KLEOPATRAS
OTE
Tourist Office ■
VASSILEOS YIORYIOU B

To Asclepion & Mastihári
GRIGORIOU TOU PEMPTOU
Bus Station
Post Office
Olympic Airways
VIRONOS
ELEFTHERIOU
HALKONOS
To Campsite

Odeion
Dionysus Temple
MITROPOLEOS
AYIOU NIKOLAOU
KORAI
VENIZELOU
KOUROUKLI

Casa Romana

▶ To Platáni

well as Kós Town. The **KTEL terminal** in town is a series of stops around a triangular park 500m back from the water; the municipality also runs a **local bus** service through the beach suburbs and up to the Asclepion, with a ticket and information office on Aktí Koundouriótou.

The *Trapeza Pisteos/Credit Bank* on the waterfront opens on Saturday morning for **exchange**; some other banks open in the evenings, and there are various ATMs. The

post office is at Venizélou 14, and may open Saturday and Sunday mornings in season, while the **OTE** at Víronos on the corner of Xánthou, is open until 11pm daily. *Happy Wash* laundry is at Mitropóleos 14.

Accommodation

If you're just in transit, then it makes sense to **stay** in Kós Town. Good budget alternatives in the centre include the *Dodekanissos* (☎0242/28 460; ③), around the corner at Ipsilándou 2; the *Elena* (☎0242/22 740; ③), at Megálou Alexándhrou 5; or the deservedly popular *Pension Alexis* (☎0242/28 798; ③), Irodhótou 9 at the corner of Omírou, across from the Roman *agora;* the same management has the *Hotel Afendoulis* (☎0242/ 25 321; ④), about 600m south at Evripílou 1. For longer stays, the rooms let by *Moustafa Tselepi* (☎0242/28 896; ③) at Venizélou 29, on the corner of Metsóvou, are a good choice, and some have cooking facilities. Across the port, along Avérof, are some other reasonable, if noisier, options: try the *Pension Popi* (☎0242/23 475; ③) at no. 37, or the *Nitsa* (☎0242/25 810; ③) at no. 41. The well-appointed **campsite** is 2500m out towards Cape Psalídhi, and can be reached by the city bus service, but is open only during the warmer months.

Eating, drinking and nightlife

Eating out well and cheaply is likely to pose more problems. You can pretty much write off most of the waterfront tavernas, though the *Romantica*, one of the first as you come from the ferry jetty, and its neighbour the *Limnos*, are within the bounds of reason. Inland, the least expensive and most authentic establishments are the *Australia Sydney* at Vassiléos Pávlou 29, with an amazingly well-stocked bar and an ample menu, and the *Olimpiadha* at Kleopátras 2, both near *Olympic Airways*. You might also try the *Ambavris*, 800m south out of town, and the atmospheric *Anatolia Hamam*, housed partly in an old Turkish bath off Platía Dhiagóras. If you're craving an English – or even American – **breakfast**, various cafés serve that or just coffee under giant trees on Platía Ayías Paraskevís, behind the produce market: expensive but worth it.

In terms of **nightlife**, you need look no further than the inland pedestrian way joining Platía Eleftherías and the castle; every address is a bar, just choose according to the crowd and the noise level. Otherwise there is one active **cinema**, the *Orfevs* with summer and winter premises.

The Asclepion and Platáni

Hippocrates is justly celebrated on Kós; not only does he have a tree named after him, but the star exhibit in the town museum is his statue, and the Asclepion (city bus via Platáni 8.30am–2.30pm, to Platáni only 2.30–11pm; or a 45-minute walk) is a major tourist attraction. Treatments described by Hippocrates and his followers were still used as recently as a hundred years ago, and his ideas on medical methods and ethics remain influential.

The **Asclepion** whose ruins can be seen (Tues–Sun 8.30am–3pm; 600dr) was actually built after the death of Hippocrates, but it's safe to assume that the methods used and taught here were still his. Both a temple to Asclepius (son of Apollo, god of medicine) and a renowned centre of healing, its magnificent setting on terraces levelled from a hillside overlooking the Anatolian mainland reflects early doctors' recognition of the importance of the therapeutic environment: springs still provide the site with a constant supply of clean fresh water. There used to be a rival medical school in the ancient town of Knidos, on the Asia Minor coast southeast of Kós, at a time when there was far more traffic across the straits than today. Incidentally, there are no facilities at the Asclepion.

HIPPOCRATES

Hippocrates (c 460–377 BC) is generally regarded as the father of medicine, and through the Hippocratic oath – which probably has nothing to do with him, and is in any case much altered from its original form – still influences doctors today. He was certainly born on Kós, but otherwise details of his life are few and disputed; what seems beyond doubt is that he was a great physician who travelled throughout the Classical Greek world but spent at least part of his career teaching and practising at the Asclepion on the island of his birth. To Hippocrates were traditionally attributed a vast number of medical writings, only a small portion of which he could actually have written; in all probability they were the collection of a medical library kept on Kós. Some probably were Hippocrates' own work – in particular *Airs, Waters and Places*, a treatise on the importance of environment on health, is widely thought to be his. This stress on good air and water, and the holistic approach of ancient Greek medicine, can in the late twentieth century seem positively modern.

A mild social segregation still prevails close at hand in the bi-ethnic village of **PLATÁNI** (*Kermete* in Turkish), on the road to the Asclepion; the Greek Orthodox stay in their *kafenía* while the Muslim minority still manage the three establishments dominating the crossroads. All of the latter – particularly *Arap* – serve excellent, relatively cheap, Turkish-style food, far better than anything you generally get in Kós Town. There's a working Ottoman fountain nearby, and the older domestic architecture of Platáni is strongly reminiscent of rural styles in provincial Crete, from where many of Platáni's Turks came early this century.

Just outside Platáni on the road back to the harbour, the Jewish cemetery stands in a dark pine grove, 300m from the Muslim graveyard. Dates on the headstones stop ominously after 1940, after which none were allowed the luxury of a natural death. The old synagogue, locked and crumbling since the 1944 deportations to the concentration camps, is back in Kós Town between the ancient *agora* and the waterfront.

Eastern Kós

If you're looking for anything resembling a deserted **beach** near the capital, you'll need to make use of the city bus line connecting the various resorts to either side of town, or else rent a vehicle. Closest is **Lámbi**, 3km north towards Cape Skandhári with its military watchpoint, the last vestige of a vast army camp which has deferred to the demands of tourism. On the same coast, 12km west of the harbour, **TIGÁKI** is still just about a village, easily accessible by *KTEL* bus or rented push-bike (a popular option in the flat east end of Kós). As a result it's crowded until evening, when everyone except those lucky enough to have rented a room has disappeared.

The far end of the city bus line beginning at Lámbi is Áyios Fokás, 8km out, with the unusual and remote **Brós Thermá** 5km further on, easiest reached by moped. Here **hot springs** trickle over black sand into the sea, warming it up for early or late-season swims. There's a small seasonal café but no other facilities.

Inland, the main interest of eastern Kós resides in the villages of **Mount Dhíkeos**, a handful of settlements collectively referred to as Asfendhíou, nestling among the slopes of the island's only forest. They are accessible either via the curvy side-road from Zipári, or a more straightforward turning signed as "Píli".

Modern **PÍLI** is sprawling and unattractive, and the lack of tourist amenities seems an admission that no-one will stop here. **Old Píli**, signposted inconspicuously as such on a house corner in Amaníou, the next hamlet east, gets more attention; a paved road leads up a wooded canyon, stopping by a spring at the base of a crag with a Byzantine castle and the ruined houses of the abandoned village tumbling away from it. The frescoes in the handful of medieval churches are in bad condition, however, and all told the place is more impressive from a distance.

From Amaníou the main dirt track leads northeast via the untouristed hamlet of Lagoúdhi to **EVANGELÍSTRIA**, where there's a taverna and an interesting "suburb", **ASÓMATI**, with fine whitewashed houses. **ZIÁ**, further up the now paved road, is the hapless target of up to six tour buses per night; several rather commercialized tavernas take advantage of the spectacular sunsets, but it's a good idea to clear out immediately afterwards.

Beyond Ziá the way deteriorates to dirt once more, continuing to **ÁYIOS YIÓRYIOS**, where only around thirty villagers and a handful of foreigners and Athenians renovating houses dwell; there is one tiny store where you can get a drink. **ÁYIOS DHIMÍTRIOS**, 2km beyond, on an exceedingly rough track, was abandoned entirely during the junta years, when the inhabitants went to Zipári or further afield. Indeed, the best reason for coming up this way is to get some idea of what Kós looked like before tourism and ready-mix concrete took root.

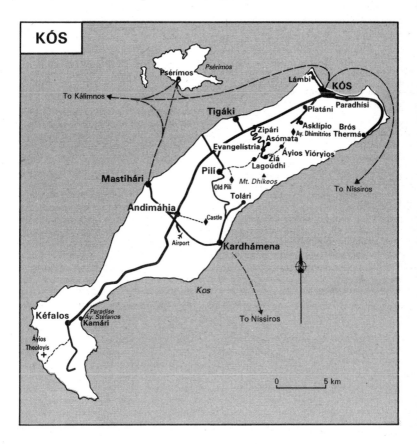

Western Kós

Near the centre of the island, a pair of giant roundabouts by the airport funnels traffic northwest towards Mastihári, northeast back towards town, southwest towards Kéfalos, and southeast to Kardhámena.

The beach at **MASTIHÁRI** is smaller than those at Tigáki or Kardhámena, and the small town is increasingly built up, but it is the port for the least expensive *kaíkia* to Kálimnos and the tiny Greek islet of Psérimos (see below), so you may want to come here; there are plenty of rooms to rent if you need to stay. In season there are daily morning and mid-afternoon sailings, with an extra late-night departure when charter landings warrant it – though be warned that boats can be fully occupied by package clients.

KARDHÁMENA, on the southeast-facing coast, is the island's second-largest package resort, packed in season; runaway local development has banished whatever redeeming qualities it may once have had. A beach stretches to either side of the town, backed on the east with ill-concealed military bunkers and a road as far as Tolári, where there is a massive hotel complex. Halfway back towards Andimáhia an enormous **castle** (the Knights' again) sprawls atop a ridge. Like Mastihári, Kardhámena is most worth knowing about as a place to catch inter-island *kaíkia*, in this case to Níssiros. There are supposedly two daily sailings in season, at approximately 9am and 5pm, but in practice the afternoon departure takes place any time between 1.30 and 6.30pm, depending on when the Nissirians have finished their shopping.

Outside high season, there are generally a few **rooms** not taken by tour companies and prices, at ②–③ depending on the facilities and number of people, are not outrageous. The one reasonable **taverna**, *Andreas*, is right on the harbour; inland, a **bakery** (signed with red arrows) does homemade ice cream, yogurt and sticky cakes; *Peter's* across the street is one of the more flexible **moped rental** outfits.

The end of the line for buses is the inland village of Kéfalos, which squats on a mesa-like hill looking back down the length of Kós. Most visitors will have alighted long before, either at **KAMÁRI** or **ÁYIOS STÉFANOS**, where the exquisite remains of a fifth-century basilica overlook tiny Kastrí islet; both places have plenty of accommodation. The beach begins at Kamári and runs five kilometres east, virtually without interruption, to the cliff-framed and aptly-named **Paradise beach**. Unfortunately the entire area between Kamári and Áyios Stéfanos has been overshadowed by a huge Club Med complex of bungalows surrounding the main luxury hotel.

Kéfalos itself is rather dull but is the staging point for expeditions into the rugged southwest peninsula. To the west, around the monastery of **Áyios Theológos**, you can still find deserted stretches of coastline, but the nearest cove is about 6km distant over rough tracks – and none are as sheltered as the bays on the island's southeast flank.

Psérimos

If it weren't for its proximity to Kós and Kálimnos, which results in day-trippers by the boatload every day of the season, **Psérimos** could be an idyllic little island. Even in April and October, however, you can be guaranteed at least 100 outsiders a day (which doubles the population), so imagine the scene in high season as visitors spread themselves along the main sandy beach, which stretches around the bay in front of the twenty or thirty houses that constitute **PSÉRIMOS VILLAGE**. There are a couple of other, less attractive pebbly beaches, no more than thirty walking minutes distant – in fact nowhere on Psérimos is much more than half an hour's walk away.

When the day-trippers have gone you can, out of season, have the place to yourself and even in season there won't be too many other overnighters, since there's a limited number of **rooms** available. Of the three small "hotels", the best for value, cleanliness and friendliness is the one run by Katerina Fyloura above her taverna on the eastern side of the harbour. She has a total of thirteen beds apportioned over five rooms (③) and the food's good too. Katerina also acts as postmistress if you want to write home, since the island can't support a post office. There's just one small **store**, not very well-stocked, and most of the island's supplies are brought in daily from Kálimnos. **Eating out**, however, won't break the bank and there's plenty of fresh fish in the handful of tavernas.

The island is easily reached from either Kálimnos or Kós: most Kós Town–Kálimnos and Mastihári–Kálimnos excursion *kaíkia* make a stop at Psérimos in each direction.

Astipálea

Both geographically and architecturally, Astipálea would be more at home among the Cyclades – on a clear day the island can be seen quite clearly from Anáfi or Amorgós, and it looks and feels more like them than its neighbours to the east. Despite its butterfly shape, it's not the most beautiful of islands: the barren coastline gives way in parts to fields, citrus groves and decent, mountainous walking country, but the beaches are often stony and litter-strewn.

In antiquity the island's most famous citizen was Kleomedes, a boxer disqualified from an early Olympic Games for killing his opponent. He came home so enraged that he demolished the local school, killing all its pupils. Things have calmed down a bit in the intervening 2500 years and today the capital is a quiet fishing port – the catch is locally consumed, as the island is too remote for it to be shipped to the mainland. This is also a reflection of the notoriously poor ferry links; things have improved recently with the introduction of two new services to the Cyclades, but you still risk being marooned here for an extra day or three. Despite the relative isolation, plenty of people find their way to Astipálea in summer, though relatively few are English-speaking – it seems more popular with French, Italian and Athenian second-home owners.

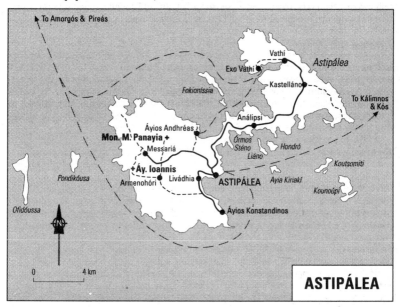

Yialós and Hóra

The main harbour of **YIALÓS** dates from the Italian era (Astipálea was the first island the Italians occupied in the Dodecanese) and most of the settlement between the quay and the line of nine windmills is even more recent. As you climb up beyond the port towards **HÓRA**, though, the neighbourhoods get progressively older and their steep streets are enlivened by the *poúndia* or colourful wooden balconies of the whitewashed houses. The whole culminates in the fourteenth-century *kástro*, one of the finest in the Aegean. Until well into this century over 3000 souls dwelt within, but depopulation and wartime damage have combined to leave only a desolate shell today; the fine groin vaulting over the entrance and a couple of maintained churches remain an attraction, though restoration is now beginning.

There are several inexpensive **hotels** down in the port – the *Astynea* (☎0243/61 209; ③), the *Paradisos* (☎0243/61 224; ③), the *Vangelis* (☎0243/61 281; ③) and the *Egeon* (☎0243/61 236; ③) – but if you can get them, **rooms** in the upper town near the windmills that mark the *platía* in Hóra are better. Further up the scale, *Viva Mare* (☎0243/61 292; ⑤) are well-appointed studio units a bit inland from Yialós. Finally, there's a **campsite** halfway along the 5km to Analípsi, easily reached by bus.

Toh Akroyiali, *Babis* and *Karlos* **tavernas** are the local haunts, *Astynea*, on the wharf, *Australia* and *Iy Monaxia*, behind the ferry dock, are also good. The stepped hill of Maltezána constitutes the business district; here you'll find more places to eat, several discos, shops, the **OTE** and a **travel agency** arranging boat excursions to remote beaches. The **post office** is well up in the Hóra, as are some subdued clubs like *Kastro Bar* and *Artemis*. You can change money at the post office or a bank agent (there's no actual bank).

A **bus** runs regularly between Hóra, Skala, Livádhia and Analípsi in July and August, less frequently out of season – the posted timetables are far from reliable. There are only two official **taxis**, far too few in season when lots of Athenians visit; several places rent out mopeds. The island **map** sold locally is grossly inaccurate.

Around the island

Half an hour's walk (or a short, frequent bus journey) from the capital is **LIVÁDHIA**, a fertile green valley with a popular, good beach and shaded restaurants by the water-side. You can **camp** here or **rent a room** or bungalow in the beach hamlet – for example from the Nikos Kondaratos family (☎0243/61 269; ②), which has been known to offer a mattress in the local citrus and banana orchards when they're full inside. Among the **tavernas**, *Yiesenia*, *Thomas* and *Kalamia* are all decent.

If the beach here is not to your liking, continue southwest on a footpath to **Tzanáki**, with nude bathing and fewer people. Continuing to **Áyios Konstandínos** cove is well worthwhile, where a taverna plus the shade from the fringing orchards are a plus.

The best outing on the island, however, has to be the two-hour walk from Astipálea to the oasis of **Áyios Ioánnis**. Walk one hour along the dirt track beginning from the sixth or seventh windmill, then bear left at the fork (right leads to the anchorage of **Áyios Andhréas**: one ramshackle taverna, good swimming and snorkelling). After a while, you pass another path going right towards the uninspiring monastery of Panayía Flevariotíssas; carry on above **Arménohori** (a pillaged ancient site) and the farming hamlet of Messariá, before turning left, at the top of a pass, on to a footpath heading for some bony-white rock outcrops. Soon the walled orchards of the farm-monastery of Áyios Ioánnis (not to be confused with a seaside cloister of the same name to the north) come into view. Just below, a ten-metre waterfall plunges into deep pools fine for bathing. A rather arduous trek down the valley ends at a fine pebbly bay, and proper paths lead back towards Armenohóri if you don't fancy a reprise of the jeep tracks you arrived on.

Northeast of the harbour, a series of bays nestle in the "body" of the "butterfly". Of the two coves known as **Marmári**, one is home to the power plant, and the next one hosts the island's only organized **campsite**. Beyond, at **Stenó**, the middle beach, with clean sand and fresh-water wells, is the best.

ANÁLIPSI, universally known as Maltezána after Maltese pirates, is about a five-kilometre taxi-ride or walk beyond the campsite. Although the second-largest settlement on Astipálea, there's little for outsiders save a narrow, sea-urchin-speckled beach and two small **tavernas** (*Obelix* is excellent), plus quite a few **rooms**. At the edge of the surrounding olive groves are the well-preserved remains of **Roman baths**, with floor mosaics of zodiacal signs and the seasons personified. In high season, Análipsi can be a welcome escape – once you find your way around, there are other beaches accessible around the bay. The road ends at **VATHÍ**, an even sleepier fishing village with a single taverna and a superb harbour, which is where the ferry docks in winter when Astipálea Town is battered by the prevailing southerly winds. At such times, and only then, there is a bus between Vathí and Astipálea. Occasional *kaíkia* shuttle back and forth in season between Vathí and either Áyios Andhréas or Yialós.

Kálimnos

Most of the population of **Kálimnos** lives in or around the large port of Pothiá, a wealthy but not conventionally beautiful town famed for its sponge divers. Sadly almost all the Mediterranean's sponges, with the exception of a few deep-water beds off Italy, have been devastated by disease, and only three or four of the fleet of thirty or more boats can currently be usefully occupied. In response to this economic disaster, the island is attempting to establish a tourist industry – so far confined to several tiny beach resorts – and has customized its sponge boats for deep-sea fishing. The warehouses behind the harbour, however, still process and sell sponges (imported from Asia and America) to tourists all year round. During the Italian occupation houses here were painted blue and white to keep alive the Greek colours and irritate the invaders. The custom is beginning to die out, but is still evident; even some of the churches are painted blue.

Since Kálimnos is the home port of two hydrofoil lines, and of the very useful local ferry *Nissos Kalimnos* (see "Travel Details"), and is also where the long-distance ferry lines from the outer Cyclades and Astipálea join up with the main Dodecanesian ones, many travellers unwittingly find themselves here, and are initially most intent on how to move on quickly. The islanders have remained welcoming nonetheless, and indulgent of short stays, perhaps realizing that the place won't hold most people's interest for more than a day or two.

Pothiá

POTHIÁ, without being particularly picturesque, is colourful and authentically Greek, the overwhelming impression being of the phenomenal amount of noise engendered by the cranked-up sound systems of the dozen waterfront cafés, and the exhibitionist motorbike traffic. **Accommodation** is rarely a problem, since pension proprietors usually meet the ferries; otherwise the *Hotel Patmos* (☎0243/22 750; ③), in a relatively quiet sidestreet at the west end of the front near the **EOT** booth, or the *Pension Greek House* (☎0243/29 559; ②), 200m to the north in Amoudhára district, are dependable fall backs. Slightly to the south, the well-signposted *Hotel Panorama* (☎0243/23 138; ③) perches above *Greek House*.

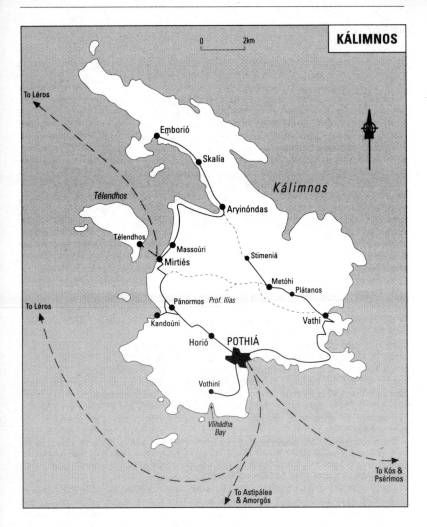

For **eating out**, the best strategy is to follow the waterfront west past the Italian-built municipal "palace" to a line of **fish tavernas and ouzerís**. The first, nameless joint under the tamarisks is okay, *Barba Petros* at the far end is a bit glitzy, while *Psarouzeri O Kambourakis* in between represents fair value. Sticky-cake fans will want to take three paces west to *Zaharoplastiki O Mihalaras*, while still further in the same direction, *Apothiki* is currently the coolest waterfront bar/café. The local speciality is octopus croquettes.

The **OTE** and the **post office** are virtually opposite each other inland on Venizélou; all **boat and hydrofoil agents** line the waterfront as you bear right out of the pier-area gate, and there's an *Olympic Airways* office at Patriárhou Maxímou 17. Finally, waterfront branches of the *National* and *Ionian* **banks** both have autotellers.

Around the island

Buses run as far as Aryinóndas in the northwest and Vathí in the east, while for more freedom there are plenty of places to rent a **moped**. Chances are you'll want to escape, at least during the day, to one of the smaller coastal settlements.

Heading northwest across the island, the first place you come to is the old capital, **HORIÓ**, sandwiched between an eroded **castle** of the Knights of Saint John and the miniature Byzantine precinct of **Péra Kástro**. The crumbling ruins of the latter are peppered with conspicuously white churches, but it's the Knights' castle (known locally as *Kástro Hrissoherías*) that especially merits a visit, with its stupendous views over the entire west coast of the island.

From the ridge at Horió the road dips into a cultivated ravine, heading for the consecutive beach resorts of Kandoúni, Pánormos, Mirtiés and Massoúri. All of them are far more developed than is warranted by the scanty shelves of grey sand or pebbles in the vicinity; at **MIRTIÉS** and **MASSOÚRI** there is scant possibility of finding a room amid the package-holiday paraphernalia. The trip across the strait to the striking, volcanic-plug island of **TÉLENDHOS** is arguably the best reason to come to Mirtiés; little boats shuttle to and fro constantly throughout the day. On the islet you'll find a ruined monastery, a castle, a couple of tiny beaches and several tavernas and pensions, all in or near the single village; if you want to book ahead, try *Pension Uncle George* (☎0243/47 502; ②), *Dhimitris Harinos* (☎0243/47 916; ②), or *Foukena Galanomati* (☎0243/47 401; ②). It's also possible to go from Mirtiés directly to Léros aboard the daily *kaíki*.

Beyond Mirtiés, **ARYINÓNDAS** and **EMBORIÓ** both have relatively empty, decent beaches, the latter alongside a couple of good tavernas which have rooms (*Harry's*, ☎0243/47 434 and *Themis*, ☎0243/47 277). If the bus fails you, there is sometimes a shuttle boat back to Mirtiés.

East from Póthia, an initially unpromising, forty-minute ride ends dramatically at **VATHÍ**, whose colour provides a startling contrast to the lifeless greys elsewhere on Kálimnos. A long, fertile valley, verdant with orange and tangerine groves, it seems a continuation of the cobalt-blue fjord which penetrates finger-like into the landscape. In the simple port, known as Rína, there are a handful of *kafenía* and tavernas to choose from, as well as a the *Galini* **hotel** (☎0243/31 241; ③) and a few **rooms**. For **walkers** the lush valley behind, criss-crossed with rough tractor-tracks and paths, may prove an irresistible lure, but be warned that it will take you the better part of three hours, most of it shadeless once you're out of the orchards, to reach points on the opposite coast. The only facilities en route lie in the hamlets of Plátanos and Metóhi at the head of the valley; once past these, the route divides, with one option going to Massoúri, the other to Aryinóndas via the third hamlet of Stiménia.

Southwest of Pothiá, the attractive little sandy bay of **Vlihádha**, with the village of **VOTHINÍ** perched above, is plainly visible from most ferries coming or going, and considerably less crowded than the northwestern beaches. Local *kaíkia* make well-publicized excursions to the southerly caves of **Kéfalos**, **Skaliá** and **Ayía Varvára**, all nearly as impressive as the photographs they use to tempt you to go there.

Léros

Léros is so indented with deep, sheltered anchorages that during the last world war it harboured, in turn, the entire Italian, German, and British Mediterranean fleets. Unfortunately, these magnificent fjords and bays seem to absorb rather than reflect light, and the island's relative fertility can seem unruly when compared to the crisp lines of its more barren neighbours. These characteristics, coupled with the island's absence until recently from the lists of most major tour operators, mean that barely

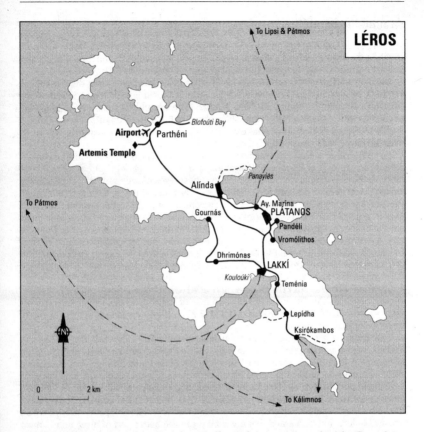

To Lipsi & Pátmos

LÉROS

Blofoúti Bay

Airport Parthéni

Artemis Temple

Panayiès

Alínda

Ay. Marína
PLATANOS

Gournás

Pandéli

Vromólithos

Dhrimónas

LAKKÍ

Kouloúki

Teménia

Lepídha

Ksirókambos

To Pátmos

N

0   2 km

To Kálimnos

10,000 foreigners a year (many of them Italians who grew up on the island), and not many more Greeks, come to stay. Although lacking spectacularly good beaches, Léros is on the verge of being "discovered" by those in search of more understated pleasures, such as gentle walks, botanizing and the company of islanders unjaded by mass tourism. Things should stay that way until or unless the extension to the airport runway that will enable it to accommodate jets, mooted for years, takes place.

Not that the island needs, nor particularly encourages, tourism; various prisons and sanitariums have long dominated the Lerian economy. Under the junta the island was the site of an infamous detention centre, and today mental hospitals on Léros are still the repository for many of Greece's more intractable psychiatric cases; another asylum is home to hundreds of mentally handicapped children. The island's domestic image problem is compounded by its name, the butt of jokes by mainlanders who pounce on its similarity to the word *léra*, connoting rascality and unsavouriness. Islanders are in fact extremely friendly to those who visit, but their island's role and image seem unlikely to change. In 1989 a major scandal burst forth concerning the administration of the various asylums, with EC maintenance and development funds found to have been embezzled by administrators and staff, and the inmates kept in degrading and inhumane conditions. By 1991 EC inspectors pronounced themselves satisfied that the abuses had stopped, and there have been drastic improvements in the treatment of patients, including the establishment of halfway houses across the island. Although Léros will be a long time overcoming this additional stigma, the institutional identity is not as pervasive as you might expect.

More obvious is the legacy of the Battle of Léros late in 1943, when overwhelming German forces displaced a British division: unexploded bombs and shells turn up as gaily painted garden ornaments in the courtyards of churches and tavernas, or have been pressed into service as gateposts.

Unusually for a small island, Léros has abundant groundwater. This, combined with the avenues of eucalyptus trees planted by the Italians, makes for a horrendously active mosquito contingent, so come prepared. The island is small enough to walk around, but there is a bus service and several bike-rental outfits.

Lakkí and Ksirókambos

All large **ferries**, and *Ilio Line* hydrofoils arrive at the main port of **LAKKÍ**, once the headquarters of a bustling Italian naval base, which accounts for the extraordinary look of the place. Wide boulevards, laid out around little parks and statues, are lined with some marvellous Art Deco edifices – most notably the round-fronted cinema (closed since 1985), the school and the defunct *Leros Palace Hotel*.

Buses don't meet the ferries; instead, there are taxis that charge set fares to standard destinations. Accordingly, few people stay in Lakkí, preferring to head straight for the resorts of Pandéli or Vromólithos (see below), though you can **eat** very well at *Sotos*, a Swedish co-run place with plenty of choice for vegetarians. The nearest **beach** is at Kouloúki, 600m west, where there's a seasonal snack-bar.

KSIRÓKAMBOS, nearly 5km from Lakkí at the extreme south of the island, is the point of arrival for *kaikía* from Mirtiés on Kálimnos. Billed as a resort, it's essentially a fishing port where people also happen to swim – the beach here is poor to mediocre, improving as you head west. **Accommodation** is available at *Villa Maria* (☎0247/22 827; ③) or, a bit inland, at *Yianoukas Rooms* (☎0247/23 148; ②); the island's **campsite** is in an olive grove at the village of Lepídha, 750m back up the road to Lakkí. **Meals** can be had at *Taverna Tzitzifi*es, just by the jujube trees at the east end of things, where the road hits the shore.

Pandéli and Vromólithos

Just under 3km north of Lakkí, Pandéli and Vromólithos together form the fastest-growing resort on the island – and are certainly the most attractive and scenic places to stay.

PANDÉLI is still very much a working port, with a negligible beach, but is a good bet for non-package **accommodation**, such as *Pension Roza* (☎0247/22 798; ②) or *Pension Kavos* (☎0247/23 247; ③), further east, with a pleasant breakfast terrace. Up on the ridge dividing Pandéli from Vromólithos, the peace at the *Hotel Rodon* (☎0247/23 524; ③) is disturbed only by wafts of R&B or soul from the *Beach Bar*, perched on a rock terrace some distance below. The other, long-lived bar is the civilized *Savana*, at the opposite end of Pandéli, but the soul of the place is its waterfront **tavernas**, which come alive after dark. These get less expensive and less pretentious as you head east, culminating in *Maria's*, a local institution, decked out in coloured lights and whimsically painted gourds – try the grilled octopus. *Zorba's* offers large portions of well-prepared food, with vegetarians well catered for.

VROMÓLITHOS boasts the best easily accessible beach on the island, hemmed in by hills studded with massive oaks. The **beach** is gravel and coarse sand, and the water's fine, but a nasty reef must be crossed before you reach a sharp dropoff to deeper water. Two tavernas behind the beach trade more on their location than their cuisine, but the standard of **accommodation** here is higher than at Pandéli, with the result that it tends to be monopolized by package companies; *Tony's Beach Rooms & Studios* (☎0247/27 742; ④) is worth a try.

Plátanos and Ayía Marína

The Neoclassical and vernacular houses of **PLÁTANOS**, the island capital 1km west of Pandéli, are draped gracefully along a saddle between two hills, one of them crowned by the inevitable Knights' castle. Locally known as the **Kástro**, this is reached either by a rough road peeling off the Pandéli road, or a more scenic stair-path from the central square; the battlements, and the views from them, are dramatic, especially at sunrise or sunset. Except for the *Hotel Eleftheria* (☎0247/23 550; ③), elevated and quiet enough to be desirable, it's not really a place to stay or eat, although it's admirably provided with **shops and services** – including seven hairdressers. *Leros Travel* acts as a ferry-ticket agent and is conveniently located next door to *Olympic Airways* (☎0247/24 144), while the **post office** and short-hours **OTE** are down the road towards Ayía Marína. **Buses** ply four to six times daily between Parthéni in the north and Ksirókambos in the south.

Plátanos merges seamlessly with **AYÍA MARÍNA**, 1km north on the shore of a fine bay. Although there's no accommodation here, *DRM* and *Kastis* travel agencies can book rooms elsewhere, as well as arranging tickets for ferries and hydrofoils. On the water, *Taverna Ayia Marina* has the broadest menu, while *Garbo's* (evenings only in summer), on the road to Plátanos, seems to have hit upon a winning formula of English food (including curries) and movie-poster decor.

The north

ALÍNDA, 3km northwest of Ayía Marína, ranks as the longest-established resort on Léros, with development focused around a narrow strip of pea-gravel and hotels block-booked by package companies. Seven kilometres further along the main route north is the marked side track for the **Temple of Artemis**. In ancient times, Léros was sacred to the goddess, and the temple here was supposedly inhabited by guinea fowl – the grief-stricken sisters of Meleager, metamorphosed by Artemis following their brother's death. All that remains now are some jumbled walls, but the view is superb. The onward road skims the shores of sumpy and reed-fringed Parthéni Bay, until the paved road runs out at **Blefoúti**, a rather more inspiring sight with its huge, virtually land-locked bay with greenery-flecked hills behind. The beach is fairly ordinary, but there are tamarisks to shelter under and a decent taverna, *Iy Thea Artemi*, for lunch.

Pátmos

Arguably the most beautiful, certainly the best known of the smaller islands in the Dodecanese, **Pátmos** is unique. It was in a cave here that Saint John the Divine (in Greek, *O Theologos*), had his revelation (the Bible's Book of Revelation) and unwittingly shaped the island's destiny. The monastery which commemorates him, founded here in 1088, dominates the island both physically – its fortified bulk towering high above anything else – and, to a considerable extent, politically. While the monks no longer run the island as they did for more than 700 years, their influence has nevertheless stopped Pátmos going the way of Rhodes or Kós. Despite vast numbers of visitors, and the island's firm presence on the cruise, hydrofoil and yacht circuits, tourism has not been allowed to take the island over. There are a number of clubs and even one disco around Skála, the port and main town, but everywhere else development of any kind is appealingly subdued.

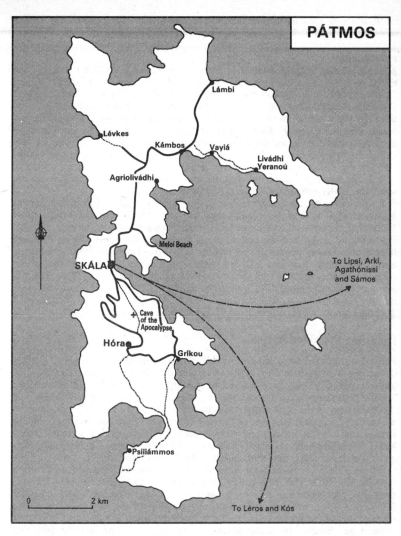

Skála and around

SKÁLA seems initially to contradict this image of Pátmos. The waterside, with its ritzy-looking cafés and clientele, is a little too sophisticated for its own small-town good, and it must be said that some of the world-weary service personnel are none too civil at times. In season it's crowded by day with excursionists from Kós and Rhodes; by night with well-dressed cliques of visitors. In winter the shops and restaurants close and most of their owners and staff leave for Rhodes; the town itself taking on a somewhat depressed air, with no place for the kids to roar their motorbikes towards. If you feel like moving straight out, the most obvious possibility is **Méloï Beach**, 1500m to the north, and one of the most convenient and popular on the island; Hóra, a bus or taxi-ride up the mountain, is a more attractive base but has few rooms.

Practicalities

Accommodation in Skála itself is in demand but, for noise-avoidance reasons, you might be better off away from the centre. Good mid-range hotels are the *Galini* (☎0247/31 740; ④) or the *Blue Bay* (☎0247/31 165; ④), a quiet place just to the east of town; the *Rex* (☎0247/31 242; ②) is a central but rather noisy cheapie. More likely, however, you'll end up in rooms, hawked vociferously on the quay; they are mostly higher than usual quality, though with correspondingly higher prices, too. There are plenty of places for **meals**, subject to sudden rushes when the cruise boats arrive – among the best are *Pandelis*, behind the *Café Arion* (see below), for fish, *Grigori's*, on your left as you disembark from the ferry, and the *Skorpios Creperie* and *Platanos* grill, both on the way to Hóra. The trendiest **bar** is currently the barn-like *Café Arion* on the waterside, its deceptively small entrance easily missed.

If you're keen to stay nearer to a beach, there's a good but overpriced **campsite** at **Méloï**, together with some **rooms** – best are those run by *Loula Koumendhourou* (☎0247/32 281; ③), on the slope south of the bay – and a couple of tavernas.

Everything else is near the police station: the boat docks right opposite; **bus and boat timetables** are posted outside; and the fairly helpful municipal **tourist information** (daily except Sun, 9am–1pm & 5–8pm) is at the back. Moped and **motorbike rental** outfits are common, with lowish rates owing to the modest size of the island; at the south end of the front, *DRM* is about the most useful **ferry-ticket agent**, representing the *Nissos Kalimnos*, *Miniotis Lines*, *G&A*, and one of the hydrofoil companies. There are **banks**, a **post office** and an **OTE** (closed at weekends).

Hóra and the monasteries

For cruise-ship passengers and overnighters alike the first order of business is likely to be heading up to the Monastery of Saint John, sheltered behind massive defences in the hilltop capital of Hóra. There is a bus up, but the half-hour walk by a beautiful old cobbled path puts you in a more appropriate frame of mind. Just over halfway, pause at the **Monastery of the Apocalypse** (Mon Wed & Fri 8am–2pm & 4–6pm, Tues Thur Sat & Sun 8am–2pm; free) built around the cave where Saint John heard the voice of God issuing from a cleft in the rock, and where he sat dictating His words to a disciple. A leaflet left for visitors points out that the "fissure . . . (divides) the rock into three parts, thus serving as a continual reminder of the Trinitarian nature of God".

This is merely a foretaste of the **Monastery of Saint John** (erratic hours, but theoretically Mon Tues Thur & Sun 8am–2pm & 4–6pm, Wed Fri & Sat 8am–2pm; the cloister of the Apocalypse adheres to the same schedule; "modest" dress essential; 500dr admission to treasury). Behind its imposing fortifications have been preserved a fantastic array of religious treasures dating back to the earliest days of Christianity: relics, icons, books, ceremonial ornaments and apparel of the most extraordinary richness.

Outside Saint John's stout walls, **HÓRA** is a beautiful little town whose antiquated alleys shelter over forty churches and monasteries. The churches, many of them containing beautiful icons and examples of the local skill in wood carving, are almost all locked, but someone living nearby will have the key. Among the best are the church of **Dhiassozoússas** and the monastery of **Zoödhóhou Piyís**.

You can **eat** well at *Vangelis* on the inner square, which has the edge over nearby *Olympia* in terms of freshness and variety. There are, however, very few **places to stay**; foreigners here are mostly long-term occupants, and almost a third of the crumbling mansions have been bought up and restored in the past two decades. Getting a short-term room can be a pretty thankless task, even in spring or autumn; the best strategy is to contact *Vangelis* taverna early in the day, or phone ahead for reservations at *Yioryia Triandafyllou* (☎0247/31 963; ④) or *Marouso Kouva* (☎0247/31 026; ④).

Finally, don't miss the **view** from Platía Lótzas, particularly at dawn or dusk: the land-masses to the north, going clockwise, include Ikaría, Thímena, Foúrni, Sámos with the brooding mass of Mount Kérkis, Arkí, and the double-humped Samsun Dag (ancient Mount Mikale) in Turkey.

The rest of the island

Pátmos, as a locally published guide memorably proclaimed, "is immense for those who know how to wander in space and time". The more conventionally propelled may find it easier to get around on foot, or by bus. This is a rewarding island for **walking** with a network of paths, while the overworked **bus** which connects Skála with Hóra, Kámbos and Gríkou is still fairly reliable – the terminal, with a posted-up timetable, is right in front of the main ferry dock.

After the extraordinary atmosphere and magnificent scenery, it's the **beaches** that are Patmos' principal attraction. From Hóra a good trail heads southeast to the sandiest part of generally overdeveloped and cheerless **Gríkou** within forty minutes. From either Gríkou or Hóra, you can ride a moped over dirt roads as far as Stavrós Church on the Dhiakoftí isthmus, beyond which a thirty-minute walk leads to **Psilí Ámmos** beach, the only all-sand cove on the island, with shade lent by tamarisks and a good taverna. There's also a summer *kaíki* service here from Skála. More good beaches are to be found in the north of the island, most of them accessible on foot by following the old paths which (with the exception of some paved or cross-country stretches) parallel the startling, indented eastern shore.

The first beach beyond Méloï, **Agriolivádhi**, has a strip of sand at its centre and a taverna; the next, **Kámbos**, is popular with Greeks, and the most developed strand on the island, with seasonal watersports facilities and tavernas, though the shore is rocky underfoot. If you head east from Kámbos, **Vayiá** and **Livádhi Yeranoú** are less-visited, although the latter can be subject to drifting rubbish. From Kámbos you can also head north to the bay of **Lámbi**, best for swimming when the prevailing wind is from the south, and renowned for an abundance of multicoloured stones. A hamlet of sorts here has rooms and two adjacent tavernas which are among the best on the island. This is also the most northerly port of call for the daily excursion *kaíkia* which shuttle constantly around the coast in season.

As is so often the case, you'll find the island at its best in spring or autumn. It can get cold in winter, but there is a hard core of foreigners who live here year-round, so things never entirely close down. Many of the long-term residents rent houses in **Léfkes**, a fertile valley just west of Kámbos with a lonely and sometimes wild beach at its end.

Lipsí

Of the various islets to the north and east of Pátmos, **Lipsí** is the largest and most populated, and the one that is beginning to get a significant summer tourist trade; now also a port of call for main-line ferries between the Cyclades and the larger Dodecanese, Lipsí can be crowded out in August. Deep wells water many small, well-tended farms, but there is only one spring, and pastoral appearances are deceptive – four times the relatively impoverished full-time population of 450 is overseas (many in Tasmania, for some reason). Most of those who stayed cluster around the fine harbour, as does most of the food and lodging.

Accommodation choices include *Rooms Panorama* (☎0247/41 279; ③), *Angeliki Petrandi* (③), and *Studios Barbarosa* (☎0247/41 312; ③), just up the stairway into the town centre. The best **tavernas** are the *Mongos Brothers'* premises affiliated to the *Kalypso*, and *Toh Dhelfini*, next to the police station. A Lipsian quirk are the bizarre local **kafenía**: some seem to have a double life as bars and the front rooms of private dwellings; others have garish posters or juke boxes, and there are fishermen's joints with nonexistent decor where you'll be served grilled seafood *mezédhes*. There is a **post office** and an **OTE**, and the combination **tourist office** and **Ecclesiastical Museum** is hilariously indiscriminate, featuring such "relics" as oil from the sanctuary on Mount Tabor and water from the Jordan River.

The island's **beaches** are rather scattered: closest is Liendoú, just west of town, but the most attractive is **Katsadhiá**, a collection of small, sandy coves south of the port, with a very good taverna, *Andonis* (May–Sept only), just inland from an eyesore of a music bar, *Dilaila*. **Kohlakoúras**, on the east coast, is by contrast rather grubby shingle with no facilities. An hour's walk along the road leading west from town brings you to **Platís Yialós**, a small, shallow, sandy bay with no development but sheltered from winds. In high season enterprising individuals run pick-up trucks, with bench seats, to the various coves.

A number of paths provide opportunities for a variety of **walks** through the undulating countryside, dotted with blue-domed churches – you can walk from one end of Lipsí to the other in less than two hours. A **carpet-weaving school** for girls operates sporadically on the quay, and some evenings a *santoúri* (Levantine hammer-dulcimer) player performs. Other than that there's absolutely nothing to do or see, but you won't find many better places to do nothing.

Arkí, Maráthi and Agathónissi

Arkí is considerably more primitive, lacking both electricity and a ferry dock, with no discernible village centre. About half the size of Lipsí, just thirty inhabitants cling to life here; most are engaged in fishing. It's an elective stop on the route of the **Nissos Kalimnos**: if you want to stay here, you must warn the captain well in advance, so he can radio for the shuttle service from the island. A desperately poor place, its complete depopulation seems conceivable within the next decade. While there is a seasonal taverna with rooms, there's not even a proper beach; the nearest one just offshore is on the islet of **Maráthi**, where a taverna caters to the day-trippers who come a couple of times a week from Pátmos – links with Arkí are unreliable. The pair of tavernas here both rent some fairly comfortable **rooms**, making Maráthi a better option than Arkí for acting out Robinson Crusoe fantasies.

Agathónissi is sufficiently remote – much closer to Turkey than Pátmos, in fact – to be out of reach even of these excursions; just 150 people live here, fishing and raising goats. Pebble beaches can be found west of the harbour settlement of Áyios Yióryios, and at **Katholikó** and **Hokhliá**, reached by walking to opposite ends of the island. There's a bona fide inland village, **MEGÁLO HORIÓ**, a hundred or so people, two stores, and one pension run by the Katsouleri family (☎0247/24 385; ②); the *Kafenio Dhekatria Adhelfia* does generous home-style lunches. There are three **places to stay** in Áyios Yioryios, in descending order of preference: *Theoloyia Yiameou* (☎0247/23 692; ②), *Maria Kamitsa* (☎0247/23 690; ②), and some rooms above *George's Taverna* (☎0247/24 385; ②). For **meals** out, *George's* and *Yiannis* are both good bets; George does meat and game dishes, while Yiannis offers fish and meat grills. Of late, Agathónissi has begun to attract some intrepid backpackers, and with hydrofoil connections dovetailing fairly well with the appearances of the *Nissos Kalimnos*, you needn't be marooned here for more than two or three days during the tourist season.

travel details

To simplify the lists below, the *Nissos Kalimnos* has been left out. Since 1989, this car ferry has been the most regular lifeline of the smaller islands – it visits them all at least once a week between March and December. Its schedule is currently as follows: Monday and Friday morning, leaves Kálimnos for Kós, Níssiros, Tílos, Sími, Rhodes and Kastellórizo. Tuesday and Saturday morning, departs Rhodes for Sími, Tílos, Níssiros, Kós, with an evening out-and-back trip to Kálimnos; Wednesday and Sunday departs Kálimnos for Léros, Lipsí, Pátmos, Agathónissi, Pithagório (Sámos), and back to Kálimnos via the same islands; Thursday morning from Kálimnos to Kós and back, then to Astipálea and back, then to Kós and back once more to Kálimnos;. This ship is often poorly publicized on islands other than its home port; for current, disinterested information you're strongly advised to phone the central agency on Kálimnos (☎0243/29 612).

Ferries

AGATHONÍSSI 1 weekly to Lipsí, Pátmos, Sámos.

ASTIPÁLEA 2–3 weekly to Amórgos, Náxos, Páros, Síros, Pireás; 1–2 weekly to Kós, Kálimnos, Rhodes, Níssiros, Tílos, Míkonos, Tínos.

HÁLKI Twice weekly to Kárpathos and Rhodes Town; once weekly to Crete and select western Cyclades, subject to cancellation in bad weather. Once-daily **kaíki** to Rhodes (Skála Kamírou).

KÁLIMNOS Similar **ferry** service to Kós, but with fewer to Páros and Pireás and no services to Thessaloníki. Morning **kaiki**, afternoon **speedboat** to Kós Town; 2 or 3 daily **kaikía** to Mastihári, usually via Psérimos. Daily **kaíki** from Mirtiés to Ksirókambos on Léros.

KÁRPATHOS (PIGÁDHIA) AND KÁSSOS Twice-weekly connections between the islands, and to Rhodes, Hálki, Crete (Iráklion and Sitía), Mílos and Pireás; once to Crete (Áyios Nikólaos), Sími, Thíra, Páros, Náxos, Folégandhros, Síkinos and Sífnos.

Note: Dhiafáni is served by only one weekly mainline ferry to Crete, select western Cyclades and Rhodes, subject to cancellation in bad weather until the new pier is completed.

KASTELLÓRIZO (Méyisti) 3 weekly to Rhodes; 1 weekly to Pireás indirectly, via select Dodecanese and Cyclades.

KÓS 10–17 weekly to Rhodes and Pireás; 7–10 weekly to Kálimnos; daily to Léros and Pátmos; 2 weekly to Tílos and Níssiros; 1 weekly to Thessaloníki; 1 weekly to Astipálea, Sími, Lipsí, Náxos, Páros, Síros. **Excursion boats** 3 daily in season from Mastihári to Psérimos and Kálimnos, daily from Kós Town to Kálimnos via Psérimos, and Rhodes; 1 or 2 daily from Kardhámena to Níssiros, 4–5 weekly from Kós Town to Níssiros; 3 weekly to Pátmos.

LÉROS Daily to Pireás, Pátmos, Kálimnos, Kós and Rhodes; 1 weekly to Lipsí, Náxos, Páros, Míkonos, Síros. Seasonal daily **excursion boats** from Ayía Marína to Lipsí and Pátmos, and from Ksirókambos to Mirtiés on Kálimnos.

LIPSÍ 1–2 weekly to Síros, Páros, Náxos, Pireás, Pátmos, Sími, Tílos, Níssiros, Kós, Kálimnos, Léros.

NÍSSIROS AND TÍLOS Same as for Sími, plus 1 weekly between each other, Rhodes, Kós, Kálimnos, Astipálea, Páros, Síros. **Excursion boats** between Níssiros and Kós as follows: to Kardhámena 2 weekly at 4pm and the islanders' "shopping special" at 8am; 4–5 weekly to Kós town (seasonal and expensive).

PÁTMOS Similar **ferry** service to Léros, with the addition of 2 weekly to Foúrni, Ikaría, Sámos; seasonal **tourist boats** to Sámos, Lipsí, and Maráthi on a daily basis; less often to Arkí.

RHODES 10–12 weekly to Kós and Pireás; 7–10 weekly to Kálimnos; daily to Léros and Pátmos; 4 weekly to Crete (Áyios Nikólaos/Sitía or Iráklion); 1–2 weekly to Sími, Lipsí, Tílos, Níssiros, Astipálea, Hálki, Kárpathos, Kássos; once weekly to Folégandhros, Mílos, Sífnos, Síros, Thessaloníki. **Excursion boats** twice daily to Sími.

SÍMI 1 weekly to Rhodes, Tílos, Níssiros, Kós, Kálimnos, Léros, Lipsí, Pátmos, Náxos, Páros and Pireás. **Excursion boats** twice daily to Rhodes.

Hydrofoils

Two hydrofoil companies, *Ilio Lines* and *Nearhos Mamidhakis* (aka Dodecanese Hydrofoils) serve the Dodecanese between May and mid-October, operating out of Rhodes and Kálimnos. For current schedule information, phone ☎0241/24 000 or 0242/25 920 for *Nearhos Mamidhakis*, and ☎0273/27 337 or 0273/61 914 for the agent for *Ilio Lines*.

Flights

KÁRPATHOS 2–7 daily to Rhodes; 2–4 weekly to Kássos; 2 weekly to Athens; 1 weekly to Crete (Sitía).

KÁSSOS 2–4 weekly to Kárpathos; 3–7 weekly to Rhodes; 1 weekly to Crete (Sitía).

KASTELLÓRIZO (Méyisti) 2/3 weekly to Rhodes.

KÓS 2–3 daily to Athens; 2–3 daily to Rhodes.

LÉROS 3 –7 weekly to Athens.

RHODES 4–5 daily to Athens; 4 weekly to Iráklion; 2 weekly to Thessaloníki.

International ferries

KÓS 1–14 weekly to Bodrum, Turkey (45min).

RHODES Daily to Marmaris, Turkey (1–2hr) by Greek hydrofoil or more expensive Turkish car ferry; 2–3 weekly to Limassol, Cyprus (18hr) and Haifa, Israel (39hr). Services to Egypt are currently suspended.

CHAPTER FIVE

THE EAST AND NORTH AEGEAN

T he seven substantial islands and four minor islets scattered off the coast of Asia Minor and northeast Greece form a rather arbitrary archipelago. Although there is some similarity in architecture and landscape, virtually the only common denominator is the strong individual character of each island. Despite their proximity to modern Turkey, members of the group bear few signs of an Ottoman heritage, especially when compared to Rhodes and Kós. There's the odd minaret or two, and some of the domestic architecture betrays obvious influences from Constantinople, Thrace and further north in the Balkans, but by and large the enduring Greekness of these islands is testimony to the 4000-year Hellenic presence in Asia Minor, which only ended in 1923.

This heritage is regularly referred to by the Greek government in its propaganda war with the Turks over the sovereignty of these far-flung outposts. The tensions here are, if anything, worse than in the Dodecanese, aggravated by potential undersea oil deposits in the straits between the islands and Turkey. The Turks have also persistently demanded that Límnos, astride the sea lanes to and from the Dardenelles, is demilitarized, but so far Greece has shown no signs of cooperating.

The heavy military presence can be disconcerting, especially for lone woman travellers, and large tracts of land are off-limits as military reserves. But, as in the Dodecanese, local tour operators do a thriving business shuttling passengers for absurdly high tariffs (caused partly by the need for payoffs at both ends) between the easternmost islands and the Turkish coast with its amazing archeological sites and watering holes. Bear in mind, if you're thinking of making the journey, that, if you have travelled to Greece on a charter flight, your ticket will be invalidated by an overnight stay in Turkey. Many of the islands' main ports and towns are not the quaint picturesque places you may have become used to in other parts of Greece; indeed a number are relatively large and uninteresting university, military and commercial centres. In most cases you should suppress your initial impulse to take the next boat out and press on into the worthwhile interiors.

Sámos is the most visited of the group and, if you can leave the crowds behind, is perhaps also the most verdant and beautiful. **Ikaría** to the west is relatively unspoiled, and nearby **Foúrni** is a haven for determined solitaries. **Híos** is culturally interesting, but its natural beauty has been ravaged and the development of tourism has until recently been deliberately retarded. **Lésvos** is an acquired taste, though once you get a feel for the island you may find it hard to leave – the number of repeat visitors grows yearly. By contrast virtually no foreigners and few Greeks visit **Áyios Efstrátios**, and with good reason. **Límnos** is considerably better, but its appeal is confined mostly to the area around the pretty port town. To the north, Samothráki and Thássos are totally isolated from the others, except via the mainland port Kavála, and it's easiest to visit them en route to or from Istanbul. **Samothráki** has one of the most dramatic seaward

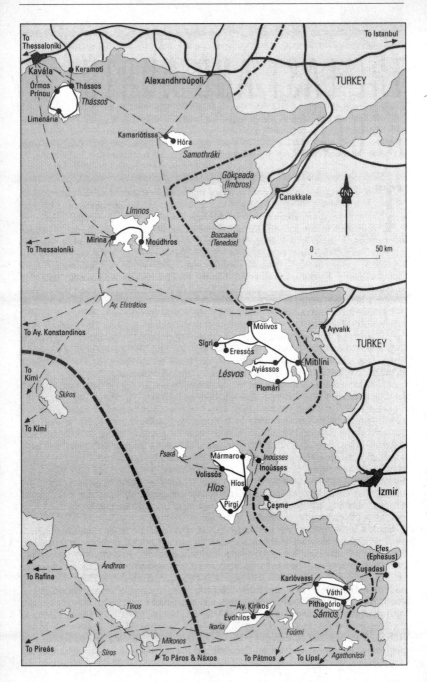

approaches of any Greek island, and one of the more important ancient sites. The appeal of **Thássos** is rather broader, with a varied offering of sandy beaches, forested mountains and minor archeological sites. Easily accessible from the mainland, however, it can be overrun in high season.

Sámos

The lush and seductive island of **Sámos** was formerly joined to the Asia Minor until sundered from Mount Mycale opposite by Ice Age cataclysms. The resulting 2500-metre strait is now the narrowest distance between Greece and Turkey, and, accordingly, military watchpoints bristle on both sides.

There's little physical evidence of it today, but Sámos was once the wealthiest island in the Aegean and, under the patronage of the tyrant Polycrates, home to a thriving intellectual community; Epicurus, Pythagora, Aristarchus and Aesop were among the residents. Decline set in when the star of Classical Athens was in the ascendant, though its status was improved somewhat in early Byzantine times when Sámos constituted its own *theme* (imperial administrative district). Later, towards the end of the fifteenth century, Turkish pirates pillaged the island, which then remained empty for more than a hundred years until an Ottoman admiral received permission from the sultan to repopulate it with Greek Orthodox settlers, a role which goes far to explaining the local identity crisis and a rather thin topsoil of indigenous culture. Most of the village names are either clan surnames, or adjectives indicating origins elsewhere – constant reminders of refugee descent. There is no genuine Samiote music, dance or dress, and little that's original in the way of cuisine and architecture (the latter, in particular, is a blend of styles from northern Greece and Asia Minor).

The Samiotes compensated somewhat for their deracination by fighting fiercely for independence during the 1820s, but, despite their accomplishments in decimating a Turkish fleet in the narrow strait and annihilating a landing army, the Great Powers handed the island back to the Ottomans in 1830, with the consoling proviso that it be semi-autonomous, ruled by an appointed Christian prince. This period, referred to as the *Iyimonía* (Hegemony), was marked by a mild renaissance in fortunes, courtesy of the shipping and tobacco trades. However, union with Greece, the ravages of a bitter World War II occupation and mass emigration effectively reversed the recovery until tourism appeared on the horizon during the 1980s.

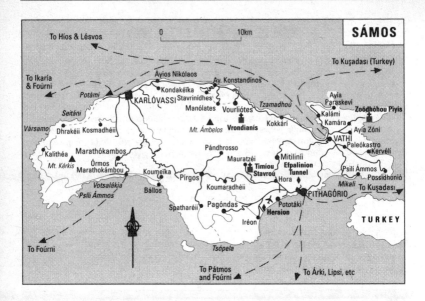

Today, the Samian economy is increasingly dependent on package **tourism**, far too much of it in places; the eastern half of the island has pretty much been surrendered to the onslaught of holidaymakers, although the more rugged western part has retained much of its undeveloped grandeur. The rather sedate clientele is overwhelmingly Scandinavian, Dutch and German, and a far cry from the singles scene of the Cyclades. The absence of an official campsite on such a large island, and phalanxes of self-catering villas, tell you exactly what sort of custom is expected.

Getting there and getting around

Sámos has no less than three **ferry ports** – Karlóvassi in the west, Vathí and Pithagório in the east – as well as an **airport**, which is 14km southwest of Vathí and just 3km west of Pithagório. All ferries between Pireás, the Cyclades and Sámos call at both Karlóvassi and Vathí, as do the smaller *Miniotis Line* ferries linking the island with Híos, Foúrni, Ikaría and Pátmos, and the *Gianmar* and *Ilio Line* hydrofoils to the Dodecanese and north Aegean. In addition, Vathí receives the once-weekly *NEL* sailing between northern Greece and the northern Dodecanese, via all intervening islands, as well as the lion's share of hydrofoils and small ferries from Kuşadası; Pithagório siphons off a bit of the Turkey shipping in high season, and additionally sees two regular weekly ferry connections from as far south as Kós in the Dodecanese.

The **bus terminals** in Pithagório and Vathí lie within walking distance of the ferry dock; at Karlóvassi, a bus is occasionally on hand to take you the 3km into town from the port. There is no *Olympic* shuttle bus to and from the airport; you are at the mercy of the numerous taxi drivers, who shouldn't charge you more than 2000dr for the trip to Vathí. In high season, **taxis** to the airport or docks must be booked several hours in advance (☎0273/28 404 in Vathí) – have your hotel do it for you.

The bus service itself is excellent along the Pithagório–Vathí and Vathí–Karlóvassi via Kokkári routes, but poor otherwise. However, you're almost certain to have to **rent a motorbike** or **car**, and with literally dozens of outlets – at least for bikes – there's little problem in finding good deals.

Vathí

Lining the steep northeast shore of a deep bay, **VATHÍ** is the provincial capital, founded after 1830 to replace Hóra as the island's main town. It's of minimal interest for the most part – although the pedestrianized bazaar and tiers of Neoclassical houses have some attraction – and the only real highlight is the excellent **Archeological Museum** (daily except Mon 8.30am–3pm; 500dr), set behind the small central park beside the derelict old town hall. One of the best provincial collections in Greece is housed in both the old *Paskallion* building and a modern wing across the way, specially constructed to house the star exhibit: a majestic, five-metre-tall *kouros*, discovered out at the Heraion sanctuary (see p.259). The *kouros*, the largest free-standing effigy to survive from ancient Greece, was dedicated to Apollo but found together with a devotional mirror to Hera from a Nile workshop, only one of two discovered in Greece.

In the *Paskallion*, more votive offerings of Egyptian design – a hippo, a dancer in Nilotic dress, Horus-as-Falcon, an Osiris figurine – prove trade and pilgrimage links between Sámos and the Nile valley going back to the eighth century BC. Visible Mesopotamian and Anatolian influences in other artwork confirm the exotic trend, most tellingly in a case full of ivory miniatures: Perseus and Medusa in relief, a kneeling, perfectly formed mini-*kouros*, a pouncing lion, and a drinking horn terminating in a bull's head. The most famous artefacts are the dozen or so bronze **griffin-heads**, for which Sámos was the major centre of production in the seventh century BC; mounted on the edge of bronze cauldrons, they were believed to ward off evil spirits.

The provincial authority's plans for the **waterfront** have been stalled for lack of funds. However, near the much-needed car park and new fishing harbour you can see the fishermen peddle their catch on the flagstone quay mornings before 10am. The dumping of raw sewage in the bay has ceased, but still nobody in their right mind goes swimming at Vathí; the closest appealing beaches are some way distant. One waterfront curiosity is the old French Catholic church, labelled "ECCLESIA CATOLICA" in Latin, which has stood disused except for monthly masses since 1974, when the last nuns departed Sámos after having schooled several elite generations for nearly a century.

Strolls inland can be more rewarding. You might visit the museum-like **antique store** of Mihalis Stavrinos, just off the central Platía Pithagóra (the so-called "Lion Square"), where you can invest in assorted precious baubles or rescue rare engravings from the silverfish. Even better is **ÁNO VATHÍ**, 150m above sea level, an officially preserved community of tottering, tile-roofed houses that's the goal of many a day-stroller. The village's late medieval churches are neglected, but still worth a look: the tiny chapel of **Áyios Athanásios**, near the main cathedral, boasts a fine *temblon* and naïve frescoes.

Arrival, information and facilities

From the **ferry dock** the shore boulevard, Themistokléous Sofoúli, describes a 1300-metre arc around the bay. About 400m along is Platía Pithagóra, distinguished by its lion statue; while 800m along is the major turning inland to the **bus terminal**, merely a chaos of vehicles at a perennially cluttered intersection, next to a booking office. The two most comprehensive **ferry/travel agents** are *By Ship* on the front (☎0273/27 337) and *Samina Tours* at Themistokléous Sofoúli 67 (☎0273/28 841); between them they sell tickets for just about every boat or hydrofoil, domestic or international (except *NEL* lines to the North Aegean and mainland, and the *Agapitos Lines* ferry towards Pireás); they also have money-exchange facilities.

The municipal **tourist information office** is on Ikostipémptis Martíou (summer Mon–Fri 8am–8pm, Sat–Sun 9am–1pm; winter variable hours), not especially cheerful but worth a stop for leaflets, comprehensive bus and ferry schedules and accommodation listings – staff do not make reservations for you.

Vathí is chock-a-block with **bike-and-car-rental** franchises, which keeps rates reasonable. Try *Europe Rent a Car* (two outlets, near the bus station, and near *Number Nine* pub), *Louis* (just behind the waterfront, 400m south of the dock), or for cars only, *Budget* at Themistokléous Sofoúli 31 (☎0273/28 856) or *Autoplan* at no. 67 (☎0273/23 555). Other amenities include the **post office** (Mon–Fri only) on Smírnis, 150m inland from the *Olympic* offices; **OTE** across the way from the cathedral and street produce market; three waterfront **banks**; and two automatic **laundries** – *Alex* at Yimnasiárhou Katevéni 17 is the friendlier, providing service washes.

Accommodation

Most **accommodation** establishments catering for independent travellers cluster in the hillside district of Katsoúni, more or less directly above the ferry dock. Their proprietors tend not to meet arriving ferries, since even these rooms are partly block-booked by tour groups. However, hunting for yourself, affordable options are surprisingly numerous, except in August. They include the waterfront *Hotel Parthenon*, oldest in town but clean and acceptable other than bar noise from below (☎0273/27 234; ②; open all year); the somewhat more comfortable *Hotel Artemis*, just off "Lion Square" (☎0273/27 792; ③); *Pension Ionia*, inland at Manoli Kalomíri 5 (☎0273/28 782; ②; open all year); the *Pension Trova* around the corner at Kalomíri 26 (☎0273/27 759; ②); or the *Pension Avli*, a wonderful period piece up a nearby stair-street at Aréos 2 (☎0273/22 939; ②). This is the former convent school of the French nuns, so the rooms, arrayed around a courtyard (*avlí* in Greek) are appropriately institutional.

None of these outfits are palaces by any means; for more luxury you'll have to spread your net a bit wider. Start at the surprisingly affordable *Hotel Galaxy*, at Angéou 1, near the top of Katsoúni (☎0273/22 665; ③), set in garden surroundings, with a small pool. *Samos Hotel* (☎0273/28 377; ④), right by the ferry dock, frequently drops its rates in winter, and is open all year. Only the front rooms of the *Hotel Paradise* at Kanári 21 (☎0273/23 911; ④–⑤) look out over the bus stop – side and rear rooms have views of local orchards and the pool.

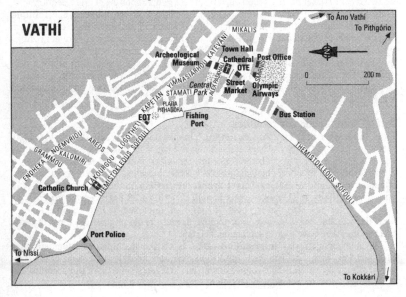

Eating and drinking

The only waterfront **tavernas** worth a second glance are *Ta Dhiodhia*, 1km south along Sofoúli, next to the military headquarters, serving pricey but well-prepared seafood and *mezédhes* (evening only); *Stelios*, 150m north of the dock on the right, ideal for a no-nonsense, pre-ferry meal; and finally *Ouzeri Apanemia*, at the far west end of the shore boulevard, where slightly above-average prices are justified by the appetizing fare from the Athenian chef. Up in Áno Vathí, the only place to eat is the popular *Agrambeli*, whose menu varies nightly.

Vathí nightlife revolves around a half-dozen **bars**, longest lived of these being *Number Nine*, on a sea-view terrace at Kefalopoúlou 9 (north of the jetty). Another standby is the inconspicuously marked *Cleary's Pub*, just behind Platía Pithagóra, run by Desireé, aka "Spooky", who played one of the naked witches in Polanski's *Macbeth*. *Metropolis*, in the orchards behind the *Hotel Paradise*, is Vathí's recently built **disco**.

Around Vathí

The immediate environs of Vathí offer some modest beaches and small hamlets with tavernas, ideal targets for day trips.

Two kilometres **east** of (and above) Vathí spreads the vast inland plateau of Vlamarí, devoted to vineyards and supporting the hamlets of **AYÍA ZÓNI** and **KAMÁRA**. Of the two simple tavernas in Kamára, *O Kriton* is recommended. From Kamára you can climb up a partly cobbled path to the cliff-top **monastery of Zoödhóhou Piyís**, for views across the end of the island to Turkey.

Heading **north** out of Vathí, the narrow, street threads through beachless **KALÁMI** – formerly the summer retreat of rich Vathiots and now home to resort hotels – before ending after 7km at the pebbly bay and fishing port of **AYÍA PARASKEVÍ** (or Nissí), with two tavernas and good (if rather unsecluded) swimming.

As you head southeast from Vathí along the main island loop road, the triple chapel at **Treis Ekklisíes** marks an important junction, with another fork 100m along the left-hand turning. Bearing left twice takes you through the hilltop village of **PALEÓKASTRO**, remarkable only for its evening-only taverna *Ta Dhilina*, for which Vathiots regularly undertake the special six-kilometre trip out here. After another 6km you reach the quiet, striking bay of **Kervéli**, with a small gravel beach, a pair of expensive tavernas and two new luxury hotels. It's not worth continuing to the road's end at **POSSIDHÓNIO**, whose tavernas are mediocre and beach negligible.

Turning right at the second junction leads to the beaches of Mikáli and Psilí Ámmos. **Mikáli**, a kilometre of windswept sand and gravel, has been recently developed. **Psilí Ámmos**, further east around the headland, is a crowded, sandy cove, whose best and longest-established namesake taverna is on the right as you arrive. If you swim to the islet, a tempting target, beware of strong west-to-east currents which sweep through the narrow straits even in the shallows. There's a bus service out here up to five times daily in season.

Pithagório and around

Most traffic south of Vathí heads for **PITHAGÓRIO**, the island's premier resort, renamed in 1955 to honour its native ancient mathematician, philosopher and mystic. Prior to that it was known as Tigáni (Frying Pan) – in mid-summer you'll learn why. The sixth-century BC tyrant Polycrates had his capital here, and beyond the village core of cobbled lanes overshadowed by thick-walled mansions lie acres of currently suspended archeological excavations – which have had the effect of forcing modern Pithagório to expand northeastward and uphill. The small **harbour**, fitting more or less perfectly into the confines of Polycrates's ancient port, and still using his jetty, is today devoted almost entirely to pleasure craft and overpriced cocktail bars.

Sámos's principal surviving attempt at a **castle**, the nineteenth-century *pírgos* (tower-house) of Lykourgos Logothetis, overlooks both the town and the shoreline where this local chieftain oversaw decisive victories by "Kapetan Stamatis" and Admiral Kanaris over the Turks in the summer of 1824. The final battle was won on Transfiguration Day (August 6), and accordingly the church beside the tower bears a huge sign in Greek announcing that "Christ Saved Sámos 6 August 1824".

More ancient antiquities include the fairly dull **Roman baths** west of town (Tues, Wed, Fri 9am–2.30pm; Thurs & Sun 11.30am–2.30pm; Sat 10.30am–2.30pm; free) and a miniscule **archeological collection** in the town hall (Tues, Thur & Fri 9.30am–12.45pm; Wed 11am–12.45pm; Sun 9am–12.45pm; free). Rather more interesting is the **Efpalinion tunnel** (Tues & Fri 11am–12.45pm; Wed, Thur & Sun 9.30am–12.45pm; Sat 10.30am–12.45pm; free), an aqueduct bored through the mountain just north of Pithagório at the behest of Polycrates. Its mid-section has collapsed but you should be able to explore the intial portion of its one-kilometre length with a flashlight. To get there, take the signposted path from the shore boulevard at the west end of town.

If you're keen, you can also climb to the five remaining chunks of the Polycratian **perimeter wall** enclosing his citadel. There's a choice of routes: one leading up from the Glífa lagoon west of Pithagório, past an **ancient watchtower** now isolated from any other fortifications, and the other – which is easier – leading from the monastery of **Panayía Spilianí** and the adjacent ancient **amphitheatre**.

Practicalities

If there are any **accommodation** vacancies – and it's best not to count on it in mid-season – proprietors meet incoming ferries. Otherwise it's a matter of phoning ahead or chancing on a spot as you tramp the streets. The **tourist information booth** (☎0273/61 389), on the main thoroughfare, Likoúrgou Logothéti, can help in finding rooms.

Quietly located at the seaward end of Odhos Pithagóra, south of Likoúrgou Logothéti, the modest *Tsambika* and *Sydney* (②) pensions are worth considering as nocturnal noise can be a problem elsewhere. Another peaceful area is the hillside north of Platí Irínis, where the *Hotel Galini* is one of the better small outfits here (☎0273/61 167; winter ☎01/98 42 248; ④–⑤). Further uphill, on the road to Vathí, the rear units of *Studios Anthea* (☎0273/62 086; ④) are fairly noise-free and allow you to self-cater.

Eating out can be frustrating in Pithagório, with value for money often a completely alien concept here. Away from the water, *Taverna Platania*, under two eucalypts opposite the town hall, is a good choice for a simple meal; *Maritsa*, on the first side street above the quay, south of Likoúrgou Logothéti, does fish for about as reasonably as you can expect in a tourist resort. For waterside dining, you're best off at the extreme east end of the quay, near what passes for a town beach, at either of two *ouzerís*, *Remataki* or *Odysseas*.

If none of this appeals, the **bus stop** to get you away is just west of the intersection of Likoúrgou Logothéti and the road to Vathí. Two **banks** and the **post office** also line Likoúrgou Logothéti, while the **OTE** is on the quay below the *Hotel Damo*. The flattish country to the west is ideal for pedal-bike touring, a popular activity, though if you want to rent a **moped**, *Evelin's* – 1500m out of town by the airport junction and namesake hotel – is reasonable and helpful.

Around Pithagório

The main local beach stretches for several kilometres west of the Logothetis castle, punctuated about halfway along by the end of the airport runway, and the cluster of hotels known as **POTOKÁKI**. Just before the turnoff to the heart of the beach sprawls the ultra-luxurious *Doryssa Bay* complex, which includes a meticulously concocted fake village, guaranteed to confound archeologists of future eras. No two of the units, joined by named lanes, are alike, and there's even a *platía* with an expensive café. If you actu-ally intend to stay in the area, however, the *Fito Bungalows Hotel* (☎0273/61 58; ⑤–⑥) is more affordable, with breakfast included in the price. If you don't mind the crowds generated by these two hotels, the sand-and-pebble **beach** here is well groomed and the water clean; misanthropes will have to head out to the end of the road for more seclusion.

The Potokáki access road is a dead end, with the main island loop road pressing on from the turnoff for the airport and Iréon hamlet. Under layers of alluvial mud, plus today's runway, lies the Sacred Way joining the ancient city with the **Heraion**, the massive shrine of the Mother Goddess (daily except Mon 8.30am–3pm; 500dr). Much touted in tourist literature, this assumes humbler dimensions – one re-erected column and assorted foundations – upon approach. Yet once inside the precinct you sense the former grandeur of the temple, never completed owing to Polycrates's untimely death at the hands of the Persians. The site chosen was the legendary birthplace of the goddess, near the mouth of the still-active Imvrassós stream; in the far corner of the fenced-in zone you glimpse a large, exposed patch of the paved processional Sacred Way.

The modern resort of **IRÉON** nearby is a nondescript grid of dusty streets, unobjec-tionable enough except in midsummer. The clientele seems a bit younger, more active and less packaged than in Pithagório, with more independent rooms in evidence. The most locally patronized **taverna** is the westernmost on the shore, and there are a series of bars behind the coarse-shingle beach.

The island loop road continues from the Iréon/airport turnoff to another junction in long, narrow **HÓRA**, the medieval capital and still a large, noisy village packed with mili-tary personnel and employees in the local tourist industry. It's worth knowing about principally for a handful of tavernas, such as *Iy Sintrofía*, on the road in from Pithagório; a grill on Platía Ayías Paraskevís; and *O Andonis* on the square with the running fountain. None are especially cheap but they are at least more down-to-earth than anything in Pithagório.

Heading north from the crossroads takes you through a ravine to **MITILINIÍ** which initially seems an amorphous sprawl; a brief exploration, however, turns up a fine main square with some atmospheric *kafenía*, the unmarked *Dionyssos* taverna opposite them – by itself worth the trip up from the coast – and the island's last remaining indoor cinema, down a side street. A **Paleontological Museum** on the top floor of the community offices (Mon–Fri 8.30am–2pm; 200dr) is essentially a room of barely sorted bones from an Ice-Age animal dying-place nearby, and not worth the bother.

Southern Sámos

Since the circum-island bus only passes through or near the places below once or twice daily, you really need your own vehicle to explore them.

Some 4km west of Hóra an inconspicuous turning leads uphill to the monastery of **Timíou Stavroú**, currently the island's most important monastery, although the annual festival (September 14) is more an excuse for a tatty bazaar in the courtyards than any for music or feasting. A similarly poorly marked detour takes off a kilometre further ahead to **MAVRATZÉII**, one of the two Samian "pottery villages"; this one specializes in the *Koúpa tou Pithagóra* or "Pythagorean cup", supposedly designed by the sage to leak over the user's lap if he over-indulged beyond the "fill" line. More prac-tical wares can be found in **KOUMARADHÉII**, back on the main road, another 2km along.

From here you can descend a dirt track through burnt forest to the sixteenth-century monastery of **Megális Panayías** (daily 10am–1pm or at the whim of the care-taker), re-opened after a lengthy restoration and containing the finest frescoes on the island. The track, accessible to the average car, continues to the village of **MÍLI**, submerged in lemon groves – you can also get here from the Iréon road. Four kilometres above sprawls **PAGÓNDAS**, a large hillside community with a splendid main square and an unusual communal laundry house. From here, a wild but scenic dirt road curls 9km around the hill to **SPATHARÉII**, set on a natural balcony offering the best sea views this side of the island. From Spatharéii a paved road leads back 6km to **PÍRGOS** on the main road, lost in pine forests at the head of a ravine, and the centre of Samian honey production. A short distance down the gorge, **KOÚTSI** is a small oasis of plane trees – seventeen of them, according to a sign – shading a gushing spring and a taverna that's an excellent lunch stop if the tour buses haven't beaten you to it.

The rugged and beautiful coast south of the Pagóndas–Pírgos route is largely inaccessible, glimpsed by most visitors for the first and last time from the descending plane bringing them to Sámos; **Tsópela** is the only beach here with marked road access. The western reaches of this shoreline are approached via the small village of **KOUMÉÏKA**, with a massive inscribed marble fountain and a pair of *kafenía* on its square. Below extends the long, pebbly bay at **Bállos**, with sand, a cave and naturists at the far east end. Bállos itself is merely a sleepy collection of summer houses, several **rooms** to rent and a few **tavernas**, best of which is the *Cypriot*. Much of the food here is oven-cooked in limited portions; the garrulous couple running it prefer advance notice (☎0273/36 394).

Returning to Kouméïka, the apparently dodgy side road just before the village marked "Velanidhiá" is in fact quite passable to any vehicle, and a very useful short cut if you're travelling towards the beaches beyond Órmos Marathókambos (see "Western Sámos", overpage).

Kokkári and around

Leaving Vathí on the north coastal section of the island loop road, there's little to stop for until you reach **KOKKÁRI**, the third major Samian tourist centre after Pithagório and the capital. It's also the prime prompter of nostalgia among Sámos regulars; while lower Vathí and Pithagório had little beauty to sacrifice, much has been irrevocably lost here. The town's profile, covering two knolls behind twin headlands, is still recognizable, and even today several families doggedly untangle their fishing nets on the quay, lending some credence to brochure-touting of the place as a "fishing village". But in general the identity of what is now merely a stage set has been altered beyond recognition, with constant inland expansion over vineyards and the abandoned baby-onion fields that gave the place its name. With exposed, uncomfortably rocky beaches adjacent buffeted by near constant winds, Kokkári seems an unlikely candidate for further gentrification, although its Germanic promoters seem to have made a virtue of necessity by developing it as a highly successful windsurfing resort.

Practicalities

As in Vathí and Pithagório, a fair proportion of Kokkári's **accommodation** is block-booked by tour companies; one establishment not completely devoted to such trade is the pleasant *Hotel Olympia Beach* (☎0273/92 353; ④), on the western beach road, co-managed with the *Olympia Village* (☎0273/92 420; ⑤ for apartments). Otherwise *Yiorgos Mihelios* (☎0273/92 456; ③–④) has a wide range of rooms and apartments to rent. If you get stuck, seek assistance from the seasonal **EOT post** (☎0273/92 217), directly seaward from the main church.

Most **tavernas** line the waterfront, and most charge above the norm – even *Toh Kyma*, oldest and westernmost, still with a considerable local clientele. At the eastern end of things, *Ta Adhelfia* is as close as you'll get to a simple, unpretentious *psistariá* (although even it has credit-card stickers on display), while for a blow-out, the Athenian-run *Kariatidha*, a few doors down, is worth the extra cost. Inland, *Farmer's* – on the village through-road, a few steps east of the summer **cinema** – is highly regarded for its locally grown food, and in autumn may offer *moustalevriá* (grape must dessert).

Other amenities include a short-hours **bank** on the through road, a **post office** in a Portakabin on a lane to seaward, and a **laundrette** next to that.

West of Kokkári: the coast

The closest half-decent beaches are thirty to forty minutes' walk away to the west. The first, **Lemonákia**, is a bit too close to the road, with an obtrusive café; the graceful crescent of **Tzamadhoú** (as in Coleridge's Xanadu) figures in virtually every EOT poster of the island. It's a bit more natural, with path-only access and the west end of the saucer-shaped pebble beach by tacit consensus a nudist zone. Unfortunately a spring just inland has been fenced off to discourage the colonies of freelance campers who used to congregate here, and to encourage everyone to patronize the fairly pricey **taverna** signposted up in the vineyards. There's one more pebbly bay west of Avlákia (a mostly Greek resort 6km from Kokkári) called **Tzábou**, but unless you're passing by and want a quick dip it's not worth a special detour.

The next spot of any interest along the coast road is **Platanákia**, essentially a handful of tavernas and rooms for rent at a plane-shaded bridge and turn-off for Manolátes (see overpage). Platanákia is actually the eastern suburb of **ÁYIOS KONSTANDÍNOS**, whose surf-pounded esplanade has at long last been repaved. However, there are no usable beaches within walking distance, so the collection of warm-toned stone buildings (increasingly adulterated by concrete structures) serves as a more peaceful alternative to Kokkári. In addition to modest **hotels** such as the *Ariadne* (☎0273/94 206; ④), the *Four Seasons* (③) or the *Atlantis* (☎0273/94 329; ③), along the highway, there's a new generation of luxury bungalows and rooms in the new buildings; the **tavernas** of Platanákia are 1500m distant if the two here don't appeal.

Once past "Áyios" (as the bus conductors habitually bellow it out), the mountains hem the road in against the sea, and the terrain doesn't relent until near **KONDAKÉÏKA**, whose *platía*-with-*kafenío* is worth a visit at dusk for its fabulous sunsets, after which you can descend to its diminutive shore annexe of **ÁYIOS NIKÓLAOS** for excellent fish suppers, particularly at the westernmost of the two **tavernas** here. There's also a reasonable beach here, not visible from the upper road – walk east, ten minutes past the last studios.

Hill villages

Inland between Kokkári and Kondakéïka, an idyllic landscape of pine, cypress and orchards is overawed by dramatic, often cloud-shrouded mountains, so far little burned. Excursions into this quintessentially Romantic countryside are accordingly popular. Despite destructive nibblings by bulldozers, some of the trail system linking the various **hill villages** is still intact, and you can walk for as long or as little as you like, returning to the main highway to catch a bus home. Failing that, most of the communities can provide a bed at short notice.

The monastery of **Vrondianís** (Vrónda), directly above Kokkári, is a popular destination, although since the army now uses it as a barracks, the place only really comes alive during its annual festival (September 7–8), when *yiórti* – a special cereal-and-meat porridge – may be served. **VOURLIÓTES**, 2km west of the monastery, has beaked chimneys and brightly painted shutters sprouting from its typical tile-roofed houses. On the photogenic central square, the best established of several tavernas is *Snack Bar Iy Kiki*, serving two local specialities: *revithokeftédhes* (chickpea patties), and homemade *moskháto* dessert wine, so syrupy that you'll want to make a spritzer of it with soda. (The other Samian delicacy worth trying if you've access to a kitchen are the excellent sausages available from select butchers between September and May).

MANOLÁTES, further uphill and an hour-plus walk away via a deep river canyon, also has a pair of simple snack bars, and is the most popular trailhead for the five-hour round-trip up **Mount Ámbelos** (Karvoúnis), the island's second highest summit. From Manolátes you can no longer easily continue on foot to Stavrinídhes, the next village, but should plunge straight down, partly on a cobbled path, through the shade-drenched valley known as **Aïdhónia** (Nightingales) to Platanákia. Aïdhónia has a couple of mock-rustic tavernas under its trees, popular targets of "Greek Nights Out".

Karlóvassi

KARLÓVASSI, 37km west of Vathí and the second town of Sámos, divides into no less than four, occasionally unattractive, neighbourhoods: Néo well inland, whose untidy growth was spurred by the influx of post-1923 refugees; Meséo, across the usually dry river bed, draped appealingly on a knoll: and postcard-worthy Paleó (or Áno), above Limáni, the small harbour district. Undistinguished as it generally is, Karlóvassi makes an excellent base from which to explore the west of the island. The name, incidentally, despite a vehement lack of Ottoman legacy elsewhere on Sámos, appears to be a corruption of the Turkish for "snowy plain" – the plain in question being the conspicuous saddle of Mount Kérkis overhead, which is indeed snow-covered in a harsh winter.

Limáni

Most tourists stay at or near **LIMÁNI**, which has a handful of rooms and several expensive hotels. The **rooms**, all in the inland pedestrian lane behind the through road, are quieter – try those of *Vangelis Feloukatzis* (☎0273/33 293; ③) or *Ioannis Moskhoyiannis* (③). The port itself, its quay pedestrianized at night, is an appealing place with a boat-building industry at the west end and all the **ferry-ticket agencies** grouped at the middle; often a shuttle bus service operates from Néo Karlóvassi, timed to boat arrivals and departures. Tavernas and bars are abundant, but by far the best and most reasonable place to **eat** is *Steve's*, run by a genial South-African Greek and easily worth a special trip for lunch or dinner.

Paleó and Meséo

Immediately overhead, the partly hidden hamlet of **PALEÓ** is deceptively large, its hundred or so houses draped on either side of a leafy ravine. The only facilities are the sporadically functioning café *Toh Mikro Parisi*, and a seasonal taverna on the path down towards **MESÉO**. The latter is a conceivable alternative base to Limáni, with one pension just behind the playground, and other **rooms** scattered through the intervening half-kilometre between here and the sea. Lost in the residential streets near the top of Meséo's hill is a simple but satisfying **taverna**, *O Kotronis*, while down on the small square there's a small year-round bar-*ouzerí*, *Para Pende*, which attracts a mix of locals and tourists. Following the street linking the square to the waterfront, you pass one of the improbably huge, turn-of-the-century churches, topped with twin belfries and a blue-and-white dome, which dot the coastal plain here. Just at the intersection with the coast road you'll find the friendly, good-value *Ouzeri Toh Kima* (April–Oct), the best place in town to watch the sunset over a selection of *mezédhes*.

Néo

NÉO has little to recommend it, except for a wilderness of derelict stone-built warehouses and mansions down near the river mouth, reminders of the long-vanished leather industry which flourished here during the first half of this century. However, if you're staying at Limáni, you'll almost certainly at some point visit one of the two **banks**, the **post office**, the **OTE** or the **bus stop** on the main lower square. Some, though not all, of the buses coming from Vathí continue down to the harbour.

While waiting for a bus, one of two traditional *kafenía* might interest you: *O Kleanthis*, on the lower *platía*, or *O Kerketevs*, by the upper square. Any enforced halt in Néo, or Karlóvassi in general, is mitigated somewhat by the fact that the people here are appreciably friendlier than in the east of the island.

Western Sámos

Visitors put up with the dullness of Karlóvassi partly for the sake of western Sámos' excellent **beaches**. The closest of these is **Potámi**, forty minutes' walk away via the coast road from Limáni or an hour by a more scenic, high trail from Paleó. This broad arc of sand and pebbles, flecked at one end with tide-lashed rocks, gets crowded at summer weekends, when seemingly the entire population of Karlóvassi descends on the place. Near the end of the trail from Paleó stands *Toh Iliovasilima*, a friendly fish taverna; there are also a very few **rooms** signposted locally, but most individuals staying camp rough along the lower reaches of the river which gives the beach its name.

A path leads twenty minutes inland, past the eleventh-century church of **Metamórfosis** – the oldest on Sámos – and the campers' tents, to an apparent dead end. From here on you must swim and wade in heart-stoppingly cold water through a fern-tufted rock gallery to a series of **pools and waterfalls**; bring shoes with good tread and perhaps even rope if you want to explore above the first cascade. You probably won't be alone until the trail's end, since the canyon is well known to locals and even included in certain "Jeep Safaris".

Just above the Metamórfosis church, a clear path leads up to a small, contemporaneous **Byzantine fortress**. There's little to see inside other than a subterranean cistern and badly crumbled lower curtain wall, but the views out to sea and up the canyon are terrific, while in October the place is carpeted with pink autumn crocus.

The coast beyond Potámi is the most beautiful and unspoiled on Sámos. The dirt track at the west end of Potámi bay ends after twenty minutes of walking, from which you backtrack a hundred metres or so to find the well-cairned side trail running parallel to the water. Within twenty minutes' walking along this you'll arrive at **Mikró Seïtáni**, a small pebble cove guarded by sculpted rock walls. A full hour's walk from the trailhead, through partly fire-damaged olive terraces, brings you to **Megálo Seïtáni**, the island's finest beach, at the mouth of the intimidating Kakopérato gorge. You'll have to bring food and water along, though not necessarily a swimsuit – there's no dress code at either of the Seïtáni beaches.

Beach resorts

Heading south out of Karlóvassi on the island loop road, the first place you'd be tempted to stop off is **MARATHÓKAMBOS**, a pretty, amphitheatrical village overlooking the eponymous gulf; there's a taverna or two, but no short-term accommodation.

Its port, **ÓRMOS MARATHOKÁMBOU**, 18km from Karlóvassi, has recently been pressed into service as a tourist resort, though some character still peeks through in its backstreets. The port has been improved, with *kaíkia* offering day trips to Foúrni and the nearby islet of Samiopoúla, while the pedestrianized quay has become the centre of attention. A curiosity at its western end is the island's only stop light, installed to control entry to a one-lane alley. Three or four tavernas seem pretty indistinguishable, although *Trata* at least offers bulk wine, a Sámos rarity.

The beach extending immediately east from Órmos is hardly the best; for better ones you'll need to continue 2km west to **VOTSALÁKIA**, Sámos' fastest-growing resort, straggling for 2km more behind the island's longest – if not its most beautiful beach. Its appeal as an overwhelmingly family resort has been diminished in recent years by the solid carpet of rooms, apartments and often rather poor tavernas behind. But Votsalákia is still a vast improvement on the Pithagório area, and the hulking mass of 1437-metre Mount Kérkis overhead rarely fails to impress. As far as **accommodation** goes, *Emmanuil Dhespotakis* (☎0273/31 258; ③) seems to control a good quarter of the beds available, with most of his premises towards the quieter, more scenic western end of things. Also in this vicinity is *Akroyialia*, the most traditional **taverna**, with courtyard seating and fish and meat grills; *Loukoullos*, on the ocean side of the road near the last of the Dhespotakis rooms, is a fancier, enjoyable bistro-bar. Other facilities include branches of nearly all the main Vathí travel agencies, offering **vehicle rental** (necessary, as only two daily buses call here) and money exchange.

If Votsalákia (officially signposted as Kámbos) is not to your taste, you can continue 3km past to **Psilí Ámmos**, more aesthetic and not to be confused with its namesake beach in the southeast corner of Sámos. The sea shelves gently here – ridiculously so, as you're still only knee-deep a hundred paces out – and cliffs shelter clusters of naturists at the east end of 600m of sand. Surprisingly there are only a few **taverna/room** outfits: one fair-sized apartment complex in the pines at mid-beach, the other two back up on the road as you approach, both of these fine for a simple lunch.

German interests have more or less completely taken over **Limniónas**, a smaller cove 2km further west, by constructing a large villa complex rather grandiosely labelled as "Samos Yacht Club". Yachts do occasionally call at the protected bay, which offers decent swimming away from a rock shelf at mid-strand, two **tavernas** at the east end and a few short-term accommodation facilities.

Mount Kérkis

Gazing up from a supine seaside position, some people are inspired to go and climb **Mount Kérkis** (Kerketévs). The classic route begins at the west end of the Votsalákia strip, along the bumpy jeep track leading inland towards the Evangelistrías convent. After 30 minutes on the track system, through fire-damaged olive groves and past charcoal pits (a major industry hereabouts), the path begins, more or less following power lines steeply up to the convent. A friendly nun will proffer an *oúzo* in welcome and point you up the paint-marked trail, continuing even more steeply up to the peak.

The views are tremendous, though the climb itself is humdrum once you're out of the trees. About an hour before the top, there's a chapel with an attached cottage for sheltering in emergencies and, just beyond, after a wet winter, a welcome spring. Elation at attaining the **summit** may be tempered somewhat by the knowledge that on August 3, 1989, one of the worst Greek aviation disasters ever occurred here, when an aircraft flying out of Thessaloníki slammed into the mist-cloaked peak with the loss of all 34 aboard. All told, it's a seven-hour outing from Votsalákia and back, not counting rest stops.

Less ambitious walkers might want to circle the flanks of the mountain, first by vehicle and then by foot. The road beyond Limniónas to Kallithéa and Dhrakéii, truly back-of-beyond villages with views across to Ikaría, has recently been paved as far as Kallithéa, making it possible to venture out here on an ordinary motorbike. The bus service is better during the school year, when a vehicle leaves Vathí daily at 11.30am bound for these remote spots; during summer it only operates two days a week (currently Mon & Fri).

From **DHRAKÉII**, the end of the line with just a pair of very simple *kafenía* to its credit, a ninety-minute trail descends through partly burned forest to Megálo Seïtáni, from where it's easy enough to continue on to Karlóvassi within another two-and-a-half hours. People attempting to reverse this itinerary often discover to their cost that the bus (if any) returns from Dhrakéii early in the day, at 2pm, compelling them to stay overnight at two rather expensive **rooms** establishments (summer only) in **KALITHÉA**, and dine there at either the simple *psistariá* on the square or a newer taverna on the western edge of the village.

From Kallithéa, a newer track (from beside the cemetery) and an older trail lead up within 45 minutes to a spring, rural chapel and plane tree on the west flank of Kérkis, with path-only continuation for another half-hour to a pair of cave-churches. **Panayía Makriní** is free-standing, at the mouth of a high, wide but shallow grotto, whose balcony affords terrific views of Sámos' west end. **Ayía Triádha**, a ten-minute scramble overhead, has by contrast most of its structure made up of cave wall; just adjacent, another long, narrow, volcanic cavern can be explored by flashlight some hundred metres into the mountain, and perhaps further with proper equipment and a willingness to crab along on hands and knees.

After these subterranean exertions, the closest spot for a swim is **Vársamo** (Válsamo) cove, 4km below Kallithéa and reached via a well-signposted dirt road. The beach here consists of wonderful multicoloured volcanic pebbles, and there's a single rooms/snack bar place and two caves to shelter in.

Ikaría

Ikaría, a narrow, windswept landmass between Sámos and Míkonos, is little visited and invariably underestimated. Its name is supposed to derive from the unexpected appearance of Icarus, who fell into the sea just offshore after the wax bindings on his wings melted; and (as some locals are quick to point out) the island is clearly wing-shaped. For years the only substantial tourism was generated by a few radioactive hot springs on the south coast, some reputed to cure rheumatism and arthritis, some to make women fertile, though others are so potent that they've been closed for some time. The unnerving dockside sign which once read "Welcome to the Island of Radiation" has now been replaced by one proclaiming "Welcome to Icarus' Island".

Ikaría, along with Thessaly on the mainland, western Sámos and Lésvos, has traditionally been one of the Greek Left's strongholds. This tendency was accentuated during the long decades of right-wing domination in Greece, when the island was used as a place of exile for political dissidents. Apparently the strategy backfired, with the transportees outnumbering, and proseletyzing, their hosts; at the same time, many

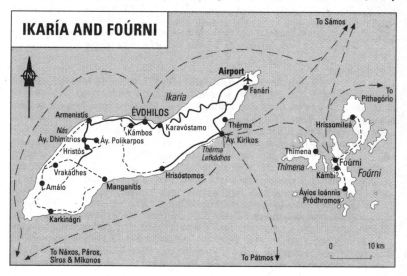

IKARÍA AND FOÚRNI

Ikarians emigrated to North America, and ironically their regular capitalist remittances help keep the island going. It can be a bizarre experience to be treated to a monologue on the evils of US imperialism, delivered by a retiree in perfect Alabaman English.

These are not the only Ikarian quirks, and for many the place is an acquired taste. It is not a strikingly beautiful island except for the forested portions of the northwest; the north face is less sheer than the south shore, but nonetheless furrowed by deep canyons which deflect the road system into sinuosities extreme even by Greek standards. The southern coastline drops steeply in cliffs and most of the landscape is scrub-coated schist, though there is ample ground water. Neither are there many picturesque villages, since the rural schist-roofed houses are generally scattered so as to be next to their famous apricot orchards, vineyards and fields, while the community store or taverna is equally hidden. Finally, the people, while not unfriendly – quite the contrary in fact – have resisted most attempts to develop Ikaría for conventional tourism, which splutters along principally between July and September. An airport in the northeast, its runway graded right across the tip of the island into the sea to permit approaches in any wind, is due to begin operation in the near future. Long periods of seemingly punitive neglect by Athens have made the locals profoundly self-sufficient and idiosyncratic, and tolerant of the same characteristics in others.

Áyios Kírikos

Most, though not all, ferries call at the south-coast port and capital of **ÁYIOS KÍRIKOS**, about 1km southeast of the island's main thermal resort. Because of the spa trade, beds are at a premium in town; arriving in the evening, as is often the case, accept any reasonable offers of rooms at the jetty, or – if in a group – proposals of a taxi ride to the north coast, which won't be much more than 6000dr *per vehicle* to the end of the line. A cream-and-green-coloured **bus** sets out across the island from the main square, daily at 10am (to Armenistís; in practice, any time from 9–11am), weekdays at noon (to Évdhilos only), and additionally at 1.30pm Monday and Friday to Armenistís.

The baths in **Thérma** are rather slimey, open 8am–1pm only. A far better bet if you're after a soak are the more natural hot springs at **Thérma Lefkádhos**, 3km south-west of Áyios Kírikos, below a cluster of villas. Here the seaside spa is derelict, leaving the water to boil up right in the shallows, mixing with the sea between giant volcanic boulders to a pleasant temperature. The only drawback is the landward setting; a 1993 fire devastated all the trees hereabouts, besides killing fourteen people.

Practicalities

There are several **hotels**, like the *Isabella* (☎0275/22 238; ④), or the friendly, basic but spotless *Akti* (☎0275/22 694; ②–③), on a knoll east of the fishing quay, with views of Foúrni from the garden. Otherwise, **rented rooms** fill fast and are not especially inexpensive: *Adam's Pension* (☎0275/22 418; ③) is about the fanciest, while those of *Ioannis Proestos* (☎0275/23496; ③), above the sweet shop next to *Iy Sinandisis* (see below), are squeaky clean and excellent value; there are two more quiet, well-placed establishments directly behind the base of the ferry jetty and a little to the west. In desperation, you might try one of the three unmarked, spartan outfits grouped around the **post office** on Dhioníso, the inland high street. There are also two **banks**, a limited-hours **OTE**, and assorted ferry **agents**, such as *Ikariadha* and *Dolihi Tours* – though all are coy about the daily noontime *kaíki* to Foúrni, whose tickets are sold on board. You can **rent** motorbikes and cars here, too, but both are cheaper in Armenistís.

Eating out, you've slightly more choice than in lodging. On the way from the ferry to the main square you'll pass the barn-like *Ta Adhelfia* and *Ta Votsalsa*, open only in the evenings; *Ouzeri Psistaria*, inland towards the post office, is a very good and reasonable combination *ouzerí* and *loukoumádhiko*. Just around the corner from the latter, *Iy*

Klimataria is no culinary marvel but worth noting because, unlike most, it operates year-round. Finally, the giant *Iy Sinandisis* on the tree-shaded esplanade is utterly unlike any other *kafenío* in the Greek islands: in a reversal of the norm, young adults play *távli* and cards inside, while outside their elders and assorted foreigners suck on sweets or watch each other – better entertainment by far than anything dished up at the summer cinema.

Évdhilos and around

The twisty, 41-kilometre road from Áyios Kírikos to Évdhilos is one of the most hair-raising on any Greek island, and the long ridge which extends the length of Ikaría often wears a streamer of cloud, even when the rest of the Aegean sky is clear. **KARAVÓSTAMO**, with its tiny, scruffy port, is the first substantial north coast place, and has a series of three beaches leading up to **ÉVDHILOS**. Although this is the island's second town and a ferry stop at least three times weekly in summer, it's considerably less equipped to deal with visitors than Áyios Kírikos. There are two **hotels**, the *Evdoxia* on the slope west of the harbour (☎0275/31 502; ③) and the *Georgios* (☎0275/31 218; ③), plus a few **rooms**. Of the trio of waterfront **restaurants**, *O Kokkos* has the largest menu but is expensive; try *O Flisvos* next door instead. A **post office** and **OTE**, and a surprisingly good town **beach** to the east, are also worth knowing about.

KÁMBOS, 2km west, sports a small museum in the village centre with finds from nearby **ancient Oinoe**, the twelfth-century church of Ayía Iríni next to the museum, the sparse ruins of a Byzantine palace (just above the road) used to house exiled nobles, as well as a large beach. **Rooms** are available from the store run by *Vassilis Dhionysos* (☎0275/31 300; ②), which also acts as the unofficial tourist office for this part of Ikaría, and meals from a **taverna** (dinner only).

Kámbos is also the start and end point of a road loop up through the hamlet-speckled valley inland: **MARATHÓ** isn't up to much but **FRANDÁTO** has a summer-time taverna; **STÉLI** and **DHÁFNI** are good, attractive examples of the little oases which sprout on Ikaría.

Armenistís and around

Most people don't stop until reaching **ARMENISTÍS**, 57km from Áyios Kírikos, and with good reason: this little resort lies in the heart of Ikaría's finest wooded scenery, with two enormous, sandy beaches – **Livádhi** and **Messakhtí** – five and fifteen minutes' walk to the east respectively. Campers in the marshes behind each stretch set the tone for the place, but the islanders' tolerance doesn't yet extend to nude bathing, as signs warn you; a semi-official campsite is in the process of being set up.

A dwindling number of older buildings lends Armenistís the air of a Cornish fishing village; it's a tiny place, reminiscent of similar youth-oriented spots on the south coast of Crete, though lately gentrification has definitely set in. A "music bar" operates seasonally behind the nearer beach, but nightlife is mostly about extended sessions in the tavernas and cafés overlooking the anchorage. The *Paskhalia* taverna/**rooms** (☎0275/71 302; winter ☎01/24 71 411; ③) is the cleanest in both categories, with doubles with bath; the food, including full breakfasts, is good, too, and not exorbitant. Should you require more luxury, there's the *Armena Inn* (④) well up the hillside or the luxury *Cavos Bay Hotel* (☎0275/71 381; winter ☎01/76 40 235 ④–⑤), 1km west. A giant bakery/cake shop caters to sweet teeth for the entire west end of the island, and the *Marabou Travel Agency* changes money and rents clapped-out **mopeds** and somewhat sturdier jeeps, although you don't really need either, since the best of Ikaría lies within an hour's walk of the port.

The sole drawback to staying in Armenistís is **getting away**, since both taxis and buses are elusive. Theoretically, **buses** head at least as far as Évdhilos – all the way to Áyios Kírikos on Mondays and Fridays – at 7am, and to Évdhilos daily at 3pm, but school kids have priority on the early departure, and the second one is unreliable even by Ikarian standards.

Beyond Armenistís: the southwest

Armenistís is actually the shore annexe of three inland hamlets – Áyios Dhimítrios, Áyios Políkarpos and Hristós – collectively known as **RÁHES**. Despite the modern dirt roads in through the pines, they still retain a certain Shangri-La quality, with the older residents speaking a positively Homeric dialect. On an island not short of foibles, Hristós is particularly strange, inasmuch as the locals sleep much of the day, but shop, eat and even send their children to school at night; in fact most of the villages west of Évdhilos adhere to this schedule, defying central-government efforts to bring them in line with the rest of Greece. Near the small main square there's a **post office** and a **hotel/restaurant**, but for lunch you'll have to scrounge something at one of two unusual *kafenía*. The slightly spaced-out demeanours of those serving may be attributable to over-indulgence in the excellent home-brewed **wine** which everyone west of Évdhilos makes – strong but hangover-free, and stored in rather disgusting goat-skins which are also used as shoulder bags, sold in some shops.

By tacit consent, Greek or foreign hippies, naturists and dope-fiends have been allowed to shift 4km west of Armenistís to **Nás**, a tree-clogged river canyon ending in a small but sheltered pebble beach. This little bay is almost completely enclosed by weirdly sculpted rock formations, and it's unwise to swim outside the cove's natural limits – there are drownings nearly every year in the open sea here, as well as at Messakhtí closer to Armenistís. The crumbling foundations of the fifth-century temple of **Artemis Tavropoleio** (Patroness of Bulls) overlook the permanent deep pool at the mouth of the river; people who used to camp rough just upstream are now encouraged to use the semi-official site at *Snack Bar River*. If you continue inland along this, Ikaría's only year-round watercourse, you'll find secluded rock pools for freshwater dips. Back at the top of the path leading down to the beach from the road are two or three tavernas and as many **rooms** – try the *Pension Nas* (☎0275/41 255; ②).

Should you be persuaded to rent a vehicle from *Marabou* in Armenistís, or join one of their jeep safaris, you can run through half a dozen villages at the southwest tip of the island. **VRAKÁDHES**, with two *kafenía* and a natural-balcony setting, makes a good first or last stop on a tour. A sharp drop below it, the impact of the empty convent of **Evangelistrías** lies mostly in its setting amidst gardens overlooking the sea. Nearby **AMÁLO** has two summer tavernas; just inland, **Langádha** is not a village but a hidden valley containing an enormous and seasonally popular *exohikó kéndro* (rural taverna).

The puny mopeds will go down *from* Langádha *to* Kálamos, not the other way around; in any case it's a tough bike that gets all the way to **KARKINÁGRI**, built at the base of cliffs near the southern extremity of Ikaría and a dismal anticlimax to a journey out here. The only thing likely to bring a smile to your lips is the marked intersection of Leofóros Bakunin and Odhós Lenin – surely the only two such streets in Greece – at the edge of town, which boasts a couple of sleepy, seasonal tavernas and a rooms establishment near the jetty. Before the road was opened (the continuation to Manganítis and Áyios Kírikos is stalled at an unblastable rock-face), Karkinágri's only easy link with the outside world was by **ferry** or *kaíki*, both of which still call once or twice a week in mid-summer.

Satellite islands: Foúrni and Thímena

The straits between Sámos or Ikaría are speckled with a number of spidery-looking islets. The only ones permanently inhabited are Thímena and Foúrni, the latter home to a huge fishing fleet and one of the more thriving boatyards in the Aegean. As a result of these, and the improvement of the jetty to receive car ferries, Foúrni's population is stable, unlike so many small Greek islands. The islets were once the lair of Maltese pirates, and indeed many of the islanders have a distinctly North African appearance.

Foúrni

Apart from the remote hamlet of Hrissomiliá in the north, where the island's main motorable road goes, most of the inhabitants of **Foúrni** are concentrated in the **port** and Kámbi hamlet just south. The harbour community is larger than it looks from the sea, and there are several **rooms** establishments, the most desirable being those run by *Manolis and Patra Markakis* (☎0275/51 268; ②–③), immediately to your left as you disembark – they have both cold-water rooms in front and all-mod-cons units in the rear. If they're full (usually the case in August), you can head inland to the modern blocks of *Evtihia Amoryianou* (☎0275/51 364; ③) or *Maouni* (☎0275/51 367; ③).

Of the three waterfront **tavernas**, the local favourite is *Rementzo*, better known as *Nikos'*; if you're lucky the local *astakós* or Aegean lobster, actually an oversized saltwater crayfish, may be on the menu. The central "high street", fieldstoned and mulberryshaded, ends well inland at a little *platía* with a handful of more conventional *kafenía*, a modern snack bar, and a **post office** where you can change money.

A fifteen-minute walk south from the port, skirting the cemetery and then slipping over the windmill ridge, brings you to **KÁMBI**, a scattered community overlooking a pair of sandy, tamarisk-shaded coves which you'll share with chickens and hauled-up fishing boats. There are two cafés, the upper one providing filling snacks, the lower one controlling seven **rooms** that are admittedly spartan but have arguably the best views on the island; another family also has some cottages to let. A path continues to the next bay south, which like Kámbi cove, is a preferred anchorage for wandering yachts.

Continuing further south along the coast is problematic on foot; best to arrange boat trips in the harbour to **Marmári** cove, so named for its role as a quarry for ancient Ephesus in Asia Minor; you can still see some unshipped marble blocks lying about. From Marmári, a faint trail climbs up to the spine of the island, emerging onto the dirt road just south of Theológos chapel. Most of the old ridge path can still be followed south of the chapel, shortcutting the road as it drops to the hamlet and monastery of **ÁYIOS IOÁNNIS PRÓDHROMOS**. There are no facilities whatsover here – sometimes not even reliable fresh water – but you'll find two tiny, secluded beaches below the hamlet to either side of the jetty.

Heading north from the harbour via steps, then a trail, there are more **beaches**: an average one by the fish-processing plant, and two better ones further on, following the path. At the extreme north of the island, idyllic **HRISSOMILEÁ** is again usually approached by boat as the dirt road in is so bad. The village, split into a shore district and a hill settlement at the top of a canyon, has a decent beach; even better, less accessible, ones flank it to either side. Near the dock are very rough-and-ready combination *kafenía*/tavernas; equally simple **rooms** can be arranged.

Thímena

Thímena has one tiny hillside settlement, at which the regular *kaíki* calls on its way between Ikaría and Foúrni, but no tourist facilities, and casual visits are explicitly discouraged. The *kaíki*, incidentally, leaves Ikaría at about 1pm (five days a week), stays overnight at Foúrni and returns the next morning. The twice-weekly *kaíki* from

Karlóvassi and the larger car ferries which appear at odd intervals are likewise not tourist excursion boats but exist for the benefit of the islanders. The only practical way to visit the island on a day trip is by using one of the summer morning hydrofoils out of Sámos (Vathí or Pithagório).

Híos

"Craggy Híos", as Homer aptly described his (probable) birthplace, has an eventful history and a strong sense of place. It has always been relatively prosperous, in medieval times through the export of gum mastic, a trade controlled by Genoese overlords, and later by virtue of several shipping dynasties. The maritime families and the military authorities did not encourage tourism unitl the late 1980s, but with the worldwide shipping crisis, and the saturation of other, more obviously "marketable" islands, resistance has dwindled. Increasing numbers of foreigners are discovering a Híos beyond its large port capital: fascinating villages, important Byzantine monuments and a respectable complement of beaches. While unlikely ever to be dominated by tourism, the local scene has a definitely modernized flavour – courtesy of numerous returned Greek-Americans – and English is widely spoken.

Unfortunately, the island has suffered more than its fair share of catastrophes during the past two centuries. The Turks perpetrated their most infamous, if not their worst, anti-revolutionary atrocity here in 1822, massacring 30,000 Hiots and enslaving or exiling even more. In 1881, much of Híos was destroyed by a violent earthquake, and throughout the 1980s the natural beauty of the island was markedly diminished by several devastating forest fires, compounding the effect of generations of tree-felling by boat-builders. Nearly two-thirds of the majestic pines are now gone, with patches of woods persisting only in the far northeast and at the exact centre of Híos.

In 1988 the first charters from northern Europe were instituted, an event that signalled equally momentous changes for the island. There are now perhaps 10,000 guest beds on Híos, the vast majority of them in the capital or the nearby beach resort of Karfás. Tourist numbers are evenly divided between a babel of nationalities – Austrian, Belgian, Norwegian, Swiss, Dutch, German, plus a small British contingent brought in by specialist operators. Further expansion, however, is hampered by the lack of direct air links between Britain and Híos, and the refusal of property owners to part with land for the extension of the airport runway.

Híos Town

HÍOS, the harbour and main town, will come as a shock after modest island capitals elsewhere; it's a bustling, concrete-laced commercial centre, with little predating the 1881 quake. Yet in many ways it is the most satisfactory of North Aegean ports; time spent exploring is amply rewarded with a large and fascinating bazaar, a museum or two, some authentic tavernas and, on the waterfront, Greece's best-attended evening *vólta* (promenade). Because of its central location on the island's east shore, and preponderance of tourist facilities, Híos is the obvious base for explorations, especially if you're without a vehicle. Although it's a sprawling town of about 30,000, most things of interest to visitors lie within a hundred or so metres of the water.

South and east of the main *platía*, officially Plastíra but known universally as Vounakíou, extends the marvellously lively tradesmen's **bazaar**, where you can find everything from live monkeys to cast-iron woodstoves. Híos must feature more varieties of bread than any other town in Greece – corn, whole wheat, multi-grain, so-called "dark" and "village" – and most bakers in the marketplace were will offer at least two or three from this list.

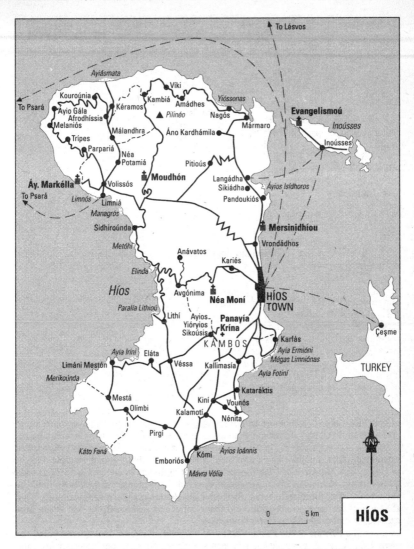

The grandiosely titled "Byzantine Museum", occupying the old **Mecidiye Mosque** (daily except Mon 10am–1pm; free), opposite the Vounakíou taxi rank, is little more than an archeological warehouse and workshop, awash in marble fragments such as Turkish, Jewish and Armenian gravestones. The official Archeological Museum located on Mihálon is currently closed, and its collection was never very compelling anyway.

More worthwhile is the **Argenti Museum** (Mon–Fri 8am–2pm, also Fri 5–7.30pm, Sat 8am–12.30pm; free), housed on the top floor of the Koraï Library building at Koraïï 2 and endowed by a leading Hiot family. Accordingly there's a rather ponderous gallery

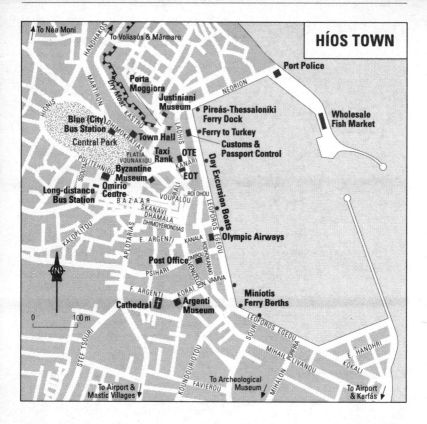

HÍOS TOWN

To Néa Moni

To Volissós & Mármaro

HANDHAKOS

MARTIRON

HIONIS

Dry Moat KÁSTRO

DHIMOKRATIAS

SOUTAFILIATO

POLITEHNIOU

KALOPLITOU

APLOTARIAS

N

0   100 m

STEF TSOURI

FAVIÉROU

KOUNDOURIOTOU

Porta Moggiora

Justiniani Museum

NEORION

Port Police

Wholesale Fish Market

Blue (City) Bus Station

Central Park

Town Hall

Taxi Rank

LADHIS

Pireás-Thessaloníki Ferry Dock

Ferry to Turkey

Customs & Passport Control

OTE

KANARI

EOT

Day Excursion Boats

PLATÍA VOUNAKÍOU

Byzantine Museum

Omírio Centre

Long-distance Bus Station

BAZAAR

VOUPALOU

ROÍ DHOU

LEOFOROS EGEOU

SKANAVI
DHAMALA
DHIMOYERONDIAS

E. ARGENTI

KANALA

RODHOKANAKI

Olympic Airways

Post Office

PSIHARI

OMIROU KANARI

VENIZELOU

VAMVA

F. ARGENTI

KORAÍ

Cathedral

Argenti Museum

Miniotis Ferry Berths

LEOFOROS EGEOU

MIHAIL LIVANOÚ

SOUR

MIHALON

E. HANDHRI

KOKALI

To Airport & Mastic Villages

To Archeological Museum

To Airport & Karfás

of genealogical portraits, showing if nothing else the local aristocracy's compulsion to ape English dress and artistic conventions in every era. The other wing boasts a hall of costumes and embroidery, kitsch figurines in traditional dress, and carved wooden implements from the time when the island was more forested. Among multiple replicas of Delacroix's *Massacre at Hios* are engravings of eighteenth-century islanders as seen by assorted Grand Tourists, plus several views of the Genoese *kástro* which, until the earthquake, was completely intact; thereafter developers razed the seaward walls, filled in much of the moat to the south and made a fortune selling off the real estate thus created around present-day Platía Vounakíou.

Enter the **Kástro** at the Porta Maggiora, the gate giving on the square behind the town hall. A small tower just inside is home these days to the Justiniani Museum (closed for repairs; theoretically daily except Mon 9am–8pm; free), up some stairs and housing a satisfying collection of unusual icons and mosaics rescued from local churches. The small dungeon adjacent briefly held 75 Hiot notables before their execution as hostages by the Turks in 1822. The old residential quarter inside what remains of the castle walls, formerly the Muslim and Jewish neighbourhoods, is well worth a wander; among the wood-and-plaster houses you'll find assorted Ottoman monuments in various states of decay, including a cemetery, a small mosque, several inscribed fountains and a former dervish convent converted into a church after 1923.

Arrival, information and services

The **airport** lies 4km south along the coast at Kondári; any of the blue urban buses labelled "Kondári Karfás", departing from the station on the north side of the park, passes the airport gate. The green-and-cream long-distance **buses** leave from a parking area on the opposite side of the park, behind the Omirio Cultural Centre. **Ferry** agents cluster to either side of the customs building, towards the north end of the waterfront Egéou and its continuation Neoríon. *Miniotis Lines*, at Neoríon 21–23 (☎0271/24 670 or 41 073), operates a regular morning service to Çeşme, small ferries to many neighbouring islands, and excursions to Inoússes. The Turkish evening ferry to Çeşme is currently handled by *Faros Travel* (☎0271/27 240), while the *Gianmar* **hydrofoil** agent is *Omiros Tours*, on Egéou at the corner of Kanári (☎0271/41 319).

The helpful municipal **tourist office** (May–Sept Mon–Fri 7am–2.30pm & 6–9.30pm; Sat 10am–1.30pm; Sun 10am–noon; Oct–April Mon–Fri 7am–2.30pm) is at Kanári 18, near the *Ionian Bank*. The conspicuous "Hadzelenis Tourist Information Office" (☎0271/26 743) on the quay is a private entity geared to accommodation placement.

While **bus services** to the south of Híos are adequate, those to the centre and northwest of the island are almost non-existent. For such excursions it's well worth renting a powerful **motorbike** (not a moped) or a car, or **sharing a taxi** (a common practice) – uniquely in Greece, they're bright red. **Car rental agencies** sit in a row along Evyenías Handhrí, behind the *Chandris Hotel*; of these, *George Sotirakis/European Rent a Car* at no. 3 (☎0271/29 754) can be recommended.

The **OTE** (daily 7am–midnight) is directly opposite the tourist office, while the **post office** is on Omírou. **Banks** are numerous, as you'd expect for such a well-off island. A Hiot idiosyncrasy is the complete lack of afternoon **shopping hours** during summer – if you want to buy anything, make sure you do so before 2pm.

Accommodation

Híos Town has a relative abundance of affordable accommodation, rarely – if ever – completely full. Most of it lines the water or the perpendicular alleys and parallel streets behind, and almost all of it is plagued by traffic noise to some degree – we've listed some of the more peaceful establishments.

Anesis, corner of Vasilikári and Aplotariás, in the bazaar (☎0271/44 801). Rooms with bath, fridges and air conditioning; quiet after dark. ③

Apollonio, Roídhou 5 (☎0271/24 842). Fairly quiet hotel tucked onto a tiny plaza just inland from the water. A seaward annexe, the *Acropolis*, has simpler rooms in the next category down. ③.

Faidra, Mihaíl Livanoú 13 (☎0271/41 130). Well-appointed pension, in an old mansion complete with stone arches in the downstairs winter bar; in summer the bar operates outside, so ask for a rear room to avoid nocturnal noise. Prices vary according to season and length of stay. ④–⑤.

Hios Rooms, Kokáli 1, corner Egéou (☎0271/27 295 or 26 743). Clean, antique rooms above a ships' chandler's; relatively quiet for a seafront locale. ②

Kyma, east end of Evyenías Handhrí (☎0271/44 500). A Neoclassical mansion with a modern extension, splendid service and big breakfasts. The old wing saw a critical moment in modern Greek history in September 1922, when Colonel Nikolaos Plastiras commandeered it as his HQ after the Greek defeat in Asia Minor, and announced the deposition of King Constantine I. ⑤.

Pelineon Rooms, Omírou 9, corner of Egéou (☎0271/28 030). Many rooms have sea view (though not the singles), and the owner also does bike and car rental. ②–③.

Rodhon, Zaharíou 17 (☎0271/24 335). The owners can be crotchety, and the more basic rooms are a bit steeply priced, but this is virtually the only place inside the *kástro*, and very quiet. ③

Rooms Alex, Mihaíl Livanoú 29 (☎0271/26 054). The friendly proprietor often meets late-arriving ferries; otherwise ring the bell. There's a roof garden above the well-furnished rooms, which come with and without bath. ②–③.

Eating

Eating out in Híos Town can be more pleasurable than the rash of obvious, mostly bogus, *ouzerís* on the waterfront would suggest; it is also usually a fair bit cheaper than on the neighbouring islands of Sámos and Lésvos.

Estiatorio Dhimitrakopoulos, corner of Sgoúta and Vlatariás, near KTEL station. Simple, inexpensive oven-cooked lunches in a tiny hole-in-the-wall, which attracts an interesting mixed clientele of locals and foreign residents. Lunch only.

Iakovos Pavtas, beside the wholesale fish market at far northeast end of harbour jetty. Go early for the best quality at this *ouzerí*; mostly seafood, pricier than *Theodhosiou*, but blissfully free of exhaust fumes. Dinner only.

No-name, corner of Roídhou and Venizélou, immediately behind the *Apollonio* lodgings. Small milkshop, which serves sheep's-milk yogurt from Lésvos, *loukoumádhes* and rice pudding.

O Hotzas, Yioryíou Kondhíli 3, near Stefánou Tsoúri. Long the premier taverna in Híos Town, this has now moved to new premises featuring an arcaded interior and summer garden. The cooking has deteriorated of late, but you might still catch them on a good night. Dinner only; closed Sun.

Ouzeri Theodhosiou, junction of Egéou and Neoríon. The genuine article, with a good, inexpensive, huge menu, though it's best to wait until the ferries which dock immediately opposite have departed. Dinner only.

Drinking, nightlife and entertainment

Iviskos, on the quay. The most tasteful café on the quay, with a range of juices, coffees and alcoholic drinks.

O Kavos, south end of the quay, near the "kink" in Egéou. The best (and oldest) bar in terms of music, decor and crowd.

Omírio, south side of the central park. Cultural centre and events hall well worth stopping in at: frequently changing exhibitions, and foreign musicians often come here after Athens concerts to perform in the large auditorium.

Beaches around Híos Town

Híos Town itself has no beaches worth mentioning and the closest one of interest is at **KARFÁS**, 7km south past the airport and served by frequent blue buses. Most of the recent growth in the Hiot tourist industry has occurred here, to the considerable detriment of the 500-metre-long beach itself, but the one bright spot is a unique **pension**, *Markos' Place* (☎0271/31 990; ②–③), installed in the former pilgrims' cells at the **monastery of Áyios Yióryios and Áyios Pandelímon**, on the hillside south of the bay. The church still functions as such, separate from the activities of the many groups who book the place; individuals (there are several single "cells") are more than welcome, though advance reservations are strongly suggested. At the south end of the beach, *O Karfas* (locally known as *Yiamos*' after the proprietor) is a fair bet for cheap and abundant **food**. Service and atmosphere are better at the more expensive *Karatzas* at mid-beach, whose seaview **hotel** upstairs (☎0271/31 180; ③) is one of the few establishments here that still is geared to non-package-tour custom. However, the best food of all is to be had at *Toh Dholoma*, 3km back towards town at Kondári, on a side road between the swimming pool and the *Morning Star Hotel*.

Some 2km further along the coast from Karfás, **AYÍA ERMIÓNI** is less of a beach than a fishing anchorage surrounded by a handful of tavernas and rooms to rent. The actual beach is at **Mégas Limniónas**, a few hundred metres further, even smaller than Kárfas but rather more scenic, especially at its south end where low cliffs provide a backdrop. Both Ayía Ermióni and Mégas Limniónas are served by extensions of the blue bus route to either Karfás or Thimianá, the nearest inland village.

The coast road loops up to Thimianá, from where you can (with your own transport only) continue 3km south towards Kalimassiá to the turning for **Ayía Fotiní**, a 700-metre pebble beach with exceptionally clean water. There's no shade, however, unless you count shadows from the numerous blocks of rooms under construction behind the main road; there is a small cluster of **tavernas** around the parking area where the side road meets the sea.

The last settlement on this coast, 5km beyond Kalimassiá and served by long-distance bus, is **KATARÁKTIS**, remarkable mainly for its pleasant waterfront of balconied houses, its fishing port and a few tavernas. There are no appreciable beaches nearby, and inland explorations of the nearby narrow-alleyed hill villages of **NÉNITA** (same bus service) and **VOUNÓS** may be more rewarding.

Southern Híos

The olive-covered, gently rolling countryside in the **south of the island** is also home to the mastic bush, *Pistacia lentisca* to be precise, which here alone in Greece produces an aromatic gum of marketable quantity and quality. The resin scraped from Híos branches was for centuries the base of paints, cosmetics and chewable jelly beans which became a somewhat addictive staple in the Ottoman harems. Indeed the interruption of the flow of mastic from Híos to Istanbul by the revolt of spring 1822 was one of the root causes of the brutal Ottoman reaction. The wealth engendered by the mastic trade supported a half-dozen *mastikhohoriá* (mastic villages) from the time the Genoese set up a monopoly in the substance during the fourteenth and fifteenth centuries, but the end of imperial Turkey, and the industrial revolution with its petroleum-based products, knocked the bottom out of the mastic market. Now it's just a curiosity, to be chewed – try the sweetened *Elma* brand gum – or drunk as a liqueur called *mastíha*, though it has had medicinal applications since ancient times. These days, the *mastihohoriá* live mainly off their tangerines, apricots and olives. The towns themselves, the only settlements on Híos spared by the Turks in 1822, are architecturally unique, laid out by the Genoese but distinctly Middle-Eastern-looking.

The mastic villages

ARMÓLIA, 20km from town, is the first, smallest and least imposing of the mastic villages. Its main virtue is its pottery industry – the best shops are the last two on the right, driving southwest – and there are three snack bars: two on the road, and another in the centre, all open year-round. Out of season it can be difficult to find open places to eat in the south of the island.

PIRGÍ, 25km from the port, is perhaps the liveliest and certainly the most colourful of the communities, its houses elaborately embossed with *ksistá*, geometric patterns cut into the plaster and then outlined with paint. On the northeast corner of the central square the twelfth-century Byzantine church of **Áyii Apóstoli** (Tues–Thurs & Sat 10am–1pm), embellished with much later frescoes, is tucked under an arcade. The giant **Cathedral of the Assumption** on the square itself boasts a *témblon* in an odd folk style dating from 1642, and an equally bizarre carved figure peeking out from the base of the pulpit. Pirgí has a handful of **rooms**, many of them bookable through the *Women's Agricultural and Tourist Cooperative* (☎0271/72 496; ③). Otherwise, there's *Rita's Rooms*, on the main bypass road (☎0271/72 479; ②), with a noisy pub nearby. In the medieval core you'll find a bank, a post office, a miniscule OTE stall on the *platía* and a couple of **tavernas**, best of these *Iy Manoula*, right next to OTE.

OLÍMBI, 7km further along the same bus route serving Armólia and Pirgí, is the least visited of the villages but not devoid of interest. The characteristic tower-keep, which at Pirgí stands virtually abandoned away from the modernized main square, here looms bang in the middle of the *platía*, its ground floor occupied by two *kafenía*. By now you will have grasped the basic layout of a mastic village: an originally rectangular warren of stone houses, the outer row doubling as the town's perimeter fortification, and pierced by just a few gates. More recent additions, although in traditional architectural style, straggle outside the original defences.

MESTÁ, 11km west of Pirgí, has a more sombre feel and is considered the finest example of the genre. From the main square, dominated by the **church of Taxiárhis** (the largest on the island), a bewildering maze of cool, shady lanes, provided with anti-earthquake buttresses and tunnels between the usually unpainted houses, leads off in all directions. But most streets end in blind alleys, except the critical half-dozen leading to as many gates; the northeast one still has an iron grate installed. If you'd like to stay, there are half a dozen **rooms** in restored traditional dwellings managed by *Dhimitris Pipidhis* (☎0271/76 319; ③); those run by the *Zervoudhi* (☎0271/76 240; ②) and *Yialouri* (☎0271/76 137; ②) households are somewhat less costly. Of the two **tavernas** on the main *platía*, *O Morias sta Mesta* is renowned for its tasty rural specialities, including edible mountain weeds and the locally produced raisin wine: heavy, semi-sweet and sherry-like.

The south coast

One drawback to staying in Mestá is the dearth of good beaches nearby. Its harbour **LIMÁNI MESTÓN** (or Passá Limáni), 3km north, has come down considerably in the world since the ferry service here ceased some years ago. With no beach of any sort in sight, you wonder who stays in the handful of rooms; it's only worth a trip for the two **fish tavernas**. The closest beach worthy of the name is at **Merikoúnda**, 4km west of Mestá.

Reached by a rough seven-kilometre side road just east of Olímbi, the little beach of **Káto Faná** is popular with Greek summer campers, who blithely disregard signs forbidding the practice; there are no facilities. A vaunted Apollo temple in the vicinity amounts to scattered masonry around a medieval chapel built atop it, by the roadside some 400m above the shore.

Pirgí is actually closest to the two major beach resorts in this corner of the island. The nearest of these, 6km distant, is by **EMBORIÓS**, an almost landlocked harbour with a few mediocre tavernas (most passable of these *Ifestio*); there's a scanty, British-excavated archeological zone nearby, the ancient Hiots not having been slow to realize the advantages of the site as a trading-post. For swimming, follow the road to its end at an oversubscribed car park and the beach of **Mávra Vólia**, then continue by clear trail over the headland to two more dramatic pebble strands of red and black volcanic stones, twice the length and backed by impressive cliffs.

If you want sand you'll have to go to **KOMÍ**, 3km northeast, also accessible from Armólia via Kalamotí. It's bidding to become a sort of Greek-pitched Karfás, though so far there are just a few fairly undistinguished tavernas and summer apartments behind the brown sand. The bus service, at least, is fairly good in season, often following a loop route through Pirgí and Emboriós.

Central Híos

The **central** portion of Híos, extending west from Híos Town, matches the south in terms of monumental interest, and a recently improved road network makes touring under your own power an easy matter. There are beaches as well, on the far shore of the island, still not the best on Híos (see "Northern Híos" overpage) but serviceable for a dip at the end of the day.

The Kámbos

The **Kámbos**, a vast, fertile plain carpeted with citrus groves, extends southwest from Híos Town almost as far as the village of Halkío. The district was originally settled by the Genoese during the fourteenth century and remained a preserve of the local aris-tocracy until 1822. Exploring it with a bicycle or motorbike is apt to be less frustrating than going by car, since the poorly marked roads form a web of lanes sandwiched between high walls, guaranteeing disorientation and frequent backtracking. Behind these walls you catch fleeting glimpses of ornate old mansions built from a tawny, peanut-brittle-pattern masonry. Courtyards are paved in pebbles or alternating light-and-dark tiles, and most still contain a *mánganos*, or water-wheel, onced used to draw water up from thirty-metre-deep wells.

Many of the sumptuous three-storey dwellings, constructed in a hybrid Italo-Turco-Greek style, have languished in ruins since 1881, but a few have been converted for use as unique accommodation. Most famous of these is the *Villa Argenti* (☎0271/31 599; fax 31 465; or in Milan, ☎02/49 88 254), ancestral home of the Italo-Greek counts Argenti de Scio. Initially restored early this century, it has become the most exclusive accommodation in Greece, consisting of four self-contained apartments installed in outbuildings in the orange orchards, plus a few luxury double rooms in the main mansion. If you have to ask how much, you can't afford it.

Lesser mortals can stay at the contrastingly well-marked and publicized *Hotel Perivoli* (☎0271/31 513 ⑤), just 100m north of *Villa Argenti*, whose orchard is also home to a popular **restaurant** (dinner only). The rooms, no two alike, are equipped with fireplaces and (in most cases) en-suite baths and sofas. Blue urban buses bound for Thimianá pass just 200m to the east.

Not strictly speaking in Kámbos, but most easily reached from it en route to the *mastikhohoriá*, the thirteenth-century Byzantine **church of Panayía Krína** is well worth the effort required to find it. Starting from Vavíli village, 9km from town, follow a maze of vaguely marked dirt tracks to the church, isolated amidst orchards and woods. It is usually closed for snail's-pace restoration, but you get a fair idea of the finely fres-coed interior, sufficiently lit by a twelve-windowed drum, through the apse window. The alternating brick-and-stonework of the exterior alone justifies the trip out, though harmony is marred by a clumsy lantern over the narthex, added later.

Néa Moní

Almost exactly in the physical centre of the island, the **monastery of Néa Moní**, founded by the Byzantine Emperor Constantine Monomakhos (The Dueller) IX in 1042 where a wonder-working icon had been discovered, is among the most beautiful and important monuments on any of the Greek islands. Its mosaics rank with those of Dháfni and Óssios Loukás as being among the finest art of their age, and its setting – high in still partly forested mountains west of the port – is no less memorable. **Bus excursions** are provided by the KTEL on Tuesday and Friday mornings; otherwise come by motorbike, or walk **from Kariés**, 7km northeast, to which there is a regular blue-bus service. Taxis from town, however, are not prohibitive at about 5000dr round-trip per carload, and a suitable wait while you look around is included in the price.

Once a powerful and independent community of 600 monks, Néa Moní was pillaged during the events of 1822 and most of its residents put to the sword. The 1881 tremor caused comprehensive damage (skilfully repaired), while a century later a forest fire threatened to engulf the place until the resident icon was paraded along the perimeter wall, miraculously repelling the flames. Today the monastery, with its giant refectory and vaulted water cisterns, is inhabited by just two elderly nuns and a similar number of lay workers; when the last nun dies, Néa Moní will be taken over by monks.

Just inside the **main gate** (daily 8am–1pm & 4–8pm) stands a chapel/charnel house containing the bones of those who met their death here in 1822; axe-clefts in children's skulls attest to the savagery of the attackers. The *katholikón*, with the cupola resting on an octagonal drum, is of a design seen elsewhere only in Cyprus; the frescoes in the exonarthex are badly damaged by holes allegedly from Turkish bullets, but the **mosa-ics** are another matter. The narthex contains portrayals of the *Saints of Hios* sand-wiched between *Christ Washing the Disciples' Feet* and *Judas' Betrayal*; in the dome of the sanctuary, which once contained a complete life-cycle of Christ, only the *Baptism*, part of the *Crucifixion*, the *Descent from the Cross*, the *Resurrection* and the *Evangelists Mark and John* survived the earthquake.

The west coast

With your own transport, you can proceed 5km west of Néa Moníto **AVGÓNIMA**, a jumble of houses on a knoll perched above the coast; the name means "Clutch of Eggs", an apt description of the clustered houses as seen from the ridge above. Since the 1980s, the place has been almost totally restored as a summer haven by descendants of the original villagers, though the permanent population is just seven. A returned Greek-American family runs an excellent, reasonable **taverna**/*kafenío* on the main square, *O Pyrgos*, but as yet there's no place to stay. A paved side road continues another 4km north to **ANÁVATOS**, whose empty, dun-coloured dwellings, soaring above pistachio orchards, are almost indistinguishable from the 300-metre-high bluff on which they're built. During the 1822 insurrection the 400 inhabitants threw themselves over this cliff rather than surrender to the besieging Ottomans, and it's still a preferred suicide leap. Anávatos itself is two persons less populous than Avgónima, and, given a lack of reliable facilities plus an eerie, traumatized atmosphere, it's no place to be stranded at dusk.

West of Avgónima, the main road descends 6km to the coast in well-graded loops; in the wake of recent surfacing this also makes a good alternative approach to the northwest of Híos. Turning right (north) at the junction leads first to the much-advertised beach at **Elínda**, alluring from afar but rocky-shored and murky-watered up close; better to continue towards more secluded coves to either side of Metóhi, or below **SIDHIROÚNDA** (snack bar), the only village hereabouts, which enjoys a spectacular hilltop setting overlooking the coast.

All along this coast, as far southwest as Limáni Mestón, loom round **watchtowers** erected by the Genoese to look out for pirates; one of these has furnished the name of **Kastélla**, the first swimmable cove you reach by turning left from the junction. The weekday-only bus service resumes 7km south of the junction at **LITHÍ**, a friendly village of whitewashed buildings perched on a wooded ledge overlooking the sea. There are tavernas and *kafenía* near where the bus turns around, but the only places to stay are down at windswept, dreary **Paralía Lithioú** 2km below, a weekend target of Hiot townies for the sake of its large but garbage-fringed beach.

Some 5km south of Lithí, the valley-bottom village of **VÉSSA** is an unsung gem, more open than Mestá or Pirgí but still homogeneous. Its honey-coloured buildings are arrayed in a vast grid punctuated by numerous belfries; there's a simple taverna, and you can stay at an old inn, *Toh Petrino* (☎0271/25 016 or 41 097; ④). The ridgetop village of **ÁYIOS YIÓRYIOS SIKOÚSSIS**, nearly 8km east and above on the way back to Híos Town, has had its architectural profile spoilt by new construction, but a popular and well-marked taverna near the church offers sweeping views. Your last chance for a swim near Véssa is provided by a series of secluded sandy bays along the 16-kilometre road west to Limáni Mestón; only that of **Ayía Iríni** has a taverna, and all suffer from periodic wind and rubbish attacks owing to the northerly exposure.

Northern Híos

Northern Híos never really recovered from the Turkish massacre, and the desolation left by the fires of 1981 and 1987 will further dampen the spirits of inquisitive travellers. Since early this century the villages have languished all but deserted much of the year, which means that bus services are correspondingly sparse. About one-third of the former population now lives in Híos Town, venturing out here only on the dates of major festivals or to tend grapes and olives, time which barely adds up to four months of the year. The balance of the northerners or their descendants, based in Athens or the US, visit their ancestral homes for just a few weeks at mid-summer, this brief but intense season being used to arrange marriages between local families.

The road to Kardhámila

Blue city buses run north from Híos Town only as far as **VRONDÁDHOS**, an elongated coastal suburb which is the favourite residence of the island's many seafarers. Homer is reputed to have lived and taught here, and just above the little fishing port and pebble beach you can visit his purported lectern, more probably an ancient altar of Cybele and surrounded by terraced parkland. Accordingly many of the buses out here are labelled *Dhaskalópetra* (Teacher's Rock).

If you have transport, by all means make a stop at the **monastery of Panayía Mirsinidhíou** (Mirtidhiótissis) – of little intrinsic interest but most photogenically set overlooking the sea. Some 5km along, the route swoops down to the tiny hamlet at **Pandoukiós** bay, bereft of amenities but economically important by virtue of several offshore fish nurseries raising bass and gilt-head bream. A side road just north leads to stony **Áyios Isídhoros** cove, home to the rather inconveniently located island campsite, though the site itself is shaded and faces Inoússes islet across the water.

Travelling by bus, **LANGÁDHA** is probably the first point on the eastern coast road where you might be tempted to alight. Set at the mouth of a deep valley, this attractive little harbour settlement looks across its bay to a pine grove, and beyond to Turkey. There are three **rooms** establishments (try *Eleni Sidheri*, ☎0271/74 637; ③), but most night-time visitors come for the sake of the excellent seafood at the two surviving **tavernas** at the start of the quay; the remainder of the esplanade has been taken over by patisseries, bars and cafés. There is no proper beach anywhere nearby; **Dhelfíni** bay just to the north is an off-limits naval base.

Just beyond Langádha an important side road leads 5km up and inland to **PITIOÚS**, an oasis in a mountain pass presided over by a tower-keep; continuing 4km more brings you to a junction allowing quick access to the west of the island and the Volissós area (see below).

Kardhámila and around

Most traffic proceeds to **ÁNO** and **KÁTO KARDHÁMILA**, the latter 37km out of the main town. Positioned at opposite edges of a fertile plain rimmed by mountains, they initially come as welcome, green relief from Homer's crags. Káto, better known as **MÁRMARO**, is the larger, its waterside streets flanked by the hillside neighbourhood districts of Ráhi and Perivoláki, and indeed it's the second largest town on the island, with a bank, post office, OTE branch and filling station (the only one in the entire north). However, there is little to attract a casual visitor: the port, mercilessly exposed to the *meltémi*, is strictly businesslike, and there are few tourist facilities. One exception is the *Hotel Kardamyla* (☎0272/23 353; ⑤–⑥), co-managed with Híos Town's *Hotel Kyma* by Theodhore Spordhilis. The hotel sits behind the bay's only pebble beach, and its **restaurant** is a reliable source of meals for non-guests as well.

For better swimming head west – by car from the signposted junction by the church, on foot past the harbour-mouth windmill for an hour along a cemented coastal driveway – to **Nagós**, a gravel-shore bay at the foot of an oasis. The lush greenery is nourished by active springs up at a bend in the road, enclosed in a sort of grotto and flanked by a *psistariá*, all overawed by tall cliffs. The place name is a corruption of *naós*, after a large Poseidon temple that once stood near the springs, but centuries of orchard-tending, antiquities-pilfering and organized excavations after 1912 mean that nothing remains visible. Down at the shore the swimming is good, if a bit chilly, and there are two tavernas, one renting **rooms** (☎0272/23 540; ③). Several more are under construction, and your only chance of relative solitude in July or August lies fifteen minutes' walk west at **Yióssonas**. This is a much longer beach, but less sheltered, rockier and with no facilities.

Northwestern villages

Few outsiders venture beyond Yióssonas; an afternoon bus occasionally covers the distance between Mármaro and Kambiá village, 20km west. Along the way, **AMÁDHES** and **VÍKI** are attractive enough villages at the base of 1297-metre **Pilinéo**, the island's summit, easiest climbed from Amádhes. **KAMBIÁ**, overlooking a chapel-strewn ravine, has very much an end-of-the-line feel, despite the recent paving of the onward road south through Spartoúnda and Kipouriés to its union with the trans-island road to Volissós.

Around 4km north of this junction, you can detour to visit the sixteenth-century **monastery of Moudhón**, once ranked second on the island after Néa Moní before its partial destruction in 1822. Among its naive frescoes is one of the *Ouranódhromos Klímax* (Stairway to Heaven), a trial-by-ascent in which ungodly priests are beset by demons who hurl them into the mouth of Leviathan, while the righteous clergy are assisted upwards by angels. In an era when illiteracy was the norm, such panels were intended quite literally to scare the hell out of simple parishioners.

If without transport, go to one of the *kafenía* by the main church in Kambiá to be pointed along the one-hour path across the canyon to the abandoned hamlet of Agrelopó; from the church there a system of jeep tracks leads in another ninety minutes to the tumbledown pier and seaweed-strewn beach at **AYIÁSMATA**. This is one of the strangest spots on Híos, consisting of perhaps twenty buildings (four of them churches), including the miraculous hot springs after which the place is named. The spa is currently in the throes of restoration, so it's best not to count on staying or eating here.

Roads **south of Ayiásmata**, paved once more, pass through strikingly beautiful countryside up to the villages of Kéramos and Afrodhíssia. Here the surfaced road system splits: the southerly turning continues south through Hálandhra and Néa Potamiá – the latter an ugly prefab village built to replace an older one destroyed by landslide – for 20km towards Volissós.

A northwesterly turning from Afrodhíssia is more worthwhile, approximating a coastal road for this part of the island. **KOUROÚNIA**, 6km along, is beautifully arranged in two separate neighbourhoods, looking out from thick forest cover. After 10km more, you reach **ÁYIO GÁLA**, where a disproportionate number of old ladies in headscarves hobble about; there's a single telephone in the *kafenío*, whose proprietor summons those called over a loud hailer. The place's claim to fame is a grotto-church complex, built into a palisade at the bottom of the village. Except on the August 23 festival date, you'll need to find Petros the key-keeper, who lives beside a eucalyptus tree at the top of the stairs leading down to it. The larger of the two churches occupies the mouth of the cave system; it's originally fifteenth century but has had an unfortunate pink exterior paint job that makes it look like a recent villa. Inside, however, a fantastically intricate *témblon* vies for your attention with a tinier, older chapel, built entirely within the rear of the cavern. Its frescoes are badly smudged, except for a wonderfully mysterious and mournful Virgin holding a knowing Child in the apse.

Volissós and around

VOLISSÓS, 42km from Híos Town by the most direct route, was once the most important of the northwestern villages, and its old stone houses still curl appealingly beneath the crumbling hilltop Byzantine fort. The Genoese improved the towers, and near the top of the village you may be shown an utterly spurious "House of Homer". Today Volissós can seem depressing at first, with the bulk of its 250 remaining, mostly elderly, permanent inhabitants living in newer constructions around the main square – impressions improve with longer acquaintance.

Grouped around the *platía* you'll find a **post office** (but no bank), two shops and three evening-only **tavernas**, none especially noteworthy. Since the **bus** only comes out here on Sundays on a day-trip basis, and on Monday and Thursday in the afternoon, you should plan on **staying overnight**. This should cause no dismay, since the area has the best beaches on Híos, unspoiled because most inland property owners have thus far refused to sell land to developers. Houses in the village itself are, however, for sale, and eleven have been meticulously restored by *Stella Tsakiri* (☎0274/21 421; ③–④) and accommodate from two to four persons – all have terraces, fully equipped kitchens and original features such as tree trunks upholding sleeping lofts.

Otherwise, there are four conventional rooms 2km south at **LIMNIÁ**, the port of Volissós, above the single permanent **taverna** on the jetty (☎0274/21 315; ③). Limniá itself is a lively working fishing anchorage, with *kaíki* skippers coming and going from Psará (Mon, Wed & Fri at mid-morning) and very occasionally to Plomári on Lésvos.

At Limniá you're not far from the fabled beaches either. A kilometre's walk southeast over the headland brings you to **Managrós**, a seemingly endless sand-and-pebble beach where nudism is tolerated; the nearest **lodgings** are the bungalows of *Marvina Alvertou* (☎0274/21 335; ③). The more intimate **Lefkáthia** lies just a ten-minute stroll along the jeep track threading over the headland north of the harbour; amenities are limited to a seasonal snack bar on the sand, and *Ioannis Zorbas* apartments (☎0274/21 436; ④), sited just where the jeep track joins a paved road down from Volissós. This is headed for **Límnos** (not to be confused with Limniá), the next protected cove 400m east of Lefkáthia, with a seasonal *psistariá* operating behind the sand.

Ayía Markélla, 5km further west of Límnos, stars in many local postcards: a long, stunning beach fronting the monastery of the same name, the latter not especially interesting, or useful, to outsiders. Its cells are reserved for Greek pilgrims, while in an interesting variation on the expulsion of the money changers from the temple, only religious souvenirs are allowed to be sold in the holy precincts, while all manner of plastic junk is on offer just outside. There's a single snack bar as well, and around July 22 – the local saint's festival and biggest island celebration – the "No Camping" signs doubtless go unenforced. Some old maps show **hot springs** at one end of the beach; these, actually twenty minutes' walk away around the headland, turn out to be tepid seeps into pot-sized cavities at the tidal zone, not worth the bother. A handier bit of intelligence is that the dirt road past the monastery grounds is passable to any vehicle, emerging up on the paved road between Melaniós and Volissós.

Satellite islands: Psará and Inoússes

There's a single settlement, with beaches and a lone rural monastery, on both of Híos's satellite isles, but each is surprisingly different from the other, and the main island, too. **Inoússes**, the closer one, has daily *kaíkia* from the main harbour in season; **Psará** is served six days a week, with ferries or *kaíkia* on alternate days from Híos Town and Limniá.

Psará

The birthplace of revolutionary war hero Admiral Kanaris, **Psará** devoted her merchant fleets – the third largest in 1820s Greece after Ídhra and Spétses – to the cause of independence, and paid dearly for it. Vexed beyond endurance, the Turks landed overwhelming forces in 1824, to stamp out this nest of resistance. Perhaps 3000 of the 30,000 inhabitants escaped in small boats which were rescued by a French fleet, but the majority retreated to a hilltop powder magazine and blew it, and themselves, up rather than surrender. The nationalist poet Solomos immortalized the incident in famous stanzas:

> *On the Black Ridge of Psará,*
> *Glory walks alone.*
> *She meditates on her heroes,*
> *And wears in her hair a wreath*
> *Made from a few dry weeds*
> *Left on the barren ground.*

Today the year-round population barely exceeds four hundred, and it's a sad, stark place, never having really recovered from the holocaust; the Turks burned whatever houses and vegetation the blast had missed. The only positive recent development was a decade-long revitalization project instigated by a French-Greek descendant of Kanaris and a Greek team. The port was improved, mains electricity and pure water provided, a secondary school opened, and cultural links between France and the island established, though so far this has not been reflected in increased tourism or tourist facilities.

Arriving can be something of an ordeal: the regular ferry from Híos Town takes four hours to cover the 35 nautical miles of habitually rough sea. Use the port of Limniá to cross in at least one direction if you can; this route takes half the time at half the price.

Since few buildings in the east-facing harbour community predate this century, it's a strange hotchpotch of ecclesiastical and domestic architecture that greets the eye on disembarking. There's a distinctly southern feel, more like the Dodecanese or the Cyclades, and some strange churches, no two alike in style, in and out of town.

If you **stay overnight**, your choices are limited to a single studio behind the dock-side string of *kafenía* and tavernas; some rooms let by the priest's wife; the municipal (and overpriced) inn (②), and the EOT *ksenónas* in a restored prison (☎0274/61 293; ③). For **eating**, the best and cheapest place by far is the EOT-run *Spitalia*, housed in a restored medieval hospital at the edge of town. A **post office**, bakery and shop complete the tally of amenities; there's no bank.

Psará's **beaches** are decent, getting better the further northeast you walk from the port. You quickly pass Káto Yialós, Katsoúni and Lazoréta with its off-putting power station; **Lákka**, fifteen minutes along, seems to be named after its grooved rock forma-tions in which you may have to shelter, as much of this coast is windswept, with a heavy swell offshore. **Límnos**, 25 minutes out along the coastal path, is big and pretty, but there's no reliable taverna here, or indeed at any of the other beaches. The only other thing to do on Psará, really, is to walk north across the island to the **monastery of the Assumption**; this – uninhabited since the 1970s – comes to life only during the first week of August when its revered icon is taken in procession to town, and then back again on August 6, with great ceremony.

Inoússes

Inoússes has a permanent population of about three hundred – down from more than twice that number since World War II – and a very different history from Psará. For generations, this medium-sized islet has provided the Aegean with many of her wealthi-est shipping families: the richest Greek shipowner in the world, Kostas Lemos, was born here, and virtually every street or square here is named for one member or other of the numerous Pateras clan. This helps explain the large villas and visiting summer yachts in an otherwise sleepy Greek backwater – as well as a sporadically open **Maritime Museum** near the quay, endowed by various shipping magnates and devoted to nautical exhibits and souvenirs. The bigwigs have also funded a large nauti-cal academy to train future seamen, at the west end of the quay.

Only on Saturdays and Sundays can you make an inexpensive **day-trip** to Inoússes from Híos with the locals' ferry *Inousses*; on other days of the week this arrives at 3pm, returning early the next morning. On weekdays during the tourist season you must participate in the pricey excursions offered from Híos, with return tickets running up to three times the cost of the regular ferry.

Two church-tipped islets, each privately owned, guard the unusually well-protected harbour; the **town** of Inoússes is surprisingly large, draped over hillsides enclosing a ravine. Despite the wealthy reputation, it's of unpretentious appearance, with the houses displaying a mix of vernacular and modest Neoclassical style. There is just one, fairly comfortable **hotel**, the *Thalassoporos* (☎0272/51 475; ④), on the main easterly hillside lane. **Eating out** is similarly limited to *O Glaros*, a simple *ouzerí* just below the nautical academy. It's best to come equipped with picnic materials, or be prepared to patronize one of the three shops (one on the waterfront, two up the hill). Beside the museum is a **post office** and a **bank**, with the **OTE** a few paces further west.

The rest of this tranquil island, at least the southern slope, is surprisingly green and well tended; there are no springs, so water comes from a mix of fresh and brackish wells, though there are mutterings of a reservoir in the offing. The sea is extremely clean and calm on this lee shore; among the sheltered southerly beaches, choose from **Zepága**, **Biláli** or **Kástro**, five, twenty and thirty minutes' walk west of the port respectively, or the more secluded **Farkeró**, 25 minutes east: first along a cement drive ending at a seaside chapel, then by path past pine groves and over a ridge. As on Psará, there are no reliable facilities at any of the beaches.

At the end of the westerly road, beyond Kástro, stands the somewhat macabre convent of **Evangelismoú**, endowed by the Pateras family. Inside reposes the mummified body of the lately canonized daughter, Irini, whose prayers to die of cancer in place of her terminally ill father Panagos were answered early in the 1960s on account of her virtue and piety; he's entombed here, also, having outlived Irini by some years. The abbess, presiding over some twenty nuns, is Mrs Pateras. Only women are allowed admission, and even then casual visits are not encouraged.

Lésvos (Mitilíni)

Lésvos, the third largest Greek island after Crete and Évia, is not only the birthplace of Sappho, but also of Aesop, Arion and, more recently, the Greek primitive artist Theophilos, the poet Odysseus Elytis and the novelist Stratis Myrivilis. Despite these artistic associations, it may not at first strike the visitor as particularly beautiful or interesting; much of the landscape is rocky, volcanic terrain, dotted with thermal springs and alternating with vast grain fields, salt pans or even near-desert. But there are also oak and pine forests as well as vast olive groves, some of these over five hundred years old. With its balmy climate and suggestive contours, the island tends to grow on you with prolonged acquaintance.

Lovers of medieval and Ottoman **architecture** certainly won't be disappointed. Genoese castles survive at the main town of Mitilíni, at Mólivos and near Ándissa: these date from the late fourteenth century, when Lésvos was given as a dowry to a Genoese prince of the Gatelouzi clan following his marriage to the niece of one of the last Byzantine emperors. Along with Crete, Lésvos was the only Greek island where Turks settled significantly in rural villages (they usually stuck to the safety of towns), so driving along you frequently encounter the odd Ottoman bridge or crumbling minaret in the middle of nowhere. Again, unusually for the Aegean islands, there was an approximation of a post-Byzantine Greek Orthodox urban aristocracy here, who built rambling mansions and tower-houses, some of which have survived the destruction which claimed the rest in this century.

Social and economic idiosyncrasies persist: anyone who has attended one of the lengthy village *paniyíria*, with music for hours on end and tables in the streets groaning with food and drink, will not be surprised to learn that Lésvos has the highest alcoholism rate in Greece. Breeding livestock, especially horses, is disproportionately important, and traffic jams caused by mounts instead of parked cars are not unheard of – signs reading "Forbidden to Tether Animals Here" are still part of the picture.

Historically, the olive plantations, *oúzo* distilleries, animal husbandry and a fishing industry supported the inhabitants, but with these enterprises relatively depressed, mass-market **tourism** has made considerable inroads. However, there are few large hotels outside the capital or Mólivos, rooms still just outnumber villa-type accommodation, and the first official campsites opened only in 1990. While Lésvos is far more developed than Híos, it is far less so than Sámos, a happy medium that will accord with many people's tastes. Public buses tend to radiate out from the harbour for the benefit of working locals, not tourists who may want to do an out-and-back day trip. Carrying out such excursions is next to impossible anyway, owing to the size of the island – about 70km by 45km at its widest points – and the occasionally appalling roads (at long last being improved, along with their signposting). Furthermore, the topography is complicated by the two deeply indented gulfs of Kalloní and Yéra, which means that going from A to B usually involves an obligatory change of bus at either the port capital, on the east shore, or the town of Kalloní, in the middle of the island. In short, it's best to decide on a base and stay there for at least a few days, exploring its immediate surroundings on foot or by vehicle, rather than constantly trying to move on.

Mitilíni Town

MITILÍNI is the port and capital, and in Greek fashion sometimes doubles as the name of the island, something to watch out for when travelling by ferry or plane. The town sprawls between and around two broad bays divided by a promontory where the **Genoese fortress** sits – open much of the day but not to be photographed since it's a military area. Further inland, the town skyline is dominated in turn by the Germanic spire of **Áyios Theodhóros** and the mammary dome of **Áyios Therápon**, together expressions of the post-Baroque taste of the nineteenth-century Ottoman Greek bourgeoisie. They stand more or less at opposite ends of the **bazaar**, whose main street, Ermoú, links the town centre with the little-used north harbour. On its way there Ermoú passes half a dozen antique shops near the roofless **Yeni Tzami**, now a venue for art exhibits. Between Ermoú and the castle lies a maze of atmospheric lanes lined with grandiose Belle Epoque mansions and elderly houses.

More formal stimulation is provided by the excellent **Archeological Museum** (daily except Mon 8.30am–3pm; 400dr), currently housed partly in the mansion of a large estate just behind the ferry dock (although a large modern installation is under construction). Among the more interesting of the well-labelled and well-lit exhibits are a complete set of mosaics from a Hellenistic dwelling, rather droll terracotta figurines, votive offerings from a sanctuary of Demeter and Kore excavated in the castle, and Neolithic finds from present-day Thermí. A specially built annexe at the rear contains stone-cut inscriptions of various edicts and treaties, and – more interesting than you'd think – *stelae* featuring *nekródhipna* or portrayals of funerary meals.

There's also a **Byzantine Art Museum** behind Áyios Therápon, containing various icons (Mon–Sat 9am–1pm; 100dr), and a small **Folk Art Museum** (sporadic hours; 150dr) on the quay next to the blue city-bus stop.

All of the foregoing may sound like a lot but in fact the town's pleasures are easily exhausted in half a day. Most visitors, repulsed by the general urban bustle, get out as soon as possible; Mitilíni returns the compliment by being in fact a very impractical and expensive place to base yourself.

Arrival, transport and information
You should pause long enough to stop at the jointly housed **tourist police/EOT post** (daily 8.30am–5.30pm), behind the customs building, in order to get hold of their excellent town and island maps, plus other brochures.

There are two **bus stations** in town. The *astikó* (blue bus) service departs from the middle of the quay, while *iperastikó* (standard *KTEL*) buses leave from a small station near Platía Konstandinopóleos at the southern end of the harbour, all the way around from where ferries dock. There is no bus link with the **airport**, and a shared taxi (they're expensive) for the 8km into Mitilíni is the usual method. If you're intent on getting over to Ayvalık in Turkey, book **ferry tickets** through either *Aeolic Cruises*

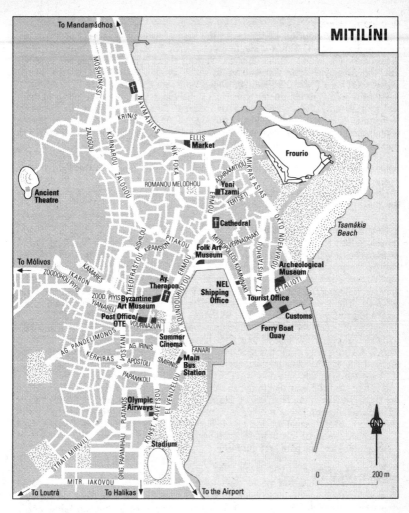

(☎0251/23 960) or *Mytilana Travel* nearby at Koundouriótou 69 (☎0251/41 318). Agencies for standard *NEL* and *Nomicos* ferries, and *Ilio Line* hydrofoils, are bunched together on the easterly reach of Koundouriótou, the quay street; *Olympic Airways* is southwest of the bay and central park, at Kavétsou 44.

Car rental is best arranged through reputable chain franchises like *Payless* or *Europcar* – though it's generally cheaper to rent at the resort of your choice. Mopeds or even proper motorbikes will make little impact on this huge island, and will certainly go for a spill on some of the rougher dirt roads.

Other amenities include the **OTE** and **post office**, next to each other on Vournázon, a block behind the central park, and three **banks** with autotellers: the *Ethniki* (*National*), *Pisteos* (*Credit*) – both on Koundouriótou – and the *Emboriki* (*Commercial*) on Ermoú.

Accommodation

Finding **accommodation** is difficult at the best of times: the waterfront hotels are noisy and exorbitant, with few single rooms to speak of. It's best to hunt for rooms between the castle and Ermoú. Yioryíou Tertséti street in particular has two possibilities: the friendly *Pelayia Koumniotou* at no. 6 (☎0251/20 643; ②), or the fancier *Dhiethnes* at no. 1 (☎0251/24 968; ③), whose rooms are en-suite.

Past the Yeni Tzami, quieter, cheaper establishments between the north harbour and fortress advertise themselves – for example *Cuckoo's Nest*, near the corner of Navmahías Ellís and Nikifóro Foká (☎0251/23 901; ②), or *Salina's Garden Rooms*, behind the Yeni Tzami at Fokéas 7 (☎0251/42 073; ③). The Neoclassical *Hotel Rex* at Katsakoúli 3, behind the Archeological Museum (☎0251/28 523; ③), looks inviting from the outside, but the en-suite rooms (no singles) are gloomy and overpriced. For Belle Epoque character you're better off in the far south of town, at the *Villa 1900*, a restored mansion with period furnishings and ceiling murals, at P. Vostáni 24 (0251/43 437; ④), where you may be able to bargain the price down a little. There's another similar, if less preserved, outfit nearby at E. Vostáni 24 (③).

Eating, drinking and nightlife

Lunch is best had at the *Iy Lesvos* on Ermoú. Further down, beside the Yeni Tzami, *Albatross* has a bizarre interior, with a human clientele to match, and the food – pickled *krítama* herb and grilled sardines, served up by the wild-eyed owner himself, and washed down by peculiar wine – seems incidental. Another example of a dying breed is the *Ouzeri Krystal*, on the seafront Koudourióti betwen the *Ionian Bank* and the *Bank of Greece*. The cavernous, wood-floored interior has walls lined by mirrors and bench seats and gaming tables at the centre, with more contemporary seating outside.

Options for more conventional dining are somewhat limited; the obvious venue for a seafood blowout is the line of four **fish tavernas** on the southerly quay known as Fanári. All are pretty comparable in price and food, though *Stratos* and *Strofi* at the seaward end are the most popular. Right around the port from here at Koundouriótou 56, the *Asteria* is a safe option for more involved, meat-and-veg oven casseroles.

If you're stuck here involuntarily, awaiting a dawn-departing ferry, some consolation can be derived from the town's good **nightlife** and **entertainment**. *Hot Spot* is a fairly accurate self-description of the bar at Koundouriótou 63, near the *NEL* agency, with good music. More formal musical events form the heart of the *Lesviakó Kalokéri*, held in the castle from mid-July to mid-September. The summer **cinema** *Pallas* is between the post office and the park on Vournázon.

Around Mitilíni

Heading north along the coast from Mitilíni, the beaches are negligible but the startling views across the straits to Turkey make the trip towards Mandamádhos worthwhile. On the way you can detour to see a Roman aqueduct at **MÓRIA**, and various *pírgi* (tower-mansions), relics of the nineteenth-century gentry, at **PÁMFILLA** and **PÍRGI THERMÍS**. However, the most compelling attraction is the **baths** at **LOUTRÓPOLI THERMÍS**, sunken indoor hot-spring pools overarched by great vaults. There's a half-hourly blue bus service to them, but enquire first before boarding since the spa is periodically closed for repairs.

Just south of the town, on the road to the airport, you can visit more tower-mansions at **HRISSOMALOÚSSA** and **AKLIDHÍOU**. Beyond the airport, but reached easiest by taking a blue city bus as far as the village of Loutrá (and then a taxi), the remote double-cove beach of **Áyios Ermoyénis** is attractive, but it's crowded on weekends and for pleasant immersions near Mitilíni (the fee-entry town "beach" at Tsamákia is mediocre) you're best advised to make for **Loutrá Yéras**, 8km along the main road to

Kalloní. These public baths (summer daily 8am–7pm, winter daily 10am–6pm; 150dr) are just the thing if you've spent a sleepless night on a malodorous ferry, with three ornate spouts that feed just-above-body-temperature water into a marble-lined pool in a vaulted chamber; there are separate facilities for each sex. A snack-bar/café operates seasonally on the roof of the bath house, overlooking the gulf, and there is even an old **inn** nearby (☎0251/21 643; ②).

The Variá museums
Perhaps the most rewarding single targets near Mitilíni are a pair of museums at **VARIÁ**, 3km south of town (regular half-hourly buses). The **Theophilos Museum** (daily except Mon 9am–1pm & 4.30–8pm; 250dr) honours the naïve painter born here in 1868, and presents four rooms of wonderful, little-known compositions specifically commissioned by his patron Thériade (see below) in the several years leading up to his death in 1934; virtually the only familiar piece is likely to be *Erotokritos and Arethousa* in Room 3. Theophilos brought a wealth of accurate sartorial detail to bear on the pastoral Lésvos which he obviously knew best, in such elegiac scenes as fishing, reaping, olive-picking and baking; there are droll touches also, such as a cat slinking off with a fish in *The Fishmongers*. In classical scenes – such as *Sappho and Alkaeos* in Room 4, a landscape series of Egypt, Asia Minor and the Holy Land, and historical episodes from wars historical and contemporary – Theophilos was clearly on shakier ground. *Abyssinians Hunting an Italian Horseman*, for instance, is clearly fantastic, being nothing more than Native Americans chasing down a Conquistador.

The adjacent **Thériade Museum** (daily except Mon 9am–2pm & 5–8pm; 500dr) is the brainchild of another native son, Stratis Eleftheriades. Leaving the island at an early age for Paris, he Gallicized his name to Thériade and went on to become a renowned art publisher, convincing some of the leading artists of the twentieth century to participate in his ventures. The displays consist of lithographs, engravings, woodblock prints and watercolours by the likes of Miró, Chagall, Picasso, Léger, Rouault and Villon, either annotated by the painters themselves or illustrations for the works of prominent poets and authors – an astonishing collection for a relatively remote Aegean island. Near the two museums is an enterprising snack bar.

Southern Lésvos

The southernmost portion of the island is indented by two great inlets, the gulfs of **Kalloní** and **Yéra** – the first curving in a northeasterly direction, the other northwesterly, thus creating a fan-shaped peninsula at the heart of which is the 968-metre Mount Ólimpos. Both shallow gulfs are in turn almost landlocked by virtue of very narrow outlets to the open sea.

Plomári and around
PLOMÁRI is the only sizeable coastal settlement in the south, the second largest on Lésvos, and presents an odd mix of beauty and its famous *oúzo* distilling industry. Despite a lack of sandy beaches nearby, it's besieged in summer by hordes of Scandinavian tourists, but you can usually find a **room** – they are signposted literally everywhere – at the edge of the old, charmingly dilapidated town. Unfortunately, rustling up a decent meal is considerably harder, with the dinner-only *Platanos* taverna at the central plane tree often unbearably busy, and nothing special at that. Best of a very mediocre bunch on the waterfront is *D'Annelise*, within sight of the bus stop.

You'll probably do no worse at **ÁYIOS ISÍDHOROS**, 3km east, which is where most tourists actually stay; try *Iy Mouria*, where the road turns inland to cross the creek draining to the long, popular pebble beach. The closest sandy beach is ninety minutes' walk west of Plomári, past isolated coves in the direction of **Melínda**. Back in

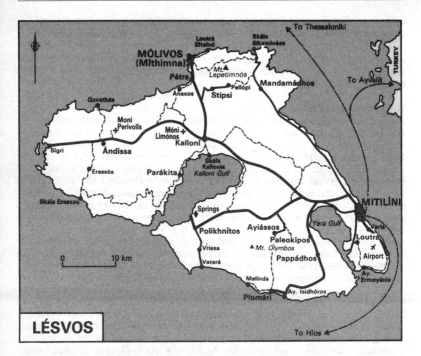

To Thessaloniki

Loutrá Eftaloú
Skála Sikaminéas
MÓLIVOS (Míthimna)
Pétra
Mt. Lepetimnós
Pellópi
Anaxos
Stípsi
Mandamádhos
To Ayválik
TURKEY
Gavathás
Moni Perivolís
Móni Limónos
Kallöní
Sígri
Ándissa
Eressós
Parákita
Skála Kallonía
Kalloni Gulf
Skála Eressoú
MITILÍNI
Springs
Polikhnítos
Ayiássos
Yera Gulf
Vrissa
Paleókipos
Mt. Olymbos
Loutrá
Vaterá
Pappádhos
Airport
Melinda
Ay. Isidhóros
Ay. Ermoyénis
0   10 km
Plomári

LÉSVOS

To Híos

town the *Okeanis Hotel* (☎0252/32 469; ③) is one of several local outlets for car rental and runs boat trips to the still-better beaches of **Tárti** (24km east; food and lodging) and Vaterá (see below). The local *paniyíri* season kicks off in mid-July with the **Oúzo Festival**, culminating on the 27–28 of the month with celebrations in honour of Áyios Harálambos, featuring such rurally focused activities as horse races and a bull sacrifice.

The bus line into Plomári runs via the pretty villages of Paleókipos and Skópelos (as well as Áyios Isídhoros), but if you're hitching or have your own two-wheeler (no cars carried) you can take a slight shortcut by using the daytime-only ferry at **PÉRAMA**, across the neck of the Yéra Gulf. The road north from Plomári to Ayiássos has paving and public transport only up to Megalohóri – rough dirt and your own conveyance thereafter, though the surface should improve in future years.

Ayiássos

AYIÁSSOS, nestled in a remote, wooded valley under the crest of Mount Ólimbos, is the most beautiful hill town on Lésvos – the ranks of traditional houses lining the narrow, cobbled streets are all protected by law. On the usual, northerly approach, there's no clue of the enormous village until you see huge ranks of parked cars at the southern edge of town (where the bus also leaves you).

Don't be put off by the huge phalanxes of wooden and ceramic kitsch souvenirs, aimed mostly at Greeks, but continue past the central **church of the Panayía Vrefokratoússa** to the old bazaar, with its *kafenía*, yogurt shops and unusually graphic butcher's stalls. Video-game arcades have made certain inroads, but in some cafés bands of *santoúri*, clarinet, lap-drum and violin play on weekend afternoons, accompanying inebriated dancers on the cobbles outside. Rather more packaged are the products of *santoúri* player Ioannis Kakourgos, who plays and sells cassettes from his little studio underneath the church, built in the twelfth century to house an icon supposedly painted by the Evangelist Luke. With such a pedigree, the local August 15 festival is one of the liveliest in Greece, let alone Lésvos, and makes clear the country-fair element in a traditional *paniyíri*, where pilgrims came to buy and sell as well as perform devotions.

There are a very few **rooms** available for the increasing number of visitors. The best **restaurants** are *Dhouladhelli*, on your left as you enter the village from the extreme south (bus stop) end, or *Dhayielles*, further along. At either of these spots you can eat for a fraction of the prices asked at the coastal resorts.

Vaterá – and its approaches

A different bus route from Mitilíni leads to Vaterá beach via the inland villages of Polihnítos, whose spa has long been closed for repairs, and more attractive Vríssa. If you're after a bath, try the working **hot springs of Áyios Ioánnis** (100dr), fairly well signposted 2km below the village of Lisvóri. Flanking the chapel are two vaulted-chamber pools, though the water is odiferous, iron-stained and best enjoyed on a cool evening.

VATERÁ itself is a huge, seven-kilometre-long sand beach, backed by vegetated hills; the swimming is delightfully calm, clean and warm. The west end of this strip has several accommodation options, the nicest of the **hotels** clustered here the Greek- and American-run *Vatera Beach* (☎0252/61 212; open winter by arrangement; ④–⑨). It also has a good attached restaurant with shoreline tables from where you can gaze on the cape of Áyios Fokás, whose **temple of Dionysus** and early Christian basilica are finally being properly excavated. The **campsite** here lies slightly inland from the portion of the beach east of the T-junction, where studio/villa units predominate. Here several more **tavernas** line the shore road, and because the clientele are mostly local weekenders, they're reasonably priced and good – for example, *Ta Kalamakia*. **Nightlife** – thus far a pub or two, and the *Arena Disco* – is rather low-key, reflecting Vaterá's status as a family resort. If you intend to stay here you'll probably want your own transport, as the closest shops are 4km away at Vríssa, and the bus appears only three times daily.

To the east, a fair-to-poor dirt road leads via Stavrós and hidden Ambelikó to either Ayiássos or Plomári within an hour and a half. A direct coastal road to Melínda is on the cards, though Plomári is opposing this, fearful of losing tourist trade to the infinitely superior beach at Vaterá. Leaving the area going north towards Kallóní, the short cut via the coast guard base at **Ahladherí** is well worth using and passable in its present state to all but the more underpowered mopeds – moreover, it should be paved shortly.

Western Lésvos

The main road west of Loutrá Yéra is surprisingly devoid of settlement, with little to stop for before Kallóní other than the traces of an ancient **Aphrodite temple** at Mési (Messon), signposted just east of the Ahladherí cutoff and about 1km north of the main road. At the site (daily except Mon 8.30am–3pm; free) just the eleventh-century BC foundations and a few column stumps remain, plus the ruins of a fourteenth-century Genoese-built basilica; it was once virtually on the sea but a nearby stream has silted things up in the intervening millennia. All told, it's not worth a special trip, but certainly make the short detour if passing by – and brace yourself for the manically voluble caretaker.

Some 7km beyond lies the turning for the **AYÍA PARASKEVÍ**, where a famous bull-sacrifice rite is observed at the end of June or beginning of July; at other times the village presents an intriguing tableau of nineteenth-century bourgeois architecture.

KALLONÍ itself is an unembellished agricultural and market town more or less in the middle of the island, but you may spend some time here since it's the intersection of most bus routes. If you have a lot of time to spare, you might make the three-kilometre walk to SKÁLA KALLONÍS, a principally Dutch and English package resort with a long, if coarse, beach on the lake-like gulf. None of the handful of restaurants merits a mention, and **push-bike rental** – ideal for the flat terrain hereabouts – is the resort's only distinction.

Inland monasteries and villages

West of Kalloní the road winds 4km uphill to the **monastery of Limónos**, founded in 1527 by one Ignatios. It is a huge complex, with just a handful of monks and lay workers to maintain three storeys of cells ringing the giant courtyard, adorned with strutting peacocks and huge urns sporting potted plants. Beside, behind and above are respectively an old-age home, a lunatic asylum, and a hostel for pilgrims; the *katholikón*, with its carved-wood ceiling and archways, is built in Asia-Minor style and traditionally off-limits to women. A former abbot established a **museum** (daily 9am–1pm & 5–7.30pm; 100dr) on two floors of the rear wing; the ground-floor ecclesiastical collection is fine enough, but you should prevail upon the warden (easier done in large groups) to open the upper, ethnographic hall. The first room is a re-created Lesvian salon, while the next is crammed with an indiscriminate mix of kitsch and priceless objects – Ottoman copper trays to badly stuffed, rotting egrets by way of brightly painted trunks – donated since 1980 by surrounding villages. An overflow of farm implements is stashed in a corner storeroom below, next to a chamber where giant *pithária* (urns) for grain and olive oil are embedded in the floor.

Beyond, the road west passes through Fília, where you can turn off for a time-saving short cut to Skoutáros and the north of Lésvos; the dirt surface has recently been regraded and should be passable to any car. Most traffic continues through to the unusually neat village of **SKALOHÓRI**, its houses in tiers at the head of a valley facing the sea and the sunset, and **VATOÚSSA**, the most landlocked but also the most beautiful of the western settlements.

Eight kilometres beyond Vatoússa, a short track leads down to the sixteenth-century **monastery of Perivolís** (daily 8am–7pm; pull on the bell rope for admission), built as the name suggests in the midst of a riverside orchard. You should appear well before sunset, as only natural light is available to view the fine if faded frescoes in the narthex. In an apocalyptic panel worthy of Bosch, *The Earth and Sea Yield Up Their Dead*, the *Whore of Babylon* rides her chimaera and assorted sea-monsters disgorge their victims. On the north side you see a highly unusual iconography of *Abraham, the Virgin, and the Good Thief of Calvary in Paradise*. Further interest is lent by a humanized icon of Christ, under glass at the *témblon*.

ÁNDISSA nestles under the west's only pine grove; at the edge of the village a sign implores you to "Visit our Central Square", and that's not a bad idea, for the sake of its three enormous plane trees, shading several cafés and tavernas. Directly below Ándissa, a paved road leads 6km north toward the fishing hamlet of **GAVATHÁS**, with a narrow, partly protected beach and a few places to eat and stay – such as the *Hotel Restaurant Paradise* (☎0253/56 376; ③) – among its 25 or so buildings. A dirt side track leads to the huge, duned but wave-battered beach of **Kámbos**, one headland east; you can keep going in the same direction, following signs pointing to "Ancient Andissa". Where they actually lead you to is **Ovriókastro**, the most derelict of the island's Genoese castles, evocatively placed on a promontory within sight of Mólivos and a goodly swathe of coast to either side. Dirty exposed beaches adjacent are unlikely to appeal, though there is a small snackbar. The locals mistakenly identify the castle with the ancient town, but the latter is actually a fair way inland, and difficult to find.

Just beyond modern Ándissa there's an important junction. Keeping straight ahead leads you past the still-functioning **monastery of Ipsiloú**, founded in 1101 atop an extinct volcano and still home to four monks. The *katholikón*, tucked in one corner of a large, irregular courtyard, has a fine wood-lattice ceiling but had its frescoes repainted to worsening effect in 1992 and no longer ranks as meritorious art; more intriguing are bits of Iznik tiles stuck in the facade. Upstairs you can visit a fairly rich museum of ecclesiastical treasure (donation in exchange for a postcard). Ipsiloú's patron saint is John the Theologian, a frequent dedication for monasteries overlooking apocalyptic landscapes like the surrounding parched, boulder-strewn hills.

Near here is one of the main concentrations of specimens from Lésvos' rather over-rated **petrified forest**, indicated by forest service placards which also warn of severe penalties for pilfering souvenir chunks. For once contemporary Greek arsonists cannot be blamed for the state of the trees, created by the combined action of volcanic ash and hot springs some 15 million years ago. The other main cluster is south of Sígri, but locals seem amazed that anyone would want to trudge though the barren countryside in search of them; upon arrival you may agree, since the mostly horizontal, three-metre-long chunks aren't exactly one of the world's wonders. If you're curious, there are a fair number of petrified logs strewn about the courtyard of Ipsiloú.

Sígri

SÍGRI, near the western tip of Lésvos, has an appropriately end-of-the-line feel. The bay here is guarded both by a Turkish **castle** and the long island of Nissopí athwart its mouth, which protects the place somewhat from prevailing winds; very occasionally, in what seems an experimental programme, a *NEL* ferry plying the line between Skíros and Límnos is diverted to call here. The castle sports the sultan's monogram over the entrance, something rarely seen outside Istanbul and a token of the high regard in which this productive island was held. A vaguely Turkish-looking church is in fact a converted **mosque**, while the town itself is an uneasy mix of old and cement dwellings. The town **beach**, south of the castle headland, is narrow and scrappy; there's a better one – glimpsed on the way in – 3km north at a river mouth, as well as an even better one 2km south at another creek mouth, just off the one-lane track to Eressós.

If you want to **stay**, there's a mid-range hotel and a handful of **rooms**, including *Nelly's Room and Apartments* (☎0253/54 230; ③), looking right at the castle. Among several **tavernas**, *Remezzo* may have the best view of the town beach and the fanciest menu, but *Galazio Kyma* – the unmarked white building with blue trim, opposite the jetty – gets first pick of the fishermen's catch and can offer unbeatably fresh seafood.

Skála Eressoú and Eressós

Most visitors to western Lésvos park themselves at **SKÁLA ERESSOÚ**, a growing resort accessible via the southerly turning between Ándissa and Ipsiloú. The beach here, given additional character by an islet that's within easy swimming distance, runs a close second to the one at Vaterá, and consequently the place is beginning to rival Plomári and Mólivos in numbers of visitors – who form an odd mix of Brits, Scandinavians, Greek families, neo-hippies and lesbians (of whom more overpage). Behind stretches the largest and most attractive agricultural plain on Lésvos, a welcome green contrast to the volcanic ridges above. Coming south the 15km from the junction there's no hint of the approaching oasis, something that adds to its idyllic quality as it erupts suddenly just beyond the inland town of **ERESSÓS**. This supports a contented colony of expatriates who have bought or rented property, and a stroll along lanes flanked by the vernacular houses is well worthwhile, but only during the cooler hours of the day. During summer half of the population is down at Skála, in the older cottages on the slope leading up to Vígla hill.

There's not much to Skála – just a roughly rectangular grid of perhaps five streets by eight, including the waterfront pedestrian zone (officially Papanikolí). A café-lined square at mid-waterfront is dominated by a bust of Theoprastus – a renowned botanist who originally hailed from **ancient Eressos**. This was not, as you might suppose, on the site of the modern village, but atop Vígla hill at the east end of the beach; you can still see some remaining crumbled bits of citadel wall from a distance. Once on top the ruins prove even scantier, but it's worth the scramble up for the comprehensive views – you can discern the ancient jetty, submerged out beyond the modern fishing anchorage.

A rather more famous (reputed) native of ancient Eressos was **Sappho**, and there are usually appreciable numbers of gay women here paying homage, particularly at the campsite and in the clothing-optional zone of the beach west of the river mouth. In the river itself live about a hundred terrapins who have learned to come ashore for bread-feedings.

Skála has countless **rooms**, most of the sea-view ones block-booked in advance by tour companies; in high season, often the best and quietest you can hope for is something inland overlooking a garden or fields. At such times it's wise to entrust the search to an agency, such as *Snapi Travel* on the east waterfront (☎0253/53 855;); you pay a small commission but it saves trudging about for vacancies. There are few bona fide **hotels**; longest established of these, well placed on the front if a bit noisy, is *Sappho the Eressia* (☎0253/53 233; ③), open all year. Otherwise, there's a free **campsite** at the west edge of town, under some trees behind the sand, with toilets, a shower and sinks.

Most **tavernas**, with elevated wooden dining platforms, crowd the beach; the best, both on the eastern walkway, are *Iy Gorgona*, with friendly service and a large menu of Greek standards, and the British-run *Bennett's*, at the extreme east end of things opposite the islet. Inland, on the way to the museum, the *Aphrodite Home Cooking* taverna is as described. Canadian-run *Yamas* is the place for pancake breakfasts; they also rent out mountain bikes and function as an Anglophone bar at night. *Sympathy*, a few doors down, has an arty-Greek clientele and an uncanny double for Charles Manson serving behind the bar. The gay women's contingent favours *Marianna's*, near the bust of Theophrastos; a summer **cinema** rounds out the nightlife.

Skála has an adjacent **post office** and **OTE**, a coin-op **laundrette** near the church, but no bank; exchange rates offered at the various travel agencies are disadvantageous, so come prepared.

Moving on

If you're returning to the main island crossroads at Kalloní, you can complete a loop from Eressós along the western shore of the Gulf of Kalloní via the hill villages of Mesótopos and Ágra; this route is currently all paved except for the first 11km out of Eressós, with that stretch scheduled for completion soon.

A marked track leads down from **MESÓTOPOS** to beaches at **Tavári** and **Kroússos**, both popular with Greeks and offered as destinations of boat-trips from Skála Eressoú. The only settlement of any consequence on the gulf's west shore is **PARÁKILA**, which boasts a ruined mosque, an Ottoman bridge and a fair proportion of Lesvos' citrus groves; nearby beaches are unlikely to prompt a halt.

Northern Lésvos

The main road north of Kalloní winds up a pine-flecked ridge and then down the other side into increasingly attractive country, stippled with poplars and blanketed by olive groves. Long before you can discern any other architectural detail, the silhouette of Mólivos castle indicates your approach to the oldest established tourist spot on Lésvos.

Mólivos (Míthimna)

MÓLIVOS (officially Míthimna), 61km from Mitilíni, is arguably the most aesthetically pleasing spot on Lésvos. Tiers of sturdy, red-tiled houses, some standing defensively with their rear walls to the sea, mount the slopes between the picturesque harbour and the **Genoese castle** (daily except Mon 7.30am–sunset; free), which provides interesting rambles around its perimeter walls, and views of Turkey across the straits. Closer examination reveals a dozen weathered Turkish fountains along flower-fragrant, cobbled alleyways, a reflection of the fact that before 1923 Turks constituted 35 percent of the local population, and owned most of the finest mansions. You can try to gain admission to the Greek-built **Krallis** and **Yiannakos mansions**; a small municipal library, in the rather vaguely signposted town hall, is usually open during weekday working hours. Until proper excavations begin, **ancient Mithymna** to the northwest is of essentially specialist interest, though a necropolis has been unearthed next to the bus stop; it's mainly the use of the Classical name that has been revived. The motivation for this, as so often in the Balkans, is political; *Mólivos* ("Graphite", of which there is none locally) is a futile Hellenization of the Turkish name *Molova*.

Modern dwellings and hotels have been sensibly banned from the preserved municipal core – a powerful Athenian watchdog group, "Friends of Molyvos", has seen to that – but this has inevitably sapped all the authentic life from the upper bazaar; just one lonely tailor still plies his trade amongst the redundant souvenir shops, and the last locals' *ouzerí* shut down in 1990. Having been cast as upmarket, there are no phallic postcards or other tacky accoutrements in Mólivos, but there are still constant reminders that you are strolling through a stage-set for mass tourism. Yet, except in August, the town's vine-canopied streets seem readily to absorb all who make their way here.

The **town beach** is mediocre – rocky and riddled with sea-urchins in the shallows – though it improves somewhat as you head towards the southern end and a clothing-optional zone. Advertised **boat excursions** to bays as remote as Ánaxos and Tsónia (see overpage for descriptions) seem a frank admission of this failing; there are also eight daily **minibus shuttles** in season, not appearing on any printed bus schedules, linking all points between Ánaxos and Eftaloú.

There are plenty of **rooms** (② & ③) available in town, most easily reserved through the municipal **tourist office** by the bus stop (daily 9am–1pm, 2.30–4pm & 6–8pm), which operates a no-fee telephone booking service. The main sea-level thoroughfare, straight past the tourist office, heads towards the harbour, where a couple of small **hotels** overlook the water; of these, the *Sea Horse* (☎0253/71 320; ④) is fine if you're not interested in making an early night of it. At some hotels in town, you may come upon an insistence that you take mandatory half-board. Otherwise, take the street heading upwards from just beyond the tourist office, past houses with shaded courtyards and – if you're lucky – you'll find room vacancies here; look for placards with the blue-on-white official EOT logo of a face in profile. One of the nicest and quietest (but highest up) are the three kept by *Varvara Kelesi* (☎0253/71 460; ②); few such houses, incidentally, have more rooms than that. There is now also an official **campsite**, *Camping Methymna*, 2km northeast of town.

Around the tourist office you'll find an automatic foreign-money-changing machine, and several **moped and car rental** places. The **post office** is near the top of the upper commercial street, Kástrou, while the **OTE** and a **bank** stand opposite each other on the lower market lane, Dhekátou Évdhomou Noemvríou, at the intersection with the shore road.

Choose carefully when **eating out**. You're usually better off forsaking the sea-view panoramas for Australian-run *Melinda's* at no. 52 of the lower market lane, where the partially vegetarian food is good; it's also the only place open between October and May. On the harbour itself, *Toh Khtapodhi* is the oldest outfit, while *The Captain's Table* at the far end, offers seafood, *mezédhes* and meat. *Medusa*, an *ouzerí* behind *Toh Khtapodhi*, has some highly unusual dishes such as seafood turnovers and cream-stuffed peppers. For dessert, try the pudding-and-cake shop *El Greco*, across the street and downhill from *Melinda's*, where Panayiotis the proprietor is a wonderful ranconteur (in several languages) and acts as a sort of mother hen to aspiring foreign artists, as the numerous paintings on the wall testify.

Midsummer sees a short **festival** of musical and theatrical events up in the castle. As fas as **nightlife** goes, the dancing bar *Q*, one of several down near the old port, and the state-of-the-art outdoor disco *Gatelouzi* near Pétra – the place to be seen on Saturday night – easily outstrip the attractions offered by the perennially empty disco on the water directly below *El Greco*. There's also a summer cinema next to the tourist office; the old mosque spanning the bazaar street supposedly functions as a movie house in winter.

Pétra and Ánaxos

Since there are limits to the expansion of Mólivos, many package companies are now shifting their emphasis towards **PÉTRA**, 5km due south and marginally less busy. The town is beginning to sprawl untidily behind its broad sand beach and seafront square, and diners on the square regularly get sprayed by the exhaust fumes from buses, but the core of old stone houses, many with Levantine-style balconies overhanging the street, remains. Pétra takes its name from the giant rock monolith located some distance inland and enhanced by the eighteenth-century church of the **Panayía Glikofiloússa**. Other local attractions include the sixteenth-century church of **Áyios Nikólaos** and the intricately decorated **Vareltzidhena** mansion (daily except Mon 8.30am–3pm; 200dr).

There are plenty of **rooms** plus a few small hotels, and as at Pirgí on Híos a *Women's Agricultural Tourism Cooperative*, formed by Pétra's women in 1984 to offer something more unusual for visitors. In addition to operating a lunchtime-only **restaurant** on the square (which also serves as a **tourist office**, crafts shop and general information centre; Mon–Sat 9am–3.30pm), they arrange accommodation where it's possible to participate in the proprietors' daily routine and learn a bit about village life. Advance reservations are usually needed (☎0253/41 238 or 41 340; ③). Aside from the cooperative's eatery, **tavernas** (like those behind the north beach) are generally a bit tatty, and you're better off either at the *Ouzeri Pittakos* (dinner only) 100m south of the square, or the *Grill Bar* right on the *platía*, ideal for a quick *souvláki* or tentacle of octopus.

ÁNAXOS, 3km south of Pétra, is a bit overdeveloped but still by far the cleanest beach in the area. Half-a-dozen or so restaurants sit behind a kilometre of sand dotted with pedalos and sunloungers; the **rooms** here seem unaffiliated with any tour company, making Ánaxos a good bet for short-notice accommodation in high season, though you may be plagued by mosquitoes from the river mouth. From anywhere along here you enjoy beautiful sunsets between and beyond three offshore islets.

Around Mount Lepétimnos

East of Mólivos, the villages of **Mount Lepétimnos**, marked by tufts of poplars, offer a day or two of rewarding exploration. The first stop, though not exactly up the hill, might be **Loutrá Eftaloú**, some rustic (and painfully hot) **thermal baths** 5km along the road passing the campsite. These are housed in an attractive old domed structure, which has remained open while much-need renovation proceeds on the adjacent inn; there's a 200-drachma fee if the caretaker is about. Nearby, there are a considerable number of luxury hotels and bungalow complexes, some surprisingly reasonable – try the *Aeolis* (☎0253/71 772; ⑤). In the opposite direction, behind the baths, is a pebble beach for taking a cooling-off dip (clothing optional).

The main road around the mountain first heads 6km east to **VAFIÓS**, with one of two well-advertised **tavernas** featuring live music some nights, before curling north around the base of the peaks. This stretch is in the process of being surfaced, but currently the asphalt, and twice-daily bus service back toward Mitilíni, does not resume until Áryennos, 6km before the exquisite hill village of **SIKAMINIÁ** (Sikamiá), the birthplace of the novelist Stratis Myrivilis. Below the "Plaza of the Workers' First of May", with its two traditional *kafenía* and views north to Turkey, one of the imposing basalt-built houses is marked as his childhood home. A trail shortcuts the twisty road down to **SKÁLA SIKAMINIÁS**, easily the most picturesque fishing port on Lésvos. Myrivilis used it as the setting for his best-known book, *The Mermaid Madonna*, and the tiny rock-top chapel at the end of the jetty will be instantly recognizable to anyone who has read the novel.

On a practical level, Skála has a few **pensions** (such as the sea-view *Gorgona*), and three or four **tavernas**, best and longest-lived of these *Iy Mouria* (aka *Iy Skamnia*), with seating under the mulberry tree in which Myrivilis used to sleep on hot summer nights. In addition to good seafood courtesy of the active local fleet, you can try the late-summer speciality of *kolokitholoúloudha yemistá* (stuffed squash blossoms). The only half-decent local beach, however, is the rather average one of **Káyia** just to the east, so Skála is perhaps better as a lunch stop rather than a base. A fairly rough, roller-coaster track follows the coast west back to Mólivos.

Continuing east from upper Sikaminiá, you soon come to **KLIÓ**, whose single main street leads down to a *platía* with a plane tree, fountain, *kafenía* and views across to Turkey. The village is set attractively on a slope down which six kilometres of dirt road, better than maps suggest, descend to **Tsónia** beach. This proves to be 600 metres of beautiful pink volcanic sand, with just a single taverna and another café at the fishing-anchorage end. Tsónia is essentially the summer annexe of Klió, with the entire population down here at weekends in season.

South of Klió, the route forks at **KÁPI**, from where you can complete a loop of the mountain by bearing west along a partly paved road. **PELÓPI**, where the asphalt currently runs out, is the ancestral village of the unsuccessful 1988 US presidential candidate Michael Dukakis, and sports a former mosque now used as a warehouse on the main square. Garden-hidden **IPSILOMÉTOPO**, the next village along, is punctuated by a minaret (but no mosque) and hosts revels on July 17, the feast of Ayía Marína.

By the time you reach sprawling **STÍPSI**, you're almost back to the main Kalloní–Mólivos road; consequently there's a sporadic bus service out again, as well as a large **taverna** at the edge of town where busloads of tourists descend in season for "Greek Nights". There are also **rooms** to let, so Stípsi makes a good base for rambles along Lepétimnos' steadily dwindling network of trails; in recent years donkey-trekking has become more popular than walking, and you'll see outfitters advertising throughout the north of the island.

The main highway south from Klió and Kápi leads back to the capital through **MANDAMÁDHOS**. This attractive inland village is famous for its pottery, including the Ali-Baba style *pithária* (olive-oil urns) seen throughout Lésvos, but more so for the "black" icon of the Archangel Michael, whose enormous **monastery** (daily summer 6am–10pm, winter 6.30am–7pm), just to the north, is the powerful focus of a thriving cult and a popular venue for baptisms. The image – legendarily made from a mixture of mud and the blood of monks slaughtered in a massacre – is really more idol than icon, both in its lumpy three-dimensionality and in the manner of veneration which seems a holdover from pagan times. First there was the custom of the coin-wish, whereby you pressed a coin to the Archangel's forehead; if it stuck, then your wish would be granted. Owing to wear and tear on the image, the practice is now forbidden, with supplicants referred to an alternative icon by the main entrance.

It's further believed that in carrying out his various errands to bring about the desires of the faithful, the Archangel wears through enough footwear to stock a small shoeshop. Accordingly the icon was until recently surrounded not by the usual *támmata* (votive medallions) but by piles of miniature gold and silver shoes left by those he had helped. The ecclesiastical authorities, perhaps embarrassed by these "primitive" practices, had all of the little shoes removed in 1986. Of late, a token substitute has re-appeared, taking the form of several pairs of tin slippers which can be dedicated (ie filled with money) and left in front of the icon. Exactly why his devotees should want to encourage these perpetual peripatetics is uncertain, since in Greek folklore the Archangel Michael is also the one who comes for the souls of the dying.

Límnos

Límnos is a prosperous agricultural island which has only recently awoken to tourism; its remoteness and inconvenient ferry schedules have until now protected it from the worst excesses of the holiday trade. Most summer visitors are Greek, and as a foreign traveller, you're still likely to find yourself an object of curiosity and hospitality, though the islanders are becoming increasingly used to numbers of German and British visitors. Accommodation tends to be comfortable and pricey (④–⑤ is the norm), with a strong bias towards self-catering units.

Among Greeks, Límnos has a reputation for being dull, largely due to its unpopularity as an army posting, and there is a conspicuous **military** presence. In recent years, the island has been the focus of disputes between the Greek and Turkish governments; Turkey has a long-standing demand that Límnos should be demilitarized and Turkish aircraft regularly overfly the island, serving to worsen already tense Greek–Turkish relations.

The bays of Pourniá and Moúdhros, the latter one of the largest natural harbours in the Aegean, almost divide Límnos in two. The west of the island is dramatically bare and hilly, with the abundant volcanic rock put to good use as street cobbles and the walls of the village houses and rural cottages. Like most volcanic islands, Límnos produces excellent **wine**: a dry white of denomination quality, and some of the best retsina in Greece, neither exported unfortunately. The east is low-lying and speckled with ponds or marshes popular with duck-hunters, where it's not occupied by cattle, combine harvesters and vast cornfields.

Despite popular slander to that effect, Límnos is not flat, barren or treeless; much of the countryside consists of rolling hills, well vegetated except on their heights, and with substantial clumps of almond, jujube, poplar and mulberry trees. The island is, however, extremely dry, with irrigation water pumped from deep wells, and a limited number of potable springs. Yet somehow various terrapin-haunted creeks bring sand to the many long, sandy **beaches** around the coast, where it's easy to find a stretch to yourself – though there's no escaping the stingless jellyfish which periodically pour out of the Dardanelles and die here in the shallows. On the plus side, the beaches shelve gently, making them ideal for children, and thus warm up early in summer, with no cool currents except near the river mouths.

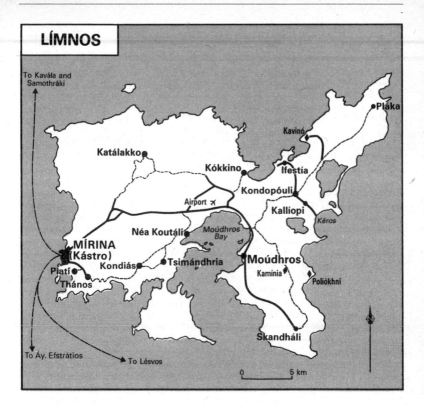

LÍMNOS

To Kavála and Samothráki

Pláka

Kavinó

Katálakko

Kókkino

Ifestía

Kondopóuli

Airport ✈

Kalliópi

Kéros

Néa Koutáli

Moúdhros Bay

MÍRINA (Kástro)

Platí

Kondiás

Tsimándhria

Moúdhros

Thános

Kamínia

Poliókhni

Skandháli

To Áy. Efstrátios

To Lésvos

0   5 km

Mírina

MÍRINA (also called Kástro), the capital and port on the west coast, with its five thousand inhabitants, has the atmosphere of a provincial market town rather than of a resort. It's pleasant enough, if not especially picturesque apart from a core neighbourhood of old stone houses dating from the Ottoman occupation. Few explicitly Turkish monuments have survived – there's no mosque, for example – though a fountain at the harbour end of Kídha retains its inscription and is still highly prized for its drinking water. Mírina is fairly large for an island town, but most things of interest are on the main shopping street, Kídha – stretching from the harbour to **Romeïkós Yialós**, the beach and esplanade to the north of the castle – or its perpendicular offshoot, roughly halfway along, Garoufalídhou.

The originally Byzantine **castle** (access unrestricted), located on a headland between the ferry dock and Romeïkós Yialós, is quite ruinous despite later additions by the Genoese and Ottomans, but warrants a climb at sunset for views over the town, the entire west coast and – in exceptional conditions – over to Mount Áthos, 35 nautical miles west.

The **Archeological Museum** (daily except Mon 8.30am–3pm; 400dr) occupies an old mansion behind Romeïkós Yialós, not far from the site of Bronze-Age Myrina in the suburb of Ríha Nerá. Finds are assiduously labelled in Greek, Italian and English, and the entire premises are exemplary in terms of presentation – the obvious drawback being that the best exhibits have been spirited away to Athens, leaving a collection that's often of scholarly interest and no more. The south ground-floor gallery is mainly devoted to pottery from Polióhni (Polychni); the north wing contains more of the same, plus items from ancient Myrina; while upstairs are galleries of post-Bronze-Age artefacts from Kavírio (Kabireio) and Ifestía (Hephaestia). The star upper-storey exhibits are votive lamps in the shape of **sirens**, found in an Archaic sanctuary at Hephaestia. Seeming rather less vicious than the harpie-like creatures described in Homer, they are identified more invitingly as the "muses of the underworld, creatures of superhuman wisdom, incarnations of a nostalgia for paradise". An entire room is also devoted to metal objects, of which the standouts are gold jewellery and bronze items, both practical (cheese graters) and whimsical (a vulture, a snail).

Arrival, transport and other facilities

The **airport** is 22km east of Mírina, almost at the exact geographic centre of the island, sharing space with an enormous air force base. Límnos is one of the few remaining destinations with a shuttle bus to the *Olympic* town terminal. **Ferries** dock at the southern end of the town, in the shadow of the castle.

The **bus station** is on Platía Eleftheríou Venizélou, at the north end of Kídha. One look at the sparse schedules (only a single daily afternoon departure to most points except more frequently to Kondiás and Moúdhros) will convince you of the need to **rent a vehicle**. Cars, motorbikes and bicycles can be had from either *Myrina Car* (☎0254/24 476), *Petridou Tours* (☎0254/24 787) or the hopefully named *Rent a Reliable Car* (☎0254/24 587); rates for bikes are only slightly above the island norm, but cars are expensive. A motorized two-wheeler is generally enough to explore the coast and the interior, as there are few steep grades but many perilously narrow village streets.

Among three **banks**, the *Ethniki Trapeza*, just off Kídha next to the **OTE**, has an autoteller; the **post office** and *Olympic* airlines terminal are adjacent to each other on Garoufalídhou.

Accommodation

You may be met off the boat with offers of a **room**. Otherwise, try the simple but friendly *Hotel Aktaion* (☎0254/22 258; ③), somewhat noisily located by the harbour, or the secluded *Apollo Pavillion* on Frínis (☎0254/23 712), a cul-de-sac about halfway along Garoufalídhou, with options ranging from pricey hostel-type facilities in the basement (②–③) to large studios on the upper floors (③–④), whose balconies have views of either the castle or the mountains. Romeïkós Yialós has several rooms-only **pensions** installed in its restored houses, though all are plagued to some extent by evening noise from the bars below; best value of the bunch is *Kosmos*, above the namesake pizzeria (☎0254/22 050; ④). One block inland at Sakhtoúri 7, the *Pension Romeïkós Yialos* (☎0254; 23 787; ④) is quieter and a bit less expensive. Just north of Romaïkós Yialós, the areas of Ríha Nerá and Áyios Pandelímonas are likely bets for **self-catering units**; *Poseidon Apartments* (☎0254/23 982 or 51 304; ④) is one possibility, set a little behind the beach, though the best positioned are the hilltop *Afroditi Apartments* at Áyios Pandelímonas (☎0254/23 489; ⑤). Finally, the *Akti Myrina* (☎0254/22 310; winter ☎01/41 37 907) is a self-contained, luxury complex of 110 wood-and-stone bungalows at the north end of Romeïkós Yialós, with all conceivable diversions and comforts at hand. It's horribly expensive, but costs considerably less if booked through a British tour operator.

There's **no official campsite** on Límnos, though Greek caravanners and campers tend to congregate at the north end of Avlónas and Platí beaches (see opposite for accounts).

Eating and drinking

About halfway along Kídha, *O Platanos* serves traditional oven food on an atmospheric little square hemmed in by old houses; while *Avra*, on the quay next to the port police, makes a good choice for a pre-ferry meal or an evening grill. This close to the Dardanelles and its seasonal migrations of fish, **seafood** is excellent on Límnos; accordingly there are no less than five tavernas arrayed around the little fishing port. There's little between them, and in any case all the proprietors (and proprietresses) are related by blood or marriage, though *O Glaros* at the far end is considered the best – and works out slightly more expensive.

Not too surprisingly given the twee setting, the restaurants and bars along Romeïkós Yialós are pretty poor value except for a drink in sight of the nocturnally illuminated castle. For **beachside eating**, it's better to walk further north to *Iy Tzitzifies* with its tree-shaded tables. Finally, worth a mention – though not a taverna – is an unusual **shop** next to *O Platanos* in the bazaar, devoted to top-grade Cretan products such as wine, honey, oil and spices.

Western Límnos

As town beaches go, Romeïkós Yialós is not at all bad, but if you're looking for more pristine conditions strike out further north, past *Akti Myrina*, to the beach at **Avlónas**, unspoiled except for a new luxury complex flanking it on the south. Some 6km from town you work your way through **KÁSPAKAS**, its north-facing houses in pretty, tiled tiers, before plunging down to **Áyios Ioánnis**. Here, the island's unusual taverna features seating in the shade of a volcanic outcrop, with a sandy beach stretching beyond.

PLATÍ, 2km southeast of Mírina, is a village of some character – athough since it becomes very busy at night, rooms here are a bad proposition. However, you'll find an excellent and popular *ouzerí* on the smaller *platía*, the *Zimbabwe*, where the quality of the food (and the prices) belie its humble appearance. The long and sandy **beach**, 700m below, proves popular and usually jellyfish-free; except for the luxury compound at the south end, the area is still resolutely rural, with sheep parading to and fro at dawn and dusk. In the middle of the beach, the low-rise *Plati Beach Hotel* (☎0254/23 583; ④) has an enviable position; there are also scattered rooms available, like those behind *Tzimis Taverna* (☎0254/24 142; ③). More expensively, both for rooms and food, there's the poolside bar/restaurant attached to the tastefully landscaped *Villa Afroditi* (☎0254/23 141 or 24 795; winter ☎01/96 41 910; ⑤), which offers what could be the best buffet breakfast in Greece.

THÁNOS, roughly 2km to the southeast, is little more than a bigger version of Platí village, with only a few tavernas and rooms in evidence; **Paralía Thánous**, a rough track ride below the village, is perhaps the most scenic of the southwestern beaches, with two tavernas, one (*O Nikos*) renting studio-apartments (☎0254/22 787; ③). Beyond Thános, the road curls over to the enormous beach at **Áyios Pávlos** (Nevgátis), flanked by weird volcanic crags on the west and reckoned to be the island's best.

The closest amenities – such as they are – lie 3km further along (11km from Mírina) at **KONDIÁS**, the island's third largest settlement, cradled between two hills tufted with Limnos' only pine forest. Stone-built, red-tiled houses combine with the setting to make Kondiás the most attractive inland village, though facilities are limited to a few noisy **rooms** above one of two *kafenía*. **Eating** is better at the two simple tavernas of **Dhiapóri**, 2km east, the shore annexe of Kondiás; the beach is unappealing, with the main interest lent by the narrow isthmus dividing the bays of Kondiás and Moúdhros.

Eastern Límnos

The shores of **Moúdhros bay**, glimpsed south of the trans-island road, are muddy and best avoided; the bay itself enjoyed considerable importance during World War I, including Allied acceptance of the Ottoman surrender aboard the British warship *HMS Agamemnon* on October 30, 1918. The port of **MOÚDHROS**, the second largest town on Límnos, is a dreary place, with only a once-weekly ferry to Samothráki and a wonderful kitsch church to recommend it. Yet there are three **hotels** here, including *Toh Kyma* (✆0254/71 333; ⑤) and *Blue Bay* (✆0254/71 041; ④), both with **tavernas**, at the harbour; and some **rooms** just outside the town on the main paved road to Roussopoúli (✆0254/71 470 or 71 422; ③), all of use as bases for visiting the archeological sites and beaches of eastern Límnos.

A little further along the Roussopoúli road, you unexpectedly pass an **Allied military cemetery** (unlocked) maintained by the Commonwealth War Graves Commission, its neat lawns and rows of white headstones incongruous in such parched surroundings. In 1915, Moúdhros Bay was the principal base for the disastrous Gallipoli campaign. Of the 36,000 Allied dead, 887 are buried here, with 348 more at another graveyard near Portianós – mainly battle casualties who died after having been evacuated to the base hospital at Moúdhros.

Indications of the most advanced Neolithic civilization in the Aegean have been unearthed at **Polióhni (Polyochni)**, 3km by dirt track from the gully-hidden village of **KAMÍNIA** (7km east of Moúdhros; two simple grill-tavernas). Since the 1930s, Italian excavations have uncovered four layers of settlement, the oldest from late in the fourth millennium BC, pre-dating Troy on the Turkish coast opposite; the town met a sudden, violent end from war or earthquake in about 2100 BC. The actual **ruins** (9.30am–5.30pm daily; free) are of essentially specialist interest, though a *bouleuterion* (assembly hall) with bench seating, a mansion and the landward fortifications are labelled. During August and September the Italian excavators are about, and if they are free to show you around the place may become that much more interesting. The site occupies a bluff overlooking a long, narrow rock-and-sand beach flanked by stream valleys, the mouth of one of these comprising the old port.

Ifestía and Kavírio, the other significant ancient sites on Límnos, are most easily reached via the village of Kondopoúli, 7km northeast of Moúdhros. Both sites are rather remote, and only feasible to visit if you have your own transport.

Ifestía (Hephaestia), in Classical times the most important city on the island, took its name from Hephaistos, god of fire and metal-working. According to legend, Hephaistos landed on Límnos after being hurled from Mount Olympus by Zeus, the fall leaving him lame forever. Much of the site (daily 9.30am–3.30pm; free) remains unexcavated, but there are scant remains of a theatre and a temple dedicated to the god.

Kavírio (Kabireio), on the opposite shore of Tigáni Bay from Ifestía, is a little more evocative. The **ruins** (daily 9.30am–3.30pm; free) are those of a sanctuary connected with the cult of the Kabiroi on Samothraki (see p.302), although the site on Límnos is probably older. Little survives other than the groundplan, but the setting is undeniably impressive. Eleven column stumps stake out a stoa, behind eight spots marked as column bases in the main *telestirio* or shrine where the cult mysteries took place. More engaging, perhaps, is a nearby sea grotto identified as the Homeric **Spiliá tou Filoktíti**, where the Trojan war hero Philoctetes was abandoned by his comrades-in-arms until his stinking, gangrenous leg had healed. The cave has landward access as well, via the steps leading down from the caretaker's sunshade.

The east-coast beach at **Kéros**, 4km by dirt road below **KALLIÓPI** (two snack bar/tavernas), in turn 2km from Kondopoúli, is one of the best on the island. A long stretch of sand with dunes and shallow water, it attracts a number of Greek tourists and Germans with camper vans and windsurfers, but is large enough to remain uncrowded. By contrast, mediocre beaches near the village of **PLÁKA** at the northeastern tip of the island, are not worth the extra effort, and the adjacent hot springs appearing on some maps are actually warm mud baths.

Áyios Efstrátios (Aï Strátis)

Áyios Efstrátios is without doubt one of the most isolated islands in the Aegean. Historically, the only outsiders to stay here have been those who were compelled to do so – it served as a place of exile for political prisoners under both the Metaxas regime of the 1930s and the various right-wing governments that followed the civil war. It's still unusual for travellers to show up on the island, and, if you do, you're sure to be asked why you came.

You may well ask yourself the same question, for **ÁYIOS EFSTRÁTIOS** village – the only habitation on the island – is one of the ugliest in Greece. Devastated by an earthquake in 1967, it was grimly rebuilt as rows of concrete prefabs, attended by a concrete church and an underused shopping centre. The remains of the old village – some two dozen houses which escaped damage – overlook the modern village from a neighbouring hillside. Sadly, most of the destruction was caused by army bulldozers rather than the earthquake: the re-building contract went to a company with junta connections, and the islanders were prevented from returning to their homes, although many could have been repaired. All in all, the village constitutes a sad monument to the corruption of the junta years. If you're curious, there's an old photograph of the village, taken before the earthquake, in the *kafenío* by the port.

Architecture apart, Áyios Efstrátios still functions as a very traditional fishing and farming community, with the prefabs set at the mouth of a wooded stream valley draining to the harbour beach. Tourist amenities consist of just two very basic **tavernas** and a single **pension** in one of the surviving old houses, which is likely to be full in the summer, so call in advance (☎0254/93 202; ②). Nobody will object, however, if you **camp** at the far end of the town beach.

As you walk away from the village – there are hardly any cars and no real roads – things improve rapidly. The landscape, dry hills and valleys scattered with a surprising number of oak trees, is deserted apart from wild rabbits, sheep, an occasional shepherd, and some good beaches where you can camp in desert-island isolation – perhaps the only reason you're likely to visit Áyios Evstrátios. **Alonítsi**, on the north coast, a ninety-minute walk from the village following a track up the north side of the valley, is a two-kilometre stretch of sand with rolling breakers and views across to Límnos.

A little to the south of the village, there's a series of greyish sand beaches, most with wells and drinkable water, although with few proper paths in this part of the island, getting to them can be something of a scramble. **Lidharío**, at the end of an attractive wooded valley, is the first worthwhile beach, but again, it's a ninety-minute walk, unless you can persuade a fisherman to take you by boat. Some of the caves around the coast are home to the rare Mediterranean monk seal, but you're unlikely to see one.

Ferries between Límnos and Kavála to either Rafína, Kími or Áyios Konstandínos call at Áyios Efstrátios every two or three days throughout the year; in summer, there's also a *kaíki* from Límnos twice a week. Despite harbour improvements, it is still a very exposed anchorage, and in bad weather you could end up stranded here far longer than you bargained for.

Samothráki (Samothrace)

After Thíra, **Samothráki** has the most dramatic profile of all the Greek islands. Originally colonized by immigrants from Sámos (hence the name), it rises abruptly from the sea in a dark mass of granite, culminating in 1600-metre Mount Fengári. Seafarers have always been guided by its imposing outline, and in legend its summit provided a vantage point for Poseidon to watch over the siege of Troy. The forbidding coastline provides no natural anchorage, and landing is still very much subject to the vagaries of the wind. Yet despite these difficulties, for over a millennium pilgrims journeyed to the island to visit the **Sanctuary of the Great Gods** and to be initiated into its mysteries. The Sanctuary is still the outstanding attraction of the island, which, home to under 3000 people and too remote for most tourists (although July and August can be busy), combines an earthy simplicity with its natural grandeur.

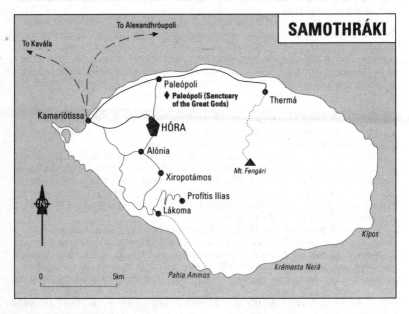

Kamariótissa and Hóra

Ferries and the new hydrofoils dock at the little port of **KAMARIÓTISSA**, where there are three hotels on the seafront and numerous **rooms** for rent in the maze of streets behind. Turning left as you step ashore, the first – and cheapest – hotel is the homely *Kyma* (☎0551/41 263; ②–③), which also has a good, family-run restaurant. The seafront is lined with **tavernas**, the best of which are the *Klimataria* and *Horizon*, which, with a couple of nearby bars and discos, constitute the island's only real nightlife. There's a **bank** and *Niki Tours* (☎0551/41 465), which rents out **motorbikes and mopeds**, and can also help with accommodation. Otherwise, Kamariótissa isn't a picturesque or particularly interesting village, and you're unlikely to want to stay long.

Buses run hourly in season (but only twice weekly in winter) along the north coast to Thermá via Palaeópoli (the site of the Sanctuary) and Kariotes, or inland to **HÓRA**, the only other village of any size, an attractive community of whitewashed Thracian-style houses overshadowed by the western flanks of Mount Fengári and the ruins of a Byzantine fort. Hóra has no accommodation, but there are two popular **tavernas** with fine views down the valley and out to sea. There's also another bank, the **post office**, the **OTE** branch and **tourist police** (☎0551/41 203).

The Sanctuary of the Great Gods

A track leads north from Hóra to the hamlet of Paleópoli (see below), and, in a stony ravine between it and the plunging, northeasternmost ridgeline of Mount Fengári, lie the remains of the **Sanctuary of the Great Gods**. From the late Bronze Age to the last years of the Roman occupation, the mysteries and sacrifices of the cult of the Great Gods were performed on Samothráki. The island was the spiritual focus of the northern Aegean, and its importance in the ancient world was comparable (although certainly secondary) to that of the Mysteries of Eleusis.

The religion of the Great Gods revolved around a hierarchy of ancient Thracian fertility figures: the Great Mother, a subordinate male deity known as Kadmilos, and the potent and ominous twin demons, the *Kabiroi*. When the Samian colonists arrived (traditionally c700 BC) they simply syncretized the resident deities with their own – the Great Mother became Demeter, her consort Hermes, and the *Kabiroi* were fused interchangeably with the *Dioskouroi*. Around the nucleus of a sacred precinct the newcomers made the beginnings of what is now the Sanctuary.

The mysteries of the cult were never explicitly recorded, since ancient writers feared incurring the wrath of the *Kabiroi*, but it has been established that two levels of initiation were involved. Incredibly, both ceremonies, in direct opposition to the elitism of Eleusis, were open to all comers, including women and slaves. The lower level of initiation may, as is speculated at Eleusis, have involved a ritual simulation of the life, death and rebirth cycle; in any case, it's known that it ended with joyous feasting and it can be conjectured, since so many clay torches have been found, that it took place at night by their light. The higher level of initiation carried the unusual requirement of a moral standard (the connection of theology with morality – so strong in the later Judeo-Christian tradition – was rarely made at all by the early Greeks). This second level involved a full confession followed by absolution and baptism in bull's blood.

The site

The **site** (daily except Mon 8.30am–3pm; 400dr) is well labelled, simple to grasp and strongly evokes its proud past. It's a good idea to visit the **museum** (open same hours as the site, admission with the same ticket) first, where sections of the buildings have been reconstructed and arranged with friezes and statues to give you an idea of their original scale. An excellent guide by Karl Lehmann – the American site excavator – is on sale.

The first structure you come to is the **Anaktoron**, the hall of initiation for the first level of the mysteries, dating in its present form from Roman times. Its inner sanctum was marked by a warning *stele* (now in the museum) and at the southeast corner you can make out the libation pit. Next to it is the **Arsinoeion**, the largest circular ancient building known in Greece. Within its rotunda are the walls of a double precinct (fourth century BC) where a rock altar, the earliest preserved ruin on the site, has been uncovered. A little further on, on the same side of the path, you come to the **Temenos**, a rectangular area open to the sky where the feasting probably took place, and, edging its rear corner, the conspicuous **Hieron**. Five columns and an architrave of the facade of this large Doric edifice which hosted the higher level of initiation have been erected; dating in part from the fourth century BC, it was heavily restored in Roman times. Its stone steps have been replaced by modern blocks but the Roman benches for spectators remain in situ, along with the sacred stones where confession was heard.

To the west of the path you can just discern the outline of the **theatre**, and above it on a ridge is the **Nike fountain**, famous for the exquisitely sculpted marble centrepiece – the *Winged Victory of Samothrace* – which once stood breasting the wind at the prow of a marble ship. It was discovered in 1863 by the French and carried off to the Louvre, with a copy belatedly forwarded to the local museum. Higher up along the ridge, opposite the rotunda, is an elaborate medieval fortification made entirely of antique material. Finally, on the hill across the river stands a monumental **gateway** dedicated to the Great Gods by Ptolemy II; many of its blocks lie scattered across the ravine.

The rest of the island

The only accommodation near the site itself is in the hamlet of **PALEÓPOLI**, where the old and basic *Xenia Hotel* (☎0551/41 166; ③–④) tries hard to compete with the *Kastro Hotel* (☎0551/41 001; ⑥), which comes with pool and restaurant. Four kilometres east, near Kariotes, is the much smaller *Elektra* (☎0551/98 243; ④–⑤), though despite the family feel here, the lack of a restaurant means you may prefer to be nearer the action – such as it is – in **THÉRMA** (Loutrá), a further 2km east.

With its running streams, plane trees and namesake hot springs, Thérma is one of the better places to stay on Samothráki, although it's packed in July and August (mainly with an odd mixture of German hippies and elderly Greeks here to take the waters). It's a rather dispersed place, with a small harbour under construction to accommodate the ferries and recently introduced hydrofoils – up in the woods, are the well-established *Kaviros Hotel* (☎0551/98 277; ⑤), open May to October, and – 700m from the beach – the bungalows of the *Mariva Hotel* (☎0551/98 258; ④). The nearby *Restaurant Iphestos* is lively and popular; try the spit-roast goat or chicken. The *Shelter* café-pub, in the old schoolhouse, attracts a younger crowd.

Beyond Thérma, on the wooded coastline, are two municipal **campsites**, open June to September. The first, 1500m from the village, although large, has no facilities except toilets; the second, 2km from the village, is more expensive but has hot water, electricity, a small shop, restaurant and bar. The bus from Kamariótissa passes both sites.

The lush countryside beyond Thérma is fine for walking, and the more ambitious can climb the highest mountain in the Aegean, **Mount Fengári** (the Mountain of the Moon, also known as *Sáos*), in a six-to-eight hour round trip. (You could also start from Horá but the route is more difficult.) From the top, a clear day permits views from the Trojan plain in the east to Mount Áthos in the west.

Beaches on Samothráki's north shore are uniformly pebbly and exposed; for better ones head for the warmer south flank of the island. A couple of daily buses go as far as **PROFÍTIS ILÍAS**, an attractive hill village with good tavernas but no place to stay, via Lákoma, where you alight for the beautiful two-hour walk to **Pahiá Ámmos**, an 800-metre sandy beach with a hidden freshwater spring at its eastern end. The nearest supplies are at **LÁKOMA**, but this doesn't deter big summer crowds who also arrive by excursion *kaíki*. These also continue past the Krémasta Nerá coastal waterfalls to **Kípos**, another good sandy beach with fresh water nearby, at the extreme southeast tip of the island.

Thássos

Just twelve kilometres from the mainland, **Thássos** has long been a popular resort for northern Greeks, and in recent years has been attracting considerable numbers of foreign tourists. Without being spectacular, it's a very beautiful island, its almost circular area covered in gentle slopes of pine, olive and chestnut that rise to a mountainous backbone and plunge to a line of good sandy beaches. It's by no means unspoiled, but visitors tend to be spread over six or seven fair-sized villages as well as the two main

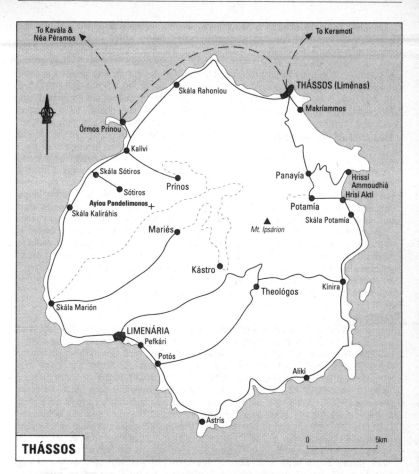

To Kavála &
Néa Péramos

To Keramotí

Skála Rahoníou

THÁSSOS (Liménas)

Makríammos

Órmos Prínou

Kalívi

Skála Sótiros

Sótiros

Prínos

Panayía

Hrissí
Ammoudhiá
Hrisi Aktí

Ayíou Pandelímonos

Skála Kaliráhis

Potamía

Potamía

Skála Potamía

Mariés

Mt. Ipsárion

Kástro

Kínira

Theológos

Skála Marión

LIMENÁRIA

Pefkári

Potós

Alikí

Astrís

0   5km

THÁSSOS

towns, so enclaves of bars and discos haven't swamped the ordinary Greek life of marble-quarrying, beekeeping and harvesting nuts, olives or fruit. Beehives often line the roadsides, and local honey can be bought all over the island, as can thick, treacle-like walnut jam. Among the less pleasant wildlife is the ubiquitous mosquito, so come prepared. Also, most of the inland forests were ravaged by fire in 1985, so do heed the many forest-fire prevention warnings and be extra careful if camping.

Thássos Town

THÁSSOS TOWN, or Liménas/Limín as it's also known, is the island capital and nexus of life, though not the main port. Kavála-based ferries usually stop down the coast at Órmos Prínou, but a few each day continue on here – a trip worth making for the pine-clad mountain views. The town, though largely modern, is partly redeemed by its pretty fishing harbour, a popular sand beach just to the east, and the substantial remains of the ancient city which pop up between and above the streets.

Ancient Thássos abounded in mineral wealth, controlled goldmines on the Thracian mainland and had two safe anchorages, assets which ensured prosperity through Classical, Macedonian and Roman rule. The ruins surrounding the modern town – Limín, incidentally, means "the harbour" – show traces from each phase of this development. The main excavated area is the **agora**, the entrance is beside the town **museum** (Tues–Fri 8am–7pm, winter closes at 5pm, Sat & Sun 8.30am–3pm; 400dr), a little way back from the modern harbour. The site is fenced but not always locked and, taking advantage of this, is best seen towards dusk when a calm, slightly misty air often descends. Prominent are two Roman *stoas* but you can also make out shops, monuments, passageways and sanctuaries from the remodelled Classical city. At the far end of the site (away from the sea) a fifth-century BC passageway leads through to an elaborate sanctuary of Artemis, a good stretch of Roman road and a few seats of the *odeion*.

Above the town, roughly in line with the smaller fishing port, steps spiral up to a **Hellenistic theatre**, fabulously positioned above a broad sweep of sea. On the same corner of the headland as the theatre, you can still see the old-fashioned *kaíkia* being built, and gaze across to the uninhabited islet of Thassopoúla. It's possible to **rent boats** from the fishing harbour, self-skippered or not, to take you there and elsewhere.

Beyond the theatre, a path winds on to a **Genoese fort**, constructed out of numerous stones from the ancient acropolis. From here you can follow the circuit of **walls** to a high terrace supporting the foundations of a temple of Apollo and onwards to a small rock-hewn sanctuary of Pan. Below it a precarious, sixth-century BC "secret stairway" descends to the outer rank of walls and back into town. It's a satisfying itinerary, which gives you a good idea of the structure and extent of a fairly typical Classical city.

Practicalities

If you want to stay, there are lots of **hotels and pensions** from which to choose, and plentiful **rooms** to rent, too, though in summer you should take the first thing offered on arrival. If you get the choice, the *Acropolis* on the landward side of the main square (☎0593/22 488; ③–④), is worth seeking out, a traditional house built in 1900. Also recommended is the central, small and friendly *Astir* (☎0593/22 160; ③); the pleasant *Diamanto* (☎0593/22 622; ②), which is a right turn from the ferry; and the *Hotel Athanaria* (☎0593/22 545; ②), hidden in an orchard – to find this, turn right on leaving the ferry, make for the *Xenia* hotel beyond the end of the quay and just before the *Xenia* turn left (inland) and follow the lane. There's the usual complement of waterfront **tavernas and cafés** and while there's nothing outstanding, you can eat reasonably well if you shop around. In and around the main square, try *Iy Piyi* or *Zorba's*.

Car rental is available from *Thassos Tours* (☎0593/23 250), towards the fishing harbour, or *Thassos Rent-a-Car* (☎0593/22 535) on the main square; **mopeds and motorbikes** from *Thassos Tours* or the widely advertised *Billy's Bikes*. **Bicycles** are also available, though be aware that there's little flat terrain. The **bus station** is on the front, near the ferry mooring. The service is good, with about five buses per day doing the full island circuit in season, and several more to and from different villages, with a bias towards the west coast. The **tourist police** (May–Sept daily 9am–10pm; ☎0593/23 111) are in the police station on the front, near the bus station.

Around the coast

The first beach clockwise from Liménas, **Makriámmos**, is an expensive, limited-access playground for package tourists, and it's best to carry on to **PANAYÍA** or **POTAMIÁ**, two attractive villages situated on a mountainous ledge overlooking Potamiá Bay. Panayía is a bustling and pretty mountain village where life revolves around the central square with its large plane tree and fountain. There are a few souvenir shops, two small **hotels** – the *Helvetia* (☎0593/61 231; ③) and the *Chrysalis* (☎0593/61 979; ④) – and

rooms for rent, but you'll also see sheep and goats being herded through the middle of the village. This is an ideal place for a drink and a meal in the lively evenings, and food tends to be less expensive than elsewhere – try the *Kostas* or *Ethitrio* restaurants. Potamiá has one of the best marked paths up to the 1204-metre summit of **Mount Ipsárion**; and by the lovely church there is a small **art museum** (Tues–Sat 9am–1pm, summer also 6–9pm, Sun 10am–2pm; free).

There are more tavernas, two more hotels and a campsite at the excellent, sandy **Hrissí Ammoudhiá** beach, 4km downhill from Panayía at the north end of the bay. No buses go here but it's easy enough to walk from Panayía (though not with heavy luggage) or cheap enough to get a taxi. Once you get there you can choose between the *Villa Chrysalis* (☎0593/61 979; ③), the hugely expensive *Hotel Dionysus* (☎0593/61 822; ⑥) or the *Golden Beach* **campsite** (☎0593/61 472), the only one on this side of the island. **SKÁLA POTAMIÁS**, at the southern end of the bay, is less attractive with its rocky beach; every building seems to be a souvenir shop, hotel, cafeteria or "rooms to let". Skála's main virtue is the local fishing fleet and the corresponding quality of the seafood restaurants.

KÍNIRA is a tiny hamlet further south with a moderate beach, a couple of grocery stores and hotels – cheapest is the *Villa Athina* (☎0593/41 214; ②–③) – a few rooms and a lot of beehives. **Paradise Beach**, nicely situated, sandy, and mainly nudist, lies 1km south, and there are more beautiful and deserted coves beyond in the same direction if you're willing to explore.

The south-facing coast of Thássos has most of the island's best beaches. **Aliki** (32km from Thássos Town) faces a double bay which almost pinches off a headland. The mixed sand-and-pebble spit gets too popular for its own good in high season, but the water is crystal-clear and the four beachside tavernas offer good food. The roadside hamlet here is at least worth a stopover and there are several **rooms** to rent; *Suzanna's*, above the road, are clean, basic and cheap. Nearby, on the headland, were ancient marble quarries which supplied the Greek city-states and later the Romans, and on the western cove the pillars of a Doric sanctuary are still visible. It is possible to walk away from the crowds and find some excellent spots for snorkelling, sunbathing and picnics, using the slabs of marble that are scattered around the headland, both above and below the waterline; these have occasionally been eroded into convenient bathtub shapes.

At the extreme south tip of Thássos, **ASTRÍS** is a quiet village with some rooms, a sandy beach, and a couple of restaurants, but the best-appointed local resort is **Potós**, where there are two modest **hotels**, the *Io* (☎0593/51 216; ②) and *Katerina* (☎0593/51 345; ②), and a fine one-kilometre sandy beach facing the sunset. **Pefkári**, 1km west, is essentially an annexe of Potós but the manicured sand has been overwhelmed by the touristic development behind.

As an alternative to Thássos Town you can base yourself in the marginally quieter and quainter **LIMENÁRIA**, the island's second town, built to house German mining executives brought in by the Turks at the turn of the century. Their remaining mansions lend some distinctive character, but this apart it's a rather ordinary tourist resort, handy mainly for its **banks**, **post office** and **OTE** station. There are a few **hotels**, the best of which is the *Menel* (☎0593/51 396; ③), and numerous **rooms**, so you'll eventually find something affordable and vacant. There's also a **campsite** between Limenária and Pefkári: the *Pefkari* (☎0593/51 190; April–Sept).

Continuing clockwise from Limenária to Thássos town, the bus service is more frequent, but there's progressively less to stop off for. The various *skáles* (coastal annexes of villages built inland during piratic ages) such as Skála Marión, Skála Kaliráhis and Skála Sotíros, are bleak, straggly and windy, uninviting even on the rare occasions when the shore is sandy.

ÓRMOS PRÍNOU has little to recommend it, other than the ferry connections to Kavála. Buses are usually timed to coincide with the ferries, but if you want to stay, there are numerous **rooms**, quayside **tavernas** and an EOT **campsite** (☎0593/71 171; May–Sept). There's a better **campsite** near **SKÁLA RAHONÍOU**, between here and Thássos Town (though the beach is mediocre), as well as rooms, hotels and fish restaurants.

The interior

Few people get around to exploring inland Thássos, but there are several worthwhile rambles around the hill villages besides the aforementioned walk up Mount Ipsárion from Potamiá. From Potós you can hitch or take a bus up to **THEOLÓGOS**, a linear community of old houses founded by refugees from Constantinople, which was the island's capital under the Turks (the last of whom only departed after 1923). It has a small square with a couple of cafés under a tree, and a few **rooms** are available (though none are advertised) – there are some above one of the cafés and the baker on the square has rooms near the *Restaurant Lambiris*.

From Theológos you can walk down to Kínira on the east coast on a gravel jeep track, or take your chances with narrower trails leading north through whatever remains of the forest. The most interesting return to Potós involves a westward trek, on a variety of surfaces, to **KÁSTRO**, the most naturally fortified of the anti-pirate redoubts. Thirty houses and a church surround a rocky pinnacle which is a sheer drop on three sides; summer occupation is becoming the rule after total abandonment in the last century. You could perhaps be put up for the night – there's one taverna, one phone, no power – but without transport you will have to walk or hitch 15km down a dirt road to Limenária.

From Kalívi on the west coast a minor road leads 4km up to **PRÍNOS**, start of the signposted, one-hour walk up to Ayíou Pandelímonos nunnery. From there you can press on to **SOTÍROS**, an untouched old village to the west, or take the much more confusing way (on lumber roads) to **MARIÉS** in the direction of the Kástro. You can often hitch down from the inland villages with people who've been tending their beehives, but take food along for the day – there are often no facilities at all.

travel details

To simplify the lists that follow we've excluded a regular sailing of the *NEL* company, which once a week runs a ferry in each direction, usually the *Alcaeos*, linking Thessaloníki or Kavála with Límnos, Áyios Efstrátios, Lésvos, Híos, Sámos and Pátmos. Each one-way trip takes about 24 hours – exact days subject to change according to season.

SÁMOS (Vathí) 3–7 weekly to Ikaría, Páros, Pireás (14hr); 2–3 weekly to Híos and Náxos; 1–2 weekly to Foúrni, Míkonos, Tínos, Síros.

SÁMOS (Karlóvassi) As for Vathí, plus 2 weekly *kaíki* departures, usually early Mon and Thurs afternoon, to Foúrni.

SÁMOS (Pithagório) 1–2 weekly to Foúrni, Ikaría, Pátmos; 1–2 weekly (usually Wed and Sun afternoon) to Agathónissi, Lipsí, Pátmos, Léros, Kálimnos, with onward connections to all other Dodecanese (see the *Nissos Kalimnos* ferry summary in *The Dodecanese* chapter). Also expensive excursion *kaíkia* daily in season to Pátmos.

IKARÍA 3–7 weekly to Sámos (both northern ports), Páros and Pireás (at least 2 weekly services via Évdhilos year-round); 2–3 weekly to Náxos; 1–2 weekly to Híos, Foúrni, Pátmos, Míkonos, Tínos, Síros; 4–5 weekly, from Áyios Kírikos, to Foúrni.

FOÚRNI 1–2 weekly ferries, usually Wed or Sun, to Sámos (northern ports), Páros and Pireás; smaller ferries twice weekly (often Tues and Fri) to Sámos (Pithagório), Ikaría, Pátmos, Híos; morning *kaíki* to Ikaría, Mon, Wed, Fri, Sun, and on Sat only by demand; twice weekly (usually Mon and Thur) morning *kaíki* to Karlóvassi (Sámos).

HÍOS 4–7 weekly to Pireás (10hr) and Lésvos (3hr 30min); 3 weekly to Límnos and Thessaloníki; 2–3 weekly to Sámos (5hr); 1–2 weekly to Foúrni and Pátmos; 1 weekly to Rafína, Psará, Áyios Efstrátios, Kavála. Daily *kaíki* to Inoússes; 3 weekly to Psará (4hr), 2 weekly on different days from Limniá to Psará (2hr).

LÉSVOS 4–13 weekly to Pireás (12hr direct, 14hr via Híos); 4–9 weekly to Híos (3hr 30min); 4 weekly to Límnos (7hr); 3 weekly to Thessaloníki (17hr); 2 weekly to Áyios Efstrátios (4hr 30min); 1 weekly to Kavála (15hr) and Rafína.

LÍMNOS 5 weekly to Kavála, Lésvos, Híos, Pireás; 3 weekly to Thessaloníki, Áyios Efstrátios and Rafína; 1 weekly to most of the Sporades, Rafína, and either Kími (Évvia) or Áyios Konstandínos (Thessaly). Also a summer-only *kaíki* to Áyios Efstrátios twice weekly.

ÁYIOS EFSTRÁTIOS 3 weekly to Límnos, Rafína; 2 weekly to Kavála, Mitilíni, Híos; 1 weekly to Skíros.

SAMOTHRÁKI 2–5 daily ferries to/from Alexandhroúpoli (2hr) in season, dropping to 5–6 weekly out of season. Also a connection with Moúdhros on Límnos once a week throughout the year (originating in Alexandhroúpoli), and with Kavála (and therefore other North Aegean islands) once a week, currently on Fri, returning on Sat.

THÁSSOS 7–15 ferries daily (depending on season) between Kavála and Órmos Prínou (1hr), with a few of these services extending to Liménas. Similar frequencies between Liménas and Keramotí (45min). No direct connections with any other island; usually you must travel via Kavála.

Hydrofoils

Two companies – *Ilio Lines* and *Gianmar* – divide the **hydrofoil** trade between them in the east Aegean. *Gianmar* craft are based on Híos, operating almost-daily morning runs to Sámos, Ikaría and Pátmos to the south, Lésvos (Plomári) and Límnos to the north, with occasional trips to Psará. *Ilio Lines* link Sámos (Vathí and/or Pithagório) with Pátmos, Lipsí, Léros, Kálimnos and Kós (in the Dodecanese) daily in season; Lésvos and Híos five times weekly; and Ikaría, Foúrni, Agathónissa (Dodecanese) and Alexandhroúpoli (Thrace) twice weekly. Many of the craft are actually based on Lésvos, from where there are services 6 weekly (indirectly) to

Alexandhroúpoli, 5 weekly to Híos and Sámos (Vathí), 2 weekly to Kavála and 1 weekly to Límnos. All routes reverse themselves exactly on the return leg, so frequencies between all points are the same in each direction.

In addition to the domestic lines, there is also an **international hydrofoil** service twice daily (in theory), June–Sept between Vathí (Sámos) and Kusadaşı (Turkey), and several times weekly between Híos and Çeşme (Turkey). Fares are currently much the same as for a conventional ferry (see below).

International ferries

Vathí (Sámos)–Kusadaşı (Turkey) At least 1 daily, late April to late October; otherwise a Turkish boat only by demand in winter, usually on Fri or Sat. Morning Greek boat (passengers only), afternoon Turkish boats (usually 2 in season – they take 2 cars apiece). Rates are £32/US$48 one way including taxes on both the Greek and Turkish sides, £41/$61 return all-in; no day return rate. Small cars £30/$45 one way. Journey time 1hr 30min. Also regular (3–4 weekly) services in season from **Pithagório**.

Híos–Çeşme (Turkey) 2–12 boats weekly, depending on season. Thurs night and Sat morning services tend to run year-round. Rates are £31/$47 one-way, £40/$60 return, including Greek taxes; no Turkish taxes. Small cars £36/$54 each way. Journey time 45min.

Mitilíni (Lésvos)–Ayvalık (Turkey) 5–9 weekly in season; winter link unreliable. The current rates are about £25/$38 one way, £33/$49 return including Greek taxes; no Turkish tax on this crossing. Small cars cost £30/$45 each way. Journey time 1hr 30min. Once weekly in high season there is also a link with **Dikili**, a few kilometres south of Ayvalık (same prices and crossing time).

Flights

Sámos–Athens (3–4 daily; 1hr)
Híos–Athens (4–5 daily; 50min)
Lésvos–Athens (3–4 daily; 45min)
Lésvos–Thessaloníki (10 weekly; 1hr 10min)
Límnos–Athens (2–3 daily; 1hr)
Límnos–Lésvos (1 daily; 40min)
Límnos–Thessaloníki (1 daily; 50min)

CHAPTER SIX

THE SPORADES AND ÉVVIA

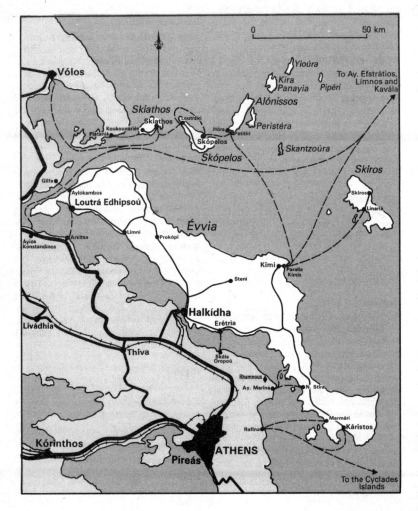

The three northern **Sporades**, Skíathos, Skópelos and Alónissos, are scattered (as their Greek name suggests) head-to-tail, just off the mainland, their mountainous terrain betraying their origin as extensions of Mount Pelion in Thessaly. They're archetypal holiday islands, with a wide selection of good beaches, transparent waters and thick, pine forests. They are all very busy in season, and both Skíathos and Skópelos have sacrificed their entire character to tourism. None has any prominent historical sites, nor much history until the Middle Ages – Skíathos Town is nineteenth century, while the oldest area of Skópelos sits within its thirteenth-century *kástro*. There is, therefore, no pressure to do much sightseeing.

Skíathos has the best beaches, and is still the busiest island in the group, though these days **Skópelos** gets very crowded, too. **Alónissos** is the quietest of the three, and has the wildest scenery, but it's only really worth a visit if you stay outside the ugly, post-earthquake main town. **Skíros**, further southeast, retains more of its traditional culture than the other three islands, though development is now well under way. The main town doesn't yet feel like a resort, but is not uncommercialized either. Unlike the other three islands, the only good beaches are those close to the main town. To the south, the huge island of **Évvia** (or Euboea) runs for 150km alongside the mainland. It is one of the more attractive Greek islands, with a forested mountain spine and a rugged, largely undeveloped coast. Perhaps because it lacks any real island feel or identity due to its proximity to the mainland, Évvia is explored by few foreign tourists. Athenians, in contrast, visit in force, unbothered by such scruples and attracted to half a dozen or so major resorts.

The Sporades are well connected by bus and ferry both with Athens (via Áyios Konstantínos or Kími) and with Vólos, and it's easy to island-hop in the northern group. The only ferry connection to Skíros is from Kími, plus a *Flying Dolphin* service in summer from Vólos via the other Sporades. Évvia is linked to the mainland by a bridge at its capital Halkídha, and by a series of shuttle-ferries.

Skíathos

The commercialization of **Skíathos** is legendary among foreigners and Greeks – it's a close fourth to that of Corfu, Míkonos and Rhodes. But if you've some time to spare, or a gregarious nature, you might still break your journey here in order to sample the best, if most overcrowded, **beaches** in the Sporades. Along the south and southeast coasts, the road serves an almost unbroken line of concrete villas, hotels and restaurants, and although this isn't enough to take away the island's natural beauty, it makes it difficult to

---

ROOM PRICE SCALES

All establishments in this book have been price-graded according to the scale outlined below. The rates quoted represent the cheapest available room in high season; all are prices for a double room, except for category ①, which are per person rates. Out of season, rates can drop by up to fifty percent, especially if you negotiate rates for a stay of three or more nights. Single rooms, where available, cost around seventy percent of the price of a double.

Rented private rooms on the islands usually fall into the ② or ③ categories, depending on their location and facilities, and the season; a few in the ④ category are more like plush self-catering apartments. They are not generally available from late October through the beginning of April, when only hotels tend to remain open.

① 1400–2000dr (£4–5.50/US$6–8.50) ④ 8000–12000dr (£22–33/US$33–50)
② 4000–6000dr (£11–16.50/US$17–25) ⑤ 12000–16000dr (£33–44/US$50–66)
③ 6000–8000dr (£16.50–22/US$25–33) ⑥ 16000dr (£44/US$66) and upwards
For more accommodation details, see pp.32–34.

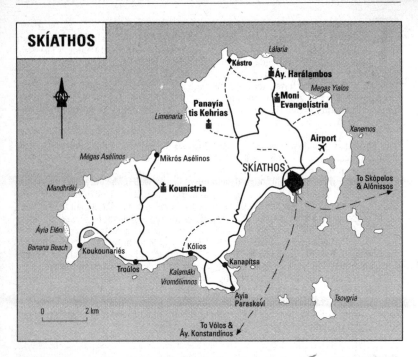

find anything unspoilt or particularly Greek about it all. As almost the entire population lives in Skíathos Town, a little walking soon pays off. However, camping outside official sites is strongly discouraged, since summer turns the dry pine-needles to tinder, and you should be aware of the risk of fire on each of the Sporades islands.

Skíathos Town

SKÍATHOS Town, where the ferries dock, looks great from a distance, but as you approach, the tourist development becomes all too apparent. Even the little offshore **Boúrtzi fortress**, surrounded by crumbling segments of Venetian wall, houses a taverna, and the old quarters (on the slopes away from Alexándhrou Papadhiamándi street) are in danger of being overwhelmed by ranks of hotels, restaurants and "English" pubs. Skíathos is very like Corfu – a tourist sprawl around the coast, and a very busy *hóra*.

As for sights, there aren't many, apart from the excellent **Galerie Varsakis** (open usual shop hours), near the fishing port on Platía Tríon Ierarhón. This is one of the best folklore displays in Greece, and many of the older items on display would do the Benaki Museum proud; Mr Varsakis neither expects, nor wants, to sell the more expensive of these, which include antique textiles, handicrafts and jewellery.

Arrival, transport and other facilities

Buses and **taxis** ply from near the **ferry harbour**. To Koukounariés, the bus is the cheapest option; it runs roughly every thirty minutes in summer and the last one returns at 12.30am. Also in summer, *Aselinos Tours* run a private bus to Asélinos beach once a day, leaving at 11am from outside their office, close to the official bus stop and returning at 4.30pm (300dr). If shared among a few people, taxis should work out to be only a little more expensive – though ask the fare first.

A large number of competing **rental outlets** in town, most on the front behind the ferry harbour, offer bicycles, mopeds, motorbikes, cars and motorboats. The lowest priced, beach buggy-type cars go for around 12,000dr a day, motorboats for 15,000dr a day; fuel and insurance are extra. At a slower pace, several travel agents organize "round the island" **mule trips** (5200dr a day), or there's horse riding at the *Pinewood Riding Club* on the road to Tróulos to Mégas Asélinos, 1km north of the junction.

Most other facilities are on Alexándhrou Papadhiamándi, including the **OTE**, **post office**, **banks** and *Olympic Airways* office.

Accommodation

Most of the island's accommodation is in Skíathos Town. The few reasonably priced **hotels** or **pensions** will be full in season, though you can usually find a room, albeit slightly more expensively than on most islands. At other times, supply exceeds demand and you can find very cheap **rooms** with a little bargaining. There is no official accommodation bureau but there are several tourist agencies. For an honest and helpful approach, try Dimitris Mathinos, a former sea captain with an office at the bottom of Alexándhrou Papadhiamándi, though avoid lodgings in the flatlands to the north as they tend to be noisy. Also ask at the *Art Café* (opposite the ferry gates), which serves a good breakfast and runs a network of good **pensions**, including *Dina Rooms* (☎0427/21 508; ③), *Adonis Stamelos Rooms* (☎0427/22 962; ④) and the *Pension Kvouli* (☎0427/21 082; rooms ④, maisonettes ⑤). The best location for accommodation is beyond the *Stamatis* taverna, overlooking the fishing harbour. There's another concentration of good rooms on Kapodhistríou 14. If you're looking for more **upmarket accommodation** in high season – say the *Alkyon Hotel*, on the seafront at the commercial port end (☎0427/37 002; ⑥), or the *Meltemi Hotel*, on the front near the taxi rank (☎0427/21 593; ⑥) – try and book a season ahead, or a month ahead for April, May and October.

The island now has four official **campsites** – at Koliós, Koukounariés, Asélinos and Xanémos beach. Koliós is okay, but Koukounariés and Asélinos are probably the best choices. Xanémos beach is 3km northeast of Skíathos Town, right next to the airport runway, and, apart from being within walking distance of the town, has little to recommend it.

Eating, drinking and nightlife

You're spoilt for choice for **eating places**, but nothing's particularly cheap apart from the few burger/*gyros* bars. One of the best and cheapest tavernas is *Zorba's*, opposite the taxi rank, while *Toh Trigono*, on Alexándhrou Papadhiamándi, does good pasta. If you fancy a change, there's an Italian restaurant, *La Piazza*, up the steps at the end of the harbour. The English-run *Lemon Tree Restaurant*, with its vegetarian food and *tapas*, now has a nearby rival, the *Daskalio Cafe Bar*, whose laid-back Brits serve excellent curries. For more elegant dining, head for the area above and to the west of Plátia Tríon Ierarhón, where you'll find *Le Bistrot* and *Alexanders'* (for excellent moussaka and chicken dishes). Further along, above the flat rocks where people sunbathe, *Tarsanas* is a converted boatbuilders' yard with a picturesque veranda – the best place in town for an evening drink as the harbour lights come on.

Nightlife centres on the clubs on or near Politechníou – the new *West* and *Borzoi* are the latest favourites, the *Apothiki Music Hall* has live music and a good atmosphere, while *BBCE* on the seafront rocks till dawn. Bars show more musical variety – places like the *Banana* are pop-oriented and popular, the pricey *Kirki* and *Kentavros* play jazz and blues, *Adagio* has classical music in the evenings, and stalwart *Admiral Benbow* belts out classic Sixties soul.

Around the island

As an alternative to the buses, or bike rental, you could get your island bearings on a **boat trip** around Skíathos. These cost around 2500dr per person and leave around 10am; boats also run to the islet of Tsougriá (opposite Skíathos Town), where there's a good beach and a taverna. Both leave from the fishing harbour beyond the Boúrtzi, and not the yacht anchorage to the north of the ferry harbour; east coast *kaíki* leave from the quay area in front of the bus station.

If you're interested in seeing more of Skíathos **on foot**, the locally produced Skíathos guide by Rita and Dietrich Harkort (available in larger tourist shops) has detailed instructions and maps for walks all over the island. It's a good way to escape the crowds, although you're never going to get away from it all completely.

Monasteries and Kástro

The **Evangelístria monastery** (daily 8am–noon & 4–8pm), more than an hour on foot out of Skíathos Town, is also accessible by rented moped, car or mule. The Greek flag was raised here in 1807, and, among other heroes of the War of Independence, Kolokotronis pledged his oath to fight for freedom here. It is exceptionally beautiful, even beyond the grandeur of isolation you find in all Greek monasteries. To reach it, walk 500m out of the centre of town on the road towards the airport until, at the point where the asphalt veers to the right, you take a prominently signposted tarmac track that veers left; be careful to stick to the tarmac and not to wander off onto the dirt roads.

Beyond Evangelístria, a mule track continues to the abandoned **monastery of Áyios Harálambos**, from where it's possible to walk across the island to the old ruined capital of Kástro along another dirt road, taking about two hours. To reach Kástro from Skíathos Town, it's quicker to take the direct road, though in all it's still a hard five- to six-kilometre uphill slog; the turning is signposted on the road behind town, some distance beyond the turning for Evangelístria.

Just over halfway between Evangelístria and Kástro, a well-used dirt track (signposted) turns left and heads towards the abandoned fifteenth-century monastery of **Panayía tis Kehrias**, three hours' walk from town. It's said to be the oldest on the island and has a colony of bats inside. It's a beautiful walk (or organized donkey-ride), and there are two pebbly beaches below, one with a welcoming stream that powers a cool shower. Ignoring this excursion, the paved road continues to within a thirty-minute walk of **Kástro** – a spectacular spot, built on a windswept headland. In the past, the entrance was only accessible by a drawbridge (now ruined), which has been replaced by a flight of steps. The village was built in the sixteenth century, when the people of the island moved here for security from pirate raids. It was abandoned 300 years later in 1830, following independence from Turkey, when the population moved back to build the modern town on the site of ancient Skíathos. The ruins are largely overgrown, and only three churches survive intact, the largest still retaining some original frescoes. From outside the gates, a path leads down the rocks to a good pebble **beach**. With a stream running down from the hills and a daytime café (with slightly overpriced food and drinks), it wouldn't make a bad place to camp. However, for an apparently inaccessible spot, it does attract a surprising number of people. All the island excursion boats call here, and even when they've gone, there's little chance of having the ruins or beach to yourself.

Finally, the seventeenth-century **Kounístria monastery**, can be reached by turning right off the road that runs from Tróulas to Asélinos. It's a very pretty spot, with a beautiful carved temple, spendid icons, a grape arbour and a taverna.

The beaches

The real business of Skíathos is **beaches**. There are reputed to be more than sixty of them on the island, even so hardly enough to soak up the numbers of summer visitors:

at the height of season, the local population of 4000 can be eclipsed by up to 50,000 outsiders. The beaches on the northeast coast aren't easily accessible unless you pay for an excursion *kaíki*. Reaching them on foot requires treks more arduous than those described above. The bus, though, runs along the entire south coast, and from strategic points along the way you can easily reach a good number of beaches. The prevailing summer *meltémi* wind blows from the north, so the beaches on the south coast are usually better protected. Most of the popular beaches have at least a drinks/snacks stall; those at Vromólimnos, Asélinos and Troúlos have proper tavernas.

The beaches before the **Kalamáki peninsula** are unexciting, but on the promontory itself, flanked by the campsite and Kanapítsa hamlet, **Rígas, Ayía Paraskeví** and **Vromólimnos** are highly rated, the last offering windsurfing and waterskiing. The water along this stretch, however, is cloudy and appears contaminated, though it improves after Troúlos. For scuba enthusiasts, there is the new *Dolphin Diving Centre* (☎0427/22 520) at the *Nostos* hotel, on the eastern side of the Kalamáki peninsula.

Just before Troúlos you can turn right up a paved road, which runs 4km north to **Mégas Asélinos**, a very good beach with a campsite and a reasonable taverna. A daily bus and excursion boats stop here, so it's crowded in season. A fork in the paved road leads to Kounístra monastery (see above) and continues to **Mikrós Asélinos**, just east of its larger neighbour and somewhat quieter.

The bus only goes as far as **KOUKOUNARIÉS**, a busy resort, though the three beaches are excellent if you don't mind the crowds. There's a majestic sandy bay of clear, gradually deepening water, backed by acres of pines, and despite its popularity it merits at least one visit if only to assess the dubious claim that it's the best beach in Greece. The road runs behind a small lake at the back of the pine trees, and features a string of **hotels, rooms and restaurants**, as well as a good campsite. The *Strofilia* apartments here (☎0427/49 251; ⑤) are particularly nicely furnished. If you feel like entering into the spirit of things, jet-skis, motorboats, windsurfing and waterskiing are all available off the beach.

Banana Beach (also known as Krássa), the third cove on the far side of Poúnda headland, is the trendiest of the island's nudist beaches. For the less adventurous, the turning for **Ayía Eléni** (the penultimate bus stop), leads one kilometre to the pleasant beach (with a drinks kiosk). Or ask the driver to set you down before here, at the start of the thirty-minute path to **Mandhráki** and **Elia** beaches, which have similar facilities.

The famed **Lalaria beach**, on the northern stretch of coast, can be reached by "taxi-boats" from the town. It's beautiful, with steep cliffs rising behind it and excellent swimming, but beware of the undertow. The island's three natural grottos – Skotini, Glazia and Halkini – are nearby and are included in many of the "round-the-island" trips. Southwest of Kástro are the greyish sands of **Megas Yialos**, one of the less crowded beaches, and **Xanemos**, another nudist beach, though both suffer from airport noise.

The only real way to get away from the crowds is to persuade a boat owner to take you out to one of Skiáthos' **islets**. Tsougriá, in particular, has three beaches, with a snack bar on the main one.

Skópelos

Bigger, more rugged and better cultivated than Skiáthos, **Skópelos** is, in its way, just as busy. As you approach the island from the sea, it appears a peaceful place, but once on land, little has remained immune to tourism. Most of the beaches have sunbeds, umbrellas and some watersports, despite the island-wide jellyfish problem. Inland, it is a well-watered place, harvesting olives, plums, pears and almonds. Glóssa and Skópelos, its two main towns, are also among the prettiest in the Sporades, clambering uphill along paved steps, their houses distinguished by attractive wooden balconies and grey slate roofs.

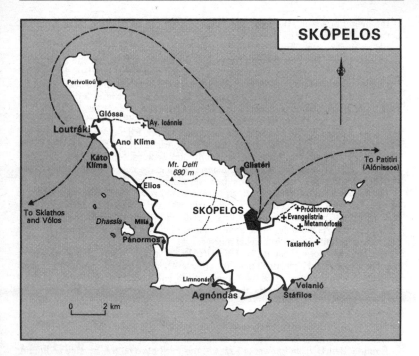

A number of nationalities have occupied the island at various stages of its history, among them the Romans, Persians, Venetians, French and, of course, the Turks. Indeed the Turkish admiral, Barbarossa (Redbeard), had the entire population of the island slaughtered in the sixteenth century.

Loutráki, Glóssa and the west

Most boats call at both ends of Skópelos, stopping first at the small port of **LOUTRÁKI** with its thin pebble beach, filthy water, couple of hotels and few rooms for rent. The town has been spoilt a little by developments at either end, but it's still not a bad place to stay if you're after peace and quiet; try *O Stelios* (②), a simple pension above the taverna *Flisvos*, or the *Avra* (☎0424/33 550; ④), a fancier hotel. Unfortunately most of the quayside tavernas are a rip-off, although the café/shop in the *platía* by the harbour is shaded by beautiful chestnut trees and sells a highly recommended, home-made retsina; the *Flisvos* isn't bad either, a friendly place with decent pasta dishes.

High above Loutráki, **GLÓSSA** is perhaps a preferable base, a sizeable and quite beautiful, totally Greek town, with several *kafenía*, a taverna and rooms to let – some of which are hot and musty, with erratic water pressure. *Kostas and Nina's* place (☎0424/33 686; ②) has simple, clean rooms, some with a view; they also rent out studios longer term. You could also try *H. Tsoukala* (☎0424/33 223 or 33 767; ③), near the bus stop for rooms, or the *Pension Valentina* (☎0424/33 694; ③). There's one taverna, *Toh Agnandi*, which is a lively and authentic place to eat, and full most evenings. Incidentally, it's a good idea to accept offers of a taxi ride up to Glóssa from Loutráki; it's a stiff walk up even if you know the path short cuts, and taxi drivers will know which pensions have vacancies. If it's really high season, though, and even Glóssa is packed, three nearby villages, Athéato, Káto Klíma and Paleo Klíma all have rooms, while Neo Klíma has two hotels and *O Xenos,* a decent *ouzerí.*

Ninety minutes' walk from Glóssa, up to the north coast, will bring you to a **beach** the locals call Perivolioú. The walk itself is worthwhile, passing a **monastery** next to a hollow stone cairn containing masses of human bones and skulls. There's also a huge hollow oak tree here, in the heart of which is a small tank of drinking water. The beach, when you get there, is nothing out of the ordinary, but there's spring water for drinking and a cave for shade.

East of Glóssa, a new dirt road leads to the splendidly sited monastery of **Áyios Ioánnis**, perched on the top of a rock high above a small sandy cove where you can swim. The buildings themselves are modern and rather ugly, but the walk from Glóssa (again, about 90min) is beautiful and peaceful, with hawks and nightingales for company.

Skópelos Town

If you stay on the ferry beyond Loutráki – and this is probably the best plan – you reach **SKÓPELOS** town, sloping down one corner of a huge, almost circular bay. The best way to arrive is by sea, with the town revealed slowly as the boat rounds the final headland. Be prepared for the crowds though, since Skópelos Town has seen enormous commercialization over recent years, with a huge increase in visitors and prices. The centre is a mass of boutiques and pricey tavernas, with an untidy sprawl of new hotels to the southeast. Spread below the oddly whitewashed ruins of a Venetian **Kástro**, are an enormous number of churches – 123 reputedly, though some are small enough to be mistaken for houses and most are locked except for their annual festival day.

Outside town, perched on the slopes opposite the quay, are two convents, **Evangelístria** (daily 8am–1pm & 4–7pm), which is within view of the town, and **Pródhromos** (daily 8am–1pm & 5–8pm). The nearby monastery of **Metamórfosis** was abandoned in 1980 but is now being restored by the monks and is open to visitors. You should dress respectfully, although the hospitable nuns at the two convents will lend you leg-covering if necessary. Access is simplest by following an old road behind the line of hotels in town to Evangelístria (an hour's walk). From there it's an extra half hour's scramble over mule tracks to Pródhromos, the remotest and most beautiful of the three. Ignore the new road that goes part way – it's longer and takes away most of the beauty of the walk.

Practicalities

The **ferry quay** is at the western end of a long promenade, lined with an array of boutiques, bars, stores and restaurants. Where the quay meets the main road, turn left and follow the sea until you pass the children's swings and the second *períptero*; at the point where the road divides around a car park, you'll find the **bus station**. Opposite the bus station entrance, a short road leads into a maze of lanes, though signposts lead you to the **post office**. There is a branch of the *Commercial Bank* about 50m from the quay.

In the main body of the town there are dozens of **rooms** for rent; take up one of the offers when you land, since most are otherwise unadvertised. Alternatively, try the *Lina Guest House* on the front (☎0424/22 637; ④) or, among the allotments, the very pleasant *Hotel Captain* (☎0424/22 110 or 22 980; ③) – both have clean, if basic, rooms with private bathrooms; some rooms have balconies. For more **expensive hotels**, you're unlikely to find a space without having booked through a tour operator, but if you fancy the likes of the *Elli* (☎0424/22 549; ⑤), *Aperiton* (☎0424/22 322; ⑥) or *Dionysos* (☎0424/23 210; ⑥) – each with a pool – ask about vacancies at *Madro Travel* on the quay (☎0424/22 145); they're also the local *Flying Dolphin* agents.

There's a wide variety of **places to eat**, ranging from the good to the truly terrible. Those at either end of the harbour are a rip-off, while the clutch along the main prom, near the park, are in stiff competition in terms of price and variety of dishes offered. Best of these is definitely *Toh Aktaion*, with exceptionally pleasant staff and big, delicious, reasonably priced portions. Otherwise, *La Costa* is average but friendlier than most, *Pirate's* (follow the signposts) does curries and vegetarian food. There's a creperie, the *Greca*, and the best *yíros* are from *O Platanos*, near the post office. It's also worth heading a couple of kilometres towards Stáfilos to the *Terpsis* taverna for their stuffed-chicken speciality – book twelve hours in advance.

Nightlife in Skópelos is on the increase, but is more the late-night bar than nightclub variety. That said, the *Disco 52*, neighbouring *Labikos* and *Kounos* are popular in season, and the *Skopelitissa* plays Greek pop music till the early hours.

Around the rest of the island

Buses cover the island's one paved road between Skópelos Town and Loutráki (via Glóssa) about six times daily between 7am and 10.30pm, stopping at the paths to all the main beaches and villages. **Stáfilos**, 4km south of town, is the closest beach, if small and rocky. It is getting increasingly crowded, but the *Terpsis* taverna, which rents **rooms**, is a very pleasant spot shaded by a vast pine tree.

There's a very prominent "No Camping" sign at Stáfilos, but if you walk five minutes around the coast north to **Velanió**, there is spring water and a campsite near the beach. Here the pines and surf always draw a small, summer (often nudist) community.

Further around the coast to the west, the very touristy, beachless, fishing anchorage of **AGNÓNDAS** (with a combination restaurant/rooms) is the start of a fifteen-minute path (2km by road) or half-hourly *kaíki* to **LIMNONÁRI**, 100m of fine sand set in a rather grim and shadeless rock-girt bay. There are a couple of places to stay and eat, but camping would be a bit cramped, and it's all a bit commercial and rather tatty. However, the *Takonis* taverna here isn't bad, serving good, fresh fish.

PÁNORMOS is very much a full-blown resort, with rooms, tavernas, a campsite (where people of all income levels may find themselves at times when Skópelos is choc-full) and watersports. The beach here is gravelly and steeply shelving, but there are small secluded bays close by. The enormous *Panormos Beach Hotel*, a stalwart of package holidays, has a beautiful garden and fine views – it's worth trying for space at *Madro Travel* in Skópelos Town (see "Practicalities" above). Slightly further on at **MILIÁ**, there is a tremendous, 1500m sweep of tiny pebbles beneath a bank of pines, facing the islet of Dhassía. There's one taverna and just a couple of houses with rooms (☎0424/22 735 for both; ③) in this languid setting; nudist swimming is possible at a lovely 500-metre-long beach a little way north, though the sea both here and at Miliá teems with jellyfish.

Further north, **ELIOS**, 9km short of Glóssa, is a medium-sized resort in its own right, and not a particularly pleasant one either, although its usually crowded beach is nice and there's a reasonable taverna, *Theophilos*, with good, if pricey fish. Beyond here, the virtually abandoned village of Paleo Klíma marks the start of a beautiful fortyminute **trail** to Glóssa, via the earthquake-ruined settlement of Áyii Anaryiri and the oldest village on the island, Athéato.

West of Skópelos town various jeep tracks and old paths wind through olive and plum groves toward **Mount Dhélfi** and the Vathiá forest, or skirt the base of the mountain northeast to Revíthi hill with its fountains and churches, and the site of **Karyá**, with its *sendoúkia* or ancient tombs. Tracks on the north flank of Dhélfi, beyond Karyá, might just conceivably lead all the way to the Klíma villages, but the main, old trans-island donkey track ends disappointingly in the vicinity of Elios.

To the northwest of Skópelos Town, **Glistéri** is a small pebble beach with no shade but a taverna much frequented by locals on Sundays. **Sáres**, reached by half-hourly *kaíkia* from town, is also a popular beach. A fork off the Glistéri and Mount Dhélfi tracks can – in theory – be followed across the island to Pánormos within ninety minutes; it's a pleasant walk though the route isn't always obvious. As usual, local maps of the island are mostly very inaccurate, a situation aggravated by the many new tracks bulldozed across the island since the maps were printed, making exploration interesting but sometimes frustrating.

Alónissos and some minor islets

The most remote of the Sporades, **Alónissos** is also, on initial appearance, the least attractive. It has an unfortunate recent history. The vineyards were wiped out by disease in 1950 and the *hóra* was damaged by an earthquake in 1965. Although its houses were mostly repairable, corruption and the social control policies of the new junta were instrumental in the forcible transfer of virtually the entire population down

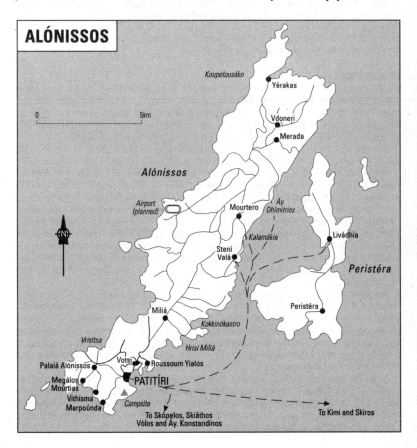

to the previously unimportant anchorage of Patitíri. The result is a little soulless, but on closer acquaintance the island turns out to be one of the most traditional in Greece, though this can leave single, female travellers open to hassle. That said, if you're polite and dress respectably, the people are charming. Take time and explore.

Patitíri and the old town

PATITÍRI is not a good introduction to the island. The flat-roofed concrete buildings are relieved only by a row of bars and near-identical restaurants along the seafront. Although Alónissos attracts fewer visitors than Skíathos or Skópelos, most of those who do come stay in Patitíri, and from mid-July to the end of August it can get very crowded. Travelling independently, there seems little reason to stay longer than you have to, though it's the easiest place for picking up connections for beaches and the old town.

PALAIÁ ALÓNISSOS is a fine but steep fifty-minute walk via a donkey track – signposted on the left just outside Patitíri. Alternatively, there's a bus (theoretically 4 daily, though it actually runs every 15min from late morning until lunch and 7–9pm if there are enough passengers). Although many houses are still derelict, much of the village has been restored, mainly by the English and Germans who bought the properties at knock-down rates. Only a few local families continue to live here, which gives the village a rather odd and un-Greek atmosphere, but it is picturesque, and the views make the trip worthwhile. Most of the owners only come here in July and August, and for the rest of the year their houses are closed up.

Practicalities

All the important facilities are in Patitíri; the OTE is on the seafront, buses and taxis congregate next door, the post office is on the *hóra* road, while *kaíki* leave from the quay beside the *Pension Flisvos* (see below). You can rent a moped or motorbike at reasonable prices, although beyond Vótsi the roads are unpaved and should be ridden with care. A couple of the rental places also rent out motorboats and dinghies.

Rooms are easy to find, though you'll probably be approached with offers as you get off the ferry, sometimes by older women wearing traditional blue and white costumes. Try *Nikolaos Dimakis* (☎0424/65 244; ③), *Elini Athanasiou* (☎0424/65 240; ②), *O M Kyriazis* (☎0424/65 229; ③) or the *Ioulieta* pension (☎0424/65 463; ③), all of which make an effort to please. Finally, ask at the third supermarket on the left on Pelasgon for access to a brand new, as yet unnamed, building of rooms. The local room-owners' association (☎0424/65 577) has an office on the front, and can find you a room in Patitíri or nearby Vótsi, but you'll end up paying more. *Alonissos Travel* (☎0424/65 511) can do bookings for a limited number of rooms and apartments in the old town, though accommodation here is in short supply so expect to pay well over the odds, particularly in season. Otherwise, ask around; few people put up "room for rent" signs, but try *Fadasia House* (☎0424/65 186; ④), simple and clean, and the least unfriendly of a rather sullen bunch.

Restaurants along the front of Patitíri are reasonably priced, but the food is nothing special. Of the bunch, the best place for breakfast is the *Balcony Bar* (signposted), which serves delicious fresh peach juice; and in the evenings, try the friendly *Pension Flisvos*, or *Naffilos*, which has occasional musicians. The old town has a bar, two shops, and a few tavernas. The *Paraport* taverna is good, though not especially cheap, but it does have one of the best views on the island. The *Aloni* has good views out to sea plus occasional art exhibitions.

Nightlife is low key. There's a pool room, and several bars; the best of the seafront cluster is *Pub Dennis*, whose ice-cream concoctions are divine, though both *Nine Muses* and *La Vie* are popular. Club-wise, *Borio* and the *Disco 4 x 4* are fairly European, while the *Disco Rocks* plays Greek music (and is not for solo females), as does the superior *Rembetika*, on the road to the old town.

The island's beaches

Alónnisos has some of the cleanest water in the Aegean, but it's sadly lacking in good beaches. There's only one really sandy beach on the island (Vithísma), the rest varying from rough to fine pebbles. There's no bus, but *kaíki* run half-hourly from Patitíri north to Hrisí Miliá, Kokkinókastro, Stení Vála, Kalamákia and Áyios Dhímitrios, and south around the coast to Marpoúnda, Vithísma and Megálos Moúrtias. *Kaíki* also sail occasionally to Livádhia and the Peristéra islets.

Patitíri itself has a grimy stretch of shingle, but decent swimming can be had from the rocks around the corner to the north, past the cranes; pick your way along a hewn-out path and you're there (ladder provided). To the north, above the headlands, Patitíri merges into two adjoining settlements. **Roussoúm Yialós** holds nothing of interest, but fancies itself as a budding resort. There's an attractive harbour, tavernas and a few rooms – try the unnamed building on the front (☎ 0424/65 334; ③). **Vótsi** is still being built. The best beaches, however, are well to Patitíri's north, mostly on the eastern side.

Hrisí Miliá, the first good beach, has pine trees down to the sand and a taverna; there are a couple of new hotels on the hillside above, and it can get crowded in summer. At **Kokkinókastro**, over the hill to the north, excavations have revealed the

---

THE MEDITERRANEAN MONK SEAL

The Mediterranean Monk Seal has the dubious distinction of being the European mammal most in danger of extinction. Perhaps 800 survive in total worldwide, the majority around the Portuguese Atlantic island of Madeira and the coast of the West African state of Mauritania, and in small numbers in the Ionian and Aegean seas, having disappeared entirely from the Mediterranean. The largest population, an estimated 25–30 seals, lives around the deserted islands north of Alónissos.

Monk seals can travel up to 200km a day in search of food, but they usually return to the same places to rear their pups. They have one pup every two years, and the small population is very vulnerable to disturbance and the possibility of mother seals being separated from and losing their pups. Originally, the pups would have been reared on sandy beaches, but with increasing disturbance by man, they have retreated to isolated sea caves, particularly around the coast of the remote islet of Pipéri.

Unfortunately, the seals compete with fishermen for limited stocks of fish, and, in the overfished Aegean, often destroy nets full of fish. Until recently it was common for seals to be killed by fishermen. This occasionally still happens, but in an attempt to protect the seals, the seas around the northern Sporades have been declared a marine wildlife reserve: fishing is restricted in the area north of Alónissos and prohibited within 5km of Pipéri. On Alónissos, the conservation effort and reserve have won a great deal of local support, mainly through the efforts of the Hellenic Society for the Protection of the Monk Seal (HSPMS), based at Stení Vála. The measures have won particular support from local fishermen, as tighter restrictions on larger, industrial-scale fishing boats from other parts of Greece should help preserve fish stocks and benefit them financially.

Despite this, the government has made no serious efforts to enforce the restrictions, and boats from outside the area continue to fish around Pipéri. There are also government plans to reduce the prohibited area around Pipéri to 500m. On a more positive note, the HSPMS, in collaboration with the Pieterburen Seal Creche in Holland, has reared three abandoned seal pups, all of which have been successfully released in the seas north of Alónissos.

For the moment, your chances of actually seeing a seal are remote, unless you plan to spend a few weeks on a boat in the area. It's recommended that you shouldn't visit Pipéri or approach sea caves on other islands which might be used by seals, or encourage boat owners to do so. Spear fishing, by tourists or professional fishermen, is a particular threat near caves used by seals and is strongly discouraged.

site of ancient Ikos and evidence of the oldest known prehistoric habitation in the Aegean. There's nothing much to see, but it's a beautiful spot with a good pebble beach, and, in July and August, a daytime taverna.

STENÍ VÁLA, opposite the island of Peristéra, is perhaps the most obvious place to stay. It's almost a proper village, with a shop, a few houses, a bar, rooms and three tavernas, one of which stays open more or less throughout the year. There's a campsite (☎0424/65 258) in an olive grove by the harbour, a long pebble beach and other beaches within reasonable walking distance in either direction. **KALAMÁKIA**, to the north, also has a couple of tavernas, and a few rooms.

If you want real solitude, **Áyios Dhímitrios**, nearby **Megaliamos** (where fossils have been found), **Yérakas** (an old shepherds' village much further north) and **Koupelousáko** are recommended, but be aware that currents along this stretch can be treacherous. However, before committing yourself, take one of the round-the-island trips available, and return the next day with enough food for your stay – there are no stores outside the port.

In the opposite direction from Patitíri, **Marpoúnda** features a large hotel and bungalow complex and a rather grim beach. Better to turn left after the campsite towards **Megálos Moúrtias**, a pebble beach with several tavernas linked by dirt track with Palaiá Alónnisos, 200m above. Just before Megálos Moúrtias, a path heads down through the pine trees to **Vithísma**, a much better sand and shingle beach that's hardly visible from above. A windsurfing school operates from here in summer.

Further north, visible from Palaiá Alónnisos, **Vrisítsa** is tucked into its own fingerlike inlet. There's sand and a sometime taverna, but little else.

Beyond Alónissos: some minor islets

Northeast of Alónissos half a dozen tiny islets speckle the Aegean. Virtually none of these has any permanent population, nor any ferry service, and the only way you can reach them – at least Peristéra, Kirá Panayía and Yioúra – is by excursion *kaíki*, and even then only in high season (the excursion boats serve primarily as fishing boats from September to May) and as weather permits. Considerable powers of persuasion will be required to get the fishermen to take you to the other, more remote islets. It is possible to be left for a night or more on any of the islands, but when acting out your desert-island fantasies, be sure to bring more supplies than you need: if the weather worsens you'll be marooned until such time as small craft can make it out to you.

Peristéra is the closest islet to Alónissos, to which it was once actually joined, but subsidence (a common phenomenon in the area) created the narrow straits beween the two. It is graced with some sandy beaches and there is rarely anyone around, though some Alónissans do come over for short periods to tend the olive groves, and in season there are regular evening "barbecue boats" from the main island. As on Alónissos, a few unofficial campers are tolerated, but there is only one spot, known locally as "Barbecue Bay", where campfires are allowed.

Kirá Panayía (also known as Pelagós) is the next islet out and is equally fertile. It's owned by the Orthodox Church and there are two monasteries here, one inhabited as recently as 1984. Boats call at a beach and anchorage on the south shore, one of many such sandy stretches and coves around the island, which is popular with yachtsmen. There's no permanent population other than the wild goats. The island boasts a stalactite cave reputed to be that of Homer's Polyphemus (the Cyclops that imprisoned Odysseus).

Nearby **Yioúra** has a similar, larger cave with perhaps better credentials as the lair of Polyphemus. The main feature, though, is a herd of rare wild goats, distinctive enough to have earned the island the status of a reserve. Two middle-aged couples live here as wardens; part of their job is to unlock the cave for visiting parties and provide a hurricane lamp. You'll need more than a single source of illumination to see much, however, and getting down into the cavern is fairly strenuous. Apart from the tourist boats, the wardens' only contact with the outside world is a twice-monthly mail-and-provisions boat, which, like all other craft, cannot land at the primitive jetty in rough seas.

Pipéri, near Yioúra, is a sea-bird and monk seal refuge, and permission from the EOT (in Athens) is required for visits by non-specialists. Tiny, northernmost **Psathoúra** is dominated by its powerful modern lighthouse, although here, as around many of these islands, there's a submerged ancient town, brought low by the endemic subsidence. Roughly halfway between Alónissos and Skíros, green **Skantzoúra**, with a single monastery (still inhabited by one monk) and a few seasonal shepherds, seems a lesser version of Kirá Panayía.

Skíros (Skyros)

Despite its closeness to Athens, **Skíros** had until recently remained a very traditional and idiosyncratic island. Any impetus for change had been neutralized by the lack of economic opportunity (and even secondary schooling), forcing the younger Skyrians to live in Athens and leaving behind a conservative gerontocracy. A high school has at last been provided, and the island has been "discovered" in the past decade. It's now the haunt of continental Europeans, chic Athenians and British, many of whom check in to the "New Age" Skyros Centre, catering to those who feel Skíros by itself isn't enough to "rethink the form and direction of their lives".

Meanwhile, Skíros still ranks as one of the most interesting places in the Aegean. It has a long tradition of ornate woodcarving, and a *Salonáki Skiriani* (handmade set of chairs) is still considered an appropriate partial dowry for any young Greek woman. A very few old men still wear the vaguely Cretan traditional costume of cap, vest, baggy trousers, leggings and *trohádhia* (Skyrian clogs), but this is dying out. Likewise, old women still wear the favoured yellow scarves and long embroidered skirts.

The theory that Skíros was originally two islands seems doubtful, but certainly the character of the two parts of the island is very different. The north has a greener and more gentle landscape, and away from the port and town it retains much of its original pine forest. The sparsely inhabited, south is mountainous, rocky and barren; there are few trees and the landscape is more reminiscent of the Cyclades than the Sporades. Compared to Skíathos, Skópelos and Alónissos, Skíros isn't a great place for out-of-the-way beaches. Most **beaches** along the west coast attract more than their fair share of sea-borne rubbish, and, although the scenery is sometimes spectacular, the swimming isn't that good. The beaches on the east coast are all close to Skíros Town, and the best option is probably to stay here rather than heading for somewhere more isolated.

GOAT DANCES AND WILD PONIES

Skíros has some particularly lively, even outrageous festivals. The *Apokriatiká* (pre-Lenten) carnival here is structured around the famous "Goat Dance" performed by masked revellers in the village streets. The foremost character in this is the Yéros, a menacing figure concealed by a goatskin mask and weighed down by garlands of sheep bells. Accompanying him are Korélles and Kyriés (transvestites – only the men participate) and Frangi (maskers in "Western" garb). For further details, read Joy Koulentianou's *The Goat Dance of Skyros*, available in Athens and occasionally on the island.

The other big annual event takes place near Magaziá beach on August 15, when children race domesticated members of the wild pony herd native to Skíros and said to be related to the Shetland pony (if so, it must be very distantly). They are thought, perhaps, to be the diminutive horses depicted in the Parthenon frieze, and at any time of the year you might find some of the tame individuals tethered and grazing near Skíros Town.

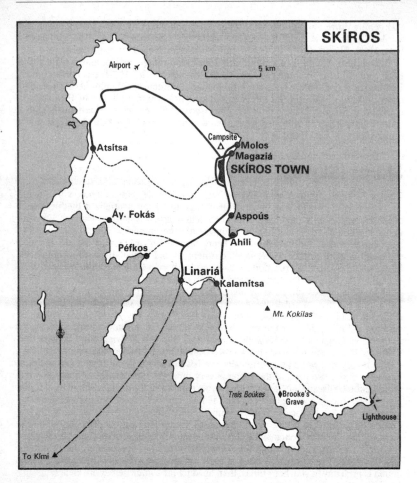

Linariá

After crossing a seemingly endless expanse of sea, the boat docks at the tiny port of
LINARIÁ, a functional place on the island's west coast. Most buildings are in the
modern Greek-concrete-box style, and while it's a pleasant place to while away time
waiting for the ferry, there's little else to keep you. If you do stay the night, there are
two tavernas (one with rooms) and a bar around the harbour. In high season, *kaíki* ply
from Linariá to the Pentekali and Yerania **grottos**, and to the **islet of Skiropoúla**,
which has a cave and some of the Skyrian wild ponies. There's a reasonable sandy
beach called Kalóyeros a few minutes' walk along the main road from Linariá, and
there should be no problem if you want to camp here.

A road connects Linariá to Skíros town, 10km away, and then continues round, past
the airport, to Atsítsa; the **bus to Skíros** leaves from the quay. Midway up the Linariá
to Skíros-town route, a side road links Ahíli with Kalamítsa. Most other roads are passable on a rented moped, apart from the direct track between Skíros town and Atsítsa.

Skíros Town

SKÍROS Town (also known as Hóra), with its decidedly Cycladic architecture, sits on the landward side of a high rock rising precipitously from the coast. According to legend, King Lycomedes pushed Theseus to his death from its summit. It has a work-aday atmosphere without feeling like a resort or being especially picturesque. The older and more intriguing parts of town are higher up, climbing towards the **Kástro**, a mainly Byzantine rather than Venetian building, built on the site of the ancient acropolis. There are few traces of this, although remains of the Classical city walls survive below on the seaward side of the rock. The *kástro* is open to visitors; to reach its upper parts you pass through a rather private-looking gateway into the monastery, then through an attractive shaded courtyard and up a whitewashed tunnel. There's little to see at the top, apart from a few churches in various states of ruin, but there are great views over the town and this part of the island, and the climb up takes you through the quieter and more picturesque part of town, with glimpses into traditionally decorated houses.

Perhaps equally striking, and splendidly incongruous, is the **Memorial to Rupert Brooke** at the northern end of town. It takes the form of a bronze statue of "Immortal Poetry" and its nakedness caused a scandal among the townspeople when it was first set up. Brooke, who visited the south of the island very briefly in April 1915, died shortly after of blood poisoning on a French hospital ship anchored offshore and was buried in an olive grove above the bay of Treis Boukés. (The site can be reached on foot from Kalamítsa, by *kaíki*, or, less romantically, by taxi.) Brooke has become some-thing of a local hero, despite his limited acquaintance with Skíros, and ironically was adopted by Kitchener and later Churchill as the paragon of patriotic youth, despite his forthrightly expressed socialist and internationalist views.

Just below the Brooke statue are two museums. The **Archeological Museum** (Tues–Sat 9am–3.30pm, Sun 9.30am–2.30pm; 400dr) has a modest collection of pottery and statues from excavations on the island, and a reconstruction of a traditional Skíros house interior. The privately run **Faltaitz Museum** (daily 10am–1pm & 5.30pm–8pm; free), in a nineteenth-century house built over one of the bastions of the ancient walls, is more interesting with a collection of domestic items.

Practicalities

Arriving in Skíros Town, the **bus** from Linariá leaves you by the school, just below the main *platía*; the **OTE**, **post office** and **bank** are all nearby. *Skiros Travel* (☎0222/91 123 or 91 600), on the main street above the *platía*, can provide **information** and advice and can find a room or hotel; in high season, it's a good idea to telephone them in advance. There are a few **moped and motorbike** rental places in the area around the *platía*.

You'll probably be met off the bus with offers of **rooms**, which it's as well to accept. *Anna Stergiou* (☎0222/91 657; ③–④) on Ayía Mena has clean, homely rooms, some in her house and some with kitchens nearby. Or call *Vangeliou Mavrikos* (☎0222/91 115; ②–④) for dormitory-type rooms with shared bathroom or more private ones. There's a **campsite** at the bottom of the steps below the archeological museum, with basic amenities but a good bar.

The *platía* and the main street running by it are the centre of village life, with a couple of noisy pubs and a wide choice of *kafenía*, tavernas and fast-food places. There are few outstanding **places to eat;** most are overpriced, or serve rather average food. *O Glaros*, just below the *platía*, is an exception, and many of the local people eat here. It's a very basic taverna with a limited menu, but the owners are friendly and the food is good and reasonably priced. Also the *psistariá, O Skyros,* is worth a try for its hefty portions, *Moraiti* on Agoras is cheap and cheerful, *Sisyphos* has vegetarian specialities and the *Sweets Workshop* does some wonderful cakes.

The town's **nightlife** is mostly bar-based until very late, when the few clubs get going. The *Pub Bar* is the most popular meeting place, while *Kalypso* is mellow and uncrowded. Best clubs include the *Skyropoula*, *On The Rocks* and *Apocalypsis*. At high-season weekends though, it can be more fun to join in the dancing at the Magaziá campsite.

Magaziá and Mólos and some beaches

A path leads down past the archeological museum towards the small coastal village of **MAGAZIÁ**, coming out by the official campsite (see above). From there, an 800-metre-long sandy beach stretches to the adjacent village of **MÓLOS**. In recent years, a sprawl of new development between the road and the beach has more or less joined the two villages together. Despite this, the beach is good, and if you don't feel like walking down from Skíros Town to go swimming, it would be a good place to stay. There are lots of **rooms** down here, reflecting the young crowd that uses the beach's watersports and volleyball facilities. *Stamatis Marmaris* (☎0222/91 672; ④) and *Manolis Balotis* (☎0222/91 386; ③), near the campsite, are both popular. The beachfront **tavernas** compare favourably with those in town: a small taverna in a converted windmill at the Mólos end of the beach has good food and the best view, and the taverna *Akti*, also in Mólos, does a cheap and filling moussaká.

For quieter beaches, take the road past Mólos, or better, try the excellent and undeveloped beach directly below the *kástro*. The path down to it is 150m beyond the disco *Skyropoula* – it isn't obvious from above. However, following the road beyond here, the beaches are disappointing until **Méalos beach** (known more commonly as **Aspoús**), which has a couple of tavernas and rooms to rent. To the south, **Ahíli**, had one of the best beaches on the island until it was effectively destroyed by the construction of a new marina. South of Ahíli, the coast is rocky and inaccessible, although you can take a *kaíki* trip down to the bay of **Treis Boukés**, passing some picturesque sea caves on the way.

Kalamítsa, on the west coast across from Ahíli, lacks character and the beach and sea aren't that clean. There's a better and more remote beach halfway along the road to Treis Boukés, though it has absolutely no facilities.

Around the rest of the island

In summer, the whimsical bus service visits the more popular beaches if that's all you want to do. Otherwise, from Skíros Town it's best to direct your footsteps (or moped) due west, following Kifissós Creek into the pine-filled heart of this half of Skíros, which contrasts sharply with the barren rockiness of the south.

Just north of town, turn right off the airport road onto a track leading to **Ayía Ekaterína**, a pretty, small beach with its own chapel. There are also two nice beaches near the airport, and **Kalogrias**, further on, is quiet but pleasant. You can reach them via a track beyond Áyios Dhimítrios.

The dirt track from Skíros Town across to **Atsítsa** is well worth the effort (3–4hr walk), but isn't practical with a moped. Atsítsa is an attractive bay with pine trees down to the sea (tapped by the Skyrian retsina industry), and an increasing number of rooms. The beach is rocky and isn't great for swimming; there's a small sandy beach fifteen minutes' walk to the north at **Kirá Panayiá**, but it's nothing special.

Elsewhere in the coniferous north, **Áyios Fokás** and **Péfkos** bays are easiest reached by a turning from the paved road near Linariá, though there is (more difficult) access from Atsítsa. Both are in the process of being discovered by villa companies, but each has a few rooms. Áyios Fokás is quite primitive, but Péfkos boasts a taverna (it's only open in season, as are all other tavernas away from Linariá, Skíros Town, Magaziá and Mólos). The bay is beautiful and the beach reasonable but not that clean – the beaches around Skíros Town are much better for swimming.

Évvia (Euboea)

Évvia is the second-largest Greek island (after Crete), and seems more like an extension of the mainland to which it was in fact once joined. At **Halkídha**, the gateway to the island, the connecting bridge has only a forty-metre channel to span, the island reputedly having been split from Attica and Thessaly by a blow from Poseidon's trident (earthquakes and subsidence being the more pedestrian explanations). There are ferry crossings at no fewer than seven points along its length, and the south of the island is closer to Athens than it is to northern Évvia.

Nevertheless, Évvia *is* an island, in places a very beautiful one. But it has an idiosyncratic history and demography, and an enduringly strange feel that is not to most foreigners' tastes. A marked Albanian influence in the south, and scattered Lombard and Venetian watchtowers can make it seem "un-Greek". Indeed, the island was the longest-surviving southerly outpost of the Ottoman Turks, who had a keen appreciation of the island's wealth, as did the Venetians and Lombards before them. The last Ottoman garrison was not evicted until 1833, hanging on in defiance of the peace settlement that awarded Évvia to the new Greek state. Substantial Turkish communities, renowned for their alleged brutality, remained until 1923.

Economically, Évvia has always been prized. By Greek standards, it's exceptionally fertile, producing everything from grain, corn and cotton to kitchen vegetables and livestock (the Classical name "Euboea" means "rich in cattle"). High-quality meat is far easier to come by than fish, reinforcing the continental feel; retsina from the many vineyards is held in similar high regard, flavoured by lately fire-ravaged pine trees. Despite the collapse of much of its mining industry, the island remains relatively prosperous, so there has been no need or inclination to encourage mass foreign tourism. Accordingly, Greeks predominate, especially in the north around the spa of **Loutrá Edhipsoú**. In high season, Évvia can seem merely a beach annexe for much of Thessaly and Athens.

In the rolling countryside of the **north**, grain-combines whirl even on the sloping hay-meadows between olive groves and pine forest. This is the most conventionally scenic part of the island, echoing the beauty of the smaller Sporades. The **northeast coast** is rugged and largely inaccessible, its few sandy beaches surf-pounded and often dirty; the **southwest** is gentler and more sheltered, though much disfigured by industrial operations. The **centre** of the island, between Halkídha and the easterly port of Kími, is mountainous and dramatic, while the far **southeast** is mostly denuded and poor.

Public **transport** consists of seasonal hydrofoils along the protected southwest coast from Halkídha upwards, and passable bus services along the main roads to Káristos in the southeast and Loutrá Edhipsoú in the northwest. Otherwise, explorations are best conducted by rented car; any two-wheeler will make little impact on the enormous distances involved.

Halkídha

The heavily industrialized island-capital of **HALKÍDHA** (the ancient Halkís, an appellation still used) is the largest town on Évvia, with a population of 50,000. A shipyard, rail sidings and cement works make it a dire place apart from the old Ottoman quarter of **Kástro**, still home to gypsies, some Turks from Thrace and, at most, a hundred Jews – all that remains of the oldest Jewish community in Greece.

The entrance to the *kástro* – on the right as you head inland from the old *Euripos* bridge – is marked by the handsome fifteenth-century **mosque**, nominally a museum of Byzantine artefacts, but permanently locked. Beyond lie the remains of the old fortress, an arcaded aqueduct and the unique basilican **church of Ayía Paraskeví**

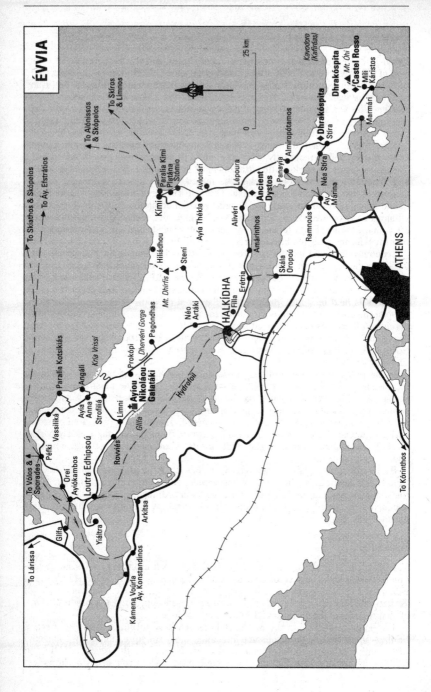

ÉVVIA

0   25 km

To Lárissa

To Vólos & Sporades

To Áy. Efstrátios

To Skíathos & Skópelos

To Alónissos & Skópelos

To Skíros & Límnos

Gliffa

Yfáltra

Kámena Voúrla
Áy. Konstandinos

Arkítsa

Péfki

Vassiliká

Orei

Ayiókambos

Loutrá Edhipsoú

Rovíes

Limni

Ayia Anna

Strofiliá

Angáli

Paralía Kotsikiás

Kría Vríssi

Prokópi

Dhirvéni Gorge

Pagóndhas

Glifa

Áyiou Nikoláou
Galatáki

Hydrodoi

Néo
Artáki

HALKÍDHA

Filla

Erétria

Mt. Dhírfis

Steni

Hiliádhou

Ayía Thékla

Skála
Oropoú

Ramnoús

Amárinthos

Alivéri

Avlonári

Lépoura

Ancient
Dystos

Panayía

Áy.
Marína

Néa Stíra

Almiropótamos

Stíra

Dhrakóspita

Kími

Paralía Kími

Platána
Stómio

ATHENS

To Kórinthos

Dhrakóspita

Castel Rosso

Mt. Óhi

Míli

Káristos

Marmári

Kavodóro
(Kafiréas)

(also generally shut). The church is an odd structure, converted by the Crusaders during the fourteenth century into a Gothic cathedral. In the opposite direction, in the new town, an **archeological museum**, Venizélou 13 (daily except Mon 8.30am–3pm; 400dr), contains finds principally from nearby ancient Erétria.

The waterside overlooks the **Evripós**, the narrow channel dividing Évvia from the mainland, whose strange currents have baffled scientists for centuries. You can stand on the bridge that spans the narrowest point and watch the water swirling by like a river. Every few hours the current changes and the "tide" reverses. Aristotle is said to have thrown himself into the waters in despair at his inability to understand what was happening, so if you're puzzled you're in good company; there is still no entirely satis-factory explanation.

Practicalities

For most visitors, though, such activities are strictly time-fillers, with much the best view of the place to be had from the bus, train or hydrofoil on the way out. **Trains** arrive on the mainland-side of the channel, beneath the seventeenth-century Ottoman fortress of Kara Baba; given numerous, quick rail links with Athens, there's no conceiv-able reason to stay overnight. Most other services of interest lie within sight of the old Evripós bridge. The **hydrofoil** terminal sits just northeast, on the mainland side of the channel. The **bus station** is 400m from the bridge along Kótsou, then 50m right; no schedules are posted, but you should get a connection for any corner of the island as long as you show up by 2pm. The **OTE** is on Venizélou, near the museum.

Options for **eating out** are not brilliant, least of all at the obvious quayside tourist-traps; the immediate vicinity of the bus station has a handful of acceptable grills serv-ing adequate lunches.

East from Halkídha

The coast road heading east out of Halkídha is an exceptionally misleading introduc-tion to the interior of Évvia. Just what British and German package-tour companies see in the disappointing scenery around Erétria and Amárinthos is hard to imagine. There are some intriguing **Frankish towers** at Fílla, worth a detour inland from Vasilikó if you have a car, and some easy connections to Athens, but little else.

Modern **ERÉTRIA** is a rather dreary resort laid out on a grid plan; for non-packaged travellers its main asset is a well-advertised ferry service across to Skála Oropoú in Attica. The **site of ancient Erétria** is more distinguished, though much of it lies under the town. A few scanty remains are dotted around the town centre, most conspic-uously an **agora** and a **Temple of Apollo**, but marginally more interesting are the excavations in the northwest corner, behind the small museum (rarely open). Here a **theatre** has been uncovered; steps from the orchestra descend to an underground vault used for sudden entrances and exits. Beyond the theatre are the ruins of a **gymnasium** and a **sanctuary**. While most of the "highlights" are diligently signposted, all appear to be suffering from years of neglect and are currently fenced off.

Just before Aliveri, an enormous modern power plant and a virtually intact medieval castle seem incongruously juxtaposed, and more Fílla-type towers look down from nearby hills; thereafter, the route mercifully heads inland. Beyond Lépoura, where the road branches north and south, the scenery improves drastically. Take the north fork towards Kími, and cross some of the most peaceful countryside in Greece.

Twelve kilometres north of Lépoura, at Háni Avlonaríou, stands the Romanesque thirteenth- or fourteenth-century **basilica of Áyios Dhimítrios**, Évvia's largest and finest, though unhappily locked. **AVLONÁRI** proper, 2km east, is dominated by a hill that commands most of the island's centre. At its crown is a huge Lombard or Venetian tower, rearing above the Neoclassical and vernacular houses that tier the lower slopes. This is the first place you'd probably choose to break a journey from Halkídha, if you have your own vehicle; there's a single taverna below the *platía*, though no accommodation.

This part of Évvia is particularly well endowed with Byzantine chapels, since Avlonári was an archiepiscopal see from the sixth century onwards. Back on the road to Kími, a left fork just north of Háni Avlonaríou (the bus goes this way) leads past the hamlet of Ayía Thékla, where a small, shed-like **chapel** of that saint, probably slightly later than Áyios Dhimítrios, hides in a lush vale below the modern church. Inside, enough fresco fragments remain with their large-eyed faces to suggest that some fine art has been lost over time. The right fork leads towards the coast and takes you past Oxílithos, with its somewhat more elaborate **chapels of Áyios Nikólaos** and **Ayía Ánna**, both at least a century older than Áyios Dhimítrios.

The road hits the coast at the fine beach of **Stómio** (known also, and confusingly, as Paralía or "Beach"), some 1500m of sand closing off the mouth of a river, which is deep, swimmable and often cleaner than the sea. To the north and east you glimpse the capes enclosing the broad bay of Kími. Up on the road, there are a couple of cafés and a small pension; most facilities, however, are further round the coast at **PLATÁNA**, where another river is flanked by a line of older houses, many with rooms or flats to rent.

Despite its name, the extremely functional port of **PARALÍA KÍMIS** has no real beach, and does not make a particularly congenial place to be stuck overnight waiting for a ferry or hydrofoil to the Sporades or Límnos. The most substantial and traditional **taverna** is *Spanos/Toh Egeo*, at the south end of the front; the two **hotels**, *Coralli* (☎0222/22 212; ④) and *Beis* (☎0222/22 604; ④), will work out more expensive than anything in Platána or Kími proper.

Most travellers get to **KÍMI** (the main ferry port to Skíros) by bus, which takes the inland route via Ayía Thékla. The upper part of town is built on a green ridge overlooking both the sea and Paralía Kími, 4km below. At the bottom of town, on the harbour-bound road, you can visit the **Folklore Museum**, which has an improbably large collection of costumes, household and agricultural implements and old photos recording the doings of Kimians both locally and in the USA, where there's a huge community. Among the emigrants was Dr George Papanikolaou, deviser of the "Pap" cervical smear test, and there's a statue honouring him up in the upper-town *platía*. Nearby are a couple of cheapish **hotels**, the *Kimi* (☎0222/22 408; ③) and the *Krineion* (☎0222/22 287; ③), plus some unadvertised **rooms**, and good **tavernas** where you can sample the products of the local vineyards.

To get up into the rugged country west of Kími, you must negotiate jeep tracks through the forest, or return to Halkídha for the bus service up to **STENÍ**, a large and beautiful village at the foot of Mount Dhírfis. The village has a few cheap *psistariés* and two **hotels**, the *Dirfys* (☎0228/51 217; ③) and the *Steni* (☎0228/51 221; ④). It's a good area for hiking, most notably up the peaks of Dhírfis and Ksirovoúni, and beyond to the isolated beach hamlets of Hiliádhou and Ayía Iríni, though you'll need a good map or hiking guide to find your way.

South from Halkídha

The extension of Évvia southeast of Lépoura, usually so narrow that you can sometimes glimpse the sea on both sides simultaneously, has a flavour very distinct from the rest of the island. Often bleak and windwept, it forms a geological unit with neighbouring Ándhros, with shared slates and marble. Ethnically, the south has much in common with that northernmost Cyclade: both were heavily settled by Albanian immigrants from the early fifteenth century onwards, and *Arvanítika* (a medieval dialect of

Albanian) was until recently the first language of the remoter villages here. Even non-*Arvanítika* speakers often betray their ancestry by their startlingly fair colouring and aquiline features. For a place so close to Athens, the south is often surprisingly rural; some of the houses have yet to lose their original slate roofs, and the few fields on the steep slopes are far more often worked by donkeys and horses than by farm machinery.

Immediately southeast of Lépoura, most foreign maps persist in showing the lake of Dhístos in bright blue. In fact, the lake area has been almost totally drained and reclaimed as rich farmland, much to the detriment of the migratory birds who used to stop off here, and to the annoyance of Greek and foreign environmentalists who would prefer that they still did so. Atop the almost perfectly conical hill in the centre of the flat basin are the sparse fifth-century-BC ruins of **ancient Dystos**, and a subsequent medieval citadel.

Beyond the Dhístos plain, the main road continues along the mountainous spine of the island to Káristos at the southern end of the paved road system and bus line. If you have your own transport, it's worth stopping off at **STÍRA**, above which are a cluster of **Dhrakóspita** (Dragon Houses), signposted at the north edge of the village and reached by track, then trail. They are so named after the only semi-mythological beings thought capable of shifting into place their enormous masonry blocks, and the structures' origins and uses have yet to be definitively established. The most convincing theory holds that they are sixth-century-BC temples built by immigrants or slaves from Asia Minor working in the nearby marble and slate quarries.

The shore annexe of **NÉA STÍRA**, 5km downhill from the hill village, is a fairly standard package resort, worth knowing about only for its handy ferry connection to Ayía Marína (which gives access to ancient Rhamnous) on the Attic peninsula. Much the same can be said for **MARMÁRI**, 19km south, except in this case the ferry link is with Rafína.

Káristos and around

At first sight **KÁRISTOS** is a bleak grid, courtesy of nineteenth-century Bavarian town-planners, which ends abruptly to east and west and is studded with modern buildings. Your opinion will improve with prolonged acquaintance, though this is still unlikely to be for more than a few days. What Káristos can offer to a handful of independent travellers is its superb (if often windy) beach of **Psilí Ámmos** to the west, and a lively, genuine working-port atmosphere. Only one plot of fenced-in foundations, in the central bazaar, bears out the town' ancient provenance, and the oldest obvious structure is the fourteenth-century Venetian **Bourtzi** (permanently locked) on the waterfront. This small tower is all that remains of once-extensive fortifications. Every evening the shore road is blocked with a gate at this point to permit an undisturbed *vólta* or promenade by the locals.

Practicalities

Rafína-based **ferries** and **hydrofoils** also serve Káristos, docking rather obviously at mid-quay; **buses** arrive inland, above the central *platía* and below the *National Bank*, near a tiny combination grill/ticket office labelled *KTEL*. This has information on the extremely infrequent (once daily at best) departures to the remote villages of the Kavodoro (Kafiréas) cape to the east.

Affordable **accommodation** can prove to be a headache. Very close to the Bourtzi on the shore road, the *Hironia* (☎0224/22 238; ④) is in need of maintenance but undeniably well placed, with quiet rear rooms. The *Als*, just inland at mid-esplanade (☎0224/22 202; ④), will be pretty noisy; perhaps the best strategy is to follow up signs in restaurant windows advertising **rooms** inland.

By contrast, you're spoilt for choice when **eating out**, as Káristos must have more restaurants than the rest of Évvia put together. One of the best choices is the *Kavo Doros*, a friendly and reasonable taverna on Párodos Sachtoúri just behind the front, which serves oven food; another is the cheap, filling and popular lunchtime option, *Ta Kalamia*, at the west end of the esplanade by the start of Psilí Ámmos beach.

Around Káristos

The obvious excursion from Káristos is inland towards **Mount Óhi** (1399m) Évvia's highest peak after Dhírfis and Ksirovoúni. **MÍLI**, a fair-sized village around a spring-fed oasis, 3km straight inland, makes a good first stop, with its few tavernas. Otherwise, the medieval castle of **Castel Rosso** beckons above, a 20-minute climb up from the main church (longer in the frequent, howling gales). Inside the castle is a total ruin, except for an Orthodox **chapel of Profitis Ilías** built over the Venetians' water cistern, but the sweeping views over the sea and the town make the trip worthwhile.

Behind, the ridges of Óhi are as lunar and inhospitable as the broad plain around Káristos is fertile. From Míli, it's a three-hour-plus hike up the largely bare slopes, mostly by a path cutting across the new road, past a little-used alpine-club shelter (fed by spring water) to the summit and yet another *dhrakóspito*, even more impressive than the three smaller ones at Stíra. Built of enormous schist slabs, seemingly sprouting from the mountain, this one is popularly supposed to be haunted.

North from Halkídha

The main road due north from Halkídha crosses a few kilometres of flat farmland and salt marsh on either side of ugly Néa Artáki, after which it climbs steeply through forested hills and the **Dhervéni gorge**, gateway to the north of Évvia.

The village of **PROKÓPI** lies beyond the narrows, in a valley defined by the rich and beautiful woods that make it famous. A counterpoint, in the village itself, is the eyesore pilgrimage church of **Saint John the Russian**, which holds the saint's relics. The "Russian" was actually a Ukranian soldier, captured by the Turks in the early eighteenth century and taken to Turkey where he died. According to locals, his mummified body began to sponsor miracles, and the saint's relics were brought here by Orthodox Turks from Cappadocian Prokópi (today Ürgüp) in the 1923 population exchange – Evvian Prokópi is still occasionally referred to by its old name of Ahmetága.

Following a shady, stream-fed glen for the 8km north of Prokópi, you suddenly emerge at Mandoúdhi, much the biggest village in the north of the island, though now squarely in the doldrums following the collapse of the local magnesite industry; ignore signs or depictions on certain maps of a beach at Paralía Mandoúdhi, which is nothing more than abandoned quarries and crushing plants. The closest serviceable beach is at **Paralía Kírinthos**, better known as **Kría Vrissí** (take a right-hand turning off the main road, 3km beyond Mandoúdhi). At the coast, two rivers – one salt-water, one fresh – bracket a small beach, with the headland south of the sweet river supporting the extremely sparse remains of **ancient Kirinthos**. The hamlet of Kirinthos, just inland, is edged by cornfields and consists merely of a cluster of summer houses, with one sporadically functioning taverna and no short-term accommodation.

Back on the main road, a fork at Strofiliá, 8km north of Mandoúdhi, offers a choice of routes: continue north to the coastal resorts that curl round the end of the island, or head west for Límni.

Límni

If you're hunting for a place to stay, **LÍMNI**, on the west coast 19km from Strofiliá, is by far the most practical and attractive base north of Halkídha. The largely Neoclassical, tile-roofed town, built from the wealth engendered by nineteenth-century shipping prowess, is the most appealing on the island, with serviceable beaches and a famous convent nearby.

There is a regular **hydrofoil** service to Halkídha and the Sporades, and buses from Halkídha stop at the north side of the quay. Límni has an **OTE**, a **post office** and two **banks**, all inland just off the main through-road into town from Strofiliá.

As yet, Límni gets few package tours, and vacancies at the two **hotels** are usually available except during August. At the extreme south end of the waterfront, and thus quieter, the *Limni* (☎0227/31 316; ③) is good value, with singles and doubles; the *Plaza* beside the bus stop, (☎0227/31 235; ②), is even more reasonable, but has no singles and gets some noise from nocturnal revels outside. The *Pirofanis* (☎0227/31 640; ③), an *ouzerí* beyond the *Plaza,* rents some **rooms** upstairs and apartments north of town. The best **place to eat** in terms of setting, menu and popularity is *O Platanos* (under the enormous quayside plane tree). *Toh Astron*, 3km south of town on the coast road past the *Limni*, is a well-regarded taverna, specializing in meat dishes.

Around Límni

The outstanding excursion from Límni is 7km south (under your own steam) to the **convent of Ayíou Nikoláou Galatáki**, superbly set on the wooded slopes of Mount Kandhíli, overlooking the north Evvian Gulf. To get there, veer up and left at the unsigned fork off the coast road; there's no formal scheme for visiting, but don't bother showing up between 3pm and 5pm when all of Greece – secular and monastic – sleeps. Though much rebuilt since its original Byzantine foundation atop a Poseidon temple, the convent retains a thirteenth-century tower built to guard against pirates. One of a dozen or so shy but friendly nuns will show you frescoes in the *katholikón* dating from the principal sixteenth-century renovation. Especially vivid, on the the right of the narthex, is the *Entry of the Righteous into Paradise*; they ascend a perilous ladder, being crowned by angels and received by Christ – the wicked miss the rungs and fall directly into the maw of Leviathian.

Below Ayíou Nikoláou Galatáki, and easily combined with it to make a full half-day outing, are the pebble-and-sand **beaches of Glífa**, arguably the best on Évvia's south-west-facing coast. There are several in succession, leading up to the very base of Mount Kandhíli, with path-only access to the last few. The shore is remarkably clean, considering the number of summer campers who pitch tents here for weeks on end; a single roadside spring, 2km before, is the only facility in the whole zone.

The are no recommendable beaches in Límni itself, though if you continue 2500m northwest from the town you reach the gravel strand of **Kohíli**, with a basic but leafy **campsite** out on the cape, 500m beyond mid-beach.

ROVVIÉS, some 10km further in the same direction, doesn't stand out, but with its medieval tower, grid of weekenders' apartments and services is the last place of any sort before Loutrá Edhipsoú.

Northern coastal resorts

Returning to the junction at Strofiliá, take the main road north for 8km to **AYÍA ÁNNA** (locally and universally elided to Ayiánna), which has long enjoyed the unofficial status of Évvia's most folkloric village by virtue of some lingering traditional costumes on the older women, and an assiduous local ethnographer, Dimitris Settas, who died in 1989. The place itself is nothing extrordinary, and most passers-by are interested in the prominently marked turnoff for **Angáli beach**, 5km east. This is billed as the area's best, and it's sandy enough, but like this entire coast it's exposed and garbage-strewn, the low hills behind lending little drama. A frontage road, set back 200m or so, is lined by a few kilometres of anonymous villas and apartments, with the "village" at the north end.

Ten kilometres beyond Ayía Ánna, a side road heads downhill for 6km, past the village of Kotsikiá, to **Paralía Kotsikiás**. The small cove with its taverna and rooms serves primarily as a fishing-boat anchorage, and its tiny, seaweed-strewn beach will interest few. **Psaropoúli beach**, 2km below Vassiliká village (13km north of the Kotsikiá turnoff), is more usable in its three-kilometre length, but like Ayía Ánna it seems flotsam-scruffy and shadeless, with a smattering of rooms, self-catering units and tavernas not imparting much sense of community. **Elliniká**, the next signposted beach, lies only 800m below its namesake village inland; it's far smaller than Angáli or Psaropoúli, but cleaner and certainly the most picturesque spot on this coast, with a church-capped islet offshore as a target to swim to. The approach driveway has a very limited number of facilities comprising a minimarket, one taverna and a few studios.

Beyond Elliniká the road (and bus line) skirts the northern tip of Évvia to curl southwest towards **PÉFKI**, a seaside resort, mobbed with Greeks in summer, which straggles for some two kilometres along a mediocre beach. The best **restaurants**, near the north end of this strip, include *Ouzeri Ta Thalassina* and *Psitopolio O Thomas*, while *Zaharoplastio O Peristeras* proffers every decadent sweet known to Greek man. **Accommodation** is the usual Évvian mix of self-catering units and a few fancy hotels, all resolutely pitched at mainlanders; the **campsite**, *Camping Pefki*, is 2km north of town behind the beach, rather pricey and of most interest to those in caravans.

The next resort (14km southwest), **OREÍ**, is so poorly signposted from the bypass road that one suspects that they don't especially want any casual trade. A detour yields a grid-planned, not especially attractive place, with only its role as the last **hydrofoil stop** en route to Vólos and the Sporades to recommend it. Some 7km further along the coast, **AYIÓKAMBOS** has a frequent ferry connection to Glífa on the mainland opposite, whence there are buses to Vólos. Ayiókambos itself proves suprisingly pleasant considering its port function, with a patch of beach, two or three tavernas and a few rooms for rent.

The trans-island bus route ends 14km south of Ayiókambos at **LOUTRÁ EDHIPSOÚ**, which attracts older Greeks (filling more than a hundred creaky hotels and pensions) who come to bathe at the **spas** renowned since antiquity for curing everything from gallstones to depression. There are less regimented **hot springs** at Yiáltra, 15km west around the head of Edhipsós bay, where the water boils up on the rocky beach, warming the shallows to comfortable bath temperature. From Loutrá Edhipsoú, the coast road heads southeast to Límni, permitting a loop of northern Évvia while based there.

travel details

Alkyon Tours (in cooperation with *Nomicos* ferry lines), and the competing *Goutos Lines*, provide expensive **conventional ferry** services out of Vólos, Áyios Konstandínos and Kími, with fares almost double those on Cyclades or Dodecanese lines. On the plus side, *Alkyon* maintain an Athens office (Akadhimías 97) for purchase of ferry, *Flying Icarus* and combined bus-and-ferry tickets.

Between April and October, *Flying Dolphin* and *Flying Icarus* **hydrofoils** operate between various mainland ports and the Sporades. These are pricier than the ferries but cut journey times virtually in half.

SKÍATHOS, SKÓPELOS AND ALÓNISSOS

Ferries

Áyios Konstandínos: to Skíathos (9 weekly; 3hr); Skópelos (7 weekly; 5hr, 3 continuing to Alónissos, 6hr).

Kími: to Alónissos (4 weekly; 3hr) and Skópelos (4 weekly; 3hr 30min), 2 continuing to Skíathos (5hr 30min).

Vólos: to Skíathos (3–4 daily; 3hr) and Skópelos (3–4 daily; 4hr); Alónissos (at least daily; 5hr; this is the most consistent service out of season, and is always the cheapest).

Ceres *Flying Dolphins* (April–Oct only)

Áyios Konstandínos: to Skíathos, Glóssa, Skópelos and Alónissos (April, May & early Oct 1–3 daily; June–Sept 3–5 daily).

Néos Marmarás (Halkidhikí): to Skíathos, Skópelos, Alónissos and Skíros (June–Aug daily).

Plataniás (Pílion): to Skíathos, Skópelos and Alónissos (June–Aug 2 daily).

Thessaloníki: to Skíathos, Glóssa, Skópelos and Alónissos (June–Aug daily).

Tríkeri (Pílion): to Vólos (June–mid-Oct daily); Skíathos (June–mid-Sept 2 daily); Skíathos, Skópelos and Alónissos (April–Oct daily).

Vólos: to Skíathos, Glóssa and Skópelos (April, May & Oct 2 daily; June–Sept 4 daily); at least 2 daily (April–Oct) continue from Skópelos to Alónissos.

Flights

Athens: to Skíathos (3 daily; 40min).

SKÍROS

Ferries

Skíros is served by conventional ferry, the *Lykomides*, from **Kími** ((2hr 20min). Services are at least twice daily mid-June to mid-Sept (usually at around noon & 5pm), once daily (5pm) the rest of the year; ☎0222/22 020 for current information. There is a connecting bus service for the afternoon boat, from the Liossíon 260 terminal in Athens (departs 12.30pm).

Flying Dolphins

A daily **hydrofoil** (June–Aug) links Skíros with Skíathos, Skópelos and Alónissos, as well as Néos Marmarás on Halkidhikí.

Flights

Athens: to Skíros (June–Oct; 5 weekly; Nov–May 2 weekly).

ÉVVIA

Buses

Athens (Liossíon 260 terminal): to Halkídha (every 30min 7.45am–9pm; 1hr 40min); Kími (4–5 daily; 3hr 40min).

Halkídha to: Káristos (1–2 daily; 3hr); Límni (4 daily; 1hr 30min); Loutrá Edhipsoú (4 daily; 3hr); Kími (4 daily; 1 hr 45 min)

Trains

Athens (Laríssis station): to Halkídha (18 daily; 1hr 25min).

Ferries

Arkítsa: to Loutrá Edhipsoú (12 daily 6.45am–11pm; 50min).

Ayía Marína: to Néa Stíra (summer 12–20 daily; 50min); Panayía (summer 3–4 daily; 50min).

Glífa: to Ayiókambos (8 daily; 30min).

Rafína: to Káristos (Mon–Thurs & Sat 3 daily, Fri & Sun 4 daily; 2hr); Marmári (2 daily; 1hr).

Skála Oropoú: to Erétria (hourly 5am–10pm; 25min).

Ceres *Flying Dolphins*

Halkídha: to Límni, Loutrá Edhipsoú, Oreí, Skíathos and Skópelos (May to mid-Oct 5 weekly; usually late afternoon).

Oreí: to Vólos, Skópelos and Alónissos (June to mid-Sept daily); Skíathos (June to mid-Oct 2 daily).

Ilio Line Hydrofoils

Rafína: to Káristos (mid-June to late Sept 4 weekly).

Tínos/Míkonos (Cyclades): to Káristos (mid-June to late Sept 3 weekly).

*Connecting buses **from Athens** run to Rafína (every 30min; 1hr 30min), Ayía Marína (5 daily; 1hr 15min) and Skála Oropoú (hourly; 2hr) all from the Mavromatéon terminal, and to Arkítsa and Glífa from the Liossíon 260 terminal.*

CHAPTER SEVEN

THE IONIAN

The Ionian islands comprise a core group of six – **Corfu** (Kérkira), **Páxi** (Paxos), **Lefkádha** (Lefkhas), Itháki (Ithaca), Kefalloniá (Cephallonia) and Zákinthos (Zante) – which shepherd their satellites down the west coast of mainland Greece. In addition, the group takes in the islands of **Kíthira** and **Andíkithira**, miles adrift at the foot of the Peloponnese, and to all intents a different sphere of island-hopping.

The six core islands will come as quite a shock to those used to the stark outlines of the Aegean. Afloat on the haze of the Adriatic, they are characterized by green, even lush, landscapes – a fertility that is a direct result of the heavy rains which sweep over the archipelago (especially Corfu) from October to March. If you visit in the off-season, come prepared. From April to September, however, the climate is a delight – gentler and a few degrees cooler than the Aegean.

The islands were the Homeric realm of Odysseus, centred on Ithaca (modern Itháki) and here alone of all modern Greek territory the Ottomans never held sway. After the fall of Byzantium, possession passed to the **Venetians** and the islands became a keystone in that city state's maritime empire from 1386 until its collapse in 1797. Most of the population must have remained immune to the establishment of Italian as the official language and the arrival of Roman Catholicism, but Venetian influence remains evident in the architecture of the island capitals, despite damage from a series of earthquakes.

On Corfu, the Venetian legacy is mixed with that of the **British**, who imposed a military "protectorate" over the Ionian at the close of the Napoleonic Wars, before ceding the archipelago to Greece in 1864. There is, however, no question of the islanders' essential Greekness: the poet Dionissios Solomos, author of the National Anthem, hailed from the Ionians, as did Nikos Mantzelos, who provided the music, and the first Greek president, Ioannis Kapodistrias.

Today, **tourism** is the dominating influence, especially on **Corfu**, one of the first Greek islands established on the package-holiday circuit. Its east coast is one of the few stretches in Greece with development to match the Spanish *costas*, and in summer even its distinguished old capital, Kérkira Town, wilts beneath the onslaught. However, the island is large enough to retain some of its charms and is perhaps the most scenically beautiful of the group.

Parts of **Zákinthos** – which with Corfu has the Ionians' best beaches – seem to be going along the same tourist path, following the introduction of charter flights from northern Europe, but elsewhere the pace and scale of development is a lot less intense. Little **Páxi** is a bit too tricky to reach and lacks the water to support a large-scale hotel, although a number of British companies have moved in offering villa holidays. **Lefkádha** – which is connected to the mainland by a causeway and "boat bridge" – has, so far at least, a quite low-key straggle of resorts, although it has excellent beaches and bays, which are particularly good for novice sailors and windsurfers.

Perhaps the most rewarding duo for island-hopping, however, are **Kefalloniá** and **Itháki**, the former with a series of "real towns" and a life in large part independent of tourism, the latter, Odysseus's rugged capital, protected by an absence of sand. The Ionian islands' claims to Homeric significance are manifested in some apt if fanciful sights on Itháki, and other islands, as well as countless bars, restaurants and streets named after characters in the Odyssey.

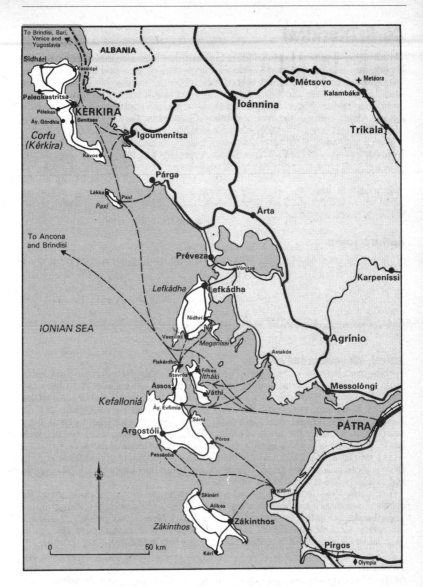

There are no ferry connections from these islands to **Kíthira**, which is most easily visited as part of a tour of the Peloponnese. If you make it – and you can get a weekly ferry on to Crete – the rewards are low-key: a very "Greek" island, with little foreign tourism and no special sights to attract it. Which may, of course, be just what you're after. For true isolates, there is also a twice weekly link to Andíkithira, an island visited, to our knowledge, by just one reader of this book in the past ten years.

Corfu (Kérkira)

The seductive beauty of **Corfu** (Kérkira in Greek) has been a source of inspiration for generations. It is thought that Shakespeare took tales of the island as his setting for *The Tempest*; Lawrence Durrell echoed this tribute by naming his book about the island *Prospero's Cell*; and Edward Lear enthused that it made him "grow younger every hour". Henry Miller, totally in his element, became euphoric, lying for hours in the sun "doing nothing, thinking of nothing". Some claim Corfu to be Homer's kingdom of Phaeacia where Odysseus was washed ashore and met the beautiful Nausicaa.

With a reputation as the "greenest Greek island", its natural appeal, the shapes and scents of its lemon and orange trees, its figs, cypresses and, above all, its three million olive trees, all remain an experience – if sometimes a beleaguered one, for Corfu has more package hotels and holiday villas than any other Greek island. Yet for all the commercialism – and the wholesale spoiling of its northeast coast – it remains an island where you can still leave the crowds behind, and where almost everyone seems to end up having a good time.

Kérkira Town

Corfu's scale of tourism is apparent the moment you arrive in **KÉRKIRA TOWN** (or Corfu Town). It is a graceful, elegant town – almost a city – sandwiched between a pair of **forts** and with a gorgeous esplanade, the **Spianádha**, where the Corfiotes play cricket most Sundays – one of the town's more obvious British legacies. The town even reminded Evelyn Waugh of Brighton, as he noted in his diary. However, the crowds in summer are overpowering and in season, at least, you'll probably find a night or two here at the beginning or end of your stay is time enough.

Arrival, information and services

Ferries from Italy dock at the New Port to the west of the Néo Froúrio (New Fort); those to and from the mainland (Igoumenitsa, Párga, etc) arriving slightly further west. The Paleó Froúrio (Old Fort) dock is now only used for excursions and by some ferries to Paxos. If in doubt, check with the ticket agent or the **port police** (☎0661/32 655). Coming from the **airport**, 2km south of the centre, you can walk (about 40min), get a taxi (1200dr, but agree the fare in advance; ☎0661/33 811 for radio taxis), or catch local bus #5 or #6 blue bus, which leave from 500m north of the terminal gates.

The **tourist office** is 800m east of the New Port, at Zavitsianou 17 (☎0661/37 520). Here you can pick up free maps of the town and island, bus timetables, a list of hotels and campsites and information on rooms for rent.

The *Corfu News* (published by and available from the tourist office) is useful for details of **services** (launderettes, doctors and dentists, etc); branches of most of the major **banks** are dotted throughout the town. *Greek Skies Travel* (☎0661/30 883) are the agents for *American Express* at Kapodhistríou 20. The central **post office** is at Alexandros 19; while **OTE** is at Montzarou 9 (daily 6am–midnight).

Transport

All the island's **buses** start and finish in town. There are two terminals: one on Platía San Rócco for numbered **blue bus** routes to the suburbs and across the island; the other at 9 Paradhos, I Theotóki, second left up this street from the New Port, for **green buses** to more remote destinations. For schedules, consult the tourist office or check the terminal boards. If you are heading for Athens, you can buy combination bus and ferry tickets for the trip (at least daily in season) from the KTEL bus terminal just off I Theotóki.

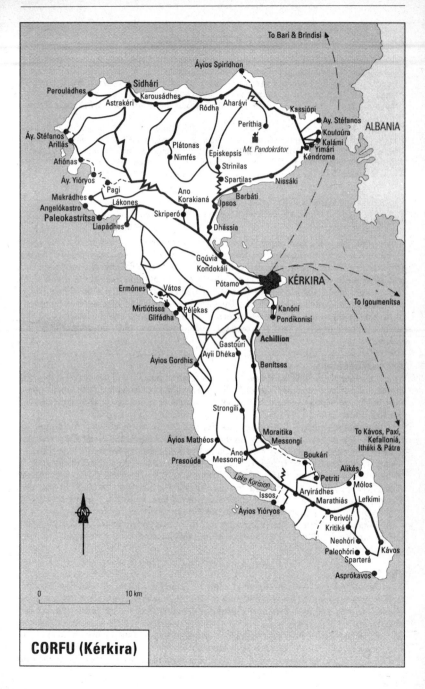

CORFU (Kérkira)

Mopeds, bicycles and cars are available for rent in the town, with most of the agencies found around the Old and New Ports and along Xenofondos Stratigou. Try *Top Cars* (☎0661/35 237) for reasonable rates. Motorbikes are more reliable than mopeds and less likely to have been pushed beyond their capacity but only take them if you're an experienced rider. An incredible number of people have accidents on the gravelly, potholed tracks. Note that almost all of the garages on the island are closed on Sundays.

In season there are also a few excursion **kaíkia** boats to certain beaches on the southern coast of the island – providing easier and more pleasant access than the buses.

Accommodation

There are usually **accommodation** touts meeting the boats – and taxi drivers, too, will often know of places to stay. Alternatively, pick up a list of rooms from the tourist office (see p.338), which can point you in the right direction; rooms are mainly located near the New Port.

Things fill so quickly in high season, that it's barely worth offering recommendations. If space is available, the best mid-range option by far is the *Hotel Kypros*, Áyion Patéron 13 (☎0661/40 675; ③). Other **hotels** worth phoning ahead for include: *Pension Anthis*, Kefalomandoúkou (☎0661/25 804; ④); *Hotel Arcadian*, Kapodistríou 44 (☎0661/37670; ④); *Hotel Bretagne*, Georgáki 27 (☎0661/31 129; ⑤); *Hotel Dalia*, 7 Ethnikou Stadiou (☎0661/36 048; ⑤); *Hotel Europa*, Yitsiali 10, New Port (☎0661/39 304; ③); *Hotel Hermes*, Markóra 14 (☎0661/39 268; ④); *Hotel Ionian*, 46 Xen. Stratigou (☎0661/39915; ④); and *Hotel Phoenix*, H. Smírnis 2 (☎0661/42 290; ④).

At Kondokáli village, 4.5km north of town, there is a **youth hostel** (☎0661/9 1292) and **campsite** (☎0661/91 202), neither in an ideal location for the town but certainly inexpensive enough.

The Town

A stroll around the old parts of town offers a fascinating blend of Venetian, French, British and occasional Greek architecture. The most obvious sights are the forts, the **Paleó Froúrio** and **Néo Froúrio**, whose designations (*paleó* – "old", *néo* – "new") are a little misleading since what you see of the older structure was begun by the Byzantines in the mid-twelfth century, a mere hundred years before the Venetians began work on the newer citadel. They have both been modified and damaged by various occupiers and besiegers since, the last contribution being the Neoclassical shrine of **St George**, built by the British in the middle of Paleó Froúrio during the 1840s. The Paleó Froúrio is open daily from 8am to 7pm (free) and hosts a sound-and-light show most evenings; the Néo Froúrio is home to the Greek navy and off-limits to the public.

The **Spianádha** (Esplanade) has a leisured and graceful air, and many are ensnared by one of the cafés facing the **Listón**, an arcaded legacy of the brief French occupation, built by the architect of the Rue de Rivoli in Paris. If paying high prices for your *tsíntsi bírra* (ginger beer – another British influence) puts you off, stroll along the far side of the promenade close to the fort, where in the splendid flower gardens you can join groups of women chatting and lace-making in the evening sun.

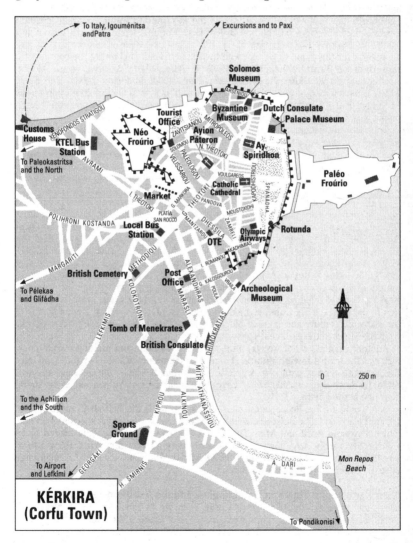

KÉRKIRA
(Corfu Town)

Fronting the north end of the Spianádha is the **Palace of St Michael and St George** (Tues–Sat 8.30am–3pm, Sun 9.30am–2.30pm; 500dr, students 200dr), a solidly British edifice built as the residence of their High Commissioner, one of the last of whom was the future Prime Minister William Gladstone, and later used as a palace by the Greek monarchy. Its former staterooms house a large collection of Asiatic art, together with Byzantine relics from the island. Outside is a row of Doric columns bookended by monumental arches, with reliefs of the Ionian islands and Odysseus's rudderless ship. Through the archway is the loggia of the *Corfu Reading Society*, which has exhibitions of manuscripts, maps and art (daily 9am–1pm, plus 5–8pm Thurs & Fri), and close by is a Venetian landing stage and city gate, framing the Vido islet.

Towards the south of the Spianádha is the **Maitland Rotunda**, a graffiti-covered bandstand commemorating the first British High Commissioner, and, just beyond it a **statue of Ioannis Kapodistrias** (1776–1831), first president of modern Greece and an agitator for the union of Greece with the Ionian islands. Following the coast south, turn right on Vrála St just after the *Corfu Palace Hotel* and you come to the **Archeological Museum** (Tues–Sun 9am–3pm; 400dr, students 200dr, free Sun), which houses a modest collection whose prize exhibit is a 2500-year-old gorgon's-head pediment. Keep heading south from here and you reach **Mon Repos**, the town's public beach, a sand and shingle strip with a little jetty and a snack bar.

The most atmospheric part of town is the area known as **Campiello** – a maze of Venetian-era alleyways between the Palace of St Michael and St George and the old port. At the edge of the quarter, on the waterfront at Arseníou 41, is the **Solomos Museum** (Mon–Fri 5–8pm), former home of the Greek national poet and housing his archives and memorabilia. Nearby is the sixteenth-century Antivouniótissa church, which houses a little **Byzantine Museum** (Tues–Sun 9am–3pm) of icons.

To the southwest of the quarter is Corfu's **Cathedral**, packed with icons, including a fine sixteenth-century painting of *St George Slaying The Dragon* by the Cretan artist Michael Damaskinos. The building shares religious precedence with the church of **Áyios Spirídhon**, a few blocks to the east on Vouthrótou, where you will find the silver-encrusted coffin of the island's patron saint, Spirídhon – Spiros in the diminutive – after whom about half the male population is named. Four times a year (Palm Sunday and the following Saturday; August 11; and first Sunday in November), to the accompaniment of much celebration and feasting, the relics are paraded through the streets of Kérkira. Each of the days commemorates a miraculous deliverance of the island credited to the saint – twice from plague during the seventeenth century, from a famine of the sixteenth century and (a more blessed release than either of those for any Greek) from the Turks in the eighteenth century.

Another twisted grid of streets, south from the cathedral and backing onto the new fort, was the town's **Jewish quarter**, home to a community of some five thousand from the sixteenth century until 1940, when they were rounded up by the Germans and sent off to the death camp at Auschwitz. A **synagogue** survives on Velissáriou, at the southern edge of the ghetto.

South of Platía San Rócco, at the start of Kolokotroni, is the **British Cemetery**. It's a tranquil place and a botanist's heaven, well known for its numerous species of orchids which flower in April and May. The graves and gardens are lovingly tended to by George Psáilascoho who has lived and worked here for over fifty years. He will show you the memorial to the 44 British soldiers who died in 1946 when an Albanian mine destroyed their ship in the Corfu channel.

Near Corfu Town: Vlahérna, Pondikoníssi and the Achillion Palace

The most popular excursion from Corfu Town is to the islets of Vlahérna and Pondikoníssi, just offshore from the plush suburb of **Kanóni**, 4km south of town (take blue bus #2 from end of G.Theotóki, next to Platía San Rócco, every 30min). The closer is **Vlahérna**, capped by a small monastery and joined to the mainland by a short cause-way. Just beyond, a boat trip, swim or pedalo-push will bring you to **Pondikoníssi** (Mouse Island). Tufted with greenery and a small chapel, this is legendarily identified with a ship from Odysseus's fleet, petrified by Poseidon in revenge for the blinding of his son Polyphemus. The Homeric echoes are somewhat marred by the thronging masses and low flying aircraft from the nearby runway.

Three kilometres further to the south, past the resort sprawl of Peramá, is a rather more bizarre attraction: the **Achillion**, a palace built in a (fortunately) unique blend of Teutonic and Neoclassical styles in 1890 by Elizabeth, Empress of Austria. Henry Miller considered it "the worst piece of gimcrackery" that he'd ever laid eyes on and thought it "would make an excellent museum for surrealistic art". It is today a casino by night, though you can just visit the gardens in the daytime. If you are driving, you might combine a visit with a **meal** at the *Taverna Tripas* – one of the island's most imaginative, and not overpriced for the quality of its food– at the village of Kinopiástes, 3km inland.

Eating and drinking

Eating out, you need to pick your way through the tourist joints if you want to find anywhere vaguely Greek in style and price; for picnics, the best place is the produce **market** on G.Markóra.

Good **restaurant** choices include the *Averof*, at the Old Port, for traditional Greek dishes – it's a bit pricey but the food is well-prepared and presented. For a fine open-air setting next to Old Port, try the *Restaurant Skouna*, on Plateía Mitropóleos. *Yisdhakis*, Solomoú 20, off N. Theotóki, is as authentic as they come; while *Naftikon*, N.Theotóki 150, is unpretentious, with typical Greek and Corfu specialities. There's excellent seafood at *Orestes*, Stratigoú 78, by the New Port; and consider *Psistaria Ninos*, Sevastianoú 44, just off Kapodhistríou, a pleasant backstreet restaurant, or *Psistaria Poulis*, Arvanitáki 11, off G.Theotóki, for those of carnivorous taste.

For **drinks** and snacks, you are spoilt for choice with tourist-oriented bars and pubs. For a more local flavour, try Platia San Rocco and especially the *Café Espresso* there. *Café Plakádha*, in Platía Ayíou Spiridhóna, is enclosed by elegant architecture; while *The Cubby Hole*, Cotardou 42, just off N. Theotóki, is a cosy, friendly bar.

Nightlife and entertainment

Corfu Town has no shortage of **bars and clubs**, and during the summer there's a fair number of **open-air concerts** and **cultural events**. Indeed brass bands can some-times be heard practising around the old town. For details of events, check the *Corfu News*, or tune into *Radio Rama* (96.3 FM; Mon–Sat 3–5pm), with news and chat in Greek and English and spirited DJ-ing. Best of the town's **cinemas** – all of which show undubbed English/American films – is the one on G. Theotóki.

The most popular **clubs** are to the west of the New Port. *Coco Flash* and *Apokalypsis* are two of the best, the latter with wildly over-the-top decor of pyramids and Olympic torches. The *Hippodrome* has a pool and giant video screen but a reputation for attract-ing *kamákia* (lecherous locals on the hunt for women tourists).

The northeast coast

The coastline **north of Kérkira** has been remorselessly developed and the initial stretches are probably best written off. The concentration of hotels, villas and camp-sites give little sense of being in Greece, the beaches vary between pebbly and rocky and are often sullied with rubbish washed up from the mainland, and the sea looks murky and polluted, too. Things improve considerably, however, as you progress north and especially once you round the coast beyond Kassiópi.

Kérkira Town to Píryi

The first resort past Kérkira's suburbs is **KONDOKÁLI**, where the island's youth hostel and the town's nearest campsite are located (see Corfu Town "Accommodation"). Their siting is uninspired, to say the least– a built-up area, with the stench of a sewage plant blowing in on the wind. Tourists are shuttled through en route to the **Danilia Village** (daily 9am–1pm & 6pm–dawn), five minutes up the main road, a slick operation supposed to look like nineteenth-century Corfu, with workshops and museum, and evening entertainment.

Next stop around the bay is **GOÚVIA**, off the main road but on the routes of most green buses (plus blue bus *Dhassia #7*) and with lots of rooms for rent. The resort hugs the edge of the huge bay, once used by the French fleet to hide from Nelson, though the downflow from Kondokáli means that the sea here is absolutely filthy. Still, it's a friendly place and has an attractively low-key nightlife compared with the next resorts along the coast.

Continuing north, it's best to bypass **Cape Komméno**, which looks lovely from the distance, with thick foliage on the promontory, but up close turns out to be just a trio of dirty beaches, fronted by *Dionysos Camping* and a cluster of large hotels. There are more campsites at the next resort, **DHÁSSIA**, a touristic sprawl with little to recommend it. For a bit more life, you'd do better at **ÍPSOS**, every inch the package resort, with an esplanade, fish and chips, water-slides, and bars named *Irish Shamrock*, *Wurzeis* and *Pig and Whistle*. There are quite a few **rooms** for rent and two **campsites**; *Corfu Camping* (☎0661/93 246) and *Ipsos Ideal* (☎0661/93 583). To swim, wander over to **PÍRYI**, a village which has more or less merged with Ípsos, fronted by a better and sandy beach. From Píryi, too, a road trails up Mount Pandokrátor.

North to Áyios Stéfanos

North of Píryi, a rather different island emerges, as you move from hotel to villa country. The resorts are smaller, and the sea is cleaner, too – indeed, away from the main road, there's still a hint of the Corfu of Gerald Durrell's books, some of which were set on this coast.

BARBÁTI is the first place of note – a former fishing hamlet, surrounded by hills and woods, and still identifiably Greek, despite a sizeable hotel and taxi-boats to and from Ípsos. The few rooms for rent here are mainly located in the new hamlet area, a hundred steep metres above the sea. A kilometre to the north is **Glífa**, a pebble beach with a taverna.

The next focal point is **NISSÁKI**, a rather spread-out village with a number of coves, the first and last accessible by road, the rest only by track. There's a vast hotel, a *Club Med* complex and a tiny, stony beach, plus good watersports. Rooms in summer are like gold dust, but if you can find a bed, it's a good base. If you're prepared to walk, you can pick your way along the coast to find a number of quiet bays. **Kéndroma**, a kilometre out, has a few rooms for rent. Beyond here, there are more rooms at the villages of **YIMÁRI** – though this has poor swimming and a pebble beach – and **KAMINÁKI**, where there's a limestone cave full of bats.

KALÁMI, set on a curved bay, was the site of Lawrence Durrell's *Prospero's Cell* – which he wrote at the *White House*, where there is now an excellent taverna. A once-pretty hamlet, it's being developed fast, with a rash of garish, pink villas stamping out the charm of the grand old houses. There are a number of expensive rooms – including, if you're organised and reasonably affluent, the *White House* itself (bookable by the week through *CV Travel* in London, ☎0171/581 0851).

There are more little coves around the headland between Kalámi and **KOULOÚRA**, a tiny harbour that has retained its charm, set beside a deep, U-shaped bay enclosed by tall cypresses, palm and eucalyptus trees. It's postcard-pretty and has a small, shingle beach, a lovely taverna, but no rooms for rent. Another good taverna, *Nikos's*, is to be

---

DAY TRIPS TO ALBANIA

Since 1991, and the collapse of Communist rule in Albania, it has been possible to take day trips from Corfu to the Albanian coast – little more than a nautical mile from northern Corfu. These can be arranged at the resorts of Áyios Stéfanos, Kalámi and Kassiópi, though all involve a bus transfer to Corfu Town where you clear customs and board.

The main operator is *Petrakis Shipping Company*, next to the Old Port at Elefthériou Venizélou 9 (☎0661/31 649). The boats dock at the Albanian seaside town of Sarandë, a predominantly Greek-speaking settlement. The trip costs around 7000dr, plus US$30 which covers the entry permit to Albania and port taxes. The excursion includes a visit to the Roman archeological site at Vouthrota. *Petrakis* may also be running longer tours, depending on Albanian political conditions – which at present are extremely volatile.

---

found at the tiny nearby hamlet of Agnistíni, and there are lovely beaches down some of the tracks around; **Kerásia**, down a very grotty track, is a large shady cove with a beach café.

The deep bay of **ÁYIOS STÉFANOS** looks better from the distance. It's a pretty cove with clear water but flanked by a well-heeled resort, marred by some insensitive hotels.

Kassiópi and around the coast to Ródha

Set in a sheltered bay, **KASSIÓPI** has a resort history dating back to Tiberius, who had a villa here. Recently it has become very developed and anglicised, but retains pockets of old village life and has an ancient plane tree dominating its main square. Accommodation is often block-booked, but there are a few rooms for rent and some excellent **restaurants** – try the *Kassiopi Star* or the harbourside *Three Brothers*. Nightlife includes some decent **bars**; the *Wave Bar* is by a small jetty and *Bar Tropicana* has pop quizzes and bingo. There are also two **discos**, *Unicorn* and *Axis*, and, fifteen minutes' walk out of town, a *bouzoukia* joint, the *Kan Kan*.

People bathe from the promontory below Kassiópi's fortress, around the promontory to the west, but all the beaches are out of town. The closest, around ten minutes' walk, is known as **Imerólia**; beyond it is **Avlídhi**, stony, more secluded and reached from a rough track off the main road. Footpaths and boat excursions give access to other rocky coves and sand.

West of Kassiópi, the coast is initially barren, and forms one of the quietest stretches in Corfu. **Avláki**, a long stretch of mixed sand and shingle, has a taverna and attracts a few windsurfers; **Kalamáki** has a pebbled beach but little accommodation. Just beyond here a road (near the garage) turns off up **Mount Pandokrátor**, past the tumbledown and overgrown village of **PERITHÍA**, with its beehives, nut trees and a taverna, the *Capricorn Grill*; from the village a footpath leads to the summit.

Back on the coast, the first settlement of any size is **ÁYIOS SPIRÍDHON**, where there are a few rooms, a small, sandy beach and an ugly hotel. If you continue on a little way you'll see a sign to **Almirós** beach, the start of a continuous strand that sweeps around to Ródha. At this end it's very quiet, with just one taverna and the occasional camper van ignoring conspicuous "No Camping" signs. Nearby, a small channel leads to the Antinióti lagoon, an oasis-like cove with tepid water and wild birds.

Halfway to Sidhári is **AHARÁVI**, a staid tourist community that straggles along a huge, sandy beach. It's purpose-built and a bit soulless, the hotels and beach packed to the brim with young families. There are two decent bars, *Skandros* and *The Barn*, but little in the way of rooms for rent, and camping is not encouraged.

South from Aharávi a road heads back to Píryi, skirting the western foothills of Mount Pandokrátor. It runs past **EPISKEPSÍS**, a farming community strung out along a ridge, with a couple of cafés and a three-storey Venetian manor, and on to **SPARTÍLAS**, whose square and bar (with superb local wine) is shaded by a vast elm tree. Off the main route a side road leads up to Pandokrátor's 906-metre summit, via **STRINÍLAS**, which is served by a twice daily bus from Corfu Town. This unspoilt village sits in an exposed position and the stone buildings have a very weatherbeaten look about them.

Ródha and around

RÓDHA was once a small village but has been taken over by tour operators, whose clients revel in the watersports on the narrow, shelving beach, and snap up the opportunity to go horse-riding and play tennis. Motorboats can be rented for fishing trips from *Sam's* (☎0663/93258). Hotels are generally block-booked but there's a fair **campsite**, *Roda Camping* (☎0663/63 120).

A pleasant road heads inland from here, passing nearby traditional villages like **NIMFÉS** (with a nice taverna, and a nearby cave-chapel and spring) and **VALANIÓN** (with an abandoned monastery and lovely pool). Between Nimpés and Plátonas a small factory produces bottles and sells ouzo, wine and the local liquor, *Kum Kuat*.

Just down the coast from Ródha, **ASTRAKÉRI** has the first "Rooms for Rent" signs for miles, a trio of **hotels** – best value are the *Sandra* (☎0663/31 120; ④) and *Astrakeri Beach* (☎0663/31 238; ④) – and a campsite. It's a little windswept but has some nice coves nearby as well as a fishing harbour. The west end of the bay merges into the beginning of Sidhári's resort development (see below).

Paleokastrítsa and the northwest

The topography of **PALEOKASTRÍTSA** – a perfect, sand-fringed natural harbour between cliff-headlands – has led it to be identified with Homer's *Scheria*, where Odysseus was washed ashore and escorted by Nausica to the palace of her father Alcinous, King of the Phaeacians. It's a stunning site, though as you would expect, one that's long been engulfed by tourism. The hotels spread ever further up the hill around the bay, and have been boosted by the construction of a marina, invaded during the day by hordes of day trippers. On the plus side, there are excellent watersports: the bay is superb for snorkelling and there's one of the few Greek opportunities for scuba diving (equipment and lessons from the *Baracuda Club*; ☎0663/41 211).

For **accommodation**, there's the *Green House* (☎0663/41 311; ③), with less expensive places up the hill or hidden in the olive groves on either side of the main road. The best **campsite** is *Paleokastritsa Camping* (☎0663/41 204) but it's a long walk down to the sea. Paleokastrítsa also boasts excellent fish restaurants, mopeds for rent, and an impressive range of boat trips.

If you're staying in town, boat rides provide the easiest access to **beaches to the south** – such as cliff-backed Áyia Triádha, Yérifa and Stiliári; by road, these can be reached via Liapádhes (which has rooms for rent). Attached to the small promontory is the impressive **Theotokos Monastery** (daily 7am–1pm & 3–8pm), inhabited by four monks who still produce olive oil from a working press. More enjoyable is a walk up to the Byzantine fortress of **Angelókastro**, reached by following a narrow road (making it off limits to tourist buses) from Kríni and up a cobbled path. Perched on a rocky outcrop it has a tremendous setting and dramatic views of the coast.

North of Paleokastrítsa

To the north of Paleokastrítsa are the inland villages of **LÁKONES**, increasingly a suburb of Paleokastrítsa, and **MAKRÁDHES**, with its fading whitewashed alleys; both have rooms for rent. Six kilometres of winding, often unsurfaced, road brings you to the superb bay of **Áyios Yióryios**, a long sweep of sand set beneath towering limestone cliffs. There's no village as such at Áyios Yióryios, but a fair bit of package accommodation, a line of tavernas (best are the *Marina* and *Nafsika*), two discos, a relaxed atmosphere and lots of watersports.

Around Áyios Yióryios bay to the north is **AFIÓNAS**, a tiny village up on the cape. *Taverna Bardhis* has rooms with views of Ionian sunsets and Gránia islet, said to be the Phaeacian boat that was turned to stone by Poseidon. Up the coast from here, **ARILÁS**, is a fairly low-key resort backing another wide bay, with a narrow beach and friendly atmosphere. Nearby **MAGOULÁDHES** is a small village with an old convent, **Móni Ithamíni**, and a monk's hermitage, **Móni Ipsí**, which has some valuable icons.

At windswept **ÁYIOS STÉFANOS** (not to be confused with the east coast resort), there are enjoyable breakers – making this an up-and-coming watersports centre. At present the resort boasts a handful of hotels and a fair scattering of **rooms** for rent. Day-trippers descend most mornings, but leave the village almost empty at night. Stroll north for seclusion, or into the hills for coastal views.

PEROULÁDHES, around the corner, is quite a surprise. For a start it's a genuine, if somewhat run-down, village. Then there's the beach, reached by a steep path to the brick-red sand below spectacular, wind-eroded cliffs. *Sunset Taverna* and *Panorama Restaurant* have views across to some of the islets off Corfu's northwest coast. The lack of a bus service, plus afternoon shade over the beach, keeps the place distinctly underfrequented.

All of which is in dramatic contrast to **SIDHÁRI**, whose long beach, shallow water and picturesque rock forms have made it a favourite family resort. It's not, in fact, very attractive: there are lots of mosquitoes, tacky gift shops and fast food joints; murk seeps from the river onto the beach, and crowds fill the two main roads. The best restaurants are *Oasis* (a little way out of town) and *Sophocles*, the best bar *Legends*, and the best disco *Remezzos*. As it's a flat part of the island, there are bicycles for rent. You can also escape by excursion boat to the offshore islets of Othóni, Erikoússa and Mathráki (see overpage).

Central and southern Corfu

Two natural features divide the centre and south of Corfu. The first is the **Plain of Rópa**, whose bleak landscape harbours an inaccessible coast. Settlements and development stop a little to the south of Paleokastrítsa and only resume around **Ermónes** and **Pélekas** – a quick bus ride across the island from Corfu Town. Down to the south, a second dividing point is the **Korissíon lagoon**. The sandy plains and dunes that skirt this natural feature are great places for botanists and ornithologists. Beyond, a single road trails the interior, with sporadic side roads to resorts on either coast. The landscape here is flat, with salt pans forming an undistinguished backdrop for a series of relatively undefiled beaches – and, in the far south, **Kávos**, Corfu's big youth resort.

Ermónes to Koríssion lagoon: the west coast

ERMÓNES has one feature that must be unique in Greece: a lift down to the beach, linked to the *Corfu Golf Club* and a large hotel complex. The beach, below heavily wooded cliffs, has pebbly sand and freshwater streams; another strand at nearby **Kóndo Yiálo** is small, sheltered and beautiful.

Just inland is **VÁTOS**, an unspoilt village with **rooms** for rent and a **campsite**, *Vatos Camping* (☎0661/94 393); both tavernas are called *Spiro's*. Opposite a small church near these tavernas, a tiny path leads to a steep track cut into the cliffs down to **Mirtiótissa** beach, one of the best on the island. It has a nudist section at one end, a monastery at the other, and rooms halfway down the path. Take snacks and water as there are no facilities. It's far preferable to the next resort, **GLIFÁDHA**, dominated by a huge hotel, and with scores of apartments seemingly under permanent construction.

PÉLEKAS is also busy, since it's the main crossroads in the west-centre of the island, and its beach is usually packed solid. *Spirós Taverna* has a travel agency and a few rooms. The village above the beach, however, has remained quite pleasant, with unpretentious tavernas such as *Acropolis* and *Panorama*. Cheapish **rooms** can be found at *Pension Alexandros* (☎0661/94215; ③) and *Jimmys* next door. During the evenings, tourists arrive to watch the sunsets; if you're not the tour-bus type, take the #11 bus from Platía San Rócco in Corfu Town. Signs point to the place where the Kaiser used to watch the sunset (*iliovasílema*) on a small hill above the town. The aptly named *Sunset Restaurant* is a little pricey but its position merits a drink at least.

Heading south, the next real resort is ÁYIOS GÓRDHIS and it's arguably the nicest on the island. Vines spread down from pine-clad cliffs to a mile-long, sandy coastal strip, with Plitíri point behind, and jagged rocks thrusting skyward below the one big hotel. The resort is dominated by the bizarre *Pink Palace* (③), an American-run holiday complex that claims to cater for backpackers – the price includes room, breakfast, dinner as well as volleyball, watersports and cliff diving.

Mount Áyii Dhika – Corfu's second peak – casts its shadow over this central part of the island, and the roads on its west side are a bit erratic. Edging through a landscape of cypresses, citrus and olive groves, you eventually reach a long swathe of beaches beside a calm sea leading down to the Korissíon lagoon. On its north side is PARAMÓNAS, with rooms for rent and a sand and pebble beach. A little further on is **Prasoúda**, an amphitheatre-shaped beach with a single taverna. The road south of here becomes a track, leading to a more isolated beach with another taverna, and to the thirteenth-century **Gardiki castle**, an octagonal structure on a low knoll, still partly intact.

Benítses to Boukári: the east coast

The **east coast** of the island, from Corfu Town's suburb-resorts of Kanóni and Pérama south to Messónghi is almost as developed as the stretch north of the capital. South of the suburbs is BENÍTSES, which used to be *the* Corfu package resort. Only slightly more bearable for having engulfed a genuine village, it has a very mediocre beach adjacent to the busy main road, and an olive grove with a fish-and-chip shop and a go-kart track. The clientele is mainly British families with teenagers; bars advertise British beers and discos have names like *Summer Lovers* and *G-Spot*. The only redeeming feature – and not much of one at that – is a small **shell museum**.

Things don't improve much until you reach MESSÓNGÍ, set beneath Hlomós mountain, which is fast merging with MORAÍTIKA, along a sandy stretch of beach, separated from the road by a line of low-rise hotels, restaurants and discos. There are, at least, a lot of **rooms** for rent – some of the best value at the *Hotel Three Stars* (☎0661/92 457; ③) – and a **campsite**, *Sea Horse Camping* (☎0661/75 364).

The road immediately south of Messónghi is due to be surfaced before long, though at present it's a bit rough. If you make it, BOUKÁRI rewards with a small hotel, some rooms and Spiro's friendly **taverna**, and fishermen who still fish. For swimming, walk some way around the coast towards the north, as there are various crude sewage outlets near the village.

Alternatively, head for PETRITÍ, a working fishing port – reached on an unsurfaced road from Boukári or by a side road off the Boukári–Aryirádhes road – where you can share a rather modest strand with a few villa dwellers. Fishermen here still spread their nets under the olive trees. *Pension Egripos* (☎0661/51 949; ③) is worth trying and **rooms** are quite easy to find.

Southern Corfu

The roads from west and east coasts join at ARYIRÁDHES, a small town that could make a nice inland base if you have transport to visit the local beaches. It has a few rooms for rent advertised, as does KOUSPÁDHES, on the Boukári road.

At **ÁYIOS YIÓRYIOS**, on the west coast, 3500m from Aryirádhes, a short walk north will take you to a beautiful undeveloped stretch of surf-pounded sand known as **Issos Beach**. The village proper is an expanding straggle of hotels, apartments and restaurants, with a few rooms for rent. Its drawback is daily excursion-boat invasions from Paleokastrítsa. The island is only about 5km wide at this point and it would be feasible to spend the morning on the east coast and walk to the west for the afternoon.

Further south down the central main road is **MARATHIÁS** whose beach merges with Santa Barbara and Maltas Beach, a long trek down a dirt road from the delapidated village of Perivóli. The strand is a continuation of the one at Áyios Yióryios, but made somewhat unenticing by a couple of open sewers. It's better to stay at one of the rooms places a little inland, and walk to the far end of the beach to swim; there are several tavernas.

There isn't much to see at **LEFKÍMI**, the main town and administrative centre of the south, which has a dirty beach to the east. In season there is a daily ferry service to Igoumenitsa (75min) from the port, 2km to the south. **ALIKÉS** is to the north – still small-time, with a sandy beach; **MÓLOS**, is plain, simple and dominated by a German-run hotel.

At **KÁVOS**, near the southern tip of the island, young British package tourists have made the place the nightlife capital of Corfu: most of the "rave" crowd that come here don't leave until it's time to go home. The resort is huge, stretching for several kilometres and encompassing eighty bars and clubs. Good **restaurants** include *O Naftis* and *Mandella's* (which offers Greek dishes and roast dinners); among **bars** catering for the young party animal are the *Ship Inn, JC's* and numerous video bars; while for **discos** there's *The Venue, Limelight* and – perhaps the country's best – the *Future Pace*. The beach is fair, with lots of watersports on offer.

An hour's walk from Kávos, following the path just before *Spiros Bar*, at the south end of the village, brings you to **Cape Asprókavos** and the ruined **monastery of Arkoudhílas**. This path also offers a view of Arkoudhílas beach, which can be reached on foot via quiet **SPARTÉRA**, a hamlet which rents rooms to the respectable. If you take this road, and loop around to the west coast, you reach the village of **DRAGOTÍNA**, which has a handful of rooms for rent and a couple of tavernas. A half-hour's walk along a track (impossible for mopeds) leads to one of Corfu's best beaches – secluded, isolated and reasonably empty, with just a single summer beach-taverna.

Corfu's satellite islands: Eríkousa, Mathráki and Othoní

Northwest of Corfu are three small and little-known satellite isles – **Eríkousa**, **Mathráki** and **Othoní**. They get few visitors and, if you go, you'll probably have to stay a couple of days between ferries. There'll be little to do besides swim, lie on the beach and relax; choices of accommodation and places to eat are very limited, and there's nowhere to change money. These are islands for those in search of peace and solitude – *isikhía*, as the Greeks put it. Each is connected to Corfu Town by **car ferry** and to Sidhári by **kaíki** (see "Travel Details" at the end of this chapter for schedules).

Development of the islands has been restricted largely by their scarcity of water rather than anything lacking in the way of scenery and beaches. Without much land or tourism, job prospects on the islands are few and, since the 1950s, most of the island populations have left – a good proporton of them for New York. Many of those still living here have spent part of their lives in America, and almost everybody speaks a few words of English.

Eríkousa (Merlera)

Of the three islands, **Eríkousa** attracts most visitors. **Kaíkia** from Sidhári bring day-trippers several times a week, while the *Hotel Erikousa* (☎0663/71 555; ④) and a few cheaper rooms cater for those staying longer. There's a good, long sandy beach in front of the island port and village, and even when the excursion boats have arrived, you can walk further on and have the end of the beach to yourself. If this isn't isolated enough for you, there's a longer and totally empty beach beyond the headland to the east.

The small village is pleasant enough, without being particularly picturesque. There's a shop, a couple of *kafenía* and a single **taverna** on the beach which takes advantage of its monopoly by charging over the odds. Inland, a couple of smaller, more traditional settlements stand amid hills covered by cypress and olive trees.

Mathráki (Samothráki)

Mathráki is smaller than Eríkousa, and apart from returning Greek-Americans, who swell the population in summer, very few people come here. This is quite fortunate, for its sandy beach, stretching from the harbour for the length of the eastern side of the island, is a nesting site for the endangered **loggerhead turtle** (see p.362). It's important not to camp anywhere near the beach – and not to make any noise there at night.

From the harbour, a road climbs the hillside up to the tiny village of **KÁTO MATHRÁKI**, where brightly painted houses are scattered amongst the olive groves. There are very few rooms to rent – don't count on finding one – and a combination shop-*kafenío*-taverna at the top of the hill overlooking the sea; the food is good, but the choice is limited to say the least, and you'd do well to bring some supplies with you. The scenic island road takes you to the slightly larger village of **ÁNO MATHRÁKI** at the other end of the island, with a single, old-fashioned *kafenío* next to the church. From here, a path leads down to the far end of the beach.

Othoní (Fano)

Othoní is the largest, and, at first sight, the least inviting of Corfu's satellite isles. Around the harbour, the landscape is dry and barren, and the village has a definite end-of-the-line feel. There are no great sandy beaches, and most people swim from the shingle in front of the village. Inland, however, there's some fine scenery, and on closer acquaintance you'll find that the village has an enjoyable atmosphere. A small foreign community usually gathers during the summer, and there are always a few yachts moored in the bay. Among a handful of *kafenía* and **tavernas**, try *O Mikros* for Greek standards, and the Italian-run *La Locanda dei Sogni* for pricier meals – and nice **rooms** (☎0663/71 640; ③). In addition, there are a few cheaper private rooms in the village.

To explore the island, follow the donkey track up the valley left of the harbour, which leads to the main inland village, **HORIÓ**. This route takes you through rocky peaks and valleys with hillsides cloaked by cypress trees. Horió, like other inland villages, is heavily depopulated – only about sixty people still live on the island through the winter – but it's very attractive, and the architecture is completely traditional. From the road, a track leads down to the far side of the island and some more rocky and isolated beaches.

Paxí (Paxos) and Andípaxi (Antipaxos)

Paxí is just 12km by 4km in extent and devoted almost completely to olive cultivation. Like Corfu's northern satellite isles, a dire water shortage has prevented construction of all but one luxury hotel, though the island is not exactly remote – or unvisited. There are **ferries** almost every day in season from Corfu and from Igoumenitsa, Sívota and Párga on the mainland, and seats on the latter crossing must be reserved a day ahead in summer. The island's population of just over two thousand is often matched in season by visitors. Paxos is popular with the yachting fraternity and villa crowd so has quite an exclusive air. Late July and August are best avoided when the island swarms with designer-clad tourists, prices are bumped up and rooms are scarce. However, there are plenty of places to escape to, and by evening most of the calm has returned.

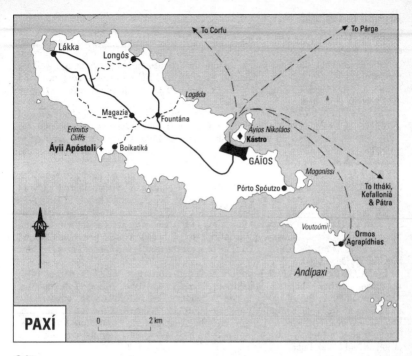

To Corfu
To Párga
Lákka
Longós
Logáda
Magaziá
Fountána
Erímitis
Cliffs
Áyii Apóstoli
Boikatiká
Áyios Nikoláos
Kástro
GÁIOS
Mogoníssi
Pórto Spóutzo
To Itháki,
Kefalloniá
& Pátra
Voutoúmi
Ormos
Agrapídhias
Andípaxi

PAXÍ

0   2 km

Gáios

Most people stay in or around the main harbour and village of **GÁIOS**, whose three-
and four-storey, pastel-tinted houses front a channel of water, giving the impression of
being built on a river. Opposite is the islet of **Áyios Nikoláos**, endowed with an inevitable ruined Venetian fort; it can be reached by boat and offers the best view of the town
– one not much changed since it was sketched by Edward Lear last century.

Unless it's the height of the season, you should be able find a **room** in or around
Gáios. If you're not met on arrival with offers, go through the square away from the
waterside and take the road that leads out of the town. When you get to the edge of the
built-up area, turn left at the crossroads/bus stop up a steep concrete road and keep an
eye out for the signs. Don't be afraid to haggle.

Food is slightly overpriced, but no more than you would expect on a small island
with a short tourist season. Some of the best-value meals are to be had at *Spiro's* (also
called *Beautiful Paxi*), *Volcano* and *Andreas'* fish taverna, all in or around the square.
For **drinks**, try the *Akteion Kafeniou* on the corner of the main square, where you'll
pay about one-fifth of the price charged at the trendier bars used by the foreign yachting crowds.

The island's only sandy beach is **Mogoníssi**, 45 minutes' walk to the south, set in a
pleasant bay and flanked by the *Kingfisher* bar and taverna. En route to the beach you
pass numerous rocky covelets with fun-sized shingle beaches. Above one of these is
Taverna Klis which advertises Greek dancing and "crayfish". A free bus/boat service
leaves Gáios for the beach every evening at 7.30pm, and there's unofficial camping
behind the beach.

Around the island

Paxí's single main road splits halfway up the island, with one branch leading from Gáïos to Lákka and the other to Longós. A **bus** travels between these three main communities about six times a day, though they're also within easy enough walking distance – as is everywhere on the island. Plentiful olive trees provide shade; the island homes are scattered, forming many tiny communities; and there are also said to be over seventy churches.

The *Greek Islands Club* – one of the main operators to this island – puts out a useful wildflower and walking guide, available in Gáïos and Lákka, which details hard-to-find paths. Get an early start on your ramblings, as all of Paxí's beaches are exposed to prevailing summer afternoon winds. Inland you will pass redundant olive presses and beautiful white houses with green shutters and doors.

Midway point on the road to Lákka is **MAGAZÍA**, which has a friendly taverna with rooms. A pleasant trail from here leads to the enormous chalk-coloured cliffs of **Erimítis**, which can also be viewed from behind Ayii Apóstoli church in Boikatiká which is a good viewpoint for sunsets. **LÁKKA** itself is set in a small, almost circular, bay with a pebbly cove for swimming, though the bay in general is rather stagnant. Short-term **accommodation** is quite difficult to find but there are a few rooms to rent; ask at *Planos Travel* (☎0622/31 103). The best **restaurant** is the *Rose of Paxos* and best **bar** *The Harbour Light*.

LONGÓS facing northeast, is prettier, with better tavernas – like *Kakarántzas* (with vegetarian dishes such as mushroom *stifádo*) and the *Nassos* fish taverna. Accommodation in the village is limited to holiday villas, but this doesn't concern the multitudes at the island's premier unofficial **campsite**, one cove to the south. That, and two more coves southwest of Longós, including Logáda beach, constitute the highest concentration of (pebbly) swimming spots on Paxí, along with a similar concentration of Italian and Greek holidaymakers.

Andípaxi

Andípaxi island is connected several times daily by speedboat (15min) or ordinary *kaíki* service from Gáïos. The trip – a very popular day excursion – seems expensive for what it is, but the route takes in the spectacular caves on the rocky southern tip of Paxí on the way, and you might see a few flying fish into the bargain. The boat stops at a couple of superb beaches (sandy and better than any on Paxí) before going on to the main anchorage and village – such as it is – known as Órmos Agrapídhias.

There are two tavernas at the first beach (one has a **campsite**), while the second has a bar with food and a panoramic view. The beaches are connected by a dirt road and there are paths all over the island. There are no rooms to be rented and, if you camp, the tavernas are not likely to stay open just for you in the evening, so bring provisions. Small vineyards abound on Andípaxi and the sweet red *krasí* is sold in Gáïos (behind the square) and packs a powerful punch.

Lefkádha (Lefkas)

Lefkádha is an oddity. Connected to the mainland by a long causeway through salt marshes, it barely feels like an island – and in fact, historically it isn't. It is separated from the mainland by a canal cut by Corinthian colonists in the seventh century BC, This has been redredged (after silting up) on various occasions since and today is connected by a thirty-metre boat-drawbridge built in 1986.

Lefkádha was long an important strategic base, and approaching the causeway you pass a series of fortresses, climaxing in the fourteenth-century castle of **Santa Maura** – the Venetian name for the island. These defences were too close to the mainland to avoid an Ottoman tenure, which began in 1479, but the Venetians wrested back control a couple of centuries later. They were in turn overthrown by Napoleon in 1797 and then the British took over as Ionian protectors in 1810. It wasn't until 1864 that Lefkádha, like the rest of the Ionian archipelago, was reunited with Greece.

At first glance Lefkádha is not overwhelmingly attractive, although it is a substantial improvement on the mainland just opposite. The whiteness of its rock strata – *Lefkás* means "white" – is often brutally exposed by roadcuts and quarries, and the highest ridge is bare except for ugly military and telecom installations. With the marshes and sumpy inlets all around, both mosquitoes and foul smells can be a midsummer problem. On the other hand, the island is a verdant place, supporting cypresses, olive groves and vineyards, particularly on the western slopes, and life in the mountain villages remains relatively untouched, with the older women still wearing traditional local dress – two skirts (one forming a bustle), a dark headscarf and a rigid bodice.

Lefkádha has been the home of various literati, including two prominent Greek poets, Angelos Sikelianos and Aristotelis Valaoritis, and the short-story writer Lefcadio Hearn, son of American missionaries. Support of the arts continues in the form of a well-attended international **festival** of theatre and folk-dancing lasting the bulk of each August, with most events staged in the Santa Maura castle. On a smaller scale, frequent village celebrations accompanied by *bouzouki* and clarinet ensure that the strong local wine flows well into the early hours.

Lefkádha Town and around

The island's main town, **LEFKÁDHA**, lies just south of the shallow lagoon, opposite the mainland fortress. It was badly hit by earthquakes in 1948 and 1953, and its **houses** have been rebuilt in an extraordinary fashion, with the upper storeys typically constructed of plywood and corrugated metal to lay as little stress as possible upon the foundations; indeed the erection of anything over two floors in height is supposedly forbidden, although a few hotels seem to flout this law. The tilted shutters and porches on stilts, the numerous **fish traps** out in the lagoon, and summer flotillas of yachts, complete a portscape that could almost be Caribbean.

The business district, festive at night with strings of light bulbs overhead, lines the town's long, narrow thoroughfare, with narrow alleys disappearing to either side. Scattered about are a score of Italianate **churches**, most of them dating from just after the start of the Venetian occupation, though much altered in the wake of various earthquakes. If you manage to gain entrance you'll find, as elsewhere in the Ionian, that the icons and frescoes show Renaissance rather than Byzantine influences. Take a look also at the self-styled *Mousio Fonografou*, an antique shop specialising in old 78rpm records and wonderful horn-machines.

Practicalities

The **bus station** faces the southern yacht anchorage. There are regular services to the main resorts of Nidhrí, Vassilikí and Aï Nikítas, as well as the interior settlement of Kariá. To get anywhere else efficiently you'll need to **rent** a car or a very tough motorbike. For hardy cyclists mountain bikes are also available. Most of the rental agencies are on Aristotélous Valaóriti. Incidentally, Lefkádhan road-signing is atrocious, so get a good, detailed map and don't be shy about asking for directions.

Hotels in town are on the pricey side. Two decent, budget choices are the *Vyzantion*, near the entry to town on the main street at Dorpfeld 4 (☎0645/22 692; ③),

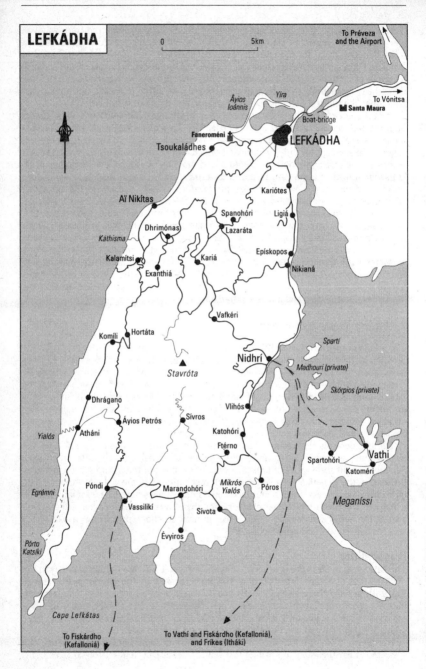

LEFKÁDHA

0   5km

To Préveza
and the Airport

To Vónitsa

Áyios
Ioánnis

Yíra

■ Santa Maura

Boat-bridge

Faneroméni ♠

LEFKÁDHA

Tsoukaládhes

Kariótes

Aï Nikítas

Spanohóri

Ligiá

Dhrimónas

Lazaráta

Káthisma

Epískopos

Kalamítsi

Kariá

Nikianá

Exanthiá

Vafkéri

Komíli

Hortáta

Sparti

Nidhrí

Madhouri (private)

Stavróta ▲

Skórpios (private)

Dhrágano

Vlihós

Áyios Petrós

Sívros

Katohóri

Yialós

Atháni

Ftérno

Spartohóri

Vathi

Katoméri

Egrémni

Póndi

Marandohóri

Mikrós
Yialós

Póros

Meganíssi

Vassilikí

Sívota

Pórto
Katsíki

Évyiros

Cape Lefkátas

To Fiskárdho
(Kefaloniá)

To Vathí and Fiskárdho (Kefaloniá),
and Fríkes (Itháki)

and the *Patras* on the main square (☎0645/22 539; ③). More upmarket is the *Santa Maura*, again on Dorpfeld (☎0645/22 342; ⑤). There are also a few signs pointing towards **rooms** on the lagoon shore-road, including those run by a friendly family at Stefaníssi 14 (☎0645/23 118; ③).

Among town centre **restaurants**, try *Regantos* at Dhimárhou Verióti 17 (a minor street going north from the main square), or the cosy *Eftikia Taverna* on Kerfákis near the town's entrance. *Romantica Taverna* at Mitropoleos 11 and *The Lighthouse* (*O Faros*) on Filarmónikis have reasonable food in pleasant little gardens. At the start of the road to Aï Nikítas is the *Adriatica*, one of the more elegant restaurants on the island; it's not cheap but it features unusual vegetarian dishes, an excellent fish pie and various seafood dishes. Swanky cafés predominate in the main square – *kafenío* culture becomes more evident closer to the junction at the top of the street. *Barbarosa* is one of the best **bars**.

Around Lefkádha Town

The closest decent beach to the capital is at **Áyios Ioánnis**, the spit bordering the Yíra lagoon on its west – about 45 minutes away if you choose to walk. It's sandy but also has pebbles that the wind-churned surf can hurl with bruising force. Continuing clockwise past a couple of stone windmills around the Yíra from here would bring you to a calmer, north-facing bay and the inexpensive *Estiatorio/Psitopolio Yira*, serving good food to a mainly local clientele. From there it's easy enough to complete a loop back to town, past the bridge.

West of the harbour, you can follow the Aï Nikítas road up to **Faneroméni monastery** (closed 2–4pm). It's no longer inhabited but has beautiful views and retains its old *símandro* (oxen's yoke and hammer), which was used to call the monks to prayer when first the Turkish, and later German, occupying forces forbade the use of bells.

Inland, a confusion of roads lead from the port to a welter of tiny villages in the north-centre of the island, overlooking a broad agricultural upland whose existence you hardly suspect gazing up from sea level. Possible targets here include the rickety hilltop hamlet of **SPANOHÓRI**, near the thriving crossroads town of **LAZARÁTA** with its *platía* tavernas, or the embroidery centre of **KARIÁ**, with expensive lace for sale and a few rooms for rent. It also has a fine *platiá* enclosed by plane trees and *kafenios*, making it an excellent lunchtime or evening excursion.

The east coast to Vassilikí

Heading south from Lefkádha town along the eastern shore, there's little initially to demand a halt except for **campsites** at Kariótes (☎0645/23 594) and Epískopos (☎0645/71 388), where there's a rocky beach. Only **LIGIÁ**, with its fishing port, has retained any village feel, and most of this coast is dotted with small, nondescript resorts patronised mostly by Greeks. Hotels charge well over the odds; if you choose to stop, there is a veritable plethora of rooms on offer, while the village also has the superbly named taverna, *The Breath of Zorba*.

Few foreigners, in fact, stop before **NIDHRÍ**, built on the site of a drained swamp. Useful as a ferry port to other islands and in a marvellous setting, the town itself has little character. The swimming off the tiny beach here is very average, and the only redeeming feature is the view out over various islets. **Rooms** are generally reserved in advance, but the tourist agencies on the front might turn up something for you. There is no shortage of cocktail bars, discos or **restaurants**, though the last present few gastronomic surprises.

The German archeologist **Wilhelm Dörpfeld** believed Nidhrí, rather than Itháki, to be the site of Odysseus's capital, and did indeed find Bronze Age tombs on the plain nearby. His theory identifying ancient Ithaca with Lefkádha fell into disfavour after his death in 1940, although his obsessive attempts to give the island some status over its neighbour are honoured by a statue on Nidhrí's quay. His tomb is tucked away at Ayía Kiriakí on the opposite side of the bay, near the house in which he once lived, visible just above the chapel and lighthouse on the far side of the water.

VLIHÓS, 3km south of Nidhrí at the head of an all-but-landlocked bay, is essentially an annexe of the bigger resort, though the presence of more old buildings, a quieter setting away from the road, and summer *bouzouki* events count in its favour. The bay is unsuitable for swimming; there is a **campsite** on the far side at Desími.

Beyond Vlihós, the main island road twists through or past the attractive hill villages of Katohóri, Ftérnos and Póros, all of which have at least one evening taverna apiece. The main resort in this corner of the island is the deep bay of **Mikrós Yialós** below **PÓROS**, which has **rooms** and a rather luxurious **campsite**. It's a scenic spot but the pebble beach gets both busy and dirty in July and August. Heading inland from here **SÍVROS** is neither the picturesque mountain village one had hoped for nor does it have a decent taverna or *kafenío*.

The next inlet to the west, **SÍVOTA**, has no beach to speak of and is really just a yacht harbour – albeit a fairly scenic one. A brief evening visit is perhaps best, when the five fish tavernas get going. A more functional swimming beach and a semi-official **campsite** can be found at **Kastrí**, 4km down a very rough side road between Marandohóri and Kondaréna. Looking down on the valley is the quiet village of **ÉVYI-ROS** with the odd room and one taverna.

The southeastern bus route ends around 40km from Lefkádha Town at **VASSILIKÍ**, which enjoys a fine setting with the island's largest agricultural strip just behind the broad bay. However, the beach is drab and the town tacky, dominated by a role as one of Europe's premier windsurfing centres. If you've not come on an instructional package, you can usually find a stray board to rent, but beginners may be forced to confine their efforts to the morning hours, since afternoon gusts off the plain behind sweep all except experts from the water.

In the end, Vassilikí is probably of most interest for its **ferry connections** south to Kefalloniá. The **campsite** behind the beach is well appointed but relatively expensive; alternatively there are various rooms, a **post office** (with an exchange), and an **OTE** station with handy evening and Sunday afternoon hours. **Eating out**, you're advised to try **Póndi**, a quieter district a kilometre distant on the far side of the bay, where the *Kamares Restaurant* is recommended.

ÁYIOS PÉTROS, 4km inland and to the north, has some unusual half-timbered houses and a lively main square, on and around which are several tavernas. *Ta Batsanakia* is a good, characterful grill with palatable local wine.

The west coast

Starting out from Lefkádha Town, the west coast begins with rather more promise. Past the Faneroméni monastery (see above) and the village of Tsoukaládhes, you arrive at **AΪ NIKÍTAS**, a fine, little-developed hamlet, with a single, flagstoned main street flanked by a half-dozen **tavernas**, about as many **rooms**, a campsite (just inland) and a few bars leading down to a tiny beach. It's not exactly traditional but makes a superb base and a ten-minute boat ride around the headland, or an hour's hike through scrub and bushes, will bring you to **Mílos beach** – a mile-long sweep of sand and shingle.

The next stop south is **Káthisma beach**. This attracts large numbers of freelance campers, though thus far there is just one proper taverna-rooms establishment, plus a trio of mobile canteens with showers and toilets. More substantial facilities are to be found (well up the hill) at **KALAMÍTSI**, host to dozens of **rooms** and a few **tavernas**. The tiled roofs, pleasant setting – facing a terraced hillside – and friendly locals make it an agreeable spot. This has its own large beach, too, 3km away, connected by a particularly steep track. There is no road directly between Káthisma and Kalamítsi beaches; between the two main bays, however, you can walk through several inviting coves frequented by nudists, and past a freshwater spring.

Visible just inland from Kalamítsi are two unspoilt communities reachable by meandering roads: **DHRIMÓNAS**, something of an architectural showcase with its uniform, old stone houses, and **EXANTHIÁ**, as good or better in its amphitheatrical arrangement. Neither has any tourist facilities.

Heading south again on the main route, a right turn at Komíli leads to **ATHÁNI**, another popular village, with plenty of **rooms** and **tavernas**. The choice of nearby beaches consists of **Yialós**, 4km south and marked after a fashion; **Egrémni**, 6km distant; and, most picturesque (but also most crowded), **Pórto Katsíki**, 10km along an increasingly bumpy road, at the base of high cliffs and with a single taverna. It's not as isolated as it first appears – *kaíkia* ferry in sun-worshippers from Vassiliki, just around the headland.

If the west wind is up, none of these coves will be inviting, and you might make the best of things and drive past the monastery of Áyios Nikólaos to the Lefkadhan "Land's End" at **Cape Lefkátas** (Doukato), which drops 75 abrupt metres into the sea. Byron's Childe Harold sailed past this point, and "saw the evening star above, Leucadia's far projecting rock of woe: And hail'd the last resort of fruitless love". The fruitless love is a reference to Sappho, who in accordance with the ancient legend that you could cure yourself of unrequited love by leaping into these waters, leaped – and died. In her honour the locals termed the place *Kávos tis Kirás* (Lady's Cape), and her act was imitated by the lovelorn youths of Lefkádha for centuries afterwards. And not just by the lovelorn, for the act (known as *katapontismós*) was performed annually by scapegoats – always a criminal or a lunatic – selected by priests from the Apollo temple whose sparse ruins lie close by. Feathers and even live birds were attached to the victim to slow his descent and boats waiting below took the chosen one, dead or alive, away to some place where the evil banished with him could do no further harm.

The rite continued into the Roman era, when it degenerated into little more than a fashionable stunt of decadent youth. These days, Greek hang-gliders hold a tournament from the cliffs every July. Weather permitting, there are *kaíki* trips out of Vassilikí for the more sedentary or those without vehicles capable of reaching the cape overland.

Lefkádha's satellites

Lefkádha has a string of satellite islets – Spartí, Madhourí, Skórpios and Meganíssi – over to the east of the island. **Meganíssi** is the only one with a village population and public access, from the port of Nidhrí. Of the other Lefkádha satellites, **Skórpios** is the retreat of the (now almost extinct) Onassis family and its staff, with landing still strictly forbidden. It was here that Aristotle married Jackie Kennedy. Landing is also forbidden on **Madhourí**, the property of the poet Nanos Valaoritis and his family. **Spartí** is uninhabited and covered in scrub.

Meganíssi

Meganíssi, a twenty-minute ferry or excursion-boat crossing from Nidhrí, has been for some time a closely guarded secret among island aficionados, without a postcard or souvenir shop in sight. A severe water shortage, and little scope for more ambitious building, is likely to thwart any of the major operators from moving in and for the present, rented rooms are readily available and cheap.

The main ferry stop is **VATHÍ**, a fishing port, whose harbour entrance is flanked by chapels to bless all boats and grant safe passage. That aside, it's a rather scruffy place, moving at its own slow pace. A road leads up from here to the more attractive village of

KATOMÉRI, with a welcoming taverna and the island's first **hotel**, the *Meganisi* (☎0645/51 240; ④) – small, simple and very pleasant.

The road continues in a westerly loop to **SPARTOHÓRI**, an immaculate village with whitewashed buildings and an abundance of bougainvillea. The locals – many returned emigrés from Australia – live from farming and fishing and are genuinely welcoming. There are a few tavernas, with limited choice, but excellent cooking and decent prices; the best is *Taverna Lakis*. Through the village and at the end of the island road is Pórto Spílio, a stop for some of the Nidhrí excursion boats. A minibus service meets the ferry at Vathí to connect the three villages but the distances are easily walkable.

Several tracks lead over the hills of the island and down through the olive-grove terracing to secluded bays. The most popular of these is **Ambelákia**, which attracts visiting yacht flotillas. You might also persuade a boat to take you to the caves on the southwest coast which reputedly sheltered submarines during World War II.

Lefkádha's satellites

Somewhat further to the east of Lefkádha – moored, in fact, just off the mainland coast – is one further island, **Kálamos**, with its own satellite islets, **Kástos** and **Átokos**. The only regular access is from the village of Mítikas, on the mainland south of Vónitsa; this is connected by local caique with Léfkadha in summer.

Mítikas itself is a sleepy little settlement, with a few rows of rickety houses strung along a pebbly shore. It is a pleasant place in which to break your journey, with a smattering of rooms, a small hotel, the *Simos* (☎0646/81 380; ③), and some tavernas pitched at locals; inland is a wall of amphitheatric mountainside.

Kálamos

The island of **Kálamos** is essentially a bare mountain that rises abruptly from the sea. In summer there are usually a few yachts moored in the small fishing harbour below the main port and village, Hóra, but otherwise the island sees few visitors. The only regular connection is the daily *kaíki* from Mitikas; this leaves Mítikas at noon and returns from the island at 7am the next day. The few **rooms** in Hóra, the island's village, are usually booked through the summer, so come prepared to camp.

HÓRA is spread out among gardens and olive groves on the south coast. It's quite a good-looking village, having largely survived the 1953 earthquake. There's a basic *kafenío*/taverna and a "supermarket" by the harbour, and two more **cafés** higher up, next to a **post office** where you can change money. The village **beach**, to the southwest, has a couple of tavernas behind a long stretch of shingle; in summer a few people camp beyond the windmills at the end. There's a much better, but less accessible pebble beach fifteen minutes to the east of the harbour.

KÁSTRO, the old fortified main village, is a ninety-minute walk from Hóra. Its walls are surrounded by roofless and abandoned houses and its *platía i*s overgrown, used by villagers to keep their hens and sheep. Down towards its harbour, more of the houses are still inhabited, though there's no shop or café.

There are more good beaches between Hóra and Episkopí, on the north coast facing Mítikas. The island's strip of road runs this way but the beaches can be reached more easily by boat than by scrambling down the forested slopes from the road. To the southeast of Hóra, a mule track leads to the village of Pórto Leóne, deserted since the 1953 earthquake. It's a two-hour walk across scrub-covered mountainside, with views across to the neighbouring island of Kástos.

Kástos and Átokos

The island of **Kástos** has one village with a harbour and taverna. Only a few families still live here permanently and there's no regular *kaíki*. If you want to get across, you could ask around in Mítikas or Kálamos to see if anybody is planning a trip, but you'll probably have to hire a *kaíki* to take you. Normally the only visitors are from the occasional yachts calling in at the harbour.

The islet of **Átokos**, to the southwest, has a few ruined houses, but is now completely uninhabited, as are the other islets scattered to the south.

Kefalloniá (Cephallonia, Kefallinía)

Kefalloniá is the largest of the Ionian islands – a place that has real towns as well as resorts and which, until the late 1980s, paid scant regard to tourism. Perhaps this was in part a feeling that the island could not easily be marketed. Virtually all of its towns and villages were levelled in the 1953 earthquake, and these masterpieces of Venetian architecture had been the one touch of elegance in a severe, mountainous landscape. A more likely explanation, however, for the island's late emergence on the Greek tourist scene is the Kefallonians' legendary reputation for insular pride and stubbornness.

Having decided on the advantages of an easily exploitable industry, however, Kefalloniá is at present in the midst of a tourism boom. Long favoured by Italians – its occupiers for much of the last war – it has now begun attracting British package companies, for whom a new airport terminal has been constructed, while virtually every decent beach has been endowed with a sprinkling of restaurants. There are definite attractions here, too, with some beaches as good as any in the Ionian, and a fine, if pricey, local wine, the dry white *Rombola*. Moreover, the island seems able to soak up a lot of people without feeling at all crowded, and the magnificent scenery can speak for itself, the escarpments culminating in the 1632-metre bulk of **Mount Énos**, declared a national park to protect the fir trees (*Abies cephalonica*) named after the island.

The size of Kefalloniá, a poor bus service and a distinct shortage of summer rooms makes **moped or car rental** almost essential. Fortunately, most of the towns, beaches and larger resorts have a rental outlet. If you are depending on the buses, be warned that there's only a basic grid of services: Sámi, the main port, to Argostóli, the island capital, and Fiskárdho (in the north); and Argostóli to the resorts of Skála and Póros in the southeast. Using a moped, take care as the terrain is very rough in places – almost half the roads are unsurfaced – and the gradients can sometimes be a bit challenging for underpowered machines.

Sámi and around

Most boats dock at the large, and not very characterful, port and town of **SÁMI**, built and later rebuilt near the south end of the Ithaki straits, more or less on the site of ancient Sámi. This was the capital of the island in Homeric times, when Kefalloniá was part of Ithaca's maritime kingdom: today the administrative hierarchy is reversed, Itháki being considered the backwater. With ferries to most points of the Ionian, and several companies introducing direct links to Italy – and one even to Piraeus, Samos and Turkey – the town is clearly preparing itself for a burgeoning future.

For the moment, though, most arriving passengers tend to get out as fast as possible. In addition to **moped rentals** (available on the waterfront), there are three daily **buses** to Argostóli, plus one bus (change at Dhivaráta) and a ferry to Fiskárdho. If you need or decide to stay, the town has a few **rooms** for rent and the four cheapest hotels are the waterfront *Hotel Kyma* (☎0674/22 064; ③), *Hotel Melissani* (☎0674/22 464; ③), *Hotel Ionion* (☎0674/22 035; ④) and *Hotel Krinos* (☎0674/32 002; ③). Best of the rather mediocre **restaurants** are *Faros* and *Dolphin* on the Paralia.

Four kilometres to the east of Sami, along a track that climbs and descends a steep hill is the excellent **Andisámos** beach, renowned for its clear water.

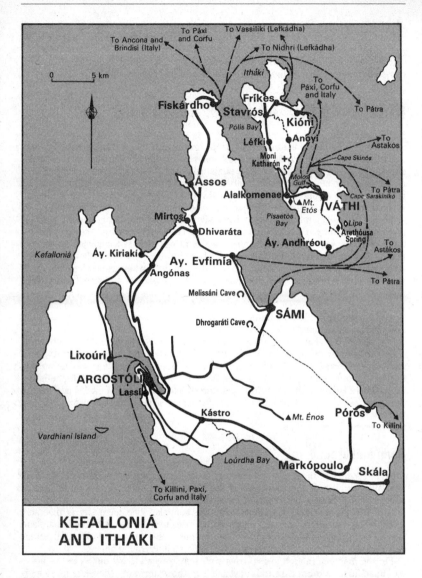

To Páxi and Corfu
To Vassiliki (Lefkádha)
To Ancona and Brindisi (Italy)
To Nidhri (Lefkádha)
Itháki
To Páxi, Corfu and Italy
To Pátra
Fiskárdho
Fríkes
Stavrós
Kióni
Pólis Bay
Léfki
Anoyí
To Astakós
Moni Katharón
Cape Skinós
Ássos
Molos Gulf
To Pátra
Alalkomenae
VÁTHI
Cape Sarakinikó
Mírtos
▲Mt. Etós
Pisaetós Bay
Dhivaráta
◊Lipa
Arethóusa Spring
Kefalloniá
Áy. Kiriakí
Áy. Andhréou
To Astákos
Ay. Evfimía
Angónas
To Pátra
Melissáni Cave
Dhrogaráti Cave
SÁMI
Lixoúri
ARGOSTÓLI
Lassí
Kástro
▲Mt. Énos
Póros
To Killíni
Vardhiani Island
Loúrdha Bay
Markópoulo
Skála
To Killíni, Paxi, Corfu and Italy

0   5 km

KEFALLONIÁ AND ITHÁKI

Karavómilos beach and the Melissáni and Dhrogaráti caves

More rooms and a **campsite**, *Karavomilos Beach* (☎0674/21 680), are to be found at **Karavómilos beach**, 2km to the north of Sámi. The beach itself is not very exciting but there is the opportunity of a boat ride to the **Spíli Melissáni** (daily 9am–8pm; 700dr), a blue-tinged sea-cave partly submerged in brackish water. You're taken into an inner lake-grotto, whose waters, amazingly, emerge from an underground fault which leads the whole way under the island to a point near Argostóli. At this point, known as

Katavóthres, the sea gushes endlessly into a subterranean channel – and, until the 1953 earthquake disrupted it, the current was used to drive seamills. That the water, now as then, still ends up in the cave has been shown with fluorescent tracer dye. The lake grotto can also be reached from the village itself.

Another, more conventional, cavern, the **Spíli Dhrogaráti** (daily, dawn to dusk; 600dr), is to be found 4km inland of Sámi, just off the main road to Argostóli. A very impressive stalagmite-bedecked chamber, it was previously used for concerts thanks to its marvellous acoustics – Maria Callas once sang here.

Áyia Evfimía

At **ÁYIA EVFIMÍA**, 10km north of Sámi, the road (and bus) turns inland towards Fiskárdho. You could do worse than stop at this pretty port town, which seems to have just about the right mixture of locals and visitors, and boasts the best **restaurant** on the island, *Stavros Dendrinos's Taverna*. To find it, walk round the harbour past the main dock and 500m on to the so-called **Paradise beach**. The small pebble beach is fine for swimming, and, on a terrace above, the multilingual Stavros serves an unusual range of excellently prepared food – and great house wine. There are **rooms** (②–③) available above the premises (and a few more a short walk further on), but they suffer from the heat and noise generated by a busy restaurant. This is a shame, because the view is superb, and rooms back in Áyia Evfimía are not easy to find, especially for short stays. *Hotel Pilaros* (☎0674/61 210; ④) on the promenade is one possibility.

Note that in summer there is a useful daily **ferry link** from Áyia Evfimía to Itháki and on to Astakós on the mainland.

Southeast Kefalloniá

Heading directly **southeast from Sámi** by public transport is impossible; to get to **Skála** or **Póros** you need to take one bus to Argostóli and another on from there; five daily run to Skála, three to Póros. With your own vehicle, the backroads route from Sámi to Póros is an attractive option. It's eighty percent dirt track but negotiable with a decent moped; the road is signposted to the left just before the Dhrogaráti cave.

Póros

PÓROS was one of the first resorts on the island to wake up to the idea of tourism, providing the shortest and most popular ferry link with the mainland (to Killíni in the Peloponnese, with three boats a day in season). The port is just over the headland from the main village. Several foreign tour operators maintain offices in the village, and a few **rooms** to rent are available for independent tourists but the place hasn't really changed that much. With its houses encroaching onto the dark green hillsides, the long beach, a small separate bay for boats, and nearby shady coves, it's a more attractive entry point than Sámi. To **eat**, a good choice is *Dionysos Taverna* which can be found by heading west from the small, palm-fringed square.

A dirt road twists 12km around the rocky coastline from **Póros to Skála** at the southern extremity of the island. It's a lovely, isolated road, with scarcely a building en route, save for a small chapel, 3km short of Skála, next to ruins of a **Roman temple**.

Skála

The village of **SKÁLA** has well and truly arrived as a thriving, albeit not unpleasant, beach resort. Alongside the standard bars and restaurants, a fair proportion of the decent stretch of sand is covered by sunbeds and parasols. At the north end of town, opposite the *Hotel Skala*, the remains of a **Roman villa** are on show, featuring finely detailed mosaics. **Rooms** aren't easy to find in summer, as tour operators have cleaned up on accommodation in both hotels and village houses. If you're stuck, ask at the

LOGGERHEAD TURTLES

The Ionian islands harbour the Mediterranean's main concentration of loggerhead sea turtles (*Caretta caretta*). These creatures, which lay their eggs at night on sandy coves, are under direct threat from the tourist industry in Greece.

Each year, many turtles are injured by motorboats, their nests are destroyed by bikes ridden on the beaches, and the newly hatched young die entangled in deckchairs and umbrellas thoughtlessly left out at night on the sand. The turtles are easily frightened by noise and lights, too, which makes them uneasy cohabitants with freelance campers and late-night discos.

The Greek government has passed laws designed to protect the loggerheads, including restrictions on camping at some beaches but, in addition to the thoughtlessness of visitors, local economic interests tend to prefer a beach full of bodies to a sea full of turtles.

On Kefalloniá, the turtles' principal nesting ground is Potomákia beach, 5km to the west of Skála. Other important locations for the loggerhead turtles include Zákinthos, although numbers have dwindled to half their former strength in recent years, and now only about 800 remain. Nesting grounds are concentrated around the fourteen-kilometre bay of Laganás, but Greek marine zoologists striving to protect and study the turtles are in dispute with locals and the burgeoning tourist industry.

Ultimately, the turtles' main hope of survival may rest in their being appreciated as a unique tourist attraction in their own right.

small *Kinotikó Grafío* (Council Office) on the main street, or try at Ratzíkli, 3km from Skála on the Argostóli road – a little inland from the sea.

Skála to Argostóli

Skála is edged by a fine stretch of sand, which continues around the headland and on to the south coast of the island. For the first few kilometres, the road runs a little inland and there is little development. At **Potomákia Beach**, 5km along the coast from Skála and reached by a turning at Ratzíkli, there are breeding grounds of loggerhead turtles (see box above). The sands and dunes are popular with locals at weekends and development looks set, with large clearings of land in preparation for tavernas and hotels. If you visit, or stay, leave the beach to the turtles at night.

The Argostóli road meets the sea midway around Loúrdha Bay at **KÁTO KATELION**, where an absurd number of restaurants compete for the seasonal occupants of unsightly, purpose-built apartments and a few freelance campers. One possible attraction is that the local **moped rental** agency arranges **scuba dives**.

Continuing west, the road heads inland again, past **MARKÓPOULO**, where the **Assumption of the Virgin festival** (Aug 15) is celebrated in unique style at the local church with small, harmless snakes with cross-like markings on their heads. Each year, so everyone hopes, they converge on the site to be grasped to the bosoms of the faithful; a few, in fact, are kept by the priests for years when they don't naturally arrive. The celebrants are an interesting mix of locals and gypsies – some of whom come over from the mainland for the occasion. It's quite a spectacle.

Further on, rooms are available at Vlaháta and Moussáta, and from the former a track winds its way up to the 5000-foot summit of Mount Énos. On a clear day, you might not quite see forever, but should at least get a glimpse of neighbouring Zákinthos. Note that the main access route is from the Argostóli–Sámi road.

There are more rooms and unofficial summer camping at **LOURDHÁTA**, a little village just inland from its one-kilometre-long beach – which is flanked by a trio of tavernas. It's an attractive base, and just beyond the beach, across some rocks, a tall overhanging tree directs a trickling freshwater-fall into the sea. Further west, there's another good beach and a taverna at **ÁYIOS THOMÁS**. At **PESSÁDHA** a ferry plies in the summer months to Ayios Nikoláos on Zákinthos; the tiny, uninhabited harbour is some way below the village.

Argostóli and around

ARGOSTÓLI, Kefalloniá's capital, is a large and thriving town, virtually a city, with a marvellous site on a bay within a bay. The stone bridge, connecting the two sides of the bay, was initially constructed by the British in 1813. A small obelisk remains, but the plaque commemorating "the glory of the British Empire" has disappeared. The town was totally rebuilt after the earthquake but has an enjoyable, defiantly Greek streetlife, especially during the evening *volta* around Platía Metaxá – nerve centre of the town.

A couple of museums near each other on Rokou Veryoti are worth a little time. The **Historical and Cultural Museum** (Mon–Sat 8.30am–2.30pm; 500dr) is strong on photographic documentation of Argostóli, including the British and French occupations and the 1953 earthquake and its aftermath. A bit less imaginative is the **Archeological Museum**, a block down on G. Veryóti (Tues–Sun 8.30am–3pm; 400dr); it consists mainly of pottery, including pieces from a number of Mycenaean tombs discovered in the village to the south.

Practicalities

The **EOT**, on the waterfront Metaxá street, keeps a list of **rooms for rent** and will phone to book for you – assuming there are vacancies. If you'd rather look around yourself, try *Spiros Rouhatas* at Metaxá 44 (☎0671/23 941 or 24 936; ③), who has rooms above his café opposite the Lixoúri ferry quay, or the *Adherfi Tzivras* (②) restaurant, on the side street V. Vandaroú, opposite the petrol pumps by the bus station. Two budget **hotels** exist, *Hotel Pantheon*, Zakínthou 4 (☎0671/22246; ②), next to the post office, and *Hotel Chava* (☎0671/22427; ③), up from the bridge. Close to the bus station, *Hotel Allegro* (☎0671/22268; ④) is also reasonably priced.

More mundane and harder work is the **campsite**, a two-kilometre walk (no bus) to the end of the promontory at Fanári. The site is just after the **Katavóthres**, the point at which the sea drains into the ground to re-emerge at Karavómilos (see "Sámi and around").

For **meals**, the *Adherfi Tzivras* (see above) is very good value, though *Kalafitis* and *Taverna Anonymous* have better locations facing the bay. *Patsoura's* has a good reputation, too, while for a highly recommended splurge, go for the *mezédhes* at the *Cyprus Taverna*. The liveliest **bars** are *Phoenix* and *Allodi* in Platia Metáxa.

Buses run from Argostóli to most points of the island and *KTEL* tries to make up for (or exploit) the shortcomings of its network by offering tours, and trips to nearby islands and Olympia. There is one daily **boat** to Killíni and a daily **hydrofoil** to Zákinthos, then Patras. The walk-on **ferry to Lixoúri** (see below) leaves every hour. Numerous agencies rent out **cars and mopeds**: *Express Cars* in the main square is one of the most reliable.

South of Argostóli: beaches and Kástro

For a swim, locals and visitors alike take a bus to **LÁSSI**, across the headland from Argostóli. Flanking the village, on either side of a hill, are two excellent but crowded beaches: **Platís** (wide) and **Makrís Yiálos** (long). Both are lined with hotels and tavernas, with Lássi itself developing rapidly whilst trying to absorb the increase in volume of tourists, generated by improvements to the airport a few kilometres south.

With a moped, the best inland excursion is to **KASTRO** (also known as Áyios Yióryos or San Giorgio), the medieval Venetian capital of the island. The old town here supported a population of 15,000 until its destruction by an earthquake in the seventeenth century: substantial ruins of its castle (daily except Mon 8.30am–3pm), churches and houses can be visited on the hill above the modern village of Travliatata. Byron was impressed by the view from the summit in 1823, when he lived for a few months in the village of Metaxáta, some kilometres below; sadly, as at Messolónghi, the dwelling where he stayed no longer exists. Two kilometres south of Kastro is a fine collection of religious icons and frescoes kept in a restored church that was part of the nunnery of Ayios Andréas.

Lixoúri

A quick ferry hop across the bay will bring you to **LIXOÚRI**, the only sizeable centre on Kefallonía's rugged western peninsula. The town itself is a bit downbeat, but would be a quiet and inexpensive base if you could get one of the rooms at the *Estiatorio Maria* on Kósti Palamá (②), near the main square. The restaurant is basic to the point of scruffy, and won't suit all tastes. For a bit more class try *Antony's* opposite the quay, or the *Ocean Breeze* at the end of the promenade. On the road south, the *Bella Vista Pension* (☎0671/91 911; ③) has a few rooms.

Walking south of Lixoúri, Lepídha beach is the first of a series of sand-and-seaweed beaches, reached after about thirty minutes. Proceed along these (and along tracks where necessary), and eventually you'll reach **Cape Áyios Yióryios**. Around the cape, ninety minutes' walk from Lixoúri, are the red sands of Mégas Lákos, facing Vardhiani island. Largely undeveloped, save for a small cluster of apartments, it's advisable to bring provisions as there is no café for miles around. The same strand continues to the more publicised **Xi Beach**, now dominated by a modern hotel complex.

The west coast and the road north

From Argostóli, most people board a bus bound for **Fiskárdho** in the north – a highly scenic journey that passes side roads to several excellent beaches. The first of these is **Áyia Kiriakí**, reached by a 2km track from Angón. The next, **Mírtos**, is signposted just past Dhivaratá and reached along a steep track. Seen from the cliff road above, it is one of the most spectacular and most photographed beaches in Greece – a splendid strip of pure white sand and pebbles – and in summer it attracts a fair number of day-trippers and campers. It's not an ideal place to stay, however, as it has no shade (apart from the cave at one end), and no toilet facilities. A seasonal bar rustles up sandwiches and drinks – overpriced, of course, but the alternative is a 4km slog up to Dhivaratá's two grills and a shop.

The main road, hacked out of the palisades on this road, continues north to **ÁSSOS**, a fishing village built on a narrow isthmus that links it with a castle-crowned headland. It's a placid place with a few cafés and tavernas, and plenty of daytime visitors, but it is far from spoilt and would make a fine base if you could get one of the few rooms for rent.

Fiskárdho

Kefallonía's picture-postcard village, **FISKÁRDHO**, is notable mainly for having escaped damage in the earthquake, preserving intact its eighteenth-century Venetian houses. It is pretty, but also totally dominated by tourism, with a yacht club, lots of boutiques, and restaurants serving expensive fish and bottled wine. If you're going to eat anywhere, try *Nikolas's Taverna*; at least service here is with good grace and a twinkle in his eye. **Rooms** in season are like gold dust, with only the odd cancellation from a package company on offer. Particularly nice ones are offered by *Anna Barzouka* (☎0674/51 572; ④); to find her, ask, as the streets are not named. *Hotel Panorama* (☎0674/51 340; ④) is likely to be full, but worth a try.

Close to the town, there's reasonable swimming off a mixture of rock and pebble beaches, One of the most popular, **Emblísi**, one kilometre away, has slanted slabs of rock, good to sunbathe on and snorkel from. On the hill above, the *Herodotus Taverna* is a decent place to eat and, apart from one unsightly pylon, has a panoramic view of Lefkáda, Itháki and the mainland. Daily **ferries** run to Vassilikí and Nidhrí on Lefkádha, as well as to Itháki and down the coast to Sámi. There are also **kaíkia** to Itháki in season.

Itháki (Ithaca)

Rugged **Itháki**, Odysseus's legendary homeland, has had no substantial archeological discoveries but it fits Homer's description to perfection: "There are no tracks, nor grasslands . . . it is a rocky severe island, unsuited for horses, but not so wretched, despite its small size. It is good for goats." In Cavafy's splendid poem *Ithaca*, the island is symbolised as one's journey and destination to life:

> *When you set out on the voyage to Ithaca*
> *Pray that your journey may be long*
> *full of adventures, full of knowledge.*

Despite the romance of its name, and its proximity to Corfu, very little tourist development has arrived to spoil the place. This is doubtless in part accounted for by a dearth of beaches, though the island is good walking country, with a handful of small fishing villages and various pebbly coves to swim from. In the north, apart from the ubiquitous drone of mopeds the most common sounds are sheep bells jangling and cocks (a symbol of Odysseus) crowing.

Váthi

Ferries from Pátra, Kefalloniá, Astakós, Corfu or Italy land at the main port and capital of **VÁTHI** (Itháki Town), sited at the mouth of a bay so deep it seems to close completely around. The small capital features old tiled houses, either undamaged or faithfully rebuilt after the terrible 1953 earthquake, and a small archeological museum on Odhos Kalliniko (daily 9am–3pm; free). Dozens of yachts and cruise ships stop here for a couple of hours but not many people actually stay – tourist development is for once at a virtual standstill.

Rooms for rent are, however, inconspicuous and in very short supply. If nobody meets you off the ferry, try looking around the backstreets south of the ferry quay. Alternatively, head for one of the two hotels, the *Odysseus* (☎0674/32 381; ④) and the *Mentor* (☎0674/32 433; ⑤), at opposite ends of the long quay. There's a little more choice for meals, with seven or eight **tavernas**, though all seem remarkably similar in price and fare. Among the more reliable are the *Psistaria Athinaiki Gonia*, *Toh Trehandiri* (authentic food in the bazaar) and *Toh Kantouni* (next to the water, near the ferry dock). Further around the bay, *Gregorys* and *Tsiribis* face the town and are popular with foreign nautical types. The island speciality, is *ravaní*, a syrupy sponge cake.

In season the usual small boats shuttle tourists from the harbour to a series of tiny coves along the peninsula northeast of Váthi – a service that's particularly useful, as road links around the island are very poor. The pebble-and-sand **beaches** between Cape Skinós and Sarakinikó Bay, such as Filiátro and Gidháki, are excellent, many people learning of them too late as the ferry they're departing on steams past. Most of those closer to town are little more than concrete diving platforms, though you might reflect that Byron enjoyed daily swims off the Lazzaretto islet in mid-harbour during his visit of 1823.

With some determination, you can walk out to the better beaches when the *kaíkia* aren't running. However, as long as you have good footwear you may prefer to spend your time hiking out to a handful of nearby sites tentatively identified with Homeric locations, or to head further north on Itháki for swimming or more sedentary pastimes.

Odysseus sites

Two paths to "Odysseus sites" are signposted from Váthi and either of them makes for an easy morning's walk across beautiful country of cypress, olives and vineyards. Both walks lack shade, so take a hat and plenty of water.

The Arethoúsa spring and Perahóra

The **Arethoúsa spring**, ninety minutes' walk south from the port, is down to a trickle in summer but interestingly positioned. Immediately above towers a crag known locally as *Korax* (the raven), exactly as described by Homer in the meeting between Odysseus and his swineherd Eumaeus, on his return to the island to fight the suitors. To reach it, take the signposted track south out of Váthi, and turn down and left on to a narrower path after an hour; the final approach is signalled by occasional green markings on the stones.

If you miss the turning, the main thoroughfare continues on to the **Maráthia plateau** (today called Perapigádhi after its capped well), where Eumaeus had his pigsties, but fails to reach remote **Ayíou Andhréou Bay** (accessible only by sea), where Telemachus disembarked to avoid Penelope's suitors who were lying in ambush for him on Asteris Island (the modern Dhaskalío). Below Arethoúsa, more tiny paths drop down to a pair of good swimming coves in the lee of Lípa islet.

Perapigádhi shouldn't be confused with **PERAHÓRA**, an old pirate-proof inland village some 2km above Váthi. The upper settlement – with one *kafenío*/taverna and a rooms place – makes a good return option from Arethoúsa or a trip in itself; obvious paths lead up to it from the olive-swathed plain or there's a direct track, signposted from Váthi's Odhós Penelópis.

The Grotto of the Nymphs and ancient Alalkomenae

Of equally questionable authenticity but fun to visit in any case is the **Grotto of the Nymphs** (known locally as *Marmarospíli*), a large cavern about 2500m southwest of Váthi, where local lore suggests Odysseus, on the advice of Athena, hid the treasure he had with him on his return to Ithaca. It was certainly known in ancient times and seems to have once been used as a place of worship. If its attribution is correct then the **Bay of Dhexiá** (west of Váthi and below the cave) would be where the Phaeacians put in to deposit the sleeping Odysseus and which he failed to recognise as his homeland.

Further to the north, **Mount Etós** looms over the head of the Molos gulf. On its summit are the ruins of **ancient Alalkomenae**, excavated by Schliemann (of Mycenae fame) and mistakenly declared to be the "Castle of Odysseus"; in fact it dates from at least five centuries after Homer. The site is almost impossible to find, and the search for others is complicated by the studiously inaccurate "Odysseus maps" sold on Itháki.

A side road skirts the base of the mountain and crosses the narrowest point on the island to get to pebbly **Pisaetos Bay**, nearly 7km in all from Váthi but with some of the best swimming near town. From the tiny quay, there are three or four daily ferries to Sami on Kefalloniá. Buses don't go to Pisaetos but the short half-hour crossing justifies a taxi ride from Váthi (1500dr).

Northern Itháki

The main road out of Váthi continues across the isthmu____
to the northern half of Itháki, serving the villages of **Léfk**___
There are three evenly spaced daily **buses**, though the ___
moped country. Likewise the close proximity of the set___
Homeric interest make it suitable rambling country. Once a ___
last two of those communities – a cheap and scenic ride use____
alike to meet the main-line ferries in Váthi. As with the rest o___
limited amount of accommodation.

Stavrós

STAVRÓS, near the base of arid Mount Korífi (or officially Mount Nisíti – a re-adoption of its old Homeric name), is a fair-sized village with a couple of rather pricey tavernas (the best is *Fatouro*) and some rooms. **Pólis Bay**, fifteen minutes' walk below it, has rocky swimming; people camp here, though there are no facilities whatsoever. Supported by a few nearby Mycenaean remains, the bay is the archeologists' current candidate for the main port of ancient Ithaca.

One kilometre north of Stavrós, more Mycenaean remains have been found amid the ruins of a Venetian fort, on a hill known as **Pelikáta**. This could perhaps have been the site of Odysseus's palace and capital: speculation that is supported by the fact that it enjoys a marvellous simultaneous view over Pólis Bay and Fríkes Bay. The tiny Stavrós **museum** (daily except Mon 9am–3pm) has a modest collection of terracotta jugs, bronze figurines and a fragment of a clay face mask claimed to be a votive offering to Odysseus.

Make your way up the four-kilometre track to the all-but-abandoned village of **EXOYÍ** in the northwest corner of the island and climb the belltower next to the blue-domed church for even more stunning views of this part of Itháki.

Fríkes, Kióni and Anoyí

FRÍKES is a half-hour walk downhill beyond Stavrós, smaller but with a handful of tavernas, a hotel (*Nostos*, ☎0674/31 644; ⑤), a few rooms and a pebbly strip of beach. Seasonal ferries to and from Lefkádha and Fiskárdho on northern Kefalloniá dock here. The port is linked by bus to Váthi. The very helpful *Kiki Travel* (☎0674/31 726) rents mopeds, boats and can help finding accommodation. From Fríkes a lovely coastal path leads to a couple of reasonable beaches; Mamakás beach, over the hill, is even better. Try and get to them early as a strong wind blows from mid-afternoon onwards.

Around three kilometres east, at the end of the road, is the village of **KIÓNI**, one of the more attractive bases on the island, though its few rooms (including the luxurious *Kioni Apartments*, ☎0674/31 362; ⑥) seem to be permenantly occupied during summer. There's good swimming nearby, free of sea urchins, at the end of the path to Áyios Ilías chapel to the southeast.

With Kióni as your starting point, you can also walk or go by moped due south to the still inhabited **monastery of Katharón**, via the inland village of **ANOYÍ**, where the proprietress of the one taverna will lend you the keys to the fourteenth-century village church and its excellent frescoes. From the monastery, the vista of Vathí in its horse-shoe bay must rank as one of the most magnificent in all the Ionian.

Zákinthos (Zante)

Zákinthos, which once exceeded Corfu itself in architectural distinction, was hit hardest by the 1953 Ionian earthquake, and the island's grand old capital was completely destroyed. Rebuilt, it feels a rather sad, soulless town and the island's attractions lie

yards, orchards and olive groves of the interior, and some excel-
tered about the coast. Although the forests are inevitably depleted
el the sense of Homer's description of "wooded Zákinthos".
er, in contrast to Itháki, the island is one of the fastest-growing tourist resorts
eece. Pessimists mutter darkly of Zákinthos being turned into another Corfu, and
with upwards of 300,000 visitors a year that's understandable. Most tourists, though,
are conveniently housed in one place – Laganás, on the south coast. As well as the
foreign visitors, July and August also sees an influx of Greek holidaymakers, particularly Athenians, attracted by the island's proximity to the mainland. If you avoid those
months, and steer clear of Laganás and the developing resort villages of Argási and
Tsilívi, there is still a peaceful Zákinthos to be found.

Spring's the time to see the **flowers**, and autumn if you want to eat the produce. Any
time's a good time for the local **wines**, such as the white *Popolaro*, which is among the
best in the Ionians. For dessert or a snack, try *mandoláto*, the ubiquitous and delicious
honey/egg/almond nougat, or the very strong and pungent *grapéria* **cheese**. You may
see temporary stalls by the roadside selling *fitouri* and *pasteli*, sweet, fried local delicacies.
From late August to mid-March, beware the local **hunting season** – everywhere in the
island you'll see what look like little playhouses on stilts; these are the hunters' blinds.

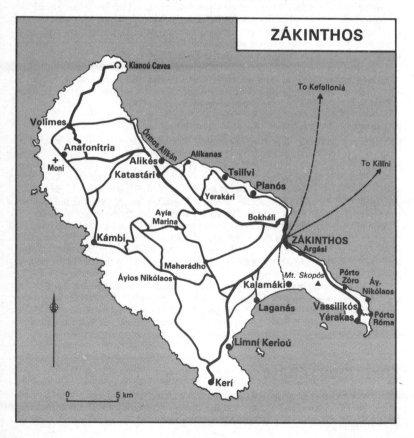

Zákinthos Town

The town, like the island, is known as both **ZÁKINTHOS** and Zante. This former "Venice of the East" (*Zante, Fior di Levante*, "Flower of the Levant", in an Italian jingle), rebuilt on the old plan, has bravely tried to recreate some of its style, though reinforced concrete can only do so much.

The most tangible hints of former glory are to be found in **Platía Solómou**, the grand and spacious main square. At its north (waterside) corner stands the beautiful fifteenth-century sandstone church of **Áyios Nikólaos**, while paintings and icons salvaged from here and other island churches are displayed in the imposing **Neo-Byzantine Museum** (Tues–Sun 8.30am–3pm; 400dr, students 200dr) by the town hall. This collection is exceptional for during the seventeenth and eighteenth centuries Zante became the centre of an Ionian School of painting, given impetus by Cretan refugees unable to practise under Turkish rule.

The square itself is named after the island's great poet **Dionissios Solomos**, who was responsible for introducing demotic Greek (the spoken language of the people) as a literary idiom and who also wrote the words to the Greek national anthem. A small museum (daily 9am–2pm; free) is dedicated to him in the nearby Platía Ayíou Márkou, two blocks up; it is worthwhile for its glimpses of Zante's strong artistic life as well as to see photographs of the town taken both before and after the earthquake.

Elsewhere in town, look in at the large church of **Áyios Dhioníssios** (daily 7am–noon & 4.30–9pm), one of the very few buildings left standing after the earthquake, and with impressive frescoes. And, if you've a few hours to fill, walk up an old cobble path to the town's massive **Venetian fortress** (daily 8am–8pm; 400dr), which has views south to Pílos and north to Messolóngi and is a great picnic spot. En route to the fortress lies the suburb village of **Boháli**, occupying a natural balcony overlooking the harbour, and with a number of popular if slightly expensive tavernas. In season these are the venues for *kantádhes*, an Italianate style of trio-singing accompanied by guitars and mandolins. At the edge of the town, on the road to Kalamáki, take a peep at the charming blue and white church Ayios Elípios, virtually hewn out of a small, rocky hill.

Practicalities

The flatlands of south and east Zákinthos are ideal places to rent a **pedal bike**, available along with **mopeds** and **motorcycles** from *Stainatis* at Desila 9, *Sky Rentals* at A. Makri 7, and other agencies. **Buses** depart from a station on Odhós Filitá (one block back from the *Fina* pump on the main waterside road), with a frequent service to Laganás, and reasonable ones to Tsilí…ví and Alikés.

Since most people stay closer to the beaches, **accommodation** in Zákinthos Town is relatively easy to come by and reasonably priced. It tends to be hotel-based, however, with rooms for rent not much in evidence. In town, try *Pension Zenith* at Tertséti 44 (✆0695/22 134; ③), *Hotel Oasis* on Koutoulist (✆0695/22 287; ③) or *Hotel Ionian* at Alex Roma 18 (✆0695/42 511; ③). For a bit of a splurge, the *Xenia* at Róma 60 (✆0695/42 666; ④) and *Hotel Bitzaro* at Dion Roma 46 (✆0695/23 644; ⑤) are worth trying. If a short man with a Mexican bandit moustache meets you off the ferry and offers you a lift in his red Opel Manta it is worth accepting – this will be Fotis Giatvas whose rooms are some of the best value on Zákinthos (✆0695/23 392; ②). They lie 2km out of town towards Planos but the mobility issue is easily solved by renting a moped.

The one time you'll stand little chance of finding a room is around August 24, the feast of Áyios Dioníssios, when even some of the Greek visitors have to resort to sleeping outside the church for lack of a room. The **tourist police** have information about accommodation (and bus services); they're to be found in the police station on the front, sandwiched between Tzouláti and Merkáti streets, next to the helpful travel agency *Spring Tours*, which offers round the island boat tours.

There's an adequate selection of **restaurants and tavernas**. One of these, *Taverna Arekia,* east of Platía Solómou at Kryeneniou 80, is a must – great food, barrelled wine and an earthy atmosphere make it popular with Greeks and tourists alike. Just before it is *Alivizos,* another good choice. You can also work up an appetite by walking a good way in the opposite direction to Ayíou Dhionissíou (an approach road to the church) – here, *Malvetis* and the *Grill House,* two almost identical *psistaries,* have limited menus but offer good, cheap food. More central is *Bukios* restaurant, the best value of the places on the main square.

The south and west

The road heading southeast from Zákinthos harbour passes under Mount Skopós on its way to some of the finest scenery and best beaches on the island. If you're just after a quick swim, head for the beach at **Pórto Zóro**, just to the northeast of the road with two seafront bars.

Vassilikó and around to Laganás

Further south, **VASSILIKÓ** lies within easy striking distance of a series of good-to-excellent beaches and has a few modest hotels and a scattering of rooms for rent. There is a long stretch of sand known as the Ionian beach and the *Ionian Taverna* offers rooms (☎0695/35 211; ④). Nearby is the enticing *Costas Brothers Taverna,* set in a beautiful garden and featuring quality food and folk music. Through a wood the next turning takes you to **St Nicholas beach** with watersports and good snorkelling.

Campers congregate under the trees at the popular **Pórto Róma** beach, just to the east – a pleasant enough strand, but nothing more. There are rooms here, too, but the seasonal tavernas are oversubscribed and overpriced.

Yérakas – signposted straight ahead – is a good beach and the impressive rock strata and formations of the peninsula make a fine backdrop. There are **rooms** for rent on the way down to Yérakas, though camping is strictly illegal both here and on the beaches to the west – Dephní and Kalamáki – as they are the nesting grounds of **loggerhead turtles** (see feature on p.362). Zákinthos is the most important Ionian location for the turtles, though local numbers today are down to about 800, roughly half of what they were as recently as the mid-1970s.

West of tourist-dominated **Kalamáki**, the beach becomes progressively muddier and more commercialized until new heights (or depths) are demonstrated at the resort of **LAGANÁS** proper. Around the bay, there are further nesting grounds for the **loggerhead turtles**, though the majority now lay their eggs on two small beaches, whereas until recently they used the whole of the fourteen-kilometre bay. In recent years, Greek marine zoologists, attempting to protect and document the turtles, have come into violent dispute with locals, uneasy at restrictions on developing their land for tourism. All things considered, one can't help feeling pessimistic about the turtles' future. As for Laganás itself – there's little to be said, save that if you're not already booked into a hotel here, you probably won't find a room.

Kerí

KERÍ, in the southwest corner of the island, retains some of its pre-earthquake houses and, more curiously, natural **tar pools** commented on by both Pliny and Herodotus and still used for caulking boats. You can also visit the lighthouse by following a dusty track, which leads to spectacular views at the tip of the peninsula where limestone cliffs plunge into turquoise waters. There is a passable beach at **Limní Kerioú**, a few kilometres east, where as at Kerí you can stay, eat and drink inexpensively and in generally local company. Small *kaikia* take people to Keri Cave and Marothonissi island.

Maherádho, Kilioméno and Kámbi

If you have transport, an enjoyable route away from Laganás or Kerí is the mountain road, which leads ultimately to Alikés in the north. Around 15km from either is the village of **MAHERÁDHO**, which shelters the spectacularly ornate church of Ayía Mávra. It is certainly the place to be if you're on the island for her feast day, which usually falls on the first weekend in July.

The road from here to the rural mountain village of **KILIOMÉNO** (sometimes known as Ayios Nikólaos after its grand old church) has recently been improved and is just about passable for a 50cc scooter. However, a sturdier, more powerful bike – not a moped – is more suitable for traversing some of the mountain roads west, over to Kámbi. As well as the state of the roads, you also have the local maps to contend with – roads rated as major on these are often little more than goat tracks, or even non-existent; some of the newer and better roads are not shown, while others are placed inaccurately.

The effort of such safaris can be worth it, though, as the sunsets to be viewed from the clifftops on the rocky western coast are spectacular. **KÁMBI** is the favoured place for organised "Sunset Trips", when the busloads turn up at the taverna, teetering 300m above the sea on the cliff's edge; there's no denying that the performance here is stunning. Even higher than the taverna is an enormous cross, erected to commemorate the deaths of islanders who were thrown off the cliffs during the 1940s, some say by the Nazis, others by nationalist troops in the civil war.

The north

North and west from Zákinthos Town, the roads thread their way through luxuriantly fertile farmland, punctuated with tumulus-like hills. **TSILÍVI**, 4km out, is the closest beach to town worthy of the name, shallow and sandy with warm water, though the evening breeze whips up the surf. It's another settlement riding on the wave of the tourist boom, and there are plenty of rooms, eateries and cocktail bars. Slightly further north is *Camping Zante* (☎0695/24 754).

A pleasant cycle ride from Tsilívi takes inland back roads through lemon groves to Alíkanas. En route you pass the quiet, hilltop village of **ÁNO YERAKÁRI**, one of three settlements within a few hundred metres of each other and offering a couple of rooms. From the church there are fine 360-degree vistas. Ammoúdhi beach is an unspoilt place for a quick dip.

Alikón bay

Ormós Alikón, 13km further north of Tsilívi, is a huge, gently sloping expanse of sand washed by good breakers. At its eastern end is the village of **ALÍKANAS**. Villas are block-booked here by a couple of tour companies, and there's an alarming amount of building going on. Nearby, however, are two excellent **restaurants**. *Ta Neraidha*, with a great setting on Alíkanas harbour, always has fresh, well-cooked fish; while a friendly family runs *Mantalena*, on the road to Alikés, which serves a variety of delicious traditional dishes from the kitchen, a genuine house wine from the proprietors' own grapes, and water from a well on the premises.

Towards the northwest end of the bay, **ALIKÉS** is an increasingly busy package resort with rooms, restaurants and mopeds for rent. There are half a dozen hotels, but as yet nothing on the scale of Laganás, possibly because of the presence of rats and mosquitoes, aggravated by the stagnant water from the river.

A pleasant excursion by moped – or even on foot – from Alikés is to the small cove of **Koróni**, where sulphur springs discharge into the sea. Swimming is quite an experience, if you don't mind the smell, with a few inches of cool, fresh seawater on the surface and warm tracts below. Butterflies abound here in summer.

Further north, **Ayíos Nikólaos** functions as a port for the short, twice-daily crossing to Pessada on Kefallonía. From here another good trip is a ride by **kaíki** (1000dr) to the extreme northern tip of the island, where the **Kianoú (Blue) Caves** are some of the more realistically named of the many contenders in Greece. They're terrific for snorkelling, and when you go for a dip here your skin will appear bright blue. The road snakes onwards through a landscape of gorse bushes and dry stone walls until it ends at the lighthouse of **Cape Skinani**. With one cafeteria, and a view of the mountainous expanse of Kefallonia, it's a good spot for unofficial camping.

Inland: Katastári, Volímes and Ayía Marina

KATASTÁRI, the island's largest community after the capital, lies just inland from Alikés. It's a workaday place, of interest for a chance to witness ordinary island life; stop here and you're likely to be waved over to the *kafenío*.

With a moped, you might be tempted to head 18km northwest to **Anafonítria monastery**. This withstood the earthquake remarkably well and is today tenanted by a few nuns who will show you the frescoed *katholikón*, a medieval tower, and the purported cell of Saint Dhionissios, the patron of Zákinthos whose festivals are on August 24 and December 17. Well represented on postcards, there's a shipwreck (*Toh Navágio*) 3500m from the village down a very rough track. The rusty remains lie embedded on a fantastic beach which isn't accessible by foot, but can be viewed from above. The cliff top vantage point is assuredly not recommended for those with vertigo. A little further north is the large village of **VOLÍMES**, renowned for its embroidered handicrafts. You'll know when you've arrived – mats, rugs and linen hang by the roadside and local women holler "oriste!" at passing tourists.

AYÍA MARÍNA, a few kilometres south of Katastári, has a church with an impressive Baroque altar screen, and a belfry that's being rebuilt from the remnants left after the 1953 earthquake. Like most Zákinthos churches, the belltower is detached, in Venetian fashion. Just above Ayía Marína is the *Parthenonas Taverna* rightly boasting one of the best views on the island. From it you can see the whole of the central plain from beyond Alikés in the north to Laganás Bay in the south.

Kíthira

Although isolated at the foot of the Peloponnese, the island of **Kíthira** is considered part of the Ionian group and shares their history of Venetian, and later, British rule; under the former it was known as Cerigo. For the most part, though, the similarities end there. The island architecture, whitewashed and flat-roofed, looks more like that of the Cyclades, albeit with a strong Venetian influence. The landscape is different, too: wild scrub- and gorse-covered hills or moorland sliced by deep valleys and ravines.

Depopulation has left the land underfarmed and the abandoned fields overgrown, for, since the war, most of the islanders have left for Athens or Australia, giving Kíthira the reputation of being a classic emigrant island; it is known locally as "Australian Colony" or "Kangaroo Island", and Australia is referred to as "Big Kíthira". Many of the villages are deserted, their *platías* empty and the schools and *kafenía* closed. Kíthira was never a rich island, but, along with Monemvassía, it did once have a military and economic significance – which it likewise lost with Greek independence and the opening of the Corinth Canal.

These days, tourism has brought a little prosperity (and a few luxury hotels), but most summer visitors are Greeks and especially Greek-Australians. For the few foreigners who reach Kíthira, it remains something of a refuge, with its fine and remarkably undeveloped beaches the principal attraction. A word of warning, though: out of season, very little stays open outside of Potámos.

Arriving – and getting around

If you arrive by **boat or hydrofoil** from Pireás or Neápoli in the Peloponnese, you'll normally disembark at Ayía Pelayía in the north of the island. In bad weather, for example when the *meltémi* is blowing from the north (common during July and August), boats – particularly hydrofoils – may use Kapsáli, below Kíthira's capital, Hóra, in the south. The **airport** is deep in the interior, 8km southeast of Potamós; taxis meet arrivals.

You can generally find a **taxi** at either harbour, but don't hope for public transport – in summer, the island **bus** runs just once a day between Ayía Pelayía, Potamós, Hóra and Kapsáli, and out of season reverts to its role as the school bus – although you can generally flag it down if you don't mind joining the kids. In fact, most places on Kíthira, beaches in particular, are difficult to reach without your own transport, so you're well advised to rent a **car** or **moped**, bearing in mind that there is no reliable service station south of Potamós.

Ayía Pelayía and northern Kíthira

There's a reasonable choice of **tavernas** and **rooms** in **AYÍA PELAYÍA**; the *Faros Taverna* (☎0735/33 282; ③) offers both, from its waterfront location. The clean and comfortable *Hotel Kytheria* (☎0735/33 3221; ④) is more luxurious, as are the more recent *Filoxenia Apartments* (☎0735/33 100; ⑥), with striking blue shutters and an imaginative layout around small courtyards. Ferry and hydrofoil **tickets** are available from *Conomos Travel* (☎0735/33490), on the ground floor of the *Kytheria*.

Potamós and around

From Ayía Pelayía, the main road winds up the mountainside towards **POTAMÓS**, Kíthira's largest village. A pleasant and unspoilt village which, if you have a rented vehicle, makes a good base for exploring the island. It has a few **rooms**, the *Pension Porfyra* (☎0735/33 329; ④), together with **tavernas**, a **bank**, a **post office**, Olympic Airways office (☎0735/33 688) and two petrol stations. Most of the shops on the island are here, too, as is the **Sunday market**, Kíthira's liveliest regular event.

From Logothetiánika, just south of Potamós, an unpaved road leads down to **Áyiou Eleftheríou**, a good sandy beach on the west coast, backed by high cliffs.

Paleohóra

The main reason for visiting Potamós is to get to **PALEOHÓRA**, the ruined medieval capital of Kíthira, 3km to the east of the town. Few people seem to know about or visit these remains, though they constitute one of the best Byzantine sites anywhere on the Greek islands. The most obvious comparison is with Mystra in the Peloponnese: although Paleohóra is much smaller, a fortified village rather than a town, its natural setting is equally spectacular. Set on a hilltop at the head of the Káko Langádhi gorge, it is surrounded by a sheer 100m drop on three sides.

The site is lower than the surrounding hills and invisible from the sea and most of the island, something which served to protect it from the pirates that have plagued the island through much of its history. The town was built in the fourteenth century by Byzantine nobles from Monemvassía, and when Mystra fell to the Turks, many of its noble families also sought refuge here. Despite its seemingly impregnable and perfectly concealed position, the site was discovered and sacked by Barbarossa, commander of the Turkish fleet, in 1537, and the island's 7000 inhabitants were sold into slavery.

The town was never rebuilt, and tradition maintains that it is a place of ill fortune, which perhaps explains the emptiness of the surrounding countryside, none of which is farmed today. The hills are dotted with Byzantine chapels, which suggests that, in its heyday, the area must have been the centre of medieval Kíthira; it is rumoured to have once had 800 inhabitants and 72 churches.

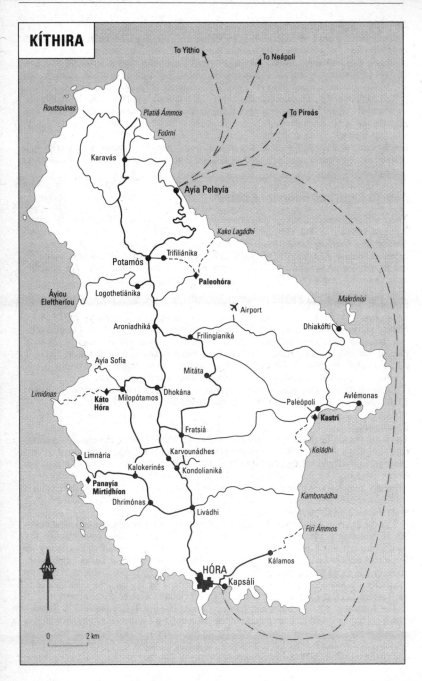

KÍTHIRA

Routsoúnas
Platiá Ámmos
Foúrni
Karavás
Ayía Pelayía

To Yíthio
To Neápoli
To Pireás

Kako Lagádhi
Potamós · Trifiliánika
Paleohóra

Áyiou
Eleftheríou
Logothetiánika

Airport

Makrónisi

Aroniadhiká
Frilingianiká
Dhiakófti

Ayía Sofía
Mitáta

Limiónas
Káto
Hóra · Milopótamos · Dhokána
Avlémonas
Paleópoli
Kastrí

Fratsiá
Keládhi

Limnária
Karvounádhes
Kalokerinés · Kondolianiká
Panayía
Mirtidhíon
Dhrimónas
Livádhi
Kambonádha

Firi Ámmos

HÓRA
Kálamos
Kapsáli

0   2 km

These days the principal remains are of the surviving churches, some still with traces of frescoes, and the castle. The site is unenclosed and has never been seriously investigated, although excavations are now planned.

There's a rough dirt road to Paleohóra, signposted off the main road from Potamós to Aroniadhiká and feasible for mopeds. On foot, it's quicker and more interesting to take the path from the tiny village of Trifiliánika, just outside Potamós – look out for a rusting sign to the right as you enter the village. The path is overgrown in parts and not easy to follow; the ruins only become visible when you join the road above the gorge.

Karavás

KARAVÁS, 6km north of Potamós, is untypical of the island's villages – its architecture and the setting, in a deep wooded valley with a stream, are more reminiscent of the other Ionian islands. One of Kíthira's most pleasant villages, it would be a superb base, though there is (as yet) nowhere to eat or stay.

Platiá Ámmos, at the end of the valley, is a sandy beach with a seasonal fish **taverna**. The little pebble beach at **Foúrni**, 2km south, is quieter and more attractive.

Kapsáli

KAPSÁLI, in addition to its harbour function, is the one place on Kíthira largely devoted to tourism. Most foreign visitors to Kíthira stay here, and it's a popular port of call for yachts heading from the Aegean to the Ionian islands and Italy. Set behind double pebble-sand bays, it is certainly picturesque. The larger of its two bays has a line of **tavernas**; the *Magus*, nearest the harbour, has good food at reasonable prices. As for nightlife, there are a couple of lively **bars**: *Bikini Red* and *Yacht Inn*.

The best **accommodation** is usually booked up in summer by a British holiday company; rooms for more casual visitors can be hard to find, and expensive when you do. Phoning ahead, you might try for a stay at the apartments owned by Kalokerines Katikies (☎0735/31 265; ④), Byron Duponte (☎0735/31 245; ④) or the Megalondis (☎0735/31 340; ④); more luxury is to be had at the sophisticated *Hotel Raikos* (☎0735/31 629; ⑤). A basic **campsite** (June–Sept) nestles in the pine trees behind the village.

There's a mobile **post office** in summer, and a couple of travel agents near the harbour: *Kythoros International* (☎0735/31 925) deals with travel, accommodation and vehicle rental, while *Roma Travel* (☎0735/31 561) deals with accommodation only. *Panayiotis* (☎0735/31 600) and *Nikos* (☎0735/31 5700) both rent **cars, motorbikes and mopeds**. Some of these operate in summer only; if closed, you could try their Hóra branches – see below.

Hóra

HÓRA (or Kíthira town), a steep 2km haul above Kapsáli, has an equally dramatic site, its Cycladic-style houses tiered about the walls of a Venetian castle. Within the **castle**, most of the buildings are ruined, but there are spectacular views of Kapsáli and, out to sea, to the islet of Avgó (Egg), legendary birthplace of Aphrodite. Below the castle are the remains of older Byzantine walls, and 21 Byzantine churches in various states of dereliction. A small **museum** (Tues–Fri 8.45am–3pm; Sun 9.30am–2.30pm) houses modest remnants of the island's numerous occupiers, in particular Minoan finds from excavations at Paleópoli.

Compared to Kapsáli, Hóra stays quiet and many places are closed out of season. A few **tavernas** open in summer, of which *Zorba* is by far the best, but the climb from Kapsáli discourages the crowds. Out of season, only one café/fast-food place stays open, near the square. **Accommodation** is slightly easier to find than in Kapsáli. Two good possibilities are the *Hotel Kathy* (☎0735/31 318; ②) or the *Pension Kythira*, at

Manitohóri, 2km further inland (☎0735/31 563; ③). Back in Hóra, are the *Castello Studios* (☎0735/31 068; ④; year-round) and the old-style *Hotel Margarita* (☎0735/31 711; ⑥). Other facilities include a couple of **banks**, an **OTE**, **post office**, and branches of *Panayiotis* (☎0735/31 004) and *Nikos* (☎0735/31 767) vehicle rental.

The southeast coast

The beach at Kapsáli is decent but gets very crowded in July and August. For quieter, undeveloped beaches, it's better to head out to the east coast, towards Avlémonas. Be warned, however, that the roads are unpaved and can be hazardous on moped.

Fíri Ámmos and Kambonádha

Fíri Ámmos, the nearest good sand beach to Kapsáli, is popular but not overcrowded, even in summer. To get there, you can follow a paved road as far as the sleepy village of Kálamos (take the northerly side road between Kapsáli and Hóra); the beach is signposted down a dirt track on the far side of the village. Fíri Ámmos can also be reached from the inland village of Livádhi, on the Hóra–Arodhiánika road – as can **Kambonádha**, the next beach north.

Paleópoli and Avlémonas

PALEÓPOLI, a hamlet of a few scattered houses, is accessible by a paved road from Aroniádhika. The area is the site of the ancient city of **Skandia**, and excavations on the headland of **Kastrí** have revealed remains of an important Minoan colony. There's little visible evidence, apart from shards of pottery in the low crumbling cliffs, but happily, tourist development in the area has been barred because of its archeological significance. Consequently, there's just one solitary **taverna**, the *Skandia* (June–Sept), on the excellent two-kilometre, sand-and-pebble **beach** that stretches to either side of the headland.

The surrounding countryside, a broad, cultivated valley surrounded by wild hills, is equally attractive. **Paleokástro**, the mountain to the west, is the site of ancient Kíthira and a sanctuary of Aphrodite, but again, there's little to be seen today. Heading across the valley and turning right, an unpaved road leads up to a tiny, whitewashed church above the cliffs. From there, a track leads down to **Keládhi**, a beautiful pebble beach with caves and rocks jutting out to sea.

AVLÉMONAS, 2km east of Paleópoli, is a tiny fishing port with two tavernas, a few rooms and a rather unimpressive Venetian fortress. The coast is rocky, the scenery bleak and exposed, and the village has something of an end-of-the-world feel.

Dhiakófti

DHIAKÓFTI, over the mountain to the north of Avlémonas, is equally bleak and remote, but surprisingly has developed into something of a resort for Greek families. The main attraction is a tiny white sand beach, which is picturesque, but crowded in summer; backed by a few fishermen's cottages, it has fine views across to the islet of **Makrónisi**. The village is well supplied with plenty of **rooms**, a few **tavernas** – and prominent "No Camping" signs.

North and west of Hóra

LIVÁDHI, 4km north of Hóra, has **rooms** and, on the main road, the newish *Hotel Aposperides* (☎0735/31656; ⑤) which, together with the Toxotis reataurant opposite, would make a good base if you had transport. At Katouni (2km out), there is an incongruous arched bridge; a legacy of the nineteenth century when all the Ionian islands were a British protectorate, it was built by a Scottish engineer. From the village, a fork heads west to Kalokerinés, and continues 3km further to the island's principal monastery, **Panayía Mirtidhíon**, set among cypress trees above the wild and windswept west coast. Beyond the monastery, a track leads down to a small anchorage at Limnária; there are few beaches along this rocky, forbidding shore.

Milopótamos, Káto Hóra and the Áyia Sofía cave

North of Livádhi, the main road crosses a bleak plateau whose few settlements are near-deserted. At Dhokána it's worth making a detour off the main road for **MILOPÓTAMOS**, a lovely traditional village and a virtual oasis, set in a wooded valley occupied by a small stream. Nearby is a waterfall, hidden from view by lush vegetation – follow the sign for "Neraidha" past an abandoned restaurant. The valley below the falls is overgrown but contains the remains of the watermill that gave the village its name.

Káto Hóra, 500m down the road, was Milopótamos's predecessor. Now derelict, it remains half-enclosed within the walls of a Venetian fortress. The fortress is small and has a rather domestic appearance: unlike the castle at Hóra, it was built as a place of refuge for the villagers in case of attack, rather than as a base for a Venetian garrison. All the houses within the walls, and many outside, are abandoned. Beyond here, an unpaved and precipitous road continues 5km through spectacular scenery to **Limiónas**, a rocky bay with a small beach of fine white sand.

The reason most visitors come to Milopótamos is to see the cave of **Áyia Sofía**, the largest and most impressive of a number of caverns on the island. A half-hour signposted walk from the village, the cave is open regularly (but not necessarily every day) from mid-June to mid-September (4–8pm). When the cave is closed, you can probably find a guide in Milopótamos; ask at the village, giving a day's notice, if possible.

The cave is worth the effort to see: the whitewashed entrance has been used as a church and has a painted iconostasis. Once inside, the cave system comprises a series of chambers with stalactites and stalagmites, down to a depth of 250m; inevitably in Kíthira, the highlights include the Apartment of Aphrodite – with her bedroom and boudoir on show.

Andíkithira

The tiny island of **Andikíthira** has twice-weekly connections in summer only on the Kíthira–Kastélli run. Rocky and poor, it only received electricity in 1984. Attractions include good birdlife and flora, but it's not the place if you want company. With only fifty or so inhabitants divided between two settlements – **Potamós**, the harbour, and **Sohória**, the village – people are rather thin on the ground. A resident doctor and a teacher serve the dwindling community (there are three children at the village school, as compared with nearly forty in the 1960s).

Both places offer a few rather primitive **rooms** (no toilet/running water) in summer; out of season, they may need a bit of persuasion to open up. Those in Sohória are by the island shop, which is also basic in the extreme: no wine, produce or eggs, and bread baked once a week (on Mondays).

Elafónissos – and Neápoli

The final island in this book, **Elafónissos**, hardly merits the name, lying as it does just 400 metres off the southeasternmost "finger" of the Peloponnese.

It is reached from the little port of **Neápoli**, which itself is disappointing: a modern and surprisingly developed resort, for such an out of the way place, catering mainly to Greek holidaymakers. Besides **rooms**, the village has two modest **hotels**: the *Aivali* (☎0734/22 287; ②) and the *Arsenakos* (☎0734/22 991; ③), both small and worth booking ahead in summer. The huge new *Hotel Limara Mare* (☎0734/22 236; ⑤) is a fall-back, if an expensive one. If you are waiting for the ferry or hydrofoil, you can eat well at the *Restaurant Metaxia Manalitsi*, by the bridge on the seafront; *Captain D Alexandrakis* (☎0734/22 940), also on the seafront, acts as an agent for ferries, hydro-foils and rooms.

Neápoli **beach** extends north to the village of Vingláfia, where you can negotiate for a fishing boat across the 400-metre channel to the islet of Elafónissos. Alternatively, there are caiques direct from Neápoli.

Elafónissos island

Like Neápoli, **Elafónissos** is relatively busy in summer, and again is frequented mainly by Greek visitors. The island's lone village is largely modern and functional, but has plenty of rooms and some good fish tavernas. The two **pensions**, the *Asteri* (☎0734/61 271; ③) and *Elafonissos* (☎0734/61 210; ③), are worth booking.

Although scenically barren, the island has one of the best **beaches** in this part of Greece. This is at Káto Nísso, a large double bay of fine white sand, 5km southeast of the island village, from where a caique leaves every morning in summer. There's one basic sandwich-and-drinks stand at the beach, and usually a small community of people camping here. Another beach to the southwest of the village is quieter but less spectacular.

travel details

Corfu (Kérkira)

Year-round, there are almost hourly (5am–10pm) **ferries** between Igoumenítsa and Corfu (1hr), and there are at least daily connections between Corfu and Pátra (Patras; 9hr). Additionally, most of the ferries between Italy and Greece (Brindisi/ Pátra) call at Corfu; stopover is free, if specified in advance.

In season, there are sometimes hydrofoils between Corfu, Páxi and other Ionian islands, and Brindisi (Italy). There are also plans for a catamaran between Brindisi, Corfu, Paxos and Igoumenitsa. For details of these services contact *Charitos Shipping* (☎0661/44 611).

Several **flights** daily between Corfu and Athens (45min). Seasonal flights (twice weekly) to/from Kefalloniá and Zákinthos.

Elafónissos

Fishing boats from Vingláfia village, close by Neápoli at the foot of the Peloponnese, ply across the 400-metre channel to Elafónissos. Caiques also run to the island from Neápoli.

Eríkousa, Mathráki and Othoní

A **car ferry**, the *Alexandros II*, runs from Corfu Town to all the islands twice weekly, currently leaving Corfu on Tues and Sat at 6.30am. The route is Corfu–Eríkousa–Mathráki–Othoní– Mathráki–Eríkousa–Corfu. The ferry leaves Corfu Town from opposite the *BP* station on Eleftherioú Venizeloú street, midway between the Igoumenítsa and Italy ferries. Tickets and information from *Star Travel Agency* (☎0661/36 355), Eleftherioú Venizeloú 4, Corfu Town. *Star Travel* also run an excursion boat to Eríkousa and Othoní on Sundays in season.

Kaíkia leave Eríkousa and Othoní for Sidhári early on Mon and Thurs morning, returning to Eríkousa at about 11am, and to Othoní, via Mathráki, at about 1pm. These are primarily supply boats for the local people. To check days and times, ask at Sidhári's jetty, or call Stamatis Zoupanos (☎0663/95 141) at *Budget Travel* in Sidhári, who can also give you information on excursion boats from Sidhári to Eríkousa.

Lefkádha and its satellites

Four **buses** daily to and from Athens (6hr) and regular services from Áktio (near Préveza). At least daily **boats**, in season, from Nidhrí to Meganíssi, Kefalloniá (Fiskárdho) and Itháki (Fríkes or Pisaetós); 30min from Vassilikí to Kefalloniá (Fiskárdho and Sámi). From June to September *Ilio Line* **hydrofoils** link Lefkádha with Préveza, Paxí, Corfu, Itháki and Kefalloniá.

There is also an unreliable summer-only ferry from Mitíkas, south of Vónitsa on the mainland. Mitíkas has more regular connections with the satellite island of Kalamós.

Itháki (Ithaca) and Kefalloniá

Daily **ferry** connection between Pátra and Itháki (Váthi – 5hr) and Kefalloniá (Sámi; 6hr). Year-round daily ferries between Astakós (on the mainland south of Vónitsa) and Váthi (on Itháki), usually continuing to/from Ayía Evfimía on Kefalloniá; leaves Astakós early afternoon. Three or four daily hops from Pisaetós on Itháki to Sámi on Kefallonia (half-hour). Also 4 ferries daily in season (once daily out) between Póros (southeast tip of Kefalloniá) and Killíni (Peloponnese, 1hr); 2 daily in season (1 out) between Lixoúri on Kefalloniá and Killíni (1hr); 2 daily in season between Pessádha (Kefalloniá) and Ayios Nikoláos (Zákinthos); daily in season ferries from Fiskárdho (Kefalloniá) to Fríkes and Váthi on Itháki and Nidhrí and Vassilikí on Lefkádha.

From June to September *Europe II* hydrofoils link Argostóli (Kefallonía) with Pátras and Katakolo (mainland) and Zákinthos Town. *Almer* hydrofoils connect Póros with Lefkhádha and Itháki.

Kefalloniá is also on an international *Minoan Lines* route, whose *Ariadne* ferry runs weekly (mid-May to early October) from **Ancona** to the island, then on to Pátra and Iráklion.

Daily **flights** between Argostóli (Kefalloniá) and Athens (45min); useful seasonal flights to/from Zákinthos and Corfu.

Kíthira and Andíkithira

There is a **ferry** most days between Yíthio and Kíthira (2hr 30min); contact *Haloulakos* (☎0733/24 501) or *Rozakis* (☎0733/22 207) for current information. "Flying Dolphin" **hydrofoils** also operate between Yíthio, Neápoli and Kíthira.

A weekly (twice weekly in summer) ferry also runs between **Pireás and Kíthira/Andíkithira**, continuing on to Kastélli on Crete. Currently, this leaves Pireás on Sundays and calls at Kiparíssi, Monemvassía, Neápoli and Elafónissos on the mainland Peloponnese, before reaching Kíthira, Andíkithira and finally Kastélli; the complete trip takes about 16 hours and the boat turns around on Monday back along the same route. For current schedules, phone *Miras Ferries* (☎01/41 27 225) or *Ventouris Ferries* (☎01/41 14 911).

Twice daily **flights** between Kíthira and Athens (50min).

Paxí

Year-round there is a twice-weekly car and passenger **ferry**, the *Kamelia*, from Corfu (3hr), which in season usually calls at Sívota (also known as Moúrtos) on the mainland en route; information from *Sivota Travel* (☎0665/93 222). From June to September, there are also daily **ferries** from Corfu (3hr) and Párga (2hr), 2–3 weekly from Pátra (6hr), and **hydrofoils** from Igoumenítsa, Préveza and Lefkádha.

Zákinthos (Zante)

Up to 5 **ferries** a day in summer (2 out of season; 1hr 30min) between Zákinthos and Killíni (Peloponnese). At least four daily bus/ferry services to Athens. Unreliable, twice-daily connection in summer from Ayíos Nikoláos to Pessádha (Kefalloniá).

From June to September *Europe II* hydrofoils link Zákinthos with Kefalloniá and Pátras (see Kefalloniá, above).

Daily **flights** between Athens and Zákinthos (45min). Twice weekly **flights** to/from Kefalloniá and Corfu.

PART THREE

THE
CONTEXTS

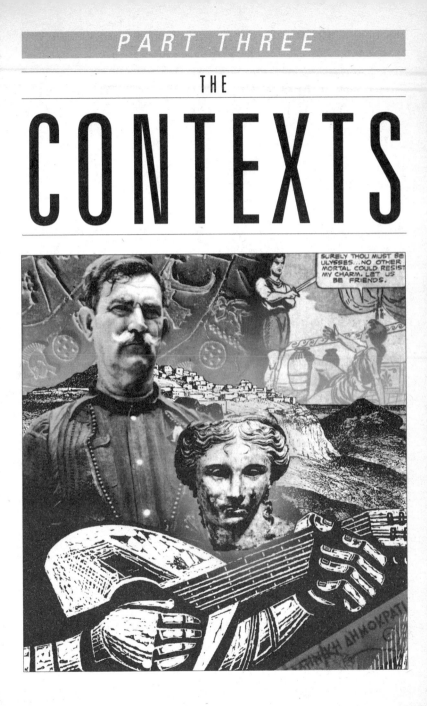

THE HISTORICAL FRAMEWORK

This Historical Framework is intended just to lend some perspective to travels in Greece, and is weighted towards the era of the modern, post-Independent nation – especially the twentieth century. Greeks are inveterate talkers-about-politics, and it won't be long before you find yourself in a taverna discussion. So, it's just as well to know the key figures.

NEOLITHIC, MINOAN AND MYCENAEAN AGES

Other than the solitary discovery of a fossilized Neanderthal skull near Thessaloníki, the earliest **evidence of human settlement** in Greece is to be found at Néa Nikomedhía, near Véria. Here, traces of large, rectangular houses dated to around 6000 BC have been excavated.

It seems that people originally came to this land in the eastern Mediterranean in fits and starts, predominantly from Anatolia. These **proto-Greeks** settled in essentially peaceful farming communities, made pottery and worshipped Earth/Fertility goddesses – clay statuettes of whom are still found on the sites of old settlements. This simple way of life eventually disappeared, as people started to tap the land's resources for profit and to compete and exchange in trade.

MINOANS AND MYCENAEANS

The years between around **2000 and 1100 BC** were a period of fluctuating regional dominance, based at first upon sea power, with vast **royal palaces** serving as centres of administration. Particularly important were those at **Knossos** in Crete, and **Mycenae**, **Tiryns** and **Argos** in the Peloponnese.

Crete monopolized the eastern Mediterranean trade routes for an era subsequently called the **Minoan Age**, with the palace at Knossos surviving two earthquakes and a massive volcanic eruption on the island of Thíra (Santoríni), at some undefinable point between 1500 and 1450 BC. The most obvious examples of Minoan culture can be seen in frescoes, in jewellery, and in pottery, the distinctive red-and-white design on a dark background marking the peak period of Minoan achievement. When Knossos finally succumbed to disaster, natural or otherwise, around 1400 BC, it was the flourishing centre of **Mycenae** that assumed the leading role (and gives its name to the civilization of this period), until it in turn collapsed around 1200 BC.

This is a period whose history and remains are bound up with its **legends**, recounted most famously by Homer. Knossos was the home of King Minos, while the palaces of Mycenae and Pylos were the respective bases of Agamemnon and Nestor; Menelaus and Odysseus hailed from Sparta and Ithaca. The Homeric and other legends relating to them almost certainly reflect the prevalence of violence, revenge and **war** as increasing facts of life; instigated and aggravated by trade rivalry. The increasing scale of conflict and militarization is exemplified in the massive fortifications – dubbed Cyclopean by later ages – that were built around many of the palaces.

The Greece of these years, certainly, was by no means a united nation – as the Homeric legend reflects – and its people were divided into what were in effect a series of splinter groups, defined in large part by sea and mountain barriers and by access to **pasture**. Settlements flourished according to their proximity to and prowess on the sea and the fertility of their land; most were self-sufficient, specializing in the production of particular items for **trade**. Olives, for example, were associated with the region of Attica, and minerals with the island of Mílos.

THE DORIAN AND CLASSICAL ERAS

The Mycenaean-era Greek states had also to cope with and assimilate periodic influxes of new peoples and trade. The traditional view of the collapse of the Mycenaean civilization has it that a northern "barbarian" people, the **Dorians**, "invaded" fom the north, devastating the existing palace culture and opening a "dark age" era. These days, archeologists see the influx more in terms of shifting trade patterns, though undoubtedly there was major disruption of the palace cultures and their sea powers during the eleventh century.

Two other trends are salient to the period: the almost total supplanting of the mother goddesses by **male deities** (a process begun under the Mycenaeans), and the appearance of an **alphabet** still recognizable by modern Greeks, which replaced the so-called "Linear A" and "Linear B" Minoan/Mycenaean scripts.

CITY-STATES: SPARTA AND ATHENS

The ninth century BC ushered in the beginnings of the Greek **city-state** (*polis*). Citizens – rather than just kings or aristocrats – became involved in government and took part in community activities and organized industry and leisure. Colonial ventures increased, as did commercial dealings, and the consequent rise in the import trade was gradually to give rise to a new class of manufacturers.

The city-state was the life of the people who dwelt within it and each state retained both its independence and a distinctive style, with the result that the sporadic attempts to unite in a league against an enemy without were always pragmatic and temporary. The two most powerful states to emerge were Athens and Sparta, and these were to exercise a rivalry over the next five centuries.

Sparta was associated with the Dorians, who had settled in large numbers on the fertile Eurotas (Évrotas) river plain. The society of Sparta and its environs was based on a highly militaristic ethos, accentuated by the need to defend the exposed and fertile land on which it stood. Rather than build intricate fortifications, the people of Sparta relied upon military prowess and a system of laws decreed by the (semi-legendary) **Lycurgus**. Males were subjected to military instruction between the ages of seven

and thirty. Weak babies were known periodically to "disappear". Girls too had to perform athletic feats of sprinting and wrestling, and even dwellings were more like barracks than houses.

Athens, the fulcrum of the state of Attica, was dynamic and exciting by contrast. Home of the administrations of **Solon** and **Pericles**, the dramatic talents of Sophocles and Aristophanes, the oratory of Thucydides and Demosthenes, and the philosophical power of Socrates and Plato, it made up in cultural achievement what it lacked in Spartan virtue. Yet Sparta did not deserve all the military glory. The Athens of the sixth and fifth centuries BC, the so-called **Classical period** in Greek history, is the Athens which played the major part in repelling the armies of the Persian king Darius at Marathon (490 BC) and Salamis (480 BC), campaigns depicted later by Aeschylus in *The Persians*.

It was also Athens which gave rise to a tradition of **democracy** (*demokratia*), literally "control by the people" – although at this stage "the people" did not include either women or slaves. In Athens there were three organs of government. The *Areopagus*, composed of the city elders, had a steadily decreasing authority and ended up dealing solely with murder cases. Then there was the Council of Five Hundred (men), elected annually by ballot to prepare the business of the Assembly and to attend to matters of urgency. The Assembly gave every free man a political voice; it had sole responsibility for law-making and provided an arena for the discussion of important issues. It was a genuinely enfranchised council of citizens.

This was a period of intense creativity, particularly in Athens, whose actions and pretensions were fast becoming imperial in all but name. Each city-state had its **acropolis**, or high town, where religious activity was focused. In Athens, Pericles endowed the acropolis with a complex of buildings, whose climax was the temple of the Parthenon. Meanwhile, the era saw the tragedies of Sophocles performed, and the philosophies of Socrates and Plato expounded.

Religion at this stage was polytheistic, ordering all under the aegis of Zeus. In the countryside the proliferation of names and of sanctuary finds suggests a preference for the slightly more mundane Demeter and Dionysus.

THE PELOPONNESIAN WARS

The power struggles between Athens and Sparta, allied with various networks of city-states, eventually culminated in the **Peloponnesian Wars** of 431–404 BC. After these conflicts, superbly recorded by Thucydides and nominally won by Sparta, the city-state ceased to function so effectively.

This was in part due to drained resources and political apathy, but to a greater degree a consequence of the increasingly commercial and complex pressures on everyday life. Trade, originally spurred by the invention of **coinage** in the sixth century BC, continued to expand; a revitalized Athens, for example, was exporting wine, oil and manufactured goods, getting corn in return from the Black Sea and from Egypt.

The amount of time each man had to devote to the affairs of government decreased and a position in political life became a professional job rather than a natural assumption. Democracy had changed, while in philosophy there was a shift from the idealists and mystics of the sixth and fifth centuries BC to the Cynics, Stoics and Epicureans – followers, respectively, of Diogenes, Zeno and Epicurus.

HELLENISTIC AND ROMAN GREECE

The most important factor in the decline of the city-states was meanwhile developing outside their sphere, in the kingdom of Macedonia.

MACEDONIAN EMPIRE

Based at the Macedonian capital of Pella, **Philip II** (359–336 BC) was forging a strong military and unitary force, extending his territories into Thrace and finally establishing control over Athens and southern Greece. His son, **Alexander the Great**, in an extraordinarily brief but glorious thirteen-year reign, extended these gains into Persia and Egypt and parts of modern India and Afghanistan.

This unwieldy empire splintered almost immediately upon Alexander's death in 323 BC, to be divided into the three Macedonian dynasties of **Hellenistic Greece**: the Antigonids in Macedonia, the Seleucids in Syria and Persia, and the Ptolemies in Egypt. Each were in turn conquered and absorbed by the new Roman Empire, the Ptolemies – under their queen Cleopatra – last of all.

ROMAN GREECE

Mainland Greece was subdued by the Romans over some seventy years of campaigns, from 215 to 146. Once in control, however, **Rome** allowed considerable autonomy to the old territories of the city-states. Greek remained the official language of the eastern Mediterranean and its traditions and culture coexisted fairly peacefully with that of the overlords during the next three centuries.

In central Greece both **Athens** and **Corinth** remained important cities but the emphasis was shifting north – particularly to towns, such as **Salonica** (Thessaloníki), along the new *Via Egnatia*, a military and civil road engineered between Rome and Byzantium via the port of Brundisium (modern Brindisi).

THE BYZANTINE EMPIRE AND MEDIEVAL GREECE

The shift of emphasis to the north was given even greater impetus by the decline of the Roman Empire and its apportioning into eastern and western empires. In the year 330 AD the Emperor Constantine moved his capital to the Greek city of Byzantium and here emerged Constantinople (modern Istanbul), the "new Rome" and spiritual and political capital of the **Byzantine Empire**.

While the last western Roman emperor was deposed by barbarian Goths in 476, this oriental portion was to be the dominant Mediterranean power for some 700 years, and only in 1453 did it collapse completely.

CHRISTIANITY

Christianity had been introduced under Constantine and by the end of the fourth century was the official state religion, its liturgies (still in use in the Greek Orthodox church), creed and New Testament all written in Greek. A distinction must be drawn, though, between perceptions of Greek as a language and culture and as a concept. The Byzantine Empire styled itself Roman, or *Romios*, rather than Hellenic, and moved to eradicate all remaining symbols of pagan Greece. The Delphic Oracle was forcibly closed, and the Olympic Games discontinued, at the end of the fourth century.

The seventh century saw **Constantinople** besieged by Persians, and later Arabs, but the Byzantine Empire survived, losing only Egypt, the least "Greek" of its territories. From the ninth to the early eleventh centuries it enjoyed an archetypal "golden age", in culture, confidence and security. Tied up in the Orthodox Byzantine faith was a sense of spiritual superiority, and the emperors saw Constantinople as a "new Jerusalem" for their "chosen people". It was the beginning of a diplomatic and ecclesiastical conflict with the Catholic west that was to have disastrous consequences over the next five centuries. In the meantime the eastern and western patriarchs mutually excommunicated each other.

From the seventh through to the eleventh centuries **Byzantine Greece**, certainly in the south and centre, became something of a provincial backwater. Administration was absurdly top-heavy and imperial taxation led to semi-autonomous provinces ruled by military generals, whose lands were usually acquired from bankrupted peasants. This alienation of the poor provided a force for change, with a floating populace ready to turn towards or cooperate with the empire's enemies if terms were an improvement.

Waves of **Slavic raiders** needed no encouragement to sweep down from the north Balkans throughout this period. At the same time other tribal groups moved down more peaceably from **central Europe** and were absorbed with little difficulty. According to one theory, the nomadic **Vlachs** from Romania eventually settled in the Píndhos Mountains, and later, from the thirteenth century on, immigrants from **Albania** repopulated the islands of Spétses, Ídhra, Ándhros and Évvia, as well as parts of Attica and the Peloponnese.

THE CRUSADES: FRANKISH AND VENETIAN RULE

From the early years of the eleventh century, less welcome and less assimilable western forces began to appear. The **Normans** landed first at Corfu in 1085, and returned again to the mainland, with papal sanction, a decade later on their way to liberate Jerusalem.

These were only a precursor, though, for the forces that were to descend en route for the **Fourth Crusade** of 1204, when Venetians, Franks and Germans turned their armies directly on Byzantium and sacked and occupied Constantinople. These Latin princes and their followers, intent on new lands and kingdoms,

settled in to divide up the best part of the Empire. All that remained of Byzantium were four small peripheral kingdoms or **despotates**: the most powerful in Nicaea in Asia Minor, less significant ones at Trebizond on the Black Sea, and (in present-day Greece) in Epirus and around Mystra in the Peloponnese (known in these times as the Morea).

There followed two extraordinarily involved centuries of manipulation and struggle between Franks, Venetians, Genoese, Catalans and Turks. The Paleologos dynasty at Nicaea recovered the city of Constantinople in 1261 but little of its former territory and power. Instead, the focus of Byzantium shifted to the Peloponnese, where the autonomous **Despotate of Mystra**, ruled by members of the imperial family, eventually succeeded in wresting most of the peninsula from Frankish hands. At the same time this despotate underwent an intense cultural renaissance, strongly evoked in the churches and the shells of cities remaining today at Mystra and Monemvassía.

TURKISH OCCUPATION

Within a generation of driving out the Franks, the Byzantine Greeks faced a much stronger threat in the expanding empire of the **Ottoman Turks**. Torn apart by internal struggles between their own ruling dynasties, the **Palaeologi** and **Cantacuzenes**, and unaided by the Catholic west, they were to prove no match. On Tuesday, May 29, 1453, a date still solemnly commemorated by the Orthodox church, Constantinople fell to besieging Muslim Turks.

Mystra was to follow within seven years, and Trebizond within nine, by which time virtually all of the old Byzantine Empire lay under Ottoman domination. Only the **Ionian islands** and the **Cyclades**, which remained Venetian, and a few scattered and remote enclaves – like the Máni in the Peloponnese, Sfákia in Crete and Soúli in Epirus – were able to resist the Turkish advance.

OTTOMAN RULE

Under what Greeks refer to as the "Dark Ages" of **Ottoman rule**, the lands of present-day Greece passed into rural provincialism, taking refuge in a self-protective mode of village life that has only recently been disrupted. Taxes and discipline, sporadically backed up by the genocide of dissenting communities, were inflicted from the Turkish Porte but estates passed into the hands of local chieftains who often had considerable independence.

Greek identity, meanwhile, was preserved through the offices of the **Orthodox church** which, despite instances of enforced conversion, the Sultans allowed to continue. The **monasteries**, often secretly, organized schools and became the trustees of Byzantine culture, though this had gone into stagnation after the fall of Constantinople and Mystra, whose scholars and artists emigrated west, adding impetus to the Renaissance.

As Ottoman administration became more and more decentralized and inefficient, individual Greeks rose to local positions of considerable influence and a number of communities achieved a degree of autonomy. Ambelákia village in Thessaly, for example, established an industrial cooperative system to export dyed cloth to Europe, paying only direct taxes to the Sultan. And on the Albanian repopulated islands of the Argo-Saronic, a **Greek merchant fleet** came into being in the eighteenth century, permitted to trade throughout the Mediterranean. Greeks, too, were becoming organized overseas in the sizeable expatriate colonies of central Europe, which often had affiliations with the semi-autonomous village clusters of Zagória (in Epirus) and Mount Pílion.

THE STRUGGLE FOR INDEPENDENCE

Opposition to Turkish rule was becoming widespread, exemplified most obviously by the **Klephts** (brigands) of the mountains. It was not until the nineteenth century, however, that a resistance movement could muster sufficient support and fire power to prove a real challenge to the Turks. In 1770 a Russian-backed uprising had been easily and brutally suppressed but fifty years later the position was different.

In Epirus the Turks were over-extended, subduing the expansionist campaigns of local ruler **Ali Pasha**; the French revolution had given impetus to the confidence of "freedom movements"; and the Greek fighters were given financial and ideological underpinnings by the *Filikí Etería*, or "Friendly Society", a secret group recruited among the exiled merchants and intellectuals of central Europe.

This somewhat moth[...] and theorists launched th[...] monastery of **Ayia Lávra** Peloponnese, where on M[...] Greek banner was openly [...] bishop, Yermanos.

THE WAR OF INDEPENDENCE

To describe in detail the course of the **War of Independence** is to provoke unnecessary confusion, since much of the rebellion consisted of local and fragmentary guerilla campaigns. What is important to understand is that Greeks, though fighting for liberation from the Turks, were not fighting as and for a nation. Motives differed enormously: landowners assumed their role was to lead and sought to retain and reinforce their traditional privileges, while the peasantry saw the struggle as a means towards land redistribution.

Outside Greece, prestige and publicity for the insurrection was promoted by the arrival of a thousand or so European **Philhellenes**, almost half of them German, though the most important was the English poet, **Lord Byron**, who died while training Greek forces at Messolóngi in April 1824.

Though it was the Greek guerilla leaders, above all **Theodhoros Kolokotronis**, "the old man of the Morea", who brought about the most significant military victories of the war, the death of Byron had an immensely important effect on public opinion in the west. Aid for the Greek struggle had come neither from Orthodox Russia, nor from the western powers of France and Britain, ravaged by the Napoleonic Wars. But by 1827, when Messolóngi fell again to the Turks, these three powers finally agreed to seek autonomy for certain parts of Greece and sent a combined fleet to put pressure on the Sultan's Egyptian army, then ransacking and massacring in the Peloponnese. Events took over, and an accidental naval battle in **Navarino Bay** resulted in the destruction of almost the entire Turkish-Egyptian fleet. The following spring Russia itself declared war on the Turks and the Sultan was forced to accept the existence of an autonomous Greece.

In 1830 Greek independence was confirmed by the western powers and **borders** were drawn. These included just 800,000 of the six million Greeks living within the Ottoman empire, and the Greek territories were for the

...art the poorest of the Classical and ...antine lands, comprising Attica, the Peloponnese and the islands of the Argo-Saronic and Cyclades. The rich agricultural belt of Thessaly, Epirus in the west, and Macedonia in the north, remained in Turkish hands. Meanwhile, the Ionian islands were controlled by a British Protectorate and the Dodecanese by the Ottomans (and subsequently by the new Italian nation).

THE EMERGING STATE

Modern Greece began as a republic and **Ioannis Capodistrias**, its first president, concentrated his efforts on building a viable central authority and govenment in the face of diverse protagonists from the independence struggle. Almost inevitably he was assassinated – in 1831, by two chieftains from the ever-disruptive Máni – and perhaps equally inevitably the great western powers stepped in. They created a monarchy, gave limited aid, and set on the throne a Bavarian prince, **Otho**.

The new king proved an autocratic and insensitive ruler, bringing in fellow Germans to fill official posts and ignoring all claims by the landless peasantry for redistribution of the old estates. In 1862 he was eventually forced from the country by a popular revolt, and the Europeans produced a new prince, this time from Denmark, with Britain ceding the Ionian islands to bolster support. **George I**, in fact, proved more capable: he built the first railways and roads, introduced limited land reforms in the Peloponnese, and oversaw the first expansion of the Greek borders.

THE MEGÁLI IDHÉA AND WAR

From the very beginning, the unquestioned motive force of Greek foreign policy was the **Megáli Idhéa** (Great Idea) of liberating Greek populations outside the country and incorporating the old territories of Byzantium into the kingdom. In 1878 **Thessaly**, along with southern Epirus, was ceded to Greece by the Turks.

Less illustriously, the Greeks failed in 1897 to achieve *énosis* (union) with **Crete** by attacking Turkish forces on the mainland, and in the process virtually bankrupted the state. The island was, however, placed under a High Commissioner, appointed by the Great Powers, and in 1913 became a part of Greece.

It was from Crete, also, that the most distinguished Greek statesman emerged. **Eleftherios Venizelos**, having led a civilian campaign for his island's liberation, was in 1910 elected as Greek Prime Minister. Two years later he organized an alliance of Balkan powers to fight the **Balkan Wars** (1912–13), campaigns that saw the Turks virtually driven from Europe. With Greek borders extended to include the northeast Aegean, nothern Thessaly, central Epirus and parts of Macedonia, the *Megáli Idhéa* was approaching reality. At the same time Venizelos proved himself a shrewd manipulator of domestic public opinion by revising the constitution and introducing a series of liberal social reforms.

Division, however, was to appear with the outbreak of **World War I**. Venizelos urged Greek entry on the British side, seeing in the conflict possibilities for the "liberation" of Greeks in Thrace and Asia Minor, but the new king, Konstantinos I, married to a sister of the German Kaiser, imposed a policy of neutrality. Eventually Venizelos set up a revolutionary government in Thessaloníki, and in 1917 Greek troops entered the war to join the French, British and Serbians in the **Macedonian campaign**. On the capitulation of Bulgaria and Ottoman Turkey, the Greeks occupied **Thrace**, and Venizelos presented at Versailles demands for the predominantly Greek region of Smyrna on the Asia Minor coast.

It was the beginning of one of the most disastrous episodes in modern Greek history. Venizelos was authorized to move forces into Smyrna in 1919, but by then Allied support had evaporated and in Turkey itself a new nationalist movement was taking power under Mustafa Kemal, or **Atatürk** as he came to be known. In 1920 Venizelos lost the elections and monarchist factions took over, their aspirations unmitigated by the Cretan's skill in foreign diplomacy. Greek forces were ordered to advance upon Ankara in an attempt to bring Atatürk to terms.

This so-called **Anatolian campaign** ignominiously collapsed in summer 1922 when Turkish troops forced the Greeks back to the coast and a hurried evacuation from **Smyrna**. As they left Smyrna, the Turks moved in and systematically massacred whatever remained of the Armenian and Greek populations before burning most of the city to the ground.

THE EXCHANGE OF POPULATIONS

There was now no alternative but for Greece to accept Atatürk's own terms, formalized by the Treaty of Lausanne in 1923, which ordered the **exchange of religious minorities** in each country. Turkey was to accept 390,000 Muslims resident on Greek soil. Greece, mobilized almost continuously for the last decade and with a population of under five million, was faced with the resettlement of over 1,300,000 Christian refugees. The *Megáli Idhéa* had ceased to be a viable blueprint.

Changes, inevitably, were intense and far-reaching. The great agricultural estates of Thessaly were finally redistributed, both to Greek tenants and refugee farmers, and huge shantytowns grew into new quarters around Athens, Pireás and other cities, a spur to the country's then almost nonexistent industry.

Politically, too, reaction was swift. A group of army officers assembled after the retreat from Smyrna, "invited" King Konstantinos to abdicate and executed five of his ministers. Democracy was nominally restored with the proclamation of a republic, but for much of the next decade changes in government were brought about by factions within the armed forces. Meanwhile, among the urban refugee population, unions were being formed and the Greek Communist Party (KKE) was established.

By 1936 the Communist Party had enough democratic support to hold the balance of power in parliament, and would have done so had not the army and the by then restored king decided otherwise. King Yiorgos (George) II had been returned by a plebiscite held – and almost certainly manipulated – the previous year, and so presided over an increasingly factionalized parliament.

THE METAXAS DICTATORSHIP

In April 1936 George II appointed as prime minister **General John Metaxas**, despite the latter's support from only six elected deputies. Immediately a series of KKE-organized strikes broke out and the king, ignoring attempts to form a broad liberal coalition, dissolved parliament without setting a date for new elections. It was a blatantly unconstitutional move and opened the way for five years of ruthless and at times absurd dictatorship.

Metaxas averted a general strike with military force and proceeded to set up a state based on **fascist** models of the age. Left-wing and trade union opponents were imprisoned or forced into exile, a state youth movement and secret police set up, and rigid censorship, extending even to passages of Thucydides, imposed. It was, however, at least a Greek dictatorship, and though Metaxas was sympathetic to Nazi organization he completely opposed German or Italian domination.

WORLD WAR II AND THE GREEK CIVIL WAR

The Italians tried to provoke the Greeks into **World War II** by surreptitiously torpedoing the Greek cruiser *Elli* in Tínos harbour on August 15, 1940. To this, they met with no response. However, when Mussolini occupied Albania and sent, on October 28, 1940, an ultimatum demanding passage for his troops through Greece, Metaxas responded to the Italian foreign minister with the apocryphal one-word answer *"óhi"* (no). (In fact, his response, in the mutually understood French, was *"C'est la guerre".*) The date marked the entry of Greece into the war, and the gesture is still celebrated as a national holiday.

OCCUPATION AND RESISTANCE

Fighting as a nation in a sudden unity of crisis, the Greeks drove Italian forces from the country and in the operation took control of the long-coveted and predominantly Greek-populated northern Epirus (the south of Albania). However, the Greek army frittered away their strength in the snowy mountains of northern Epirus rather than consolidate their gains or defend the Macedonian frontier, and coordination with the British never materialized.

In April of the following year Nazi mechanized columns swept through Yugoslavia and across the Greek mainland, effectively reversing the only Axis defeat to date, and by the end of May 1941 airborne and seaborne **German invasion** forces had completed the occupation of Crete and the other islands. Metaxas had died before their arrival, while King George and his new self-appointed ministers fled into exile in Cairo; few Greeks, of any political persuasion, were sad to see them go.

The joint **Italian–German–Bulgarian Axis occupation** of Greece was among the bitterest experiences of the European war.

Nearly half a million Greek civilians starved to death as all available food was requisitioned to feed occupying armies, and entire villages throughout the mainland and especially on Crete were burned and slaughtered at the least hint of resistance activity. In the north the Bulgarians desecrated ancient sites and churches in a bid to annex "Slavic" Macedonia.

Primarily in the north, too, the Nazis supervised the deportation to concentration camps of virtually the entire **Greek-Jewish population**. This was at the time a sizeable community. Thessaloníki – where the former UN and Austrian president Kurt Waldheim worked for Nazi intelligence – contained the largest Jewish population of any Balkan city, and there were significant populations in all the Greek mainland towns and on many of the islands.

With a quisling government in Athens – and an unpopular, discredited Royalist group in Cairo – the focus of Greek political and military action over the next four years passed largely to the **EAM**, or National Liberation Front. By 1943 it was in virtual control of most areas of the country, working with the British on tactical operations, with its own army (**ELAS**), navy, and both civil and secret police forces. On the whole it commanded popular support, and it offered an obvious framework for the resumption of postwar government.

However, most of its membership was communist, and the British Prime Minister, **Churchill**, was determined to reinstate the monarchy. Even with two years of the war to run it became obvious that there could be no peaceable post-liberation regime other than an EAM-dominated republic. Accordingly, in August 1943 representatives from each of the main resistance movements – including two non-communist groups – flew from a makeshift airstrip in Thessaly to ask for guarantees from the "government" in Cairo that the king would not return unless a plebiscite had first voted in his favour. Neither the Greek nor British authorities would consider the proposal and the one possibility of averting civil war was lost.

The EAM contingent returned divided, as perhaps the British had intended, and a conflict broke out between those who favoured taking peaceful control of any government imposed after liberation, and the hard-line Stalinist ideologues, who believed such a situation should not be allowed to develop.

In October 1943, with fears of an imminent British landing force and takeover, ELAS launched a full-scale attack upon its Greek rivals; by the following February, when a ceasefire was arranged, they had wiped out all but the EDES, a right-wing grouping suspected of collaboration with the Germans. At the same time other forces were at work, with both the British and Americans infiltrating units into Greece in order to prevent the establishment of communist government when the Germans began withdrawing their forces.

CIVIL WAR

In fact, as the Germans began to leave in October 1944, most of the EAM leadership agreed to join a British-sponsored "official" **interim government**. It quickly proved a tactical error, however, for with ninety percent of the countryside under their control the communists were given only one-third representation; the king showed no sign of renouncing his claims; and, in November, Allied forces ordered ELAS to disarm. On December 3 all pretences of civility or neutrality were dropped; the police fired on a communist demonstration in Athens and fighting broke out between ELAS and **British troops**, in the so-called **Dhekemvrianá** battle of Athens.

A truce of sorts was negotiated at Várkiza the following spring but the agreement was never implemented. The army, police and civil service remained in right-wing hands and while collaborationists were often allowed to retain their positions, left-wing sympathizers, many of whom were not communists, were systematically excluded. The elections of 1946 were won by the right-wing parties, followed by a plebiscite in favour of the king's return. By 1947 guerilla activity had again reached the scale of a full **civil war**.

In the interim, King George had died and been succeeded by his brother Paul (with his consort Frederika), while the **Americans** had taken over the British role, and begun putting into action the cold war **Truman doctrine**. In 1947 they took virtual control of Greece, their first significant postwar experiment in anti-communist intervention. Massive economic and military aid was given to a client Greek government, with a prime minister whose documents had to be countersigned by the American Mission in order to become valid.

In the mountains US "military advisers" supervised **campaigns against ELAS**, and there were mass arrests, court martials, and imprisonments – a kind of "White Terror" – lasting until 1951. Over three thousand executions were recorded, including a number of Jehovah's Witnesses, "a sect proved to be under communist domination", according to US Ambassador Grady.

In the autumn of 1949, with the Yugoslav–Greek border closed after Tito's rift with Stalin, the last ELAS guerillas finally admitted defeat, retreating into Albania from their strongholds on Mount Grámmos. Atrocities had been committed on both sides, including, from the left, wide-scale destruction of monasteries, and the dubious evacuation of children from "combat areas" (as told in Nicholas Gage's virulently anti-communist book *Eleni*). Such errors, as well as the hopelessness of fighting an American-backed army, undoubtedly lost ELAS much support.

RECONSTRUCTION AMERICAN-STYLE 1950-67

It was a demoralized, shattered Greece that emerged into the Western political orbit of the 1950s. It was also perforce American-dominated, enlisted into the Korean War in 1950 and NATO the following year. In domestic politics, the US Embassy – still giving the orders – foisted a winner-take-all electoral system, which was to ensure victory for the right over the next twelve years. All leftist activity was banned; those individuals who were not herded into political "re-education" camps or dispatched by firing squads, legal or vigilante, went into exile throughout Eastern Europe, to return only after 1974.

The American-backed, highly conservative **"Greek Rally"** party, led by General Papagos, won the first decisive post-civil war elections in 1952. After the general's death, the party's leadership was taken over – and to an extent liberalized – by **Konstantinos Karamanlis**. Under his rule, stability of a kind was established and some economic advances registered, particularly after the revival of Greece's traditional German markets. However, the 1950s was also a decade that saw wholesale **depopulation of the villages** as migrants sought work in Australia, America and western Europe, or the larger Greek cities.

The main crisis in foreign policy throughout this period was **Cyprus**, where a long terrorist campaign was waged by Greeks opposing British rule, and there was sporadic threat of a new Greek–Turkish war. A temporary and unworkable solution was forced on the island by Britain in 1960, granting independence without the possibility of self-determination or union with Greece. Much of the traditional Greek–British goodwill was destroyed by the issue, with Britain seen to be acting with regard only for its two military bases (over which, incidentally, it still retains sovereignty).

By 1961, unemployment, the Cyprus issue and the imposition of US nuclear bases on Greek soil were changing the political climate, and when Karamanlis was again elected there was strong suspicion of a fraud arranged by the king and army. Strikes became frequent in industry and even agriculture, and King Paul and autocratic, fascist-inclined Queen Frederika were openly attacked in parliament and at protest demonstrations. The far right grew uneasy about **"communist resurgence"** and, losing confidence in their own electoral influence, arranged the assassination of left-wing deputy **Grigoris Lambrakis** in Thessaloníki in May 1963. (The assassination, and its subsequent cover-up, is the subject of Vassilis Vassilikos's thriller *Z*, filmed by Costa-Gavras.) It was against this volatile background that Karamanlis resigned, lost the subsequent elections and left the country.

The new government – the first controlled from outside the Greek right since 1935 – was formed by **Yiorgos Papandreou's** Centre Union Party, and had a decisive majority of nearly fifty seats. It was to last, however, for under two years as conservative forces rallied to thwart its progress. In this the chief protagonists were the army officers and their constitutional Commander-in-Chief, the new king, 23-year-old **Konstantinos (Constantine) II**.

Since power in Greece depended on a pliant military as well as a network of political appointees, Papandreou's most urgent task in order to govern securely and effectively was to reform the armed forces. His first Minister of Defence proved incapable of the task and, while he was investigating the right-wing plot that was thought to have rigged the 1961 election, "evidence" was produced of a leftist conspiracy connected with Papandreou's son

Andreas (himself a minister in the government). The allegations grew to a crisis and Yiorgos Papandreou decided to assume the defence portfolio himself, a move for which the king refused to give the necessary sanction. He then resigned in order to gain approval at the polls but the king would not order fresh elections, instead persuading members of the Centre Union – chief among them **Konstantinos Mitsotakis**, the current premier – to defect and organize a coalition government. Punctuated by strikes, resignations and mass demonstrations, this lasted for a year and a half until new elections were eventually set for May 28, 1967. They failed to take place.

THE COLONELS' JUNTA 1967–74

It was a foregone conclusion that Papandreou's party would win popular support in the polls against the discredited coalition partners. And it was equally certain that there would be some sort of anti-democratic action to try and prevent them from taking power. Disturbed by the party's leftward shift, King Konstantinos was said to have briefed senior generals for a *coup d'état*, to take place ten days before the elections. However, he was caught by surprise, as was nearly everyone else, by the **coup of April 21, 1967**, staged by a group of "unknown" colonels. It was, in the words of Andreas Papandreou, "the first successful CIA military putsch on the European continent".

The **Colonels' Junta**, having taken control of the means of power, was sworn in by the king and survived the half-hearted counter-coup which he subsequently attempted to organize. It was an overtly fascist regime, absurdly styling itself as the true "Revival of Greek Orthodoxy" against western "corrupting influences", though in reality its ideology was nothing more than warmed-up dogma from the Metaxas era.

All political activity was banned, trade unions were forbidden to recruit or meet, the press was so heavily censored that many papers stopped printing, and thousands of "communists" were arrested, imprisoned, and often tortured. Among them were both Papandreous, the composer Mikis Theodorakis (deemed "unfit to stand trial" after three months in custody) and Amalia Fleming (widow of Alexander). The best-known Greek actress,

Melina Mercouri, was stripped of her citizenship in absentia and thousands of prominent Greeks joined her in exile. Culturally, the colonels put an end to popular music (closing down most of the *rembétika* clubs) and inflicted ludicrous censorship on literature and the theatre, including (as under Metaxas) a ban on production of the Classical tragedies.

The colonels lasted for seven years, opposed (especially after the first year) by the majority of the Greek people, excluded from the European community, but propped up and given massive aid by US presidents **Lyndon Johnson** and **Richard Nixon**. To them and the CIA the junta's Greece was not an unsuitable client state; human rights considerations were considered unimportant, orders were placed for sophisticated military technology, and foreign investment on terms highly unfavourable to Greece was open to multinational corporations. It was a fairly routine scenario for the exploitation of an underdeveloped nation.

Opposition was from the beginning voiced by exiled Greeks in London, the United States and western Europe, but only in 1973 did demonstrations break out openly in Greece. On November 17 the students of Athens **Polytechnic** began an occupation of their buildings. The ruling clique lost its nerve; armoured vehicles stormed the Polytechnic gates and a still-undetermined number of students were killed. Martial law was tightened and junta chief **Colonel Papadopoulos** was replaced by the even more noxious and reactionary **General Ioannides**, head of the secret police.

THE RETURN TO CIVILIAN RULE 1975–81

The end of the ordeal, however, came within a year as the dictatorship embarked on a disastrous political adventure in **Cyprus**. By attempting to topple the Makarios government and impose *énosis* (union) on the island, they provoked a Turkish invasion and occupation of forty percent of the Cypriot territory. The army finally mutinied and **Konstantinos Karamanlis** was invited to return from Paris to again take office. He swiftly negotiated a ceasefire (but no solution) in Cyprus, withdrew temporarily from NATO, and warned that US bases would have to be removed except where they specifically served Greek interest.

In November 1974 Karamanlis and his *Néa Dhimokratía* (New Democracy) party was rewarded by a sizeable majority in **elections**, with a centrist and socialist opposition. The latter was comprised by PASOK, a new party led by Andreas Papandreou.

The election of *Néa Dhimokratía* was in every sense a safe conservative option but to Karamanlis's enduring credit it oversaw an effective and firm return to democratic stability, even legitimizing the KKE (Communist Party) for the first time in its history. Karamanlis also held a **referendum on the monarchy** – in which 59 percent of Greeks rejected the return of Constantine – and instituted in its place a French-style presidency, the post which he himself occupied from 1980 to 1985 (and has done so again from 1990). Economically there were limited advances although these were more than offset by inflationary defence spending (the result of renewed tension with Turkey), hastily negotiated entrance into the EC, and the decision to let the drachma float after decades of its being artificially fixed at 30 to the US dollar.

Crucially, though, Karamanlis failed to deliver on vital reforms in bureaucracy, social welfare and education; and though the worst figures of the junta were brought to trial the ordinary faces of Greek political life and administration were little changed. By 1981 inflation was hovering around 25 percent, and it was estimated that tax evasion was depriving the state of one third of its annual budget. In foreign policy the US bases had remained and it was felt that Greece, back in NATO, was still acting as little more than an American satellite. The traditional right was demonstrably inadequate to the task at hand.

PASOK: 1981–89

Change – *allayí* – was the watchword of the election campaign which swept Andreas Papandreou's Panhellenic Socialist Movement, better known by the acronym **PASOK**, to power on October 18, 1981.

The victory meant a chance for Papandreou to form the first socialist government in Greek history and break a near fifty-year monopoly of authoritarian right-wing rule. With so much at stake the campaign had been passionate even by Greek standards, and PASOK's victory was greeted with euphoria both by the generation

whose political voice had been silenced by defeat in the civil war and by a large proportion of the young. They were hopes which perhaps ran naively and dangerously high.

The victory, at least, was conclusive. PASOK won 174 of the 300 parliamentary seats and the Communist KKE returned another thirteen deputies, one of whom was the composer Mikis Theodorakis. *Néa Dhimokratía* moved into unaccustomed opposition. There appeared to be no obstacle to the implementation of a radical **socialist programme**: devolution of power to local authorities, the socialization of industry (though it was never clear how this was to be different from nationalization), improvement of the social services, a purge of bureaucratic inefficiency and malpractice, the end of bribery and corruption as a way of life, an independent and dignified foreign policy following expulsion of US bases, and withdrawal from NATO and the European Community.

A change of style was promised, too, replacing the country's long traditions of authoritarianism and bureaucracy with openness and dialogue. Even more radically, where Greek political parties had long been the personal followings of charismatic leaders, PASOK was to be a party of ideology and principle, dependent on no single individual member. Or so, at least, thought some of the youthful PASOK political enthusiasts.

The new era started with a bang. The wartime resistance was officially recognized; hitherto they hadn't been allowed to take part in any celebrations, wreath-layings or other ceremonies. Peasant women were granted pensions for the first time – 3000 drachmas a month, the same as their outraged husbands – and wages were indexed to the cost of living. In addition, civil marriage was introduced, family law reformed in favour of wives and mothers, and equal rights legislation was put on the statute book.

These popular **reformist moves** seemed to mark a break with the past, and the atmosphere had indeed changed. Greeks no longer lowered their voices to discuss politics in public places or wrapped their opposition newspaper in the respectably conservative *Kathimerini*. At first there were real fears that the climate would be too much for the military and they would once again intervene to choke a dangerous experiment in democracy, especially when Andreas Papandreou assumed the defence portfolio himself in a move strongly reminiscent of his father's attempt to remove the king's appointee in 1965. But he went out of his way to soothe **military susceptibilities**, increasing their salaries, buying new weaponry, and being super-fastidious in his attendance at military functions.

THE END OF THE HONEYMOON

Nothing if not a populist, **Papandreou** promised a bonanza he must have known, as a skilled and experienced economist, he could not deliver. As a result he pleased nobody on the **economic** front.

He could not fairly be blamed for the inherited lack of investment, low productivity, deficiency in managerial and labour skills and other chronic problems besetting the Greek economy. On the other hand, he certainly aggravated the situation in the early days of his first government by allowing his supporters to indulge in violently anti-capitalist rhetoric, and by the prosecution and humiliation of the Tsatsos family, owners of one of Greece's few modern and profitable businesses – cement, in this case – for the illegal export of capital, something of which every Greek with any savings is guilty. These were cheap victories and were not backed by any programme of public investment, while the only "socializations" were of hopelessly lame-duck companies.

Faced with this sluggish economy, and burdened with the additional charges of (marginally) improved social benefits and wage indexing, Papandreou's government had also to cope with the effects of **world recession**, which always hit Greece with a delayed effect compared with its more advanced European partners. **Shipping**, the country's main foreign-currency earner, was devastated. Remittances from emigré workers fell off as they joined the lines of the unemployed in their host countries, and tourism receipts diminished under the dual impact of recession and Reagan's warning to Americans to stay away from insecure and terrorist-prone Athens airport.

With huge quantities of imported goods continuing to be sucked into the country in the absence of domestic production, the **foreign debt** topped £10 billion in 1986, with inflation at 25 percent and the balance of payments

deficit approaching £1 billion. Greece also began to experience the social strains of **unemployment** for the first time. Not that it didn't exist before, but it had always been concealed as under-employment by the family and the rural structure of the economy – as well as by the absence of statistics.

The result of all this was that Papandreou had to eat his words. A modest spending spree, joy at the defeat of the right, the popularity of his Greece-for-the-Greeks foreign policy, and some much needed reforms saw him through into a **second term**, with an electoral victory in June 1985 scarcely less triumphant than the first. But the complacent and, frankly, dishonest slogan was "Vote PASOK for Even Better Days". By October they had imposed a two-year wage freeze and import restrictions, abolished the wage-indexing scheme and devalued the drachma by 15 percent. Papandreou's fat was pulled out of the fire by none other than that former bogeyman, the **European Community**, which offered a huge two-part loan on condition that an IMF-style **austerity programme** was maintained.

The political fallout of such a classic right-wing deflation, accompanied by shameless soliciting for foreign investment, was the alienation of the Communists and most of PASOK's own political constituency. Increasingly autocratic – ironic given the early ideals of PASOK as a new kind of party – Papandreou's response to **dissent** was to fire recalcitrant trade union leaders and expel some three hundred members of his own party. Assailed by strikes, the government appeared to have lost direction completely. In local elections in October 1986 it lost a lot of ground to *Néa Dhimokratía*, including the mayoralties of the three major cities, Athens, Thessaloníki and Pátra.

Papandreou assured the nation that he had taken the message to heart but all that followed was a minor government reshuffle and a panicky attempt to undo the ill feeling caused by an incredible freeing of **rent controls** at a time when all wage-earners were feeling the pinch badly. Early in 1987 he went further and sacked all the remaining PASOK veterans in his cabinet, including his son, though it is said, probably correctly, that this was a palliative to public opinion. The new cabinet was so un-Socialist that even the right-wing press called it **"centrist"**.

WOMEN'S RIGHTS IN GREECE

Women's right to vote wasn't universally achieved in Greece until 1956, and less than a decade ago adultery was still a punishable offence, with cases regularly brought to court. The socialist party, PASOK, was elected for terms of government in 1981 and 1985 with a strong theoretical progamme for **women's rights**, and their women's council review committees, set up in the early, heady days, effected a landmark reform with the 1983 **Family Law**. This prohibited dowry and stipulated equal legal status and shared property rights between husband and wife.

Subsequently, however, the PASOK governments did little to follow through on **practical issues**, like improved child care, health and family planning. Contraception is not available as part of the skeletal Greek public health service, leaving many women to fall back on abortions – only recently made legal under certain conditions, but running (as for many years past) to an estimated 70–80,000 a year.

The **Greek Women's Movement** has in recent years conspicuously emerged. By far the largest organization is the *Union of Greek Women*. Founded in 1976, this espouses an independent feminist line and is responsible for numerous consciousness-raising activities across the country, though it remains too closely linked to the scandal-ridden opposition party, PASOK, for comfort. As a perfect metaphor for this, Margaret Papandreou felt compelled to resign from the Union following her well-publicized divorce from ex-Premier Andreas, leaving it without her effective and vocal leadership. Other, more autonomous groups, have been responsible for setting up advice and support networks, highlighting women's issues within trade unions, and campaigning for changes in media representation.

None of this is easy in a country as polarized as Greece. In many rural areas women rely heavily on traditional extended families for security, and are unlikely to be much affected by legislative reforms or city politics. Yet Greek men of all classes and backgrounds are slowly becoming used to the notion of women in positions of power and responsibility, and taking a substantial share in child-rearing – both postures utterly unthinkable two decades ago, and arguably one of the few positive legacies with which PASOK can at least in part be credited.

Similar about-turns took place in **foreign policy**. The initial anti-US, anti-NATO and anti-EC rhetoric was immensely popular, and understandable for a people shamelessly bullied by bigger powers for the past 150 years. There was some high-profile nose-thumbing, like refusing to join EC partners in condemning Jaruzelski's Polish regime, or the Soviet downing of a Korean airliner, or Syrian involvement in terrorist bomb-planting. There were some forgettable embarrassments, too, like suggesting Gaddafi's Libya provided a suitable model for alternative Socialist development, and the Mitterrand–Gaddafi–Papandreou "summit" in Crete, which an infuriated Mitterrand felt he had been inveigled into on false pretences.

Much was made of a strategic opening to the Arab world. Yasser Arafat, for example, was the first "head of state" to be received in Athens under the PASOK government. Given Greece's geographical position and historical ties, it was an imaginative and appropriate policy. But if Arab investment was hoped for, it never materialized.

In stark contrast to his early promises and rhetoric, the "realistic" policies that Papandreou pursued were far more conciliatory towards his big Western brothers. This was best exemplified by the fact that **US bases** remained in Greece, largely due to the fear that snubbing NATO would lead to Greece being exposed to Turkish aggression, still the only issue that unites the main parties to any degree. As for the once-reviled **European Community**, Greece had become an established beneficiary and its leader was hardly about to bite the hand that feeds.

SCANDAL

Even as late as mid-1988, despite the many betrayals of Papandreou, despite his failure to clean up the public services and do away with the system of patronage and corruption, and despite a level of popular displeasure that brought a million striking, demonstrating workers into the streets (February 1987), it seemed unlikely that PASOK would be toppled in the following year's **elections**.

This was due mainly to the lack of a credible alternative. Konstantinos Mitsotakis, a bitter personal enemy of Papandreou's since 1965, when his defection had brought down his father's government and set in train the events that culminated in the junta, was an unconvincing and unlikeable character at the helm of *Néa Dhimokratía*. Meanwhile, the liberal centre had disappeared and the main communist party, KKE, appeared trapped in a Stalinist time warp under the leadership of Harilaos Florakis. Only the *Ellenikí Aristerá* (Greek Left), formerly the European wing of the KKE, seemed to offer any sensible alternative programme, and they had a precariously small following.

So PASOK could have been in a position to win a third term by default, as it were, when a combination of spectacular **own goals**, plus perhaps a general shift to the Right, influenced by the cataclysmic events in Eastern Europe, conspired against them.

First came the extraordinary cavortings of the Prime Minister himself. Towards the end of 1988, the seventy-year-old Papandreou was flown to Britain for open-heart surgery. He took the occasion, with fear of death presumably rocking his judgement, to make public a year-long liaison with a 34-year-old *Olympic Airways* hostess, **Dimitra "Mimi" Liani**. The international news pictures of an old man shuffling about after a young blonde, to the public humiliation of Margaret, his American-born wife, and his family, were not popular (Papandreou has since divorced Margaret and married Mimi). His integrity was further questioned when he missed several important public engagements – including a ceremony commemorating the victims of the 1987 Kalamáta earthquake – and was pictured out with Mimi, reliving his youth in nightclubs.

The real damage, however, was done by **economic scandals**. It came to light that a PASOK minister had passed off Yugoslav corn as Greek in a sale to the EC. Then, far more seriously, it emerged that a self-made con man, **Yiorgos Koskotas**, director of the **Bank of Crete**, had embezzled £120m (US$190m) of deposits and, worse still, slipped though the authorities' fingers and sought asylum in the US. Certain PASOK ministers and even Papandreou himself were implicated in the scandal. Further damage was done by allegations of illegal **arms dealings** by still more government ministers.

United in disgust at this corruption, the other Left parties – KKE and *Ellinikí Aristerá* –

formed a coalition, the *Synaspismós*, taking support still further from PASOK.

THREE BITES AT THE CHERRY

In this climate of disaffection, an inconclusive result to the **June 1989 election** was no real surprise. What was less predictable, however, was the formation of a bizarre **"katharsis" coalition** of conservatives and communists, united in the avowed intent of cleansing PASOK's increasingly Augean stables.

That this coalition emerged was basically down to Papandreou. The *Synaspismós* would have formed a government with PASOK but set one condition for doing so – that Papandreou stepped down as Prime Minister – and the old man would have none of it. In the deal finally cobbled together between the left and *Néa Dhimokratía*, Mitsotakis was denied the premiership, too, having to make way for his compromise party colleague, **Tzanetakis**.

During the three months that the coalition lasted, the *katharsis* turned out to be largely a question of burying the knife as deeply as possible into the ailing body of PASOK. Andreas Papandreou and three other ministers were officially accused of involvement in the Koskotas affair – though there was no time to set up their **trial** before the Greek people returned once again to the polls. In any case, the chief witness and protagonist in the affair, Koskotas himself, was still imprisoned in America, awaiting extradition proceedings.

Contrary to the Right's hope that publicly accusing Papandreou and his cohorts of criminal behaviour would pave the way for a *Néa Dhimokratía* victory, PASOK actually made a slight recovery in the **November 1989 elections**, though the result was still inconclusive. This time the Left resolutely refused to do deals with anyone and the result was a consensus caretaker government under the neutral aegis of an academic called Zolotas, who was pushed into the Prime Minister's office, somewhat unwillingly it seemed, from Athens University. His only mandate was to see that the country didn't go off the rails completely while preparations were made for yet more elections.

These took place in **April 1990** with the same captains at the command of their ships and with the *Synaspismós* having completed its about-turn to the extent that in the five single-seat constituencies (the other 295 seats are drawn from multiple-seat constituencies in a complicated system of reinforced proportional representation), they supported independent candidates jointly with PASOK. Greek communists are good at about-turns, though; after all, composer Mikis Theodorakis, musical torch-bearer of the Left during the dark years of the junta, and formely a KKE MP, was by now standing for *Néa Dhimokratía*.

On the night, *Néa Dhimokratía* scraped home with a majority of one, later doubled with the defection of a centrist, and **Mitsotakis** finally got to achieve his dream of becoming Prime Minister. The only other memorable feature of the election was the first parliamentary representation for a party of the Turkish minority in Thrace, and for the ecologists – a focus for many disaffected PASOK voters.

A RETÚRNTO THE RIGHT: MITSOTAKIS

On assuming power, Mitsotakis followed a course of **austerity measures** to try and revive the chronically ill economy. Little headway was made, though given the world recession, it was hardly surprising. Greece still has **inflation** of up towards twenty percent and a growing **unemployment** problem.

The latter has been exacerbated, since 1990, by the arrival of thousands of impoverished **Albanians**. They have formed something of an underclass, especially those who aren't ethnically Greek, and are prey to vilification for all manner of ills. They have also led to the first real immigration measures in a country whose population is more used to being on the other side of such laws.

Other conservative measures introduced by Mitsotakis included laws to combat strikes and **terrorism**. The terrorist issue had been a perennial source of worry for Greeks since the appearance in the mid-1980s of a group called **17 Novemvriou** (the date of the Colonels' attack on the Polytechnic in 1973). They have killed a number of industrialists and attacked buildings of military attachés and airlines in Athens, so far without any police arrests. It hardly seemed likely that Mitsotakis's laws, however, were the solution. They stipulated that statements by the group could no longer

be published and led to one or two newspaper editors being jailed for a few days for defiance – much to everyone's embarrassment.

The **anti-strike laws** threatened severe penalties but were equally ineffectual, as breakdowns in public transport, electricity and rubbish collection all too frequently illustrated.

As for the **Koskotas scandal**, the villain of the piece was eventually extradited and gave evidence for the prosecution against Papandreou and various of his ministers. The trial was televised and proved as popular as any soap opera, as indeed it should have been, given the twists of high drama – which included one of the defendants, Koutsoyiorgas, dying in court of a heart attack in front of the cameras. The case against Papandreou gradually petered out and he was officially acquitted in early 1992. The two other surviving ministers, Tsovolas and Petsos, were convicted and given short prison sentences.

The great showpiece trial thus went with a whimper rather than a bang, and did nothing to enhance Mitsotakis's position. If anything, it served to increase sympathy for Papandreou, who was felt to have been unfairly victimized. The real villain of the piece, Koskotas, was eventually convicted of major **fraud** and is now serving a lengthy sentence.

THE MACEDONIAN QUESTION

Increasingly unpopular because of the desperate austerity measures, and perceived as ineffective and out of his depth on the international scene, the last thing Mitsotakis needed was a major **foreign policy** headache. That. is exactly what he got when, in 1991, one of the breakaway republics of the former Yugoslavia named itself Macedonia, thereby injuring Greek national pride and sparking off vehement protests at home and abroad. Diplomatically, the Greeks fought tooth and nail against the use of the name, but their position became increasingly isolated and by 1993 the new country had gained official recognition, from both the EC and the UN – albeit under the convoluted title of the Former Yugoslav Republic of Macedonia (FYROM).

Salt was rubbed into Greek wounds when the FYROM started using the Star of Veryína as a national symbol on their new flag. Greece still refuses to call its northerly neighbour

Macedonia, instead referring to it as Ta Skópia after the capital – and you can't go far in Greece these days without coming across officially placed protestations that "Macedonia was, is, and always will be Greek and only Greek!" Strong words.

THE PENDULUM SWINGS BACK

In effect, the Macedonian problem more or less directly led to Mitsotakis's **political demise**. In the early summer of 1993 his ambitious young Foreign Minister, **Andonis Samaras**, disaffected with his leader, jumped on the bandwagon of resurgent Greek nationalism to set up his own party, **Politikí Ánixi** (Political Spring), after leaving *Néa Dhímokratía*. His platform, still right-wing, was largely based on action over Macedonia and during the summer of 1993 more ND MPs broke ranks, making *Politikí Ánixi* a force to be reckoned with. When parliament was called upon to approve severe new budget proposals, it became clear that the government lacked support, and early elections were called for October 1993. Mitsotakis had also been plagued for nearly a year by accusations of phone-tapping, and had been linked with a nasty and complicated contracts scandal centred around a national company, AGET.

Many of ND's disillusioned supporters reverted directly to PASOK, and **Papandreou** romped to election victory.

THE MORNING AFTER

And so, a frail-looking Papandreou, now well into his 70s, became Prime Minister for the third time. He soon realized that the honeymoon was going to be neither as sweet nor as long as it had been in the 1980s.

PASOK immediately fulfilled two of its pre-election promises by removing restrictions on the reporting of statements by terrorist groups and renationalizing the Athens city bus company. The new government also set about improving the health system, and began to set

the wheels in motion for Mitsotakis to be tried for his alleged misdemeanours.

The thrust of popular dissatisfaction, of course, remains **the economy**, which is still in dire straits, and PASOK can hardly claim to have won any diplomatic battles over Macedonia, despite a lot of tough posturing. The only concrete move has been the imposition of a trade embargo by the Greeks, which has landed them in trouble with the European Court of Justice. There is also increased **tension with Albania**, where five ethnic Greek activists are on trial for terrorism, in retaliation for which droves of illegal Albanian workers are periodically rounded up and bussed back across the border.

At home, the Minister of Public Order, Papathemelis, has made the government extremely unpopular with the youth and bar/restaurant owners by reintroducing licensing laws and imposing, for the first time, minimum age requirements.

THE CURRENT SITUATION

Both the major parties received a good slap in the face at the **Euroelections** of June 1994, losing ground to the smaller parties. The major winner was Samaras, whose *Politikí Ánixi* almost doubled its share of the vote, while the two left-wing parties both fared quite well.

In the spring 1995 presidential elections were held to elect a successor to the 88-year-old Karamanlis. The winner, with support from *Politikí Ánixi* and *Pasok*, was Costis Stephanopoulos, a former lawyer with a clean-cut reputation, who had been put forward by Samaras and welcomed by Papandreou in a deal that would allow his party to see out their four-year term.

All is not rosy for Pasok, however, which is riven by divisions over the economy, foreign policies and, above all, by who will eventually succeed Papandreou as leader to fight the next elections in 1996. At time of writing, there is no clear candidate.

WILDLIFE

Greek wildlife – and in particular flora – may well prove an unexpected source of fascination. In spring, the colour, scent and sheer variety of wild flowers, and the resulting wealth of insect life, are breathtaking. Isolated islands have had many thousands of undisturbed years to develop their own individual species. Overall, there are some 6000 species of flowering plants (three times that of Britain, for example), many of them unique to Greece.

SOME BACKGROUND

Around 8000 years ago, Greece was thickly forested. Aleppo and maritime (Calabrian) pines grew in coastal regions, giving way to Cephallonian and silver fir or black pine up in the hills and low mountains. But early civilizations changed all that, and most of Greece, like most of Europe, is an artificial mosaic of habitats created by forest clearance followed by agriculture, either row crops or stock-grazing. As long ago as the fourth century BC, Plato was lamenting the felling of native forests on the hills around Athens. This wasn't all bad for wildlife, though: the scrubby hillsides created by forest clearing and subsequent grazing are one of the richest habitats of all.

In this century, Greece has on the whole escaped the intensification of agriculture so obvious in Northern Europe. For the most part, crops are still grown in small fields and without excessive use of pesticides and herbicides,

while flocks of goats graze the hillsides in much the same way as they have done for the last few thousand years. On the minus side is damage from rapid development of industry, logging and tourism, all carried out with little sympathy for the environment. New hotels and resorts have often destroyed rich wildlife areas, and in the Ionian, for example, the breeding grounds of the loggerhead turtle have been put under threat by tourist development of beaches.

One peculiarly Greek bonus to the naturalist is that wildlife here probably has the longest recorded history of anywhere in the world. Aristotle was a keen naturalist, Theophrastus in the fourth century BC was one of the earliest botanists, and Dioscorides, a physician in the first century AD, wrote a comprehensive book on the herbal uses of plants.

FLOWERS

What you will see of the Greek **flora** depends on where and when you go. Plants cease flowering (or even living, in the case of annuals) when it is too hot and dry for them – the high summer in Greece does the same to plants as does the winter in northern Europe. So, if you want to see flowers in high summer, head for the hills.

The best time to go is **spring** – which comes to the south coast of Crete in early March, to the Ionian a month or so later. In early **summer**, the spring anemones, orchids and rockroses are replaced by plants like brooms and chrysanthemums. The onset of summer ranges from late April to southern Crete to June/July in the Ionian.

Once the worst heat is over, there is a burst of activity on the part of **autumn** flowering species such as cyclamens and autumn crocus, flowering from October in the north into December in the south. And the first of the spring bulbs flower in January!

SEASHORE

You might find the spectacular yellow-horned poppy growing on shingled banks, and sea stocks and Virginia stocks among the rocks behind the beach. A small pink campion, *Silene colourata*, is often colourfully present.

Sand dunes are rare on the Greek islands, but sometimes there is a flat grazed area behind the beach; these can be fertile ground for orchids. Tamarisk trees often grow down to the shore, and there are frequent groves of Europe's largest grass, the giant calamus reed, which can reach 4m high.

In the autumn, look for the very large white flowers of the sea daffodil, as well as autumn crocuses on the banks behind the shore. The sea squill also flowers in early autumn, with tall spikes of white flowers rising from huge bulbs.

CULTIVATED LAND

Avoid large fields and plantations, but look for small hay meadows. These are often brilliant with annual "**weeds**" in late spring – various chrysanthemum species, wild gladiolus, perhaps wild tulips (especially in Crete), and in general a mass of colour such as you rarely see in northern Europe. (Hot summers force plants into flowering simultaneously.) Fallow farmland is also good for flowers; you can often find deserted terraces full of cyclamens, anemones and orchids.

LOW HILLSIDES

This is a versatile habitat. The trees and shrubs are varied and beautiful, with colourful brooms flowering in early summer, preceded by bushy rockroses – *Cistaceae* – which are a mass of pink or white flowers in spring. Scattered among the shrubs is the occasional tree, such as the Judas tree, which flowers on bare wood in spring, making a blaze of pink against the green hillsides, and stands out for miles.

Lower than the shrubs are the **aromatic herbs** – sage, rosemary, thyme and lavender – with perhaps some spiny species of *Euphorbia*. These occur principally on the *frígana*, limestone slopes scattered with scrubby bushes. (The other hillside type, *maquis*, with its dense prickly scrub, is better for birds.)

Below the herbs is the ground layer; peer around the edges and between the shrubs and you will find a wealth of orchids, anemones, grape hyacinths, irises and perhaps fritillaries if you are lucky. The **orchids** are extraordinary; some kinds – the *Ophrys* species – imitate insect colouration in order to attract them for pollination, and have delicate and unusual flowers. They're much smaller and altogether more dignified than the big blowsy tropical orchids that you see in florists' shops. The **irises** are beauties, too; of them, a small, blue

species called *Iris sisyrinchium* only flowers in the afternoon, and you can actually sit and watch them open around midday.

Once the heat of the summer is over, the **autumn bulbs** come into their own, with species of crocus and their relatives, the colchicums and the sternbergias, more squills and finally the autumn cyclamens flowering through into early December. Heather (genus *Erica*) provides a blaze of pink on acidic slopes around the New Year.

MOUNTAINS

These are good to visit later in the season, with flowers until June in water-scarce Crete, for example. The rocky mountain gorges are the home of many familiar garden rock plants, such as the aubretias, saxifrages and alyssums, as well as dwarf bellflowers and anemones.

The mountains are also the place to see the remaining Greek native coniferous and deciduous forests, and in the woodland glades you will find gentians, cyclamens, violets and perhaps some of the rare and dramatic lilies, such as the crimson *Lilium heldrecheii*. Above 1700m or so the forests begin to thin out, with tree line at about 1900m, and in some of these upland meadows you will find the loveliest crocuses, flowering almost before the snow has melted in spring. As in the lowlands, autumn-flowering species of crocus make a visit worthwhile later in the year.

BIRDS

Greece has a large range of the resident **Mediterranean species**, plus one or two very rare ones such as the Ruppells warbler and the lammergeier vulture, which have most of their European breeding strongholds in Greece.

The great thing about birdwatching here is that, if you pick your time right, you can see both resident and **migratory species**. Greece is on the main flyway for species that have wintered in East Africa, but breed in northern Europe; they migrate every spring up the Nile valley, and then move across the eastern Mediterranean, often in huge numbers. This happens from mid-March to mid-May, depending on the species and the weather. The return migration in autumn is less spectacular because less concentrated, but still worth watching out for.

On the outskirts of towns and in the fields there are some colourful residents. Small **predatory birds** such as woodchat shrikes, kestrels and red-footed falcons can be seen perched on telegraph wires, and lesser kestrels nest communally and noisily in many small towns and villages. The dramatic pink, black and white hoopoe and the striking yellow and black golden oriole are sparsely represented in woodland and olive groves, and Scops owls (Europe's smallest owl) can often be heard calling around towns at night. They repeat a monotonous single "poo" sound, sometimes in mournful vocal duets.

Look closely at the **swifts and swallows**, and you will notice a few species not found in northern Europe; some of the swallows will be red-rumped, for example, and you may see the large alpine swift, which has a white belly. The Sardinian warbler dominates the rough scrubby hillsides, the male with a glossy black cap and an obvious red eye.

Wetlands and coastal lagoons are excellent bird territories, especially at spring and autumn migration. Both European species of pelican breed in Greece, and there is a wide variety of herons and egrets, as well as smaller waders such as the avocet and the black-winged stilt, which has ridiculously long, pink legs. The coast is often the best place to see migration, too. Most birds migrate up the coast, navigating by the stars; a thick mist or heavy cloud will force them to land, and you can sometimes see spectacular "falls" of migrators.

The most exciting birds, however, are to be seen in **the mountain areas**. Smaller birds like blue rock thrush, alpine chough and rock nuthatch are pretty common, and there is a good chance of seeing large and dramatic birds of prey, including buzzards and smaller eagles.

MAMMALS

Greek mammals include the usual range of rats, mice and voles, and some interesting medium-sized creatures, like the beech marten. There is also a fairly typical range of European species such as fox, badger, red squirrel, hare and so on, though the Greek hedgehog is distinctive in having a white breast.

Again it's the **mountain areas** that host the really exciting species. **Wolves**, **brown bears**, **lynx**, **chamois** and **wild boar** are all present, though chances of seeing one are slim to say the least. You might, however, get a glimpse of a rare **ibex**, known locally as the *kri-kri*, in the Samaria gorge in Crete, or on one of the islets offshore.

The extremely rare Mediterranean **monk seal** also breeds on some stretches of remote coast, especially around the Sporades. If spotted, it should be treated with deference – it's endangered and easily scared from its habitat.

REPTILES AND AMPHIBIANS

A hot, rocky country like Greece suits reptiles well and there are over forty indigenous species, half of the European total. Many of these are **wall lizards**. Most of the islands have their own species, all confusingly similar: small lizards with a brownish striped back, often with an orange or yellow belly. Sit and watch a dry, sunny wall almost anywhere on the islands and you're bound to see them.

On a few islands, notably the Dodecanese and the northern Cyclades, you may see the **agama** or **Rhodes dragon**. Growing up to 30cm, though usually smaller, they really do look like miniature, spiny-backed dragons with a series of pale diamonds on a brown or grey background.

In the bushes of the maquis and *frígana* you may see the **Balkan green lizard**, a truly splendid, brightly tinted animal up to half a metre long, most of which is its tail; you can often spot it running on its hind legs, as if possessed, from one bush to another.

At night, **geckos** replace the lizards. Geckos are small (less than 10cm long), have big eyes, and round adhesive pads on their toes which enable them to walk upside down on the ceiling. Sometimes they come into houses, in which case welcome them, since they will keep down the mosquitoes and other biting insects. The **chameleon** is found infrequently in eastern Crete and some of the northern Aegean islands such as Sámos. It lives in bushes and low trees, and hunts by day; its colour is greenish but (obviously) variable.

All three European **tortoises** occur in Greece. They have suffered to varying extents from collection for the pet trade but you can still find them easily enough, on sunny hillsides. The best time is mid-morning, when they'll be basking between the shrubs and rocks. They come in all sizes depending on age – from 5cm to 30cm long. A good way to find them is by ear; they make a constant rustle as they lumber around, and if you find one, look for more, since they often seem to stick together.

A closely related reptile is the **terrapin**, which is basically an aquatic tortoise. Again, both European species occur in Greece, and they're worth looking for in any freshwater lakes or ponds. There are also **sea turtles** in the Ionian; you might be lucky and see one while you're swimming or on a boat, since they sometimes bask on the surface of the water. The one you're most likely to see is the **loggerhead turtle** (*Caretta caretta*), which can grow up to a metre long. It is endangered, and protected (see p.705).

The final group of reptiles are the **snakes**. Greece has plenty of them, but (as in most habitats) they're shy and easily frightened. Although most snakes are nonpoisonous, Greece does have a number of viper species, which are front-fanged venomous snakes,

including the nose-horned viper, as poisonous as they come in Europe.

Snakes actually cause only a handful of deaths a year in Europe but they should nonetheless be treated with respect. If you get bitten, sit and wait to see if a swelling develops. If it doesn't, then the snake was harmless or didn't inject venom. If it does, move the area bitten as little as possible, and get medical attention. Don't try anything fancy like cutting or sucking the wound, but bind the limb firmly so as to slow down the blood circulation (but not so tightly as to stop the blood flow).

Amphibians either have tails (newts and salamanders) or they don't (frogs and toads). Newts can be seen in a few alpine tarns; search for salamanders in ponds at breeding time, and under stones and in moist crevices outside the breeding season.

You can't miss the frogs and toads, especially in spring. Greece has the **green toad**, which has an obvious marbled green and grey back, as well as the common toad. **Tree**

FLORA AND FAUNA FIELD GUIDES

MEDITERRANEAN WILDLIFE

Pete Raine *The Rough Guide to Mediterranean Wildlife* (Rough Guides, UK/US). A good overview, written by the author of the preceding essay, which it expands upon, along with a site-by-site guide to the best Greek wildlife habitats.

FLOWERS

Marjorie Blainey and Christopher Grey-Wilson *Mediterranean Wild Flowers* (HarperCollins, UK). Comprehensive field guide.

Anthony Huxley and William Taylor *Flowers of Greece and the Aegean* (Hogarth Press, UK). Best book for flower identification. It doesn't describe all the Greek flowers – no book does – but it's an excellent general guide with quality photographic illustrations.

BIRDS

Petersen, Mountfort and Hollom *Field Guide to the Birds of Britain and Europe* (Collins, UK/ Stephen Green Press, US); **Heinzel, Fitter and Parslow** *Collins Guide to the Birds of Britain and Europe* (Collins, UK/Stephen Green Press, US). There are no specific reference books on Greek birds. These two European field guides have the

best coverage, with the former, ageing but excellent, retaining an edge.

MAMMALS

Corbet and Ovenden *Collins Guide to the Mammals of Europe* (Collins, UK/Stephen Green Press, US). The best fieldguide on its subject.

INSECTS

Michael Chinery *Collins Guide to the Insects of Britain and Western Europe* (Collins, UK/Stephen Green Press, US). Although this doesn't include Greece, it gives good general information about the main insects you may see.

Higgins and Riley *A Field Guide to the Butterflies of Britain and Europe* (Collins, UK/Stephen Green Press, US). A field guide that will sort out all the butterflies for you, though it's a bit detailed for the casual naturalist.

REPTILES

Arnold and Burton *Collins Guide to the Reptiles and Amphibians of Britain and Europe* (Collins, UK/ Stephen Green Press, US). A useful guide which, infuriatingly for Greek travellers, excludes the Dodecanese and eastern Aegean islands.

frogs are small, live in trees, and call very noisily at night. They have a stripe down the flank and vary in colour from bright green to golden brown, depending on where they are sitting – they can change colour like a chameleon.

INSECTS

About a third of all insect species are **beetles**, and these are very obvious in Greece. You might see one of the dung beetles rolling a ball of dung along a path like the mythological Sisyphus, or a rhinoceros-horned beetle digging a hole in a sand dune.

The **grasshopper** and **cricket** family are well represented, and most patches of grass will hold a few. Grasshoppers produce their chirping noise by rubbing a wing against a leg, but crickets do it by rubbing both wings together. **Cicadas**, which most people think of as a type of grasshopper or locust, aren't actually related at all – they're more of a large leaf-hopper. Their continuous whirring call is one of the characteristic sounds of the Mediterranean noontime, and is produced by the rapid vibration of two cavities called tymbals on either side of the body. If you have time to look closely at bushes and small trees, you might be rewarded with a stick insect or a **praying mantis**, insects that are rarely seen because of their excellent camouflage.

The most obvious Greek insects are the **butterflies**. Any time from spring through most of the summer is good for butterfly-spotting, and there's usually a second flight of adults of many species in the autumn.

Dramatic species include three species of **swallowtail**, easily distinguished by their large size, yellow and black shading, and long spurs at the back of the hind wings. **Cleopatras** are large, brilliant yellow butterflies, related to the brimstone of northern Europe, but larger and more colourful. Look out for **green hairstreaks** – a small green jewel of a butterfly that is particularly attracted to the flowers of the asphodel, a widespread plant of overgrazed pastures and hillsides.

One final species typical of the Greek islands are the **festoons**, unusual butterflies with tropical colours, covered in yellow, red and black zigzags.

Pete Raine

BOOKS

Where separate editions exist in the UK and USA, publishers are detailed below in the form "British Publisher/American Publisher", unless the publisher is the same in both countries. Where books are published in one country only, this follows the publisher's name.

O/p signifies an out-of-print – but still highly recommended – book. University Press is abbreviated as UP.

TRAVEL AND GENERAL ACCOUNTS

MODERN ACCOUNTS

Gerald Durrell *My Family and Other Animals* (Penguin). Sparkling, very funny anecdotes of Durrell's childhood on Corfu – and his passion for the island's fauna: toads, tortoises, bats, scorpions, the lot.

Lawrence Durrell *Prospero's Cell* (Faber & Faber/Penguin, the latter o/p); *Reflections on a Marine Venus* (Faber & Faber/Penguin); *The Greek Islands* (Faber & Faber/Penguin, the former o/p). The elder Durrell lived before the second world war with Gerald and the family on Corfu, the subject of *Prospero's Cell*. *Marine Venus* recounts Lawrence's wartime experiences and impressions of Rhodes and other Dodecanese Isands. *Greek Islands* is a dated, lyrical and occasionally bilious guide to the archipelagos.

Henry Miller *The Colossus of Maroussi* (Minerva/New Directions). Corfu and the soul of Greece in 1939, with Miller, completely in his element, at his most inspired.

Clay Perry *Vanishing Greece* (Conran Octopus/Abbeville Press). Well-captioned photos depict the threatened landscapes and way of life in rural Greece.

James Pettifer *The Greeks: the Land and People since the War* (Viking). A highly readable introduction to contemporary Greece – and its recent past. Pettifer roams across the country and charts the state of the nation's politics, food, family life, religion, tourism, and all points in between.

Jackson Webb *The Last Lemon Grove* (Weidenfeld, UK, o/p). Published in 1977, this is the account of an American living in the then-remote village of Paleohóra on Crete. It is as good a choice of book as you could make for a stay on the island today.

Sarah Wheeler *An Island Apart* (Abacus, UK). Entertaining chronicle of a five-month ramble through one of the least-visited islands. Wheeler has a sure touch with Greek culture and an open approach to the people she meets, whether nuns, goatherds or academics.

OLDER ACCOUNTS

James Theodore Bent *The Cyclades, or Life Among Insular Greeks* (o/p). Originally published in 1881, this remains the best account of island customs and folklore; it's also a highly readable, droll account of a year's Aegean travel, including a particularly violent Cycladic winter.

Juliet du Boulay *Portrait of a Greek Mountain Village* (Oxford UP, o/p in UK). An account of the village of Ambli, on Évvia, in the 1960s. Boulay observes and evokes the habits and customs of a fast disappearing life in an absorbing narrative.

Martin Garrett *Greece: A Literary Companion* (John Murray, UK). Brief nuggets of travel writing and the classics, arranged by region. Enjoyable and frustrating in equal measure.

Edward Lear *The Corfu Years* and *The Cretan Journal* (Denise Harvey, Athens, Greece). Beautifully illustrated journals by the famous landscape painter and author of *The Book of Nonsense*.

Terence Spencer *Fair Greece, Sad Relic: Literary Philhellenism from Shakespeare to Byron* (Denise Harvey, Athens, Greece/Scholarly Press, US). Greece from the Fall of Constantinople to the War of Independence, through the eyes of English poets, essayists and travellers.

CLASSICS AND HISTORY

THE CLASSICS

Many of the classics make good companion reading for a trip around Greece – and it is hard to beat **Homer**'s *Odyssey*, for reading when you're battling with or resigning yourself to the vagaries of island ferries. The following are all available in Penguin Classic editions:

Herodotus *The Histories*.

Homer *The Odyssey, The Iliad*.

Pausanias *The Guide to Greece* (2 vols).

Plutarch *The Age of Alexander; Plutarch on Sparta; The Rise and Fall of Athens*.

Thucydides *History of the Peloponnesian War*.

Xenophon *The History of My Times*.

ANCIENT HISTORY

A R Burn *History of Greece* (Penguin). Probably the best general introduction to ancient Greece, though for fuller and more interesting analysis you'll do better with one or other of the following.

M I Finley *The World of Odysseus* (Penguin). Good on the interrelation of Mycenaean myth and fact.

Robin Lane Fox *Alexander the Great* (Penguin). An absorbing study, which mixes historical scholarship with imaginative psychological detail.

John Kenyon Davies *Democracy and Classical Greece* (Fontana/Harvard UP). Established and accessible account of the period and its political developments.

Oswyn Murray *Early Greece* (Fontana/Harvard UP). The Greek story from the Mycenaeans and Minoans to the onset of the Classical period.

F W Walbank *The Hellenistic World* (Fontana/Harvard UP). Greece under the sway of the Macedonian and Roman empires.

BYZANTINE, MEDIEVAL AND OTTOMAN

Nicholas Cheetham *Medieval Greece* (Yale UP, o/p in US). General survey of the period and its infinite convolutions in Greece, with Frankish, Catalan, Venetian, Byzantine and Ottoman struggles for power.

John Julius Norwich *Byzantium: the Early Centuries* and *Byzantium: the Apogee* (both Penguin/Knopf). Perhaps the main surprise for first-time travellers to Greece is the fascination of Byzantine monuments. These first two volumes of Norwich's history of the empire are terrific narrative accounts.

Timothy Callistos Ware *The Orthodox Church* (Penguin). Good introduction to what is effectively the established religion of Greece.

MODERN GREECE

Timothy Boatswain and Colin Nicolson *A Traveller's History of Greece* (Windrush Press/ Interlink). Slightly dated but well-written overview of all periods Greek.

Richard Clogg *A Concise History of Greece* (Cambridge UP). A remarkably clear and well-illustrated account of Greece from the decline of Byzantium to 1991, stressing recent decades.

Michael Llewellyn Smith *Ionian Vision, Greece in Asia Minor, 1919–22* (Allen Lane/St Martin's Press, both o/p). Standard work on the Anatolian campaign and the confrontation between Greece and Turkey leading to the exchange of populations.

Mark Mazower *Inside Hitler's Greece: The Experience of Occupation 1941–44* (Yale UP). Somewhat choppily organized, but the standard of scholarship is high and the photos alone justify the price. Demonstrates how the complete demoralization of the country and incompetence of conventional politicians led to the rise of ELAS and the onset of civil war.

C M Woodhouse *Modern Greece, A Short History* (Faber & Faber). Woodhouse was active in the Greek Resistance during World War II. Writing from a right-wing perspective, his history (spanning from the foundation of Constantinople in 324 to the present), is briefer and a bit drier than Clogg's, but he is scrupulous with facts.

ARCHEOLOGY AND ART

John Beckwith *Early Christian and Byzantine Art* (Penguin/Yale UP). Illustrated study placing Byzantine art within a wider context.

John Boardman *Greek Art* (Thames & Hudson, UK). A very good concise introduction in the "World of Art" series.

Reynold Higgins *Minoan and Mycenaean Art* (Thames & Hudson). A clear, well-illustrated roundup.

Sinclair Hood *The Arts in Prehistoric Greece* (Penguin/Yale UP). Sound introduction to the subject.

Roger Ling *Classical Greece* (Phaidon, UK). Another useful and illustrated introduction.

Colin Renfrew *The Cycladic Spirit* (Thames & Hudson/Abrams). A fine, illustrated study of the meaning and purpose of Cycladic artefacts.

Gisela Richter *A Handbook of Greek Art* (Phaidon/Da Capo). Exhaustive survey of the visual arts of ancient Greece.

Suzanne Slesin et al *Greek Style* (Thames & Hudson/Crown). Stunning and stylish domestic architecture and interiors from Corfu, Rhodes and Serifos, among other spots.

R R R Smith *Hellenistic Sculpture* (Thames & Hudson, UK). Modern reappraisal of the art of Greece under Alexander and his successors.

Peter Warren *The Aegean Civilizations* (Phaidon/P Bedrick Books, the latter o/p). Illustrated account of the Minoan and Mycenaean cultures.

MODERN GREEK FICTION

Eugenia Fakinou *The Seventh Garment* (Serpent's Tail). The modern history of Greece – from the War of Independence to the colonels' junta – is told through the life stories (interspersed in counterpoint) of three generations of women. It is a rather more succesful experiment than Fakinou's *Astradeni* (Kedros, Greece), in which a young girl – whose slightly irritating narrative voice is adopted throughout – leaves the island of Sími, with all its traditional values, for Athens.

Nikos Kazantzakis *Zorba the Greek*; *Christ Recrucified* (published in the US as *The Greek Passion*); *Report to Greco*; *Freedom or Death* (*Captain Mihalis* in the US); *The Fratricides* (all Faber & Faber/Touchstone). The most accessible (and Greece-related) of the numerous novels by the Cretan master. Even with inadequate translation, their strength – especially that of *Report to Greco* – shines through.

Stratis Myrivilis *Life in the Tomb* (Quartet/New England UP). A harrowing and unorthodox war memoir, based on the author's experience on the Macedonian front during 1917–18, well

translated by Peter Bien. Completing a kind of trilogy are two later novels, set on the north coast of Lésvos, Myrivilis's homeland: *The Mermaid Madonna* and *The Schoolmistress with the Golden Eyes* (Efstathiadis, Athens, Greece). Translations of these are not so good, and tend to be heavily abridged.

Alexandros Papadiamantis *The Murderess* (Writers & Readers, US). Turn-of-the-century novel set on the island of Skíathos. Also available is a collecton of Papadiamantis short stories, *Tales from a Greek Island* (Johns Hopkins UP).

George Psychoundakis *The Cretan Runner* (John Murray/Transatlantic Arts, the latter o/p). A novel-like narrative of the invasion of Crete and subsequent resistance, by a participant, who was a guide and message-runner for all the British protagonists, including Patrick Leigh Fermor, translator of the book.

Demetrios Vikelas *Loukas Laras* (Doric Publications, UK, o/p). Classic nineteenth-century novel set mainly on Híos.

Yiorgos Yatromanolakis *The History of a Vendetta* (Dedalus). Greek magic realism as the tales of two families unravel from a murder in a small Cretan village.

GREECE IN FOREIGN FICTION

Louis de Bernières *Captain Corelli's Mandolin* (Secker & Warburg, UK). Set on Kefalloniá during the World War II occupation, this is a moving and extraordinary recreation of the era and events – at least for the first 300 pages. Then it all goes wrong, as Berniéres descends from faultless prose to soap opera sequel as he races through to the present. Nonetheless, this is still the best novel written about Greece for many years.

John Fowles *The Magus* (Picador/Dell). Fowles's biggest and best novel: a tale of mystery and manipulation, and Greek island life, inspired by his stay on Spetses, as a teacher, in the 1950s.

Mary Renault *The King Must Die*; *The Last of the Wine*; *The Mask of Apollo*; and others (Sceptre/Random). Mary Renault's imaginative reconstructions are more than the children's reading they're often taken for. The research is impeccable and the writing tight. The trio above retell, respectively, the myth of Theseus, the life of a pupil of Socrates, and that of a fourth-century BC actor.

Evelyn Waugh *Officers and Gentleman* (Penguin). This volume of the wartime trilogy includes an account of the Battle for Crete and subsequent evacuation.

SPECIFIC GUIDES

REGIONAL GUIDES

Marc Dubin *The Rough Guide to Rhodes and the East Aegean* (Penguin). Forthcoming title – due to hit the shelves in 1996 – from longtime resident of Sámos.

John Fisher *The Rough Guide to Crete* (Penguin). An expanded and practical guide to the island by the affable and eccentric contributor of the Crete chapter in this book.

Lycabettus Press Guides (Athens, Greece). This series takes in many of the more popular islands and certain mainland highlights; most pay their way both in interest and usefulness – in particular those on Páros, Pátmos, Náfplio, and the travels of Saint Paul.

WALKING

Marc Dubin *Trekking in Greece* (Lonely Planet). An excellent walkers' guide, expanding on the hikes covered in this book and adding others, including a fair number on the islands. Includes day hikes and longer treks, plus extensive preparatory and background information.

Landscapes of . . . (Sunflower Books/Hunter). A series of walking and car-tour titles devoted most usefully to Crete, Rhodes, Sámos, and Corfu. Strong on maps but a little timid in the choice of routes.

FERRIES

Frewin Poffley *Greek Island Hopping* (Thomas Cook, UK). A superb, user-friendly guide to the networks of Greek ferries, featuring full time-tables and highly imaginative maps. If only the ferries lived up to it all!

LANGUAGE

So many Greeks have lived or worked abroad in America, Australia and, to a lesser extent, Britain, that you will find someone who speaks English in the tiniest island village. Add to that thousands attending language schools or working in the tourist industry – English is the lingua franca of most resorts, with German second – and it is easy to see how so many visitors come back having learnt only half a dozen restaurant words between them.

You can certainly get by this way, but it isn't very satisfying, and the willingness and ability to say even a few words will transform your status

from that of dumb *tourístas* to the honourable one of *ksénos*, a word which can mean foreigner, traveller and guest all rolled into one.

LEARNING BASIC GREEK

Greek is not an easy language for English speakers but it is a very beautiful one and even a brief acquaintance will give you some idea of the debt owed to it by western European languages.

On top of the usual difficulties of learning a new language, Greek presents the additional problem of an entirely separate **alphabet**. Despite initial appearances, this is in practice fairly easily mastered – a skill that will help enormously if you are going to get around independently (see the alphabet box following). In addition, certain combinations of letters have unexpected results. This book's transliteration system should help you make intelligible noises but you have to remember that the correct **stress** (marked throughout the book with an acute accent) is crucial. With the right sounds but the wrong stress people will either fail to understand you, or else understand something quite different from what you intended.

Greek **grammar** is more complicated still: nouns are divided into three genders, all with different case endings in the singular and in the plural, and all adjectives and articles have to agree with these in gender, number and case. (All adjectives are arbitrarily cited in the

LANGUAGE-LEARNING MATERIALS

TEACH-YOURSELF GREEK COURSES

Breakthrough Greece (Pan Macmillan; book and two cassettes). Excellent, basic teach-yourself course – completely outclasses the competition.

Greek Language and People (BBC Publications, UK; book and cassette available). More limited in scope but good for acquiring the essentials, and the confidence to try them.

Anne Farmakides A Manual of Modern Greek (Yale/McGill; 3 vols). If you have the discipline and motivation, this is one of the best for learning proper, grammatical Greek; indeed, mastery of just the first volume will get you a long way.

PHRASEBOOKS

The Rough Guide to Greek (Penguin, UK/US). Practical and easy-to-use, the *Rough Guide*

phrasebooks allow you to speak the way you would in your own language. Feature boxes fill you in on dos and don'ts and cultural know-how.

DICTIONARIES

The Oxford Dictionary of Modern Greek (Oxford University Press, UK/US). A bit bulky but generally considered the best Greek–English, English–Greek dictionary.

Collins Pocket Greek Dictionary (Harper Collins, UK/US). Very nearly as complete as the Oxford and probably better value for the money.

Oxford Learner's Dictionary (Oxford University Press, UK/US). If you're planning a prolonged stay, this pricey two-volume set is unbeatable for usage and vocabulary. There's also a more portable one-volume *Learner's Pocket Dictionary*.

neuter form in the following lists.) Verbs are even worse.

To begin with at least, the best thing is simply to say what you know the way you know it, and never mind the niceties. "Eat meat hungry" should get a result, however grammatically incorrect. If you worry about your mistakes, you'll never say anything.

THE GREEK ALPHABET: TRANSLITERATION

Set out below is the Greek alphabet, the system of transliteration used in this book, and a brief aid to pronunciation.

Greek	Transliteration	Pronounced
A, α	a	a as in father
B, β	v	v as in vet
Γ, γ	y/g	y as in yes, except before consonants and a, o or long i, when it's a throaty version of the g in gap.
Δ, δ	dh	th as in then
E, ε	e	e as in get
Z, ζ	z	z sound
H, η	i	ee sound as in feet
Θ, θ	th	th as in theme
I, ι	i	i as in bit
K, κ	k	k sound
Λ, λ	l	l sound
M, μ	m	m sound
N, ν	n	n sound
Ξ, ξ	ks	ks sound
O, o	o	o as in hot
Π, π	p	p sound
P, ρ	r	rolled r sound
Σ, σ, ς	s	s sound
T, τ	t	t sound
Y, υ	i	ee sound, indistinguishable from η
Φ, φ	f	f sound
X, χ	h	harsh h sound, like ch in loch
Ψ, ψ	ps	ps as in lips
Ω, ω	o	o as in toad, indistinguishable from o

Combinations and dipthongs

AI, αι	e	e as in get
AY, αυ	av/af	av or af depending on following consonant
EI, ει	i	ee, exactly like η
OI, οι	i	ee, identical again
EY, ευ	ev/ef	ev or ef, depending on following consonant
OY, ου	ou	ou as in tourist
ΓΓ, γγ	ng	ng as in angie
ΓK, γκ	g/ng	g as in goat at the beginning of a word; ng in the middle
ΜΠ, μπ	b	b at the beginning of a word; mb in the middle
NT, ντ	d/nd	d at the beginning of a word, nd in the middle
ΤΣ, τσ	ts	ts as in hits
ΣΙ, σι	sh	sh as in shame
ΤΖ, τζ	ts	j as in jam

Note: An umlaut (¨) over a letter indicates that the two vowels are pronounced separately, eg Aóös is Ah-oh-s, rather than A-ooos

GREEK WORDS AND PHRASES

Essentials

Yes	*Néh*	Yesterday	*Khthés*	Big	*Megálo*
Certainly	*Málista*	Now	*Tóra*	Small	*Mikró*
No	*Óhi*	Later	*Argótera*	More	*Perisótero*
Please	*Parakaló*	Open	*Aniktó*	Less	*Ligótero*
Okay, agreed	*Endáksi*	Closed	*Klistó*	A little	*Lígo*
Thank you	*Efharistó (polí)*	Day	*Méra*	A lot	*Polí*
(very much)		Night	*Níkhta*	Cheap	*Ftinó*
I (don't)	*(Dhen) Katalavéno*	In the morning	*To proí*	Expensive	*Akrivó*
understand		In the afternoon	*To apóyevma*	Hot	*Zestó*
Excuse me, do	*Parakaló, mípos*	In the evening	*To vrádhi*	Cold	*Krío*
you speak	*miláteh angliká?*	Here	*Edhó*	With	*Mazí*
English?		There	*Ekí*	Without	*Horís*
Sorry/excuse	*Signómi*	This one	*Aftó*	Quickly	*Grígora*
me		That one	*Ekíno*	Slowly	*Sigá*
Today	*Símera*	Good	*Kaló*	Mr/Mrs	*Kírios/Kiría*
Tomorrow	*Ávrio*	Bad	*Kakó*	Miss	*Dhespinís*

Other Needs

To eat/drink	*Trógo/Píno*	Stamps	*Gramatósima*	Toilet	*Toualéta*
Bakery	*Foúrnos, psomádhiko*	Petrol station	*Venzinádhiko*	Police	*Astinomía*
Pharmacy	*Farmakío*	Bank	*Trápeza*	Doctor	*Iatrós*
Post office	*Tahidhromío*	Money	*Leftá/Hrímata*	Hospital	*Nosokomío*

Requests and Questions

To ask a question, it's simplest to start with *parakaló*, then name the thing you want in an interrogative tone.

Where is the bakery?	*Parakaló, o foúrnos?*	How many?	*Póssi or pósses?*
Can you show me the	*Parakaló, o dhrómos*	How much?	*Póso?*
road to . . . ?	*ya . . ?*	When?	*Póteh?*
We'd like a room for two	*Parakaló, éna dhomátio*	Why?	*Yatí?*
	ya dhío átoma?	At what time . . . ?	*Ti óra . . . ?*
May I have a kilo of	*Parakaló, éna kiló*	What is/Which is . . . ?	*Ti íneh/pió íneh..?*
oranges?	*portokália?*	How much (does it cost)?	*Póso káni?*
Where?	*Pou?*	What time does it open?	*Tí óra aníyi?*
How?	*Pos?*	What time does it close?	*Tí óra klíni?*

Talking to People

Greek makes the distinction between the informal (*esí*) and formal (*esís*) second person, as French does with *tu* and *vous*. Young people, older people and country people nearly always use *esí* even with total strangers. In any event, no one will be too bothered if you get it wrong. By far the most common greeting, on meeting and parting, is *yá sou/yá sas* – literally "health to you".

Hello	*Hérete*	My name is . . .	*Meh léneh . . .*
Good morning	*Kalí méra*	Speak slower, please	*Parakaló, miláte pió sigá*
Good evening	*Kalí spéra*	How do you say it in	*Pos léyeteh sta Eliniká?*
Good night	*Kalí níkhta*	Greek?	
Goodbye	*Adhío*	I don't know	*Dhen kséro*
How are you?	*Ti kánis/Ti káneteh?*	See you tomorrow	*Tha se dho ávrio*
I'm fine	*Kalá ímeh*	See you soon	*Kalí andhámosi*
And you?	*Keh esís?*	Let's go	*Pámeh*
What's your name?	*Pos se léneh?*	Please help me	*Parakaló, na me voithísteh*

Greek's Greek

There are numerous words and phrases which you will hear constantly, even if you rarely have the chance to use them. These are a few of the most common.

Éla!	Come (literally) but also Speak to me! You don't say! etc.	*Po-po-po!*	Expression of dismay or concern, like French "O la la!"
Orísteh?	What can I do for you?	*Pedhí mou*	My boy/girl, sonny, friend, etc.
Bros!	Standard phone response	*Maláka(s)*	Literally "wanker", but often used (don't try it!) as an infor-
Ti néa?	What's new?		mal address.
Ti yíneteh?	What's going on (here)?		
Étsi k'étsi	So-so	*Sigá sigá*	Take your time, slow down
Ópa!	Whoops! Watch it!	*Kaló taxídhi*	Bon voyage

Accommodation

Hotel	*Ksenodhohío*	Cold water	*krío neró*
A room . . .	*Éna dhomátio . . .*	Can I see it?	*Boró na to dho?*
for one/two/three people	*ya éna/dhío/tría átoma*	Can we camp here?	*Boróume na váloumeh ti*
for one/two/three nights	*ya mía/dhío/trís vradhiés*		*skiní edhó?*
with a double bed	*meh megálo kreváti*	Campsite	*Kamping/Kataskínosi*
with a shower	*meh doús*	Tent	*Skiní*
hot water	*zestó neró*	Youth hostel	*Ksenodhohío neótitos*

On the Move

Aeroplane	*Aeropláno*	Where are you going?	*Pou pas?*
Bus	*Leoforío*	I'm going to . . .	*Páo sto . . .*
Car	*Aftokínito*	I want to get off at . . .	*Thélo na katévo sto . . .*
Motorbike, moped	*Mihanáki, papáki*	The road to . . .	*O dhrómos ya . . .*
Taxi	*Taksí*	Near	*Kondá*
Ship	*Plío/Vapóri/Karávi*	Far	*Makriá*
Bicycle	*Podhílato*	Left	*Aristerá*
Hitching	*Otostóp*	Right	*Dheksiá*
On foot	*Meh ta pódhia*	Straight ahead	*Katefthía*
Trail	*Monopáti*	A ticket to . . .	*Éna isistírio ya . . .*
Bus station	*Praktorío leoforíon*	A return ticket	*Éna isistírio me epistrofí*
Bus stop	*Stási*	Beach	*Paralía*
Harbour	*Limáni*	Cave	*Spiliá*
What time does it leave?	*Ti óra févyi?*	Centre (of town)	*Kéndro*
What time does it arrive?	*Ti óra ftháni?*	Church	*Eklissía*
How many kilometres?	*Pósa hiliómetra?*	Sea	*Thálassa*
How many hours?	*Pósses óres?*	Village	*Horió*

Numbers

1	*énos éna/mía*	12	*dhódheka*	90	*enenínda*
2	*dhío*	13	*dhekatrís*	100	*ekató*
3	*trís/tría*	14	*dhekatésseres*	150	*ekatón penínda*
4	*tésseres/téssera*	20	*íkosi*	200	*dhiakóssies/ia*
5	*pénde*	21	*íkosi éna*	500	*pendakóssies/ia*
6	*éksi*	30	*triánda*	1000	*hílies/ia*
7	*eftá*	40	*saránda*	2000	*dhío hiliádhes*
8	*okhtó*	50	*penínda*	1,000,000	*éna ekatomírio*
9	*enyá*	60	*eksínda*	first	*próto*
10	*dhéka*	70	*evdhomínda*	second	*dhéftero*
11	*éndheka*	80	*ogdhónda*	third	*tríto*

The time and days of the week

Sunday	*Kiriakí*	Saturday	*Sávato*	Five minutes past seven	*Eftá keh pénde*
Monday	*Dheftéra*	What time is it?	*Ti óra íneh?*	Half past eleven	*Éndheka keh misí*
Tuesday	*Tríti*	One/two/three o'clock	*Mía/dhío/trís óra/óres*	Half-hour	*Misí óra*
Wednesday	*Tetárti*	Twenty minutes to four	*Tésseres pará íkosi*	Quarter-hour	*Éna tétarto*
Thursday	*Pémpti*				
Friday	*Paraskeví*				

A GLOSSARY
OF WORDS
AND TERMS

ACROPOLIS Ancient, fortified hilltop.

AGORA Market and meeting place of an ancient Greek city.

AMPHORA Tall, narrow-necked jar for oil or wine.

ÁNO Upper, as in upper town or village.

APSE Polygonal or curved recess at the altar end of a church.

ARCHAIC PERIOD Late Iron Age period, from around 750 BC to the start of the Classical period in the fifth century BC.

ATRIUM Open, inner courtyard of a house.

ÁYIOS/AYÍA/ÁYII (m/f/plural) Saint or holy. Common place name prefix (abbreviated Ag. or Ay.), often spelt AGIOS or AGHIOS.

BOULEUTERION Auditorium for meetings of an ancient town's council.

BYZANTINE EMPIRE Created by the division of the Roman Empire in 395 AD, this, the eastern half, was ruled from Constantinople (modern Istanbul).

CAPITAL The top, often ornamented, of a column.

CELLA Sacred room of a temple, housing the cult image.

CLASSICAL PERIOD Essentially from the end of the Persian Wars in the fifth century BC until the unification of Greece under Phillip II of Macedon (338 BC).

CORINTHIAN Decorative columns, festooned with acanthus florettes.

DHIMARHÍO Town hall.

DHOMÁTIA Rooms for rent in private houses.

DORIAN Northern civilization that displaced and succeeded the Mycenaeans and Minoans through most of Greece around 1100 BC.

DORIC Primitive columns, dating from the Dorian period.

ENTABLATURE The horizontal linking structure atop the columns of an ancient temple.

EPARHÍA Greek Orthodox diocese, also the smallest subdivision of a modern province.

FORUM Market and meeting place of a Roman-era city.

FRIEZE Band of sculptures around a temple. Doric friezes consist of various tableau of figures (METOPES) interspersed with grooved panels (TRIGLYPHS); Ionic ones have continuous bands of figures.

FROÚRIO Medieval castle.

GEOMETRIC PERIOD Post-Mycenaean Iron Age era named for the style of its pottery; began in the early eleventh century BC with the arrival of Dorian peoples. By the eighth century BC, with the development of representational styles, it became known as the ARCHAIC period.

HELLENISTIC PERIOD The last and most unified "Greek empire", created in the wake of Alexander the Great's Macedonian empire and finally collapsing with the fall of Corinth to the Romans in 146 BC.

HEROÖN Shrine or sanctuary, usually of a demigod or mortal; war memorials.

HÓRA Main town of an island (literally "the place"); the Hóra is also commonly known by the island name.

IERÓN Literally, "sacred" – the space between the altar screen and the apse of a church, reserved for a priest.

IKONOSTÁSI Screen between the nave of a church and the altar.

IONIC Elaborate, decorative development of the older DORIC order; Ionic temple columns are slimmer with deeper "fluted" edges, spiral-shaped capitals, and ornamental bases. CORINTHIAN capitals are a still more decorative development, with acanthus florettes.

KAFENÍO Coffee house or café; in a small village the centre of communal life and probably serving as the bus stop, too.

KAÍKI (plural KAÍKIA) Caique, or medium-sized boat, traditionally wooden and used for transporting cargo and passengers; now refers mainly to island excursion boats.

KALDERÍMI Cobbled mule- and footpaths.

KÁSTRO Any fortified hill (or a castle), but most usually the oldest, highest, walled-in part of an island HÓRA.

KATHOLIKÓN Central chapel of a monastery.

KÁTO Lower, as in lower town or village.

KENTRIKÍ PLATÍA Central square.

KOUROS Nude statue of an idealized young man, usually portrayed with one foot slightly forward of the other.

MACEDONIAN EMPIRE Empire created by Philip II in the mid-fourth century BC.

MEGARON Principal hall or throne room of a Mycenaean palace.

MELTÉMI North wind that blows across the Aegean in summer, starting softly from near the mainland and hitting the Cyclades, the Dodecanese and Crete full on.

MINOAN Crete's great Bronze Age Civilization, which dominated the Aegean from about 2500 to 1400 BC.

MONÍ Formal term for a monastery or convent.

MYCENAEAN Mainland civilization centred on Mycenae and the Argolid from about 1700 to 1100 BC.

NAOS The inner sanctum of an ancient temple; also, any Orthodox Christian shrine.

NARTHEX Vestibule or church entrance hall.

NEOLITHIC Earliest era of settlement in Greece, characterized by the use of stone tools and weapons together with basic agriculture. Divided arbitrarily into Early (c. 6000 BC), Middle (c. 5000 BC), and Late (c. 3000 BC).

NÉOS, NÉA, NÉO "New" – a common part of a town or village name.

ODEION Small amphitheatre, used for musical performances, minor dramatic productions, or councils.

ORCHESTRA Circular area in a theatre where the chorus would sing and dance.

PALAESTRA Gymnasium for athletics and wrestling practice.

PALEÓS, PALEÁ, PALEÓ "Old" – again common in town and village names.

PANAYÍA Virgin Mary.

PANIYÍRI Festival or feast – the local celebration of a holy day.

PANDOKRÁTOR Literally "The Almighty"; generally refers to the stern portrayal of Christ in Majesty frescoed or in mosaic in the dome of many Byzantine churches.

PARALÍA Beach or seafront promenade.

PEDIMENT Triangular, sculpted gable below the roof of a temple.

PERÍPTERO Street kiosk.

PERISTYLE Gallery of columns around a temple or other building.

PIRGOS Tower or bastion.

PITHOS (plural PITHOI) Large ceramic jar for storing oil, grain, etc. Very common in Minoan palaces and used in almost identical form in modern Greek homes.

PLATÍA Square, plaza.

PROPYLAION Portico or entrance to an ancient building; often used in the plural, PROPYLAIA.

SKÁLA The port of an inland island settlement, nowadays often larger and more important than its namesake, but always younger since built after the disappearance of piracy.

STELE Upright stone slab or column, usually inscribed, or an ancient tombstone.

STOA Colonnaded walkway in marketplace.

TAVERNA Restaurant.

TEMENOS Sacred precinct, often used to refer to the sanctuary itself.

THEATRAL AREA Open area found in most of the Minoan palaces with seat-like steps around. Probably a type of theatre or ritual area, though this is not conclusively proven.

THOLOS Conical or beehive-shaped building, especially a Mycenaean tomb.

ACRONYMS

ANEK *Anonimí Navtikí Etería Krítis* (Shipping Co of Crete, Ltd), which runs most ferries between Pireás and Crete, plus many to Italy.

EA Greek Left (*Ellenikí Aristerá*), formerly the Greek Euro-communist Party (*KKE-Esoterikoú*).

ELTA The postal service.

EOT *Ellinikós Organismós Tourismoú*, the National Tourist Organization.

KKE Communist Party, unreconstructed.

KTEL National syndicate of bus companies. The term is also used to refer to bus stations.

ND Conservative (*Néa Dhimokratía*) party.

NEL *Navtikí Etería Lésvou* (Lesvian Shipping Co), which runs most northeast Aegean ferries.

OTE Telephone company.

PA New nationalist party (*Politikí Ánixi* – "Political Spring").

PASOK Socialist party (Pan-Hellenic Socialist Movement).

INDEX

Islands are in bold; historic events and people in italics. There are separate index entries for towns and resorts in Corfu, Crete and Rhodes. All other large island towns and resorts are included in the main index.

A
Accommodation 32
Acronyms 414
Adhámas (Mílos) 88
Aegina – see Éyina
Agathoníssi 248
Aï Nikítas (Lefkádha) 356
Aï Strátis – see Áyios
  Efstrátios
Airlines
  in Britain 4
  in Ireland 9
  in North America 13
Akrotíri (Thíra) 139
Alexandhroúpoli (port) 12
Alíkanas (Zákinthos) 371
Alikés (Zákinthos) 371
Alikí (Kímolos) 92
Alínda (Léros) 244
Alónissos 319
Aloprónia (Síkinos) 132
American Express 41
Ammopí (Kárpathos) 204
Amorgós 126
Amphibians 402
Anáfi 140
Anafonítria monastery
  (Zákinthos) 372
Análipsi (Astipálea) 239
Anávatos (Híos) 278
Ánaxos (Lésvos) 294
Ándhros 92
Andíkithira 377
Andíparos 117
Andípaxi (Antipaxos) 352
Angístri 61
Anoyí (Itháki) 367
Anti-Paros – see Andíparos
Antipaxos – see Andípaxi

Aphaia, Temple (Éyina) 59
Apíranthos (Náxos) 123
Apocalypse, Monastery of the
  (Pátmos) 246
Apóllon (Náxos) 123
Apollonía (Sífnos) 84
Argo-Saronic islands 55–70
Argostóli (Kefalloniá) 363
Arkássa (Kárpathos) 204
Arkí 248
Armenistís (Ikaría) 267
Artemónas(Sífnos) 84
Asclepion (Kós) 233
Asélinos, Mikró/Megálo
  (Skíathos) 315
Ássos 364
Astipálea 238
Astrís 307
Atháni (Lefkádha) 357
Athens 10–11
ATMs 24
Átokos 358
Atsítsa 326
Avgónima (Híos) 278
Avlémonas (Kíthira) 376
Avlonári (Évvia) 329
Ayía Ánna (Náxos) 121
Ayía Evfimía (Kefalloniá) 361
Ayía Marína (Léros) 244
Ayía Marína (Zákinthos) 372
Ayía Pelayía (Kíthira) 373
Ayía Sofía cave (Kíthira) 377
Ayiássos (Lésvos) 288
Ayiókambos (Évvia) 334
Áyios Efstrátios (Aï Strátis)
  301
Áyios Kírikos (Ikaría) 266
Áyios Konstandínos (port) 12
Áyios Konstandínos (Sámos)
  261
Ayíou Nikoláou Galatáki
  (Évvia) 333

B
Balkan Wars 388
Banks 24
Bars 40
Batsí (Ándhros) 94
BBC World Service 43
Beer 40
Birds 400
Books 404

Breakfast 35
Bros Thermá (Kós) 234
Buses, to Greece from Britain 7
Byzantine Greece 385

C
Cafés 37
Caiques 31
Camping 34
Capodistrias, Ioannis 388
Cephallonia – see Kefalloniá
Children 50
Chios – see Híos
Cinema 47
City-states 384
Civil War 390
Classical history 385
Coffee 37
Colonels' Junta 392
Corfu (Kérkira) 336–379
  Aharávi 345
  Astrakéri 346
  Áyios Górdhis 348
  Áyios Yióryios (Corfu) 349
  Barbáti 344
  Benítses 348
  Boukári 348
  Ermónes 347
  Glifádha 347
  Kalámi 344
  Kassiópi 345
  Kávos 349
  Kérkira Town 338
  Kondokáli 344
  Kouloúra 344
  Nissáki 344
  Paleokastrítsa 346
  Pélekas 348
  Perouládhes 347
  Ródha 346
  Sidhári 347
  Vátos 347
Costs 23
Credit cards 24
Crete (KRÍTI) 144–199
  Akrotíri Peninsula 193
  Almirídha 183
  Amári Valley 185
  Anóyia 168
  Arkádhi Monastery 182
  Árvi 177
  Ayía Galíni 184
  Ayía Marína 193
  Ayía Pelayía 166
  Ayía Triádha 161
  Ayía Triádha Monastery 193

Áyia Rouméli 195
Áyii Dhéka 159
Áyios Nikólaos 170
Balí 168
Dhamnóni 183
Dhiktean Cave 170
Elafonísi 197
Élos 197
Eloúnda 172
Falásarna 197
Festós (Phaestos) 160
Fódhele 167
Frangokástello 196
Gávdhos 198
Goniá Monastery 193
Gorge of Samariá 195
Górtys 159
Goúrnes 163
Gourniá 173
Gourvenétou Monastery 193
Goúves 163
Haniá 185
Hersónisos 164
Hóra Sfakíon 196
Hrissoskalítissa Monastery 197
Ierápetra 176
Iráklion 147
Kalí Liménes 163
Kamáres 169
Kámbos 197
Kándhanos 197
Kastélli (Kíssamos) 196
Káto Zákros 176
Kefalás 183
Keratókambos 177
Kíssamos – see Kastélli
Knossós 155
Kókkino Horió 183
Kolimbári 193
Kournás, Lake 182
Kritsá 172
Lasíthi Plateau 169
Lató 173
Lefkóyia 184
Léndas 163
Loutró 196
Makriyialós 176
Mália 165
Mália Palace 165
Mátala 162
Míres 160
Mírthios 183
Mírtos 177
Móhlos 173
Mount Psilorítis – see Psilorítis
Neápoli 169
Omalós 195
Pahiá Ámmos 173
Palékastro 175
Paleohóra 198

Pánormos 168
Phaestos – see Festós
Plakiás 183
Plataniás 193
Plátanos 197
Préveli Monastery 184
Psihró 170
Psilorítis, Mount 169
Réthimnon 178
Rodhopoú Peninsula 193
Samarian Gorge 193
Sfinári 197
Sitía 174
Soúyia 196
Spíli 184
Spinalónga 172
Stalídha 165
Stavrós 193
Tílissos 168
Toploú Monastery 175
Topólia 197
Tsoútsouros 177
Tzermiádho 170
Váï Beach 175
Vorízia 169
Yioryoúpoli 182
Zákros 176
Crusades 386
Cultural festivals 47
Currency 24
Cyclades islands 71–143
Cycling 32
Cyprus crises 392–393

D

Delos 104
Departure tax 50
Despotates (Byzantine) 386
Dhiafáni (Kárpathos) 206
Dhiakófti (Kíthira) 376
Dhílos – see Delos
Dhodhekánisos – see
 Dodecanese
Dhonoússa 124
Dhriopídha (Kíthnos) 78
Dhrogaráti cave (Kefalloniá)
 361
Disabled travellers 19
Doctors 26
**Dodecanese
 (Dhodhekánisos) islands**
 200–250
Dorian history 384
Driving, to Greece from Britain
 7–9
Drug laws 49

E

EAM 390
**East and North Aegean
 islands** 251–309
Easter 45
Egiáli (Amorgós) 128
Elafónissos 378
ELAS 390
Élios (Skópelos) 318
Embassies, Greek (abroad) 20
Emborió (Hálki) 219
Emborió (Kálimnos) 241
EOT (Tourist Organization) 27
Eressós – see Skála Eressoú
 (Lésvos)
Erétria (Évvia) 329
Eríkousa (Merlera) 349
Ermoúpoli (Síros) 108
Estiatória 36
Euboea – see Évvia
Évdhilos (Ikaría) 267
Évvia (Euboea) 327
Exóbourgo (Tínos) 98
Éyina (Aegina) 57
Éyina Town 58

F

Fano – see Othoní
Fáros (Sífnos) 86
Ferries, to Greece 8–9
Ferries, within Greece 29
Festivals, Cultural 47
Festivals, Religious 44
Festivals, Traditional 44
Filóti (Náxos) 123
Fínikas (Síros) 111
Firá (Thíra) 136
Fish 36
Fiskárdho 364
Flight agents
 in Australia/New Zealand 18
 in Britain 4
 in Ireland 9
Flights
 domestic 31
 to Greece from Australasia 17
 to Greece from Britain 3
 to Greece from Canada 15
 to Greece from Ireland 9
 to Greece from USA 13
Flowers 399
Folégandhros 133
Food and drink 35–40

Football 50
Foúrni 269
Franks 386
Frí (Kássos) 200
Fríkes (Itháki) 367

G
Gáïos (Páxi) 351
Galissás (Síros) 110
Gávdhos 198
Gávrio (Ándhros) 93
Gay life 50
German occupation 389
Glóssa (Skópelos) 316
Glossary 413
Goat dances 323
Greek National Tourist Organization 27

H
Hálki 218
Halkídha (Évvia) 327
Health 25
Hellenistic Greece 385
Heraion (Sámos) 259
Híos 270
Híos Town 270
History of Greece 383–398
Hitching 32
Holiday agents (Greek specialists) 5–6
Hóra (Amorgós) 127
Hóra (Anáfi) 140
Hóra (Ándhros) 94
Hóra (Folégandhros) 133
Hóra (Íos) 130
Hóra (Kímolos) 91
Hóra (Kíthira) 375
Hóra (Kíthnos) 78
Hóra (Pátmos) 246
Hóra (Sámos) 259
Hóra (Sérifos) 81
Horió (Sími) 221
Hospitals 26
Hotels 33
Hozoviotíssas Monastery (Amorgós) 127
Hydra – see Ídhra
Hydrofoils, within Greece 30

I
Ía (Thíra) 137
Ídhra (Hydra) 64

Ídhra Town 65
Igoumenítsa (port) 12
Ikaría 265
Independence, War of 387
Information 25
Inoússes 282
Insects 403
Insurance, Travel 22
Íos 129
Ioulídha (Kéa) 76
Ipsiloú Monastery (Lésvos) 291
Iráklia 125
Ithaca – see Itháki
Itháki (Ithaca) 365

J
Jellyfish 25
Jewish holocaust 390
Johnson, Lyndon 392
Junta, Colonels' 392

K
Kafenío 37
Kaïkia 31
Kalamítsi (Lefkádha) 356
Kálamos 358
Kalávria (Póros) 64
Kálimnos 239
Kamáres (Sífnos) 83
Kamári (Kós) 236
Kamári (Thíra) 138
Kamariótissa (Samothráki) 302
Kámbi (Zákinthos) 371
Kámbos (Híos) 276
Kapsáli (Kíthira) 375
Karamanlis, Konstantinos 391, 392, 398
Karavás (Kíthira) 375
Karavómilos (Kefalloniá) 360
Karavostássi (Folégandhros) 133
Kardhámena (Kós) 236
Kardhámila (Híos) 279
Kardhianí (Tínos) 98
Karfás (Híos) 274
Káristos 331
Karlóvassi (Sámos) 262
Kárpathos 202
Kássos 200
Kastellórizo (Meyísti) 219
Kástos 358
Kástro (Kefalloniá) 363
Kástro (Sífnos) 85

Kástro (Skíathos) 314
Katápola (Amorgós) 126
Katastári (Zákinthos) 372
Káto Katelíon 362
Káto Koufoníssi 125
Kavála (port) 12
Kavírio (Límnos) 300
Kéa (Tzía) 74
Kefallinía – see Kefalloniá
Kefalloniá (Cephallonia) 359
Kerí (Zákinthos) 370
Kérkira – see also Corfu
Kérkis, Mount (Sámos) 264
Kéros 125
Kikládhes – see Cyclades
Kilioméno (Zákinthos) 371
Killíni (port) 12
Kími (Évvia) 330
Kímolos 91
Kíni (Síros) 110
Kínira 307
Kióni (Itháki) 367
Kirá Panayía (Sporades) 322
Kíthira 372
Kíthnos (Thermiá) 77
Klisídhi (Anáfi) 140
Kokkári (Sámos) 260
Kolokotronis, Theodhoros 387
Konstantinos II (Constantine), King 391
Korissía (Kéa) 75
Korthí (Ándhros) 95
Kós 230
Kós Town 231
Koskotas, Yiorgos 396, 398
Koufoníssi 124
Koukounariés (Skíathos) 315
Kríti – see Crete
Ksirókambos (Léros) 243

L
Laganás (Zákinthos) 370
Lákka (Paxí) 352
Lakkí (Léros) 243
Lambrakis, Grigoris 391
Langádha (Híos) 279
Language 408
Lássi (Kefalloniá) 363
Lefkádha (Lefkas) 352
Lefkádha Town 353
Léfkes (Páros) 116
Lefkós (Kárpathos) 205

Léros 241
Lésvos (Mitilíni) 283
Ligiá (Lefkádha) 355
Limenária 307
Límni (Évvia) 332
Limnonári (Skópelos) 318
Límnos 296
Limónos Monastery (Lésvos) 290
Linariá 324
Lipsí 247
Livádhaki (Sérifos) 81
Livádhi (Kíthira) 376
Livádhi (Sérifos) 80
Livádhia (Astipálea) 238
Livádhia (Tílos) 226
Lixoúri (Kefalloniá) 364
Loggerhead turtles 362
Longós 352
Lourdháta (Kefalloniá) 362
Loutrá Ehipsoú (Évvia) 334
Loutráki (Skópelos) 316

M
Macedonian Empire 385
Macedonian Question 397
Magaziá (Skíros) 326
Magazines, English-language 42
Maherádho (Zákinthos) 371
Maltezána (Astipálea) 239
Mammals 401
Mandamádhos (Lésvos) 295
Mandhráki (Níssiros) 228
Maps 27
Maráthi 248
Markópoulo (Kefalloniá) 362
Mastihári (Kós) 236
Mathráki (Samothráki) 350
Media 42
Megáli Idhéa 388
Megálo Horió (Tílos) 227
Meganíssi 357
Melissáni cave (Kefalloniá) 360
Menu master (Food glossary) 38
Mérihas (Kíthnos) 78
Mestá (Híos) 276
Metaxas dictatorship 389
Meyísti – see Kastellórizo
Mezédhes 38
Míkonos (Mykonos) 99
Míkonos Town 100

Miliá (Skópelos) 318
Milopótamos (Íos) 131
Milopótamos (Kíthira) 377
Mílos 87
Minoan history 383
Mírina (Límnos) 297
Mírtos (Kefalloniá) 364
Míthimna – see Mólivos (Lésvos)
Mitilíní Town (Lésvos) 284
Mitilíni – see Lésvos
Mitsotakis, Konstantinos 392, 397
Mólivos (Míthimna) (Lésvos) 293
Mólos 326
Monasteries, visits to 44
Money 24
Móni (Éyina) 61
Monk Seals 321
Moped rental 31
Mosquitoes 26
Motorbike rental 31
Moúdhros (Límnos) 300
Mount Óhi – see Óhi, Mount
Movies 47
Museums, opening hours 43
Mycenaean history 383
Mykonos – see Míkonos

N
Náoussa (Páros) 114
Náxos 118
Náxos Town 118
Néa Dhimokratía (New Democracy) 393, 397
Néa Moní (Híos) 277
Neápoli (Peloponnese) 377
Neápoli (port) 12
Neolithic history 383
Newspapers, English-language 42
Nidhrí (Lefkádha) 355
Nikiá (Níssiros) 230
Níssiros 227
Nixon, Richard 392
Nude bathing 48

O
Odysseus sites, Itháki 366
Óhi, Mount 332
Olímbi (Híos) 275
Ólimbos (Kárpathos) 205

Opening hours 43
Oreí (Évvia) 334
Otho, King 388
Othoní (Fanó) 350
Ottoman Greece 386
Ouzerí 38
Oúzo 38

P
Package holidays 5–6
Palaiá Alónissos (Alónissos) 320
Paleohóra (Kíthira) 373
Paleópoli (Kíthira) 376
Paleópoli (Samothráki) 304
Páli (Níssiros) 229
Panayiá (Thássos) 306
Pandéli (Léros) 243
Panormítis Monastery (Sími) 224
Pánormos (Skópelos) 318
Papandreou, Andreas 393–398
Papandreou, Yiorgos (George) 392–393
Paralía Kímis (Évvia) 330
Párga (port) 12
Parikía (Páros) 111
Páros 111
PASOK 393–398
Pastries 40
Patitíri (Alónissos) 320
Pátmos 244
Pátra (port) 12
Paxí (Paxos) 350
Paxos – see Paxí
Pédhi (Sími) 224
Péfki (Évvia) 334
Pérdhika (Éyina) 61
Périssa (Thíra) 138
Peristéra (Sporades) 322
Perivolís Monastery (Lésvos) 290
Pessádha (Kefalloniá) 363
Pétra (Lésvos) 294
Pharmacies 26
Phones 41
Photographic film 50
Picnic fare 35
Pigádhia (Kárpathos) 202
Pipéri 322
Pireás 10–11
Pirgí (Híos) 275
Pírgos (Tínos) 98

Píso Livádhi (Páros) 116
Pithagório (Sámos) 257
Pláka (Mílos) 88
Platána (Évvia) 330
Platáni (Kós) 234
Plátanos (Léros) 244
Platí (Límnos) 299
Platís Yialós (Sífnos) 85
Plomári (Lésvos) 287
Polióhni (Límnos) 300
Politikí Ánixi (Political Spring) 398
Pollónia (Mílos) 91
Populations, exchange of 389
Póros (Kefalloniá) 361
Póros 63
Póros Town 63
Possidhonía (Síros) 111
Postal services 41
Potamiá (Thássos) 306
Pótamos (Kíthira) 373
Póthia (Kálymnos) 239
Potokáki (Sámos) 258
Private rooms (dhomátia) 33
Prokópi 332
Prokópios (Náxos) 121
Psará 281
Psathí (Kímolos) 91
Psérimos 237
Psistariés 37
Public holidays 44

R
Radio 43
Ráhes (Ikaría) 268
Religious festivals 44
Reptiles 402
Restaurants 35
Rhodes (Ródhos) 206
  Apolakiá 218
  Arhángelos 212
  Asklípio 217
  Atáviros, Mount 216
  Áyios Isídhoros 216
  Eleóussa 216
  Émbonas 216
  Eptá Piyés 216
  Faliráki 212
  Haráki 212
  Ialyssos 215
  Kameiros 213
  Kástro Kritinías 215
  Katavía 217
  Kolímbia 212
  Láerma 216

Lárdhos 217
Líndhos 213
Monólithos 215
Péfkos 217
Petaloúdhes (Butterfly Valley) 215
Plimíri 217
Prassoníssi 217
Profítis Ilías 216
Ródhos Town 207
Síana 215
Skála Kamírou 214
Skiádhi Monastery 218
Thári Monastery 216
Tsambíkas 212
Yenádhi 217
Ródhos – see Rhodes
Roman Greece 385
Rooms (private home rentals) 33
Rovviés (Évvia) 333

S
Sailing 48
Sailing, holiday packages 6
Saint John Monastery (Pátmos) 246
Salamína (Salamis) 56
Salamis – see Salamína
Sámi (Kefalloniá) 359
Sámos 253
Samothrace – see Samothráki
Samothráki (Samothrace) 302
Samothraki, islet off Corfu – see Mathráki
Sanctuary of the Great Gods (Samothráki) 303
Santoríni – see Thíra
Scuba diving 48
Sea urchins 25
Seafood 36
Sérifos 79
Sexual harassment 49
Shops, opening hours 43
Sífnos 82
Sígri (Lésvos) 291
Sikaminiá (Lésvos) 295
Síkinos 131
Sími (Symi) 221
Síros (Syros) 107
Sites, opening hours of, 43
Skála (Kefalloniá) 361
Skála (Pátmos) 245
Skála Eressoú (Lésvos) 291
Skála Sikaminiás (Lésvos) 295

Skhinoússa 125
Skíathos 311
Skíathos Town 312
Skíros (Skyros) 323
Skíros Town 325
Skópelos 315
Skópelos Town 317
Skyros – see Skíros
Snack food 35
Soccer 50
Spetsai – see Spétses
Spétses (Spetsai) 67
Spétses Town 67
Sporades islands 310–335
Sporádhes – see Sporades
Stamps 41
Stavrós (Itháki) 367
Stení (Évvia) 330
Stení Vála (Alónissos) 322
Stíra 331
Symi – see Sími
Syros – see Síros

T
Tavernas 36
Taxis 32
Télendhos (Kálymnos) 241
Telephones 41
Television 43
Thános (Límnos) 299
Thássos 304
Thássos Town 305
Theatre 47
Theológos 308
Thérma (Samothráki) 304
Thermiá – see Kíthnos
Thessaloníki (port) 12
Thímena 269
Thíra (Santoríni) 135
Thirassía (Thíra) 139
Tigáki (Kós) 234
Tílos 225
Time 51
Tínos 96
Tínos Town 97
Toilets 51
Topless sunbathing 48
Tourist offices 27
Tragéa region (Náxos) 121
Trains, to Greece from Britain 6
Travellers' cheques 24
Triovássalos (Mílos) 89

Tripití (Mílos) 88
Truman Doctrine 391
Tsilívi (Zákinthos) 371
Turkish occupation 386
Tziá – see Kéa

V
Variá (Lésvos) 287
Vassilikí (Lefkádha) 356
Vassilikó (Zákinthos) 370
Vaterá (Lésvos) 289
Vathí (Kálimnos) 241
Vathí (Sámos) 255
Vathí (Sífnos) 86
Váthi (Itháki) 365
Venetians 386
Venizelos, Eleftherios 388
Villa rental 33

Visas 20
Vlihós (Lefkádha) 356
Volímes (Zákinthos) 372
Volissós (Híos) 280
Vólos (port) 12
Votsalákia (Sámos) 263
Vourliótes (Sámos) 261
Vromólithos (Léros) 243

W
War of Independence 387
Water sports 48
Weever fish 25
Wildlife 399–403
Windsurfing 48
Wines 37
*Women's rights and
   organizations* 395

World War I 388
World War II 389

Y
Yérakas (Zákinthos) 370
Yialós (Astipálea) 239
Yialós (Íos) 130
Yialós (Sími) 221
Yioúra (Sporades) 322
Yíthio (port) 12
Youth hostels 34

Z
Zaharoplastío 40
Zákinthos (Zante) 367
Zákinthos Town 369
Zante – see Zákinthos

DIRECT ORDERS IN THE UK

Title	ISBN	Price
Amsterdam	1858280869	£7.99
Andalucia	185828094X	£8.99
Australia	1858280354	£12.99
Barcelona & Catalunya	1858281067	£8.99
Berlin	1858280338	£8.99
Brazil	1858281024	£9.99
Brittany & Normandy	1858281261	£8.99
Bulgaria	1858280478	£8.99
California	1858280907	£9.99
Canada	185828130X	£10.99
Classical Music on CD	185828113X	£12.99
Corsica	1858280893	£8.99
Crete	1858281326	£8.99
Cyprus	185828032X	£8.99
Czech & Slovak Republics	185828029X	£8.99
Egypt	1858280753	£10.99
England	1858280788	£9.99
Europe	185828077X	£14.99
Florida	1858280109	£8.99
France	1858280508	£9.99
Germany	1858281288	£11.99
Greece	1858281318	£9.99
Greek Islands	1858281636	£8.99
Guatemala & Belize	1858280451	£9.99
Holland, Belgium & Luxembourg	1858280877	£9.99
Hong Kong & Macau	1858280664	£8.99
Hungary	1858281237	£8.99
India	1858281040	£13.99
Ireland	1858280958	£9.99
Italy	1858280311	£12.99
Kenya	1858280435	£9.99
London	1858291172	£8.99
Mediterranean Wildlife	0747100993	£7.95
Malaysia, Singapore & Brunei	1858281032	£9.99
Morocco	1858280400	£9.99
Nepal	185828046X	£8.99
New York	1858280583	£8.99
Nothing Ventured	0747102082	£7.99
Pacific Northwest	1858280923	£9.99
Paris	1858281253	£7.99
Poland	1858280346	£9.99
Portugal	1858280842	£9.99
Prague	185828015X	£7.99
Provence & the Côte d'Azur	1858280230	£8.99
Pyrenees	1858280931	£8.99
St Petersburg	1858281334	£8.99
San Francisco	1858280826	£8.99
Scandinavia	1858280397	£10.99
Scotland	1858280834	£8.99
Sicily	1858280370	£8.99
Spain	1858280818	£9.99
Thailand	1858280168	£8.99
Tunisia	1858280656	£8.99
Turkey	1858280885	£9.99
Tuscany & Umbria	1858280915	£8.99
USA	185828080X	£12.99
Venice	1858280362	£8.99
Wales	1858280966	£8.99
West Africa	1858280141	£12.99
More Women Travel	1858280982	£9.99
World Music	1858280176	£14.99
Zimbabwe & Botswana	1858280419	£10.99

Rough Guide Phrasebooks

Title	ISBN	Price
Czech	1858281482	£3.50
French	185828144X	£3.50
German	1858281466	£3.50
Greek	1858281458	£3.50
Italian	1858281431	£3.50
Spanish	1858281474	£3.50

Rough Guides are available from all good bookstores, but can be obtained directly in the UK* from Penguin by contacting:

Penguin Direct, Penguin Books Ltd, Bath Road, Harmondsworth, West Drayton, Middlesex UB7 0DA; or telephone our credit line on 0181-899 4036 (9am–5pm) and as for Penguin Direct. Visa, Access and Amex accepted. Delivery will normally be within 14 working days. Penguin Direct ordering facilities are only available in the UK.

The availability and published prices quoted are correct at the time of going to press but are subject to alteration without prior notice.

* For USA and international orders, see separate price list

DIRECT ORDERS IN THE USA

Title	ISBN	Price
Amsterdam	1858280869	$13.59
Andalucia	185828094X	$14.95
Australia	1858280354	$18.95
Barcelona & Catalunya	1858281067	$17.99
Berlin	1858280338	$13.99
Brazil	1858281024	$15.95
Brittany & Normandy	1858281261	$14.95
Bulgaria	1858280478	$14.99
California	1858280907	$14.95
Canada	185828130X	$14.95
Classical Music on CD	185828113X	$19.95
Corsica	1858280893	$14.95
Crete	1858281326	$14.95
Cyprus	185828032X	$13.99
Czech & Slovak Republics	185828029X	$14.95
Egypt	1858280753	$17.95
England	1858280788	$16.95
Europe	185828077X	$18.95
Florida	1858280109	$14.95
France	1858281245	$16.95
Germany	1858281288	$17.95
Greece	1858281318	$16.95
Greek Islands	1858281636	$14.95
Guatemala & Belize	1858280451	$14.95
Holland, Belgium & Luxembourg	1858280877	$15.95
Hong Kong & Macau	1858280664	$13.95
Hungary	1858281237	$14.95
India	1858281040	$22.95
Ireland	1858280958	$16.95
Italy	1858280311	$17.95
Kenya	1858280435	$15.95
London	1858291172	$12.95
Mediterranean Wildlife	0747100993	$15.95
Malaysia, Singapore & Brunei	1858281032	$16.95
Morocco	1858280400	$16.95
Nepal	185828046X	$13.95
New York	1858280583	$13.95
Nothing Ventured	0747102082	$19.95
Pacific Northwest	1858280923	$14.95
Paris	1858281253	$12.95
Poland	1858280346	$16.95
Portugal	1858280842	$15.95
Prague	1858281229	$14.95
Provence & the Côte d'Azur	1858280230	$14.95
Pyrenees	1858280931	$15.95
St Petersburg	1858281334	$14.95
San Francisco	1858280826	$13.95
Scandinavia	1858280397	$16.99
Scotland	1858280834	$14.95
Sicily	1858280370	$14.99
Spain	1858280818	$16.95
Thailand	1858280168	$15.95
Tunisia	1858280656	$15.95
Turkey	1858280885	$16.95
Tuscany & Umbria	1858280915	$15.95
USA	185828080X	$18.95
Venice	1858280362	$13.99
Wales	1858280966	$14.95
West Africa	1858280141	$24.95
More Women Travel	1858280982	$14.95
World Music	1858280176	$19.95
Zimbabwe & Botswana	1858280419	$16.95

Rough Guide Phrasebooks

Czech	1858281482	$5.00
French	185828144X	$5.00
German	1858281466	$5.00
Greek	1858281458	$5.00
Italian	1858281431	$5.00
Spanish	1858281474	$5.00

Rough Guides are available from all good bookstores, but can be obtained directly in the USA and Worldwide (except the UK*) from Penguin:

Charge your order by Master Card or Visa (US$15.00 minimum order): call 1-800-253-6476; or send orders, with complete name, address and zip code, and list price, plus $2.00 shipping and handling per order to: Consumer Sales, Penguin USA, PO Box 999 – Dept #17109, Bergenfield, NJ 07621. No COD. Prepay foreign orders by international money order, a cheque drawn on a US bank, or US currency. No postage stamps are accepted. All orders are subject to stock availability at the time they are processed. Refunds will be made for books not available at that time. Please allow a minimum of four weeks for delivery.

The availability and published prices quoted are correct at the time of going to press but are subject to alteration without prior notice. Titles currently not available outside the UK will be available by July 1995. Call to check.

* For UK orders, see separate price list

You are
A STUDENT

You travel
THE WORLD

You want
TO SAVE MONEY

Here's how

The International Student Identity Card

Entitles you to discounts and special services worldwide.

Available at Student Travel Offices Worldwide.